PalmPilot
The Ultimate Guide

What people are saying about PalmPilot: The Ultimate Guide

"At nearly 500 pages, the book covers a lot of ground. Pogue actually writes in English, not computerese. I came away with an understanding of the PalmPilot that my weeks of fumbling around couldn't give me. "

> — Stephen C. Miller
> *Cybertimes, New York Times*

"*PalmPilot: The Ultimate Guide* is aptly named—it's not overindulgent publisher hype. If the PalmPilot is the road warrior's 'roamin' emperor, then this book is the Gideon of Palmdom."

> — Michael Lasky
> *Computer Currents*

"Written in the same humorous, informative, entertaining style of his earlier books, Pogue's enthusiasm for PalmPilots is catching. Pogue patiently and thoroughly explains every nuance of the PalmPilot. A truly useful gift."

> — Suzanne Smith
> *San Diego Union-Tribune*

"No Dummies or Idiots at O'Reilly & Associates. Just smart people writing books for smart people. The book contains hundreds of tips and tricks to help intermediate to advanced users make the most out of their handheld computers. This book is a bible that every Pilot owner should have."

> — Richard Brill
> *TCF.NET*

"If you have a PalmPilot . . . [this book] will help you get the most out of it. In fact, it can teach you how to do things you didn't even know your Pilot was capable of doing . . . to get the most from whatever flavor of Pilot you're working with, pick up a copy of *PalmPilot: The Ultimate Guide*, polish the simple stuff, learn the fancy stuff, and tell all your friends you figured it out on your own."

> — Mike Madson
> *Computer Bits*

"David Pogue is one of my favorite authors. His writing consistently jumps off the page, with humor, solid facts, and idiosyncratic insights. This book is no exception . . . *highly recommended.*"

> — John Nemorovski
> *My Mac Magazine*

PalmPilot
The Ultimate Guide

Second Edition

David Pogue

O'REILLY®

Beijing · Cambridge · Farnham · Köln · Paris · Sebastopol · Taipei · Tokyo

PalmPilot: The Ultimate Guide, Second Edition
by David Pogue

Copyright © 1999, 1998 O'Reilly & Associates, Inc. All rights reserved.
Printed in the United States of America.

Published by O'Reilly & Associates, Inc., 101 Morris Street, Sebastopol, CA 95472.

Editor: Tim O'Reilly

Production Editor: Nancy Wolfe Kotary

Printing History:

June 1998:	First Edition.
June 1999:	Second Edition.

ISBN: 1-56592-600-5

Table of Contents

Foreword

—written by Jeff Hawkins, Handspring

When I designed the original Pilot in 1995, the goal was to create a great tool that was small, simple to use, synchronizable with your PC, and inexpensive. That's what David Pogue has done with his *Palm Pilot: The Ultimate Guide* (except maybe for the small part); read this impressive and substantial book in your office or at home. Then go forth into the world armed with your little PalmPilot.

I really like this book. It's a well-written, no-nonsense, nicely designed exploration of the Palm. Even I learned some things I didn't know before. But why does a small, simple device like the Palm need a 500-page tome, however well done? The answer is that although the Palm is easy to use, you can do a lot of things that are not mentioned in the manual that comes in the box.

What David has done here is to document all of the ways that the developer community has stretched and expanded the Palm and the tips and tricks users have come up with on their own.

I'm delighted to see this second edition expertly cover the latest Palm models, wireless Internet access with the Palm VII handheld, and pocket databases and spreadsheets. There's also coverage of things like infrared beaming, faxing, printing, telephone dialing, TV remote control (really!), and more. And there are more insider tips and tricks than ever.

I mentioned our goals in designing the Palm: small, simple, synchronizable, and inexpensive. There was one more important element, and that was our effort to aggressively court the developer community. They took the Palm and ran with it so well that today there are more than 12,000 registered Palm developers and many thousands of Palm applications.

That's one reason I'm also a fan of Tim O'Reilly, the hands-on publisher of this book and others. Tim showed up at the very first Palm Developers Conference in the fall of 1997. I was amazed; how many publishers would get down to that level of involvement in what was then an unproven product? He told me he thought the Pilot sounded cool and that he wanted to be there at takeoff. Well, he was, and his interest and understanding of the developer and user communities has paid off in this book as well.

The Palm revolution has been tremendously exciting to experience, but we're not anywhere near realizing all of its potential. I'm working now at my new company, Handspring, on products that build on all that has gone before. You can expect to see some exciting new products based upon the Palm operating system from Handspring.

But none of us would be gathered here without the support of users like you who hold this good book in your hands.

Preface

The Palm Phenomenon

In the early days of computers, when a basic four-function calculator was the size of a boxcar, pocket-size computers were just a sci-fi fantasy. Nobody dreamed that by the 1990s, computers could be *too* small.

But that's exactly the problem with most of today's pocket computers and electronic organizers—while advances in miniaturization have resulted in tiny screens and keyboards, our eyes and fingers have remained the same size. Pocket computers are simply too small to be used regularly and comfortably. So what happens? Most people who need portable information wind up buying laptop computers; nobody wants to be stuck in a meeting, hunting and pecking with pinkies on a keyboard where the dollar sign is nowhere to be found. Sure, a few of these gadgets have found cult followings—the Newton, Psion, and Wizard, to name a few— but they're small cults.

If the concept of a palmtop computer is so flawed, why is the PalmPilot such a wild success, dwarfing the sales of all its predecessors? Simple: its designers didn't *try* to create a complete computer. They assumed that you already *have* a computer. The PalmPilot is meant to be a *satellite*—an add-on to your full-sized computer, that quickly gulps down your most important information into a gizmo the size of a cassette tape.

The result is an uncannily successful piece of electronics that has stunned the industry. Millions of PalmPilots have been sold. Even after two rounds of Microsoft's best Windows CE efforts, PalmPilot OS devices still represent 80% of all palmtop sales. One mail-order company is reporting sales of 100 PalmPilots *per day*. Universally glowing reviews continue to pour forth from nearly every newspaper, business magazine, and computer magazine in the country. PalmPilot buyers become fanatics, spreading the gospel to their friends and scrabbling at the Web looking for new tips, tricks, and software. Walk down a plane aisle on your next flight, or whip open your own PalmPilot at any convention, and you'll see what I mean: these things are *everywhere,* and Palm owners feel a sense of community and togetherness.

The ironic result of the PalmPilot's popularity is that the fans have begun applying this hardy little PalmPilot to tasks normally reserved for "real" computers: sending faxes, creating artwork, playing arcade games, playing music, and even browsing the World Wide Web. Despite the PalmPilot's original intention as a simple device with a single purpose (as a PC satellite), the fans—often in the form of Palm-specialized hardware and software companies—have applied it to much more demanding tasks than 3Com, the manufacturer, ever dreamed of, and found it triumphant.

Taking your PalmPilot farther: that's what this book is about.

Why a PalmPilot?

The PalmPilot is small, light, and focused in purpose, but those are only part of its appeal. It's also a hit because:

It's inexpensive.
> Older models can be found for $100 or less; the middle of the line remains around $250; and even the wireless high-end machine, the PalmPilot VII, costs less than a fraction of a laptop's price. Everything is included: software, the cradle that connects the PalmPilot to your PC, and the synchronization software.

The batteries keep going and going.
> A pair of AAA batteries lasts most people a month or more of using the Palm-Pilot every day. *Weeks?* The average laptop battery won't run three *hours.* Even black-and-white Windows CE palmtops conk out after a week or so.

Syncing is simple.
> A single press of a single button brings your PC and your PalmPilot up to date with each other. Every name, address, appointment, or note you've jotted into your PalmPilot gets transferred to your PC—and vice versa—literally with the press of that single button. You can even synchronize your data on the road, by dialing into your home computer with a PalmPilot modem.

The software is elegantly designed.
> For example, when you're writing names and addresses, the PalmPilot capitalizes names automatically. And the day-at-a-glance calendar view concatenates empty hours, so that your entire day's agenda fits on one screen.

It talks to popular PC programs.

The PalmPilot comes with address-book, note-taking, and calendar programs for your desktop computer—software that exactly matches the software built into the PalmPilot. But most people *already* have calendar and address-book software. Fortunately, you can buy *conduit software* (plug-in modules that synchronize data with the PalmPilot's built-in programs) for almost any PC calendar or address book program, including Microsoft Outlook, Microsoft Schedule+, Lotus Organizer, Sidekick, ECCO Professional, Now Up-To-Date, Franklin Ascend, Day-Timer Organizer, Act!, GoldMine, Maximizer, and so on.

Such connectivity is, at long last, available to the Macintosh, too. Legions of Mac fans have embraced the PalmPilot as a result; after all, Windows CE palmtops can't talk to Macs at all.

There are thousands of free or inexpensive add-on programs.

3Com and US Robotics, the companies that created the PalmPilot, made it easy to write software for this machine. As a result, over 12,000 amateur and professional programmers are busily cranking out every conceivable kind of add-on software for the PalmPilot. Because they're written for the Palm OS, these programs tend to be especially fast, cleanly designed, and small; there's no such thing as a lengthy download of Palm software from the Internet! (You'll find many of these add-on programs on the CD-ROM that comes with this book.)

It's a cult.

The PalmPilot is the ultimate conversation-starter. On the train, on the plane, in the hallway—if somebody's using a PalmPilot, you've got a friend. Few other gadgets in the world have spawned so much obsessive behavior: there are PalmPilot web pages, PalmPilot conventions, and PalmPilot discussion groups on the Internet. There are also thousands of accessories, add-ons, and replacement components, from gold-plated inkless pens to calfskin carrying cases. You'll read more about them later in this book.

The History of the PalmPilot

The PalmPilot was the pet project of a young Silicon Valley entrepreneur named Jeff Hawkins. He'd watched device after device—the expensive, elegant Newton; the expensive, clunky Zoomer—bomb in the marketplace. Their failure was particularly depressing, because Hawkins's company—Palm Computing—was in the business of designing the software for such palmtops (including the Graffiti handwriting-recognition alphabet that's still used on PalmPilots).

He thought he knew why those other devices weren't successful. The experts were trying to cram too much into them. Industry experts laughed when he suggested a simpler, faster device that didn't have infrared and couldn't connect with corporate networks.

Finally, frustrated, Hawkins decided to design his *own* palmtop. He went on a personal crusade. He measured his own shirt pockets. Then, in a classic bit of engineering lore, he carved out a block of wood that's surprisingly close to the exact dimensions of today's PalmPilot. He'd walk around the company offices, seeing how it felt to write on the block's surface, honing the Graffiti alphabet, and defining the product in his head.

The design goals were to make it fast and simple; let it exchange data easily with a desktop computer; keep it shirt-pocket size; and have it cost less than $300.

Every expert and analyst argued with him over this last point. "Everyone wanted to put something else into it," Hawkins says. "Some people thought we were crazy for not having a device card slot."

For nearly a year, Hawkins shopped his prototype around to various electronics manufacturers. Most turned him down flat. Finally, US Robotics agreed to make the little device, and the first Pilots (as they were originally named) debuted in early 1996. Eventually, 3Com bought US Robotics. But Hawkins's company, Palm Computing, still works in its own protected division, making the best palmtop on Earth better every year.

Hawkins and his partner Donna Dubinski, meanwhile, left Palm Computing shortly after it became a 3Com subsidiary. Preferring the thrill of entrepreneurship to working for a huge corporation, they created a new startup company, Handspring, which is dedicated to bringing the Palm OS to new kinds of devices.

"PalmPilot" in the Name—and the Title

As with any computer, the Palm family is constantly being enhanced. The original 1996 models, the 1000 and 5000, were simply called *Pilots*. The next generation debuted in 1997 with backlit screens, improved software, email features, and the *Palm* prefix: the two models were the PalmPilot Personal and the PalmPilot Professional. (More about these model distinctions in Chapter 1, *The 3 × 5-Inch Powerhouse.*)

But the story didn't end there. In late 1997, IBM announced that it would begin selling PalmPilots under its own name: the *IBM WorkPad*. (The WorkPad is identical to the PalmPilot in nearly every way except for the color: it's black instead of PalmPilot gray.) Symbol then announced *its* own PalmPilot series—equipped with laser barcode readers—and several other companies will be joining the party.

Along the way, the lawyers of the Pilot Pen company got nervous. "We manufacture an inkless stylus for use on PalmPilot computers," they muttered. "The consumer will get confused!" After a legal tussle in a European court (where name-protection laws are more stringent than in the U.S.), 3Com was forced to drop the word Pilot from subsequent products.

That's why 3Com's products are now called the Palm III, Palm V, Palm VII, and so on—without the name Pilot. Unfortunately, instead of avoiding confusion, this change only adds to it: Microsoft calls its family of Windows CE-based PalmPilot knockoffs—*Palm PC* or *Palm-sized* computers!

So what's a poor book writer to do? What are we supposed to call this computer—and what am I supposed to call the book? I can't say "the Palm/PalmPilot/Work-Pad/Palm III" four times per paragraph. Nor does 3Com's suggestion work: they propose using "the 3Com connected organizer family" or "PalmPilot Computing ® platform devices" as the noun. No thanks—that'd bore you silly, pad the book out to 800 pages, and require the sacrifice of too many acres of rainforest.

Clearly, Pilot Pen's lawsuit has left 3Com with an intractable problem: the company no longer has a noun for its product line. "Palm" is an adjective—Palm Computing, Palm Central, and so on; few people say, "I gave my dad a Palm for his birthday." Because of this problem, most people—including, by the way, Palm Computing's own employees when they're not speaking officially—still call their handhelds PalmPilots, even though that name has been officially retired.

For the purposes of sanity and clarity, therefore, I'll call your palmtop, whatever the model, a PalmPilot, both in the text and the title. When an adjective alone would do, I'll humor Pilot Pen's lawyers by using "Palm," as in "Palm software" or "Palm accessories." Here's hoping you'll know what I mean.

Finally, there's the matter of trademarks. Palm Computing doesn't want its trademarks—HotSync, Palm V, Palm VII, and so on—to become generically used terms (like Kleenex or Rolodex). The company earnestly requests that writers about the Palm platform use its trademarks only as adjectives: "when you perform a HotSync operation" is correct, but "when you HotSync" isn't. Similarly, an author should never write: "You can beam data to any other Palm III, IIIx, V, or VII"; instead, the preferred wording is, "You can beam data to any other Palm III organizer, Palm IIIx organizer, Palm V organizer, or Palm VII organizer."

As you can see, a book-length document that stuck with Palm's guidelines would drive you quietly postal. In this book, I'll refer to individual models incorrectly—"Palm V," for example—and trust you to add the term "organizer" mentally as you read each occurrence.

What's New in the Second Edition

You might suppose that 3Com would have a hard time following up the Palm-Pilot. After all, piling on features, à la Windows CE, would threaten the very simplicity, speed, and elegance that made it a success to begin with.

Fortunately, the designers tread extremely carefully with their crown jewel. The Palm V, for example, doesn't offer a single change in its software; only the physical design has changed. Similarly, the Palm VII is identical to the Palm III in every way—with the single addition of wireless email and Web programs.

This edition of *PalmPilot: The Ultimate Guide* covers those new models, along with the third 1999 release, the Palm IIIx. (Appendix D, *Writing a Palm VII Query Application (PQA)*, even guides you through writing your own Web search programs for the Palm VII.) For Macintosh fans, 1999's big news was the long-awaited release of Palm Desktop for Macintosh, described in Chapter 9, *Palm Desktop: Macintosh*.

Recognizing the emergence of data collection as a leading PalmPilot use, you'll find a new chapter on using PalmPilot spreadsheets and databases. The new Appendix E, *Unix, Linux, and Palm*, covers the PalmPilot's connectivity with Unix and Linux, for the benefit of a growing group of passionate fans.

Finally, every chapter of this new edition offers new tricks, updates, shortcuts, and behind-the-scenes glimpses.

The only chapter you won't find in this book is the one on writing software for the PalmPilot. Because O'Reilly's full-length treatment of this topic, *Palm Programming: The Developer's Guide*, is now available, this book's programming chapter has been retired.

This book's CD-ROM has also been significantly enhanced with this new edition. This book has a new software partner—PalmCentral.com, the largest Internet site for Palm programs. The CD-ROM now features over 3,100 programs, including over 500 electronic books, hand-picked from the PalmCentral collection. It's all organized in a searchable, sortable, categorized database (the PalmCentral CD Catalog) that lets you read about, look at a picture of, and even install each of the programs onto your palmtop. (The database runs on Windows 9x, NT, and Macintosh; a text listing shows Linux and Unix users where the software is filed.) As a bonus, the PalmCentral CD Catalog even has live links to the Web pages of the software authors, plus a Show Me button that instantly opens each program's folder on the CD-ROM. See Appendix F, *About the CD-ROM*, for details.

Contents

This book covers every model of PalmPilot through June 1999, from the original Pilot model to the Palm VII. It takes you much deeper into the device's built-in programs than the manual does—and takes you far beyond them, into worlds the manual doesn't even mention, such as graphics, music, e-books, databases, spreadsheets, and the World Wide Web. The book is divided into parts, as follows:

Part I, *This Is Your PalmPilot Speaking*

> Chapter 1, *The 3×5-Inch Powerhouse*, is an introduction to the hardware itself—screen, stylus, buttons, batteries, and so on.

> Chapter 2, *Setup and Guided Tour*, tells you how to tailor the PalmPilot's preferences to suit your style and gives you a step-by-step walk-through of the PalmPilot in action.

> Chapter 3, *Typing Without a Keyboard*, answers the question, "If the Palm-Pilot has no keyboard, how do you enter text?" (By writing on its screen using the special Graffiti alphabet.) This chapter shows you how to get the most speed, accuracy, and comfort in writing in Graffiti and reviews several alternative writing systems.

> Chapter 4, *The Four Primary Programs*, explores in depth the Memo Pad, Address Book, To Do, and Date Book programs, plus other tricks and tips.

> Chapter 5, *The Other Built-In Programs*, covers the PalmPilot's less frequently discussed software: The Calculator, Find command, Expense tracker, and Security application, plus Giraffe and other games.

Part II, *Palm Meets PC*

> Chapter 6, *HotSync, Step by Step*, explores the hardware and software that let your PalmPilot talk to your desktop computer—which is one of its most important features.

> Chapter 7, *Installing New Palm Programs*, shows you how to add new programs onto the PalmPilot—and how to remove them again—using a desktop computer as a loading dock.

> Chapter 8, *Palm Desktop: Windows*, describes the functions and features of the PalmPilot's sister software, Palm Desktop, Windows version.

> Chapter 9, *Palm Desktop: Macintosh*, describes the functions and features of the PalmPilot's sister software, Palm Desktop, Mac version—part of 1999's long-awaited MacPac 2, which is included on this book's CD-ROM.

Part III, *The Undiscovered PalmPilot*

> Chapter 10, *PalmPilot: The Electronic Book*, explains how, thanks to programs like AportisDoc, the PalmPilot makes the perfect pocket novel or teleprompter.

Chapter 11, *The Secret Multimedia World*, details how, much to most people's surprise, the PalmPilot excels as a painting, drawing, photographic, and musical prodigy, using the software included with this book.

Chapter 12, *Database and Number Crunching*, reviews the leading database and spreadsheet software for the PalmPilot—and shows how you can synchronize it with your PC or Mac's database and spreadsheet programs.

Part IV, *The PalmPilot Online*

Chapter 13, *Email Anywhere*, explains how you can use your PalmPilot to do email, either directly via the Internet or using your PC as an intermediary.

Chapter 14, *The Web in Your Palm*, explains how to use the PalmPilot to surf the Web, complete with graphics, bookmarks, and other niceties.

Chapter 15, *Paging, Faxing, Printing, and Beaming*, shows how, for a computer with only one port, the PalmPilot is surprisingly adept at sharing its data.

Chapter 16, *Palm VII: Wireless Email, Wireless Web*, is exclusively for lucky owners of the Palm VII. This chapter guides you through writing and sending email, using PQAs (Palm Query Applications, which are web search miniprograms), and more—all wirelessly.

Part V, *Troubleshooting and Upgrading*

Chapter 17, *Troubleshooting*, is the place to turn on those rare occasions when something goes wrong with the PalmPilot.

Chapter 18, *The Palm Family, Model by Model*, covers the specs and upgrade options of each model.

Part VI, *Appendixes*

Appendix A, *100 Programs Worth Knowing About*, details 100 of the best of the thousands of Palm software programs out there.

Appendix B, *PalmPilot Accessories*, covers hardware add-ons for your PalmPilot: business-card scanners, global-positioning satellite systems, carrying cases, and more.

Appendix C, *Piloteers in Cyberspace*, is a listing of some of the most important web sites, discussion groups, and software archives for Piloteers.

Appendix D, *Writing a Palm VII Query Application (PQA)*, leads you through creating your own PQAs (Palm query applications), the tiny programs used by the Palm VII to search specific Web sites.

Appendix E, *Unix, Linux, and Palm*, reviews some of the leading programs that connect the PalmPilot to Unix and Linux machines.

Appendix F, *About the CD-ROM*, offers instruction in using this book's CD-ROM.

How to Contact Us

We have tested and verified all the information in this book to the best of our ability. If you have an idea that could make this book better, please let us know by writing to us at:

O'Reilly & Associates
101 Morris Street
Sebastopol, CA 95472
800-998-9938 (in the U.S. or Canada)
707-829-0515 (international/local)
707-829-0104 (fax)

You can also send messages electronically. To be put on our mailing list or to request a catalog, send email to:

nuts@oreilly.com

To ask technical questions or comment on the book, send email to the author at:

david@pogueman.com

As with any computer industry, events in the PalmPilot world move quickly. You can keep on top of the changing PalmPilot universe by visiting this book's web site, where you'll find updates and news:

http://PalmPilot.oreilly.com

Conventions Used in This Book

Italic is used for file names, functions, URLs, email addresses; text that you should type or write directly into the PalmPilot; emphasis; and to introduce new terms.

In many instances, bringing a particular option up on the Palm screen involves a trek through several menus and dialog boxes. To save paper and your patience, I'll use a notation like this:

Tap Menu → Options menu → Start Recording → OK button.

That notation means to tap the PalmPilot's Menu icon; then tap the Options menu title; from the dropped-down menu, choose Start Recording; and finally, tap the OK button in the resulting dialog box. In other words, just tap the words shown as you see them appear on the screen.

Acknowledgments

At the PalmPilot Computing division of 3Com, the spirit of openness and friendliness has made the PalmPilot OS platform a hit. The company embraces and promotes programmers, accessories, events, and *participation* in the PalmPilot business, continually fanning the fires of PalmPilot passion.

The same infectious excitement, I'm happy to say, extended to the preparation of this book. 3Com went beyond the call of duty over and over again to help. In particular, my master contact Chris Weasler repeatedly interrupted his regularly scheduled duties to answer tweaky questions, provide technical background, and much more. He orchestrated helpful briefing sessions with Palm's Mike Lundsford and Joe Sipher that paved the way for this book's Palm V and Palm VII coverage.

3Com's Maurice Sharp was my other Friend in High Places. Not only was he once again an outstanding technical reviewer for this edition (as he was for the first edition), but nobody is more fun to hang around with at trade shows. Tech reviewer Dan Royea, moderator of the weekly Internet Palm chats and knower of all things Palm, set me straight on hundreds of technical points; Chapter 17, *Troubleshooting*, especially benefitted from his wisdom.

In fact, the best part of writing a Palm book was getting to know the amazing people who work at Palm. That they've let me into the family, welcomed me to trade shows, advance briefings, and their own headquarters in Santa Clara, California, has been a head rush nonpareil. Thanks especially to Robin Abrams, Douglas Wirnowski, Liz Brookings, Andrea Butter, Amy Nemechek (of A&R Partners), Elizabeth Cardinale, David Christopher, Dawn Hannah, Mark Bercow, Gabriel Acosta-Lopez, and everyone else I've been lucky enough to meet.

Two of this book's appendixes were written by friendly experts in their fields: Appendix D, *Writing a Palm VII Query Application (PQA)*, was written by the project lead for the Palm VII's Clipper software, Dave Menconi. And Linux expert Brian Pinto was kind enough to write Appendix E, *Unix, Linux, and Palm.*

This book's completely new CD-ROM was made possible by PalmCentral.com's curator, Dr. Raymond Lau of MIT, who spent months on the project, creating screenshots and e-books where none existed, coding the auto-install and "Show Me" features, and otherwise achieving the impossible—for no money, I might add. When we reached obstacles, programmer-at-large John Holder came through, writing custom code to make the Mac and Windows installation features work smoothly.

First-edition assistance came from Neil Salkind, Fredlet, Frank Colin, Eric Cloninger, Brian Ball (ISO Productions); John Perr (Puma Technologies); David Schargel (Aportis); David Rogelberg (Studio B); John Allman (PalmPilot tech support); Dave Marks (Metrowerks); and many hardware and software companies who contributed review units and expertise.

Above all, my gratitude goes to the team at O'Reilly & Associates who shepherded this book into existence with enthusiasm and pride—Troy Mott, Katie Gardner, Tara McGoldrick, Bob Herbstman, Nancy Kotary, Maureen Dempsey, Clairemarie Fisher O'Leary, Colleen Gorman, Mike Sierra, Robert Romano, Seth Maislin, Lisa Mann, Sarah Winge, Mark Stone, and Tim O'Reilly; and the lovely Dr. Pogue and kids, who patiently waited for the actual family life that might begin when this book was finished.

I

This Is Your PalmPilot Speaking

1

The 3 × 5-Inch Powerhouse

PalmPilot Basics

Before you fall in love with your little machine, spend a moment marveling that it's actually nothing more than a pile of plastic, silicon, and glass. Most PalmPilot models are 4.7 inches tall, 3.1 inches wide, and 0.6 inches thick (the Palm V is shorter and half as thick; the Palm VII is slightly taller). It weighs between 4 and 6 ounces and has a 160-pixel-square grayscale, touch-sensitive screen. A Motorola 68328 (Dragonball) processor chip inside runs a special operating system called the Palm OS that—talk about optimized!—uses only about 40K of memory. (If you're keeping score at home, that's about one-quarter of 1 percent of the memory required by Windows 9x.)

The PalmPilot has no moving parts and doesn't accept disks of any kind; everything it knows is stored in memory, which helps explain why this machine is so fast and so rugged. Many of the usual encumbrances and trouble spots of actual computers simply don't exist on the PalmPilot. For example, there's no startup delay when you press the power button. Nor is there a Save command; your work in progress is always kept up-to-date automatically. A "launching pad" screen lists all your programs and lets you choose which to work with—but programs load instantaneously, and there's no Quit command. You eventually come to feel as though *all* your programs are always running.

The PalmPilot has no keyboard, either; to get information into it, you can either "write" on the glass, tap a tiny onscreen keyboard, or transfer stuff from your real computer. These data-input methods will be covered in depth in Chapter 3, *Typing Without a Keyboard*, and Chapter 6, *HotSync, Step by Step*.

The Buttons

Because it has no keyboard and no mouse, you operate the device by tapping its surface with two important pointing devices: (a) the *stylus,* the inkless pen tucked into a pocket at the edge of the machine, and (b) your finger.

The plastic buttons

Using your finger, you can press any of the four round buttons near the bottom of the PalmPilot. These plastic buttons are called the *hardware buttons;* they're real, physical buttons that depress when pushed, unlike the painted-on glass buttons you'll read about shortly. Each of these buttons launches one of the PalmPilot's primary built-in programs. As a handy shortcut, each of these buttons also turns the device on before launching the appropriate program, saving you a step if you're in a hurry to get going. Put another way, the PalmPilot has five On buttons. (See Figure 1-1.)

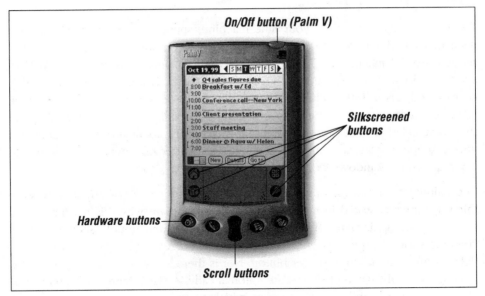

Figure 1-1. The fundamental components of the PalmPilot.

 When you first buy a PalmPilot, the four hardware buttons are assigned to the Calendar, Phone Book, To Do list, and Memo pad programs, respectively—and labeled with appropriate icons. However, you can reassign these buttons to launch other programs instead; see Chapter 2, *Setup and Guided Tour,* for details. For now, just remember that if you never use the To Do list, for example, you may as well teach it to launch, say, Space Invaders instead.

Nestled in the center of these four buttons are two smaller buttons. (On recent models, they're opposite ends of a single rocker switch.) These are the up and down *scroll buttons,* which let you view information "above" or "below" what's currently on the screen. For example, if you're reading a novel, press the bottom scroll button to see the next page of text. (Among fans of Palm books—and there are many such fans and many such books—a gripping novel isn't described as "a real page-turner"; it's called "a real button-pusher.")

The glass buttons

In addition to the four gray plastic buttons, your PalmPilot has four important "buttons" painted on the bottom part of the glass screen. These round tappable areas are sometimes called *silk buttons* or *silkscreened buttons,* because they've been painted onto the glass using a silkscreening method. On older models these icon/buttons have written labels; on the Palm IIIx, Palm VII, and so on, you'll just have to pretend. Here's what they do:

Applications

Tap this button, either with the stylus or your finger, to view the master launching-pad for all your programs, as shown in Figure 1-2.

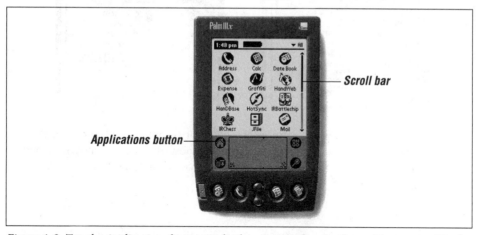

Figure 1-2. Tap the Applications button to display your application-launching screen. Use the scroll buttons to view extra programs if you have more than 12.

If you have more than 12 programs on your PalmPilot—and by the time you're finished with this book, you probably will—you'll have to scroll down to see additional screens. To scroll, either press one of the plastic scroll buttons with your finger, or tap one of the up/down triangle buttons on the scroll bar shown in Figure 1-2.

Different Screens for Different Apps

On the Palm III and later models, you can place your installed applications into *categories*—all your games on one category screen, your utilities in another, your Internet programs in another.

To switch from one category "page" to another, the long way is to tap the category pop-up menu in the upper-right corner of the screen, as shown below at left, and tap to make a choice. The short way: repeatedly tap the Applications icon (on the PalmPilot itself). With each tap, you'll be shown the next category page.

So how do you create a new category of your own? Chapter 4, *The Four Primary Programs*, contains details on the PalmPilot's Category mechanism. For now, though, just tap the pop-up Category menu in the upper-right corner of the Applications screen → Edit Categories → New and write the name of your new category.

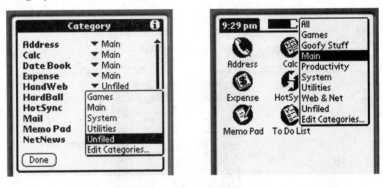

And to put an installed program *into* a category—onto a different category "page"—tap the Menu icon. Tap Category to view the screen shown above (left). Tap the pop-up menu to the right of a program's name to choose a different category for it.

The need for scrolling if you have more than 12 programs installed has inspired the world's programmers to create superior program-launching methods. For example, the program called SwitchHack (included on the CD-ROM that accompanies this book) offers you a handy list, as shown in Figure 1-3, on the left. Switching among programs is as easy as choosing from a list. (See Appendix A, *100 Programs Worth Knowing About*, for details on SwitchHack.) Similarly, on the Palm III and later models, you're offered a list view that fits many more application icons on a single screen (see Figure 1-3, right).

Figure 1-3. With one stylus stroke, summon your list of recently opened programs, bypassing the Applications screen, thanks to SwitchHack (left). Alternatively, you can use the list view of the Palm III and later models (right): tap Menu → Options → Preferences → List → OK.

Once you become skilled at the Graffiti alphabet (see Chapter 3), you don't have to press the scroll buttons to bring more applications into view on your Applications launcher screen. Instead, it's often faster to write the first letter of the program you want in the Graffiti writing area. The Applications screen scrolls instantly to the nearest alphabetical match.

Menu

Upon first inspection of the PalmPilot's tiny screen, you might not guess that its operating system uses pull-down menus, exactly as in Windows and the Macintosh. But they're there, all right, in any situation where they'd be useful—while word processing, for example. In some situations, there may be no menus at all; in others, the menus may change according to what you're doing, even within the same program.

Tapping the Menu button makes the normally invisible menu bar appear at the top of the screen, as shown in Figure 1-4. That Menu button also makes the leftmost menu drop down all by itself, serving as a foolproof reminder that you've just requested the menus' presence.

Once the first menu has dropped, you can tap the names of other menus to make them drop down. They stay down, too, exactly as in Windows or Mac OS 8. To make the menus go away, either make a selection from one of them or—if none of the commands strikes your fancy—tap anywhere else on the screen to put the menus away without making a choice.

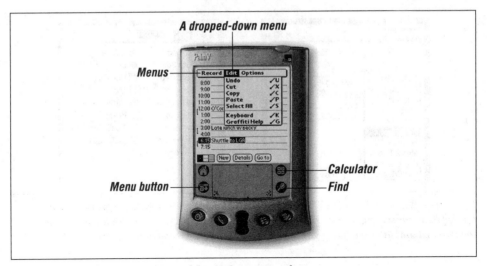

Figure 1-4. Tap the Menu icon to summon the menus, if any.

Calculator

Tapping this silk button turns your palmtop into the world's most expensive four-function calculator—with buttons so big you can use your fingers. See Chapter 5, *The Other Built-In Programs*, for a complete discussion of this minimalist application.

Find

If you've filed something away but can't remember which program it was in, tap Find. The resulting dialog box lets you specify what you want to search for—and you're shown any resulting matches regardless of which Palm program they're in. See Chapter 4's "Four Global Palm Features" section for full coverage.

If you're used to Windows or Mac menus—and you almost certainly are, since the PalmPilot is designed for people who also use a desktop computer—you'll probably find the PalmPilot's menu-summoning mechanism one of its few clunky features. After all, it's not very natural to tap the *bottom* of the screen when you want to make menus appear at the *top*.

That's why MenuHack has become so popular. It's a free, tiny, add-on program that makes the menus appear when you tap the top of the screen, exactly as in Windows or the Mac. MenuHack, included with this book's CD-ROM, is described in Appendix A, *100 Programs Worth Knowing About*.

The Serial Port

There's only one place to plug anything into the PalmPilot: at the *serial port,* the connector on the bottom. Peer into the cavity there—on some models, you must first push up the spring-loaded plastic panel at the back of the bottom—to see the ten copper contacts. Into this jack, you can plug any of the following:

The HotSync cradle

This little matching stand came with your PalmPilot. It's a sloping base into which you can place the PalmPilot itself; a cable from the cradle plugs into your PC. The cradle has one single button on it—the HotSync button—which automatically begins the process of swapping information between the PalmPilot and your PC, a process known as HotSyncing. (Details on HotSync can be found in Chapter 6.) As you'll find out in Chapter 2, you can reprogram this HotSync button to perform other handy tasks when you're not in the mood for HotSyncing.

The HotSync cable

What's nice about the HotSync cradle is that it's sturdy, simple, and free with your PalmPilot. Unfortunately, its backbone juts out at a 45-degree angle, making it unwieldy for the traveler who likes to pack light. For $15, you can buy a *HotSync cable,* which attaches to the same place on the PalmPilot but has no bulky or angular components. It plugs directly into your PC and performs exactly the same function. (See Appendix B, *PalmPilot Accessories,* for details.)

The Palm V AC adapter

Although the Palm V generally gets recharged by sitting in its HotSync cradle, that may not be a convenient arrangement if you plan to travel. In that case, $50 buys you the Palm V Travel Kit, which contains a non-bulky power cord and several outlet adapters for foreign countries.

The Palm modem

Never in a million years would you guess that this tiny gadget can actually send email, send faxes, browse the World Wide Web, and even *create* web pages, but it can. All you need is the $130 PalmPilot modem. It snaps onto the bottom of the PalmPilot, just as the cradle does, and accepts its own batteries, so as not to deplete the PalmPilot's batteries. (The Palm V requires its own, specially designed modem; see Appendix B.) As a bonus, the modem lets you synchronize the data between your PalmPilot and your PC at home—no matter where you are in the world. See Chapter 6 for more on this stunt; Part IV, *The PalmPilot Online,* for details on going online with the PalmPilot; and Appendix B for buying information.

The Palm modem cable

If you want to use your PalmPilot for online exploits, you're not obligated to buy the PalmPilot modem. You can instead buy a $20 *Palm modem cable,* which connects the PalmPilot to the external modem you already own. The modem cable can plug into most pocket modems, as well as most standard external modems.

Amazingly, the community of Palm fans isn't finished with that serial port yet. You can outfit it with a phone dialer; TV remote control; GPS (Global Positioning Satellite) receiver; voice recorder; scientific measuring probe; portable keyboard; tiny flashlight in your choice of red, white, or blue; or even a tiny vibrator that signals you silently when one of your Date Book alarms goes off—a big hit among the physicians-at-the-symphony set. (Appendix B has details on these products.)

Unfortunately, the HotSync port accommodates only one of these impressive devices at a time; the world still waits for a single, all-in-one accessory.

Tips for the Differently Handed

Only one class of customer hasn't been uniformly ecstatic about their Palm experience: left-handed people. Some grouse that Palm applications' scroll bar is on the right side, forcing the left hand to block the screen when scrolling. They complain that the left hand, when writing, tends to bump the on/off button—a definite drawback. And then there's the issue of the stylus itself: its storage slot is on the *right* side of the device (except on the Palm V, which offers slots on both sides).

Lefties aren't powerless to combat this form of manual discrimination, however. At the Lefty Pilot Users web site (*http://strout.net/info/pilot/leftypilot/intro.html*), you'll find a wealth of tips for coping. You can even download Lefty, a tiny program that makes "Lefty-aware" Palm programs automatically display scroll bars (and other right-favored elements) on the left side of the screen.

The Stylus, Screen, and Light

The PalmPilot's screen is pressure-sensitive; in other words, it's a touch screen. There's nothing magical about the stylus included with the device—it's not magnetic, or electrostatic, or otherwise gimmicked. The PalmPilot can't tell whether it's being touched by the stylus, or, say, your fingernail (although unless you've got some kind of rare genetic condition, the stylus is probably more precise than your fingernail). In other words, if you lose your stylus, almost anything will do as a replacement, including any of the fancy gold-plated inkless pens sold by Cross and others just for use with handheld computers. (See Appendix B for some replacement stylus possibilities.) Many experienced Palm addicts use an ordinary ball-point pen—with the tip retracted, of course. Ink from a pen or graphite from a pencil can damage the screen.

Generally speaking, the LCD (liquid-crystal display) screen is black-and-white. (Technically, it's *grayscale,* like a "black-and-white" TV, capable of creating four or sixteen gradations of gray—but few programs make use of this little-known feature. See Chapter 11, *The Secret Multimedia World,* and Chapter 14, *The Web in Your Palm,* for some examples.)

Therefore, the PalmPilot screen generally creates its image with tiny, solid black dots against the gray-green background. Still, this characteristic doesn't deal quite as severe a blow to the device's graphics potential as you might think. More on the PalmPilot's graphics skills in Chapter 11.

Contrast Knob

As on any LCD screen, the clarity of the PalmPilot's display varies dramatically according to the temperature of the device and the angle at which you're viewing it. The screen is actually a sandwich of glass; in the middle, 25,600 tiny individual squares float in a gooey liquid. Each little square, or *pixel,* is controlled by a minute electric current. When a particular pixel is instructed to do so, it rotates in the gooey fluid so that instead of floating parallel to your line of vision, its full square surface is facing you, blocking the transmission of light. The result: a tiny black square dot.

All this is a complicated way of saying this: whenever you turn the PalmPilot on for the first time in a work session, fiddle with the contrast knob (see Figure 1-5). A little tweaking will do wonders for your eyesight—and save on battery life, as described next.

The Backlight

One of the key differences between the original Pilot and its successors (such as the PalmPilot and Palm III) was the addition of a *backlighting* feature. You couldn't use the original Pilot in the dark—a devastating blow to the world's coal miners, theater critics, and electricians.

On more recent models, however, if you press the on/off button (see Figure 1-5) for two seconds or more, you turn on the backlight. The screen is suddenly bathed by an eerie *X-Files*-ish glow, making the PalmPilot useful to night-shift workers at last. Press the power button a second time (again, two seconds or longer) to turn the backlighting off.

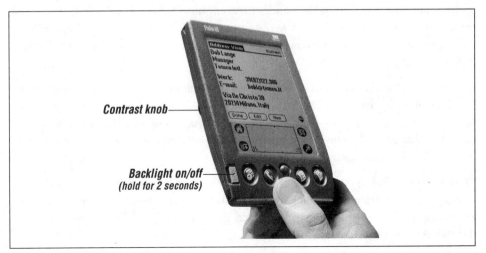

Figure 1-5. The contrast knob can make a huge difference to the PalmPilot's screen clarity. Adjust it once per day! (On the Palm V, the onscreen contrast slider appears only when you press the top-edge button.)

It's easy to understand why the original Pilot's designers didn't want to add back-lighting to begin with; one of the palmtop's most appealing features is its stinginess with battery juice. The backlight, however, more than doubles the PalmPilot's power consumption, draining the batteries like crazy. That's why you're encouraged to use the backlighting sparingly, unless you (a) use recharge-able batteries, or (b) work at Duracell.

That business about pressing the on/off button for two full seconds can be inconvenient when you're in a hurry. Fortunately, the Palm-Pilot offers a much faster method of turning the backlight on and off—you can just draw a giant line up the screen. The light springs on instantly; another slash up the glass turns the light off again. To configure your PalmPilot so that it uses the slashlight method, see Chapter 2.

Battery Notes

If you've owned a PalmPilot for more than a month or so, you've already discov-ered one of its most delicious features: you simply don't have to worry about power. A pair of AAA batteries lasts many people six weeks or more, and the Palm V's permanent lithium ion battery is charging whenever the palmtop is in its HotSync cradle. There *is* a quick, easy way to check your current batteries' remain-ing juice—just tap the Applications button to view a "fuel gauge" of remaining power—but most people don't bother. On the PalmPilot, batteries last so long that the feeling of "battery deadline panic," well known to laptop computer users, simply doesn't exist.

When you do need to change your batteries, look at the back of the machine. You'll see the battery-compartment panel just below the midline (on all models except the Palm V, of course). Press the latch with your thumb, remove the panel, and change the batteries.

How much time do you have? 3Com officially encourages you to put in new batteries within five minutes of removing the old ones. But informal tests show you've actually got longer than that; the built-in *capacitor* (an electronic component that stores a charge for a long time) actually maintains enough juice to preserve your data—even with no batteries installed—for about 11 minutes. Still, if you're paranoid, always do a HotSync (see Chapter 6), thus backing up your PalmPilot's information, before changing the batteries.

Other than the Palm V's cradle, there's no such thing as an AC power adapter for the PalmPilot. You may, however, have good luck with rechargeable batteries. On one hand, a charge doesn't last nearly as long in the PalmPilot as a pair of disposable alkaline batteries; on the other hand, you don't have to buy new ones until you've recharged yours, say, 500 times. See Chapter 17, *Troubleshooting*, for battery-conservation tips and a discussion of specific battery brands.

The Lineup of Models

The PalmPilot, like any computer, is constantly being reinvented and enhanced. Within the first three years of existence, 12 different models were available from four different companies, and the operating system had been upgraded eight times. As you read this book, and as you go on through life, identifying what model and system software you're using will be increasingly important.

Here's a brief guide to the history of Palm models; for more detail, tips and tricks for individual models, and a list of upgrading options, see Chapter 18, *The Palm Family, Model by Model.*

Pilot 1000, Pilot 5000

These original models were the first to capture the world's attention—they proved that, despite the failures of many previous gadgets from other companies, a palmtop could indeed become a mass-market best-seller.

They were boxy and limited by today's standards (see Figure 1-6). They had non-backlit screens, had no email or Internet capability, and the less expensive model had only 128K of RAM. But the HotSync process worked like a charm, the batteries lasted forever, and absolutely nobody felt overwhelmed by the software.

PalmPilot Personal, PalmPilot Professional

The newly named PalmPilot models debuted in 1997 with backlighting, greatly enhanced built-in programs (part of Palm OS 2.0), and an Expense application. As the manufacturer relaxed about the product's success in the business world, it also wrote four addictive games to include in the package (they're described in Chapter 4).

The Professional model (shown in Figure 1-6) also included TCP/IP capability, so that the device could connect to company networks or the Internet, and a built-in Mail program that could transfer email to and from your desktop computer via HotSync (see Chapter 13, *Email Anywhere*, for details). Its generous 1MB of memory made room for all this extra data.

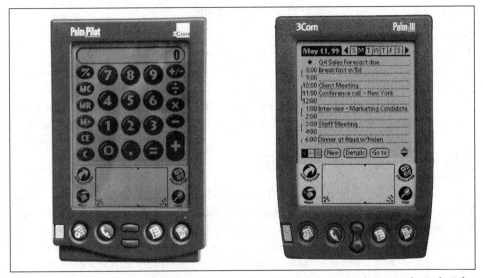

Figure 1-6. The Palm III (right) has a slightly sleeker shape than its predecessor, the PalmPilot (left).

Palm III

The 1998 model's name was the first to omit the word Pilot, although millions of befuddled fans still continue to use the word Pilot or PalmPilot to describe all of these palmtops (as this book does). Its primary features were infrared beaming (see Chapter 15, *Paging, Faxing, Printing, and Beaming*), a new operating system (3.0) that included a choice of fonts for each program, and two megabytes of memory. All of this came in a sleeker, more tapered case (see Figure 1-6)—with a flip-up lid.

IBM WorkPad

Selling its devices under the name WorkPad, IBM makes black, not gray, editions of the Palm III, Palm IIIx, and Palm V. Except for the case color, they're identical to their Palm Computing counterparts.

Symbol SPT 1500

Symbol Technologies (*http://www.symbol.com/palm*) makes portable barcode-reading machines. It's only natural, then, that the company would be attracted to the potential of the PalmPilot's sleek shape and sharp features. The result is the Symbol SPT1500, an extended Palm III whose extra height houses a laser-beam barcode reader (see Figure 1-7).

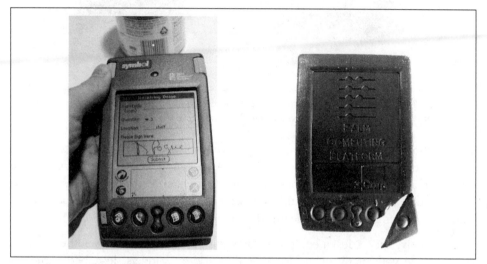

Figure 1-7. The Symbol SPT 1500 (left) adds a barcode scanner to the top of a Palm III. It's somewhat more functional than the never-released chocolate PalmPilot (right).

Palm IIIx

1999's Palm IIIx is almost identical to the Palm III—at least as far as the software and workings are concerned. But the Palm IIIx has twice the memory (a total of 4MB), a much sharper screen, and a more rugged design. It's also based on a new processor, the Motorola Dragonball EZ, which opens the way for less expensive memory upgrades down the road.

Palm V

The expensive, gorgeous, ultra-thin Palm V is the first PalmPilot to be housed in brushed aluminum, not plastic (see Figure 1-8). As with the Palm IIIx, there aren't any new features to distinguish the software—but the hardware story is exciting enough. This model is half as thick, half an inch shorter, and 25% lighter than previous models.

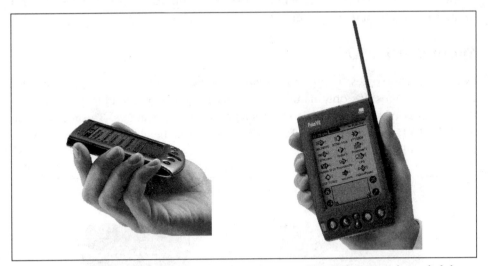

Figure 1-8. The Palm V, left, is the smallest Palm device yet. The Palm VII, right, is slightly taller than a standard PalmPilot, thanks to its built-in two-way radio circuitry.

The built-in lithium-ion battery recharges whenever the device is sitting in its HotSync cradle; Palm V owners never buy AAA batteries. The device runs for a month on a single charge, and one HotSync a day is enough time in the cradle to keep it full. Meanwhile, the Palm V's screen is the best ever to appear on a PalmPilot, better even than the Palm IIIx screen.

Unfortunately, the redesigned, power-drawing HotSync jack makes the Palm V incompatible with many of the HotSync-port add-on gadgets described earlier in this chapter, such as the vibrator and GPS receiver. (Adapters will soon be available.) And when the Palm V is carried in a tight shirt pocket, its raised scroll buttons have a tendency to turn the machine on and start chattering as pressure holds them down. Otherwise, though, the Palm V is every bit the status-symbol PalmPilot the manufacturer intended.

Palm VII

Before the Palm VII, there were ways to surf the Internet without being plugged into a phone line. You could buy a wireless modem for your laptop or PalmPilot. You could attach the proper cables, sign up for the proper $50-per-month service, and say the proper prayers.

The Code-Name Game

It's a longstanding Silicon Valley tradition for engineers to devise witty code names for their products before they're released to the public, and Palm Computing is no exception. The code name for the Palm III, for example, was Rocky, named for the Sylvester Stallone movie. Subtext: "We're the underdog who's gonna knock big bully Microsoft out of the ring." (Rumors that the Palm III was code-named for the flying squirrel on this book's cover, a reference to the classic Bullwinkle TV cartoons, have been vigorously denied.)

The Palm V was something else again. The unit is so thin, and its metal case so sharp-looking, that its original code name was a no-brainer: Razor. Unfortunately, that code name was too good, hinting too much about the then-secret project for Palm Computing's comfort. As leaks began to surface on the Internet, the company changed the code name to Sumo, so that it could now issue a truthful red-herring statement to the press that, in fact, there was no device in the works called Razor.

The Palm VII's code name, confusingly enough, was Eleven. But one rental of the movie *This Is Spinal Tap* makes all clear: In that hilarious spoof rockumentary, a spirited but none-too-bright band member exhibits a custom amplifier he's had built, featuring a volume knob whose highest setting is 11. Most amplifiers, he explains, go up only to 10—but this one goes up to 11.

Anyone who's used a Palm VII after having grown up with standard PalmPilots would have to agree—this one goes up to 11.

But the Palm VII is the first all-in-one, no-cables-necessary, ready-to-use wireless gizmo to take the world by storm. Only half an inch taller than the standard PalmPilot (see Figure 1-8), the VII's flip-up antenna instantly turns the device on. For $10 per month, you can now send or receive wireless email, or query specific web sites for useful data (such as weather, sports, news, stock quotes, cash-machine locations, flight schedules, package-tracking info, phone numbers from the White Pages, local movie showtimes, and so on). Details on these wireless features are in Chapter 16, *Palm VII: Wireless Email, Wireless Web*.

Except for its two new applications—iMessenger for email, Clipper for web queries—the Palm VII's software is otherwise identical to that of the Palm III, IIIx, and V. The engineering surprise is the built-in NiCad battery (which accounts for the extra height), which helps to counter the power drain of the built-in two-way radio.

The Secret of the Odd-Numbered Palm Models

It comes up at every cocktail party: Whatever did happen to the Palm IV and Palm VI? Why is Palm dedicated to odd-numbered models—III, V, and VII?

Answer: No modern, globally aware company would dare market a product called the Palm IV; in Japan, 4 is an ominous number foretelling bad luck.

As for the name "Palm VI"—well, if you had a revolutionary wireless Internet device to market, wouldn't "Palm VII" have a much luckier ring to it?

Qualcomm pdQ

What do you get when you cross the PalmPilot with a cell phone? The Qualcomm pdQ SmartPhone (see Figure 1-9). The Palm screen is nestled in the handset, so that the circuitry can dial, or send email to or visit the web site of anyone in your Address Book program. The device is a full-fledged PalmPilot otherwise, complete with a HotSync cradle and the usual built-in software. (For a full discussion of the email and web programs built into the SmartPhone, see Chapters 13 and 14. And see Chapter 18 for more detail on this gadget and all the others described in this section.)

Figure 1-9. It's a cell phone. It's a PalmPilot. It's a cell phone and a PalmPilot: the Qualcomm pdQ.

Future Models

Palm Computing introduced four new models in the first half of 1999 alone, and it isn't finished yet. Like any high-tech company, it keeps its products secret until they're ready. It's safe to assume, however, that the future will bring PalmPilot models with improvements in battery life, memory capacity, price, and—especially in light of the Palm V's enormous success—case designs. Future editions of this book, and its web site at *http://palmpilot.oreilly.com,* will keep you posted.

Executive Tip Summary

- If you have a lot of programs installed on your PalmPilot, also install Switch-Hack. It lets you jump to other programs directly, bypassing the Applications screen. (More on SwitchHack in Appendix A.)

- You can scroll the Applications screen by writing the first letter of the program you want on the Graffiti writing area.

- You can switch from one "category page" of applications to the next by tapping the Applications silkscreen button repeatedly. (Not available on Pilot and PalmPilot models.)

- MenuHack (see Appendix A) lets you pull down menus by tapping at the *top* of the screen, where you'd expect, instead of tapping the Menu icon at the bottom of the unit.

2

Setup and Guided Tour

Setting Up Your Palmtop

Your PalmPilot may be no bigger than a pocket calculator, but it's infinitely more flexible. Read this section with palmtop in hand; in the process, you'll not only get a gentle tour of the interface, but also tailor its operation to your own working style.

Aligning the Screen Layers

The very first time you turn on your palmtop, or after having reset it (see Chapter 17, *Troubleshooting*), you're walked through a series of setup steps. On recent models, such as the Palm IIIx, Palm V, and Palm VII, this series of startup screens forms a miniature crash course in using the device. One screen offers instructions for setting up HotSyncing; another gives you a miniature Graffiti handwriting-recognition tutorial.

No matter which model you have, however, an important part of the startup sequence is aligning the digitizer. That's when you're asked to tap three specific spots on your reading, one at a time, as shown in Figure 2-1.

The screen is actually two superimposed layers: the one you can see, which displays text and graphics, and the clear, pressure-sensitive overlay, which detects your taps and other stylus activity. Because of possible variations on the angle at which you hold the device, the PalmPilot needs to learn how the two layers are assigned at this moment on your particular unit. The "Tap center of target" routine asks you to tap three points in succession; the software notices where you tap, and adjusts its notion of the touch-sensitive layer's position accordingly.

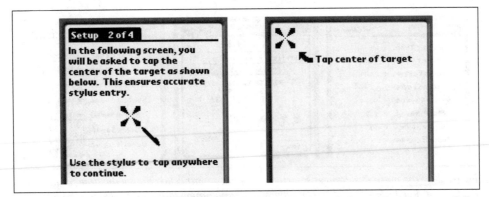

Figure 2-1. To ensure that your stylus tip is aligned correctly with the touch screen, carefully tap in the center of the targets the PalmPilot offers you.

In general, you encounter this screen-alignment business only when you turn the PalmPilot on for the very first time. On rare occasions, however, you may want to summon the screen test manually (for example, if your taps don't all seem to be registering). Tap Applications → Prefs, and on the following screen, tap the pop-up menu in the upper-right corner of the screen. Choose Digitizer to begin the alignment test. (If you're ever in the mood to play a practical joke on some uppity Palm fan, invoke the alignment routine—but deliberately tap a quarter inch to the right of the target each time. Put the palmtop back where you found it, and then wait for the hilarity to begin.)

Setting the Time and Date

Immediately after the screen-alignment test, you're asked to set the time, date, and country settings. The software assumes that you've either just purchased your PalmPilot or deliberately reset it, and so it guesses these preference settings probably need to be adjusted, too.

Setting the time and date is easy—once you figure out that you're supposed to tap *on* the time and date to set them (see Figure 2-2).

Tap the time to bring up a digital clock display, where you can adjust the numbers shown by tapping on one, and then repeatedly tapping the black up- or down-triangle buttons. Tap a.m. or p.m., if necessary, then tap the OK button.

Setting the date works the same way: Tap the currently displayed date to view the calendar shown in Figure 2-2. From here, first adjust, if necessary, the year (by tapping the left- or right-pointing triangles at the top of the screen), then the month (by tapping the correct month's name), and finally the date (by tapping on the calendar square itself). You should change the date of the month *last,* because tapping one of the individual calendar squares also acts as an OK button, returning you to the main Preferences screen.

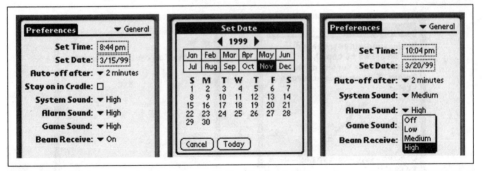

Figure 2-2. The main Preferences screen (left) offers a chance to change the time or date. Tap the time or date to bring up a screen where you can change it. For example, tap the date to bring up a calendar display (middle). The most recent models offer volume control for each sound effect (right).

If you haven't yet changed the date of the month, though, and want to back out, tap Cancel to return to the main Preferences screen without changing anything. You can safely ignore the Today button altogether. It has no purpose here—if the date were already showing today's date, you wouldn't be changing it! This calendar display is used elsewhere on the PalmPilot, in the appointment-book program, for example, and the Today button is useful in that case to mean "show me the appointments for today."

The "Sleep" Interval and Sound Control Panel

If you're using a Pilot, PalmPilot, or Palm III model, you've been using the Preferences application to set the time and date. If you have a more recent model, the end of the startup/crash-course sequence deposits you at the main Applications launcher screen. Tap Prefs.

No matter which model you have, you should now find several other useful controls before you:

Auto-off after

    If the PalmPilot notices that you haven't actually been *doing* anything for a couple of minutes, it shuts itself off automatically to conserve battery power. (Actually, it just goes into its standard "sleep" mode—all your work is preserved. Because returning to exactly what you were doing involves a single press of the on/off button, the PalmPilot's going to sleep is no big deal.) This pop-up menu lets you adjust that period of inactivity before a shutoff: your choices are one, two, or three minutes. If you're reading a PalmPilot novel, for example, and you find yourself taking more than two minutes to read a screenful before pressing the "next page" scroll button, change the auto-off time to three minutes.

The Five Components of the PalmPilot Interface

Changing the time and date, if you've been following along on your own PalmPilot, does more than teach the PalmPilot what time it is. It also teaches you about three important PalmPilot interface elements:

Dotted-outline rectangles

In Figure 2-2, you can see that a dotted-line box surrounds the time. These dotted lines are your cue that what's inside is tappable—that tapping there will *do* something.

Black triangle buttons

These up/down or left/right pairs of onscreen buttons let you increase or decrease whatever number you're seeing. On the calendar display, you can tap the left triangle to change the date to the previous year, and the right one for the next year.

Standard pushbuttons

If you've used a Mac or PC, you're familiar with these standard, oval-enclosed text buttons, like the Cancel and Today buttons shown in Figure 2-2. Tap one to execute the command displayed on the button. (When the button's name includes ellipses—the three periods shown on, for example a "Delete . . . " button—tapping the button won't do anything immediately. Instead, tapping the button will simply make a new dialog box appear, and you can take action there.)

When you change the "sleep" interval and sound controls as explained in this chapter, you'll encounter the two other recurring control elements:

Pop-up menus

The PalmPilot manual calls these mid-screen menus *pick lists,* but the idea is the same as pop-up menus on Macs and Windows machines. Wherever you see a down-pointing triangle next to a text label (see the "Auto-off after" setting in Figure 2-2, for example), you can tap the text to make a menu of options drop down. The list stays down until you tap one of the choices—or tap outside the menu to make no selection at all. Occasionally, by the way, the pop-up menu is too tall to fit on the screen. (The list of country presets on the PalmPilot models' Formats Prefs screen is one example.) In such cases, you'll see an up- or down-pointing arrow in the list of choices. Tap that arrow—or press the plastic scroll buttons—to move through the list.

Checkboxes

Tap to make the check mark appear (to turn the option on), and again to turn the option off—just as on desktop computers.

On rare occasions, you may not want your Palm device to turn itself off at all, such as when you're reading from its screen or studying a map while driving. Although it's not mentioned in the manual, a secret technique can override the auto-shutoff feature. For the complete procedure, see "Secrets of the Dot Commands" in Chapter 17, *Troubleshooting.*

Stay on in cradle

This option appears only on the Palm V. It permits the device to remain turned on, with no auto-shutoff, as long as it's sitting in its HotSync cradle. Since the Palm V's built-in batteries are recharging whenever the device is in its cradle, there's no downside to leaving it on all day (screen burn-in doesn't affect the Palm's LCD screen). This checkbox, then, presents a perfect opportunity to keep your schedule, phone book, or loved one's photo visible at all times.

System sound

The PalmPilot has a tiny but effective speaker that makes tiny but effective sounds: the clicks when you tap onscreen buttons, for example, or the little three-note melody you hear when a HotSync begins or ends (see Chapter 6, *HotSync, Step by Step*).

System Sound, in this case, doesn't include alarm and game sounds; they get their own volume controls, described next.

On original Pilot and PalmPilot models, System Sound is a checkbox that simply turns off the general clicks and HotSync sounds. On the Palm III and subsequent models—which have an enhanced, *boxed Piezo* speaker—it's a pop-up menu that lets you choose Off, Low, Medium, or High (see Figure 2-2, right).

Alarm sound

Your Date Book program (see Chapter 4, *The Four Primary Programs*) can actually double as an alarm clock, chirping to wake you or to remind you of an appointment. If you're out for a night at the opera, however, you'd probably just as soon not worry about some chirp going off in the middle of a delicate musical moment. In such a case, choose Off or Low from the pop-up menu (or, if you have an original Pilot or PalmPilot model, tap this checkbox to make the checkmark go away). Your palmtop will still turn itself on and display a text reminder of your appointments, but it won't make any noise.

Chirping isn't the only way a Palm device can get your attention. If you equip it with a tiny TaleVibes module, it can also vibrate, just like a beeper in "buzz mode." See Appendix B, *PalmPilot Accessories*, for details.

Game sound

> This category of sound includes the boops and beeps made by some Palm games, especially recent ones. You'd turn this kind of sound off if, for example, you intend to play SubHunt while in church.

Beam receive

> Palm III and later models are always on the lookout for infrared data beamed to them from other Palm devices. That's part of the beauty of the beaming feature—you don't have to do anything special to accept, say, a business card that's transmitted to you from a friend.
>
> You don't need to fear getting "junk beams," viruses, or unsolicited bloatware—your Palm gadget always asks your permission before filing any newly received data. But even so, if you're philosophically opposed to the entire concept of beams, this control lets you turn off beam reception altogether.

Time and Date Formats

After you've told the PalmPilot what day it is, you might want to tell it how the date should *look*. If you're American, never mind; but if you live in any other country, you may be used to writing November 1, 1999, as "1/11/99," for example. The PalmPilot can accommodate you.

Tap Applications → Prefs; from the pop-up menu in the upper-right corner, choose Formats. The resulting screen looks like Figure 2-3. Using the pop-up menus, you can change the way the device displays its time and date; what day of the week the Date Book program should consider the first day of the week (Sunday or Monday); and how you'd like to see numbers (with or without a comma or period in the thousands place, for example). If you lead your life with military precision, here's your chance to make the PalmPilot say "1800 hours" instead of "6:00 p.m."

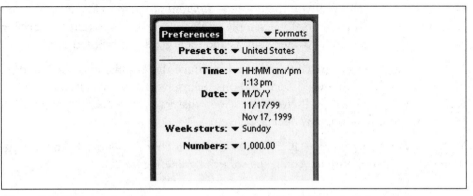

Figure 2-3. Underneath each pop-up menu is an example of the current time, date, or number display setting.

All of this may be much simpler if your country's name is already displayed in the "Preset to:" pop-up menu at the top of the screen. These presets automatically change the Time, Date, Week starts, and Numbers pop-up menus to the appropriate settings. (The original Pilot models list only Australia, Canada, United States, and United Kingdom; later models list 24 different countries, each complete with its own number and time formats. Some research assistant over at 3Com must have had a busy year.)

Shortcuts

Another item listed in the Prefs screen's pop-up menu is Shortcuts. These are abbreviations you can create that, when written in any program, automatically expand to longer versions—an important timesaver on a gadget that lacks a keyboard. See Chapter 3, *Typing Without a Keyboard*, for details on setting up and using Shortcuts.

Remapping Your Buttons

Soon after the original Pilot was introduced, Pilot zealots discovered a shortcoming. Although the Pilot came with *nine* built-in programs, there were only *four* round hardware buttons on the device itself for launching programs: one each for the Date Book, Address Book, To Do List, and Memo Pad.

For most people, those are the four most frequently used programs. But for others—especially fans who had downloaded add-on programs from the Internet—there was more to life than dates, names, to-dos, and memos. These Piloteers wanted buttons that launched, for example, their favorite medical programs, database software, games, and so on.

It wasn't long, therefore, before shareware programs like SilkHack and AppHack became available, allowing you to choose a *different* program to launch when you press the Memo Pad button, for example. Before long, people were remapping *both* their round-topped hardware buttons and their glass silkscreened buttons.

Palm Computing engineers couldn't help but notice the popularity of such add-on programs (and probably used such add-ons themselves). As a result, they added, to Palm OS 2.0 and later, a Preferences screen that lets you remap the application buttons without requiring any special software.

To do so, tap Applications → Preferences, and then choose Buttons from the pop-up menu in the upper-right. You'll see something like Figure 2-4.

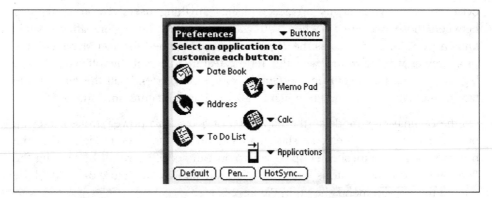

Figure 2-4. This screen shows icons representing the four hardware buttons, plus one silkscreen button—the Calculator (on the Palm VII, an additional icon appears, representing the antenna). Using the pop-up menus, you can remap these buttons to launch any Palm program.

Use the pop-up menus to redefine the programs launched by the four hardware buttons (plus the one glass program-launching button, the Calculator button; on the Palm VII, you can also redefine what happens when you raise the antenna). In fact, if you tap the HotSync button (shown in Figure 2-4), you'll get a screen where you can even redefine what the button on your HotSync cradle, or the button on your Palm modem, does when pressed! Of course, the buttons won't *look* any different; painting on a different program icon is left up to you.

The PalmPilot's built-in button-reassigning feature is useful as far as it goes. However, it doesn't let you exceed the limit of five buttons, five programs.

That's where add-on programs come in. The amazing AppHack, included on the CD-ROM accompanying this book and described in Appendix A, *100 Programs Worth Knowing About*, can actually detect which *part* of the hardware button you're pushing—for example, it can distinguish between a push on the top, bottom, left, or right quadrants—and launch a *different* program for each.

Moreover, AppHack also works on the original Pilot models, giving them at last equal footing with the modern models' button-reassigning features.

Redefining the "Ronomatic Stroke"

Under normal circumstances, your stylus does its *writing* in the Graffiti writing area below the screen and its *tapping* on the main screen area. There's only one occasion when your stylus tip accomplishes anything useful by crossing over between those two areas—when you want to invoke the feature affectionately known by Palm engineers as the *Ronomatic stroke,* named for Ron Marianetti, the programmer who came up with this terrific feature. To pull this off, you draw a big sloppy line that *begins* in the Graffiti square and extends all the way up the face of the palmtop, as shown in Figure 3-2 (and, in miniature, in Figure 2-5).

On the original Pilot models—the Pilot 1000 or 5000—this power stroke makes an onscreen keyboard appear, as shown in Figure 2-6. On later models, what the power stroke accomplishes is up to you. You can specify a result by tapping the Pen button on the Buttons preference screen shown in Figure 2-4. You'll be offered the pop-up menu shown in Figure 2-5.

Figure 2-5. This preference setting determines what happens when you drag your pen all the way up the screen.

Your choices are:

Backlight

> When you've selected Backlight from this pop-up menu, dragging your stylus up the entire face of the PalmPilot turns on the backlighting—a faster and often more foolproof method than holding down the power button for two seconds (the usual way of turning the light on and off). Repeat the power stroke to turn the backlighting off again.

Keyboard

> This is the factory setting. In other words, the power stroke summons the tiny onscreen keyboard, as shown at left in Figure 2-6, so that you can tap out your writings instead of using the Graffiti alphabet (see Chapter 3). Useful if you're in an important business meeting and can't remember the Graffiti keystroke that produces, say, the yen symbol.

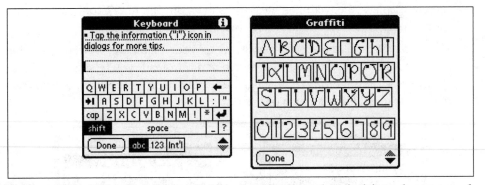

Figure 2-6. The keyboard cheat sheet (left) and Graffiti cheat sheet (right) can be summoned with a single power stroke.

Graffiti Help

When this option is selected, a power stroke makes a cheat sheet of Graffiti lettering appear on the screen, as shown in Figure 2-6. (We'll cover more about this special alphabet in Chapter 3.) If you're like most people, you carry around the white laminated Graffiti card with your PalmPilot—or have even attached the green Graffiti cheat-sheet sticker to the back of your unit. But no matter what, this onscreen cheat sheet is more convenient because it doesn't interrupt whatever you were doing.

Actually, though, the A-through-Z screen that first appears isn't the useful one; most people have mastered the basic alphabet within an hour of turning on the PalmPilot. The more useful screens are the ones that appear when you press the plastic scroll-down button or tap the down-pointing triangle—the wackier and less intuitive symbols for punctuation and international symbols. Tap the Done button to return to whatever you were doing.

Turn Off & Lock

Most people don't need this option; but if you're among those who need it, you *really* need it. With this setting, a power stroke shuts the PalmPilot off; turning it on again will require entering your password, as shown in Figure 2-7. (You set up your password using the Security application, described in Chapter 4.) This setting's usefulness is directly related to the kind of work you do on your PalmPilot. For example, it's handy if the boss walks by while you're playing MineHunt; or if you're composing your Dear John memo and John hops onto the couch next to you; or if you're a spy. (Caution to spies: while this power stroke does instantly *cover up* whatever you were doing, it doesn't hide the fact that your PalmPilot was *on*. That is, instead of actually cutting the power the instant you lift your pen, the power stroke merely displays the warning message shown in Figure 2-7; only when you then tap the Off & Lock button does the unit actually shut off.)

If you haven't yet assigned a password to your PalmPilot, by the way, this power stroke doesn't turn off the device at all. Instead, you're simply scolded, in an error message, about having tried to turn off and lock the PalmPilot without first assigning a password.

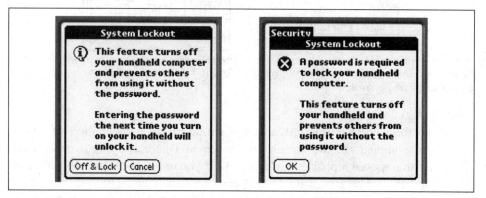

Figure 2-7. Your power stroke doesn't actually shut the PalmPilot off; instead, it presents this instructional message (left). And if you haven't given your PalmPilot a password, you don't even get that far; instead you get the message shown at right.

Beam Data

On the Palm III and later models, this pop-up menu contains an additional choice: Beam Data. If you choose this option, then whenever you do the power penstroke, the PalmPilot automatically sends the currently selected memo, To Do item, calendar appointment, or Address Book entry to any nearby Palm devices within infrared range. Your savings: one trip to a menu command.

The Ronomatic Stroke is delightful and efficient. Its only fault, really, is that there's only one of it; if you use it to turn on your backlight, you can't use it to produce the Graffiti cheat sheet.

That's the beauty of Swipe, a shareware program included on this book's CD. Swipe gives you, in essence, six Ronomatic Strokes. You can summon up to six different functions (backlight, cheat sheet, beam data, and so on), depending on which direction you drag your stylus.

Modem, Network, and Wireless

Three of the commands in the Preferences pop-up menu pertain to making connections. The Modem command lets you specify what kind of modem (if any) is hooked up to your PalmPilot (see Part 4, *The PalmPilot Online*). The Network item is useful when you want to HotSync over a corporate network (see Chapter 6, *HotSync, Step by Step*). And Wireless is an option only on the Palm VII; its primary value is reminding you what your Palm VII's email address is. (The "Warn when sending ID or location information" checkbox makes the Palm VII alert you before transmitting your present location to the Web. It normally sends this information for the purposes of getting data pertinent to your precise location, such as weather, news, traffic, or local movie showtimes. See Chapter 16, *Palm VII: Wireless Email, Wireless Web*, for details.)

Owner

The Owner preferences screen (Figure 2-8) is the easiest feature of the entire Palm universe to grasp: it simply provides a place to jot down your own name and contact information. The idea is that if you somebody finds your lost PalmPilot, they'll know where to return it.

At first glance, you might question the value of this feature—after all, its success seems to require that the finder of your lost palmtop (a) know how to use a PalmPilot enough to find this screen, which is buried in the Preferences program, and (b) not be interested in simply keeping your extremely cool palmtop.

But that's where the Ronomatic Stroke comes in. If you set this power penstroke to Turn Off & Lock, as described in the previous section, then the Owner screen is the first thing to appear when anyone tries to turn on the device. Better still, the password requirement is, to the even marginally honest soul, a further deterrent to simply keeping your lost machine.

Figure 2-8. The Owner screen holds your contact information. If you ever hope to see your PalmPilot again, consider using this space to specify a reward for its safe return.

A Ten-Minute Tour

In Chapter 1, you met the PalmPilot's hardware; in this chapter, you've had a taste of its software. Chapter 4 will walk you through the individual software programs, but if you're like most new PalmPilot owners, you're eager to get going. This section builds on what you know about the PalmPilot's basic operation to illustrate how a typical work session might go.

Adding a Name

You're on the phone. Somebody's giving you an important phone number. If this were last week, you might have begun scrambling for paper and pencil; now that you have a PalmPilot, however, you shove the stylus out of the right-side pocket with your thumb. Without even turning the device on, you're ready to receive the information.

1. **Press the Address Book button**—the button with the tiny white telephone icon. The device simultaneously turns on and opens up the Address Book program.

2. **Tap the New button.** The screen shown in Figure 2-9 appears. For the moment, let's say you don't know how to write using the Graffiti alphabet (because you haven't read Chapter 3 yet). Therefore, you'll have to input your new name and phone number using the keyboard screen.

3. **Tap the dot in the corner of the Graffiti writing area,** as shown in Figure 2-9. When the onscreen keyboard appears, tap out the name Simms. Don't worry about capitalizing the S; the PalmPilot is smart enough to assume that you're inputting a name and to capitalize the word automatically. Tap the onscreen keyboard's Done button when you're finished. (The original Pilot models lack this special dot. Summon the keyboard by tapping Menu → Edit → Keyboard instead.)

4. **Tap the First Name blank.** Again make the keyboard appear; now tap out Frank and tap Done to close the keyboard.

5. **Tap on the blank labeled Work.** You're about to enter this guy's work phone number. Even if you haven't learned the Graffiti alphabet and number set, the next step shouldn't give you any trouble; in the area shown in Figure 2-9, write the phone number 331-7702. Just write one digit after another within the same space. The only tricky part is making the hyphen, which requires *two* stylus actions: first *tap* the writing area, and then draw the dash, left-to-right as usual.

6. **Tap the Done button.** You return to the complete list of names and numbers—which, if this is a brand new PalmPilot, now contains three or four entries. Frank Simms is one of them.

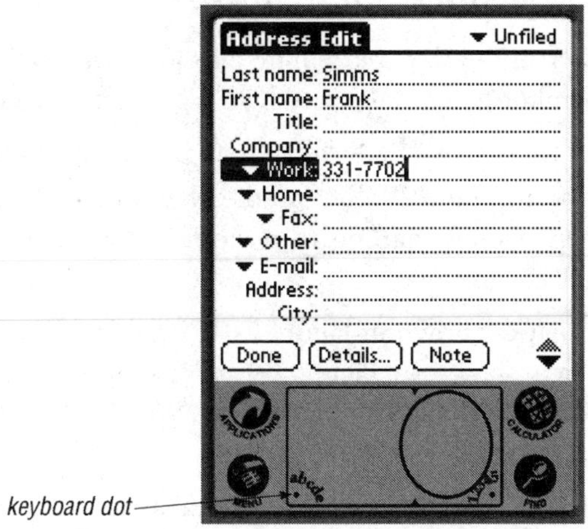

keyboard dot

Figure 2-9. Write each digit of the phone number here. Tap the dot (left) to summon the keyboard.

Menu Shortcuts for the Terminally Busy

In general, the PalmPilot's menus work just as they do on the Mac or in Windows—right down to the *keyboard shortcuts* that save you mousing on your desktop computer.

In Figure 2-12, you'll see that to the right of nearly every menu command is its *Graffiti menu shortcut*—a two-stroke Graffiti gesture that triggers the command without your actually having to open the menu. Mastering this technique can save you a lot of time and fumbling, especially when word processing.

To trigger a menu shortcut, begin by drawing a slash—from bottom to top—in the Graffiti writing area. (You can see this slash listed in the menu itself in Figure 2-12. Although the slash symbol is omitted from the menus of the original Pilots, you must still draw the slash symbol.)

When you draw the slash, you'll see the word Command: appear at the bottom of the screen. You have exactly two seconds to follow your slash with the Graffiti letter that corresponds to a menu command.

If you write the letter in time, you trigger the menu command. If not, the word Command: disappears from the bottom of the screen, and any Graffiti writing you do now is interpreted as regular writing, not as menu shortcutting.

Writing a To Do, Doing Some Math

Now suppose it's later in the day. Mr. Simms has just sent you an important client, so you want to remember to send the guy his 15 percent referral kickback.

1. **Press the To Do button** (second from the right at the bottom of your Palm-Pilot). If you have an original Pilot, tap the New button. (On later models, you can skip this step. Simply starting to write tells the device that you mean to begin a new To Do item.)

2. **Make the letter shapes shown in** Figure 2-10, one after another, in the left half of the writing area shown in Figure 2-9, even if you don't quite understand why. You're using the Graffiti alphabet now, which you'll read more about in the next chapter, to write *Send payment of $*.

   (Uh-oh . . . now you need to make a quick calculation.)

3. **Tap the Calculator button on the lower-right side of the glass.** Don't worry about your To Do item in progress; it's automatically saved.

4. **When the Calculator screen appears, figure out Simms' 15 percent commission on the $235 sale.** Do this by tapping out (with your actual fingers, if you wish): *235 X 15%=*. The answer, 35.25, should appear at the top of the screen. But now, because this is such a staggeringly difficult number to remember, you'd better copy it to the invisible Clipboard (a temporary storage area).

5. **Tap Menu → Edit → Copy.**

6. **Again push the hardware To Do button at the bottom of the PalmPilot.** Return to your To Do item in progress. Tap after the words *Send payment of $*; tap Menu → Edit → Paste.

   "Press the space bar" before continuing; to do so, draw a left-to-right dash in the left side of the Graffiti writing area.

7. **Write the words "to Simms," using the letter shapes shown in Figure 2-11.** Now comes a fancy trick that works only on recent models, not on the original Pilot 1000 and 5000.

8. **Tap Menu → Options → Phone Lookup.** See Figure 2-12. Amazingly enough, the guy's complete name and phone number has now replaced the word Simms, as shown at right in Figure 2-12. Your PalmPilot did the dirty work (of consulting the phone book program) automatically.

In just a short time, you've experienced the highs and lows of PalmPilot owner-ship: you've entered a new name into the Address Book, and then incorporated that information into another program, the To Do list. Along the way, you encoun-tered the onscreen keyboard, experimented with the PalmPilot's handwriting

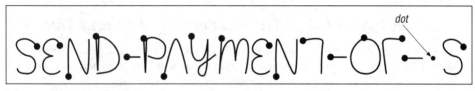

Figure 2-10. Make the shapes shown to write "Send payment of $".

Figure 2-11. Finish up your first Graffiti-alphabet sentence.

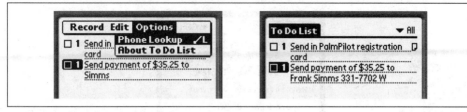

Figure 2-12. Use the Lookup command on recent models (left) to replace a partial name with the full name and phone number (right).

recognition (and the mandatory Graffiti alphabet), pulled down menus and tapped onscreen buttons, switched among three different programs, and got to know Frank Simms pretty darned well.

Executive Tip Summary

- If your screen taps sometimes don't seem to register, go to the Applications screen; tap Prefs; and choose Digitizer from the upper-right pop-up menu. You'll be led through the process of realigning the display with its touch screen.

- You can turn the PalmPilot's various sounds on or off in the General screen of Preferences.

- If you don't often use one of the four plastic buttons at the bottom of the PalmPilot (or the Calculator silkscreen button, or the Palm VII antenna), by all means remap them to launch a program you *do* use. The Buttons panel of the Preferences command lets you do this remapping.

- Draw a line from the Graffiti area straight up onto the screen. That's the *Ronomatic stroke*—and you can define its effect. The Buttons panel of the Preferences screen lets you set up the power stroke to (a) make the onscreen

Easter Eggs #1 & 2: The "Easter Egg" Egg and Taxi

An Easter egg, in computer parlance, is a tiny credits screen or secret surprise buried by a programmer, designed to appear only when you perform some incredibly improbable sequence of keystrokes and mouse clicks. The PalmPilot is loaded with 'em—the hallmark of a product whose designers love their jobs.

As though to hint at the seething carton of hidden Easter eggs, one Easter egg in particular has endured through generations of Palm models: the Easter egg Easter egg. To view this simple surprise, tap Applications → Prefs and choose General from the upper-right pop-up menu. Just above the Calculator button, draw a pea-sized circle (counterclockwise). Surprise! The Palm Easter egg itself makes an appearance exactly at your pen tip, as shown below.

(To make the Easter egg disappear, draw the same circle in the same spot again.)

The appearance of that Easter egg is the ON Switch for many other classic Palm Easter eggs, including one of the greatest Easter eggs of all: the animated taxi (also shown above). Start by switching to the Memo Pad. Now, while pressing the Scroll Down plastic button, draw a line from the middle of the Graffiti area directly to the left, all the way to the plastic border between the Applications and Menu icons. Look fast—there, putting its way across your screen emitting cute little puffs of exhaust, is the elusive Taxi. (Taxi was the Pilot's working name, even before it was the Pilot).

---

keyboard appear, (b) summon the Graffiti cheat sheet, (c) turn the backlight on or off, (d) turn off and lock the PalmPilot, or (e) beam the current data (Palm III and later).

- Menu commands are easily triggered without actually having to tap them. Instead, learn to use the faster *Graffiti menu shortcuts*—draw a slash (bottom to top) and then the initial of the command you want.

3

Typing Without a Keyboard

The PalmPilot's creators had their first design meetings at a particularly useful point in history—*after* the debut of the Apple Newton. The Newton was a much larger, much heavier, much more expensive machine, but it, too, lacked a built-in keyboard. To input text, you were supposed to write on its glass screen, just as with the PalmPilot. The Newton was designed to recognize your handwriting and convert it into neatly typed, editable text.

Unfortunately, the original Newton's fledgling handwriting-recognition skills wound up serving as *Doonesbury* comic-strip fodder. (Man writes: "Does this work?" Newton transcribes his scrawl: "Egg freckles?") There are simply too many different writing styles for one handheld computer to understand.

That's why Palm's designers decided not to train their handheld to understand you; instead, they'd train *you* to understand *it*.

Graffiti: The Sure-Fire Alphabet

To pull this off, they designed a special alphabet called Graffiti. If you learn to write using the letter shapes the PalmPilot expects, it responds with perfect accuracy. Some people grumble at first—isn't technology supposed to serve *us?*—but after a day or so of practice, the Graffiti alphabet becomes second nature for most people.

The Graffiti system isn't limited to the PalmPilot, by the way; you can also buy it as an add-on for other handheld devices, such as the MagicCap and the Motorola Envoy—even the Apple Newton.

The Logic of Graffiti

If you examine the charts on the inside covers of this book, you'll discover that almost every letter of the Graffiti alphabet is formed by a single stroke of the pen. That requirement explains the mutant shapes of the A, F, K, T, Q, and number 4, each of which is lacking the traditional finishing stroke. (Strangely enough, in forming the letter X, you're *supposed* to use two separate strokes. Don't let the inconsistency trouble you—just be glad there's one less mutant character to learn.)

The great thing about forming your letters with single strokes is that printing is faster this way. Many PalmPilot-inspired programmers, engineers, and other technical people have actually adopted the Graffiti alphabet for use even when they're not writing on the PalmPilot! Poke your head into a staff meeting, for example, and you may well see a white board or chalkboard with writing like that shown in Figure 3-1.

Figure 3-1. Don't be surprised to see writing like this in the boardrooms of corporate America.

Letters versus numbers

The PalmPilot makes its own recognition task even easier by requiring you to form your *letters* on the left side of the drawing area and your *numbers* on the right. (You can create punctuation in either space.) In your first forays into Graffiti-land, you may sometimes forget this important distinction; but the PalmPilot's attempt at recognition, every bit as nonsensical as those early Newton efforts, will quickly train you to keep your letters and numbers segregated.

Space, backspace, return, and shift

As you learn Graffiti, you'll become increasingly pleased with the common sense of some of its assignments. For example, to make a space, you just draw a quick horizontal line, as though you're scooting the next word over to the right. To backspace, draw the same dash backward, from right to left, just as though you're striking over a manuscript typo with a red pen.

What would be the Return key on a computer is a slash, made from upper-right to lower-left. This movement, too, is logical; think of the slash as an arrow pointing to the next typing area—down and to the left.

To capitalize a letter, precede it by drawing a straight vertical line from the bottom, as though drawing an arrow upward. Only the next letter you write will be affected; if you want a Caps Lock effect, in which *all* subsequent letters are capitalized, draw *two* such upward strokes. Draw another single upward stroke to exit Caps Lock mode.

Punctuation

To pop into punctuation-mark mode, tap the writing area as though you're making a period. You'll see a fat black dot appear just above the area where you write numbers. This dot is the PalmPilot's way of saying, "I understand you're in punctuation mode. Now what symbol do you want?" At this point, you make the symbol that represents the desired punctuation mark: a single tap for a period, a vertical bar (in the lower half of the writing area) for a comma, and so on. The Graffiti cheat sheet inside the front and back covers of this book shows the complete list of punctuation characters.

Most novices slow down dramatically when they approach punctuation. They make the single tap to enter punctuation mode—and then stop dead while they look up, or try to remember, the correct gesture for the marking they want. With time, though, you'll begin to conceive of the most common punctuation marks as integrated two-stroke gestures: for example, experienced PalmPilot pilots make two quick taps, in place, to produce a period.

How to Learn Graffiti

The best way to learn the Palm alphabet is to struggle through writing a paragraph or two. As you go, remember that you have four different Graffiti cheat sheets available for reference:

- The white laminated bifold card included with your palmtop.

- The dark green sticker, also included in the original package. The manual suggests that you slap the A through Z sticker onto the underside of your Palm-Pilot until you've learned those letters. After you've got those learned, replace that sticker with the punctuation sticker.

- The built-in, onscreen Graffiti table. If yours is a relatively recent-model PalmPilot, making this handy quick-reference screen appear is easy: draw a slash up the *entire* face of the glass, starting in the writing area and extending upward, as shown in Figure 3-2.

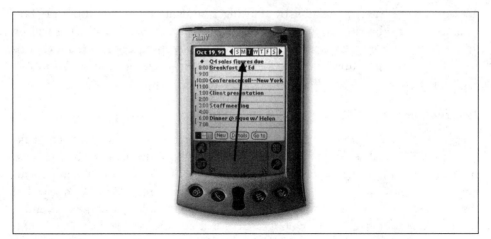

Figure 3-2. If you have the Palm OS 2.0 or later, you can make the Graffiti cheat sheet appear with one simple stroke.

If, on the other hand, you have an earlier model (a Pilot 1000 or 5000), getting to the onscreen cheat sheet is slightly harder. Tap the Applications button to the left of the writing area; on the screen that then appears, tap Graffiti.

In either case, you make the Graffiti screen go away simply by tapping anywhere on it.

- There's a Graffiti cheat sheet on the inside covers of this book. It's much more comprehensive than the 3Com cheat sheet—this book's chart lists numerous undocumented alternate character shapes.

If slogging through actual writing fries your brain too quickly, you can relax by playing a round or two of Giraffe, the Space Invaders of handwriting practice. It's a little game in which you blast letters as they fall out of the sky—each time you successfully *write* each letter, you launch a perfectly aimed missile. You'll never see this baby available as a Nintendo cartridge, but it's a good drill. For details on installing and using Giraffe, see Chapter 5, *The Other Built-In Programs.*

 If you're having trouble mastering one letter or another, install the ingenious program called TealEcho. (It's included on the CD-ROM with this book, and it's described in Appendix A, *100 Programs Worth Knowing About.*) When you form a letter in the Graffiti writing area, TealEcho actually *draws* the shape you're making. By glancing at the screen, you can see how well the letter *you're* drawing matches the ideal Graffiti shape—and you can often pinpoint the problem with your character at a glance.

Graffiti Tips and Tricks

Getting good at Graffiti is critical to your enjoyment of the PalmPilot. Therefore, it's worth spending a few more minutes mastering its nuances.

The ground rules are simple:

- Make your letters big. The bigger the gesture, the more material there is for the Palm analyzer to study.

- Writing speed doesn't affect recognition. Writing slowly at first, however, may help you confirm that you're forming your characters correctly.

- Don't write on a slant.

- If you begin the penstroke *outside* of the Graffiti writing area, the PalmPilot will ignore you.

- Suppose you've just made the Shift stroke to capitalize the next letter—a vertical stroke from bottom to top. The fat black arrow appears on the screen near the bottom, indicating that it's ready to capitalize the next letter. But now you change your mind: the next letter should be lowercase after all.

  You can "backspace over" your Shift stroke just as though it's any ordinary letter. In other words, just draw a right-to-left horizontal dash. You'll see the black arrow vanish from the screen, and the next letter you write will be lowercase as usual.

  Actually, there's a second way to cancel a Shift stroke: draw *two more* of them. That's because each successive Shift stroke cycles between three modes: Capitalize the Next Letter; Caps Lock (all letters capitalized); or Lowercase. Two vertical strokes puts you in Caps Lock mode, in other words, and a third cancels all shifting.

- Graffiti understands alternative shapes for many letters that actually save you time and increase accuracy. While some of them look even less like the traditional alphabet than the "primary" shapes, they're worth adopting if some letters are consistently giving you trouble.

  Table 3-1 offers hints, tips, and alternative shapes for the most commonly cursed letters in the Graffiti lineup. As always, the little dot (in the character map shapes) represents where your stylus should begin the stroke.

Table 3-1. Graffiti Writing Tips

Desired Letter	Graffiti Gesture	Tip
B	B B 3	For speed and accuracy, omit the downstroke. Just write the numeral 3 in the letters writing area.
C	C ⟨	The standard shape works fine. But adding a corner in the middle may help the accuracy.
D	D Q ℓ	You can omit the initial downstroke, if you like. Simply draw the shape from the lower-left corner and proceed upward. Or, fastest of all, draw a cursive lowercase L backwards—that is, starting from the end, as shown at right.
E	ℰ ≤ ℚ	If the standard "backwards numeral 3" configuration isn't cutting it for you, you can also make your E out of straight strokes, like a W on its side.
G	G 6	Speed stroke: Just write the numeral 6 in the letters area. You can make it fast and sloppy. You're also welcome to make a traditional capital G shape; either way, the PalmPilot seldom gets this letter wrong.
J	J J	Don't worry about the curve, if it slows you down; a corner, as in a backward L, works well, too. (But don't curl upward again, or the PalmPilot will think you want a U.)
K	∝	Think fish. The more you enlarge the loop, the more speed and accuracy you'll get.
L	L ⟋	If you make the first stroke perfectly vertical, you'll have to make a sharp corner at the lower-left. If you slant your L shape, though, from upper-right to lower-left, you can actually afford to be sloppier with your right angle. You can even curve it like a C, and the PalmPilot will still understand that you want an L. (If you're having trouble, make the bottom stroke longer and angle it downward.)
N	N ᴎ ∿	Precision isn't necessary; there's not much the PalmPilot can confuse with an N shape. Round the corners, if you like; even a ~ shape will work. If, for some reason, the PalmPilot doesn't recognize your N, slant it to the right.
P	P P P	As shown in the second shape, you can omit the initial downstroke; you'll take less time and get better accuracy. The top loop can be quite small.
Q	Ö U	If you're getting a P or an O, it's because you're giving short shrift to the oddball curlicue at the end of the stroke. The change of direction is more important than the closure of the big O shape; the second shape shown at left is more reliable than the standard one.
R	R R R	As with the P, you're welcome to omit the initial downstroke. As with the P, the top loop needn't be big.
S	S ⟩ 5	There are three alternatives: consider making a 5 shape; a 5 shape without the top horizontal; or a backward Z.
V	V̄ V	Remembering to draw the added top-right tail strikes many people as unnatural—since when is a V a square-root symbol? Consider drawing a traditional V shape instead—from the right side. This method is speedy, more accurate, and doesn't even require a pointy bottom; a right-to-left U shape is perfectly OK.
X	X ⤨	X is a fascinating character; it's the only one where you're allowed to use two strokes. (If you watch the screen, you'll see what's really happening: the first stroke makes a special slash character appear at the lower edge of the screen, indicating that the PalmPilot is in waiting mode. The second stroke ends the anticipation.) However, you may find it faster not to lift your stylus between strokes, as shown at left; if you're in a hurry, the X shape turns into more of a fish.
Y	y ⅄ r	There are two speed shortcuts: either draw a figure 8 in the letter area, or draw a single loop—a tiny purse shape—starting from top left. As a bonus, these alternate shapes are likely to be more accurate than the traditional lowercase y shape.
2, 5	⟨ S	Don't worry about the sharp angles. A quick, sloppy S shape (or, for the 2, backward S) in the numbers writing area does the trick.

Table 3-1. Graffiti Writing Tips (continued)

Desired Letter	Graffiti Gesture	Tip
4	L C <	Either a C or L shape in the numbers area will do the job.
7	7 ⊃	A backwards C, drawn in the numbers area, is close enough.
8	8 / 8	Speed freaks don't need to bother closing the top loop. Make the same purse shape described for the Y above, starting from top left. Or, faster still: make a skinny V that slants to the right—just down-up, and the deed is done.
'	• ↑	The apostrophe and comma are among the trickiest symbols in the Graffiti alphabet. The PalmPilot uses two factors to figure out which you've drawn: the position and the slant. Make the comma low and slanted, and the apostrophe high and straight, and you'll have no further trouble.

The Best Graffiti Tip in the Book

Put a piece of tape over the Graffiti writing area!

On the Internet, you'll hear Piloteers talk a lot about Scotch Tape #811 ("Magic"), in the blue package. Its silky surface provides a subtle, paper-like drag to the writing surface, making your stylus less likely to slip, giving you more control, and often improving your Graffiti recognition accuracy—and you can easily remove the tape if necessary. (The Scotch "Satin" variety is also great—smoother and clearer than #811.)

Other Palm fans cover the Graffiti area with Post-It notes (or Post-it Tape Flags) cut to the right shape; you can even buy special clear-plastic overlays for the entire screen (see Appendix B, *PalmPilot Accessories*).

But Scotch Tape is the greatest.

The Onscreen Keyboard

If you're caught on a pay phone during your first month with the PalmPilot and somebody's rattling off a phone number to you, and you just can't remember how to make the parenthesis symbols, it's time to bring up the onscreen keyboard. The klutzy or panicked can tap away on a tiny virtual keyboard instead of using the Graffiti system.

To make your keyboard appear, tap the tiny dot in the lower-left corner of the Graffiti writing area, shown in Figure 3-3. (On original Pilot models, tap Menu → Edit → Keyboard instead.)

Once the keyboard is on the screen, just tap to type; there's even a little Backspace key (marked by the left-pointing arrow) and Tab key (right-pointing arrow).

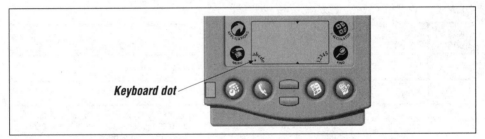

Figure 3-3. When Graffiti is just too much to handle, tap the magic dot, shown here, to make the keyboard appear.

You'll probably find the onscreen keyboard most useful for its collections of symbols and foreign-language diacritical marks, which you can access by tapping one of the three character-set buttons shown in Figure 3-4.

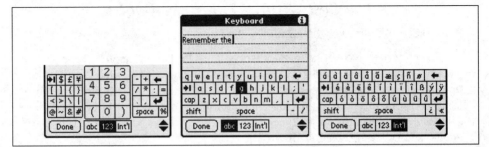

Figure 3-4. The onscreen keyboard offers three different screens full of symbols. Tap one of the three buttons as shown to switch among the panels.

To get rid of the keyboard, tap the Done button.

If your writing often involves the Graffiti alphabet's hard-to-remember symbols, consider installing SymbolHack. (It's described in Appendix A and included on the CD-ROM that comes with this book.) This program works much like the PalmPilot's own pop-up keyboard, except that it places your choice of commonly used symbols onto a palette that you design. Tap a symbol to insert it into your writing.

Graffiti Alternatives

As good as Graffiti is, it's not the only 100%-accurate handwriting-recognition system available for the PalmPilot. Software companies have raced to the cause with specially shaped alphabets of their own. Only single-digit percentages of Palm fans use these replacement systems, but what matters is that you have a choice.

Jot

The Jot alphabet's claim to fame is that it's the official alphabet of Windows CE palmtops (the PalmPilot's rival). It offers several immediately apparent advantages over the Graffiti alphabet. First, most punctuation marks require only a single pen-stroke. Second, you can write on the upper portion of the screen, not just in the Graffiti area (although the shareware Palm program ScreenWrite, on this book's CD-ROM, offers the same feature). As you write, the shape of each letter appears on the screen, to provide feedback (as the shareware TealEcho does)—great for refining your letter-making skills. Finally, many of the letter shapes are more "normal-looking" than Graffiti's. As Table 3-2 illustrates, Jot's shapes for A, E, F, K, T, and V are much more recognizable than the corresponding Graffiti shapes. (If your name is Eva Teffakeva, install Jot this minute.)

Jot also has some downsides, however: it costs $40 (from *http://www.cic.com*), takes up 120K of memory, and doesn't permit you to turn off the "shape-echo" feature when you've outgrown it. Still, it's one of the most ingenious solutions to the making-machines-understand-printing problem; it's worth trying out the demo version included on this book's CD-ROM.

TealScript

If you like the concept of Graffiti, but think you could have done a better job designing the letter shapes, TealScript may be your Holy Grail: it lets you make up your own letter shapes. You can use it to redefine only the letters that give you trouble (to make the A, E, F, K, T, V, and 4 look more like Jot's, for example). Also as in Jot, you can tell the program to give you capital letters without having to shift first—by writing the letter on the dividing line between the letter and number areas. You can choose to have certain punctuation marks appear with a single penstroke instead of requiring two. Or you can create a new alphabet entirely of your own design, one that fits better with your existing handwriting.

TealScript isn't simple to figure out; its main screen is crammed with controls, statistics, and variables like "Squelch" and "Cutoff." Its 124K memory appetite isn't puny, either. And once you've gotten used to your own custom alphabet, trying to write on someone else's (TealScript-less) PalmPilot can be disastrous.

But the result—a handwriting-recognition alphabet tailored precisely to your tastes—is quickly addictive, and makes almost every Palm program more comfortable to use. (As always, a demo version is on this book's CD; the full version is $17 from *http://www.tealpoint.com.*)

Table 3-2. The Jot alphabet ($40) is, in many ways, more natural than Graffiti. Write lowercase letters on the left half of the screen (or Graffiti area), numbers on the right, and capital letters on the dividing line.

Fitaly

This $25 software (*http://www.twsolutions.com/palm/palmfitaly*) isn't a replacement alphabet—instead, it's a replacement for the onscreen keyboard, the one used by Palm fans who haven't learned Graffiti (or who are fumbling for a Yen symbol). Textware Inc. claims that the letters on this keyboard (see Figure 3-5) are cleverly arranged to minimize stylus travel, with the most frequently used letter combinations together and near the center. As a result, the company claims that you can tap away at up to 50 words per minute. (The average Graffiti user gets about 20 words per minute.)

A good deal of practice is required to get anywhere close to those speeds. And, unfortunately, this keyboard doesn't stay out of the way of the writing area, as the built-in Palm keyboard does—instead, it's a floating window that you have to adjust frequently. On the other hand, it lets you type all 220 symbols and letters in the standard ASCII character set, far more than the usual Graffiti keyboard. For the curious, a demo of this program is on this book's CD-ROM.

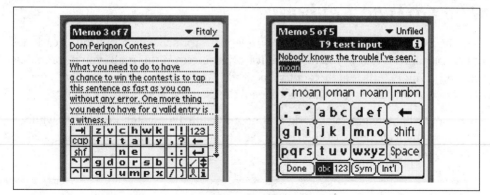

Figure 3-5. At left: the Fitaly keyboard is named for the arrangement of the second row of "keys" on this virtual keyboard. At right: the T9 keypad tries to complete your words as you tap.

T9

This software, too, offers a tappable onscreen keyboard to replace the built-in one—after installation, the T9 keyboard appears when you tap the keyboard dot in the corner of the Graffiti area—but the approach is radically different. The entire alphabet is arranged on nine "keys" (see Figure 3-5). The idea is not to tap on the precise letter you want, but anywhere on its three-letter key, which is a bigger target; as you build the word, T9 tries to deduce which word you're going for. If it displays the word you intend, you tap the "Space" key to accept the choice and move on.

If the proposed word isn't what you were shooting for, several next-best guesses appear. And if your word isn't part of the program's 60,000-word dictionary at all—a name or email address, for example—you can spell it, this time by typing exactly on the letters you want (rather than just the keys on which they appear).

Unfortunately, T9's guessing algorithm won't win any spelling bees. For example, if you tap out Frid, it's not smart enough to guess that you're going for Friday; indeed, its word guesses at that point include "Frie," "Frid," and "Drif," but no "Friday." In other words, the word-guessing algorithm is used exclusively to make sense of the three-letters-per-key combinations, not to predict what longer word you're in the process of typing—a missed opportunity. (And if you mis-tap, the results are even less useful; tap "eartquake" by mistake, and T9 offers a choice of "dartstbal" or "ebrurubbk.") The software takes up 177K of memory, plus extra memory for words you add to its dictionary.

Fortunately, you can write using Graffiti (or call up the Palm keyboard) at any time during text input, mixing and matching as suits your whim. As with any of these Graffiti alternatives, you lose nothing by trying T9 out; a demo is on this book's CD-ROM. (The full version is $30 from Tegic, *http://www.t9.com/palmpilot.html*.)

The GoType Keyboard

Graffiti and the onscreen keyboard are adequate for scratching out the occasional name or address. But if you're a novelist or reporter on the road, you're probably craving a more efficient text-entry method. Fortunately, Landware (*http://www. landware.com*) makes just what you need: the GoType keyboard.

This sleek, lightweight, $80 gadget contains a full typewriter keyboard (without Fkeys or other elements of the "extended" keyset) in the smallest possible shape. (See Figure 3-6.)

Figure 3-6. Graffiti getting you down? Attach a GoType keyboard for a compact, full-speed typing solution.

To use the keyboard, you must first install the included software. Next, open the hard lid that protects the keyboard in transit. Slide out the back-side foot that lends stability. Finally, snap your palmtop onto the HotSync-like connector, which holds it solidly in place—and begin to type away at full speed, in any Palm program.

Special features include six pushbuttons that launch the built-in Palm programs (Memo, Address Book, Mail, Find, and so on); a ShortCut key for triggering your text macros, as described later in this chapter; cursor keys; a Done key that closes most dialog boxes; and protruding cylindrical openings on each end of the keyboard that hold your stylus upright and ready. The keyboard even has Command and Alt keys, so that you can use one of GoType's most useful features: the ability to program keystrokes that launch any number of your favorite Palm programs.

The GoType has been a huge hit with PalmPilot addicts, offering most of a laptop's word processing capabilities at a fraction of the cost and weight. The 1999 models, one of which accommodates the Palm V, can even double as a full HotSync cradle. Your palmtop need never leave its spot.

Doc Files

If your challenge is reading a lot of text, not writing it, you need a Doc reader. These little Palm applications are text readers, complete with search-and-replace, bookmarking features, a choice of display fonts, and much more generous document lengths than in the built-in Memo Pad program (which limits each page to 4K of text).

Several such programs, including TealDoc, SmartDoc, and AportisDoc, are included on the CD-ROM that comes with this book; see Chapter 10, *PalmPilot: The Electronic Book*, for a complete discussion of these programs and Palm reading material. Chapter 10 also describes how to make your *own* Doc-format documents. Once you've begun dumping your email, articles, web page text, and other readable goods into Doc files destined for your PalmPilot, you'll quickly discover two huge advantages to this system: first, you can now indirectly use your computer's keyboard as a fast and familiar text-input device. And second, you'll find that you can make even the most boring business meetings pass more quickly when you can be reading entertaining material on the tiny screen in front of you without risk of detection.

Where Are My Fonts?

Fonts are getting more attention as the PalmPilot grows up. The Palm III, for example, was the first to offer a choice of three different fonts in each Palm program. Its Palm OS 3.0, meanwhile, offers "hooks" that will make it easy for programmers to add new fonts.

If you have an older model, you can always install FontHack Plus (included on the CD-ROM that accompanies this book); it lets you change the font of any program. And where do these new fonts come from? You can make your own (or adapt existing Mac or Windows ones), for starters. Visit *http://www.palmglyph.com/font.html* for instructions in making new Palm fonts.

ShortCuts: Little Strokes for Big Words

No matter how you're entering text into the PalmPilot—using Graffiti, the onscreen keyboard, or a GoType keyboard—you can save time and effort by using the ShortCuts feature. ShortCuts automatically expand abbreviations into longer phrases of up to 45 letters and spaces. The PalmPilot comes with several such entries already established: for example, you can type *me*, which the PalmPilot automatically replaces with the complete word *Meeting*. This instantaneous expansion can take place anywhere you can use Graffiti: in the Memo Pad or Address Book, for example.

Fortunately for those who might like to use the word *me* in its more common context, the PalmPilot only treats an abbreviation as a ShortCuts trigger if you precede it with the ShortCut symbol, the cursive lowercase L shape shown in Figure 3-7.

Figure 3-7. The ShortCuts character (left) tells the PalmPilot to be ready for the abbreviation to come. The result: the fully expanded text phrase (right).

The PalmPilot comes with the following built-in ShortCuts expressions:

Abbreviation	Expands to
br	Breakfast
lu	Lunch
di	Dinner
me	Meeting
ds	Today's date
ts	The current time
dts	The current date and time

To add your own ShortCuts, tap Applications → Prefs. From the pop-up menu at the upper-right corner of the Preferences screen, tap ShortCuts. You'll see the screen shown in Figure 3-8. Tap New, write the abbreviated and expanded version of your phrase, and click Done.

 When you design a ShortCut of your own, include a space after the expanded word. That way, whenever the word itself appears in your writing, you're saved the effort of drawing the space character.

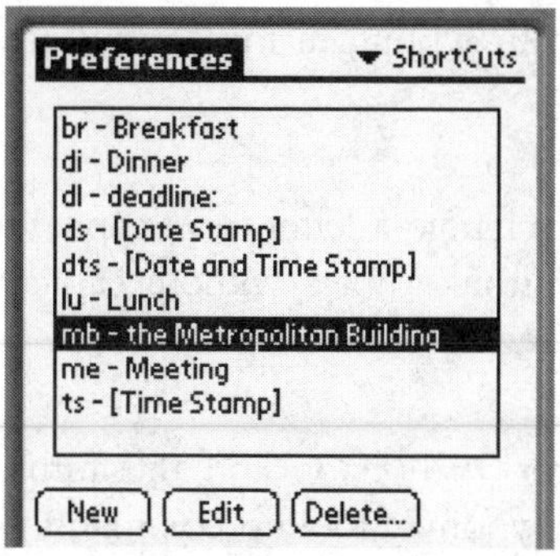

Figure 3-8. The list of ShortCuts. To add a new one, tap New; to edit one of the existing ones—either the abbreviation or its expanded form—tap it, then tap Edit.

The PalmPilot as Word Processor

Because of its lack of keyboard, the PalmPilot actually makes a fairly lousy word processor. Sure, Graffiti makes brief notes possible. And a few word processing conventions are present: for example, you can drag across text to highlight it (in readiness for cutting, copying, or replacing by "writing over" it).

But otherwise, the PalmPilot's text programming omits nearly all standard word processor niceties.

Fortunately, shareware fills in some of the holes in the PalmPilot's text programming. Consider these add-ons, for example, to make your editing life easier. (All of these programs are included with this book and are described more fully in Appendix A.)

SelectHack

Lets you "double-click" a word to highlight the entire word, just as on your Mac or Windows machine. You can even triple-tap to highlight an entire paragraph.

MiddleCaps

Generates a capital letter when you write on the dividing line between the Graffiti writing areas for letters and numbers exactly as when using the Jot alphabet described earlier. You save one penstroke every time you make a capital letter. (Despite the lack of the word Hack in its title, MiddleCaps requires HackMaster to be installed as described in Appendix A.)

DragAndDrop

Lets you edit by dragging highlighted text into new positions, exactly as you can in "real" word processors.

ScreenWrite

Instead of confining your writing in the Graffiti area, this hack lets you write directly on the screen.

CaseToggle

Lets you double-tap to change a letter from capital to lowercase, or vice-versa. In other words, you can take notes without capitalizing *anything*, and return to add capitalization later.

Thesaurus

An actual spell checker, dictionary, and thesaurus, complete with a 50,000-word dictionary and a synonym-lookup command.

SpellCheck

A pop-up spell checker that works within any Palm application.

Executive Tip Summary

- For best accuracy, make your Graffiti strokes large enough to fill the writing area.

- For even more accuracy, put a piece of Scotch tape over the Graffiti area—you get a less slippery, more controlled, more paperlike surface to write on.

- To analyze what you're doing wrong (in times of recognition inaccuracy), install TealEcho, which shows you what the PalmPilot is "seeing" you draw for each Graffiti character.

- The Graffiti alphabet is easy to learn, but if it's frustrating you, consider teaching it to recognize your own letter shapes using TealScript—or switching to a more natural-looking alphabet, such as Jot.

- Consult the inner covers of this book, which reveal over 85 alternative Graffiti shapes. Many are far faster to draw (although less recognizable as letters) than the traditional Graffiti shapes.

- Draw your V shape from the *right side* for perfect accuracy every time.

- Store frequently used phrases as ShortCuts. (Tap Applications → Prefs. From the upper-right pop-up menu, choose ShortCuts.) Include a space after each expanded word to save additional time.

4

The Four Primary Programs

Without a doubt, much of the fun of PalmPiloting is using the kinds of add-on programs included with this book. But for thousands of Palm owners, the four primary built-in programs are enough.

During the machine's development, Palm Computing programmers became obsessed over *tap counts*. They'd sit around and tally the number of stylus taps—on buttons and other controls—that were necessary to accomplish frequently used tasks, such as recording an appointment.

That attention to detail and streamlining paid off. Palm's Big Four—the programs launched by the four rounded hardware buttons at the bottom of the device—are surprisingly complete, elegant, and efficient.

The Date Book

Although there are thousands of add-on programs for the PalmPilot, few programmers have attempted to write a replacement for the Date Book program. That fact is a testimony to this program's completeness; if you've ever whipped out your PalmPilot, pressed a single button to view your next appointment, and then watched the faces of nearby laptop users who would have required three minutes to start up their machines and retrieve the same information, you know exactly what I mean.

Viewing the Day's Events

To check your upcoming appointments, press the plastic Date Book button at the lower-left corner of your palmtop. That button turns the machine on, launches the Date Book program, and flips to today's date. The display looks something like Figure 4-1.

Figure 4-1. The Date Book shows the day's events in day-at-a-glance format. At right, the time-compression feature at work. (Original Pilot models lack the ability to hide empty lines.)

The Date Book program in Palm OS 2 and later is particularly likable; as shown in Figure 4-1, time slots during the day where nothing is happening can be *hidden*. Your eye goes directly to the time slots where something is actually happening; as a bonus, omitting empty time slots means your PalmPilot can generally fit an entire day's worth of activities onto its small screen. (On the other hand, you can turn this option off if you prefer seeing all hours listed, as shown at left in Figure 4-1. To do so, tap Menu → Options → Display Options, and turn off Compress Day View.)

Palm OS 2 and later also sport tiny vertical bars at the left side of the display; they help you visualize the lengths of your appointments and, because they can overlap, help clarify simultaneous events. You can hide these bars if they get in your way; tap Menu → Options → Display Options to see the Display Time Bars checkbox.

 If you have Palm OS 2 or later, a special shortcut awaits you. Pressing the plastic Date Book button at the lower-left of the device launches the Date Book program. But if you press that same plastic button *again,* you get the week-at-a-glance screen, described in an upcoming section. Press a third time to see the month view, and a fourth to return to today's "day view" schedule. In other words, the plastic hardware button rotates among the various views of your calendar.

Changing days

To view your schedule for a different day this week, tap one of the initials at the top of the screen (S M T W T F S). You can also move forward or back a day at a time by pressing the plastic up/down buttons at the bottom of the PalmPilot. (Weirdly enough, the *up* button shows you the next *earlier* date, and the down button moves *forward* in time.) Tap the black triangle buttons on either side of the S M T W T F S header to look at this same weekday next week (or last week).

If the day you want to see isn't conveniently accessible using those buttons, tap the Go To button; you'll be able to jump to any day, past or future, in the resulting dialog box (see Figure 4-3).

Other onscreen elements

Several of the day-view screen elements are worth learning about because they appear in all of the Date Book's views. First, at the lower-left corner, you'll see three tiny squares filled with dots (see Figure 4-1). (Original Pilot models have a Week button instead.) Tap the middle button (or the Week button) to open the week view, shown in Figure 4-2. (If your display actually *looks* like Figure 4-2, you need an assistant.)

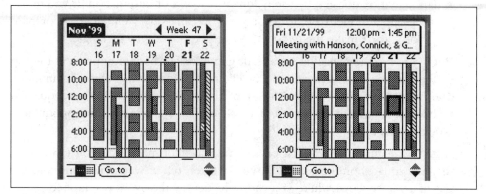

Figure 4-2. In week view (left), the dark blocks represent times that you're busy. Tap one of the gray blocks to see what you're supposed To Do (top right).

In the upper-left corner of every Date Book view, the currently viewed month and year appear in a black "tab." Tap that tab with your pen—the black tab changes to reveal the current time.

You've just read a handy two-tap trick for getting your PalmPilot to tell you what time it is, no matter what program you're using: press the Date Book button and then tap the month/year tab in the upper left.

There is, however, a quicker way to check the time, no matter what you're doing on the PalmPilot: tap the Applications button at the lower-left corner of the screen. You'll see the time displayed just next to the battery graph.

Viewing the Week's Events

While the day-at-a-glance screen shows a lot of detail, the PalmPilot can also give you a visual overview of your week ahead.

The main attraction of the week view is the gray vertical blocks that indicate chunks of busy time. As Figure 4-2 shows, the PalmPilot can even show you simultaneous (overlapping) appointments—it draws two narrow side-by-side bars. And if you're so busy that you're juggling *more* than two meetings at once, you're treated to the rare but striking *diagonal-line block* shown on the last day of the week in Figure 4-2.

In addition to the gray blocks, week view offers several other useful cues and controls:

Event details

A dark gray box doesn't, by itself, convey a world of information. If you're trying to set up a dinner date, for example, you can't very well tell your companion, "Sorry, can't make the twentieth—I've got a dark gray rectangle."

But if you tap the stylus tip *on* a dark gray block, a banner appears at the top of the screen, as shown at right in Figure 4-2, identifying that appointment. The banner remains in place for only about five seconds, so read quickly. (While the banner is displayed, a black border appears on the appointment block you tapped.)

Alas, this feature doesn't exist on the original Pilot models. If you tap one of the gray squares on these models, you're taken *out* of week view and into the day-at-a-glance view, where you can now identify the event you tapped.

Blank space

Tap any empty area on the time chart to open the corresponding day's day-at-a-glance display. For example, to open Friday's page, tap *between* gray blocks (if any). The day view opens, with the cursor already waiting at the time slot you tapped.

To move from week view into day view, you're ordinarily supposed to tap a blank area of the display. But suppose you're really busy, and there *isn't* any blank space between gray blocks. How are you supposed to open up a day-at-a-glance screen?

Tap the *header* above a particular column—one of the day-of-the-week initials (S M T W T F S) or date numbers (16 17 18 and so on). Tapping the header opens the corresponding day-view screen.

Timeless events

Some events don't occur at a certain *time,* but instead on a certain *day* (such as Aggie's Birthday or Thanksgiving). Later in this chapter, you'll learn how to add these to your Date Book. For now, note how these events appear in the week-at-a-glance view: as tiny dots just beneath the date numbers. For example, if you study the top of Figure 4-2, you'll see the dots beneath the numbers 19 and 20. November 19 and 20 each have a non-time-specific event.

The scroll triangles

The PalmPilot doesn't "collapse" empty time slots in week view, as it does in day view. You're always shown a 10-hour slice of time. To see more, tap the up- or down-triangle buttons at the right side of the screen, just below the week grid. Tapping these triangles scrolls the previous (or next) hours of the day into view.

These scroll triangles don't appear at all unless there *are* events that begin or end outside of the hours you're currently viewing. You never have to wonder *if* there are events "below the screen"—the triangles tell you so.

Off-the-screen events

The appearance of the scroll triangles isn't your only cue that events may begin or end off the current screen. Inspect your calendar grid. Is there a horizontal line at the bottom of one of the columns? (In Figure 4-2, you can see such underlines beneath the Sunday and Friday columns.) This underline signals you that you're not seeing the entire day's worth of events—that there's more, later in the day. (If the line appears above the column, of course, that means there's more to see *earlier* than the current display.) Tap the scroll triangles to see them.

The week-change buttons

The top-right corner of the screen indicates which week of the year you're viewing—Christmas generally appears in Week 52, for example—and the right- and left-pointing triangles let you view the previous and next weeks, respectively.

Instead of tapping these tiny triangles with the stylus, you can also press the plastic up/down scroll buttons at the bottom of the PalmPilot; in week view, they, too, move to the previous or next week display. (As in day view, the *downward-pointing* button takes you to the *next* week.)

The "Go to" button

At the bottom of the week grid is a button called "Go to." Tap it to make the date-selection display appear, as shown in Figure 4-3. In this special window, you can jump to any date to set up, consult, or edit your agenda. Be sure to select a month and year first, however; tapping a *day* closes this special window and opens the corresponding date's day view.

Seizing Control over Time and Space

If you're a night owl (or an early bird), you may be slightly annoyed that the PalmPilot, in all its views, insists that mornings begin at 8:00 am. You may wish that the PalmPilot would automatically display the hours when *you're* active, beginning at, for example, 10:00 a.m. (or 5:00 a.m.).

To specify what *you* consider the beginning and ending hours of the day, tap Menu → Options → Preferences. The Preferences screen appears, shown in the figure below. Tap the black triangle buttons to adjust the Starting Time (the time slot the PalmPilot's displays will put at the top of the screen) and Ending Time.

While we're at it, note that some savvy Piloteers deliberately set their Ending Time to *11:00 p.m.* Why? Suppose your day's ending time is set to 7:00 p.m. If you wish to add an appointment for 8:00, you're forced to: (1) write the appointment at some other time; (2) tap the time label of the slot you wrote on; and (3) change the time in a dialog box to 8:00. If you set your day's Ending Time to 11:00 pm, scroll arrows always appear in day view (unless you're using the "Compress Day View" option). To record an after-working-hours appointment, just tap the scroll triangles to bring the evening hours into view—no dialog box visit required.

On the other hand, a certain other population of PalmPilot users deliberately sets both the Starting Time and Ending Time to the *same time*. The result: in day view, you won't see any empty time slots displayed *at all*, as shown in the figure below at right—one small blow in the modern war against complexity. When you consult your calendar for the day, you see only a neat, clean, short list of events; if you have no events scheduled, you see only a single blank line.

—Continued—

At first, you might wonder: with no empty lines available, how can you record a new appointment? If you've adopted this ultra-collapsed display mode, you must create a new appointment by writing the first number of its *time* in the Graffiti writing area. The dialog box shown in Figure 4-6 appears, so that you can finish specifying the time—and then, when you tap OK, you'll return to the day view, where a new blank line has been created. Write the name of the appointment on it, and you're done.

Figure 4-3. Only on the Go to Date screen is time travel a reality. If you decide not to change the date displayed, tap Cancel; if you've been viewing some date in the past or future, tap This Week to return to the week display for today's date.

In Palm OS 2 or later, the Date Book offers a handy rescheduling option. Point to a gray square in week view. If you keep your stylus tip pressed against the screen, you can actually *drag* that appointment to a different time slot—or even a different day.

Unfortunately, your dragging is confined to the current screen; you can't drag an appointment out of the current week. If that's your goal, you'll have to reschedule it manually, using the techniques described in "Changing the date of an appointment," later in this chapter.

The Month View

You get to the month view by tapping the rightmost of the three "view" buttons, as shown at lower left in Figure 4-4, or by pressing the plastic Date Book button repeatedly.

Figure 4-4. The month view, available in Palm OS 2 or later, lets you see how your month is shaping up.

The PalmPilot would be somewhat larger than 3×5 inches if it had to show you the actual *names* of your appointments in this month-at-a-glance view. The squares representing appointments here are so small that only three fit on each day's square—and you can't tap one to identify it, as you can in week view.

Instead, the PalmPilot tries to show you which *chunks* of the day have events scheduled: if you've got something before noon, you see a tiny black block at the *top* right of the calendar square. If something's scheduled to begin between noon and 1:00 p.m., a black block appears at the *middle* right side; and if you have an appointment scheduled for 1:00 p.m. or later, a black block appears at the *lower* right side. Figure 4-5 should make all of this clear.

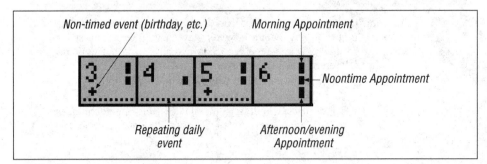

Figure 4-5. A few of the indicators you might see in the PalmPilot's month view.

Figure 4-5 also shows an example of the nearly microscopic + symbol that may appear on the *left* side of a calendar square. This symbol indicates a non-timed event, such as a birthday or holiday. Finally, you may see a horizontal dotted line running across several days of the month view—your cue that some event has been scheduled to appear on several consecutive days, such as "In Dallas through Friday."

Don't be alarmed if your month view doesn't show the tiny + symbol (for timeless events) or horizontal dotted line (for daily repeating events). As it comes from the factory, the PalmPilot is set up *not* to show these extra elements in month view. You're expected to turn them on if you want them.

To do so, tap Menu → Options → Display Options. In the resulting box, you'll see the checkboxes that control Untimed Events and Daily Repeating Events; tap to turn these features on.

Month view's interface controls—scroll triangles, Go to button, month/year tab, and so on—are mostly the same as in the week view. (In this view, your plastic up/down scroll buttons take you to the previous and next month; again, though, you might find the logic backward. The top button opens the previous month.)

There are only two differences between the month and week views. First, tapping the S M T W T F S header at the top of the calendar display *doesn't* show you the corresponding day or week view, as you might expect; second, tapping a calendar square *does* open up the day view for the date you tapped.

Setting Up Appointments

If you use a full-fledged calendar program on your desktop PC, you may never need to add events on the PalmPilot itself. You'll just transfer the information from your computer to the PalmPilot before each road trip, as described in Chapter 6, *HotSync, Step by Step*. But if you think you may want to modify your schedule on the actual PalmPilot, read on.

You can create and edit appointments only in the day-at-a-glance view, not week or month views. Simply tap the appropriate time slot (such as 3:00) and begin writing in the Graffiti area (see Chapter 3, *Typing Without a Keyboard*).

If your appointment-to-be doesn't fall squarely on the hour (for example, if it's slated for 3:35 p.m.), use one of these three methods to set it up:

- Tap the line corresponding to the correct hour, such as 3:00. Write the name of the event. Then tap the time label ("3:00") at the left side of the screen to open the box shown in Figure 4-6. Tap the 35 in the right-most column; tap End Time (plus an hour and minute) to specify an end time, if any; and then tap OK.

- Begin by writing the hour number on the right side of the Graffiti writing area (write 3 to begin an appointment for 3:35, for example).

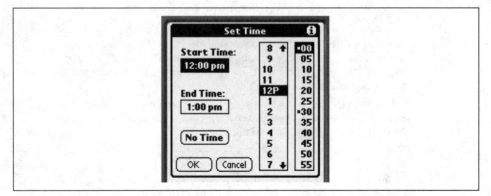

Figure 4-6. In this box, tap inside the Start Time or End Time box, and then select a time by tapping first in the hours column and then in the minutes column. (Tap the small up- and down-arrow buttons to scroll the list of hours.) No, you can't make an appointment for 3:33—only five-minute time slots are available.

Doing so automatically opens the dialog box shown in Figure 4-6, where two quick taps (on 35 and OK) will complete the time setup and return you to the day view. Now write the event's name.

This method—writing the hour number on the Graffiti area—is also a handy shortcut if the time slot you want isn't currently shown on the screen (*9*, for example); by writing in the Graffiti area, you avoid scrolling.

- In day view, tap the New button. You arrive at the Set Time screen shown in Figure 4-6. Now simply begin writing the starting time for your appointment, using the standard Graffiti number symbols. The PalmPilot does its best to guess what hour you really mean; for example, when you write the number 1, 1 p.m. is automatically selected in the scrolling list of hours (instead of the less likely 1 a.m.). But if, on the other hand, you then write a 0, 10 p.m. is now highlighted. Add a 5, and 10:50 is now selected.

As you continue to write, the PalmPilot continues to interpret. If you've set your PalmPilot to use the 24-hour, military-style clock display, for example, and you write 25, the PalmPilot automatically enters 2:50 (since there's no such time as 25:00).

Untimed events

If you'd like to jot down an *untimed event*—something associated with a particular day (like a birthday) but not a specific time—you have three options:

- Tap the New button. In the dialog box that appears, tap OK. You return to the day view, where your cursor awaits at the top of the screen. Now write the name of the event (such as "Set clocks ahead tonight").

- Tap any empty time slot and write the name of the event. When you're fin-ished, tap the time slot's label (such as "8:00") to open the dialog box shown in Figure 4-6. Tap No Time, and then OK.

- Use the easiest, fastest method of all: just start writing. (This time-saving trick isn't available on orginal Pilot models.)

In all three cases, the name of your event appears at the top of the screen. The black diamond to its left designates this event as having no special time associ-ated with it. (If you later decide this event *is* supposed to appear at a specific time, tap the black diamond. You get the Set Time box, where you can tap inside the Start Time box to set a time. Conversely, you can change an event already in a time slot *into* a nontimed event by tapping its time label, tapping No Time, and tapping OK.)

Changing the time of an appointment

To change the time for an appointment, tap the time label (such as "12:00") to its left. The dialog box shown in Figure 4-6 appears; tap an hour and minute from the two columns on the right, and then click OK to confirm the new time.

Technically, you can reach the Set Time dialog box in two other ways—either via the Event Details box (see Figure 4-7) or by writ-ing a number (in the right side of the writing area) when no Date Book event is selected (that is, the cursor isn't blinking anywhere).

But tapping a time label at the left side of the screen is much quicker.

Alternatively, you can switch to week view and drag the appointment's block to a different time slot, although you can't get much precision this way.

Changing the date of an appointment

To change the date of an appointment, tap anywhere on its line. Then tap Details. The box shown in Figure 4-7 appears; tap inside the Date dotted rectangle. A cal-endar appears, much like the one shown in Figure 4-3; tap to change the month and year first (if necessary) and, finally, the date. You return to the Details box. One final OK tap takes you back to the event you've adjusted, which is now shown on its *new* day.

To reschedule an appointment for a different time during the same week, here's a shortcut: switch to week view, and then drag the appointment's block horizon-tally to a different day (Palm OS 2 or later).

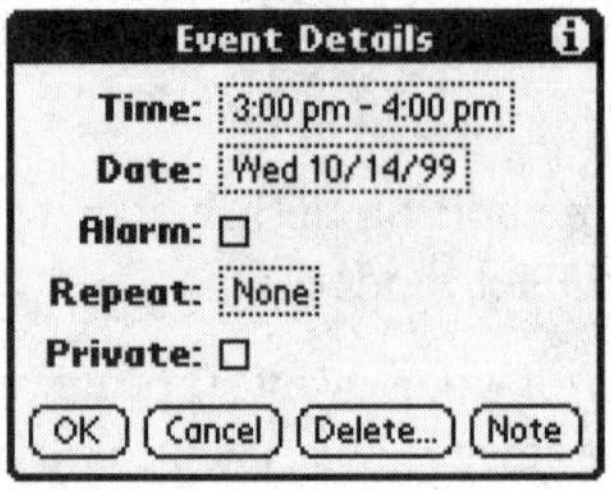

Event Details ⓘ

Time: 3:00 pm – 4:00 pm
Date: Wed 10/14/99
Alarm: ☐
Repeat: None
Private: ☐

(OK) (Cancel) (Delete...) (Note)

Figure 4-7. The Details box lets you change an event's date, set an audible alarm, schedule it to appear at regular intervals (such as once a month), add a note, or keep it safe from prying eyes.

Recurring events

You might not expect such a tiny gadget to offer a *recurring-events* feature. But if you need to schedule a once-a-month payment, or a weekly sales meeting, or your annual anniversary, you're in luck.

To create such an event, write it in on the first day of its kind. Then tap the Details button. In the Details box, tap inside the dotted "Repeat:" rectangle (where it now says None). You finally arrive at the box shown in Figure 4-8.

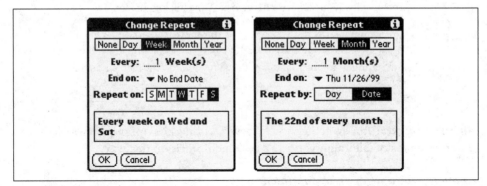

Figure 4-8. It may take you a moment to figure out what's going on in this Change Repeat box, but you'll eventually discover a great deal of flexibility.

Now specify how often this event should repeat. For example:

Every day

Tap the Day box at the top of the screen. Write (in the Graffiti area) a number into the "Every:" box to indicate the frequency—if you write *2,* for example, this event will automatically appear every *other* day on your calendar.

If this recurring event is supposed to keep going from now until doomsday, you're finished; tap OK. Otherwise, tap the "End on:" pop-up menu to specify the stop date for this repeating appointment.

The "Every day" recurring event type is the closest thing the Date Book program has to a *banner,* as found in many desktop-computer calendar programs. For example, use an "Every day" setting for a business trip, to indicate which days you'll be away.

Every week

Tap the Week box at the top of the screen. Now you see the options shown at left in Figure 4-8. By changing the "Every:" number, you can specify that this event is something that happens every week (write *1*), or every other week (write *2*), and so on. You can also tap more than one day of the week in the "Repeat on:" control—Monday, Wednesday, and Friday for your gym workouts, for example. Again, be sure to specify when this event stops, if ever, using the "End on:" pop-up menu.

Every month

This option, shown at right in Figure 4-8, is ideal for PTA meetings, mortgage-payment reminders, and other once-a-month happenings. The only new control here is the "Repeat by:" option. It lets you indicate whether this event takes place on a specific date each month (like a mortgage payment due the first of each month) or on a particular weekday (such as a computer-club meeting on the second Tuesday of each month).

How does the PalmPilot know that you mean the second Tuesday? Because that's the day on which you wrote the *first occurrence* before you even began setting up the repeat feature.

Every year

Use this option for holidays, birthdays, and anniversaries; it places a copy of this appointment on the same date of every year (December 25, for example).

When you've finished setting up the repeat feature, tap OK to return to the day view. As shown in Figure 4-9, a tiny icon (resembling, you might say, a piece of paper being duplicated) appears beside the name of the event. If you ever want to change some aspect of this event's repetition schedule, you can tap this tiny icon to open up the Details dialog box; now tap inside the Repeat box to change the repeat's setup.

Recurring events are often a complicated and inflexible feature of calendar programs. It's particularly pleasant, therefore, that the PalmPilot almost always handles such repeating appointments gracefully. If you reschedule the first event, for example, the PalmPilot offers to shift all of the repeating occurrences by a corresponding number of hours or days. If you change an event's recurrence schedule after the initial appointment has already passed, the PalmPilot thoughtfully applies the change only to current and *future* occurrences—the *past* record of your life's events is left intact.

Thanksgiving and Other Recurrent Problems

You might expect the "Every year" repeat option to be ideal for such annual events as Thanksgiving. Unfortunately, it won't work for such "Fourth Thursday in November"-type holidays; after all, Thanksgiving doesn't fall on the same numerical date of the month each year.

To schedule such an event, use the Month repeat option described earlier. Set the "Repeat by:" option to Day, and set the "Every: __ Month" option to 12. Sure enough, you'll see the plain-English translation: "The 4th Thursday of every 12th month," as shown below at left.

But what if it's not that simple? What if the 4th Thursday happens to be the last Thursday of the month? How is the PalmPilot supposed to know whether turkey-day is supposed to be the fourth Thursday or the last Thursday in November?

Easy: it asks you. After you've created the repeat, tapped OK, and tapped OK in the Event Details box, you get the message shown below. Those programmers think of everything.

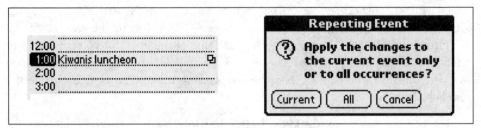

Figure 4-9. In day view, a tiny icon appears to the right of any repeating event (left). If you try to delete or change an occurrence of this repeating event, the PalmPilot is thoughtful enough to ask whether you're trying to change all occurrences or just the one you tapped (right).

Best of all, if you try to change any aspect of the appointment itself (add or delete an alarm or note, change the time of the appointment, and so on), you'll be asked the important question shown in Figure 4-9. The PalmPilot wants to know if you're adding to or changing just this one appointment—or whether this change is supposed to apply to this and all future repetitions. (The button in the Figure 4-9 message may *say* "All," but it *means* "This Event and Future Repetitions." Changing a repeating event never disturbs the occurrences prior to the one you're editing.)

Recurring Events: Breaking the Chain

When you change a recurring event's time, note or alarm status, or existence, the PalmPilot asks if you intend this change to affect all future repeats.

However, if you change the event's *name*, the PalmPilot doesn't bother consulting you. It automatically changes *every* occurrence of the event, past, present, and future. Be careful, therefore, when editing one of these events—don't delete some crucial phone-number information from its name, for example.

Fortunately, a little ingenuity can work around this potential pitfall. Whenever you adjust a recurring event's time, the PalmPilot wants to know: are you changing the time for this occurrence only, or for this and all future repetitions?

If you tap the Current button (meaning "this occurrence only"), you do more than edit that event; you also break the chain that connects it to the others of its race. In essence, you've converted it into a standalone, nonrecurring appointment. Now you're free to rename it, move it, delete it, have your way with it, without worrying that you're simultaneously making changes to subsequent occurrences of this repeating event.

Armed with this knowledge, you now know how to edit the text of one occurrence of a repeating event without affecting any others: drag it to a different time slot, tap the Current button when asked what you're changing, make your edit to the appointment's name—and finally, drag the event straight back into its original time slot.

Deleting an appointment

The PalmPilot offers three different ways to delete appointments. Each offers a tradeoff of convenience and permanence. For example:

Use the Delete Event menu command

If you're a Graffiti speed freak, write /D in the writing area (draw the slash upward). If you prefer using the menus, tap the Menu icon to make the Record menu appear; then tap Delete Event.

Either way, a message now appears: "Delete selected event?" The message box offers a checkbox labeled "Save archive copy on PC." If you select this option, the event you're deleting will disappear from your PalmPilot—but will be transferred to your desktop computer the next time you HotSync (see Chapter 6). In other words, this option lets you preserve a deleted event for recordkeeping's sake, while still freeing up memory on the PalmPilot.

Use the Details box

Tap an event's text, and then tap Details. In the dialog box that appears, tap Delete; at last you arrive at the confirmation box described earlier. This is the longest and least efficient method of deleting something.

Drag through the description of an event to highlight it, and then draw the "back-space" Graffiti stroke

The text of your calendar event disappears. When you tap anywhere else on the screen, you may even see its time slot "collapse" as subsequent events for the day slide upward to fill the gap. This is the fastest way to delete an event.

If you delete the text of a *recurring* event, you're instantly deleting *all occurrences* of that event—you won't even be warned.

Furthermore, if you delete an appointment by deleting its text, you're not offered a chance to have the deleted event archived on your desktop computer the next time you HotSync. (See Chapter 8, *Palm Desktop: Windows*, for more on archiving and HotSyncing.)

The PalmPilot as Alarm Clock

The PalmPilot's built-in speaker doesn't have the strength to wake up an entire dorm room, but it's loud enough to get your attention if you're (a) at your desk at work, hoping not to disturb your coworkers, or (b) sleeping with the PalmPilot on the bedside table. Therefore, the alarm feature is ideal for reminders and wake-up calls for the average-depth sleeper.

To set an alarm, create an appointment, as described in the previous sections. Then, with the cursor still blinking on the proper day-view line, tap Details.

As you can see in Figure 4-10, the box that now appears offers an Alarm option. Once you've tapped that checkbox to select it, a new set of controls appears; they let you specify how much advance notice you'd like. If you're reminding yourself to watch a certain show on TV, you might set the alarm to 5 Minutes, so you've got five minutes to get downstairs and find the correct channel. If you're off to Tampa for a relative's wedding, on the other hand, you might want the alarm to go off 2 Days before the "Tampa wedding" Date Book event. That way, you've got some time to shop for a wedding gift. (You can enter any number in the blank from zero to 99, replacing the 5, which is the proposed amount.)

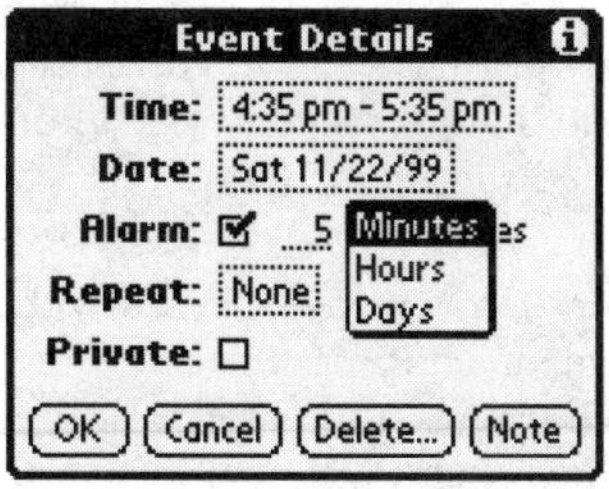

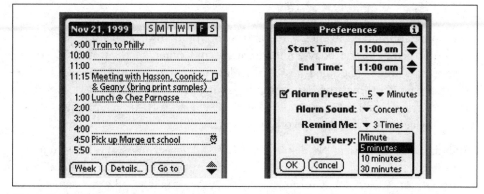

Figure 4-10. Tap the Minutes pop-up menu to see your choice of time units—Minutes, Hours, or Days—that represent the advance notice you want for your alarmed appointment.

Tap OK when you're finished. Except on original Pilots, a tiny alarm clock icon appears next to your appointment's name, as shown in Figure 4-11.

Figure 4-11. Once an alarm is set, an alarm clock icon appears next to the event's name (except on original Pilot models), as shown at 4:50 at left. On the Palm III and later models, you can control what sound the alarm makes and how insistent it is—tap Menu → Options → Preferences to access the dialog box shown at right.

How the PalmPilot gets your attention

When the designated moment arrives, the PalmPilot turns itself on automatically (if it wasn't on already). It sounds the alarm to get your attention—on the Pilot and PalmPilot, three "ding-dong!" chirps; on the Palm III and later models, whatever alarm sound you choose in the Date Book program's Preferences dialog box (see Figure 4-11, right). Meanwhile, the screen shows a no-frills, full-screen alert message whose distinguishing characteristic is an alarm-clock icon. Tap OK to make the message go away.

If a couple of missed breakfasts have convinced you that the alarm sound isn't loud enough to wake you, remember that the PalmPilot's internal speaker faces the *back* of the unit. Therefore, leaving your PalmPilot snugly wrapped in a leather case isn't the best way to maximize volume. Take it out of its case and leave it face down on your nightstand for maximum sound.

The PalmPilot's alarm isn't what you'd call a musical virtuoso, especially on pre-Palm III models: you get three two-note chirps, and that's it. If you sleep through those chirps, you'll miss your morning meeting.

AlarmHack, an add-on program included with this book, can help. It offers 10 replacement chirp sounds, one of which might be more successful in waking you. AlarmHack also lets you make the sound play more than three times, just as the Palm III and later models can do.

But if you're determined to sleep in, AlarmHack also offers an option that turns the entire screen into an Alarm Off button, so that you can shut the thing up without even having to open your eyes.

Alarms for nontimed events

By tapping an untimed event's name and then tapping the Details button, you can set up an alarm for birthdays, anniversaries, and other such events. Of course, these events aren't scheduled for a particular *time* (only for a certain *day*); therefore, the PalmPilot isn't quite as frantic in getting your attention as it is with timed alarms. For example, it doesn't turn on by itself, and it doesn't play any sound when the alert for an untimed event comes up.

Instead, the PalmPilot simply displays the full-screen alert message a few minutes, hours, or days before the beginning of the day on which your untimed event occurs. If your PalmPilot is turned on at the time, you'll see the message; otherwise, you'll see the message as soon as you turn the PalmPilot on during the day of the untimed event.

For example, if you leave the proposed alarm setting—five minutes—on your untimed "Christmas" event, your PalmPilot will show a message at 11:55 p.m. on Christmas Eve, if you're using it at the time. Otherwise, the message will appear the first time you use the palmtop on Christmas day.

Alarms for the alarm-obsessed

If you find yourself setting up alarms for *most* of the events in your Date Book, consider telling the PalmPilot to set up alarms for *all* events. (You can always turn off the alarm for the appointments for which you don't need reminders.)

To do so, tap Menu → Options → Preferences. In the dialog box that appears, tap the Alarm Preset checkbox, and then tap Done. From now on, every new appointment you notate will give you a five-minute warning alarm (unless you change the warning time, as described earlier).

Alarms for the silence lover

If you're attending a live performance or movie, do the world a favor: temporarily shut up *all* your PalmPilot alarms. To do so, tap Applications → Prefs; from the upper-right pop-up menu, choose General; and tap the Alarm Sound checkbox so that no checkmark appears.

Your PalmPilot will still display visual messages as your alarms go off—but it won't make a sound.

Forgetting the Past

Each event in your Date Book consumes only the tiniest amount of your memory. Still, as time goes by, those appointments and notes add up. After you've used your PalmPilot for six months or more, consider erasing past events so that they're not cluttering up your machine's limited memory. You lose very little by doing so—you'll still have a backup on your desktop computer in case you ever want to consult those past months' calendars (or even restore them to the PalmPilot).

To purge past events, follow these steps:

1. Tap Menu → Record → Purge. (As an alternative to this entire step, you could use the Graffiti menu shortcut: /E. Draw the slash from the bottom.)

2. In the dialog box (see Figure 4-12), use the pop-up menu to specify how far back you want your appointments preserved. For example, if you choose "1 week" from the pop-up menu, everything *older* than one week will be deleted from the PalmPilot. As long as you leave the checkbox called "Save archive copy on PC" selected, though, those calendar entries won't be gone forever. The next time you HotSync (see Chapter 6), those old events do disappear from the Palm Desktop program on your PC or Mac—but they're still retrievable in the form of a Date Book archive, as described in Chapters 8 and 9.)

3. Tap OK.

Figure 4-12. The Purge command lets you free up PalmPilot memory by deleting (but backing up) events that have already passed.

If you'd like the added satisfaction of seeing proof that you've freed up memory, tap Applications → Menu → App → Info (or on pre-Palm III models, Applications → Memory instead), and relish how much lower the Date Book memory amount is now. (This is only satisfying, of course, if you checked its memory consumption *before* doing the purge.)

If the Date Book memory amount doesn't look impressively low, it may be because you used the "Save archive copy on PC" option in Step 2. In that case, your PalmPilot is still hanging on to the older data, awaiting its next date with your PC. Only after your next HotSync will the PalmPilot truly be rid of those older appointments, and only then will you free up the memory you've worked so hard to reclaim.

When you purge old Date Book events, everything older than the date you specified is erased from the PalmPilot's memory. But what if there's some important event in your life that you want to preserve—even though it took place a while ago? Wouldn't it be nice if you could designate certain significant appointments as non-purgeable?

You can. Before you purge, tap the event and then tap the Details button. Change the event into a repeating event—that only repeats, for example, every 50 years. The PalmPilot can't purge the *first occurrence* of any repeating event whose repetitions haven't finished yet. As a result, the event you designated will be safe from purging—at least for the next 50 years! (And by then, you'll be wearing the Palm MCMVIII implanted in your earlobe.)

Four Global Palm Features

A few of the PalmPilot's features work in *any* of its built-in programs: attaching notes, finding lost bits of information, grabbing numbers from the Address Book program, and hiding sensitive data from unauthorized snoopers. Here's how you might use them in the Date Book program.

Attaching a note

The name of a particular Date Book appointment can be several lines long—255 letters and spaces, or about 40 words. But suppose you need more room; for example, suppose you want to record instructions for getting to a particular meeting. In that case, use the Notes feature. (Notes are also available in the To Do and Address Book programs.)

Here's how: After entering the name of your appointment (or Address Book name, or To Do entry), tap Menu → Record → Attach Note. (Or, if you're a shortcut-lover,

DateBk3: The Date Book on Steroids

This powerful program offers a week view that actually shows your appointments (as shown below, left), a year view, a list view, and other views. It integrates your To Do-list items with your calendar (as shown below, right), lets you associate alarms and repeats with your To Do's, adds a Snooze feature to the alarms, lets you create appointments that go on past midnight, offers a daily journal, and boasts 40 other improvements over the built-in Date Book program.

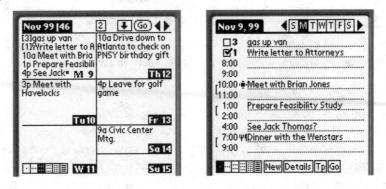

Its sole downside—its memory requirement of 245K—seems a small sacrifice for such an impressive piece of life-management software. (A trial version is on this book's CD-ROM.)

simply write /A in the Graffiti area—the menu shortcut for Attach Note. Draw the slash from bottom to top.)

A new screen appears, like that shown in Figure 4-13, where you can write up to 4,025 characters' worth of notes. Now *that's* more like it: about 670 words, roughly a single-spaced page of typing.

As you can see in Figure 4-13, the bottom of the Notes window shows two boxed letter As on the Pilot or PalmPilot. These buttons control the size of the text in the Notes window. On later models, you can choose from among several different fonts—tap Menu → Options → Font to view your choices.

Don't expect a Macintosh or Windows 95 here—you have only one font in each program—but when your eyes are bleary, it's nice to be able to magnify the text by tapping a larger font button.

For details on using the scrollbars that appear in long notes, see the "The Memo Pad" section later in this chapter.

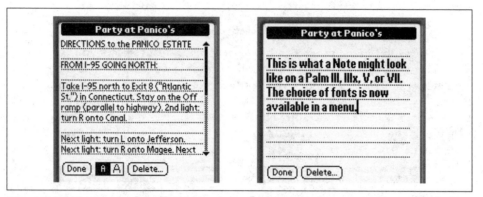

Figure 4-13. The Notes page, which holds text associated with a particular appointment. Get used to the Notes feature; a similar one is available in several other Palm programs.

Finding a scrap of information

Suppose you need to know when you last had your meeting with Joseph Schorr, but you can't remember. Don't waste your time scrolling through week after week of Date Book screens. Instead, use the Find command, which searches your *entire* PalmPilot for information—To Do list, Memo Pad, Address Book, *and* the Date Book—simultaneously.

Tap the Find icon at the lower right of the screen. A Find blank appears, as shown in Figure 4-14; type a word or phrase you're sure was part of the description of that appointment (or even part of its Notes), and then tap OK.

After a moment, the result is a list of items from all four major programs that contain the name you looked for (also shown in Figure 4-14). For example, you'll see any appointments you've had with Schorr (listed under the Date Book category), but you may also see Schorr's phone number (from the Address Book program).

Find	Find
Find: Schorr	**Matches for "Schorr"**
OK Cancel	——— Addresses ———
	Schorr, Joseph 503-844-9877 W
	——— Datebook ———
	Lunch at Joe S... 2/14/98 1:00 pm
	Schorr confere... 4/4/98 1:00 pm
	——— Memos ———
	——— To Do Items ———
	——— Mail Messages ———
	Cancel

Figure 4-14. When you tap the Find icon, you get the Find blank (left). Type what you're looking for and tap OK. Now the PalmPilot shows you a list of matches for what you sought, from all of its various programs (right).

Tap a line in this items-found window to view its full entry in the appropriate program. For example, in Figure 4-14, you could tap the second of the two Date Book entries, because it's the most recent entry in the Date Book.

To get the most out of the Find command, you should know that:

- Capitalization doesn't matter when you're searching.

- You don't have to complete the word you're looking for. You can write *base* to locate the word *baseball*.

- On the other hand, the PalmPilot searches only for matches at the *beginnings* of words. If you search for *ball*, the PalmPilot won't find the word *baseball*. (If this quirk bothers you, install FindHack, included with this book, which finds text even in the middle of words. FindHack is described in Appendix A, *100 Programs Worth Knowing About*.)

- Instead of writing what you're seeking into the Find blank, you can highlight some text you've already written (in any program) by dragging the stylus across it. (See Chapter 3 for more on editing techniques.) If you now tap the Find icon, the highlighted text automatically appears in the Find blank.

- As your PalmPilot becomes increasingly crammed with information, searching can take longer and longer. If, during a search, the item you're looking for appears in the list, tap the Stop button to cut short the search. (You can resume the search by tapping Find More.)

- The PalmPilot always searches the program you're in first. In other words, if you're looking up a phrase that you know appears in your Memo Pad, you'll save time by switching to the Memo Pad *before* tapping the Find button.

Phone book cross-references

If you tried the tutorial in Chapter 2, *Setup and Guided Tour*, you've already encountered the Phone Lookup command (a feature unique to Palm OS 2 and later). It automatically pastes the full name and phone number of a person listed in your Address Book into whatever *other* program you're using (Date Book, To Do, or Memo Pad, for example).

To use the Phone Lookup command, first take *one* of these three actions:

- Tap a blank line in your Date Book, or create a new blank Memo or To Do item.

- Write an identifiable portion of a person's name.

- Highlight a person's name (by dragging the stylus across it) anywhere you've already written it.

Next, invoke the Phone Lookup menu command. If you're in a hurry, use the menu shortcut—write /L in the Graffiti area (draw the slash upward, as usual). The longer way is to tap Menu → Options → Phone Lookup.

What happens next depends on how you set up the command:

• If you began with a new, blank entry, you're now shown a complete list of your PalmPilot's phone numbers, essentially as shown in the middle in Figure 4-15. Tap the name you want, and then tap Add; you return to the Date Book (or To Do or Memo program), where the full name and phone number now appears.

• If you had typed or highlighted a name, whatever you just typed or highlighted is now *replaced* by the full name and number of the closest-matching *last name* in your Address Book. (If there's more than one match, or no match, you're taken to the full phone number list shown in the middle in Figure 4-15. Again, tap the name you want and then Add; the name in your Date Book, To Do, or Memo program is replaced by the full name/number information.)

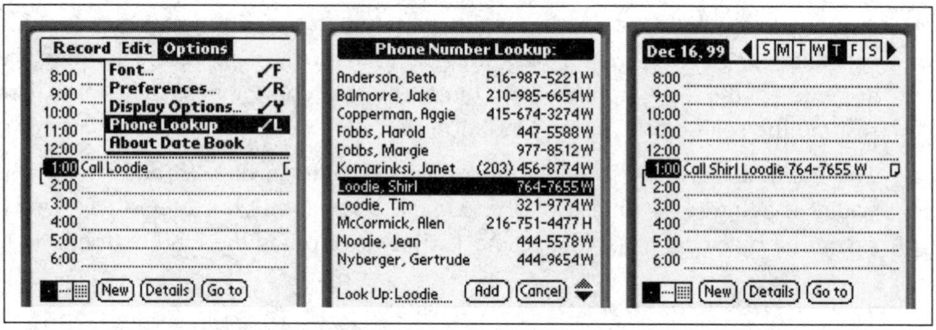

Figure 4-15. In the Date Book, To Do program, or Memo Pad, write or highlight a name (or part of a name), and then invoke the Phone Lookup command (left). If there's no obvious match with an Address Book entry, you'll be shown the full list of numbers (center), where you can make a selection and tap Add. The result is a complete name and number in the program in which you started (right).

Incidentally, the Address Book can store five or more phone numbers for each person. The phone number that appears when you use the Phone Lookup command is the *principal* one for each contact—the one you've designated as the "Show in list" number. For instructions, see "Changing the phone number labels" in "The Address Book" section of this chapter.

Keeping your appointments private

The PalmPilot's privacy feature lets you keep specified appointments (and memos, addresses, and To Do items) hidden from prying eyes. This security option is useful if, for example, you don't want a coworker snooping through the PalmPilot you leave in your desk drawer. If you pretty much keep your PalmPilot either with you or filled with declassified information, you can safely ignore this entire aspect of the machine.

To flag a particular item as private, tap it, and then tap the Details button. The Details dialog box appears, as shown in Figure 4-10. Tap the Private checkbox to put a checkmark there, and then tap OK. Now a warning message appears. It lets you know that the appointment (or To Do item, address, or memo) you've just changed *won't* disappear until you turn on the privacy master switch. Tap OK to dismiss the message.

To turn the privacy master switch on or off, tap the Applications icon. In the Applications screen, tap Security. You'll see the Show/Hide buttons; tap Hide.

Now *all* items, in all programs, that you've marked as Private are invisible. Neither you nor anyone else can see them until you tap the Show button (in that Security screen), which makes *all* of them reappear.

You can, if you wish, also specify a password that's required to hide or show all the Private items. For details (and more information about the Security program), see Chapter 5, *The Other Built-In Programs.*

The Private checkbox on certain records (appointments, addresses, and so on) is useful, as far as it goes. But it has one drawback: you can't ever *see* which appointments you've marked as private. If you go to the Security application to turn on the privacy master switch, all Private records disappear. Turn off the privacy master switch, and they all reappear—but mixed in among normal, nonprivate records.

The handy solution: Set up a category for private records in each of your PalmPilot programs. Whenever you tag a record as Private, also assign it to the Private category. From now on, all your private stuff is in one place, easy to spot, and easy to recategorize, when the time comes, as unclassified.

The Address Book

The second plastic button at the bottom of a Palm device, marked with a telephone-handset icon, launches the Address Book program. It presents a neat master list of all your contacts, sorted by last name and displaying each person's principal phone number. (See Figure 4-16.)

If your world of acquaintances includes 11 people or less, you can stop reading here: 11 names fit on a single "page" of the screen list.

Figure 4-16. The Address Book starts with a home page of all your phone numbers (left). Tap a name to open its detail view for that name (right).

If the person whose number you're looking up isn't among the first 11 listed, however, begin writing the person's last name in the Graffiti writing area. With each letter you write, the phone-book list scrolls to the name that most closely matches what you've written so far. In other words, even if you have thousands of names in the list, you can home in on a single acquaintance by writing only about three letters of the name. (In Figure 4-16, writing a single letter, N, sufficed to find Jean Noodie's entry.)

Alternatively, you can press the plastic up/down scroll buttons at the bottom of the PalmPilot—or tap the up/down black triangle buttons on the screen—to view the previous or next screens full of names.

And if you *still* can't find the name you're looking for—for example, if you can't remember some guy's name, but you know that he works at Microsoft—use the Find icon at the lower right of the screen. The Find command, as described earlier in this chapter, can locate text even among the details of an Address Book entry—not just the person's name.

After looking up a phone number by writing a few letters of the desired name on the Look Up line beneath the Address Book list, you don't have to delete what you've written before looking up a second name.

Instead, just press one of the plastic scroll buttons at the bottom of the palmtop. Doing so instantly empties the Look Up field, making it ready for your next lookup.

Changing the Sort Order

A brand-new PalmPilot sorts the names in its Address Book program alphabetically by last name. If you deal mostly with people in the corporate world, however, you may prefer to see your master list sorted by company name, as shown in Figure 4-17.

If that's the case, the PalmPilot can accommodate you. The procedure is slightly different depending on your model.

- Original Pilot models: Tap Menu → Options → List By. A box like the one shown at the right in Figure 4-17 appears.

- Later models: Write /R in the Graffiti area. The box shown at the right in Figure 4-17 appears. (If you prefer to use menus, tap Menu → Options → Preferences. The same box appears.)

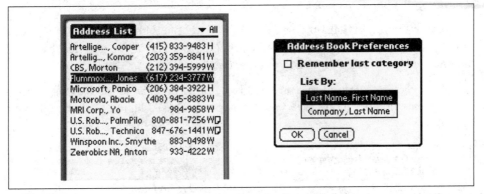

Figure 4-17. To switch between a last-name sorting order and a company-name sort (as shown at left), use the Preferences dialog box (right).

In the dialog box, select the sort order you prefer, and then tap OK.

Fortunately for your sanity, the PalmPilot isn't so rigid about sorting that it produces silly results. If you've opted to sort by last name, for example, but you also have several entries with *no* personal names—just company names—the company names will fall into alphabetical place among your other contacts' last names.

Adding Address Book Entries

To input a new Address Book entry, tap New. You arrive at the screen shown in Figure 4-18, where you can begin filling in the blanks.

There are two easy ways to move from blank to blank: either tap the stylus in each blank before writing, or use the "next field" Graffiti pen stroke shown at right in Figure 4-18. As you go, don't bother drawing the "Shift key" Graffiti stroke; the PalmPilot automatically capitalizes the first letter of every Address Book blank.

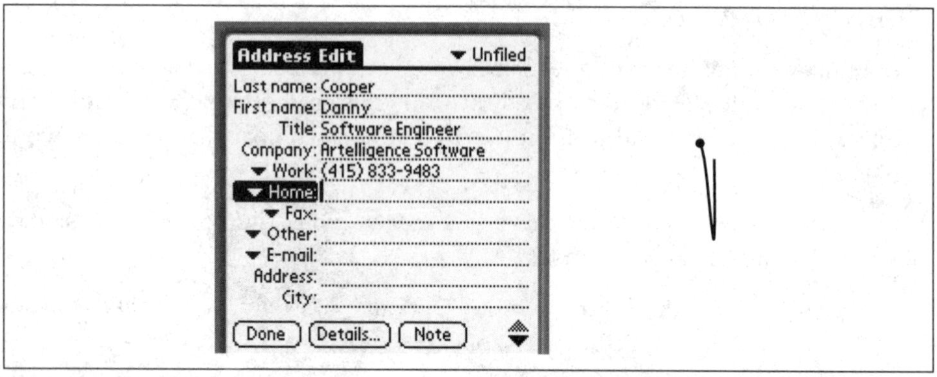

Figure 4-18. Here's the long way to enter address-book data. The short way: download existing information from your desktop computer, as described in Chapter 6. Shown at right is the Graffiti pen stroke that advances your cursor from one blank to the next.

Changing the phone number labels

These days, you'd be hard pressed to find two people with the same set of phone numbers. One may have a home phone, pager, and fax, while another may have an email address, cell phone, and work extension.

The PalmPilot gets around this problem by letting you change the various Address Book phone-number labels on a person-by-person basis. Figure 4-19 should make this clear.

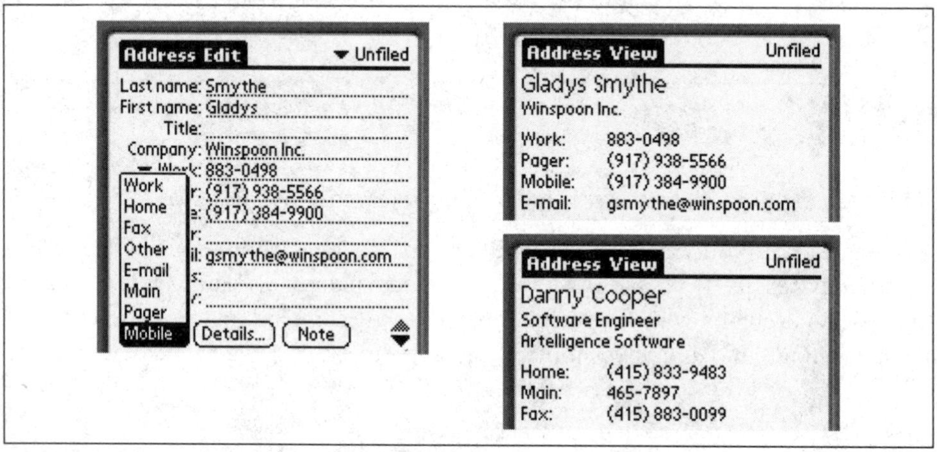

Figure 4-19. By tapping the pop-up menu beside each phone-number blank (left), you can change the labels on an address-by-address basis. The result (right): each person in your phone book might show a different set of phone-number types.

In keeping with this flexible phone-number feature, you can even specify *which* of each person's five phone numbers should appear in the master startup phone list shown in Figure 4-16. For example, Danny Cooper works at home, so you'd want his Home number to be the principal listing; but Gladys Smythe spends long hours at the office—you'd want her principal phone listing to be her Work number.

To specify which number shows up in the master list, while editing the person's information (see Figure 4-19), tap the Details button. The box shown in Figure 4-20 appears; tap the triangle next to "Show in List" to open the pop-up menu of phone numbers. Now tap the one you'd like to designate as the most important number, and then tap OK.

> ### Address Entry Details ⓘ
> **Show in List:** ▼ Main
> **Category:** ▼ Unfiled
> **Private:** ☐
> (OK) (Cancel) (Delete...) (Note)

Figure 4-20. Use the "Show in List" pop-up menu to determine which of this person's phone numbers should appear in the Address Book's main startup phone list. This setting can be different for every person in your list.

Yes, the Details dialog box lets you specify which telephone number you want to appear on the Address Book program's main index listing screen. But savvy Piloteers don't even bother with that—they know the shortcut.

It turns out that, by default, the PalmPilot displays whichever telephone number you wrote in *first* as its main phone number on the index screen. If you keep that in mind whenever you input a new person's address, you can avoid ever having to specify a "main listing" phone number.

Adding more blanks

If you're recording the names of *really* well-connected people, the PalmPilot's five phone number blanks might not be enough. For that reason, the PalmPilot also offers you four blanks that can hold any information you want: birthday, spouse's name, date of last address update, memory joggers ("bald guy on plane to LA")—whatever you want.

When you first begin filling in a person's contact information, you don't see these custom blanks—they're off the bottom of the screen. Press the lower plastic scroll button (or tap the down-pointing black triangle on the screen) to see them, as shown at right in Figure 4-21.

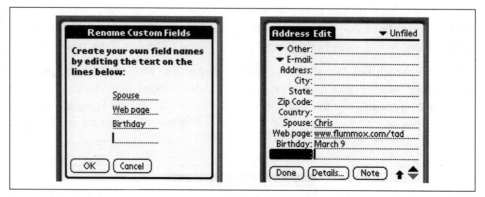

Figure 4-21. At left: you can edit the names of the custom blanks (which the PalmPilot calls "fields"). At right: your new labels appear at the bottom of every address-info screen.

To change these labels from "Custom 1," "Custom 2," and so on into something more useful, write /F in the Graffiti writing area. (The slash goes upward, as always.) That's the shortcut for tapping Menu → Options → Rename Custom Fields. The box shown in Figure 4-21 appears; delete the words "Custom 1," "Custom 2," and so on, and write in your own preferred labels for these extra-info blanks. Tap OK when you're finished.

When you return to the main data-entry screen, you'll see your new labels in place, as shown at the right in Figure 4-21.

Note that, unlike the phone-number blanks, any new labels you give to the four Custom Fields apply to *everyone in your Address Book.* You can't vary these blanks on a person-by-person basis.

> If you're using Palm Desktop 2 for Macintosh, as described in Chapter 9, store your email addresses in the fifth phone-number blank, not in the Custom fields, nor in any of the first four phone-number fields (even if they're empty). Strange as it sounds, the fifth phone-number blank's contents get HotSynced to the Palm Desktop's E-mail field, regardless of this field's actual label.

More information per blank

Although the PalmPilot displays only a single line for every phone number, address blank, and Custom Field, you can actually write more than one line of information into each blank. To create an additional line, just draw the Graffiti symbol for the Return key (a slash from the top right)—and keep writing! The blank automatically expands to accommodate the new information.

Using this trick, you could actually store, for example, several additional phone numbers in a single phone-number field—or an entire "country home" address in a single Custom Field.

Keeping addresses private

The Details box shown in Figure 4-20 offers a Private checkbox. If you turn this option on for a particular address, it can be made invisible to unauthorized users of your PalmPilot, just as a calendar entry can be. See "Keeping your appointments private" earlier in this chapter for details.

Attaching a note to an address book entry

You can attach 650 words' worth of notes to any name in your Address Book—a handy place to store directions to a client's office, a phone call history, or other text worth remembering.

To add or edit a note, tap in the narrow right margin of the main Address Book list (to the right of the H and W notations in Figure 4-17). The Note screen appears, ready for text. (This, by the way, is an utterly undocumented shortcut. Everybody else on earth takes the more laborious route to the Note editing screen: first tapping a contact name to open the editing screen, then tapping the Edit button, and finally tapping the Note button.)

After you've added Note information, you'll see a minuscule sheet-of-paper icon next to the person's name (in the startup master-phone-list view only). Henceforth, you can tap this icon to reopen the Note screen for editing.

Fortunately, you don't have to burrow to the Note screen just to read the note; the note's text shows up on your contact's main data screen—the one that appears when you tap somebody's name on the main index listing. That feature makes Notes a great place to store, for example, directions to somebody's house or office.

For more details on Notes, see "Attaching a note" in "The Date Book" earlier in this chapter.

Editing Address Book Entries

You edit names, addresses, and phone numbers the same way you input them—on the screen shown in Figure 4-16. To get there from the startup master list, tap a person's name or number, which takes you to the screen shown at right in Figure 4-19. Now tap anywhere on the screen—don't bother with the Edit button—and edit away.

Deleting Address Book entries

To cleanse your address list of somebody, tap the name on the master phone list to open that person's data screen. Now write /D in the Graffiti area (drawing the slash, as always, from the bottom). Or, if you prefer using menus, tap Menu → Record → Delete Record.

Either way, you're now asked to confirm the deletion. You're also offered the option of having this person's information backed up on your desktop computer the next time you HotSync the PalmPilot, exactly as described in "Forgetting the past," earlier in this chapter.

If you live in a province, not a state

Palm fans in Canada and other countries occasionally grumble that the Address Book seems hardwired for American users. It has blanks for, for example, State and Zip Code, which may not be appropriate in other countries.

If that's your situation, don't despair. Tap Applications → Prefs, and choose Formats from the upper-right pop-up menu. Choose your country from the pop-up menu. When you return to the Address Book, you'll see that the fields called State and Zip Code have magically changed to Province and Postal Code, or whatever's appropriate where you live.

(Conversely, the occasional American Palm user has switched to another country's formats accidentally, winding up frustrated that the currency setting on the Palm device is yen or francs instead of dollars. Now you know the secret: return to the Prefs application and change the setting back to United States.)

Categories: A Universal Palm Feature

As you go through life with your PalmPilot, you may find it convenient to categorize the people in your social circle, so that you can later view a list of people *only* in a particular group—only your business contacts or only your Christmas-card list, for example. The PalmPilot makes it easy to flag each person with a category tag—and to show you lists of people only in specific categories.

Categories are also available in the To Do list and the Memo Pad—and, on the Palm III and later, even in the Applications launcher and Expense program. In fact, you can create up to 15 different categories for *each program,* giving you a total of 45 or 75.

To place an Address Book entry into a particular category, get to the editing screen shown in Figure 4-18. (From the master startup phone list, tap a name, and then tap anywhere on the screen.) The pop-up menu for your various categories is in the upper-right corner (see Figure 4-22); tap the black triangle to choose a different category, and then tap Done.

Changing the available categories

If you're like most people, you probably find the factory-installed category list—Business and Personal (and, in the Address Book, QuickList)—a bit on the sparse side. Fortunately, you can change these labels and make up your own.

To edit your category list, tap the Category pop-up menu in the upper-right of the Address Book, Memo Pad, or To Do screen. Tap the Edit Categories command at the bottom of the list (as shown at left in Figure 4-22). The Edit Categories box appears, listing all the existing labels.

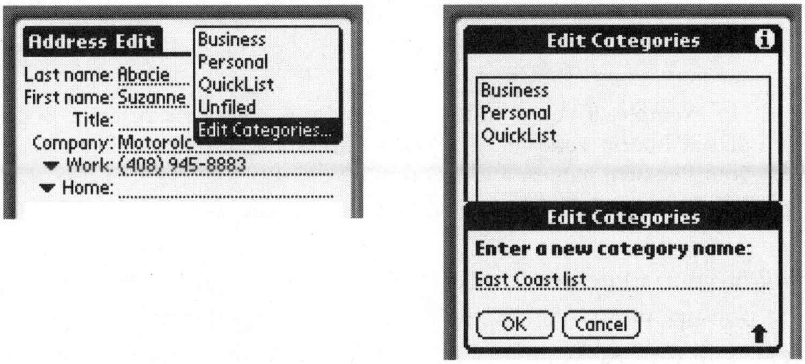

Figure 4-22. To edit the category list, use the pop-up menu in the top right of the Address Book, Memo Pad, or To Do program (left). In the Edit Categories box, tap New to create a new category label (right).

To edit one of the PalmPilot's existing labels, tap it and then tap Edit. To *add* a new category, tap New. Either way, you wind up in the box shown at the right in Figure 4-22; write the new category name and tap OK.

Henceforth, your new, improved category list will appear in the upper-right corner of the program whose category list you edited. (Again, don't be fooled by the fact that Business and Personal categories appear in all Palm programs; the category lists for each program are independent.)

If you plan to add a number of items (addresses, memos, or To Dos) that all belong to the same category, don't bother changing each one individually.

Instead, switch to the category view you want (see the next section). From now on, *every* address, memo, or To Do item you create will automatically fall into that category.

Switching category views

After you've tagged various Palm items with category labels, you can put them to use. For example, to view only your Personal addresses (or To Dos, or memos), tap the upper-right corner of the screen (where it usually says "Unfiled"), and then tap Personal in the pop-up menu. Suddenly all your names (or To Dos, or memos) that *aren't* in the Personal category are *hidden.* They're not gone—just invisible for the moment.

 Instead of using the upper-right pop-up menu to change category views, simply press the current program's plastic button at the bottom of the PalmPilot. Each press switches the list to a different category.

For example, if you're in the Address Book, press the Address Book plastic button repeatedly to view first your Business names, then your Personal names, and so on.

To view *all* of your addresses (or To Dos, or memos) again, choose All from that upper-right pop-up menu. (Alternatively, keep pressing the program's plastic hardware button until the "All" category name appears in the upper-right corner of the screen.)

Remembering the category selection when switching programs

In the Memo Pad and To Do programs, whatever category list you're viewing is what you'll see the *next* time you use the program.

The Address Book is different: in Palm OS 2 or later, you can make the Address Book either (a) behave like the other two programs, or (b) restore the category selection to All each time you return to the program.

In the Preferences dialog box (accessible from the Options menu), you'll see a checkbox called "Remember last category." (See Figure 4-17.) When that option is on, the category you last used in the Address Book will still be selected when you use it next time. Otherwise, the Address Book always shows you the names in *all* categories when you switch to it.

Manipulating categories

You can edit the list of categories without ever risking your data. For example, if you change the name of the Business category to Office, all addresses previously in the Business category are automatically flagged with the new Office label.

Similarly, if you *delete* a category, any addresses already flagged with its name rejoin the pool of Unfiled addresses, but you don't *lose* any of those names. (The PalmPilot explains this to you before proceeding.)

Finally, if you rename a category so that its name exactly matches *another* category, you effectively merge the two groups of addresses into one. (Again, the PalmPilot will explain this before acting.)

Ignoring the category feature

It's perfectly safe, by the way, to ignore the PalmPilot's category feature entirely if you don't see how it could help your particular work style. Every address, To Do item, and memo will be flagged with the "Unfiled" category name; that's perfectly OK.

Beaming from 'ere to 'ere

As Chapter 15, *Paging, Faxing, Printing, and Beaming*, explains, one of the most addictive features of the Palm III and later models (including the Palm IIIx, V, VII, IBM WorkPad, and Symbol SPT 1500) is the built-in infrared transmitter. By holding down the Address Book button for two seconds, you instantly transmit your entire "business card"—your own name, address, phone numbers, and so on—to any other Palm device within about a yard.

To tell the Address Book program which address is yours—to become your e-business card—create an entry for yourself. While editing it, tap Menu → Record → Select Business Card; tap Yes to confirm, and notice the tiny Rolodex–card icon at the top of the screen. Now you're ready to go forth and beam, using that amazing shortcut.

To deselect your Address Book entry as the business card to be beamed, you have no choice but to select a different Address Book entry as the Business Card—or to delete your own entry.

The To Do List

The To Do List opens when you press the third plastic button from the left. As shown in Figure 4-23, this simple software doodad can be a surprisingly powerful way to get control of your life.

The concept is simple: Every time you think of something else you've got to do, tap the New button and write the task down. (In fact, if you've got Palm OS 2 or later, you don't even have To Do *that;* simply begin writing in the Graffiti area.

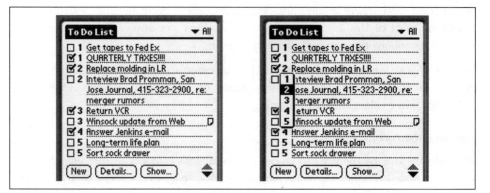

Figure 4-23. Tap a checkbox to "check off" a task you've gotten out of the way (left). To set a priority level, tap the number beside an item (right), and then tap one of the numbers (1 through 5).

The PalmPilot creates a new line automatically.) The name of a To Do item can be many lines long—up to about 100 words, in fact.

By tapping the number beside the checkbox, you can rank your To Do items in order of importance—lower numbers increase in urgency, and appear closer to the top of the list. (Don't be alarmed if the item whose priority you just changed seems to disappear. Most likely, it's just jumped into its correct sorted position, which may be off the screen.)

> The PalmPilot normally assigns Priority 1 to every new To Do item. However, if your list already contains items of various priorities, here's a timesaving tip: a new To Do item takes on the same priority level of whatever was selected *at the time you tapped the New button.*
>
> In other words, to add a new Priority 3 item, *tap* an existing Priority 3 item and then tap New. The new blank line appears automatically in its correct middle-of-the-list position.
>
> (What's more, your new To Do item also inherits the *due date* and *category* of the item you originally tapped; see the "Notating Your Deadlines" section for details on these other characteristics.)

Checking Off Tasks

As you complete the items you've listed for yourself, tap the tiny checkbox beside each item to place a checkmark there. Some people like these checked-off items to remain on the screen for awhile, reinforcing their sense of accomplishment; others prefer them to disappear immediately, bringing fresh obligations onto the screen. The PalmPilot can accommodate both kinds of people.

Delete items as they're finished

If you'd prefer each To Do item to disappear as soon as it's checked off, tap the Show button. You get the Preferences box, shown at the left in Figure 4-24. Turn off Show Completed Items, and then tap OK. From now on, an item will disappear the moment you tap in its empty checkbox.

It's not gone forever, however; if you turn the Show Completed Items option *on* again, all your completed items return to the screen.

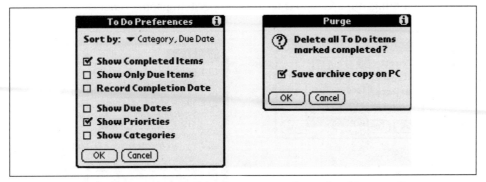

Figure 4-24. The Preferences box (left) lets you command completed items to disappear instantly. Alternatively, you can flush all completed tasks from your To Do program only when it suits you (right).

Even if you've turned off Show Completed Items, you should *also* purge your To Do data of completed tasks occasionally, as described in the next section. Doing so will reclaim memory and, in extreme cases, make your PalmPilot run faster.

Delete completed tasks en masse

Instead of having completed To Do items vanish from the screen, you may prefer that they stay in the list, complete with checkmarks. Yet you can't work this way forever; eventually, your To Do list will be so cluttered up with completed items that you can't find the *un*completed ones.

When that moment arrives (or sooner), consider telling the PalmPilot to delete completed tasks *en masse*. The short way: write /E in the Graffiti area (slash from bottom to top). The longer way: tap Menu → Record → Purge. Either way, you get the box shown at the right in Figure 4-24. It explains that you're about to delete completed items from the screen, but they can be backed up onto your desktop computer the next time you HotSync (see Chapter 6).

As in any similar dialog box, tap OK to proceed with the purging; tap Cancel to back out of this process without having actually done anything.

Notating Your Deadlines

In addition to ranking your To Do items by priority number, you can attach a due date to each item and view your tasks in deadline order, as shown in Figure 4-25.

To indicate a due date, tap within the text of a To Do item, and then tap Details. The box shown at the left in Figure 4-25 appears. The black triangle next to Due Date is a pop-up menu offering several frequently used deadline dates: Today, Tomorrow, and One Week Later, for example. There's also a Choose Date command, which brings up a calendar to use for specifying some other deadline date.

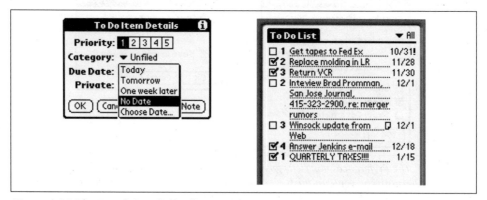

Figure 4-25. The Details box (left) offers a pop-up menu of due-date candidates. If you adjust your Show Preferences correctly, you can view your To Do items in deadline order instead of priority order (right).

Showing your deadlines

If you've just followed along, painstakingly adding due dates to your To Do items as described in the previous section, you might now be gasping in disappointment to see that the deadlines you've indicated *don't show up* in the To Do list!

Fortunately, making them appear is easy. Tap the Show button. The Preferences box appears, as shown in Figure 4-24. Turn on the Show Due Dates option, and then tap OK. Now the dates appear at the right side of the To Do screen, as shown at the right in Figure 4-25.

If you're a deadline-driven kind of person, turning on the Show Due Dates option offers a handy side effect: it adds a new narrow column to the right of the To Do list, where the due dates appear.

You can tap *in* this column to add or change an item's due date. A pop-up menu (like the one shown at left in Figure 4-25) appears right at your stylus tip—you're spared the hassle of tapping Details, opening a dialog box, tapping OK, and so on.

If a To Do item's deadline comes and goes, and you still haven't done anything about it, the due-date column adds an exclamation point to the scheduled date. (You can see an example in Figure 4-26—the first To Do item in the list.) That's the PalmPilot's quiet way of suggesting you get hopping.

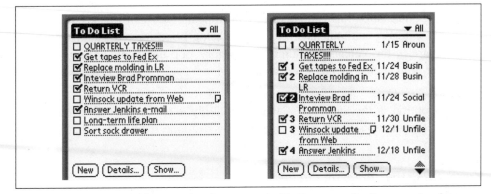

Figure 4-26. You control how much information the To Do screen displays, ranging from a minimalist display without even priority numbers (left) to a data-rich, five-column display showing due dates, priorities, and categories (right).

Sorting by deadline

The Preferences box, which you access by tapping the Show button (see Figure 4-24), offers a number of options concerning the order in which your To Do items appear. On the original Pilot models, your To Do items may be sorted either by priority number or by due date.

On later models, however, the choices are more elaborate. In the Preferences box, tap the "Sort by:" pop-up menu to view the list.

Priority, Due Date

This is the usual sorting order, used by any new PalmPilot. Items with Priority 1 appear first; within each priority level, items are sorted in due-date order. (If you haven't assigned due dates, items within a priority level appear in the order in which you created them.)

Due Date, Priority

Use this sorting option if you want the closest deadlines listed first. If several items have the same due date, they appear in priority order.

Category, Priority

As with Address Book and Memo Pad entries, you can assign a category label to each To Do item. (See the "Categories: A Universal Palm Feature" section earlier in this chapter.) This setting sorts your to dos in alphabetical category order; if several items have the same category, they're further sorted by priority.

Of course, this option doesn't make much sense unless you tell the PalmPilot to *show* your categories. To do so, tap the Show button and turn on the "Show Categories" checkbox (pictured in Figure 4-24). Now a new column appears at the right edge of the To Do screen, where the first five letters of each category label appear.

As a bonus, once this category column appears, you can quickly change an item's category without having to open dialog boxes or tap buttons. Instead, just tap *in* the category column; a category pop-up menu appears directly under your stylus. Tap to select a category.

Category, Due Date

This option is the same as "Category, Priority"—except that if several items have the same category, they're sorted by deadline date within that category clump.

Customizing your To Do list display

If you've read this section so far, you've seen that you can summon additional columns to appear on each line. In all, there are three different columns you can control, as shown in Figure 4-26: the priority number, the due date, and (on Palm OS 2 or later) the category columns.

To change the column arrangement, tap Show on the main To Do screen. You'll see the three checkboxes at the bottom of the Preferences dialog box (pictured in Figure 4-24). Turning them all on crowds your To Do descriptions, but at least you've got all your data onscreen.

The other options in the Preferences box are:

Show Completed Items

As described in the "Checking Off Tasks" section earlier in this chapter, this option governs the disappearance of To Do items you've checked off. If this option is turned off, your To Do items vanish the moment they're checked off. You can make them reappear by turning this option on again.

Show Only Due Items

When you turn on this option, To Do items whose deadlines haven't yet arrived *don't even appear*. Only deadlines due today—or deadlines that have already passed, or have no due date at all—appear in the list.

At first glance, you might suppose that this feature was added for the sole benefit of procrastinators. Actually, though, this feature opens up a very useful possibility: it means you can jot down To Do items long in advance of their actual deadlines. For example, you might schedule reminders for six and twelve months from now to get your car's oil changed. Those reminders won't appear in your To Do list until their scheduled dates roll around. In the meantime, your screen won't be cluttered up with tasks that won't become urgent for months.

Record Completion Date

When this checkbox is turned on, whenever you check off a To Do item, the PalmPilot quietly records the date of completion. (If the item had a due date, the due date is now *replaced* by the completion date.) To view the date you reached each of your goals, be sure you've turned on the Show Due Dates option in this same dialog box. (This option is available only in Palm OS 2 or later.)

 If the To Do program becomes a part of your life, consider the shareware program called ReDo. Its simple mission in life: to let you schedule recurrent To Do items, such as "file estimated quarterly taxes" or "buy a present for my spouse." (DateBk3, described earlier in this chapter, also offers this feature.)

This program is included on this book's CD-ROM and is described more fully in Appendix A.

Deleting a To Do Item

The usual life cycle of a To Do item goes like this. First, you write the item down. Eventually, you mark it as completed. Depending on your settings, the item either disappears immediately, or it disappears some time later when you use the Purge command. Finally, the To Do item is backed up onto your desktop PC for archival purposes (the next time you HotSync).

There may be times, however, when you want to interrupt this usual birth-to-death cycle and simply delete a To Do item, whether it's been checked off or not. Here are two ways to go about it:

- Drag through the text of the item and make the Graffiti "backspace" stroke. When you tap elsewhere on the screen, the remaining To Do items slide up to fill in the newly empty space.

  This method is quick and requires only two stylus strokes. The drawback is that your item is gone forever—it can't be backed up onto your PC at the next HotSync, for example, as it would be using the next deletion method.

- Tap anywhere in the text of the item and invoke the Delete Item menu command. The shortcut is /D (as usual, draw the slash from the bottom). The longer route: tap Menu → Record → Delete Item.

Either way, you're now asked to confirm the deletion. A checkbox offers you the chance to retain the item invisibly until your next HotSync, whereupon it's sent to your desktop computer for archiving.

Notes, Privacy, Phone Lookups, and Finding

In the "Four Global Palm Features" section earlier in this chapter, you can read more about these additional To Do features:

Notes

You can attach a page of detailed notes to any To Do item, just as you can with Date Book appointments and Address Book names. To do so, tap the item, tap the Details button, and then tap Note. (To remove a note without deleting the To Do item, tap the item and then use the Record menu's Delete Note command.)

Phone lookups

The PalmPilot (in Palm OS 2 or later) can automatically paste an entire name and phone number, grabbed from your Address Book program, into a To Do item. This feature works just as it does in the Date Book; write or highlight part of a name, choose Phone Lookup from the Options menu, and so on.

Privacy

This checkbox can hide a confidential To Do item from unauthorized eyes. To mark a To Do item as private, tap it; tap Details; and turn on the Private checkbox. As you read in the "Four Global Palm Features" section, however, Private To Do items don't necessarily disappear immediately—you must throw the master Hide switch in the Security program.

Find

As in the other programs, you can tap the Find icon to search for text among your To Do items (as well as the other Palm programs).

The Memo Pad

The plastic hardware button in the lower-right corner of the PalmPilot screen launches the Memo Pad. This program always starts up with a home page that lists the first line of every memo you've already written. Tap a line to open the corresponding memo page, as shown in Figure 4-27. Consult Chapter 3 for tips on word processing without a keyboard.

Memo Pad's Familiar Interface Elements

Many of the Memo Pad program's features are familiar from the other PalmPilot programs. Pilot and PalmPilot models offer two boxed As at the bottom of the

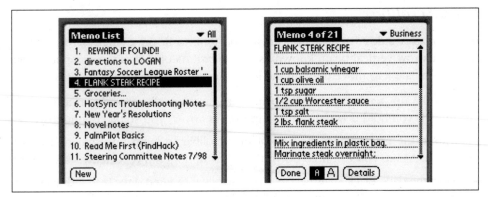

Figure 4-27. The Memo Pad greets you with an index of first lines (left). Tap one to see the complete page (right).

memo page, which switch all text (in all memos) between two type sizes; on the Palm III and later models, those boxes have been replaced by a Font command (in the Options menu) that offers a choice of additional fonts. (On such models, you can choose one font for displaying the startup home page index, and a different font for the actual memos.)

The Details button opens up the Preferences screen shown in Figure 4-28, where you can assign a memo to a particular category and mark it as private (see the "Four Global Palm Features" section earlier in this chapter). You can also use the Phone Lookup and Find commands, also described in that section.

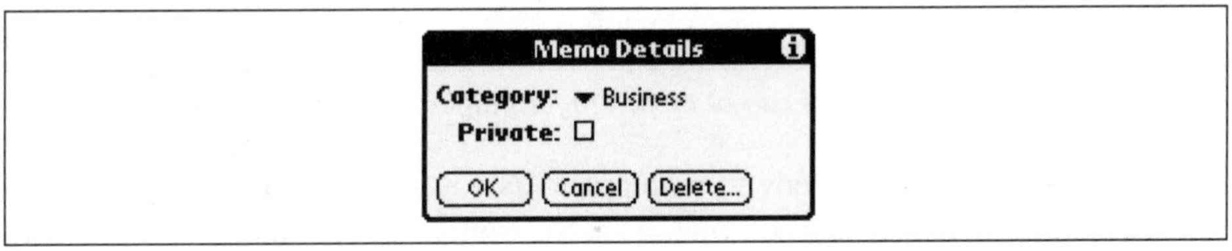

Figure 4-28. The Memo Pad Details screen is minimalist, offering access to two familiar options: Categories and the Private checkbox.

Except on original Pilot models, you can ignore the New button on the startup index screen. Instead, simply begin writing in the Graffiti area; the PalmPilot automatically opens a new memo and begins taking down what you're writing.

As in other PalmPilot programs, if you've assigned various memos to different categories, you can press the plastic Memo Pad button repeatedly to jump from viewing one category's memos to the next.

Palm Scrollbars

If your master index (or a memo) grows too long to fit on a single screen, you'll see the narrow vertical beam known as a *scrollbar.* As on a desktop computer, you can manipulate it to move through the list or memo's text, as shown in Figure 4-29:

- Tap the up- or down-pointing black triangle to scroll up or down a line at a time. If you hold down the stylus tip on this arrow, you scroll continuously.

- Tap in the gray, shaded portion of the scrollbar to jump one screenful up or down. Again, you can hold down the stylus tip to jump repeatedly.

- Drag the dark, black shaft/handle of the scrollbar to jump directly to a distant portion of the page. The scrollbar's full height is a map representing the entire page; the black portion of the scrollbar shows what relative chunk of the page you're currently viewing, and its position shows where you are relative to the full page.

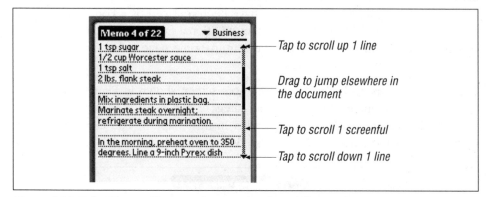

Figure 4-29. PalmPilot scrollbars can be tapped in four different places.

If you find the scrollbar too tiny to manipulate as you ride in a bouncing taxi, you can always press the plastic scroll buttons at the bottom of the PalmPilot. Each time you press the lower one, for example, the next screenful of text is brought into view—and when you reach the bottom of one memo, another press brings the *next* memo onto the screen. As legions of Palm fans know, this convenient button makes reading successive email messages or novel chapters a one-thumb affair.

If you're working with *really* long memos, you may appreciate the "Go to Top" and "Go to Bottom" menu commands, which jump instantly to the top or bottom of the memo you're currently viewing. (You're spared a lot of scroll-bar or scroll-button pushing.)

To use these commands, you can use the Graffiti ShortCuts /T or /B (for Top and Bottom, respectively; as always, draw the slash from the bottom). You can also use the usual menu-selection routine: tap Menu → Options, and tap the command you want.

Sorting Your Memos

Out of the box, the PalmPilot doesn't sort your master index. It leaves your memos
in the order in which you created them. This sorting method is known as *Manual
sorting* because it offers a rare option in the Palm kingdom: you can actually *drag*
a memo's name up or down in the index list. See Figure 4-30 for an example.

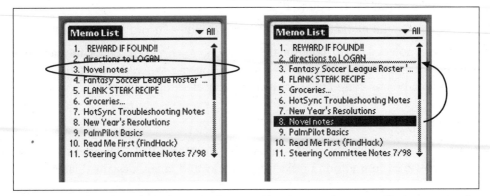

*Figure 4-30. If you keep the stylus pressed against the glass, you can actually drag a memo's
name into a new position in the list (left). As you drag, a gray horizontal line shows where
the memo's new position will be when you lift the stylus (right).*

The alternative to Manual sorting is Alphabetic, in which your memos' names
appear alphabetically. (Hint: a space comes even before the letter A. To make a
particular memo appear at the top of the alphabetically sorted list, begin it with a
space or two.)

To switch between sorting methods, write /R in the Graffiti area or tap the Menu
icon and then (in the Options menu) Preferences. You're offered a pop-up menu
containing a choice of Manual or Alphabetic sorting. If you switch to Alphabetic
sorting, you'll be warned that your manual sorting order is about to be lost
forever.

On the other hand, an alphabetically sorted list stays that way if you switch *back*
to Manual—but now you can drag *certain* memos up and down the sorted list.

Don't fall too much in love with a particular sort order for your
memos. When you HotSync, the desktop-bound copy of the Palm
software (see Chapter 6) may not preserve the customized order.

Deleting a Memo

As in the Address Book and To Do programs, if you delete all the text in a memo, the memo ceases to exist. However, because Memo Pad items are generally longer than a line or two, using this method may not save you any time over the official method:

1. Open the memo you want to delete.

2. Use the Graffiti menu shortcut /D—or tap Menu → Record → Delete Memo.

3. You're now asked to confirm the deletion. A checkbox offers to stash the deleted information away until your next HotSync, when the deleted information will be transferred to an archive on your desktop computer.

Return of the Memo Pad

As you've seen, there's not much to mastering the Memo Pad. This application will return, however, in the form of electronic books and email, described later in this book.

 Delightful as the Memo Pad is, its pages can hold no more than 4K apiece. That's fine for recipes and brainstorms, but inadequate for novel chapters and the notes from really long meetings.

Fortunately, the shareware world (and the CD-ROM that accompanies this book) is filled with alternative Palm word processors. For example, AportisDoc, BrainForest, ThoughtMill, and HiNote all free you from the Memo Pad's 4K limit. Details in Appendix A.

Executive Tip Summary

- Use the Date Book's Preferences command to control what hours' time slots are displayed in day view. For example, you may prefer to view only the hours from 10 a.m. through 5 p.m.; or you may eliminate *all* blank time slots from the Date Book's day view by specifying the same hour as the starting and ending times for the day.

- Press the Date Book plastic button repeatedly to switch among day, week, and month views. Press the To Do, Memo, or Address Book buttons repeatedly to cycle through your different catagories.

- In week view, tap a gray bar to view its label ("lunch with Harry"). Drag a gray bar to reschedule it. (To reschedule it beyond the bounds of the current week, tap it to enter day view; tap Details; and tap the date to open the calendar date-picker.)

PalmPilot Unlimited?

Although the PalmPilot seems to have unlimited potential, it isn't unlimited in its storage capacity—even if you have plenty of memory installed. The following limits are generous, but they're limits nonetheless:

Address Book:

> Maximum number of characters per field: 255
> Maximum number of characters in a note: 4,096
> Maximum number of records in Palm Desktop: 10,347

To Do List:

> Maximum number of characters per field: 255
> Maximum number of characters in a note: 4,096
> Maximum number of records in Palm Desktop: 31,113

Memo Pad:

> Maximum number of characters per record: 4,096
> Maximum number of memos in Palm Desktop: 32,767

Date Book:

> Maximum number of characters per field: 255
> Maximum number of characters in a note: 4,096

Every program:

> Maximum number of categories: 15 (plus the Unfiled category)
> Maximum number of characters for category name: 15
> Maximum number of characters that can be dropped in Word Macro at one time (in Palm Desktop): 65,536
> Maximum number of characters that can be copied to clipboard: 1,000

- In the upper-left corner of any Date Book screen, tap the black tab to see the current time.

- In day view, just begin writing numbers to set the time for a new appointment, or words to create a new untimed event.

- To create a "banner" across multiple days in the Date Book, create a repeating daily event.

- The quickest way to delete an appointment, To Do item, or Memo page is to delete all the text of the item. No menu commands or dialog boxes are required.

- Prevent a bygone Date Book appointment from being purged by changing it to a repeating event—one that only repeats every 50 years.

- The Find command searches the current application first—remember that when speed is an issue.

- If text is highlighted at the moment you tap the Find icon, that text is automatically copied into the Find blank.

- Whatever telephone number you write in first becomes the telephone number displayed on the Address Book's index listing.

- To look up a new number in the Address Book without having to delete what you've first written into the Look Up blank, just press the scroll-up or scroll-down button.

- Every Address Book field can hold more than one line of information. Just keep using the "Return key" Graffiti stroke (a top-to-bottom slash) to insert additional lines within a single field.

- Each new To Do, Memo, or Address Book item takes on the category assignment of the previous one. (Each new To Do item also inherits the due date and priority of the previously selected one.)

5

The Other Built-In Programs

Most PalmPiloteers spend most of their time in the Four Big Kahunas—the Date Book, Address Book, To Do List, and Memo Pad programs. But the second-tier programs are equally elegant, even if not important enough to merit their own plastic buttons. This chapter explores the rarely discussed supporting cast of Palm software: the Calculator, bonus games, Memory and Security programs, and—for owners of all recent models—Expense and Mail.

Except for the Calculator, these programs are accessible only from the Applications launcher screen. To see their icons, tap the Applications icon at the lower left of your screen.

Calculator

The Calculator is the only built-in program you can operate without a stylus. The buttons are so big that you can tap all the buttons with your fingers (see Figure 5-1). In other words, the Calculator makes the PalmPilot the world's most expensive five-function pocket calculator. (On the other hand, I've seen grown men pull out $5,000 laptop computers to calculate their share of the dinner tip.)

To launch the Calculator, tap the corresponding icon at the lower-right corner of the screen. There are only two significant differences between this program and an ordinary pocket calculator. First, you can paste a number into this one (copied from another program) and copy a result out of it. (The Copy and Paste commands are in the Edit menu; tap the Menu button to see it.) Sorry, Mac and Windows fans: you can't paste an entire *equation*, as you can on your computer's very similar Calculator desk accessory.

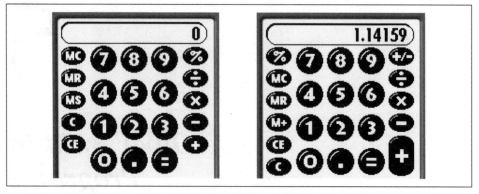

Figure 5-1. The Calculator, on the original Pilot (left) and on later models (right). Can you see the difference? Hint: compare the + buttons.

The second advantage of the software Calculator is that, if you have Palm OS 2 or later, you can review a "paper trail" of your calculation so far. To see this mathematical history, write /I in the Graffiti area (draw the slash from the bottom), or tap Menu → Options → Recent Calculations. Figure 5-2 shows the result; alas, you can't actually *edit* any of the numbers in the "tape." If you discover that you made a mistake, all you can do is say "rats" and start over.

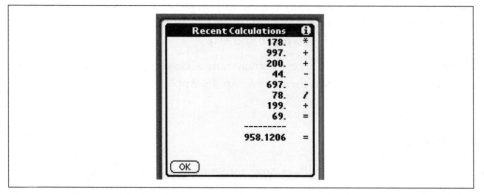

Figure 5-2. The Recent Calculations command shows you exactly where you messed up, but it doesn't give you a chance to do anything about it.

Some Sample Calculations

Although the PalmPilot's Calculator works just like a regular pocket calculator, not everyone knows *how* to use a regular pocket calculator. Here are some quick examples:

At dinner

> The total food bill was $28, and you want to know how much the tip should be. You'd launch your Calculator and type *28 × 15 %=*; the answer, 4.2,

means that $4.20 is the tip. If you're paying with a credit card, you're proba-
bly mostly interested in the grand total; in that event, you'd tap in *28 + 15%=*,
which gives you the food total *with* tip.

Planning your road trip

You're standing at the cash machine, trying to figure out how much to with-
draw for your week ahead. You figure that your first three expenses will be
$230, $40, and $125—but let's say you make a mistake typing in the third
number. (Let's say you typed 225 instead of 125.) If you tap the CE key on the
calculator just after making the mistake, you can reenter the muffed number
without having to start over. The total sequence would look like this: *230 + 40
+ 225 CE 125 =*. The PalmPilot shows 395—it's as though you never made a
mistake at all.

Two of these, two of those

Suppose you're buying antiques in sets of two. Since you can't use parentheses, how are you supposed to add together the totals of several successive
multiplications? Using the memory buttons, of course.

Palm OS 2 or later: Each time you press the M+ button, the current total is
added to an invisible running total in the machine's memory. When it suits
you, you can call up the current running total by pressing the MR (Memory
Recall) button.

Suppose the antiques, if purchased individually, cost $75, $95, and $105. Here,
then, is how you'd calculate the grand total. You'd start by punching in *75 ×
2 = M+* (that is, you want to buy *two* of the $75 items). A tiny *m* appears at the
left edge of the display, indicating that the currently displayed number (150) is
now in the memory stash. You can now press the C (Clear) key to wipe out
the current display, confident that your subtotal, 150, is still safely in memory.
Next stage: tap *95 × 2 = M+*, which adds the second subtotal (190) to the
memory stash. Finally, hit C and do the third round: *105 × 2 = M+*. To view
the grand total of your three purchases, press MR—the PalmPilot proudly
announces that you've just spent $550. Now, at last, you can press the MC
(Memory Clear) button to reset the invisible memory stash to zero.

Original Pilots: If you haven't installed the SlimCalc replacement calculator
program, your Calculator has an MS button instead of an M+ button. It works
much like the M+ button described above, with one important difference: it
stores only *one* subtotal. You can't keep adding to it by repeatedly pressing
the MS button during calculations—whenever you press the MR (memory
recall) key, you'll be shown whatever subtotal was on the screen the *last time*
you pressed MS.

Pilot: Return of the Pentium Bug?

If you inspect Figure 5-1, you'll notice something peculiar: the shape of the + key changed between the original Pilot and the current models. The new calculator also has a +/− button (to change a number from positive to negative), a new placement for the % key, and a new label (M+) for the "add to memory" key. But the new, improved buttons don't just waste less space; they also indicate that your Pilot has been cured of the *Pilot calculator bug*.

Much like the famous Pentium scandal of 1995, in which millions of Pentium chips were found to give wrong answers to certain math problems, the original Pilot calculator program had a new math all its own. Also like the Pentium bug, the Pilot's funny idea of arithmetic only exhibited itself when you made certain calculations.

Try this, for example: 1.1 − .1. The answer, of course, should be 1. Yet the Pilot misses by 90%, leaving you with the incorrect answer 0.1.

Interestingly, if you now add 1 to that answer, you get the answer 2! In other words, the Pilot may have *displayed* the answer "0.1," but it was *thinking* "1.0," the correct answer to the original problem.

If your Pilot model exhibits the telltale symptom—a shrunken + key—you can install what original 3Com calls the SlimCalc 2.0 Calculator. (It's on this book's CD-ROM.) Once you've installed it, pressing the Calculator button on your Pilot launches the new program instead of the buggy one. Unfortunately, SlimCalc doesn't simply repair the original Calculator—instead, it's a whole new program that completely *replaces* the original, eating up 17K of your Pilot's precious RAM.

If 17K is too much to devote to a fixed five-function calculator, consider installing one of the higher-powered calculators on the CD-ROM included with this book instead; see Appendix A, *100 Programs Worth Knowing About*, for details.

Technically, you're not limited to operating the Calculator with your fingers or the stylus. You can also operate the onscreen buttons by *writing,* using the regular old Graffiti alphabet. Believe it or not, you can even "press" the memory buttons by writing *MR, M+* (if you know the Graffiti stroke for +!), *MC,* and so on.

But you may live 100 years before you actually see somebody doing that. Who'd bother, except to show off?

Giraffe

When you first begin learning the Graffiti alphabet, you may find yourself frustrated. "Dog*gone* that letter K!" you might say, "I can *never* remember what its symbol is supposed to look like!"

To make Graffiti learning more fun, your PalmPilot comes with the world's tiniest arcade game: Giraffe. If you have Palm OS 2, Giraffe probably came pre-installed. On earlier models and Palm III, you have to install Giraffe from the CD-ROM that came with your package; if you have a recent model, Giraffe is probably sitting in the *Add-On* folder inside the Palm folder on your hard drive.

In either case, the idea behind Giraffe is easy, especially if you played Space Invaders as a kid. Think *Independence Day*, except that the evil marauding aliens from the sky are dressed as alphabet characters. Your job is to shoot them down before they land. The good news is that you don't have to aim; simply firing your weapon is enough to blow up an alien. The bad news is that you fire your weapon *only* when you correctly draw the Graffiti shape needed to match each falling letter. (See Figure 5-3.)

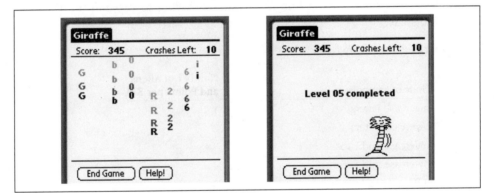

Figure 5-3. To save the world (and hone your Graffiti skills), write the letters before they touch ground (left). After a perfect round, if the PalmPilot feels generous, it might treat you to the elusive dancing palm-tree animation (right).

When you correctly write a letter or number that's falling, it blinks and disappears (accompanied by a tiny chirp). Your score increases by an amount corresponding to your current round (1 through 10). When you write an *incorrect* Graffiti symbol, the corresponding letter or number appears briefly to the right of the Help button, giving you feedback on what you're doing wrong. And if you simply can't produce the correct Graffiti symbol, the letter reaches the bottom of the screen. Your score *decreases* by the number of points indicated by the round you're in, and your Crashes counter decreases by one. If the Crashes counter reaches zero, the game's over; thanks to your lousy Graffiti skills, the world becomes overrun by the evil alien alphabet.

If you're stuck on some symbol while playing Giraffe, tap the Help button. Up pops a Graffiti cheat sheet (tap the down-pointing triangle to view additional screens full of symbols). Exit the cheat sheet by tapping the Play button.

Fortunately for you, the invading letter-aliens don't continue their invasion while you're doing Graffiti research; the game pauses for as long as you're in the Help screens. When you return to the game, you'll see that the invading symbols have been frozen in midair.

Ten Rounds, Ten Levels

A game of Giraffe has ten rounds, each increasingly difficult—and the higher levels are *unbelievably* difficult. As Table 5-1 shows, by round 10, you're attacked by 10 characters at a time, and they're ridiculously difficult Graffiti symbols, most requiring two separate pen strokes to draw—ç, ^, §, î, #, and so on. (Wondering what kind of terrific fireworks display you get if you stay alive all the way to the end of round 10? Forget it. According to the programmer, surviving to the end of the game is *impossible*, saving him the hassle of having to program in a special endgame display.)

Table 5-1. Giraffe Difficulty Levels

Level	Kinds of Symbols	Number of Aliens and Points per Kill
1	lowercase letters	1
2	lowercase letters	2
3	lowercase and caps	3
4	lowercase and caps	4
5	numbers and letters	5
6	numbers and letters	6
7	numbers and letters	7
8	symbols, numbers, and letters	8
9	symbols, numbers, and letters	9
10	foreign characters, symbols, and letters	10

Actually, though, the game may test your nerves in much earlier rounds, in a way the designers probably never foresaw: it's sometimes devilishly difficult to discern *which* letter is falling, because so many look alike. For example, the number 1, lowercase l, capital I, and the vertical stroke (l) symbol look nearly identical. The underline (_), hyphen (–), and dash (—) characters are also eye teasers, as are the zero (0) and capital O.

Now and then, after a perfect round, the PalmPilot will acknowledge your prowess by showing you a tiny movie of a swaying palm tree (because it's a *Palm*Pilot, get it?). If you're the highest scorer so far (for each level setting—Beginner, Intermediate, Expert), a dialog box pops up where you're allowed to write your initials. (To view the current high scorers in each skill category, use the Game menu's High Scores command.)

When you first play Giraffe, you may scoff at its apparent simplicity and sluggishness; it *is* very easy to knock off one lowercase letter at a time during Round 1. If you like, you can speed things up by tapping Menu → Speed, and then a different skill level: Beginner, Intermediate, or Expert. Be careful, though: a speed setting applies to the *entire* game, all the way to Round 10. You may find the Expert speed setting fine for Round 1, but you'll be dead meat by Round 7. Likewise, don't try to change the Speed setting in the middle of a great game: changing the skill level forces you to start over with Round 1.

Practice Rounds

Fortunately for easily frustrated Type A types, Giraffe offers a practice mode, where you're not penalized for crashes and the world's future isn't at stake.

To practice, tap Menu → Practice. You're now asked to choose which kinds of characters you need work on: lowercase letters, upper- and lowercase, numbers, punctuation, extended symbols (™, ¥, §, β, curly quotes, and so on), and accented symbols (é, ü, î, and the like). The round begins instantly when you make your menu selection—*don't* tap Start Game; if you do, you'll launch a normal, high-stress game of Giraffe, complete with scoring.

To end your practice round, either switch to another program (if you're finished with Giraffe), change your practice-menu setting (to keep practicing), or tap Start Game (to play a regular game of Giraffe).

The Memory/Info Screen

The Memory program (see Figure 5-4), available on every Palm model until the Palm III, serves three important functions. First, it identifies your operating-system version (see Chapter 1, *The 3×5-Inch Powerhouse*) at the very top of the window. Second, it shows how full your memory is getting. (Remember, a PalmPilot has no disk drive; the RAM capacity of your PalmPilot *is* its storage capacity.) Finally, the Memory program lets you *remove* programs you've added. It's important to remember this final feature, because you might not otherwise think to look in the Memory program for a delete-application function.

Easter Eggs # 3, 4, and 5: The Tree, the DOS, and the Dudes

Three witty Easter eggs lurk in the Giraffe game. For example, the phantom-like Sheldon the Dancing Palm Tree (Figure 5-3) usually appears only to masters of the Giraffe counterattack squad—following a perfect round, and even then only if the PalmPilot feels like it. But if you tap the Help button and then draw the Graffiti stroke for the # symbol (tap a dot and then draw a backward capital N), you summon the dancing palm whenever *you* feel like it.

But there's more. While holding the stylus tip down anywhere in the top strip of the screen (where it says Giraffe, for example), press the plastic Scroll Down button. Giraffe disappears—and in its place is the all-too-familiar DOS error message: "Not ready reading Drive C. Abort, Retry, Fail?" And here you thought you'd escaped Microsoft by buying a PalmPilot...! (To escape the phony error message, tap anywhere.)

Finally, try the only photographic Easter egg on the PalmPilot: the Photo of Two Guys. To make it appear, place your stylus tip near the lower-right corner of the Giraffe screen. While holding it down, press the plastic Scroll Up button at the bottom of the PalmPilot. Presto: a photo of two formally dressed party-goers (and, presumably, Palm Computing employees). Here they are, shown rotated 90 degrees for your viewing pleasure:

Aren't you glad to know what's using up some of your PalmPilot's precious memory?

To view your Memory information, tap the Applications button in the lower-left of your screen to bring up the Applications screen. Tap the Memory icon.

On the Palm III and later models, there's no Memory program. However, the same feature is built right into the Applications launcher—you get to the memory display by tapping Menu → App → Info.

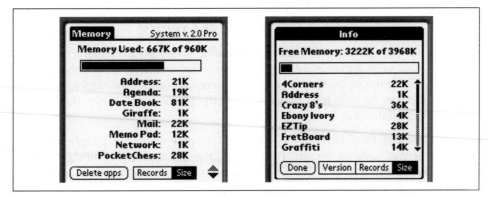

Figure 5-4. The Memory application. Left: Palm OS 2.0, with the Records button engaged. Note the Palm OS version at the top of the screen. Right: the enhanced Memory display of the Palm III and later models.

Records Versus Size

As you explore your PalmPilot and its manual, you may occasionally encounter the term *record*. A record, in Palm-speak, is one morsel of information: a Memo Pad page, for example, or one person in your Address Book, or a To Do item, or an appointment in your Date Book.

At the bottom of the Memory screen, therefore, you can see two buttons for switching the way memory usage is displayed: Records or Size. (The Palm III and later models also offer a Version button that identifies which version you have of each program.) When you tap Records, you see a list of every program installed along with the number of records you've created in that program. The memory bar at the top of the screen, in this case, shows how much memory these records take up relative to your PalmPilot's total memory capacity ("35%," for example; on the Palm III and later, you see the percentage of memory that's *free*, not used).

If you tap the Size button, on the other hand, you see a list of every program installed along with the memory its records are using up in kilobytes (K). In this view, the memory graph at the top of the screen shows you how much RAM is being used in K, plus the number of kilobytes your PalmPilot has available: "541K of 960K," for example.

In either view, if the list of programs is too long to fit on one screen, you'll see scroll-button arrows or a scrollbar at the right side of the screen. Tap them, or press your plastic scroll buttons, to view the rest of the list.

Deleting Programs

If you notice that the Memory program shows only, for example, 960K available in your 1MB PalmPilot Pro, don't be alarmed. The "missing" memory holds the

Easter Egg # 6: Roll Credits!

The names of the PalmPilot team are lurking inside your Memory or Info screen—but only a privileged few know how to see them. Here's the drill: while keeping the stylus tip pressed in the menu bar (above the screen, where it says Memory or Info, for example), press the plastic Scroll Down button at the bottom of the unit.

You're treated to a two-minute, animated display of flying programmers' names. If you have an original Pilot model, the first downward-falling credit says, "Brought to you by," and the subsequent falling objects are the hardware and software teams' names.

On Palm OS 2 or later, the top of the screen says, "PalmPilot Pro System v. 2.0 Pro By:" or "Palm OS v. 3.0 By," and the team members' names form from imploding collections of flying letters, as though they were being assembled by the world's fastest Scrabble-playing ghost. Tap to interrupt the display, if you must. (See the example below.)

The show ends with: "All the beta testers . . . And Shelldon, too!!!," and then you're returned to the regularly scheduled Memory screen.

Which makes you wonder: Who is Shelldon, and how'd he get such a good agent? Actually, Shelldon isn't a person at all—he's a palm tree, an unofficial Palm Computing mascot originally drawn by an original Palm staffer's wife. At one time, Shelldon the Palm Tree could be found painted all over Palm Computing's headquarters—on the sides of buildings, on walls, sitting on desks—and in Figure 5-3.

device's own operating software—remember, on a PalmPilot, RAM must be both memory and the hard drive.

If you consult your Memory program and notice that you're running low on free memory, consider deleting some of the add-on programs you've installed (see Chapter 7 for installation and deletion instructions). You can't delete built-in programs, such as the Calculator, Address Book, and so on, but you can certainly delete any programs you've installed yourself. If you delete a program, you delete the "disk-space" memory it takes up, along with any data associated with that program.

> If running out of memory is a worry for you, remember that you're not trapped at your original RAM limit forever. You can buy Palm-Pilot circuit boards preloaded with more memory (two, three, or eight megabytes, for example) from such companies as Technology Resources Group (*http://www.trgnet.com*). Details on your upgrade possibilities are in Chapter 18, *The Palm Family, Model by Model.*

Security

The Security program will probably strike you more as a feature than as an application. Still, if you leave your PalmPilot in your desk drawer, you may be grateful that it *has* a security feature.

As you read in Chapter 4, *The Four Primary Programs*, each Palm program lets you tag individual records (memos, addresses, to do items, or appointments) as "Private." (Tap the Details button in each of the four main programs to access the Private checkbox.)

The Private designation simply means hideable. At your command, during a visit to the Security program, *all* records in all programs that have been marked Private disappear—and reappear only when you flip the master switch in the Security program on again. If you like, you can set the PalmPilot up to require a password before flipping the master hide/show switch; you can also require a password even before turning the machine on.

How to Flip the Hide/Show Switch

To launch the Security program, tap the Applications icon. On the Applications screen, tap the Security icon. The befuddling screen shown in Figure 5-5 appears.

To engage the security feature, tap the Hide button. As shown in Figure 5-5, a warning appears; if you proceed, all Private-tagged records on your PalmPilot disappear. They won't reappear until you return to this Security program and tap Show.

For added security, tap the Password box. You'll be asked to write in a password—twice, in fact, to prevent typos. Now, if you or a snooping coworker visits the Security program and tries to flip the Hide/Show switch, the "Enter your password" screen appears. The PalmPilot won't show your private data until the password is correctly entered.

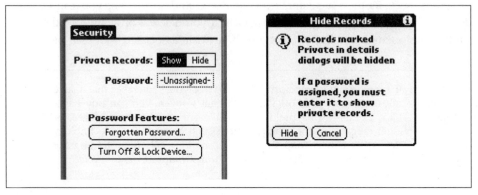

Figure 5-5. At left is the Security screen. If you tap the Hide button, the message at right explains what's going on. (A similar message appears when you switch from Hide to Show modes.)

 The Security program is fine for shielding sensitive information from casual snoopers. But if you forget your password, all the records you've marked as Private (since your last HotSync—see Chapter 6, *HotSync, Step by Step*) are gone forever.

One more caution: Hidden private records aren't encrypted; they're just temporarily out of sight. A programmer can still get at them. If you're really worried about keeping your PalmPilot safe from the evil empire, use an encoding program like the shareware CCrypt. (This means you, CIA.)

If you've already flagged certain records as Private, they vanish when you turn on the Hide switch in the Security program. But a certain weirdness awaits as you work on subsequent records. From now on, as soon as you create a memo, to do, address book entry, or appointment, when you tap the Details button and turn on the Private checkbox, your newly created record instantly disappears. Don't let this behavior freak you out; now you know that the Security program is doing what you told it to do.

How to Change or Delete Your Password

Tap inside the Password box (where, if you've set up a password, it now says "Assigned"). In the next dialog box, you'll be asked to re-enter that password so that the PalmPilot knows it's you (Figure 5-6, left). Now you'll be offered the box shown at the right in Figure 5-6—with options to change your password (by writing in a new one) or delete it entirely.

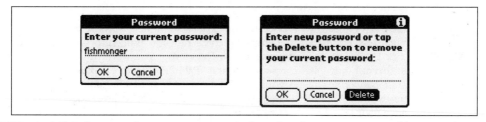

Figure 5-6. Deleting or changing your password involves first entering your old password (left), and then entering a new one or clicking Delete (right).

A useful note about passwords on the PalmPilot: Capitals don't matter. "FISH" is the same as "FisH." Spaces *do* matter, however; "Bigshot" isn't the same as "Big shot."

A useful note about passwords in general: To prevent people from using dictionary-word guessing programs to guess your password, try substituting numbers for the letters O and I when you make up your password. That is, make your password F1SS10N instead of FIS-SION. Or make your password up from the initials of a memorable sentence, such as ILTDP (for "I love this darn palmtop").

Turn Off & Lock

The remaining element on the Security screen is the "Turn Off & Lock Device" button. As the warning message explains (when you tap this button), this function turns off the PalmPilot in such a way that your password will be required to turn it back on again. (If you haven't assigned a password at all, the "Turn Off & Lock Device" button produces nothing but an error message.) The great advantage of this feature is that you don't have to fool around with tapping Details buttons, marking certain records as Private, tapping into the Security program to Hide or Show all private records, and so on. Instead, your *entire* PalmPilot is always password-protected.

If this is a feature you plan to use often, by the way, don't bother trudging off to the Security application to use the "Turn Off & Lock Device" button whenever you want to turn off your PalmPilot. Instead, use the Preferences screen to set up a full-screen penstroke as the "Turn off and lock" gesture, as described in Chapter 2, *Setup and Guided Tour.* Once that's done, you can turn off the PalmPilot quickly and easily, from within any program, simply by drawing a line up the face of the device.

The Turn Off & Lock Device button provides excellent security with much less effort than the Private-records function. But Turn Off & Lock is even more destructive if you forget your password. In such an event, only "hard resetting" your PalmPilot (see Chapter 17, *Troubleshooting*) makes your PalmPilot operable at all—but doing so erases your PalmPilot completely. Any information you've added since your last HotSync is wiped out.

Expense

The Expense program (not available on original Pilot models) is made in heaven for businesspeople who rack up travel expenses that are then reimbursed by the company (see Figure 5-7). When you return from your business trip, a HotSync transfers your expenses into a finished report, ready for tweaking, printing out, and submitting to your boss. On the Macintosh, you can HotSync this data into Informed Filler (from Shana Corp.); on Windows, Expense data flows into Microsoft Excel (several ready-to-use Excel documents came with your PalmPilot).

Expense	▼ All	**Expense**	▼ All
12/10 Taxi	$ 24.00	12/10 Taxi	¢ 24.00 ▲
12/10 Airfare	$ 348.00	12/10 Airfare	348.00
12/10 Car Rental	$ 157.00	12/10 Breakfast	157.00
12/10 Tips	$ 5.00	12/10 Bus	5.00
12/12 Business Meals	$ 57.52	12/10 Business Meals	
12/14 Incidentals	$ 60.00	12/12 Car Rental	57.52
12/15 Dinner	$ 23.17	12/14 Dinner	60.00
12/16 Supplies	$ 107.23	12/15 Entertainment	23.17
12/16 Taxi	$ 8.50	12/16 Fax	107.23
12/16 Lunch	$ 23.00	12/16 Gas	8.50 ▒
12/17 Entertainment	$ 45.30	12/16 Gifts	23.00 ▼
		Hotel	
(New) (Details...) (Show...)		(New) Incidentals ▼	

Figure 5-7. The Expense application. The home page, normal (left) and with the Expense Type pop-up menu open (right).

To open the Expense program, tap Applications → Expense. (Alternatively, you can launch Expense using any of the program-launching methods described in Chapter 1.)

Don't upgrade your Pilot just because current models offer an Expense program. The PalmPilot world offers many similar, and for some purposes superior, programs, such as Expense Director ($100 from Iambic Software) or ExpensePlus (from WalletWare).

And don't despair if you're a Quicken fan. The delightful PocketQuicken, included with this book, tracks your financial transactions until your next HotSync—at which point it exports them into your Quicken file.

Recording an Expense

The first time you use the program, you may be baffled: Expense looks like an empty screen. Once you begin recording expenditures, however, you'll see a list like the one shown in Figure 5-7. In true Palm fashion, you needn't become bogged down in nested dialog boxes to work this program—you can record the basics about all expenses right here on the main home-page view.

Recording an expense: The long way

Tap the New button to create a new expense entry. The three columns of the master list are the date (which auto-enters today's date), the expense type, and the amount.

To change the date, tap it; you're taken to a calendar. A single tap on the correct date returns to the home-page list, where the changed date now appears. (If you record your expenses like a good little trooper, of course, you'll never have to change the date, because you'll always record your expenses as they occur. The date you want in the first column is always today's date.)

To specify what the expense was, tap once where it says "-Expense type-". The longest pop-up menu yet seen on a PalmPilot now appears—it's three screens tall. Tap the up- or down-pointing arrow at the corners of this pop-up menu (Figure 5-7, right) to scroll the list—or simply press the plastic scroll arrows at the bottom of the PalmPilot. Tap a category name to select it.

If you can't find an Expense category among the 28 listed in the pop-up menu, you're out of luck—you can't edit the category list. The best workaround is to select the Other category and record the specifics by tapping the Details button.

 Don't just leave the default label, "-Expense type-", as the description for an expense. If you do, the PalmPilot will immediately *delete* whatever expense item you just recorded—date, dollar amount, and all. Choose *something* from the "-Expense type-" pop-up menu if you want to preserve your entry.

Finally, if you haven't already done so, write in the amount you spent. Writing numbers into the PalmPilot is always fun; they're easy to remember, and the PalmPilot almost never makes a handwriting-recognition error when working with numbers.

Don't bother with commas; remember to tap twice quickly if you need a decimal point; and leave off any trailing zeros. The PalmPilot will fill them in for you.

The PalmPilot also assumes that you'll generally be entering *dollars,* and so $ is the default symbol for the Amount blank. If you're doing most of your spending in a different country, by all means change the default currency symbol. To do so, tap Menu → Options → Preferences, and in the resulting dialog box, choose a different currency.

If the money symbol you need doesn't appear in the Default Currency pop-up menu, you must add it yourself. See the sidebar "Custom Currencies Step by Step by Step" later in this chapter.

Recording an expense: The short way

What's nice about the Expense screen is that if you begin writing a *word,* the PalmPilot immediately knows that you're changing the expense *type,* and automatically selects (from the pop-up menu's list) the expense type that matches what you began writing. If you write *L,* for example, the Expense type changes instantly to *Laundry;* if you continue writing *Lu,* the Expense type changes to *Lunch.* (If you've ever used programs like Quicken, you're used to this "QuickFill" feature. You can turn QuickFill off using the Expense program's Preferences command—in its Options menu—but there's no good reason to do so.)

Similarly, if you begin writing *numbers* on the number side of the Graffiti writing area, the PalmPilot knows you're inputting the amount and automatically moves the cursor to the Amount blank to receive your numbers.

In other words, the program's intelligence makes it possible to record an expense with only three penstrokes: write *E 4 0,* and you've just recorded an Entertainment expense, with today's date, of $40.00.

This example also illustrates that the New button is only for fearful beginners. Writing either a number or a letter in the Graffiti writing area *automatically* creates a new expense (*and* adds the numbers or letters you wrote to the appropriate blank).

If you do business exclusively in the U.S., you may consider the $ symbol (in every single row of your expense screen) redundant. To hide it, tap the Show button. In the resulting dialog box, tap to turn off the Show Currency checkbox, and then tap OK. Your expense screen will now show only the amounts (34.35) without the dollar signs.

Recording miles

If your company reimburses you for miles—or if you plan to deduct miles on your tax return this year—the PalmPilot is ready for you. Among the choices in the Expense Type pop-up menu is Mileage; if you choose this option, the $ in the Amount field automatically changes to say *mi*.

And what if you spend your time driving kilometers instead of miles? Tap the Show button (on the main Expense screen). In the following dialog box, change the Distance pop-up menu setting to Kilometers, and tap OK. From now on, the PalmPilot will use *km* as the units in the Amount field for any Mileage "expense."

> The Expense home-page list generally displays your expenses in chronological order. You can also view them clustered alphabetically by expense type—Airfare items first, then Business Meals, and so on.
>
> To do so, tap the Show button; you'll see the Sort By pop-up menu in the dialog box that appears. Tap either Date or Type, and then tap OK.

Recording the Details

When you're on the run, standing in line at the car-rental counter or buckling your seatbelt on the plane, the main thing is to get the essentials of your expense recorded before you forget to do so. With three or four penstrokes, you should be able to record, say, the cab fare you just spent.

When you're relaxed in your hotel room, *then* you can return to your hasty home-page notations and flesh out the details, such as when and where that taxi picked you up. To do so, select an expense item by tapping on the dollar amount. (You *could* tap the date or expense-type column instead, but then you'd trigger the calendar picker or a pop-up menu.) Now tap the Details button.

The result is shown in Figure 5-8: a special dialog box for recording the specifics of the expense. These are optional blanks; use the ones required for reimbursement and ignore the rest.

Here are your options:

Category

You can read all about the use of categories in Chapter 4. The Expense program uses categories, too—you can create a set of 15 just for use in the Expense program. You'll probably want to name your categories by trip or by time period: Vegas, MegaLith Merger, London 4/23, April Midwest trip, and so

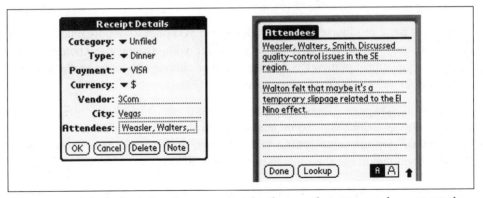

Figure 5-8. At left, the basic Details screen. At right, the page that appears when you tap the Attendees button.

on. (The list comes with two sample category names—New York and Paris. Feel free to delete them, using the Edit Categories command in the same pop-up menu, and replace them with your own expanded list.)

Type

This pop-up menu is exactly the same as the one shown in Figure 5-7. It's provided here in case, while entering the specifics of your expenditure, you decide that, for example, this was really a Dinner, not a Business Meal.

Payment

Means payment *method*; the pop-up menu lists Cash, Check, Visa, and so on. If the company has already paid for one of your expenses (your plane ticket or hotel, for example), be sure to choose Prepaid from this pop-up menu. You'll discover why when it comes time to dump your PalmPilot's records into Excel.

Currency

If you're an international traveler, this one's for you. Unfortunately, the sample currency symbols in the pop-up menu are for the U.S., England (£), and Germany (DM)—odd, since the sample *Categories* are New York and Paris!

To edit the pop-up menu, choose Edit Currencies from the pop-up menu. The resulting dialog box lets you choose from a pop-up list of 25 countries, mercifully sparing you from having to know the Graffiti penstrokes for every wacky currency symbol. The PalmPilot fills in the currency symbol automatically, based on the countries you specify.

And what if you're planning a trip to Hungary, Thailand, or any of the other places that *don't* appear in the pop-up menu? You're not sunk yet. See the sidebar "Custom Currencies Step by Step by Step" later in this chapter.

Vendor

> In this blank, you're supposed to jot down where you spent your money: the name of the cab company, airline, restaurant, theater, whatever.

City

> If it's Tuesday, this must be Detroit. Write the name of the city where this expense occurred if you're on a multi-city trip.

Attendees

> Don't think of this option as "Attendees"—think of it as "Notes." When you tap the word "Who" inside this dotted square, you get a Memo Pad-like page on which you can record any kind of freeform notes, as shown in Figure 5-8. See Chapter 4's discussion of the Memo Pad program for instructions on using the PalmPilot's built-in word processor.

> The only item worth special mention on the Attendees screen is the Lookup button: with a single button tap, you can insert the full name and phone number of anyone listed in your Address Book program. See Chapter 4 for a complete discussion of the PalmPilot's Lookup feature.

> When you return to the Details screen, you'll see the first line of your Attendees notes displayed, as shown at the left in Figure 5-8.

Transferring Your Expenses to Excel

Your PalmPilot's ability to quickly record your travel expenses is only half of its talent. Upon your return, you can connect the PalmPilot to your desktop PC and transfer all of the expense data into one of several nicely formatted reports.

For details on this transfer process, see Chapter 8, *Palm Desktop: Windows*, and Chapter 9, *Palm Desktop: Macintosh*.

Mail

The Expense program isn't the only application unique to the PalmPilot and later models; Email is another. For complete instructions for setting up and using email—no matter which model you own—see Chapter 13, *Email Anywhere*.

HotSync

For a detailed look at the HotSync program, see Chapter 6.

Custom Currencies Step by Step by Step

All right: you're in Hungary. You record a taxi ride. You tap Details to change the currency type. You tap the Currency pop-up menu—but only $ and £ are listed there. You choose the Edit Currencies command from the pop-up menu. But even in the list of 25 additional countries, you still don't find Hungary.

Just for situations like these, deep inside the Expense program, a Custom Currencies dialog box lurks; unfortunately, you could practically get to Hungary quicker. Here's how you get there:

Tap Cancel to exit the Select Currencies dialog box (if you're there), and then tap Cancel again to exit the Receipt Details box (if you're there).

Now tap Menu → Options → Custom Currencies. As shown below, you may create up to four custom money units. Tap one of the Country boxes (below, left) to open the Currency Properties window (below, right). Jot down the name of the country and the abbreviation for its money. (In Hungary, you don't spend dollars—you spend Forint, abbreviated *Ft*.) Need some wacky currency symbol you don't know the Graffiti stroke for? Tap the Menu icon to access the Keyboard command. Need a Euro symbol? If you have a Palm III or later, install Palm OS 3.3, the late-summer 1999 update described in Chapter 18. If not, you'll have to use the letter E or something; before Palm OS 3.3, there's no Euro currency symbol on the PalmPilot.

When you're finished adding the new currency, tap OK in both dialog boxes. You should be back at the main Expense home-page screen.

Unfortunately, just teaching the PalmPilot about a foreign currency doesn't add the new unit to the five symbols in the Currency pop-up menu. To do so, tap Details → Currency → Edit Currencies; tap one of the five default country names; and choose your newly created unit from the big pop-up menu. From now on, your Hungarian currency is one of the five choices in the Currency pop-up menu (in the Details dialog box); the next time you spend some Forint, you'll need only burrow a single dialog box deep—to the Details box.

Or maybe you'll just stay home next time.

iMessenger and Clipper

These programs, unique to the wireless Palm VII, are described in Chapter 16, *Palm VII: Wireless Email, Wireless Web.*

The 3Com Games Collection

As a special bonus for having purchased a post-original Pilot model, 3Com blesses you with four classic arcade games, all adapted for the PalmPilot. They're mindless, maddening, and surprisingly addictive. GameBoy, eat your heart out.

These four 3Com games don't come preinstalled, however. If you don't find them on the CD that came with your PalmPilot, you can download them from *http://www.palm.com*, and you're supposed to install them yourself. Instructions for installing programs are in Chapter 7.

Once you've installed these games, launch them by tapping the Applications icon, and then tapping the icon of the game you want.

 Regardless of your palmtop model, these games are free and available to all. Visit *http://www.palm.com* (or check out the 300 games included on this book's CD). Then see Chapter 7 for instructions on installing them.

HardBall

You'll immediately recognize this game, shown in Figure 5-9: it's Breakout, otherwise known as Brickles. Your job is to bounce the rubber ball against the bricks facing you, using the short horizontal paddle at the bottom of the screen. Each time the ball hits a brick, the brick disappears—and the ball bounces away. The object is to clear *all* the bricks from the screen and then to advance to the next, more difficult level, and continue.

To control the paddle, keep your thumbs on the plastic hardware buttons: the two left ones (Date Book and Address Book) move the paddle to the left, and the right ones (To Do and Memo Pad) move it to the right. The unlabeled buttons in the middle have a purpose, too. The Scroll Up button launches a fresh ball. (You get three balls per game; if your paddle misses all three, you have to start over with a new game.) The Scroll Down button begins a new game. As you can see, this is a game you can play even in your mittens—no stylus is involved.

122

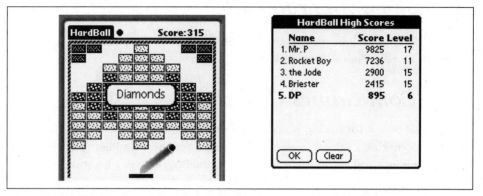

Figure 5-9. Call it Breakout, call it HardBall, but remember: it's only a game.

You'll quickly get the hang of HardBall, especially if you keep these tips in mind:

- The ball speeds up whenever it hits the top of the screen, making your job more difficult. On the other hand, getting the ball ricocheting around the top of your screen can be a great thing; pinball-like, the ball can take out a bunch of bricks with no help from you, simply by bouncing back and forth between the top of the screen and the far side of the bricks.

- This game is about *anticipation.* Start moving the paddle *before* the ball is coming at you, or you're history.

- If your paddle is still, the ball bounces off of it at the same angle at which it arrived. If your paddle is in motion at the moment the ball strikes it, however, it's theoretically possible to add some "spin" to the ball, making its departure angle larger or smaller.

- If the room is quiet, all the little beeps may drive coworkers nuts. Consider playing in silent mode. To do so, tap Applications → Preferences, and turn off either System Sound (on original Pilots) or Game Sound (Palm OS 2 or later).

- At some of the higher levels, you'll see special-looking bricks. One releases an extra ball, and another gives you a second *paddle.* Let's hope you know how to juggle.

- The special chirps you hear are chirps of congratulations; one indicates that you've just landed on the list of the nine highest scores ever attained on your PalmPilot. And if you hear the chirps twice, you've just beaten the *number one* highest score.

- Each level is different, named differently (Portcullis, Diamonds, Metro, and so on), and offers different obstacles. Can you make it all the way to level 20? (Answer: Probably not.)

MineHunt

After the stressful, adrenaline-pumped chaos of HardBall, it might be refreshing to settle down with MineHunt, where you can proceed as slowly as you like. Mine-Hunt is a thinking game, not an action game—although you *do* get blown into bloody bits if you tap the wrong spot on the screen.

The concept is simple (especially if you've ever played Minesweeper in Windows 3.1): you're on a mine field, as shown in Figure 5-10. Each time you tap a dark square, you'll either be (a) blown to smithereens because you uncovered a mine and ended the game, or (b) shown a number. The number indicates *how many* mines lie in the squares surrounding the one you clicked. For example, if you tap a square and it says 1 (as shown at right in Figure 5-10), then *one* of the squares that touches it contains a mine.

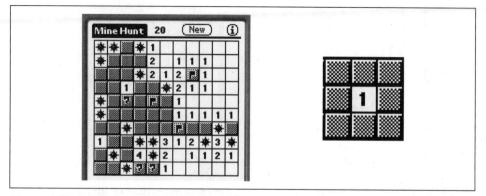

Figure 5-10. At left, the remains of a game of MineHunt. You lost. At right, you've tapped a square and unearthed the number 1. It tells you that one of the surrounding squares contains a mine.

Using your powers of logic, you're supposed to deduce which dark squares contain mines. At the outset, your best clues are the corner squares, since each has only three surrounding squares instead of eight. If a corner square turns up the number 3, for example, you know that *all three* surrounding squares contain mines. The object of the game is to tiptoe your way along until you've uncovered *all* the number squares or empty squares—but none of the mines.

Fortunately, you're allowed to make notes as you go. If you figure out that a certain square hides a mine, you plant a flag so that you'll be sure to avoid that square as the game goes on. To mark a square that you suspect is mined, tap it while pressing one of the gray plastic scroll buttons; a little flag appears.

You can make another kind of notation, too—that you don't know what's under a square. This time, while pressing one of the scroll buttons, tap the square *twice;* a question mark appears on the square. Tap a third time (with the scroll button down) to change the square back to its original, darkened state. In other words, tapping while pressing the scroll button cycles a square through its three possibilities: marked by a flag, marked by a question mark, and back to blank.

Puzzle

If this all-time simplest game doesn't drive you quietly nuts, nothing will. You see the age-old classic game: a square matrix filled with numbered tiles. One tile is missing. You're supposed to slide an adjacent tile into the gap, then slide another tile into the *new* gap, and so on, until you've restored all the numbers into their correct sequence, 1 to 15 (see Figure 5-11).

Figure 5-11. It may look simple, but it's maddening. Before (left) and after (right).

That's it. No levels, no action, no character development. Best of luck to you.

SubHunt

This arcade-ish game (see Figure 5-13), based on a classic Atari shoot-em-up, makes you the captain of a ship sailing across the surface of your PalmPilot's digital sea. Beneath you, evil submarines putter by, releasing floating mines (which look suspiciously like lowercase x's); if a mine floats all the way to the surface and strikes your ship, you suffer structural damage. Three mine hits, and your ship, smoking, slowly sinks beneath the waves, accompanied by a series of bubbling chirps

Those mines are especially distasteful, by the way, because they're so smart. For example, you can't blow one up with your own depth charges (the little torpedoes that drop from your ship). Nor, for some reason, do they ever blow up other subs—they're magic mines that work only on *your ship*. In later rounds of Sub-Hunt, you'll find yourself spending most of your time just trying to maneuver your ship so that it doesn't get struck by wave after wave of mines.

Of course, you're not defenseless; in fact, you have an unlimited supply of depth charges, which you can fire from either end of your ship, as shown in Figure 5-12. (They may *look* like small boldface periods, but they're depth charges.) You could even fire them nonstop, if it weren't for the fact that your digital sailors require some time to load them into your guns. If you fire nonstop, in other words, you'll find yourself out of ammo for several seconds. (The rows of dots flanking your score, top center of the screen, let you know how many depth charges are ready to go at each end of your ship.).

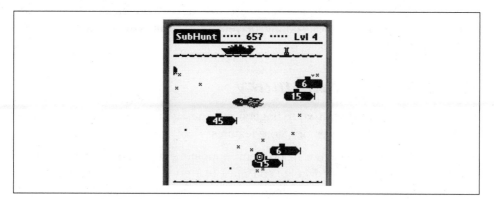

Figure 5-12. You're the ship on the surface. The x's are mines coming up to get you; the square dots are your depth charges sinking onto the enemy subs. The little oil derricks on the water surface are actually mines blowing up.

If you manage to anticipate a sub's motion correctly, your depth charge will blow it up. You get the number of points painted on the side of the sub.

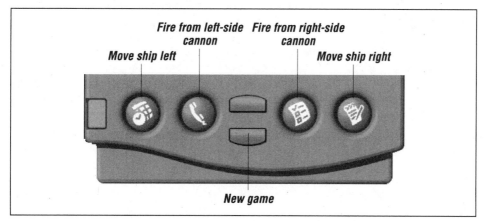

Figure 5-13. The controls for SubHunt. Put your stylus away for this one.

After you dispatch each wave of subs, the game shows you the percentage of subs you successfully sank, gives you a moment's rest, and then begins the next round, which invariably includes more subs, faster engines, and more mines. Beginning at Level 6, you'll even be treated to some aquatic life (which has been programmed to be immune to both depth charges and mines, thanks to the software-lobbying arm of the ASPCA).

As with HardBall, written by the same programmer, you may want to visit your Preferences application to turn the game sounds off if you're playing in, say, church. Similarly, you'll hear special beeps whenever you break into the pantheon of the top nine highest-scoring players—and again when you become the #1 highest scorer.

Executive Tip Summary

- Use the Calculator with your fingers, not the stylus. Don't forget about the "paper printout" and Memory Store features.

- When you mark a memo, to do item, appointment, or address as Private, it doesn't disappear immediately. You must first go to the Security program (on your Applications launcher screen) and flip the master "hide private" switch. From now on, records that you mark as private vanish immediately.

- In the Expense program, nothing is recorded unless you specify an expense type from the Expense Type pop-up menu.

- Don't bother tapping the New button in Expense—just start writing. Write a number, and the PalmPilot automatically fills in the Amount blank; write a letter, and the PalmPilot automatically selects an Expense Type to match.

II

Palm Meets PC

6

HotSync,
Step by Step

The PalmPilot's wonders would be only half as wonderful if they were confined to the tiny gadget in your pocket. What really makes the gadget spectacular is the conversations it can have with your desktop computer.

A transfer of data between PC and PalmPilot is called a *HotSync*. Officially, it's an adjective: "The HotSync process was successful." But these days, you hear people use it as every part of speech: "I performed a HotSync," "I'd better get home and HotSync this thing," "Don't interrupt the PalmPilot while HotSyncing," and so on. (As the PalmPilot's popularity has increased, the term has begun cropping up in conversations unrelated to computers: "We need to bring each other up to date on the downsizing empowerment. Let's HotSync at two o'clock.")

The concept of backing up a palmtop's data onto a PC isn't new, of course. Every kind of personal-organizer gadget—Sharp Wizard, Casio Boss, Psion, Newton, and so on—can do it to some extent. The difference is simplicity and flexibility—first, *a single button press* is all that's required to begin the transfer on a PalmPilot; and second, the transferred information on your PC isn't just a backup. It's "live" data, which you can work with just as you do while it's on the palmtop. The program called Pilot Desktop or Palm Desktop, included with the PalmPilot or the MacPac, can be your everyday calendar, address book, and so on. (See Chapter 8, *Palm Desktop: Windows*, and Chapter 9, *Palm Desktop: Macintosh*, for more on Palm Desktop.)

Moreover, the HotSync process is extremely intelligent. It doesn't simply dump the PalmPilot's contents onto the PC—it actually examines *each individual entry* on the PalmPilot and compares it with the data on your computer (and vice versa). It doesn't matter if, during the preceding week, you added some new names to your PalmPilot's Address Book and some to your computer's Address Book; after a HotSync, *both* machines match, and both are perfectly up-to-date.

Of Software Versions and Terminology

In this chapter and those to follow, you'll read about the Mac or PC-based software called Palm Desktop. This important software, with the HotSync management and installation software that accompanies it, provides your Palm organizer's data a home on your desktop PC.

This desktop software, however, is frequently upgraded by Palm Computing. Its name has changed almost as often as the version numbers—some versions were called Pilot Desktop and resided in the folder on your hard drive called Pilot or PalmPilot. Some versions were called PalmPilot Desktop. This important software, with the HotSync management and installation software that accompanies it, provides your Palm organizer's data a home on your desktop PC.

Today, all versions are called Palm Desktop, and the current versions (3.0 or higher for Windows, 2.0 or higher for Macintosh) are free to every PalmPilot owner. (You can download them from *http://www.palm.com.*) For that reason, this book's discussions apply exclusively to Palm Desktop 3.0 or later for Windows, or 2.0 or later for Macintosh.

Getting Ready to HotSync

HotSyncing requires two components: hardware and software. The hardware, of course, is the cradle that came with your PalmPilot. (When you're ready to HotSync, you set the PalmPilot firmly into the cradle's socket.)

The software is available in two versions—one each for Windows and Macintosh. The Windows version comes with every PalmPilot; the Macintosh software is a different story. It comes on the CD with this book, or you can download it from the Palm web site. (Either way, you'd be wise not to pay the requested $15 for the full Palm MacPac kit. It contains nothing more than the Palm Desktop software, which you already have, plus a Mac modem-port adapter for the end of the HotSync cradle's cable—which Palm also sells separately for $6, as described in Appendix B, *PalmPilot Accessories.* Also remember that current Macintosh models require a USB adapter as well. (The $40 Keyspan PDA Adapter is a good choice, because it doesn't even require the $6 Palm adapter.)

Installing the Desktop Software

Start by installing the software from the CD-ROM that came with the PalmPilot (or the MacPac). Your palmtop's manual, the Handbook, lists the minimum computer requirements and the usual precautions for installing new software: quit all

HotSyncing Without a Cradle

The vast majority of PalmPilot owners connect their organizers to the desktop computer using the included HotSync cradle—that is, via a serial cable. Doing so has its drawbacks for certain people, however. What if you have an original Apple iMac, which has no serial ports at all, but does have an infrared transceiver? What if you have a Windows machine whose COM ports are occupied with other devices, but has two USB ports available? Or what if you have a Windows laptop and you don't want to drag your HotSync cradle along with you on trips?

The world is hard at work addressing cases like these. Palm Computing is considering creating a USB adapter, although it won't promise a shipping date. (In the meantime, Macintosh fans whose desktop computers don't have serial ports can content themselves with a serial-to-USB adapter, such as the $40 Keyspan USB PDA Adapter.)

Infrared HotSyncing is possible, too, in which the HotSync data travels through the air, with no cables at all. To pull this off, you need a PalmPilot with an infrared jack, such as a Palm III or later model; a PC with an infrared jack, such as a laptop; and special software. For Windows, you need IrSync+ software, available from IS/Complete (*http://www.iscomplete.org*), or the Palm OS infrared software described in Chapter 15. For Macintosh, Palm has created its own infrared HotSync software, which comes with the MacPac 2 (available on this book's CD). (The company places this software emphatically in its "unsupported" category, meaning you're on your own to get it working, but the software works well for most people.)

running programs, turn off virus, screensaver, and fax programs, and don't copy files by dragging them to your hard drive—use the Installer instead.

During the installation, you'll be asked to make several important decisions. First, you'll be asked to type in a name to identify your PalmPilot. (The dialog box shown in Figure 6-1 asks you for a user name, which makes it seem as though you should enter *your* name, but you may find it more logical to type in the name of the PalmPilot instead, such as "Frank's Palm V" or "Pocketman.")

If you're a solo operator, the owner of only one PalmPilot, the user name is no big deal. If, however, you plan to sync multiple Palm-Pilots with a single desktop computer, the user name is crucial; it lets your desktop computer identify which palmtop it's talking to.

Whatever you do, *don't give two PalmPilots the same user name*. If that happens, the HotSync software becomes very confused, and may hopelessly thrash the information on both devices.

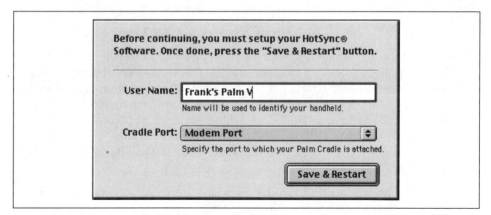

Figure 6-1. Name your PalmPilot (or yourself), but don't use this same name on a different PalmPilot.

When installing the software that accompanies the Palm VII, you'll be offered a list of additional web query applications to install. These tiny search applications each retrieve data from a particular web site: Moviefone for local movie show times, Etak for traffic reports, USA Today for news, and so on. See Chapter 16, *Palm VII: Wireless Email, Wireless Web*, for complete descriptions of these special program-ettes, and for guidance in choosing which ones to install.

When installing the Windows software for the Palm V, Palm IIIx, or a later model, on the other hand, you'll be invited to choose which desktop program you'd like the PalmPilot to communicate with—either the standard Palm Desktop or, if you have it on your hard drive, Microsoft Outlook. Make your selection (see Figure 6-2) and continue—but note that if you choose Microsoft Outlook, that program is where you'll find your PalmPilot data backed up. Your copy of Palm Desktop, as described in Chapter 8, will remain empty unless you change your mind.

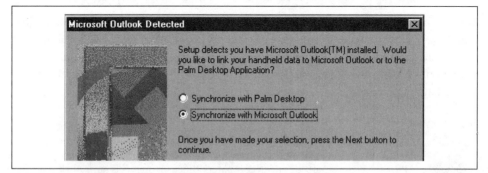

Figure 6-2. When installing a Palm V or other recent model, the installer automatically detects the presence of Microsoft Outlook on your hard drive and offers to HotSync your PalmPilot with it instead of the usual Palm Desktop.

In yet another phase of Windows installation, the installer asks you whether you'd like your email HotSynced to the PalmPilot. This feature can be useful, but it's not for everyone. See Chapter 13, *Email Anywhere*, for details; if you decide to proceed, choose your preferred email program from the list the installer offers you.

> If you decline the email hookup at this point, you can always set up email HotSyncing at a later date by running the EMailWiz application in your Palm folder.

At another point in the installation process, you'll be asked to specify which port the cradle is plugged into (in the back of your computer). On the Macintosh, you're offered a choice of modem or (if you've installed appropriate IR software) infrared ports. (If you've purchased a *serial-port expansion card,* such as those made by CSI, Keyspan, or Megawolf, you'll also see your additional ports listed here—a handy thing, if your modem and printer ports are normally occupied with other gadgets.) On Windows, select a COM port. (See Chapter 17, *Troubleshooting,* for much more discussion about COM ports.)

If you're one of the lucky few who have ports to spare, by all means specify a port, plug the cradle into it permanently, and be happy your cable-swapping is over forever. If you're like most people, however, those ports are often busy with other activities, such as accommodating your modem. If that's the case, it's OK to select the port (in the Palm Installer) that you'll use for the PalmPilot when it's plugged into the PC—and simply unplug it the rest of the time.

> On the Macintosh, you can't use the printer port for your PalmPilot cradle unless *AppleTalk* is turned off. (To turn it off, choose Chooser from the Apple menu and select AppleTalk Inactive.)
>
> AppleTalk is the Mac's networking and laser-printer feature. If your printer is an inkjet, you probably have AppleTalk turned off anyway. But if your printer is a PostScript laser printer, the modem port is a better place for your Palm connection.

What the Installer Gives Everyone

When the installation is over, you'll find a new folder called Palm on your hard drive. (Older versions of the installer may give this folder a different name, such as Pilot Desktop.) It contains several essential applications that will play an important role in managing your Palm data in the weeks and years to come. (In Windows, these programs' names are critically abbreviated as they sit in the Palm folder; however, you'll see them listed with complete names and the submenu that appears when you choose Start → Programs → Palm Desktop. This Start menu method is also the best way to launch these various programs.)

- Palm Desktop is the Windows- or Mac-based version of the built-in Palm programs. See Chapters 8 and 9 for a complete description.

- HotSync Manager is the program that oversees the exchange of data between your PC and your PalmPilot. You'll read more about this program later in this chapter.

- Install Tool is the application that lets you install new programs onto the PalmPilot, as described in the next chapter. (This program isn't present on the Macintosh; its features are incorporated into the HotSync Manager program, also described in the next chapter.)

- Mail Setup is the Windows program that lets you configure the PalmPilot to exchange email messages with your favorite Windows email program; details in Chapter 13.

- Although most people rarely interact with the Users folder (on the Macintosh) or the folder named for your PalmPilot (on Windows), these folders are extremely important. They contain your PalmPilot data, as it exists on the PC; later in this chapter, you'll find some useful tricks for manipulating or backing up your data that involve these folders.

- The Palm folder also contains a "tutorial" program called, for example, Palm Tutorial, QuickTour, or Palmtut. It's more of an ad than a tutorial, with the possible exception of the brief Graffiti-teaching section.

The installer puts all kinds of other files on your hard drive, too—on the Mac, you'll find files and folders called Scripts, Conduits, Palm OS Updates, and so on; on Windows, you'll find a million DLL files and other support documents. All of these extra files are for use by the PalmPilot itself; you can (and should) ignore them.

Setting Up the Hardware

Connect the HotSync cable to the port you specified during the software installation. If you have a Palm V, connect the AC power adapter to the end of the cradle's cable. (The Palm V must be charged by sitting in its cradle for several minutes before you can even turn it on for the first time—two hours completes the first full charge.) Mac fans: Attach the necessary adapter (such as the $6 Palm serial adapter or your USB adapter) first. Seat your palmtop in its cradle, so that the bottom edge of the PalmPilot rests tightly on the cradle.

You're ready to go—you don't even have to turn the PalmPilot on.

Setting Up the Software

When you press the single button on the cradle, you send a signal to your computer, which in turn responds by launching its Palm software and beginning the HotSync.

But the PC won't *get* the signal from the cradle unless it's *listening*. Before you actually perform a HotSync, you must tell the software when to listen. There are three ways to do so:

Always

> If you want your computer always watching the specified port for HotSync-signal activity—because the cradle is always plugged into that port—use this option. This is a dreamy arrangement; whenever you like, you can slap the PalmPilot into the cradle and press a single button to initiate the HotSync, with no other hassle or configuration. Unfortunately, while this option is in force, you can't use that port for anything else (such as modems or printers).

> *Windows:* Launch Palm Desktop; from the HotSync menu, choose Setup. In the resulting dialog box, choose Always Available (see Figure 6-3).

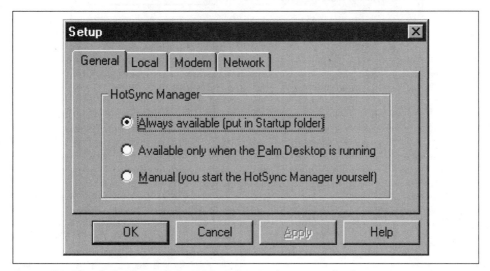

Figure 6-3. This dialog box in Pilot Desktop for Windows controls when your computer should listen for the signal to begin talking to your PalmPilot.

> *Macintosh:* Choose HotSync Manager from the green Palm icon in the upper-right of your menu bar. Turn on the "Enable HotSync software at system startup" option, and restart the computer.

> From now on, whenever you turn on the computer, a background program launches automatically. (This program, called HotSync Manager or Serial Port

Monitor, eats up about 500K of RAM all day.) The background program watches the specified port, constantly awaiting a press of the HotSync buttonOn command, Method A.

If your modem or COM port is generally in use by a modem or some other gadget, activate HotSync signal-listening only when you're ready to perform the HotSync.

Windows: Launch Palm Desktop; from the HotSync menu, choose Setup. In the resulting dialog box, choose Manual (see Figure 6-3). From now on, whenever you want to HotSync, choose Start → Programs → Palm Desktop → HotSync Manager. When the HotSync ends, exit the HotSync Manager program.

Macintosh: From the green Palm icon on your menu bar, choose HotSync Manager. Click Enabled (shown in Figure 6-4). When the HotSync is complete, click Disabled.

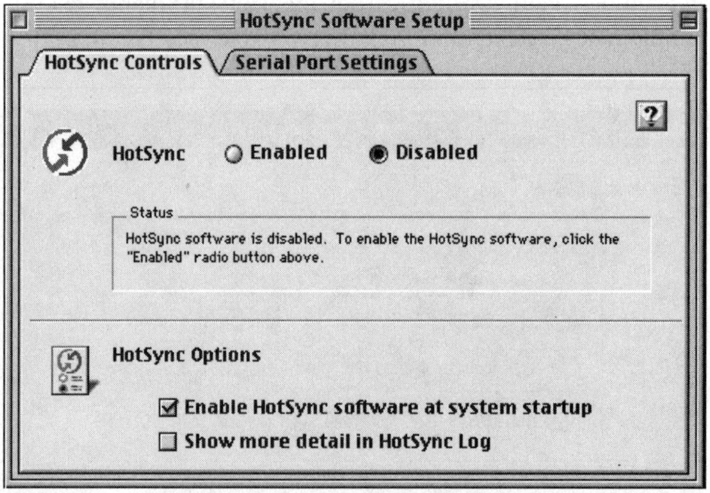

Figure 6-4. The HotSync Manager program, which debuted in early 1999, is the Macintosh way of controlling when a HotSync begins.

On command, Method B (Windows only)

Here's a second way to initiate HotSync-listening on your command.

Launch Palm Desktop; choose Setup from the HotSync menu; and choose the "Available only when Palm Desktop is running" option. From now on, whenever you run Palm Desktop, your computer will be listening for the HotSync signal. When the HotSync is complete, exit Palm Desktop.

Most people use the HotSync cradle that comes with the PalmPilot. But if you're a traveler, you might prefer the less bulky HotSync cable, available for $15 wherever fine Palm accessories are sold.

However, if you're the proud owner of said cable, you're entitled to wonder: "Hey! There's no button on this thing! How am I supposed to trigger a HotSync?"

Turn on your palmtop. Tap Applications → HotSync → Local Sync to begin the transfer.

Performing a Local HotSync

If you've configured the hardware and software correctly, here's what happens when you press the button on the HotSync cradle: First, the PalmPilot turns itself on, accompanied by the soon-to-be-familiar musical chirp shown in Figure 6-5.

Figure 6-5. The three-note chime shown here in the first measure begins a HotSync; the second three-note lick is the Palm wakeup call, announcing that the HotSync has successfully completed.

The PalmPilot begins sending its "HotSync now commencing!" signal to your PC, as shown in Figure 6-6; if there's no response from your computer, the PalmPilot will tell you so (also shown in Figure 6-6). Retrace your steps, making sure the cable is plugged into your computer and the HotSync software is installed and "listening."

The *first time* you HotSync after installing Palm Desktop, you'll be shown a list like the one in Figure 6-7; select the name you chose for your own PalmPilot when you installed Palm Desktop. Thereafter, whenever you HotSync, the PalmPilot's software will assume that it's *your* PalmPilot it's synchronizing. (If you want to HotSync somebody else's PalmPilot on the same PC, see Chapter 8 for instructions on changing the User setting.)

On the computer screen, you should next see some animated arrows flashing (at right in Figure 6-7). Status messages name each of the built-in programs (Address Book, Memo Pad, and so on) in succession as the PalmPilot compares its data with your PC's. A complete HotSync may take anywhere from 15 seconds to many minutes, depending on how many changes you've made since your last HotSync and how many add-on programs your PalmPilot has to contend with.

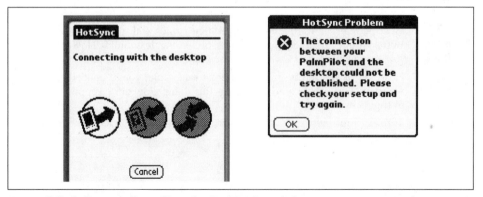

Figure 6-6. If all goes well, you'll see the HotSync logos light up one at a time on the PalmPilot screen, as shown at left. If there's a cabling or software problem, you'll get the message shown at right.

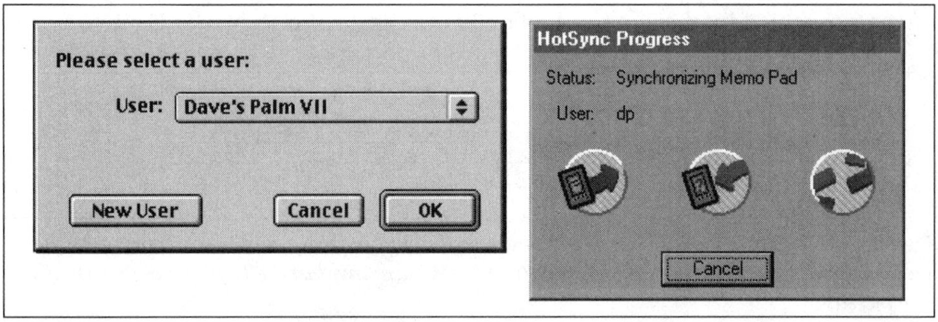

Figure 6-7. The first time you HotSync, you're supposed to tell the software whose PalmPilot is in the cradle (shown in the Macintosh version at left). If all goes well, the HotSync should then proceed, accompanied by matching status messages on your PC and PalmPilot's screens (shown on Windows at right).

When the HotSync is complete, you'll hear the "I'm done!" chirp. Pluck the PalmPilot from its cradle and inspect its contents; you'll find that any changes you've made on your PC are now intact on the PalmPilot, and vice versa.

The First HotSync: Downloading Standardized Data

If you own one palmtop and one computer, skip this section. But if you're in charge of supervising 15 or 150 employees, each with a new PalmPilot, read this information *before* you permit any HotSyncing.

As a result of corporate customers' nagging, Palm Desktop has a unique feature called *profiles*. (This feature was not available in the original versions of the Windows and Mac desktop software.) This feature lets you preload a *profile*—a canned set of information, such as company phone numbers or project deadlines—to a new PalmPilot (or a bunch of them). When these PalmPilots are later distributed, their individual users can freely name, HotSync, and add information to their new gadgets. They never need to know how their palmtops came to be prefilled with useful information.

If you have the right desktop software version, several new (or newly erased) PalmPilots, and a desire to use these profiles, see Chapter 8's section called "Profiles." You're reading about it here because you can download a profile to a PalmPilot only at the very first HotSync, before the PalmPilot has even been named. If you expect you'll use the profiles feature, now's the time to learn.

How a HotSync Works

As noted earlier, the HotSync software actually compares each record on the PalmPilot against the records on your PC. (A *record* is one address in the Address Book, one memo in the Memo Pad, one appointment in the Date Book, and so on.) If you've added new records or made changes on the PC since the last HotSync, they're automatically copied into the PalmPilot—and vice versa.

HotSync's smarts are made possible by its internal *record dating*—every single tidbit of information is quietly date-stamped when you create, delete, or change it. That's how the HotSync software decides who's "right"—your PC or your Palm-Pilot—when the data is different on each machine.

Table 6-1 shows how the HotSync software works.

Table 6-1. HotSync Functions

What You Do	What Happens at the Next HotSync
Create a record on the PalmPilot or the PC.	The new record is added to the other machine.
Delete a record on the PalmPilot or the PC.	That record is deleted from the other machine, too. (But see "Archived Records" in Chapters 8 and 9.)
Change a record on the PalmPilot or PC.	The change is made on both machines.
Change the same record the same way on both PalmPilot and PC.	Nothing.
Change the same record on PC and PalmPilot in *different* ways.	Record appears *twice* on each machine—one reflecting the PalmPilot's change, one reflecting the PC's. An error message in the HotSync Log says, "This record will be duplicated on each platform. Delete the unwanted record and HotSync again."

Table 6-1. HotSync Functions (continued)

What You Do	What Happens at the Next HotSync
Record is changed on the PalmPilot, deleted on the PC.	Record remains on each machine in its updated form; an error message in the HotSync Log says, "The following record was modified on one platform and deleted on the other. The modified version will appear on both platforms."
You change a category name on the PalmPilot or the PC.	The category name is changed on the other machine. Any records assigned to the original category are reassigned to the new name.
You add or delete a category name on the PalmPilot or PC.	The other machine is made to match.
You change a PalmPilot's name (*Windows*: use Palm Desktop's Tools → Users command; *Mac:* use HotSync Manager's Users menu).	The PalmPilot's name is changed. (This name is stored internally; there's no built-in way to change it on the PalmPilot itself.)

If you study the table, you'll see that the Palm software uniformly strives to keep everything up-to-date, tidy, matching, and safe. The only time things get sticky is when you've changed the same record in different ways on the PC and the PalmPilot; duplicate records then appear.

If duplicate records appear on your PalmPilot or PC, don't panic. The solution is easy enough: delete *one* duplicate on *one* machine, and then HotSync again.

The HotSync Log

Every time you HotSync, both PalmPilot and PC quietly keep a diary of what transpired during the inter-gadget conversation. Most people never see this *HotSync log*. But in times of troubleshooting, reading this written record can be instructive.

To view the HotSync log on the PalmPilot, tap Applications → HotSync → HotSync Log. This version of the log is very brief—it simply lists each program (Memo Pad, Address Book, and so on) preceded by OK—but it at least confirms which programs' data were successfully backed up. This standard HotSync Log looks like this:

```
HotSync started 9/23/98 00:22:37
OK Address Book
OK Date Book
OK Memo Pad
OK To Do List
OK Backup
```

On Palm Desktop, the log options can be more substantial. To view the log, launch Palm Desktop (Windows) or HotSync Manager (Mac) and choose View Log from the HotSync menu. (In Windows 95, you can also access the log by clicking the tiny HotSync icon in the Taskbar System Tray, and then choosing View HotSync Log from the pop-up menu.) Note that *each user name* (that is, each PalmPilot) has its own private log. Switch from one to the other using the User pop-up menu (Windows) or Users menu (Mac) before choosing the View HotSync Log command.

If you scroll down far enough, you'll see that the HotSync Log includes specifics about the last *ten* HotSyncs you've performed. (On the Macintosh, this log matches the PalmPilot's own log in brevity until you open HotSync Manager and turn on the "Show more detail in HotSync log" checkbox.) Here's a small excerpt of one of these more detailed logs:

```
HotSync started 9/23/98 00:12:32
Found Pilot user name
ROM Listing
System      0001 70737973 02/18/1997 02/18/1997 0003
AMX         0001 70737973 02/18/1997 02/18/1997 0003
UIAppShell  0001 70737973 02/18/1997 02/18/1997 0003
PADHTAL Library 0001 68706164 02/18/1997 02/18/1997 0003
Net Library   0001 6E65746C 02/18/1997 02/18/1997 0003
PPP NetIF    0001 7070705F 02/18/1997 02/18/1997 0003
SLIP NetIF   0001 736C6970 02/18/1997 02/18/1997 0003
Loopback NetIF 0001 6C6F6F70 02/18/1997 02/18/1997 0003
Network      0001 6E657477 02/18/1997 02/18/1997 0003
Address Book 0001 61646472 02/18/1997 02/18/1997 0003
Calculator   0001 63616C63 02/18/1997 02/18/1997 0003
Date Book    0001 64617465 02/18/1997 02/18/1997 0003
```

As you can see, the detailed logs are mostly gobbledygook, but you can generally spot dates, program names, and other telltale clues about what went on during the HotSync.

Occasionally, too, you'll find helpful, plain-English messages in the log, such as "Palm V is syncing for the first time—forcing restore" or "Failed to provide correct password." (When a HotSync goes awry, the PalmPilot's own log can be somewhat comical in its error reporting. An urgent message on the screen says, "Some of your data was NOT backed up. For details, tap HotSync Log on the HotSync screen." But when you read the Details screen, you're not exactly enlightened. It says: "Some of your data was NOT backed up.")

If some mysterious message is worth sending to 3Com's Palm tech support, it may be useful to copy the log text and paste it into another program: an email, for example, or a word processor for printing out. Just highlight the text you want by dragging through it; and then, although the Edit menu appears to be unavailable in Windows, the keyboard shortcut for Copy (Ctrl-C) still works.

The HotSync Log Nobody Knows

As you can read in the previous section, there's HotSync logging, and there's *verbose* HotSync logging. What few people realize, however, is that a completely undocumented Windows feature can provide *super*-verbose logging— a veritable War and Peace of HotSync record-keeping—that can be handy in times of troubleshooting or rampant curiosity.

The standard installation process for Palm Desktop puts a Windows shortcut in your Startup Items folder (which you can see in your Start menu's Programs command). Behind the scenes, this shortcut contains a line of DOS code that directs Windows to launch the HotSync Manager.

By editing this secret instruction, you can trigger the PalmPilot's secret super-verbose log. To do so, open your C drive → Windows → Start Menu → Programs → Startup. Right-click the HotSync Manager icon and choose Properties. In the dialog box that results, click Shortcut.

There you'll see the secret line of code, something like this:

```
C:\palm\hotsync.exe
```

Add *−v* to the end of that line, so that it now looks like this:

```
C:\palm\hotsync.exe-v
```

Quit the HotSync Manager (click its icon in your Windows 95 system tray), and then restart it (by choosing its name from your Start menu.)

When you next HotSync, your HotSync log will report every darned step that took place during the HotSync process: what was installed and where, when it happened, and so on.

You read it here first.

Specialized HotSyncs

Under normal circumstances, the PalmPilot and the PC bring each other up-to-date during a HotSync, including all the various programs' data. But you can tailor the way a HotSync works, depending on your circumstances. For example, you might decide to HotSync *only* your Address Book, that's the only data you've used all week. By limiting what gets transferred, you speed up the HotSync.

Another example: suppose somebody has completely messed up your appointments in Palm Desktop. Your PalmPilot still contains an up-to-date schedule; using a special HotSync option, you can tell your software *not* to compare the PalmPilot with the PC, but instead to *wipe out* the PC's contents, replacing it with what's on the PalmPilot now.

The Concept of Conduits

In your PalmPiloteering life, you can't avoid encountering the term *conduit.* In Palm lingo, a conduit is the piece of software responsible for HotSyncing *one kind* of data. Each Palm program—Memo Pad, Address Book, and so on—has its own conduit, which you can switch on or off independently. When you buy a program like Intelli-Sync, which lets you HotSync directly to such common PC calendar and address books as Now Contact, Outlook, ACT, and Sidekick, you're buying new *conduits.*

The master switches for the PalmPilot's own conduits are in Palm Desktop (Windows) or HotSync Manager (Mac). You can read more about these programs in Chapters 8 and 9; for now, check out the Custom or Conduit Settings command in the HotSync menu. (See Figure 6-8.) This dialog box offers at least six choices: four that correspond to the four built-in Palm programs, plus a conduit called System (which refers to Graffiti Shortcuts, network settings, and PalmPilot Preferences) and another called Install (see Chapter 7, *Installing New Palm Programs*).

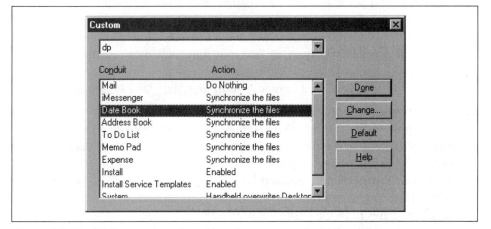

Figure 6-8. The HotSync options shown here let you control which pathways are open between your PalmPilot and your PC—and in which direction. Double-click a conduit to change its setting.

The factory setting for these options is to bring the PalmPilot and the PC up to date with each other (see Figure 6-9). However, you can specify some useful variations for each of the standard conduits. (To view these options, just double-click a conduit's name.) The options are:

Desktop overwrites handheld (or Macintosh overwrites handheld)
> This option, like the others in this dialog box, may say "overwrites Pilot" or "overwrites PalmPilot," depending on which era of Palm nomenclature your software reflects. Use it when you've made a mess of your PalmPilot data, and you want your current PC copy of this program's data transplanted into the

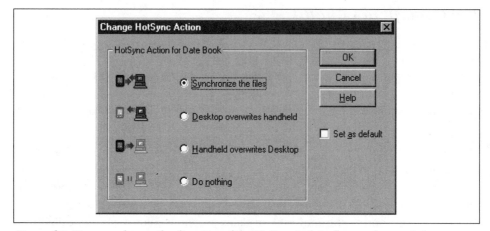

Figure 6-9. You can change the direction of the HotSync's data flow under special circumstances.

PalmPilot—you want *none* of the changes made on the PalmPilot to be preserved. You might think that this option would be useful in copying the data from your old PalmPilot onto a new one; but see "Mastering the User-Name Folders" later in this chapter to find out why that won't work. (When the Install Apps conduit is selected, this option is renamed Install Handheld Applications or Install Files. See Chapter 7, *Installing New Palm Programs.*)

Handheld overwrites Desktop (or Handheld overwrites Macintosh)

This setting means that what's on the PalmPilot now (for this particular conduit) will completely replace whatever's in the corresponding Palm Desktop module. Use this option if you've made a mess of your Palm Desktop data since your last HotSync, imported bogus names and addresses, or whatever. (This option doesn't appear for the Install Apps conduit—after all, you can't install programs from the PalmPilot to the PC.)

Do nothing

If you don't use one of the PalmPilot's programs, or if you're certain you haven't *used* one of the PalmPilot's programs since your last HotSync, you can save time with this option. At the next HotSync, this program's data won't be compared (PalmPilot-to-PC) or transferred at all. Your HotSync will finish that much faster.

For each of these options, you'll see a Set As Default checkbox or Make Default button. If you select this option, *all* future HotSyncs will operate with the modifications you've just made (for the specific conduit you changed). That is, if you never use the To Do list, choose Do Nothing and click Set As Default button.

If you don't check Set As Default, the changes you've just made will apply only to your *next* HotSync—and then they revert automatically to your previous settings.

One PalmPilot, Two PCs

It's perfectly safe to synchronize one PalmPilot with two different computers. Just install Palm Desktop on each PC, maybe buy an extra HotSync cradle for the second computer, and you're in business. (HotSyncing takes longer, but it gets done eventually.) The PalmPilot keeps everything straight, even if you make changes on both PCs simultaneously—at each HotSync, the PalmPilot simply assumes that *that* information has been updated since the *last* HotSync, regardless of which computer it's attached to.

There are two exceptions—two situations where you can get into trouble by trying to HotSync a single PalmPilot with more than one computer. The first is when you've had to *hard reset* the PalmPilot—a troubleshooting technique described in Chapter 17. Following such a drastic step, you'll want to reinstall your data onto the PalmPilot, but great confusion and data scrambling will result if you aren't careful. The correct procedure is:

1. Go to the first PC. Using the Custom or Conduit Settings command (see Figure 6-8), change all of your conduit settings to "Desktop overwrites handheld." Your PC will fill the PalmPilot with the latest data.

2. Now take the PalmPilot to your second PC. This time, reverse the custom conduit settings—change them all to "handheld overwrites desktop." At this point, all three machines should contain the same information, and you're ready to roll.

The second situation where caution is required: when you're HotSyncing to a different calendar/address book program on each of the two PCs. For example, suppose you keep your contact list in Microsoft Outlook at home, but in Sidekick at the office.

One word of advice in this situation: don't do it. Each program tracks its HotSync progress differently, and your poor PalmPilot can become hopelessly confused as to which information is current.

So you've got a Macintosh at home and a Windows machine at work. You'd love to keep your calendar and address books up-to-date at both ends, but each of your chosen software programs runs only on a single platform. What's a poor worker to do?

Get a PalmPilot. Because it can so easily speak to both Mac and Windows machines, and because it can so easily HotSync to multiple computers, the PalmPilot is the ideal go-between between incompatible computer systems. HotSync at home to the Mac, HotSync at work to the Windows machine—the PalmPilot doesn't care. Meanwhile, your data is smoothly transferred into the software of your choice at both ends.

One PC, Two PalmPilots

It's totally safe—indeed, intended by Palm as a feature—to HotSync multiple PalmPilots with a single desktop computer. As long as every PalmPilot has been given a different user name (see the section "Installing the Desktop Software" earlier in this chapter), the PC will be able to keep each PalmPilot's contents straight. See the next chapter for details.

Backing Up Your Non-Palm Data

The normal HotSync procedure backs up two categories of information: the data from the built-in Palm applications (Memo Pad, Address Book, and so on), and any applications you've added yourself ("third-party" applications), such as those on this book's CD. Several categories of data, therefore, aren't backed up at all when you HotSync: the data files from some third-party programs, databases that accompany third-party programs (the map files that go with a map-display program, for example), HackMaster files (see Appendix A, *100 Programs Worth Knowing About*, for a description of the remarkable HackMaster), and so on.

The bottom line is that the standard HotSync does not, in fact, completely back up your PalmPilot.

Fortunately, shareware comes to the rescue. The popular Backup Buddy, for example, shows you a list of all data on your PalmPilot, as shown in Figure 6-10. By clicking appropriate checkboxes—or all of them—you can specify that the additional data types get backed up on your desktop computer when you HotSync. If the worst comes to pass, you'll be able to restore all of this information your palmtop.

Backup Buddy is available for both Macintosh and Windows. However, Mac fans may be even more interested in the shareware program Palm Buddy (Mac only). It offers the same advantages of Backup Buddy—complete data backup and restore—with the added advantages of a friendly, Mac-like, hierarchical folder display (see Figure 6-10). Both Buddy programs are included on this book's CD.

Mastering the User-Named Folders

As you know, the PalmPilot stores its data entirely in RAM. But your *desktop* computer—Palm Desktop—manages to retain all your data even when the computer's turned off. Where is the data stored?

Learning the answer to this question can make you much wiser and wilier. You'll be able to manipulate PalmPilot data in surprising ways, troubleshoot, back up more effectively, and pull off sneaky stunts to amaze your friends.

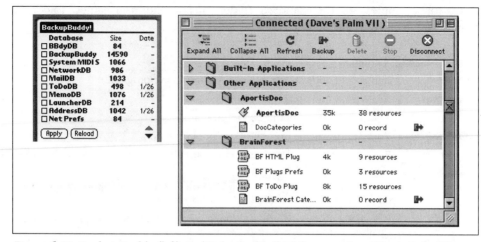

Figure 6-10. Backup Buddy (left) and Palm Buddy (right) ensure that all your PalmPilot data is backed up on your PC, including accessory files that the standard HotSync process ignores.

It turns out that Palm Desktop stores your PalmPilot's data on the hard drive, right there in the Palm folder. If you've ever performed a HotSync to your PC, you can check this out right now—open the Palm folder on your hard drive (on the Mac, these folders are inside the Users folder). Inside, you'll see that the HotSync software maintains a separate *folder* for each PalmPilot user. In each user's folder are additional folders, one for each PalmPilot program. See the extremely important Figure 6-11 for proof.

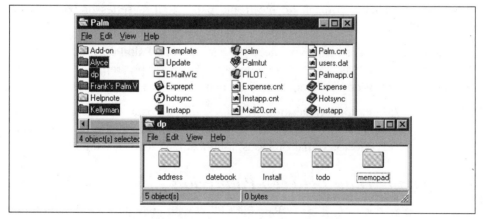

Figure 6-11. On your hard drive, inside the Palm folder, lurk individual folders for each Palm user (top). In this example, Kellyman, Alyce, dp, and Frank's Palm V store the data for four different PalmPilots. Within each user-named folder are more folders, one for each Palm program: Address Book, Memo Pad, and so on (bottom). (On the Mac, the user-named folders are inside the Users folder.)

Here, for example, are the standard folders inside the user-named folder in Windows:

Folder Name	Contents
address	Names and addresses from your Address Book program.
memopad	Notes from the Memo Pad program.
todo	Your to do lists from the To Do program.
datebook	Your appointments from the Date Book program.
install	Programs you intend to install into your PalmPilot (instructions in the next chapter).
mail	Email you've HotSynced, or will HotSync, with your desktop computer (see Chapter 12, *Database and Number Crunching*).
expense	Palm OS 2 or later: your data from the PalmPilot's Expense program (see Chapter 5, *The Other Built-In Programs*).
backup	Everything else you create or store on your PalmPilot. For example, any Graffiti Shortcuts (see Chapter 3, *Typing Without a Keyboard*); settings associated with your network (if you use network HotSyncing); add-on programs you've installed yourself (and their data); and your Preferences settings (see Chapter 2, *Setup and Guided Tour*).

How can you use this information? Let us count the ways.

Back Up Your Backup

Now that you know where the Palm data hangs out, you can easily make a backup of it by dragging it to, for example, a Zip or Jaz drive. Do this periodically, and you'll have yourself an electronic paper trail, a series of backups, of your PalmPilot's contents over the months.

Suppose disaster strikes, and you need to restore your PalmPilot's address-book data to the way it was, say, six months ago. Easy: simply replace the current "address" folder (inside the folder with your name on it) with the old one.

When you next launch Palm Desktop, you'll see the old data. Use the conduit settings shown in Figure 6-8 to specify "desktop overwrites Handheld," do a HotSync, and presto—you've restored that precious, long-lost data to your PalmPilot.

Transferring Data Between PalmPilots

Suppose you've got an old, trusty PalmPilot filled with juicy info—and then 3Com introduces a newer, better model. You buy one. Now what? How are you supposed to transfer your old PalmPilot's data to your new one?

Your first instinct might be simply to HotSync the new PalmPilot with your PC and see what happens. Unfortunately, you'll be asked to specify *whose PalmPilot* this new one is. If you choose your old PalmPilot name from the list (shown in

Figure 6-7), the HotSync software will give the new PalmPilot the old name, giving you duplicate PalmPilot names—and chaos will result.

All right then; suppose you click the New button (in the dialog box shown in Figure 6-7) and give your new PalmPilot a different user name. Ah, but now the Palm Desktop screen is empty of data—as it is for *any* brand-new user name—and you're still left with an empty PalmPilot!

The official solution

3Com suggests this approach for transferring one PalmPilot's data to another (in Windows):

1. Launch Palm Desktop. From the Tools menu, choose Users. In the dialog box (which resembles the one in Figure 6-7), click New User. Create a new user's name—let's say it's Frank.

2. Use the pop-up menu at the right side of the Palm Desktop screen to switch to your old user name (let's call it Old). At the left side of the screen, click the icon of the program whose data you want to copy—the Memo Pad, for example. (See Figure 6-12.)

3. From the Edit menu, choose Select All. You've now highlighted all the data for this particular Palm module (see Figure 6-12).

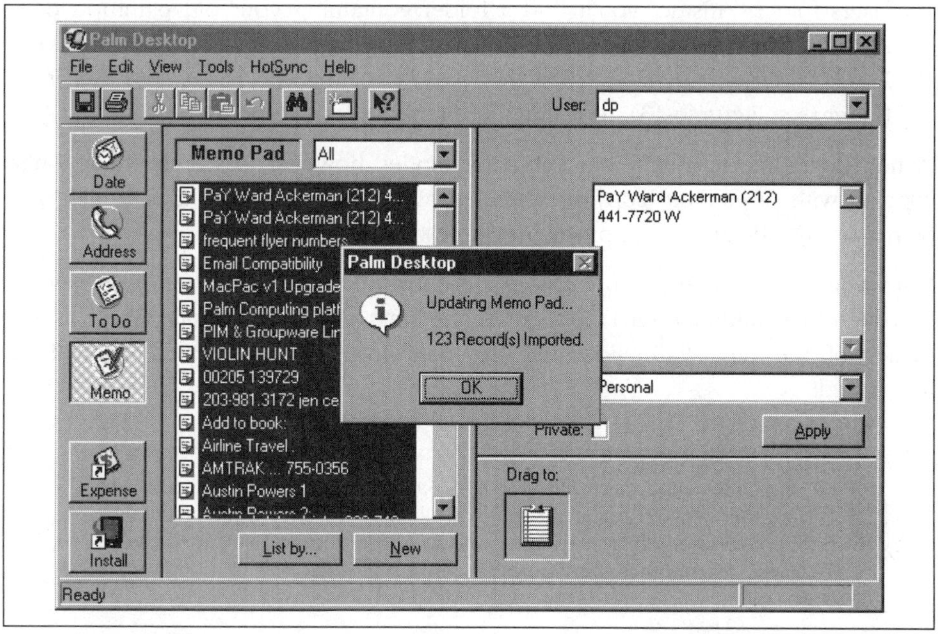

Figure 6-12. The long way of transferring data among different PalmPilot users—copy and paste. Here, you can see that the data has been highlighted.

4. From the Edit menu again, choose Copy.

5. Using the User pop-up menu at the upper right, choose Frank. You should now be looking at the empty Memo Pad screen for your newly created user name.

6. From the Edit menu, choose Paste. The data you copied from the first user name now appears as Frank's Memo Pad data.

Alas, this method is unbelievably lame. First, it takes way too many steps. Second, it doesn't work at all with the Date Book program. (In Pilot Desktop 2.0 and later, you could theoretically *export* your Date Book entries from one user's data and then *import* it into another's. That's still way too much work.)

The better solution

Here's a much sneakier, shorter way of transferring data that transfers *all* data, including calendar information:

1. *Windows:* Launch Palm Desktop. Choose Tools → Users. In the dialog box (which resembles the one in Figure 6-7), click New. *Macintosh:* Launch HotSync Manager. Choose Users → Show Palm User List. Click New User.

2. Create a new user's name—let's say it's Frank. Quit Palm Desktop.

3. Find the Palm folder on your hard drive. Open it; on the Mac, also open the Users folder. Inside, you'll find a folder containing your old pamtop's data; let's say your old PalmPilot was called Old. Open your Old folder and your Frank folder side-by-side. Copy the contents of the Old folder into the Frank folder (see Figure 6-13), replacing the Frank folder's contents.

(When upgrading to a different PalmPilot model, however, select the files you're copying with care; avoid copying system patches and preference files, which may be model-specific and cause problems on newer models.)

Now when you launch Palm Desktop and choose Frank as the user, you'll see all of your old PalmPilot's data appear. At the next HotSync, specify Frank as the owner of the new PalmPilot, and the data from the old PalmPilot will be transferred!

 If you're using Palm Desktop for Macintosh 2.1 or later, there's yet another way to transfer some, or all, of your data from one Palm-Pilot to another: by exporting and importing between Palm Desktop files. Chapter 9 contains step-by-step instructions.

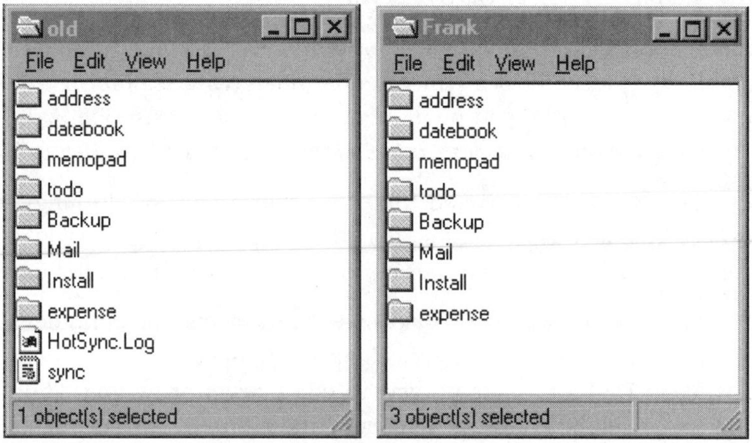

Figure 6-13. The short way of transferring data among different PalmPilot users—drag the contents of the old user-named folder (left) to the new user-named folder (right), replacing the contents.

Solving Accidental Duplicate PalmPilot Names

Despite the several hundred warnings you've read about not giving two Palm-Pilots the same name, accidents can happen. Yet there's no obvious way to change a PalmPilot's name—this information is stored in the PalmPilot's RAM in a place you can't edit. (In fact, there isn't even an obvious way of finding out your PalmPilot's name if you've forgotten. Solution: tap Applications → HotSync. Your PalmPilot's name is revealed in the upper-right corner of the screen.)

Fortunately, now that you know how the user-named folders work, you can safely correct a duplicate-name problem. Following the instructions in step 1 under "The better solution," earlier in this chapter, create a new name for the duplicate-named PalmPilot. For example, suppose you have two units called Chris's PalmPilot; create a new user named, say, Chris II.

When you return to your computer desktop, you'll discover a new folder (in the Pilot or Palm folder) called, of course, *Chris II*. Just copy the contents of the original *Chris's PalmPilot* folder into the new *Chris II* folder. Now do a "hard reset" on the second PalmPilot (a bizarre but useful procedure described in Chapter 17) to empty it completely.

When you HotSync again, identify the empty PalmPilot as Chris II. It will be filled automatically with the data you copied from Chris's PalmPilot. Presto: two PalmPilots, same data, different names.

Transfer Your Graffiti Shortcuts

Shortcuts are abbreviations that, when you make a special Graffiti penstroke, expand into longer text phrases—an essential timesaving feature of a pen-based typing system. For example, you might make the special penstroke, write *mt,* and watch your abbreviation turn into *meeting with.* See Chapter 3 for details.

Among the files in your user-named folder is a file called, of all things, *Graffiti_ ShortCuts.PRC.* This little document stores your Shortcuts. Suppose you've created a masterful set, which you wish to bestow on less fortunate PalmPilot users.

The HotSync process does indeed back up your Shortcuts; the conduit called System takes care of that. Unfortunately, backing up is *all* that conduit does. On your desktop PC, Palm Desktop offers no way to edit or even view your Shortcuts and other PalmPilot preference settings. You can't, therefore, copy and paste such data among different users, as you can with, say, Address Book data.

The only solution is to use your new knowledge of the user-named folders. In the *Palm* or folder, open the folder with your PalmPilot's name on it. Open the folder therein called Backup. Simply copy the *Graffiti_ShortCuts.PRC* file into the Backup folder of the *other* PalmPilot user, as shown in Figure 6-14, and you're done. At the next HotSync, your ingenious Shortcuts will be transferred to your comrade's palmtop.

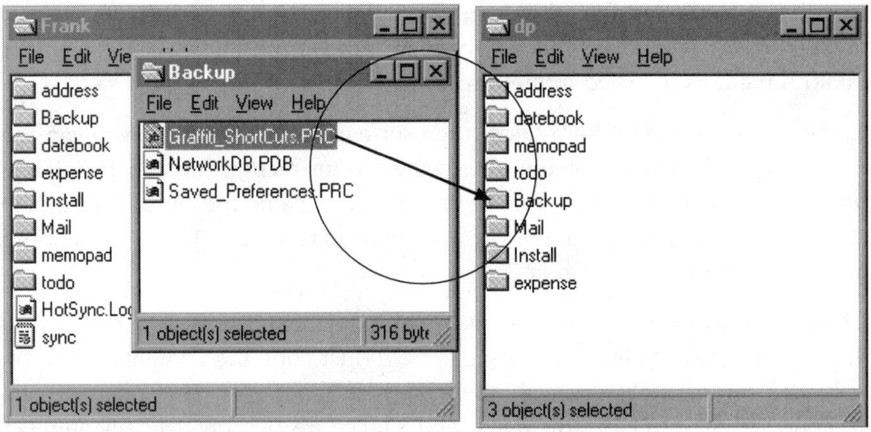

Figure 6-14. To transfer Graffiti shortcuts from user Frank to user dp, open each user-named folder. Drag the Graffiti_ShortCuts.PRC file out of Frank's Backup folder (left) into dp's Backup folder (right).

HotSync by Modem

So far in this chapter, you've read about plugging your PalmPilot directly into your PC. But you can also HotSync from the road, dialing into your home PC via modem. This feature opens up some interesting possibilities. For example, an assistant at your home office can update your calendar software while you're traveling to a business meeting in a distant city; by performing a modem HotSync, you neatly update your Date Book so that you're ready for the week's events.

This method doesn't involve the HotSync cradle. It does, however, require *two* modems—one for your PalmPilot and one for your PC. Any modem will do for your PC; the PalmPilot requires either the Palm snap-on modem or a Hayes-compatible external modem with a $15 Palm modem cable. (See Chapter 13 for details on modems.) Moreover, your home PC must be attached to its own private phone line, because it's going to answer *every call that comes in.* You don't want Aunt Ethel getting the shriek of a 56K modem in her ear when she calls to see if you got her birthday card.

 You can't do a modem HotSync on a computer with which you've never yet done a *local* HotSync. The initial HotSync must be performed via direct connection to your PC; it sets up the user-named folders on your PC hard drive, as described earlier in this chapter, which the modem HotSync will require.

How to Prepare the Desktop PC

Before leaving on your trip, you must prepare your desktop PC for the excitement to come. As mentioned above, your preparations should include a local HotSync, equipping your PC with a modem, and hooking it up to a phone line that won't be answered by any other person or device. Then:

Windows

1. Launch Palm Desktop. From the HotSync menu, choose Setup. Click the Modem tab. You'll see the options shown in Figure 6-15.

2. Use the Serial Port pop-up menu to specify the serial port your desktop PC's modem is attached to (such as a COM port).

3. From the Speed pop-up menu, specify your modem's speed. (In general, leave this setting on "As fast as possible"—change it to lower speeds only if you have trouble connecting with your PalmPilot.)

4. Use the Modem pop-up menu to indicate your desktop PC's modem brand. If your model's name doesn't appear in the list, try Hayes Basic. If that doesn't work, call the modem company to find out your model's initialization string. You'll be given a seemingly nonsensical series of letters and numbers, such as AT&F1W1S0=0S95=44. Type the initialization string into the Setup String blank in this dialog box.

5. Click OK. Now, from the HotSync menu, choose Modem. You're almost ready for the big moment; first, though, you must make sure your PC is "listening" for the HotSync signal, as described in "Setting up the software" earlier in this chapter. Because your PC will presumably be otherwise unused while you're away, you may as well turn on the "always listen" option: from the HotSync menu, choose Setup. In the resulting dialog box, choose Always Available (see Figure 6-3). Click Done.

Macintosh

1. From the green Palm menu-bar icon, choose HotSync manager.

2. Choose your modem model from the Modem pop-up menu.

 HotSync Manager's list of modems is generated according to the modem script files in your hard drive's *System* folder → *Extensions* → *Modem Scripts* folder. If your exact modem model doesn't appear in HotSync Manager's list, the easiest solution is to get the correct modem script file from the modem's software disk. (You may also, if you wish, call the manufacturer to find out the modem's initialization string.) Then, from the Modem pop-up menu, choose Custom. A new field appears, called Custom, into which you can type the string.

3. Use the lower Port pop-up menu, shown in Figure 6-15, to specify the serial port your Mac's modem is attached to (such as the printer, modem, USB, or infrared port). (If relatives are sleeping in the room where your Mac sits, you may also want to click the Modem Speaker Off button. Now, when you call in from the road to HotSync, the modem won't make its usual shrieking noises.)

4. At the top of the dialog box shown in Figure 6-15, click Modem Setup (if dial-in HotSyncing is the only kind of HotSyncing you plan to do) or Both Setups (if you'd like your Mac to monitor both incoming calls and your HotSync cradle for signals from your PalmPilot).

5. Click the HotSync Controls tab and make sure that HotSyncing is Enabled. Close the window.

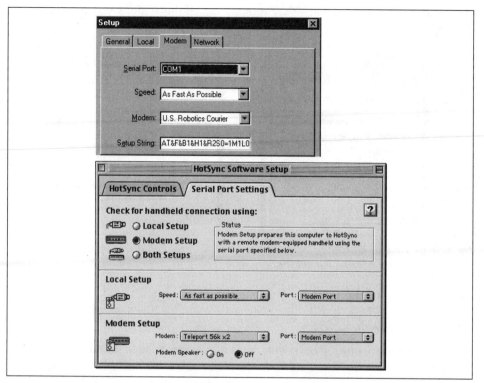

Figure 6-15. The Modem HotSync setup screen lets you teach the PC (top) or Mac (bottom) about the remote connections it'll be making.

Your computer is now ready. Do some homework, however, to make sure that nothing will interfere with your setup while you're away. For example, it's OK to turn your monitor off to save electricity, but the computer itself must stay on. (Your modem must remain on, too.) All your modem-using software, such as fax software, auto-dialing email programs, and so on, should be turned off.

Test your PC's call answering success—by running next door with the PalmPilot and dialing home, for example—before departing for that three-month trip to Afghanistan. It's a rare modem HotSync configuration indeed that works the very first time and requires no adjustments.

Setting Up the PalmPilot

When you're ready to make your PalmPilot dial, begin by tapping Applications → HotSync → Modem Setup. You should see the screen in Figure 6-16. These options should look distinctly familiar—they roughly match the settings you made on your desktop PC.

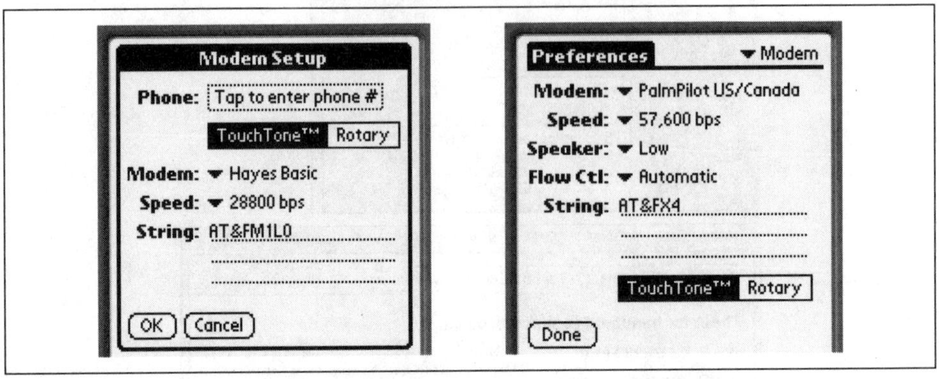

Figure 6-16. Fill in these options before dialing out with your PalmPilot. Left: the original Pilot models. Right: more recent models.

Here's how to set them up.

Modem pop-up menu

From this pop-up menu, specify what kind of modem is attached to the PalmPilot. This isn't quite as straightforward as it sounds, as the following guidelines indicate:

- If you're using the 3Com Palm modem with an *original* Pilot 1000 or 5000 model, choose Megahertz from the pop-up menu. (The PalmPilot modem didn't exist when the original Pilot models were designed; that's why you don't see an option for the PalmPilot modem in the list.)

- If you're using the PalmPilot modem with Palm OS 2 or later (a PalmPilot or Palm III model, for example), choose "PalmPilot US/Canada." If you're in the United Kingdom, the phone system is different; choose "PalmPilot UK."

- If you've purchased a PalmPilot modem cable ($15), you can also connect your PalmPilot to a standard external PC modem. "Hayes Basic" is a good setting to try if you don't see your brand listed in the pop-up menu.

- If you have a Palm V equipped with the Palm V modem, choose "Palm V Modem."

Speed, string, flow control

The original 3Com PalmPilot modem's speed is officially 14,400 bits per second; the Palm V modem is 33Kbps. But 3Com urges you to choose "57,600 bps" from the pop-up menu, on the theory that the modem's built-in data compression features will speed up your transmission.

If you're using a modem not listed in the Modem pop-up menu, you can edit the String setting. As with your desktop modem, this stream of computer codes gets sent to the modem when the dialing process begins; if you know what you're doing (or if you've called your modem manufacturer), you may be able to fill in the correct initialization codes here to accommodate modems not officially endorsed by 3Com.

For HotSyncing, leave the Flow Control set to Automatic. (It's an option only on Palm OS 2 or later.)

Speaker

This option (on Palm OS 2 or later) controls the volume of the modem's built-in speaker. The pop-up menu offers four settings—Off, Low, Medium, and High. Especially if you're using the PalmPilot modem, you may find a Medium or High setting useful when trying to troubleshoot a dialing sequence; otherwise, you may not be able to hear the dial tone, dialing sequence, calling-card confirmation beeps, and so on. On the other hand, Off is the best setting if you're in a hotel room containing a sleeping spouse.

TouchTone or Rotary

Tap to select the kind of phone system you're using: TouchTone, used by 90% of the civilized world, or rotary, used in very old phone systems.

Specifying the phone number

Now that you've instructed the PalmPilot on topics pertaining to your modem, you must tell it what number to dial—and how to dial it. The procedure varies slightly depending on your model.

Original Pilot models

If you're still looking at the Modem Setup box (see Figure 6-16), tap where it says "Tap to enter phone #".

Subsequent models

When you've finished setting up your modem, tap the Done button. You return to the main HotSync window (see Figure 6-17). Tap the "Enter phone #" box.

Now you arrive at the Phone Setup box (see Figure 6-17 again). Write the phone number—the phone number your desktop PC's modem is connected to—into the top blank. You can also control the PalmPilot's dialing process by turning on the checkboxes next to the following blanks:

Dial prefix

If the office or hotel you're in requires that you dial 8 or 9 to get an outside line, turn on this checkbox and see that it contains the proper number. In

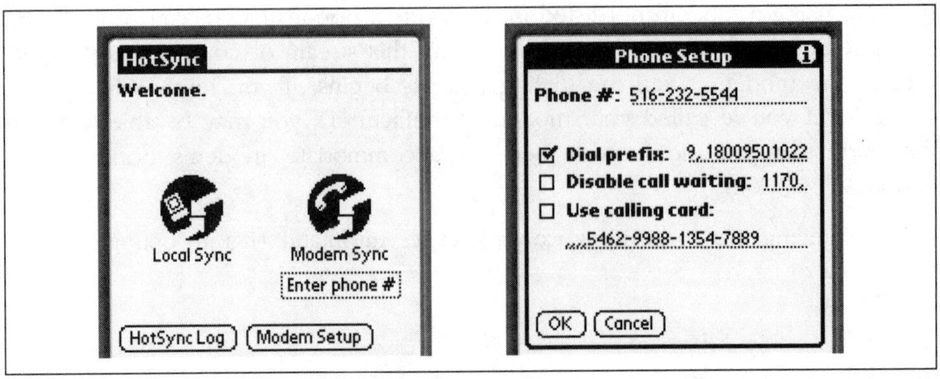

Figure 6-17. From the main HotSync screen (on all recent models; shown at left), tap the Phone # box to view the phone setup screen (right).

modem-dialing lingo, a comma means "pause for two seconds"; that's why there's a comma, by default, after the 9 in this blank.

Disable call waiting

Call waiting is the phone-company feature that interrupts your current call with a clicking sound to indicate that somebody *else* is trying to call you. Unfortunately, that clicking sound also promptly short-circuits modem-to-modem calls, such as your PalmPilot's. You can turn off call waiting on a call-by-call basis by turning on this checkbox and entering *1170* or *70*. (Although the PalmPilot's blank, by default, has a comma after this code, the comma/pause isn't generally necessary.)

Use calling card

If you use a phone card, you may be baffled by this solitary blank. Most calling cards require that you dial *three* bunches of numbers: first, an access code (such as 1-800-950-1022 for MCI); then, after a tone, zero and the phone number; and finally, after another tone, the actual card number.

The PalmPilot can accommodate you. Turn on the "Dial prefix" option and type the access phone number there. You'll quickly discover that there's not enough room on the blank to hold a full 800 number—but keep writing. Even if you can't *see* all the numbers, the blank stores the final digits invisibly. (If you have to dial 9 and *then* an 800 number, just leave the 9 and comma in place, as shown in Figure 6-17.) Add some commas after the 800 number to make the PalmPilot "wait for" the tone—each comma creates a two-second pause—and then, if your card requires a zero before the phone number, write it after the commas. A complete string in the "Dial prefix" blank, then, might look like this (only the first part will appear on the screen): 9, 1-800-950-1022,,,0.

The actual phone number, area code first, should appear in the Phone # blank as usual.

Finally, write your calling-card number in the "Use calling card:" blank (and turn on the checkbox). You'll note that four commas appear at the beginning of this blank by default—they're there to make the PalmPilot wait for the beeps from the phone company. Actually, though, you don't have to wait for this second set of tones with most calling cards; you'll probably discover that you can do without some or all of these commas, plowing directly from the phone number to the card number.

When you're finished setting up the phone number, tap the OK button. On Palm OS 2 or later, you have one final OK button to tap. You should now be at the HotSync screen, ready to dial.

> Despite the many possibilities for inclusion in your PalmPilot's dialing string—commas, calling card numbers, access numbers, and so on—the most the machine can dial is 36 digits. If the total number of numbers, commas, prefixes, country codes, and so on is more than 36, your call won't go through. That's a definite disappointment for anyone who wants to call internationally using a calling card!

Specifying what data to HotSync

In Palm OS 2 and later, you can control which *conduits* (program data types) get updated when you HotSync via modem. If you never use the Memo Pad, for example, you shouldn't waste your long-distance phone time having the Palm-Pilot and your desktop computer consult each other on that topic. (See the section, "The Concept of Conduits" earlier in this chapter, for more on conduits and controlling them.)

To turn certain data groups on or off for modem HotSync purposes, tap Applications → HotSync → Menu → Conduit Setup. The resulting window is shown in Figure 6-18. Simply tap the checkboxes to turn specific conduits on or off.

Alas, if you have a Pilot Desktop 1.0, a Macintosh, or Windows before version 95, you have no such control; *all* PalmPilot modules get HotSynced when you connect by modem.

Actually Performing the Modem HotSync

Hook up a modem to your PalmPilot, as described in Chapter 13. Connect a phone wire from your PalmPilot's modem to the telephone jack on the wall or on the phone. Your apparatus should resemble the photo in Figure 6-19.

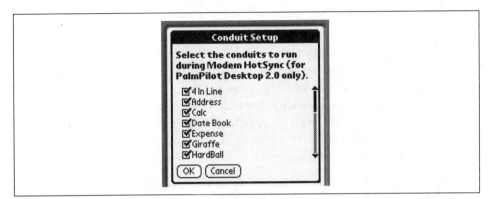

Figure 6-18. Recent models let you control which programs' data gets backed up when dialing in from afar.

Figure 6-19. With the PalmPilot modem and a phone line connected, you're ready to dial.

The phone systems in most hotels and offices are *digital lines,* which fry most modems and fax machines. The PalmPilot modem is kind enough to play three warning beeps instead of destroying itself—but either way, ask before you connect!

What you want is an *analog* line. Many modern hotels' bedside telephones have, on the side, a special jack labeled DATA or DATA-PORT; *this* jack is the one you want for plugging in your Palm modem (or laptop modem, for that matter). If there's no such jack on your bedside phone, use the jack being used by a fax machine, if you can find one; otherwise, ask the management.

You're ready to HotSync!

1. Turn on the PalmPilot. Tap Applications → HotSync. You arrive at the main HotSync screen, shown at left in Figure 6-17.

2. Tap the Modem HotSync button.

The palmtop begins dialing. If all goes well, you'll see a connection message appear on its screen, and the HotSync will proceed. You'll hear the usual musical chirps to indicate success at connecting and finishing.

Syncing with Your Favorite Windows Programs

So far in this chapter, you've read about using the HotSync software provided with your PalmPilot. In the next chapter, you'll read more about how the HotSync process loads your life's data into Palm Desktop.

But for thousands of Palm users, Palm Desktop is a poor substitute for the more fully featured calendar, address book, to do, and memo pad programs they've been using for years: Outlook, ACT, Now Up-to-Date, Agenda, Sidekick, and so on. (These programs are generically known as PIMs—personal information managers.) Does getting a PalmPilot have to mean abandoning these popular information managers and switching to the more rudimentary Palm Desktop?

Not at all. Fortunately, there's scarcely a PIM program in existence that can't sync with a PalmPilot directly, bypassing Palm Desktop entirely. To perform this kind of HotSync, you need a specialized piece of software called *conduit software;* such conduits are available for every popular PIM. Play your cards right, install the right conduit program, and you should be able to keep using the calendar or address-book software you've always used.

(This section covers conduits for major Windows PIM programs, but those aren't the only programs for which conduits are available. See Chapter 12 if you're interested in connection to database, spreadsheet, or financial desktop software; Chapter 13 for connections with desktop email programs; and Chapter 9 for coverage of Macintosh-software conduits.)

 Even if you use a different conduit program, you may want to keep Palm Desktop on your computer. It's still useful for editing certain kinds of data that aren't addressed by many third-party conduits—such as changing a PalmPilot's list of categories or user name.

Choosing the Conduit Software

Some conduit software is built into the PIM software itself; you've got nothing else to buy. For example, Starfish Software's Sidekick software talks directly to the PalmPilot, without requiring any additional software. And if you have a recent PalmPilot model, such as a Palm IIIx or a Palm V, a conduit to Microsoft Outlook is automatically installed with Palm Desktop. If you use Daytimer Organizer, on the other hand, you need to buy a specialized conduit program, such as Intelli-Sync. Table 6-2 indicates which conduits are available for the most popular desktop PIM programs.

Table 6-2. Available Conduits for PIM Programs

Your Software	Conduit Software Options
ACT 2.0	Tele-Sync for ACT
ACT 3.0	ACT PalmPilot Link CompanionLink Data-Sync for ACT IntelliSync Plus Pack
Agenda	Comes with built-in conduit
Ascend '97	Comes with built-in conduit
Daytimer Organizer 2.0, 2.1	IntelliSync
ECCO	Comes with built-in conduit IntelliSync
Eudora Planner	IntelliSync
Goldmine 3.0 and later	CompanionLink Data-Sync for Goldmine IntelliSync Plus Pack
IBM OfficeVision/VM (PROFS)	PROFS-AutoPilot
Lotus Notes	EasySync for Lotus Notes Pylon, Pylon Pro
Lotus Organizer	CompanionLink Desktop To Go EasySync for Lotus Organizer IntelliSync
Meeting Maker	MM2Pilot IntelliSync
Maximizer	Maximizer PilotLink
METZ Phones	Data-Sync for METZ Phones
Microsoft Exchange	IntelliSync

Table 6-2. Available Conduits for PIM Programs (continued)

Your Software	Conduit Software Options
Microsoft Outlook	Palm Desktop (recent models) CompanionLink Desktop To Go IntelliSync PilotMirror
Microsoft Schedule+ 7.0 and later	CompanionLink Desktop To Go IntelliSync
Netscape Calendar	Netscape Calendar Link
Novell GroupWise	SyncWise
Oracle Mobile Sales & Marketing	IntelliSync
Oracle InterOffice	IntelliSync
Schedule+	Desktop To Go IntelliSync PilotMirror
Sidekick	Comes with built-in conduit (called TrueSync) IntelliSync Plus Pack
Time & Chaos32	ChaosSync

As you can see by this table, the most capable and flexible HotSync program is Puma Technology's IntelliSync. This book's CD-ROM includes a 30-day trial version—and the back of the book has a special offer that lets you buy the full version, plus a year's worth of free updates, at a greatly discounted price.

Table 6-3 shows where to get the conduit programs listed in Table 6-2, current at this writing.

Table 6-3. Conduit Sources

Conduit	Where to Get It
ACT PalmPilot Link (free)	Download from *http://www.symantec.com/act/index_demos.html*
ChaosSync ($25)	iSBiSTER, (972) 495-6724 Web: *http://www.isbister.com/chaos32-plugins-tc2pilot.html*
CompanionLink ($75)	CompanionLink Software, (800) 386-1623 Web: *http://www.companionlink.com*
Data-Sync series ($50)	Tele-Support, (800) 386-1623 Web: *http://www.tssw.com*

Table 6-3. Conduit Sources (continued)

Conduit	Where to Get It
Desktop To Go ($50)	DataViz, (800) 733-0030 Web: *http://www.dataviz.com*
EasySync for Lotus Notes ($50)	Lotus, (800) 872-3387, ext. D669 Web: *http://www.lotus.com/calendar*
EasySync for Lotus Organizer (free)	Download from *http://www.lotus.com/home.nsf/ welcome/calendar*
ECCO Pro ($140)	NetManage, (425) 885-4272 Web: *http://www.netmanage.com*
IntelliSync ($70)	Puma, (800) 248-2795. 30-day trial version (and special offer) included with this book Web: *http://www.pumatech.com*
Maximizer PilotLink ($50)	Maximizer, (888) 629-8738 Web: *http://www.maximizer.com*
MM2Pilot (free)	Download from *http://www.palmpilotfiles.com/ original/mm2pilot.zip*
Netscape Calendar Link (free)	Download from *(http://search.netscape.com/ download/ppilot.html)*
PilotMirror ($40)	Chapura, (888) 898-2310 Web: *http://www.chapura.com*
Plus Pack ($30)	Macmillan, (800) 428-5331 Web: *http://merchant.superlibrary.com:8000/ catalog/sw/PRODUCT/PAGE/07897/bud/ 0789713594.html*
Pocket Quicken ($40)	Landware, 800-526-3977 Web: *www.landware.com*
PROFS-AutoPilot ($60)	FTB Systems, (248) 669-6943 Web: *http://www.ftbsystems.com/*
Pylon Conduit ($85)	Globalware Consulting, (773) 549-3710 Web: *http://www.gc.com/gc.nsf/($all)/products*
Sidekick 98 ($50)	Starfish, (888) 782-7347 Web: *http://www.starfish.com*
SyncWise ($50)	Toffa International, +44 (0)1922 711211 Web: *http://www.toffa.com/sync_info.html*

A Day in the Life of a Third-Party Conduit

Step-by-step instructions for HotSyncing each of the popular PIMs using each of the popular HotSync conduits would require a book in itself. But so that you get the idea, here's an example of life with a third-party conduit program, IntelliSync, shown in Figure 6-20:

1. Install IntelliSync. Spend an unusual amount of time with its Read Me file, which explains how the program handles differences in features between your desktop computer's PIM and your PalmPilot. For example, what if your

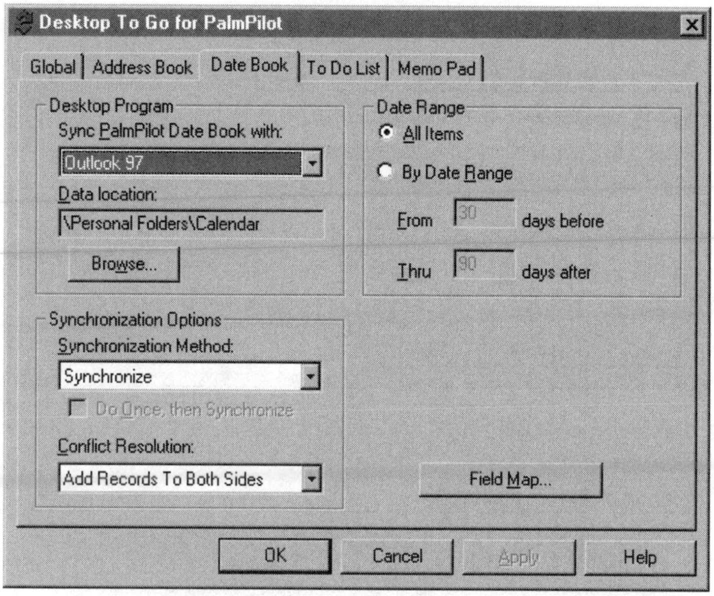

Figure 6-20. Desktop To Go (from DataViz) is flexible enough to offer numerous options for each program you'll be syncing. For example, each of the PalmPilot's programs can be synced to a different program on your desktop PC—the calendar to Schedule+, the address book to Outlook, and so on.

calendar program's to do feature lets you assign priorities from 1 to 10? How will such items show up on the PalmPilot, because its To Do program allows priority levels only up to five? (Answer: priorities from your PIM's To Do program higher than five are automatically rounded down to five.) Or what if your Windows program permits repeating To Do items—after all, the Palm-Pilot doesn't? (Answer: IntelliSync will create three to do items on the PalmPilot that correspond to the first three occurrences.)

2. Launch IntelliSync. You see the master dialog box, as shown in Figure 6-21, which should distinctly remind you of the Palm Desktop dialog box shown in Figure 6-8. In other words, you're now seeing a list of individual conduits.

3. Click a Palm program's name, and then click Choose. As shown in Figure 6-22, you get a list of every PIM program that IntelliSync knows about. Just choose the one you use.

4. One of the advantages of using a dedicated HotSync program like IntelliSync is its wealth of intelligent HotSync features. Click the Options button to open the dialog box shown in Figure 6-23; as you can see, you're offered control over every conceivable aspect of the HotSync process—which items are synchronous, what happens in the event of a conflict, and so on.

5. Click Done.

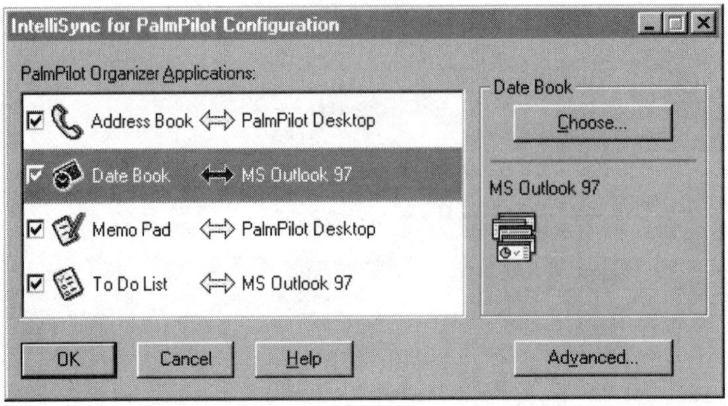

Figure 6-21. The main IntelliSync dialog box lets you assign each Palm program's data to a different Windows program.

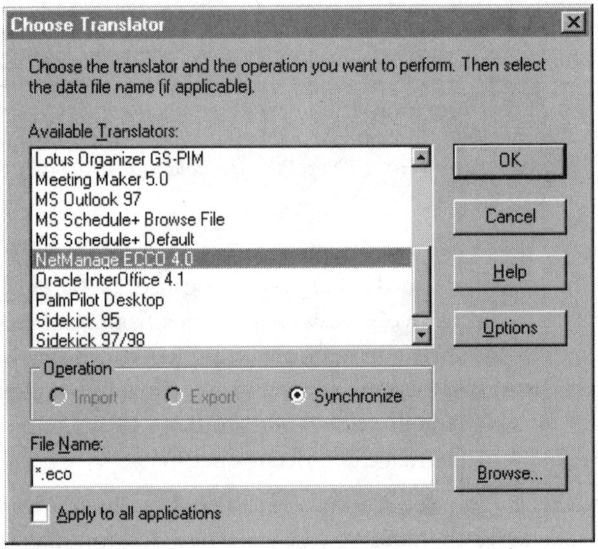

Figure 6-22. If IntelliSync doesn't display the name of the calendar, address book, to do, or note pad program that you use on your Windows machine, you must be using an off brand indeed.

That's all the setup. When you insert your PalmPilot into its cradle and press the HotSync button, IntelliSync—not the usual HotSync Manager software—takes over and manages the synchronization process. Even if you've specified a different Windows program to handle each Palm-program module, your data should now be happily up-to-date on both machines.

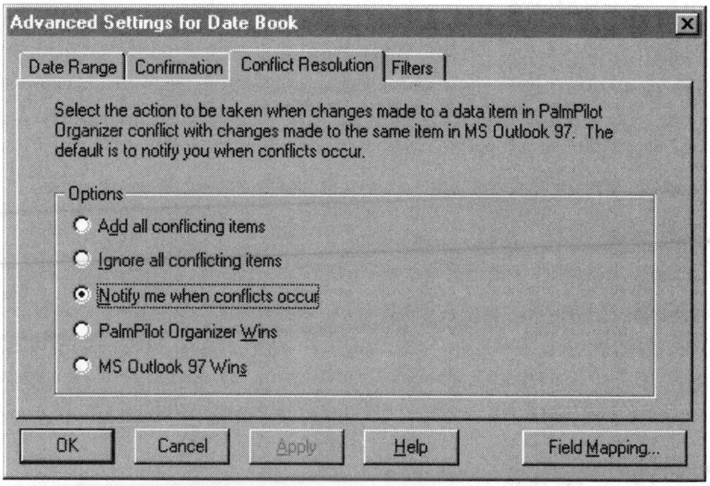

Advanced Settings for Date Book   ☒

| Date Range | Confirmation | Conflict Resolution | Filters |

Select the action to be taken when changes made to a data item in PalmPilot Organizer conflict with changes made to the same item in MS Outlook 97. The default is to notify you when conflicts occur.

Options

○ A̲dd all conflicting items

○ I̲gnore all conflicting items

◉ N̲otify me when conflicts occur

○ PalmPilot Organizer W̲ins

○ MS Outlook 97 Win̲s

| OK | Cancel | Apply | Help | Field M̲apping... |

Figure 6-23. The tabs in the Options dialog box provide additional control over the HotSync process.

Network HotSyncs

This chapter so far has covered HotSyncing to your computer *directly,* either by physically connecting your PalmPilot (via HotSync) or by directly dialing home.

3Com's Network HotSync software ($70, or free with recent models such as the Palm IIIx and V) makes several intriguing new approaches possible—for people whose PCs are part of a corporate, TCP/IP-based, local-area or wide-area network, where many computers are hooked together.

Network HotSync offers two new features: *LAN/WAN* HotSyncing and *remote-access* HotSyncing. The software kit consists of a new *.prc* program to install onto your PalmPilot; a new version of the HotSync Manager software; and several DLL files that get installed into Windows.

Don't attempt network HotSyncing unless all PalmPilots involved are PalmPilot Professional, or later, models. The desktop computers must be running Windows 95 or NT (4.0 or later), they must have TCP/IP installed, and the server must be running the Pilot/Palm Desktop software, version 2.1 or later. If you hope to dial into the network, the server must have a full-time Internet link, and you must have been assigned a *PPP account.*

LAN/WAN HotSyncs

Network HotSync lets you HotSync with *your* computer while seated at any *other* computer on your company's (or campus's) local-area network or wide-area network. That is, you can put your PalmPilot into any HotSync cradle, even if it's attached to somebody else's computer. When you press the HotSync button, your PalmPilot is smart enough to locate *your* computer over the network.

To make this work, both computers—yours and the one with the HotSync cradle, elsewhere on the network—must have TCP/IP software installed and have the latest version of the HotSync Manager program running. (See the section "Setting Up the Software," earlier in this chapter.) And if you want to do a HotSync over a *wide* area network—multiple local-area networks, joined by router boxes—those routers must be capable of transmitting *TCP/IP packets.* (Ask your local guru.)

Remote-Access HotSyncs

If your company has set up a *remote-access server*—a computer that accepts phone calls into the network from the outside—the Network HotSync software also lets your modem-equipped PalmPilot dial into the network from the road and synchronize with your desktop computer.

This kind of HotSync works with most remote-access systems: the Windows NT remote-access server (RAS); Total Control NetServers (US Robotics), the MAX Series (Ascend Communications), AS5200 (Cisco Systems); LanRover series (Shiva); and so on. You must have your own PPP or SLIP account (once again, ask whoever set up your remote-access system).

In theory, Network HotSync even lets you tap into your company's network via the Internet. In practice, however, your company has probably built *firewalls* (software protection against hackers) that prevent access from the Net.

Network HotSync Setup

How does your PalmPilot identify itself to the network? Before you attempt a network HotSync, you've tapped Applications → Preferences → Network from the menu of Preferences settings.

Setting up the PalmPilot

As shown in Figure 6-24, you've then indicated what kind of network you're dialing into (get your network administrator to tell you what settings to use), your user name, and your network password. (This user name has nothing to do with your PalmPilot's "user name," by the way. This user name is the one you use to identify yourself on your company's network.)

Now set up the HotSync options: tap the Applications icon and then the HotSync icon. A set of configuration settings awaits at the main HotSync screen. Tap the Menu icon to specify whether you're tapping into your network locally (choose "Turn LANSync on") or by dialing in ("Turn LANSync" off).

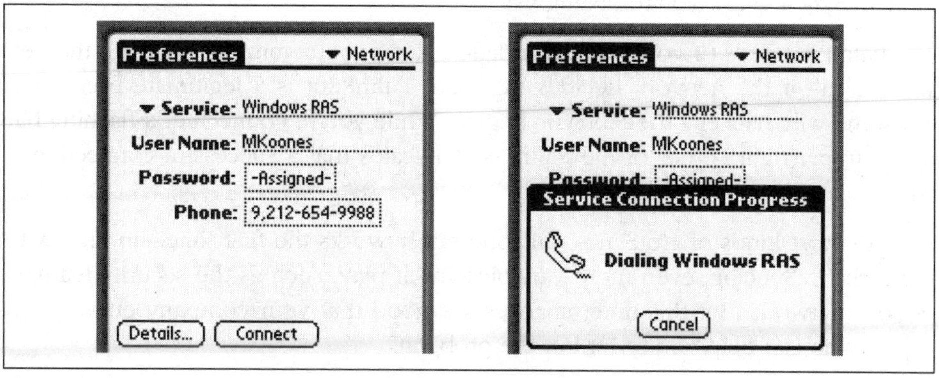

Figure 6-24. Your PalmPilot's Network Preferences screen stores your name (as you're known on the company network), password, and so on (left). Tapping Connect is one way to begin the network connection (right).

Among the most common frustrations in trying to pull off dial-in network HotSyncs are "authentication errors." That's when your company's network doesn't recognize you as a friend.

You can solve many of these problems by checking the capitalization in both the user name and password fields—it matters. Frank isn't the same as FRANK, for example. Make sure, too, that there aren't any extra spaces or return characters *after* your name or password. Delete any that you find and then try the connection again.

Before you can perform a network HotSync, you must perform a local, normal HotSync (to introduce your PalmPilot and computer to each other), exactly as with a modem HotSync, described earlier in this chapter.

Setting up the networked computers

On the desktop computers, click the HotSync Manager icon on the system tray and make sure Network is selected in the pop-up menu. These computers (yours and the one you're HotSyncing from) must be turned on and officially logged into the network before any kind of HotSyncing can take place.

Making the connection

Once everything is configured, begin the HotSync exactly the way you begin any HotSync: by pressing the cradle's HotSync button (if you're physically connected to the network) or tapping the Applications icon, the HotSync icon, and the Modem Sync icon (if you're dialing in).

The PalmPilot dials (if you're doing a dial-in HotSync), communicates with the network, and—if the network decides that your PalmPilot is a legitimate friend and not some wily hacker—the HotSync begins. While you're connected, a flashing bar in the upper-right corner of the PalmPilot indicates that a successful connection is taking place.

As with most kinds of HotSyncs, this one rarely works the first time—in fact, with network HotSyncing, even more variables are at play, such as the security features of your network. But this time, chances are good that your company employs an expert who can help you ferret out the problem.

MSCHAP Problems

If your network has a remote-access server, it likely uses one of several popular security systems, such as Password Authentication Protocol (PAP) or Challenge Handshake Authentication Protocol (CHAP).

If it uses Microsoft Challenge Handshake Authentication Protocol (MSCHAP), however, the PalmPilot will be stumped. Because of the U.S. government's restrictions on exporting encryption products, 3Com doesn't build MSCHAP features into the PalmPilot.

Instead, you're supposed to install the necessary software manually. You can obtain the free MSCHAP.ZIP file from the 3Com web site *(http://palm.3com. com/custsupp/faq/downloads/mschap.html)* or directly from 3Com Corporation. Then install the program onto your PalmPilot using the instructions in Chapter 7.

Executive Tip Summary

- It's fine to designate a port that's already in use (by a printer or modem, for example) as your HotSync port—just disconnect whatever's there when it comes time to HotSync and don't turn on the "always" port-monitoring option in Palm Desktop.

- In Palm Desktop, use the Custom command in the HotSync menu to control which programs' data are actually synchronized, and in which direction. (On the Macintosh, launch HotSync Manager, then choose HotSync → Conduit Settings to view these controls.) Doing so can cut down on HotSync time and confusion.

- The home base for your data on your PC is in the Palm folder on your hard drive—inside the folder with your name on it. Knowing about this special folder means that you can back up, replace, or otherwise manipulate your data once it has been HotSynced.

- You can't perform a modem or network HotSync until you've first performed a standard, local HotSync.

- To view your Palm device's name, tap Applications → HotSync; the name appears at the top of the screen. To change its name in Windows, launch Palm Desktop. From the User pop-up menu, choose Edit Users, click the PalmPilot's name, and click Rename. On the Macintosh, launch HotSync Manager, choose Users → Show Palm User List, click the PalmPilot's name, and click Edit.

- If you have a Palm III or later model, check out the updater to Palm OS 3.3, as described in Chapter 18. It lets you HotSync by infrared, lets HotSync Manager see more of your COM ports, offers additional preferences, and lets you HotSync at speeds up to 115 Kbps—twice as fast as the previous HotSync software.

7

Installing New Palm Programs

As this book should make emphatically clear, the four built-in Palm programs are only a starting point. With a few add-on programs, such as the 3,000 freeware and shareware programs that come with this book, your PalmPilot becomes infinitely more useful and fun.

You install a new program onto your PalmPilot by performing a HotSync. (While there's no actual synchronizing involved when you install a new program, a HotSync is the only time the PalmPilot and PC are in communication.)

Here are the *official* steps for installing a new program onto your PalmPilot. Read on, however, to find out some much quicker and simpler methods that rely on the software included with this book.

 By far the easiest method of installing new programs onto your PalmPilot is to use the CD-ROM that comes with this book. When you read about a program in the CD's searchable database that you think you'd like to try, just click the Install button; the program is automatically scheduled for installation at the next HotSync. You can ignore all subsequent instructions in this chapter. (See Appendix F, *About the CD*, for instructions on using the CD-ROM.)

Installing Add-On Programs

Where do you get new programs for your PalmPilot? Over 3,000 are included on the CD-ROM with this book. Hundreds more are available from the Internet, at sites such as PalmCentral.com (see Appendix C, *Piloteers in Cyberspace*, for a list of software-rich web sites). The quantity and quality of *commercial* Palm software is exploding, too—the catalog that comes with the Palm III family is twice as thick as the one that came with previous models.

Once you've bought or downloaded a new program, you'll probably find that its name ends with *.prc* (which stands for *Pilot resource code*). A few installable files' names end with *.pdb* (short for *Pilot database*); these aren't programs, but rather data files *used* by programs.

All that remains at this point is to get the *.prc* file from your hard drive onto your PalmPilot; read on.

If you have Windows and a Palm III, or a more recent model, dump any newly downloaded *.prc* files into the folder called *Add-On*. (It's in the *Palm* folder on your hard drive.)

The advantage of doing so is that when you indicate that you want to install something new onto your PalmPilot, you'll immediately be shown the contents of this *Add-On* folder in step 2 below. You're saved the headache of rooting around on your hard drive trying to find the downloaded file.

The Official Windows Installation Method

The simplicity of installing new software using versions 1.0 and 2.0 of Palm Desktop left something to be desired. That's why 3Com, in designing the 1998 model—the Palm III—overhauled its installation software. (You now install software from within the Palm Desktop program, instead of requiring a separate installation application.) The resulting process is far more streamlined.

The steps for installing new software onto your palmtop are far simpler if you use the latest version of Palm Desktop, whether Windows or Macintosh. This chapter assumes that you're using the latest—if not, you can download this software at no charge from *http://www. Palm.com*.

Here's how to install a new program using Palm Desktop 3.0 or later:

1. Launch Palm Desktop. Click the Install button at the lower-left corner of the screen, as shown in Figure 7-1.

2. A new dialog box appears, showing all the software you've scheduled for installation. (It's probably empty at this point.) Use the pop-up menu at the top of the screen to specify which PalmPilot you want to install onto (if you use more than one with this PC). Click the Add button.

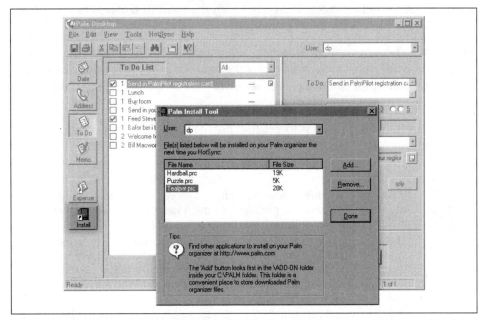

Figure 7-1. To begin installing something, click the Install button in Palm Desktop (left). The dialog box shown at center appears; click Add. (This illustration shows that several programs have already been slated for installation.)

3. You're now shown the list of waiting programs in your *Add-On* folder (which is inside the *Palm* folder), as described in the previous tip. If you see the software you want to install listed here, double-click it. If not, navigate until you do find it—once again, double-click.

4. You return to the main dialog box. If you want to specify additional programs for installation, repeat steps 2 and 3.

> If several Palm programs are listed in this dialog box—for example, the contents of your Add-on folder—you can highlight several program names simultaneously in this list box. Click the first name in the list, and then Shift-click the last one, to highlight everything between. Or, to select program names that aren't consecutive in the list, Ctrl-click their names. Finally, click Open to load them all at once into the Install dialog box.

5. Click Done. A message lets you know that the new programs will be installed at the next HotSync; click OK.

   After the next HotSync, tap the Applications icon on the PalmPilot to see your newly installed software.

If you've got several programs to install, here's a handy shortcut. In Palm Desktop, click the Install Tool icon. The dialog box shown in Figure 7-1 appears. At this point you can click your Windows desktop, locate the PalmPilot programs you want to install, and *drag their icons* into the empty Palm Install Tool window. They show up there en masse, saving you the trouble of having to select each one individually.

The Official Macintosh Installation Method

These instructions assume that you're using the 1999 MacPac software package included with this book.

1. From the small green Palm menu-bar icon, choose HotSync Manager. The HotSync Manager screen appears. (If you HotSync multiple PalmPilots on the same Mac, take a moment now to choose Users → Select Current Palm User, specify which PalmPilot you want to install these new programs onto, and click OK.)

2. Choose HotSync → Install. The dialog box shown in Figure 7-2 appears, showing all the software you've scheduled for installation. (It's probably empty at this point.) Use the pop-up menu at the top of the screen to specify which PalmPilot you want to install onto (if you use more than one with this PC).

3. *Drag-and-drop method:* Click the desktop. Locate the Palm programs (*.prc* or *.pdb* files) you want to install, and simply drag their icon into the window shown in Figure 7-2. *Dialog box method:* Click Add to List. You're shown the usual Macintosh Open File dialog box; navigate to, and double-click, the first program you want to install. Click Add to List again, and repeat as necessary.

4. When you're finished choosing files to install, close the window and, if you wish, quit HotSync Manager.

After the next HotSync, your newly installed software appears on the PalmPilot's Applications screen, ready to use.

If you find yourself installing new Palm applications fairly frequently, try this Macintosh-only timesaver. Open your Palm → Users → *your name* folder. Make an alias of the Files to Install folder. Drag the alias to your desktop.

From now on, installing a new Palm program is as easy as dragging it onto this alias—a single step. At the next HotSync, that program is automatically installed onto your palmtop.

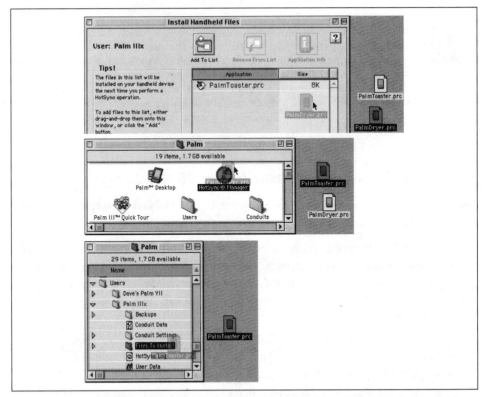

Figure 7-2. Install new programs via Macintosh by dragging into the Install window (top), onto the HotSync Manager icon (middle), or into the Files to Install folder (bottom).

How the Install Tool Works (Windows)

Behind the scenes, the Install Tool does two things. First, it puts a copy of the program-to-be-installed into your user-named folder (in a subfolder called *Install*). If you double-click the folder, then open your user-named folder (such as Frank), and then open the *Install* folder, you'll see the programs in their little transporter room, awaiting beaming to the PalmPilot (see Figure 7-3).

The Install Tool program also makes a quiet notation in your Windows System Registry that something is in the *Install* folder. It's because of this invisible on/off switch that you can't simply put new programs into the *Install* folder *manually* and expect them to get copied to the PalmPilot. Unless the "programs are waiting!" switch is turned on behind the scenes, putting programs into your *Install* folder accomplishes nothing.

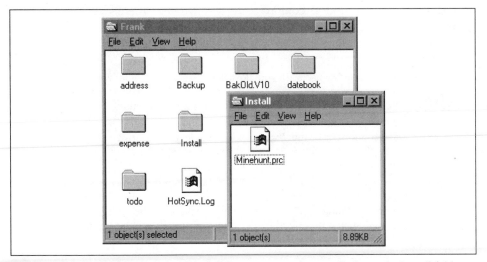

Figure 7-3. The Install Tool puts a copy of the program to be installed into the Install folder, inside your user-named folder, and inside the Palm folder.

Outsmarting InstallApp

However, knowing about the invisible "programs waiting" switch *can* save time and effort. For example, suppose you want to install 10 new programs onto your PalmPilot at once—from this book's CD, say, or from the Internet. You could, of course, repeat steps 2 and 3 in the section "The Official Windows Installation Method," earlier in this chapter.

Instead, however, the true Palm aficionado opts for the following more efficient method:

1. Click the Install button in Palm Desktop. Select for installation *one* of the new programs you want copied to your PalmPilot. After specifying that single program, exit the program or dialog box.

   At this point, you've successfully copied *one* program into your *Install* folder—*and* flipped the "programs are waiting!" switch deep inside the Windows Registry.

2. Returning to your PC's desktop, locate the *other* Palm-bound programs (whose names end in *.prc* or *.pdb*). Drag their icons into the *Install* folder (which is inside your user-named folder, which is inside the folder on your hard drive).

See the sneakiness here? In step 1, you used the Install Tool software to flip the master switch that tells Palm Desktop to copy new programs onto the PalmPilot. In step 2, you put additional programs into the *Install* folder, confident that they'll get installed right along with the first program you selected. In other words, as long as you've used the Install Tool to trigger the installation process during the next HotSync, Palm Desktop couldn't care less whether there's one or 100 programs to be installed, as long as they're in the *Install* folder.

Windows 95/98 users: If you do a lot of installing onto your Palm-Pilot—for example, if you're a regular PalmPilot web-site cruiser—you can save time by hooking up your right mouse button's Send To command.

Make a Shortcut of the *Install* folder (inside your user-named folder, inside the *Pilot* folder). Put that Shortcut inside the *Send To* folder, which is inside your *Windows* folder.

From now on, when you right-click a *.prc* or *.pdb* file's icon, use the Send To command to whisk that Palm program directly to the *Install* folder. Assuming you've successfully switched on the "programs are waiting!" switch described earlier, those programs will be installed at the next HotSync.

More Program Installation Notes for Windows

If your PC runs Windows, several time-saving shortcuts await.

The .prc double-click time-saver

If you need any additional incentive to upgrade the latest version of Palm Desktop, consider this: if version 3 or later is installed on your machine, you can launch the Install Tool automatically by simply double-clicking any Palm program on your desktop (a *.prc* or *.pdb* file). You save the time it would have taken to launch Palm Desktop and click the Install button.

Alternative installation applications

The world, the Web, and this book's CD are loaded with replacement program-installation programs. Consult the software database on this book's CD, for example, to read more about such Windows installation-related add-ons as RipCord and Backup Buddy.

How the Install Tool Works (Macintosh)

Provided you're using Palm Desktop 2.1 for the Mac or later, installing new Palm programs from the Macintosh is even easier than in Windows.

For example, on the Macintosh, you can skip the formal installation instructions provided earlier in this chapter (launch HotSync Manager, use the Install command, and so on). Instead, open the Palm folder → your user-named folder; inside, you'll see a folder called Files to Install (see Figure 7-3). There's nothing more to specifying a Palm program you want installed than dragging its icon into this folder. At the next HotSync, that file will disappear from the Files to Install folder and reappear on your PalmPilot.

Installing "Windows" Palm programs on a Mac

The beauty of Palm programs is that they're *all* available to *all* computer owners. There's no distinction between a "Windows" Palm program and a "Macintosh" PalmPilot program—the Palm operating system doesn't care what kind of computer is on your desk.

But a cruise among online Palm web sites might make you think otherwise. Some programs are listed for downloading in both "Mac" and "Windows" formats. Furthermore, upon close inspection on your Macintosh, most Palm Programs look like SimpleText documents with generic icons (also shown in Figure 7-4). Double-clicking them displays only an error message. What's going on?

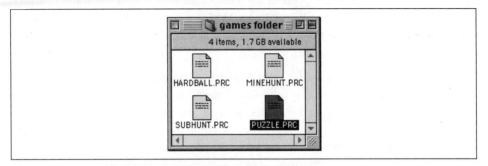

Figure 7-4. Sometimes the Mac's Install Tool can't "see" Palm programs you want to install onto your PalmPilot. In this example, 3Com's own games haven't been designed correctly to be double-clickable Palm icons.

Behind the scenes, every Macintosh program has its own customized four-letter code: the *creator code*. No two creator codes are alike. For FileMaker Pro, the creator code is FMPR. For Word, it's WDBN, and so on. Because every *document* you create is also stamped with this creator code, it always knows who its parent is. When you double-click a document icon whose creator code is FMPR, FileMaker Pro opens automatically.

Every icon also has an invisible *type* code. This piece of information specifies which kind of file it is: text, graphic, and so on. For example, depending on the options you choose in Excel's Save As dialog box, this single program can create text files (type code: TEXT), normal Excel files (XLS6), Lotus 1-2-3-exchangeable files (SYLK), Microsoft Works format (LWKS), and so on.

Some programmers, unfortunately, are unaware of Macintosh type and creator codes, and therefore don't provide their Palm programs with them. As a result, these programs show up as plain text files. (A Palm document's creator code is PITT, and the type code is "PRC ", with a space as the fourth character.)

If you plan to share your Palm programs with other Mac friends, on the other hand, you might wish to add type and creator codes so that your *friends* won't have the same problem. In the standard system software, Apple doesn't provide any way for you to change a file's type or creator code. Dozens of free or shareware programs, however, let you change this information—Drop•Info, ResEdit, TypeChanger, GetInfo Extreme, and so on. In fact, PCtoMac Install Helper, included with this book, reduces the process to a single drag-and-drop step.

Once you've changed a PalmPilot program's codes, it will forever afterward display the correct icon (and open when double-clicked).

The Secret Backups Folder

More than one Palm fan has been delighted to find that, following some catastrophe that results in an empty PalmPilot, a HotSync restores not only all personal data, such as datebook and address book info, but all previously installed add-on programs as well.

The secret is the Backups folder, which lurks in your user-named folder in the Palm folder. When you install a new Palm program, it doesn't vanish from your hard drive as it moves to your PalmPilot; instead, it's simply moved into the Backups folder, where it waits patiently. At each HotSync, your PC checks the PalmPilot to make sure that all Palm programs are still present. If not—and you didn't manually delete the program from your palmtop—the HotSync process courteously reinstalls it from the Backups folder.

This mechanism is worth knowing about for two reasons. First, as noted in Chapter 6, *HotSync, Step by Step*, not every component of every Palm application is backed up in this folder; certain categories of software, such as support databases and HackMaster files, exist only on the palmtop. In the event of disaster, no backup remains on your hard drive. (Each individual Palm programmer chooses whether to turn on the *backup bit* on each component of his or her software. That bit determines whether or not the software module will be automatically copied to the Backups folder at each HotSync. The programmer may decide not to turn on the backup bit in order to make HotSyncing faster.) Only programs like Backup Buddy, included on this book's CD in both Mac and Windows formats, are capable of making truly complete backups of all software on your PalmPilot.

The Backups folder is interesting for a second reason, too: it's a central holding tank for all your favorite add-on programs. When you want to email them to a friend or move them to a second PalmPilot, you'll know where to find them. In the latter case, in fact, you can simply copy them, on your hard drive, into the

Backups folder of the second PalmPilot; at the next HotSync, the PC will assume that such programs should be automatically "reinstalled" onto that palmtop.

Frequent the online Palm discussion groups long enough, and you'll eventually hear somebody complaining that, following a HotSync, the programs scheduled for installation don't disappear from the Install dialog box list. No matter how many times such victims manually delete those programs from the PalmPilot, they reappear after every HotSync. This anomaly arises when you've scheduled for installation a file that Windows has marked as read-only. (Sometimes a file or a folder copied from the CD-ROM is marked in this way.)

Return to the Windows desktop, right-click the icon, choose Properties, and turn off the "read-only" checkbox. Henceforth, the installable file should behave normally, disappearing from the Install list after HotSync.

How to Uninstall Programs

Removing programs from your PalmPilot is even easier than installing them.

As the confirmation box reminds you, deleting a program also deletes all *data* created by that program. That is, if you delete Super-Notepad, you also delete any writing you've done in that program.

If losing all your associated data is a concern, HotSync your Palm-Pilot before deleting a program.

Pilot and PalmPilot models

Tap Applications → Memory → the name of the program you want to remove → Delete Apps. As shown in Figure 7-5, you now see a list of programs you've installed. Tap one and then tap Delete. Now you're asked to confirm the deletion; tap Yes.

Palm III and later models

Tap Applications → Menu → App → Delete. You're shown a list of installed programs (not counting the ones that are permanently etched into the Palm-Pilot's ROM, such as the Memo Pad and Date Book). Tap the one you want to delete, tap the Delete button, and tap Yes in the confirmation dialog box.

All of this is a useful process to remember when your palmtop's memory is getting full—as Figure 7-5 illustrates, you can actually see how much RAM each of your add-on programs is consuming.

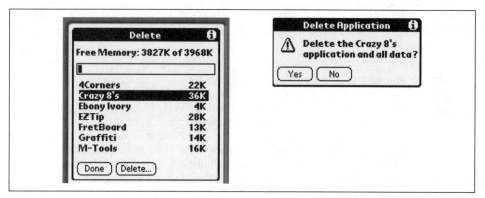

Figure 7-5. To delete a program, tap its name (left) and then confirm the deletion (right).

Executive Tip Summary

- Once you've scheduled one new program for installation using the usual Windows method, you've successfully flipped the master "programs to install" switch. You can now freely drag additional programs into the *Install* folder inside your user-named folder. They'll all be installed at the next HotSync, even though you didn't follow the usual procedure of choosing them with the Install software.

- Get into the habit of putting newly downloaded PalmPilot programs into the *Add-On* folder (which is in your Windows *Palm* folder). You'll save time when you actually go to select them for installation, because that's where Palm Desktop looks first when you click the Install button.

- On both the Mac and Windows, you can drag-and-drop Palm programs' icons from your desktop directly into the Install dialog box.

- On the Macintosh, you can drag Palm programs' icons directly onto the HotSync manager icon to install them—or into the Files to Install folder in the appropriate user-named folder. Those dragged programs will be available on your PalmPilot automatically after the next HotSync.

8

Palm Desktop: Windows

Chapter 6, *HotSync, Step by Step*, describes how data gets from your PalmPilot to your desktop computer. In this chapter, you'll find out what happens to the data when it reaches your PC. Its home there is a program called Palm Desktop. (This book assumes that you're using version 3.0 or later; if not, you can download the latest version for free from *http://www.palm.com*.)

Palm Desktop duplicates the functions of the PalmPilot on your computer—calendar, phone book, to do list, memo pad, and all. Make a change in Palm Desktop, and it's automatically updated on your PalmPilot at your next HotSync, and vice versa.

Once you begin exploring Palm Desktop, you may wonder what the fuss is about. Its calendar and address book features are adequate, but not nearly as fancy as, say, Microsoft Outlook, ACT, or Eudora Planner. Why would you use Palm Desktop to run your life?

In many cases, you wouldn't. Think of Palm Desktop as your *backup* program for the PalmPilot, or as the loading dock for your PalmPilot—not necessarily as your calendar/address book software. For example, Palm Desktop is especially handy if you want to:

- Import addresses from another program, ready to upload into the PalmPilot
- Change the options for a HotSync—for example, although HotSyncing generally updates *both* your PalmPilot and your PC, there may be times when you want your PC's data to completely replace what's on the PalmPilot, or vice versa

- Retrieve data you deleted long ago from the PalmPilot

- Manage the backing up (or loading up) of many different PalmPilots from the same PC

- Print your PalmPilot data

For details on installing Palm Desktop, see Chapter 6. (That chapter also covers the HotSync-related aspects of Palm Desktop.)

Palm Desktop Overview

When you launch Palm Desktop, you get a screen something like Figure 8-1. (If you don't, click the Date icon at the left side of the screen.)

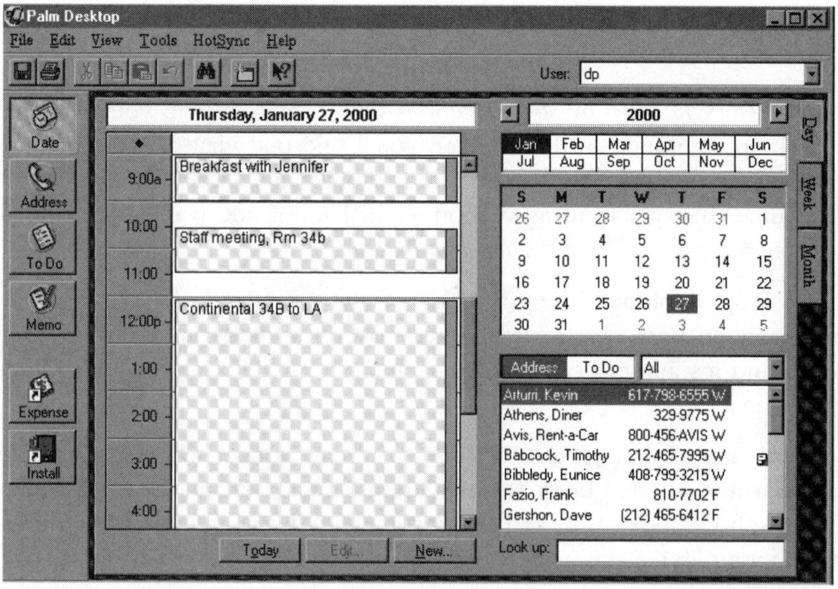

Figure 8-1. Down the left side of the screen are the icons for the main Palm programs. (The Expense icon is available only on Palm OS 2 or later; the Install icon is available only in version 3 and later.) At the upper right is the User pop-up menu, which you can ignore unless you have more than one PalmPilot.

There are two ways to control what information you're seeing. You can click the icons of the programs (Memo, Address, and so on) listed at the left side of the window. But if you HotSync more than one PalmPilot to this computer, you can also change *whose* data you're seeing by choosing from the pop-up menu in the upper-right corner of the window.

To switch among the different programs, you can click the icons at the left side of the window, choose their names from the View menu, or use the keyboard equivalents:

Program	Keystroke
Date Book	F2
Address Book	F3
To Do List	F4
Memo Pad	F5
Expense	F6
Install	F7

Once you've selected a module, the screen changes to resemble what you'd see on the PalmPilot in its corresponding program. The Date icon shows you a calendar, the Address icon opens the master list of names, and so on. Only the Expense icon works in an unexpected way; see the section "Expense," later in this chapter.

When you first launch Palm Desktop, it shows you your Date Book. You're supposed to click the left-margin icons to switch among the different PalmPilot modules.

If, however, you prefer the Address Book, To Do, or Memo Pad program to open first each time you launch Palm Desktop, choose Options from the Tools menu. You'll be shown a pop-up menu that lets you specify which module you want as your startup program.

The program also offers a toolbar—the row of tiny icons between the menu bar and the actual display area—but its icons simply duplicate the program's menu commands. Unfortunately, there's no way to hide the toolbar.

Advantages of Palm Desktop

Fortunately, there's more to Palm Desktop than a simple repetition of the Palm software. Your PC's memory, screen, printer, and other assets make Palm Desktop considerably more flexible.

For example, on the PalmPilot, each program starts up showing a home page list of your data—the Address Book, say, shows a list of names; tap one to see that person's full information screen. In Palm Desktop, however, the computer screen is big enough to show you *both* the index-list view (in the middle of the screen in Figure 8-1) *and* the actual contents of the page whose name you click.

Your PC's keyboard, hard drive, mouse, and menus also make Palm Desktop easier to work with than the actual PalmPilot, as you'll see.

Palm Desktop is designed to take advantage of your PC's monitor—not just the color and size aspects, but also the resolution options. Most monitors are designed to be set to a different resolution (or magnification level, which is determined by the number of dots visible). For example, at 640 by 480 dots (or *pixels*), you see only a few hours of the day in the Date Book program. But if you resize the display to, say, 800 by 600, Palm Desktop automatically resizes its window to show you a longer slice of the day—but everything is, of course, much smaller.

In fact, if your monitor can be changed to 1600×1200 pixels, Palm Desktop can show you the *entire* 24-hour day in its Date Book. The text of your events is nearly microscopic, but at least you can see your availability for the entire day.

In Windows 9*x*/NT, open the Control Panel called Display and use the Desktop Area slider to adjust the resolution.

PC as PalmPilot

In many ways, Palm Desktop's four or five software modules are exactly like their counterparts on the PalmPilot itself. You'll find precisely the same mechanisms for using categories, the Private checkbox, Address Book sorting options, To Do priorities, and Date Book repeat options as those described in Chapter 4, *The Four Primary Programs*.

There are, however, some important differences between these programs on the PalmPilot and on the PC. Here they are, program by program.

Date Book

Palm Desktop's Date Book shows considerably more useful information at a glance than the tiny Palm screen. Instead of seeing only gray blocks to indicate appointments in week view, for example, you can actually read what they represent, as Figure 8-2 shows.

Adding an event in Day or Week view is quicker than on the PalmPilot, too, because you don't have to open up a dialog box to do so. Just click on the calendar and begin typing. Deleting an event is simpler, too, once again avoiding a trudge through a dialog box: just click once on an event and then press the Delete key.

Week View

As Figure 8-2 demonstrates, the Date Book is extremely mouse-driven. Here are a few of the places you can click in Week view to accomplish something; in many cases, these clicks correspond to taps you'd make on the PalmPilot itself:

Palm Desktop Oddballs: Undo and Revert

Printing, screen size, and keyboard use aren't the only advantages of using Palm Desktop to edit your PalmPilot data. The PC-bound version of your Palm programs also offers a couple of productivity-software staples: Undo and Revert—but neither command works quite the way you might expect.

In theory, the Undo command, listed in the Edit menu, undoes your last action. For example, if you delete some text by accident, the Undo command should restore it.

However, Palm Desktop's Undo command is among the lamest in the industry: it *almost* never works. If you move a Date Book appointment, check off a To Do item, edit an Address Book entry, or cut a Memo Pad page, the Undo command doesn't even show up for work—it remains dimmed in the menu.

In fact, there's only one instance in which the Undo command *does* work: when you're editing text. For example, if you double-click a Memo Pad page name and begin to edit the memo itself, Undo will restore text you remove by pressing the Delete key. Undo is also available when you're typing a To Do item or Date Book appointment. It *doesn't* work when you're editing text in the Address Book, alas; it doesn't undo *anything* in the Address Book.

Therefore, if you've deleted an important date/memo/to do/address, or you've imported a huge amount of data incorrectly (there's no Undo for that, either), or you've otherwise made a mess of your Palm Desktop file, the Revert command is your sole recourse. This command, in the File menu, undoes *all* the changes you've made to the Palm Desktop file since the last time you saved it—but *only in the current module.* That is, if you're working in the Address Book, the Revert command doesn't touch the Memo Pad, Date Book, or To Do list modules; you can "revert" them independently.

Of course, Revert throws out the good changes along with the bad; but considering the program's weakling Undo command, Revert may sometimes be your only hope.

A. Click here to view the previous week's schedule. (In Month view, this button shows the previous month.)

B. Click here if you want to view a week that's too far away to be worth clicking buttons A or C. A tiny calendar display appears, much like the one in Figure 4-4 (back in Chapter 4). By clicking on that calendar display, you can jump to any day in the past or future. (See Chapter 4 for instructions on using this display.)

C. Click here to view the next week's schedule. (In Month view, this button shows the next month.)

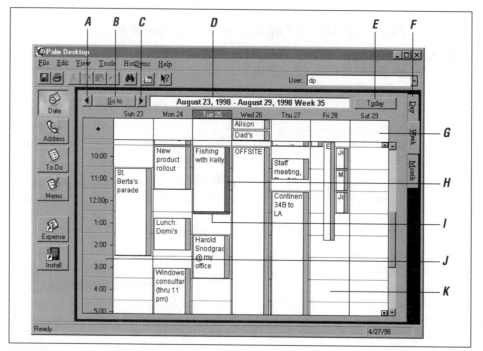

Figure 8-2. On the PC, the Date Book shows considerably more information than the PalmPilot's tiny screen. The screen is rife with mouse-clickable places; simultaneous events appear side-by-side.

D. Click a date header to highlight it. Once you've selected a day in this way, you can create a new appointment or event by clicking in the areas marked G or J. You can also double-click this date header to switch to Day view, which shows more detail about that specific date.

E. If you've been viewing your schedule for some past or future week, click the Today button to view the current week instead. (This button works the same way in Month and Day views.)

F. These tabs switch between Day, Week, and Month views. See Chapter 4 for more on these views.

G. This special rectangle is a "row heading" for untimed events—birthdays, anniversaries, and other reminders that take place on a specific *day,* but at no special time. Click here to create a new untimed event on whichever date is currently selected (as indicated by its date header, labeled D). Unfortunately, you'll never see more than the first line of text of an untimed event; however, if you continue to create additional untimed events (by clicking rectangle G again and again), the "row header" grows tall enough to accommodate the first lines of as many untimed events as you create.

So if Palm Desktop never shows more than the first line of an untimed event, how are you supposed to read the entire entry? In Week view, you can click the first line and then press the up or down arrow keys on your keyboard to scroll the text a line at a time. Alternatively, just switch to Day view (by clicking the Day tab, labeled F in Figure 8-2), where each untimed event's label stretches across the entire screen.

As in the PalmPilot's own Date Book program, you can change an untimed event into one with a time, and vice versa; to do so, double-click the "event handle" (labeled H) at the right edge of an event. The resulting dialog box (see Figure 8-8) shows "None" for the start and stop times of an untimed event, and times for a timed event—edit accordingly.

H. The *event handle*. Double-click this vertical strip to display the dialog box in Figure 8-8, where you can change an item's time, repeat schedule, and other options. Alternatively, drag this handle up or down to reschedule the event to a different time; drag it horizontally or diagonally to move the event to a different day during the week. (Actually, you can even drag to a day beyond the current week—but only in Day view. See the section "Day View," later in this chapter.)

I. The *duration handle*. This dark blue line appears only when an event is *selected*—that is, when you've clicked on it. (Another sign that you've selected an event: Its light-gray event handle turns dark.) If you move your cursor carefully over the duration handle, the cursor's shape changes to a double-headed arrow. That's your cue that you can now drag up or down to make this event taller or shorter (that is, stretching over more or less time), as shown in Figure 8-3.

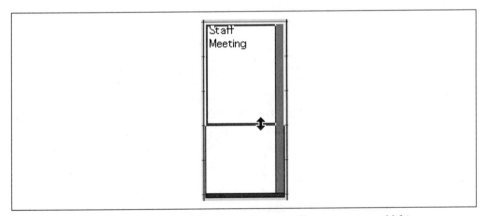

Figure 8-3. Don't you wish it were this easy to shorten staff meetings in real life?

J. The time-slot "row headers" do more than serve as a time reference; they're also buttons. Click a time to create a new event in that time slot—on the day indicated by the currently selected date header (D). You'll quickly discover the rigidity of creating new events this way: first, you have to click *twice,* once on the date header and again on the time slot you want. Second, you can only create appointments that begin on the hour.

Simply clicking *within* the master grid solves the first problem, saving you a click (see item K). As for the hour-slot problem, see the section "Changing the time," later in this chapter.

K. The quickest way to create a new event is to click in any gray unoccupied area. Palm Desktop creates a blank, one-hour, white-background appointment that begins on the hour closest to your click: 12:00, 1:00, 2:00, or whatever. Type a description for the event—don't worry if you type past the bottom of the little text area, the display scrolls automatically—and then press Return or Enter to complete your entry (and return the background color to Post-It Yellow).

To finish up, click again on your appointment to make the duration handle (I) appear, which you can drag to specify the event's duration. You can also double-click the event handle (H) to adjust the starting, ending, or repeat characteristics of your event.

Your keyboard is also useful in Week view. The right- and left-arrow keys control which date header (labeled D) is highlighted, advancing the date one day at a time.

If you add the Alt key to these arrow-key presses, you change the display one *week* at a time.

Day View

To enter Day view (shown in Figure 8-4), click the Day tab at the right edge of the screen. Alternatively, you can double-click any square in Month view (see Figure 8-7)—or double-click the date header in Week view, labeled D in Figure 8-2. The resulting display is actually fairly different from the PalmPilot's Day view—instead of a simple textual list, as on the PalmPilot, Palm Desktop shows blocks of time stretching vertically, much like Week view.

Several of Week view's mechanisms also work in Day view: you can change an appointment's time by dragging either its event handle or its center up or down, you can create a new appointment by clicking in a gray area, and you can click a time slot's "row header" (such as 10:00, 11:00, and so on) at the left side of the screen to create a new one-hour event. Exactly as in Week view, simultaneous events are shown side-by-side.

The Metaphysics of Event Handles

The true student of computer/human interface contemplates the "event handles" on appointments in Palm Desktop's Date Book and wonders: why does Palm Desktop need an "event handle" at all? After all, on the actual PalmPilot, you can reschedule an event just by clicking *inside* the block and dragging. Why not use that simpler, more natural mechanism on the PC too?

The aging teacher responds: "The difference is that on the PC, my child, you can actually read *and edit* the text for your appointments in Week view. Here, a click means *edit this appointment,* and thus may not be interpreted by the software as the beginning of a mouse drag."

The devoted student, however, replies: "But master, in Palm Desktop, a click *doesn't* activate editing! A *double*-click activates editing! You see, we *should* be able to drag an event by clicking in the middle of it. The event handle isn't necessary."

The patient tutor nods sagely. "Your logic is impeccable, my child. Why don't you try it?"

The student is befuddled, but does indeed attempt to move an appointment *not* by dragging the event handle, but instead by clicking and dragging the text itself. It works, much to the student's astonishment.

"But master, then I was right! The event handle has no purpose at all! I can drag events by their centers, exactly as on the PalmPilot—the event handle is a waste of electrons!"

The master knows that the student is ready at last to find the truth. "But then how do you open up the Event Details box, Grasshopper?"

The student is ready. "By double-clicking on the text!"

"Then how do you *edit* the text?"

The student is once again ready. "By double-clicking on the — "

There is a scowl on the student's face. "Oh, I get it. Double-clicking the text is how you signal that you want to *edit* it. I guess that's why they need an event handle."

The master smiles. "Long is the road to truth, my child."

But Day view offers a few extra goodies. For example, you can move an event to a completely different date, using the miniature calendar in the upper right, as shown in Figure 8-5. (Unfortunately, you're limited to rescheduling to another date in the *same month*. See the section "Changing the date," later in this chapter, for a workaround.)

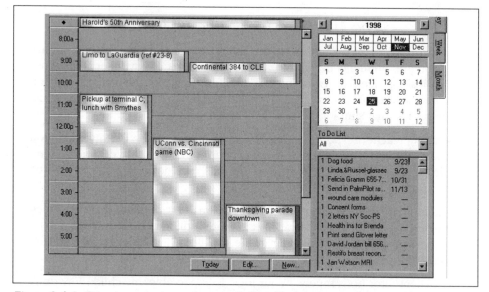

Figure 8-4. In Day view, events are shown as yellow blocks.

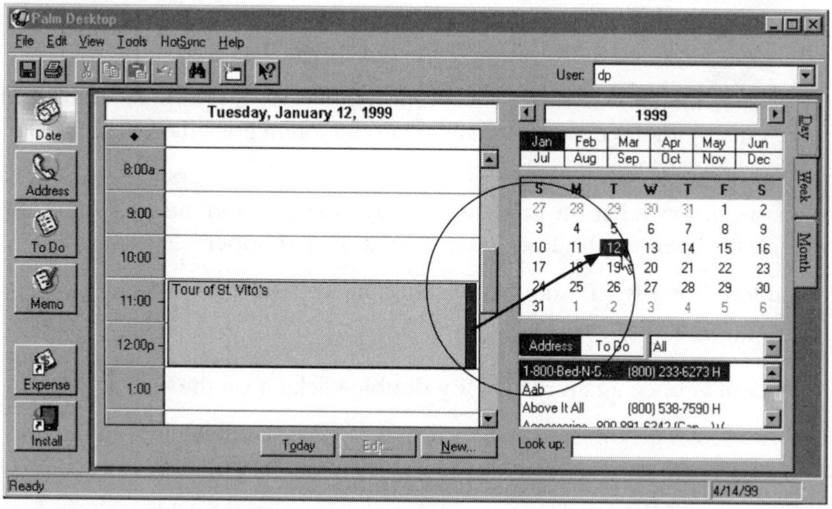

Figure 8-5. In Day view, drag an event onto a different calendar square to reschedule it.

The miniature To Do list

As a handy bonus, Day view also shows a list of To Do items in the lower-right corner. In Palm Desktop 3.0 (and later) this miniature To Do area offers two useful features. First, you can click the control just above the list, where it says Address/To Do, to change the list contents between showing your To Do list and showing your Address Book contents (see Figure 8-6).

Second, you can actually schedule an appointment by dragging a name or To Do item from this list directly onto the Day view display, as shown in Figure 8-6. Palm Desktop instantly creates a new event, with the To Do item or person's name and number neatly written and ready to go.

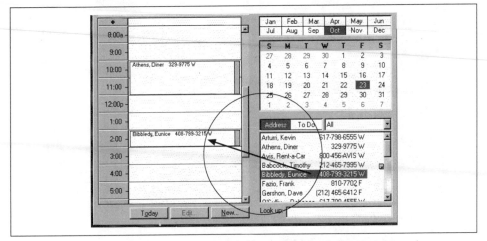

Figure 8-6. In Palm Desktop, you can control what's in the list at lower right: to dos or addresses. You can also drag from this list directly onto the main day display to schedule a new appointment or task reminder.

 As in Week view, you can change the date you're viewing in Day view by pressing the arrow keys. In Day view, however, the right- and left-arrow keys change the display one *day* at a time, exactly like the PalmPilot's own scroll buttons. The up- and down-arrow keys change the display to the same weekday in the previous or next *week*.

Month View

Palm Desktop's Month view isn't one of 3Com's masterpieces. It corresponds fairly closely to the PalmPilot's Month view: that is, it's useful for quickly checking your schedule, but you can't actually delete, edit, or move events in this view. Month view is strictly an "at-a-glance" display for checking your "busy-ness" on a particular day—and it's not even particularly good at conveying *that* information. Whereas the PalmPilot shows tiny blocks that provide a visual map of your day's schedule, Palm Desktop shows only a textual list. But because only two or three items fit in each square (on a standard monitor), you can't tell how full a particular day is. (See Figure 8-7.) If your monitor is larger, therefore, or if you choose a higher resolution (see the tip earlier in this chapter), Month view's usefulness increases dramatically.

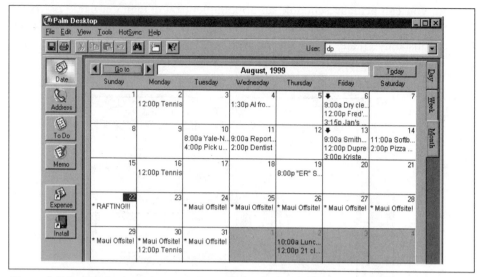

Figure 8-7. In Month view, you can't do much but look. The black down-pointing arrow indicates that a square contains additional items that don't fit.

Fortunately, you can do *one* thing in Month view: you can create a new event. Right-click the corresponding square, and then choose New Event from the pop-up menu. The Edit Event dialog box appears, described in the next section.

Double-clicking an event in Month view doesn't, as you might expect, let you see more details about that item. Instead, it simply switches you to Day view, where *another* double-click (on the event handle) opens up the details box for a particular appointment.

If you see a black down-pointing arrow in a Month-view square, Palm Desktop is trying to tell you that there are additional appointments on that day—but they don't fit in the square. Unfortunately, there's no way to view them! Clicking the black arrow doesn't scroll the square to bring the hidden items into view. All you can do is double-click the square to enter Day view, where all items appear in their glory.

You can control which date is highlighted in Month view by pressing the arrow keys (up, down, left, right). Add the Alt key to the right- and left-arrow keys, and you scroll one *month* at a time.

Once you've landed on a particular date, you can jump to the corresponding date in Day or Week view, where you can edit or adjust any event—all from the keyboard. Switch to Day, Week, or Month views by pressing Alt-D, -W, and -M, respectively.

Editing an Event

In Day or Week views, double-click an appointment's event handle (see Figure 8-3) to open up the Edit Event dialog box. (Other ways to access this box: click an event and choose Edit Event from the Edit menu; in Day view, click an event and then the Edit button; right-click an event and choose Edit Event.) You'll probably recognize the Edit Event box immediately: it's nearly identical to the PalmPilot's corresponding dialog box (see Figure 8-8).

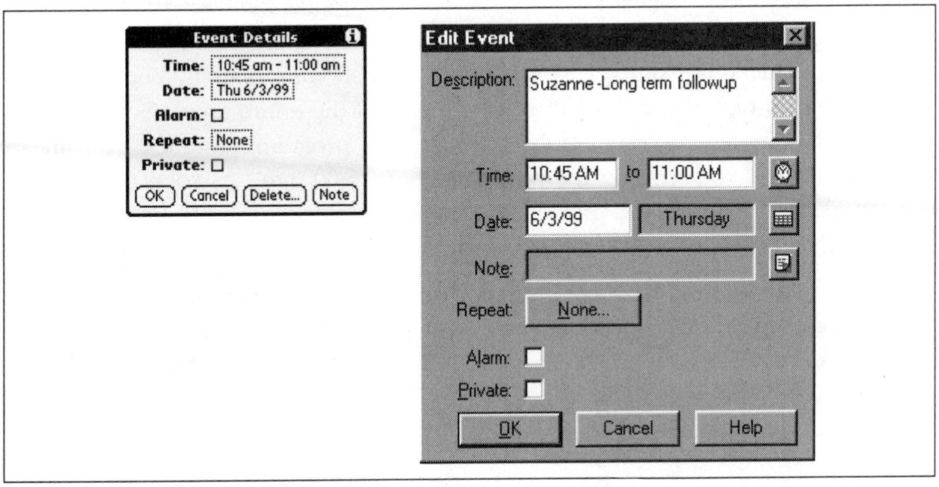

Figure 8-8. You specify an appointment's begin and end times and alarm, repeat, note, and privacy status in this dialog box (right), which closely matches the same box on the PalmPilot (left).

At the top of this dialog box is the description of your event; exactly as on the PalmPilot, the description can be 255 letters long (and you can attach a Note to record still more information).

When you're writing down a description for an event, you might wonder how to start a new line—after all, pressing Return or Enter closes the dialog box by "clicking" the OK button.

Solution: Press Ctrl-Enter (on Windows) or Command-Return (on the Mac). You create a line break without closing the dialog box.

Changing the time

Inside the Edit Event dialog box, you can modify the beginning and ending times in any of three ways—which is fortunate, because Palm Desktop's main views let you create events *only* on the hour. For all events beginning or ending during the other 59 minutes of the hour, you must use one of the following methods:

- Click in one of the Time boxes and press the + or – keys. Each press of the + key sets the time ahead 15 minutes, and the – key sets the time earlier by 15 minutes.

- Click the tiny clock icon. The Select Time dialog box appears, which is identical to the PalmPilot's own Select Time box (see Figure 4-7, and read the corresponding section of Chapter 4 for details on using this dialog box).

- Type in new times manually. While this method might seem tedious, a few shortcuts make life simpler. For example, you should generally begin by *double-clicking* one of the Time boxes (to highlight the entire time). Now type the bare minimum; if you simply type *9*, the program assumes you mean "9:00 a.m." If you type *6p*, the program stores "6:00 p.m." As soon as you click outside the box or press Tab or Enter, Palm Desktop understands your intention and completes the typing for you.

  You can also use the period instead of a colon. To specify 6:20, for example, you can type *6.2* and be done with it. If you've set your desktop computer's preference to use the 24-hour military time system, where 8:00 p.m. is displayed as 20:00, similar shortcuts await. Just type *15*, for example, to make Palm Desktop understand 15:00 (which is 3:00 p.m.).

To make your computer use military time format, choose Control Panels from your Start menu's Settings submenu. Open Regional Settings and click the Time tab; from the Time Style pop-up menu, choose "HH:mm:ss."

Now Palm Desktop displays times in the 24-hour format.

There's no other way to make Palm Desktop operate in 24-hour-clock mode, as there is on your PalmPilot.

Incidentally, if you delete the time completely, Palm Desktop writes *None* in the blank, indicating that you've just turned this event into an *untimed* one, such as a birthday or anniversary. Instead of appearing in time slot in Day or Week view, this event now appears at the very top of screen (as indicated by item G in Figure 8-2).

Changing the date

In Day view, you can reschedule an appointment by dragging its block to a different date in the same month. But to move an appointment to a completely *different* month, you have only one choice: change the event's date in the Edit Event dialog box. (You might think you could use the Edit menu's Cut and Paste commands, but you'd be wrong; they don't work in the Date Book module.)

To change the date, either edit the displayed date manually (by typing a new date), or click the tiny calendar icon to the right. Up pops a miniature calendar, which you can use to specify a different year, month, and date, all by clicking. This mini-date picker works exactly like the PalmPilot's; see Figure 4-4 and "Viewing the Week's Events" in Chapter 4.

Note, Repeat, Alarm, Private

The remaining elements of the Edit Event dialog box are exactly the same as the Details box on the PalmPilot. For details, see the section "The Date Book" in Chapter 4; for now, here's a summary:

Note

> This blank shows the first line of any note you've attached to this event (for example, directions to a party, minutes of a meeting, and so on); click the tiny note-pad icon to open the note window, where you can compose your write-up. An event with a note attached appears in Palm Desktop with the same tiny note-pad icon (see Figure 8-9), which you can click to read the note.

Figure 8-9. The small icons at the top of the event block indicate (from left to right): that an alarm has been set, that this is a repeating event, that this is a Private event, and that a note has been attached. Click the alarm-clock or note-pad icons to view the details.

 You don't necessarily have to add a note to an event by first opening the Edit Event dialog box. You can jump directly to the note-editing window by right-clicking an event and then choosing Note from the pop-up menu.

Repeat

> Click this button to open the Repeat dialog box, where you can specify that this event happens more than once (every day, once a month, and so on)—exactly as described in Chapter 4. Any repeating event shows up with a tiny "cycle" icon, as shown in Figure 8-9; to adjust the repeat settings, double-click the event handle to return to the Edit Event dialog box.

Editing alarm settings on the PC has only one tiny advantage over doing so on the PalmPilot: the Change Repeat dialog box (which appears when you click the Repeat item in the Edit Event box) lets you press the up- or down-arrow keys on your keyboard to change the repeat interval ("every 2 weeks," for example).

Alarm

Be careful with this one; Palm Desktop does *not* have an alarm feature. Instead, this feature lets you set up alarms that will go off on your *PalmPilot—* after your next HotSync (see Chapter 6). When you turn on the checkbox, you'll see the controls that govern *when* the alarm goes off: 10 minutes before the event begins, three days, or whatever, exactly as described in Chapter 4. (On your PC, absolutely nothing happens at the appointed time.)

After you've set up an alarm for an event, a tiny alarm-clock icon appears (see Figure 8-9). Click this icon to adjust (or view) the alarm settings.

Private

This checkbox lets you designate this appointment as Private, meaning it can be hidden or protected with a password. See the sections "Keeping your appointments private" in Chapter 4 or "Security" in Chapter 5, *The Other Built-In Programs,* for details. If you do turn this option on for an event, a tiny key icon appears on the description block (see Figure 8-9).

To hide all the Private-tagged appointments on your PC, choose Hide Private Records from the View menu; choose Show Private Records to bring them back.

When you create a new appointment in the Date Book in Palm Desktop, you have to turn on the Alarm option if you want one. Furthermore, Palm Desktop always proposes "5 minutes before" as the alarm setting. That is, the PalmPilot will wake up and begin chirping five minutes before the actual appointment.

But what if *most* of your appointments require an alarm? In Pilot Desktop 2.0 or later, you can specify that *all* events should start out with an alarm—and then turn the alarm setting *off* on the appointments that don't need one. Furthermore, you can change the default advance-notice time if "5 minutes" isn't appropriate.

To change these defaults, choose Tools → Options → Date Book, click the Alarm checkbox, and adjust the advance-notice controls (to, say, "1 hour before"). From now on, whenever you create a *new* appointment in Palm Desktop, it will automatically be set to have an alarm—and the "time before" setting will be preset to your new preference.

Customizing the Date Book

Exactly as on the PalmPilot, you can control which hours of the day are initially displayed when you launch the Date Book module of Palm Desktop. If you're some kind of early-riser zealot, you may want the 5:00 a.m. time slot to appear at the top of the screen; if you're a lazy slugabed, you might designate 10:00 a.m. as the official beginning of morning. Either way, Palm Desktop can accommodate you.

To adjust this setting, choose Options from the Tools menu. In the resulting dialog box, click the Date Book tab (see Figure 8-10) and choose a new start-of-the-day time from the pop-up menu.

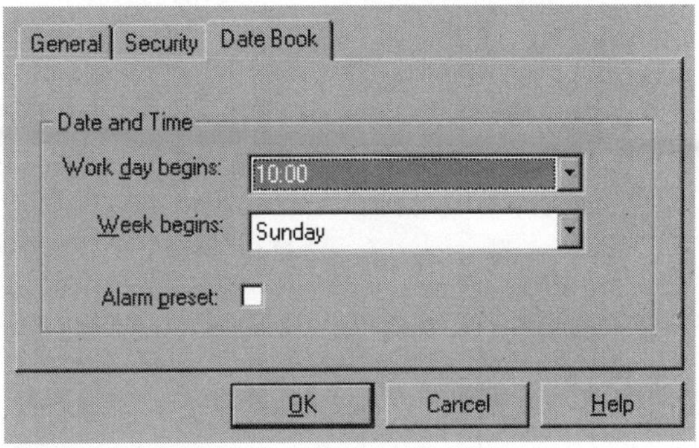

Figure 8-10. Use the "Work day begins" pop-up menu to specify the hour Palm Desktop will show at the top of the screen in Day and Week views.

While you're in this dialog box, you can also adjust which day should "begin the week"—that is, appear at the left edge of the screen in Week view—Sunday or Monday. (Use the lower pop-up menu to choose.)

Printing Your Calendar

Printing is a key role for Palm Desktop, because hooking up the PalmPilot itself to a printer isn't for the faint of heart (see Chapter 15, *Paging, Faxing, Printing, and Beaming*). Don't expect anything glamorous when it comes to printing your schedule, however. You get a neatly formatted *list* of your events, in chronological order, or a month-per-page layout (see Figure 8-12); there's no way to print pages formatted for, say, your Filofax or Day Runner.

Palm Desktop's limited printing options are especially disappointing because you can't even *export* your Date Book data to a more robust program for printing (as you can in the other three primary PalmPilot modules), such as a standalone calendar program. Pilot Desktop 2.0 and later, for Windows 95 and later, teases you by offering an Export command—but it can export only as a Palm Desktop file, not as a text file usable by other calendar software.

Still, some hardcopy is better than no hardcopy. To begin printing, it makes no difference what dates you're viewing on the screen in Palm Desktop; all that matters is that you're using the Date Book module. (If you want your Private-tagged appointments to print, be sure to choose Show Private Records from the View menu before printing.)

Choose Print from the File menu. The usual Print dialog box is enhanced by the options shown in Figure 8-11.

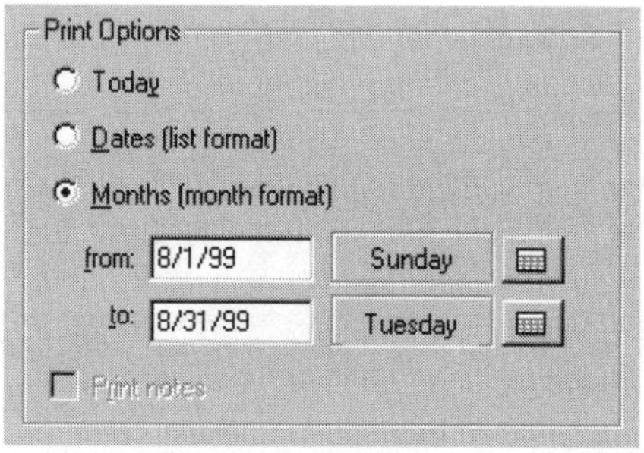

Figure 8-11. These options appear when you print the Date Book from within Palm Desktop.

Here are your options:

Today/Dates/Months

Choose one of these buttons to specify what range of dates you want included in your list-like printout. Days with nothing scheduled don't appear in your printout at all, and the printout compresses empty hours (exactly as it does on the PalmPilot; see Chapter 4). In other words, you can scarcely lose by specifying a wide range of dates—even a busy day takes up only a few vertical inches of *one side* of the printed page.

If you select the Dates button, of course, you should specify the dates whose events you want printed—either by typing or by clicking the tiny calendar icons, which summons a "date-picker" calendar like the one on the PalmPilot (see Figure 4-4).

The Months button gives you an alternative to the appointment listings of the other choices—it prints a standard monthly calendar grid.

Print Notes

When this checkbox is selected, any notes attached to your events print just underneath the event itself. (See Figure 8-12 for an example.)

When you're finished specifying your options, click OK to proceed with the printing. The result looks like Figure 8-12.

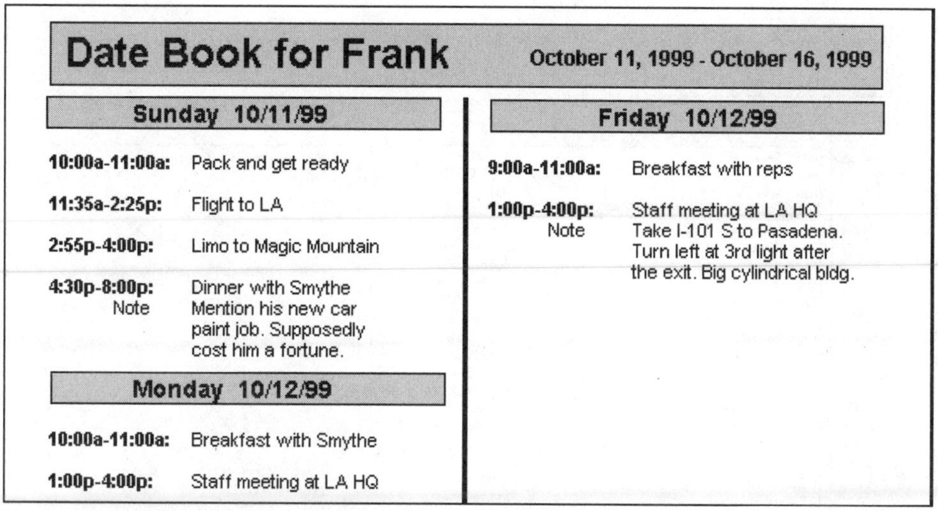

Date Book for Frank — October 11, 1999 - October 16, 1999

Sunday 10/11/99

10:00a-11:00a:	Pack and get ready
11:35a-2:25p:	Flight to LA
2:55p-4:00p:	Limo to Magic Mountain
4:30p-8:00p:	Dinner with Smythe
Note	Mention his new car paint job. Supposedly cost him a fortune.

Monday 10/12/99

10:00a-11:00a:	Breakfast with Smythe
1:00p-4:00p:	Staff meeting at LA HQ

Friday 10/12/99

9:00a-11:00a:	Breakfast with reps
1:00p-4:00p:	Staff meeting at LA HQ
Note	Take I-101 S to Pasadena. Turn left at 3rd light after the exit. Big cylindrical bldg.

Figure 8-12. Palm Desktop's printout of your calendar is essentially a nicely formatted two-column list. Empty days and empty hours are omitted (except when printing month-view format).

Address Book

Palm Desktop's Address Book module is quite similar to the PalmPilot's own. The most pleasant difference is that on the PC, you get to see both the complete list of names *and* the details screen for whichever name is currently selected (see Figure 8-13).

You can operate this primary display screen entirely from the keyboard: with the cursor in the Look Up: field below the list, just begin typing a person's last name, for example, and Palm Desktop "zeroes in" on the closest matching name in your list, exactly as the PalmPilot does.

Editing Addresses

To edit a name in the list, double-click it (or click once and then click Edit beneath the list). You get a screen that closely resembles the PalmPilot's own Address Edit screen (see Figure 4-19).

You must click each of the first two tabs in turn—Name and Address—to access all the different fields (see Figure 8-14). The third tab, Note, is equivalent to the Note button on the PalmPilot's Address Edit screen; it makes an empty window appear, into which you can record a page of notes about the person whose record you're editing.

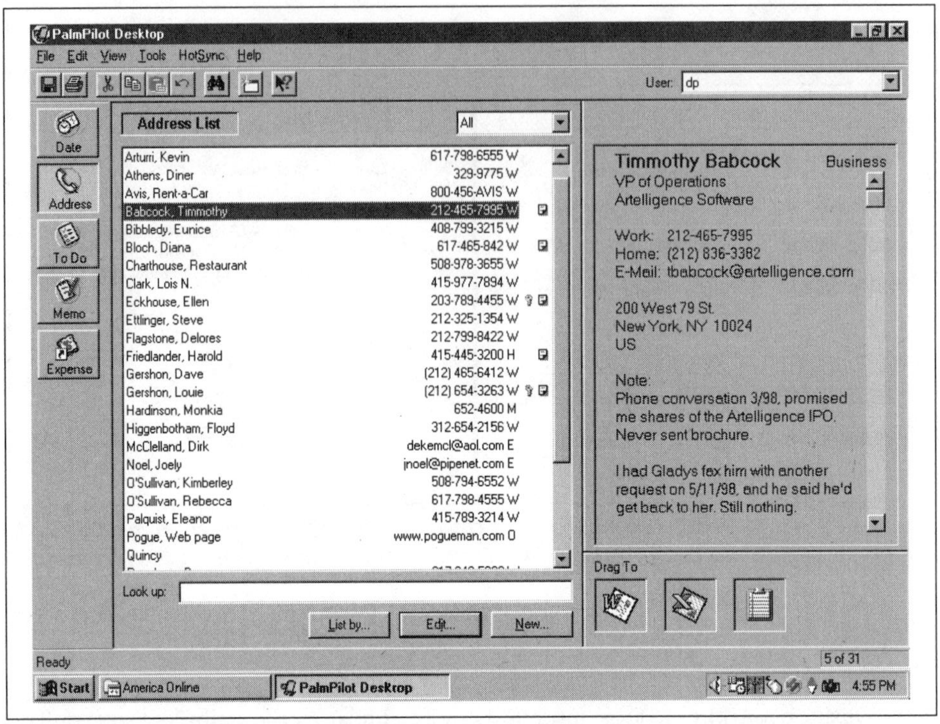

Figure 8-13. Click a name in the Address Book list (center) to view that person's complete info screen (right). The tiny key icon indicates a Private record; the tiny Note icon indicates that you've attached a note to this person's entry.

As you type, note this oddball Palm Desktop feature: you can actually fill each field with *more than one line* of information, exactly as you can on the PalmPilot itself. For example, suppose somebody's company name is actually "International Beverage Corp., A Division of Microsoft." After writing the first line, it's fine to press Return, and then to type "A Division of Microsoft" on the second line—the blank grows vertically to accommodate up to six lines of information. (Actually, *all* blanks in the Address Edit dialog box do.) This trick may pay off when it comes time to print, too, as you'll read in an upcoming tip.

If you try to type *more* than six lines, the blank will still store everything (up to 255 characters)—but it won't keep growing. After you've created six lines, you'll have to press the up- and down-arrow keys on your keyboard repeatedly to scroll the extra lines into view.

When you HotSync, the PalmPilot thoughtfully adds new lines to its own address screens to accommodate whatever extra lines you created in Palm Desktop.

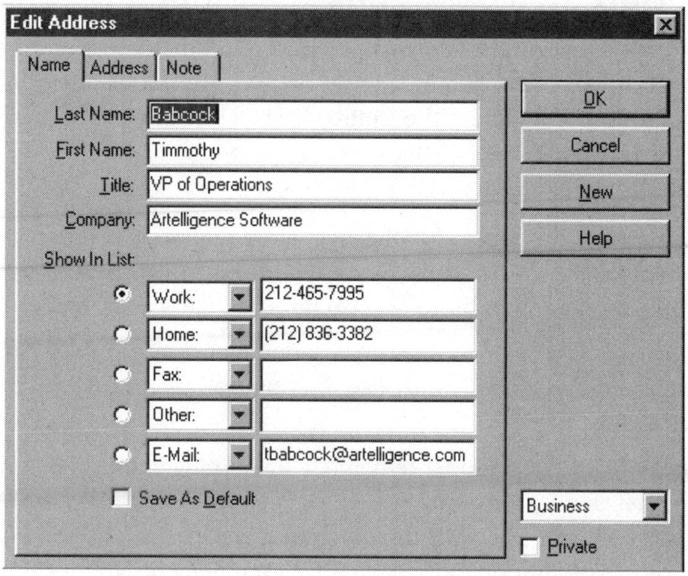

Edit Address

Name | Address | Note

Last Name: Babcock

First Name: Timmothy

Title: VP of Operations

Company: Artelligence Software

Show In List:

⦿ Work: ▾ 212-465-7995

○ Home: ▾ (212) 836-3382

○ Fax: ▾

○ Other: ▾

○ E-Mail: ▾ tbabcock@artelligence.com

☐ Save As Default

OK

Cancel

New

Help

Business ▾

☐ Private

Figure 8-14. The Address Edit dialog box is broken into multiple panels.

Adding New Addresses

To add a new address, click the New button beneath the list, or press Alt-N, or choose New Address from the Edit menu. The Address Edit window (Figure 8-14 and Figure 8-15) appears; type away, pressing Tab to jump forward through the blanks, or Shift-Tab to jump backward.

As you input this person's phone numbers, make special note of the buttons to the left of each number: click the button beside the *most often called* number for this person. That's the number that will show up in the PalmPilot's primary listing (see Figure 4-17).

If you're entering more than one person's name and address into Palm Desktop, *don't* click OK after filling in the Address Edit information! Instead, simply press Alt-N.

Doing so automatically saves the information you just typed and clears the dialog box so that it's ready for the next person's data. You've just saved several steps—including closing and reopening this dialog box—by pressing the "New Address" keystroke instead of clicking OK.

Fields, Sorting, Categories, and Other Options

As you edit your names and addresses, keep in mind that you can control several aspects of their appearance. Some of these options are independent for each person's address, and others affect the entire database at once. You can read more about these options in Chapter 4, but here's a recap:

Phone-number labels

> You can change the labels for the five phone-number blanks *independently* for every name in your Address Book. One person can have five Work numbers, while another might have one each for Mobile, Pager, and Email.
>
> To change the labels for these blanks, double-click a person's name to open the Address Edit window. Simply use the pop-up menu beside each address to reassign its label.
>
> If you *want* Palm Desktop to remember this arrangement of phone numbers for all future entries, turn on the Save As Default checkbox. Any new records you create will start out with this new arrangement of phone-number labels. Any records you import will have this arrangement, too (see the section "Importing Addresses from Other Programs," later in this chapter). (But this default setting doesn't affect new records on the *PalmPilot*—only on the PC, and only for the currently selected User Name.)

Custom fields

> You'll find four extra fields on each person's address-info screen called *Custom 1, Custom 2, Custom 3,* and *Custom 4.* You can use these blanks for anything you want: birthdays, geographical region, spouse's or kids' names, and so on.
>
> However, *Custom 1* isn't the world's clearest label for the "Spouse's name" blank; fortunately, you can edit these labels. To do so, choose Custom Field Labels from the Tools menu. A simple dialog box appears in which you can change "Custom 1," "Custom 2," and so on into more useful labels.
>
> The key fact here, however, is that changing these custom-field labels affects *every record* in your Address Book. You can't change the custom field labels independently for each person in your book. Moreover, whatever new labels you choose in Palm Desktop will be transferred automatically to your Palm-Pilot at the next HotSync, replacing whatever custom field names you had edited there.

Sort order

> You can also specify how you want your master Address Book list sorted: alphabetically by last name or alphabetically by *company* name, so that all the Microsoft employees (for example) will appear clumped together in the list.

To change the sort order, click the List By button below the list. The resulting dialog box offers only two choices: "Last Name, First Name" and "Company, Last Name"; click your selection and then click OK.

Changing the sorting order in Palm Desktop *doesn't* affect the sorting order on the PalmPilot, even if you HotSync. Nobody ever said the PalmPilot was consistent.

Categories

Exactly as on the PalmPilot itself, you can assign each name in your Address Book to a *category* (such as Business, Personal, NYC List, Xmas Cards, and so on)—up to 15 different ones *per* Palm program. (See Chapter 4 for a complete lesson on the use of categories.)

You can edit your list of category names by choosing Categories from the Tools menu; remember, though, that if you decide to change a category's label, you're also changing the category of any records already assigned to the original category. (Your new category names will be transferred to the PalmPilot at your next HotSync.)

You assign a Category to a record by choosing from the pop-up menu at the lower-right corner of the Address Edit screen (see Figures 8-14 and 8-15). You can also show only the records in a certain category by choosing from the Category pop-up menu at the top of the Address Book list (Figure 8-15).

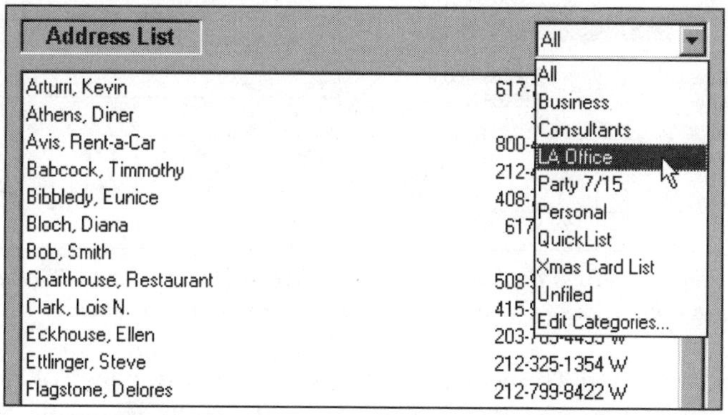

Figure 8-15. To view only the members of a certain category, choose from the pop-up menu above the master Address Book list.

Grabbing Address Book Entries for Use Elsewhere

In an ideal world, we wouldn't be condemned to having one address book for the PalmPilot, another for our email program, another for Microsoft's software, and so on—we'd just have one core Rolodex program.

Palm Desktop doesn't solve all our problems, but it takes two baby steps toward making its data available to other programs (such as your word processor, where you might find it useful to paste an address). Try the following shortcuts.

Dragging to the clipboard

Drag an address (or several selected addresses) from your master list onto the clipboard icon at the lower-right corner of the screen (you can see it in Figure 8-16). Although nothing appears to change, you've actually copied that address onto your PC's invisible clipboard. If you now switch to your Notepad, Microsoft Word, or any other word processor, you can choose Paste from the Edit menu to slap the copied address information into whatever you're working on.

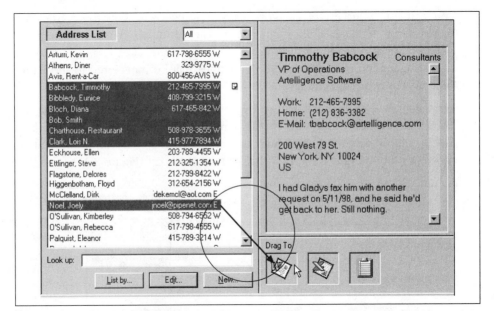

Figure 8-16. Drag an Address Book entry onto the Clipboard icon to copy it, ready for pasting into another program, or onto the Word icon to transfer it to a new letter.

Unfortunately, this Drag To mechanism copies the *entire* "page" of Address Book information—notes, custom fields, phone numbers. That means a few more moments of editing and deleting for the hapless Palm user who simply wants the mailing address.

Dragging to Microsoft Word

If you drag an address (or group of addresses) from your master list onto the Microsoft Word icon, Word launches automatically, creates a new document, and offers the options shown in Figure 8-17.

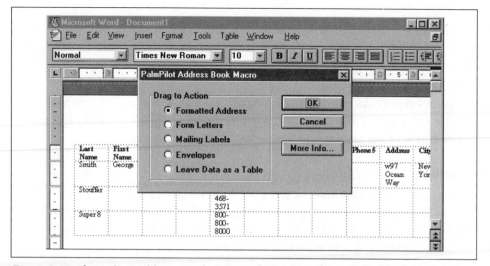

Figure 8-17. If you drag addresses to the Microsoft Word icon, this dialog box appears. It lets you format the incoming data in several different ways.

Your choices are:

Formatted address

Only the mailing-address information shows up in Word, neatly formatted. Extraneous stuff like phone numbers, notes, and spouse names are eliminated. If you dragged multiple addresses, you get one address at the top of each Word page, with forced page breaks in between.

Form letters

A form letter is set up for you, with placeholders (<<Name>>, <<Address>>, and so on) for the address at the top, the cursor waiting in the middle, and your own name signed (with "Sincerely") at the bottom. A message appears, courtesy of the Palm Desktop macro that's doing the work, telling you how to finish the job. ("After you finish editing the letter, select Mail Merge from the Tools menu.")

If you follow the instructions, you'll wind up with ready-to-print, artificially "personalized" letters to the people whose names you originally dragged.

Mailing labels

Presents a series of dialog boxes in which you specify what brand of Avery mailing labels are waiting in your printer, and which of the freshly imported address fields you want included on the label. You *could* include everything from Palm Desktop, including notes, phone numbers, spouses' names (the Custom fields), and so on; but for most purposes, the name and address are sufficient.

Envelopes

> Exactly like "Mailing labels," except that the dialog boxes require you to spec-ify what kind of envelope (and what orientation it's in) instead of which type of label.

Leave data as a table

> Your Palm Desktop address data is placed into Word as a 20-column table. The column headings are Last Name, First Name, Title, Company, and so on; each row of the table is another person from your Address Book.

Dragging to Microsoft Excel

You can also drag an address, or group of addresses, onto the Excel icon (the cen-ter icon in Figure 8-16). As long as you've got Excel installed, it launches, creates a new blank spreadsheet, and neatly plops your address data into it. It's laid out as a 20-column table, complete with row headings (Last Name, First Name, Title . . .), exactly as described in "Leave Data as a Table" in the previous section.

Format, delete, or rearrange columns, save, and print as you wish.

Printing from the Address Book

Palm Desktop gives you a great deal of control over which names print from the Address Book. For one thing, you can specify whether or not Private-flagged names print; from the View menu, choose Hide Private Records or Show Private Records. Whatever's on the screen is what you'll get when you print.

Other ways of controlling the printout:

- You can limit the printout to names belonging to a certain category. For exam-ple, if your company has offices in L.A. and Chicago, and you've assigned "LA Office" and "Chicago" as category labels to the appropriate employee listings in your Address Book, then it's simple to print a list of the people in one office or another before a trip. Just choose the appropriate category name from the pop-up menu above the Address Book list (see Figure 8-15); all *other* names are now hidden. Print away.

- You can limit the printout to names you select by hand. To do so, choose the category you want (or choose All from the category pop-up menu to include your entire address book). Now highlight individual names in the list by Ctrl-clicking them; if you want to select a group of consecutively listed names, Ctrl-click the first one and Shift-click the last one. You can also combine these techniques—for example, you can select two clumps of names by clicking the first name normally, Shift-clicking the end of the first group, Ctrl-clicking the first name of the second clump, and finally Ctrl-Shift-clicking the final name of the second clump. Figure 8-18 should make this clear.

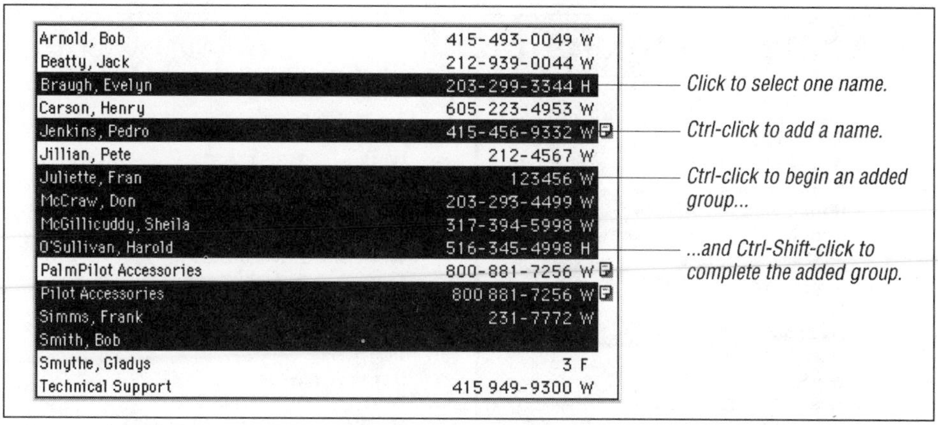
Arnold, Bob 415-493-0049 W
Beatty, Jack 212-939-0044 W
Braugh, Evelyn 203-299-3344 H
Carson, Henry 605-223-4953 W
Jenkins, Pedro 415-456-9332 W
Jillian, Pete 212-4567 W
Juliette, Fran 123456 W
McCraw, Don 203-293-4499 W
McGillicuddy, Sheila 317-394-5998 W
O'Sullivan, Harold 516-345-4998 H
PalmPilot Accessories 800-881-7256 W
Pilot Accessories 800 881-7256 W
Simms, Frank 231-7772 W
Smith, Bob
Smythe, Gladys 3 F
Technical Support 415 949-9300 W
Click to select one name.
Ctrl-click to add a name.
Ctrl-click to begin an added group...
...and Ctrl-Shift-click to complete the added group.

Figure 8-18. Three ways to manually choose names for printing or copying or deleting: individually; by Ctrl- or Command-clicking; or in clumps, by Shift-clicking.

After you've selected the names you want, choose Print from the File menu; in the dialog box, click Selection (see Figure 8-19).

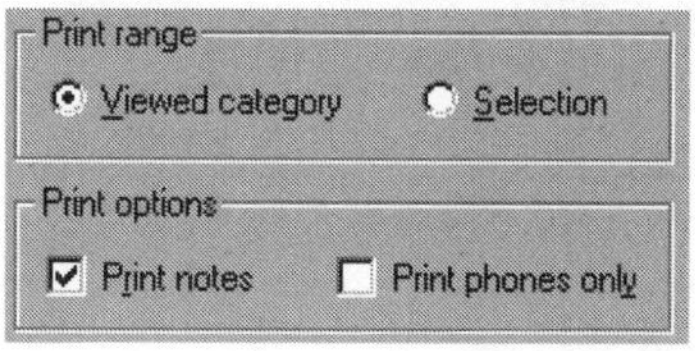
Print range
Viewed category
Selection
Print options
Print notes
Print phones only

Figure 8-19. These options control printing from the Address Book.

Two other options appear in the Print dialog box for the Address Book. First, there's Print Notes; if this box is checked, any Notes you've attached to names in your Address Book will be printed along with the names. Second, there's a Print Phones Only checkbox; turn this one on when you want a tight, concise *phone* directory printout without addresses, notes, custom fields, or even company names. The result includes the name, as many of the five phone numbers as you've typed in, and the category for each person.

Importing Addresses from Other Programs

Unlike your Date Book data, your Address Book, shown in Figure 8-18, information isn't locked forever in Palm Desktop. You can export it as a standard text file, ready to be slurped into any other address book program, database, envelope-printing software, and so on. Similarly, Palm Desktop can import text files *from* those other programs into your Address Book program.

Address Book for Frank   Abernathy - Daleford

A	C
Felix Abernathy LA Office	**Cathy Carpenter** LA Office
Artelligence Software	**Work**: 213-542-6332
Work: 213-542-6332	
Home: 213-231-3245	**Marv Chapinski** LA office
E-mail: fabernathy@lakewood.com	TeknoAge Inc.
233 East Pimlico Blvd.	**Work**: 213-626-2000
Los Angeles, CA 94341	**Fax:** 213-998-5236
Lois Ackerman LA office	
PR Director	**Harold Cooperman** LA Office
MicroTechImage Inc.	Imagineer
Work: 213-945-2000	Disnee Worldwide
Fax: 213-945-2033	**Work**: 310-285-4552
345 Hobbit Rd.	**Mobile:** 213-854-7000 x 66423
Los Angeles, CA 94341	
Peter Azrotyn	**Mindy Crausen** LA Office
CFO	Waggle & Freen
Huntington Systems	**Work**: 310-751-7755
Work: 310-319-8522	**Home:** 213-951-2345
Fax: 310-955-8522	
Pager: 310-836-3385	**Mónika Cziszar** LA Office
Mobile: 213-854-7000 x 12349	Nannys R Us/Hungary
	Work: 011-36-01-234-35877
B	**E-mail:** m_cziszar@makati.com.hu
	Fax: 011-36-01-234-58345

Figure 8-20. The Address Book's printout runs all the names together (left column)—unless you use the trick to get a blank line between names (right column).

This feature should be extremely welcome to anyone who:

- Uses an off-brand Rolodex program that doesn't have an available *conduit program* (see Chapter 6, *HotSync, Step by Step*) for synchronizing with the PalmPilot

- Owns a popular phone-book program such as Outlook or ACT, but doesn't feel like buying and setting up one of the conduit programs described in Chapter 6

- Has been using an older electronic calculator, such as a Sharp Wizard or Casio Boss, and want to transfer its contents into the PalmPilot (via an intermediary text file)

- Wants to print the PalmPilot's Address Book information in a different format than the one style cranked out by Palm Desktop (by transferring the data to a more flexible printing program, such as a word processor or database)

- Wants to take advantage of the master list of international dialing codes, airline reservation numbers, and other information provided on the PalmPilot CD-ROM

Getting a Blank Line in the Address Book Printouts

The Address Book's printout features a number of attractive elements: lightly shaded headings for each letter of the alphabet, for example, plus a banner at the top of each page that indicates what range of names are on that page ("Acme – Armada," for example). Names and phone number labels are in bold; other information is in normal type.

Only one glaring problem mars the readability of this basic listing: depending on the version you're using, Palm Desktop doesn't print a blank line between entries. In other words, the end of one person's address runs smack into the next person's name, without a break in the column.

If you're sneaky, however, you can force a blank line into the printout, as shown on the right side of the example in Figure 8-20. To make this work, you must understand the order in which Palm Desktop prints its information:

```
Name (First, Last)
Title
Company
Phone numbers
Address
Custom fields
Note
```

In other words, if you put only a space in the final field of a particular person's information, you'll get a blank line in the printout.

If you don't use the Notes, Country, or Custom fields often, then you've got an easy way out: put a space in the *Country* field. Because that's the last line of the address, Palm Desktop prints that space alone as the final line of this person's printout—thus creating an attractive empty space before the next person's listing.

If you *do* attach a Note to a person's record, once again you're home free: simply press the Return key an extra time at the end of the note. Once again, you've introduced a blank space. (Unfortunately, you can't get clever by changing your Custom fields' names to blank spaces—Palm Desktop always prints a colon [:] after each Custom field label, even if the label is nothing but a blank space.)

All of these shenanigans are necessary only when printing the full Address Book listing. If you choose the Phones Only option (see Figure 8-19), outsmarting Palm Desktop is much easier. Simply press the Return key after the *last phone number* for each person in your Address Book—yes, right there in the E-mail field (or whatever the last phone-number field is for each person), expand the blank vertically by pressing Return during data entry. And presto: neat blank lines between entries!

Understanding field order

There's only one trick to understanding the process of sending your Address Book information out of (or into) Palm Desktop: the concept of *field order*. A field, of course, is one tidbit of an address—the last name, the zip code, and the email address are three fields. (The entire address—a set of fields—is called a *record*.)

Each address-book program stores its fields in a different order. For example, suppose you use the contact database provided with ClarisWorks as a ClarisWorks Assistant template. On closer examination, you'll see that its fields don't all correspond to the PalmPilot's standard blanks, which are listed in the sidebar "Getting a Blank Line in the Address Book Printouts." See Figure 8-21 to see what Claris-Works's fields look like.

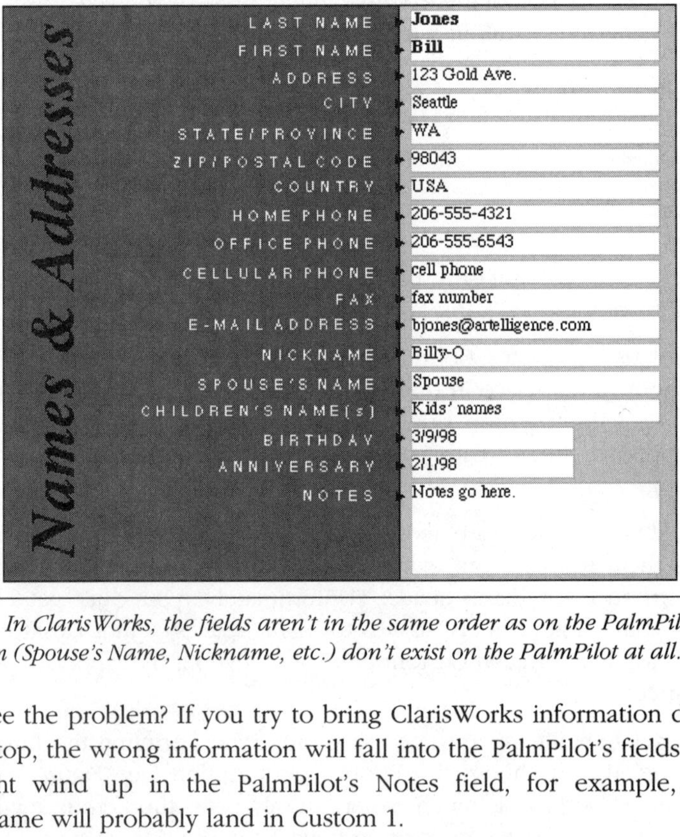

LAST NAME	Jones
FIRST NAME	Bill
ADDRESS	123 Gold Ave.
CITY	Seattle
STATE/PROVINCE	WA
ZIP/POSTAL CODE	98043
COUNTRY	USA
HOME PHONE	206-555-4321
OFFICE PHONE	206-555-6543
CELLULAR PHONE	cell phone
FAX	fax number
E-MAIL ADDRESS	bjones@artelligence.com
NICKNAME	Billy-O
SPOUSE'S NAME	Spouse
CHILDREN'S NAME[s]	Kids' names
BIRTHDAY	3/9/98
ANNIVERSARY	2/1/98
NOTES	Notes go here.

Figure 8-21. In ClarisWorks, the fields aren't in the same order as on the PalmPilot, and some of them (Spouse's Name, Nickname, etc.) don't exist on the PalmPilot at all.

Can you see the problem? If you try to bring ClarisWorks information directly into Palm Desktop, the wrong information will fall into the PalmPilot's fields. The Nickname might wind up in the PalmPilot's Notes field, for example, while the Spouse's Name will probably land in Custom 1.

For this reason, it's important that you inform *either* ClarisWorks *or* Palm Desktop that a different field order is necessary. Unfortunately for this example, Claris-Works doesn't let you rearrange the fields when you export its data; fortunately,

Palm Desktop lets you rearrange the fields when you *import* data, as you'll see in the following steps:

1. Open the program from which you want to export your addresses. (We'll use ClarisWorks in this example.) Want to save time in a later step? Fill in the first person's fields *completely,* even if you have to make up information. See Figure 8-21 for an example: Bill Jones's data has been *completely* filled in, using dummy information where necessary. (Bill doesn't have a wife or a fax machine. That's why, for example, it says "fax number" in the fax number blank and "Spouse" in the Spouse's Name field).

 If you're having any trouble at all making your importing work correctly, take the tip in step 1—filling in missing fields with dummy information—and run with it. Create a record in ClarisWorks (or whatever your starting Rolodex program is) in which *every* field contains its *own field name.*

In other words, type *First name* into the First Name field, *City* into the city field, *Zip* into the Zip Code field, and so on.

When you get down to step 6, you'll be glad you did: lining up the incoming fields with the PalmPilot's expectant fields will be child's play.

---

2. Inspect the ClarisWorks File menu: is there an Export or Save As command? If so, you're in luck. Use that command; in the next dialog box, specify what *file format* you want. In general, a *tab-delimited ASCII text file* is a good choice; it creates a standard text file on your hard drive in which each field (first name, last name, etc.) is separated by a tab, and each *record* is separated by a Return. (If you're exporting from Lotus Organizer, export as a *.csv* document instead.) Give your outgoing data file any name you want, such as *Transfer.txt,* and save it.

3. Launch Palm Desktop. Click the Address Book icon at the left side of the screen. From the pop-up menu above the list, *choose a category name!* All of the names you're about to import will be filed under whatever category name you select here. (If you don't choose a category, they'll all be marked "Unfiled.")

4. From the File menu, choose Import. From the pop-up menu at the bottom of the directory dialog box, choose the file type you're about to import (in this example, choose "Tab Separated values"), as shown in Figure 8-22.

5. Locate and double-click *Transfer.txt* (or whatever you called the file in Step 1).

6. Now the box in Figure 8-23 appears; on the left side are the names of the PalmPilot's fields, in the standard order. On the right side: your data from ClarisWorks. Your job is to make the PalmPilot's fields line up so that they'll

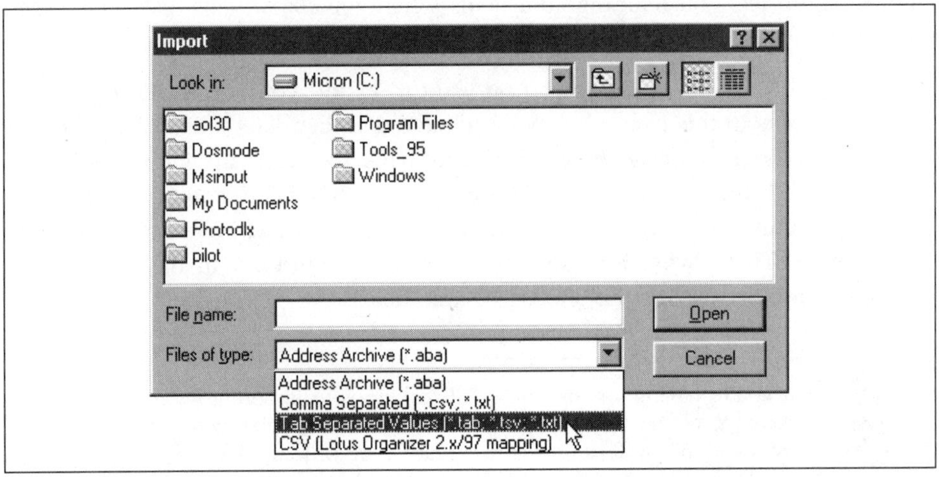

Figure 8-22. Within Palm Desktop, use the pop-up menu to specify the incoming file's type.

correctly receive the data on the right side. To do that, drag PalmPilot field names up or down. You can also uncheck a PalmPilot field name, if there's no piece of ClarisWorks data to go into it.

For example, in Figure 8-23, you can see that the fields don't line up. "123 Gold Ave." is certainly not the name of Mr. Jones's *Company,* and nor is "3/9/98" his address. After a bit of field-dragging in the left column, you should wind up with something like Figure 8-24, in which the PalmPilot fields are set to receive the corresponding information from the imported file. (Make sure you scroll up and down to check *all* the fields, because the window isn't big enough to display the complete list.)

Also apparent in Figure 8-24: certain ClarisWorks fields don't go *anywhere* on the PalmPilot. For example, one field contains nothing but the letter J— apparently some internally calculated field ClarisWorks uses to sort its names by last-name initial. There's also a blank field near the bottom of the window; that doesn't go into the PalmPilot, either. The birthdate has been lined up with the PalmPilot's Custom 1 field—you can always rename that field "Birthday" when the importing is over. (Although you'd have to scroll down to see it, the kids' names have been lined up with Custom 2, the nickname to Custom 3, and the spouse's name to Custom 4.)

7. Check the pop-up menu at the bottom of the window. Make sure it says either Windows, DOS, or Macintosh, according to the computer your imported file came from. (This is to ensure the correct translation of accent marks and other nonalphabet symbols, which are generated differently on each computer.) Also click the right and left Scan Records buttons to make sure you've lined up the *other* imported records correctly. When everything looks good, click OK.

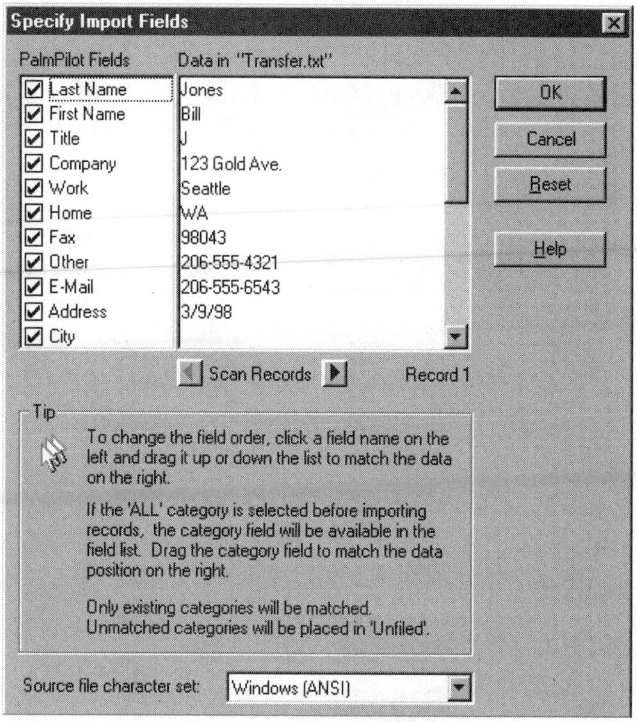

Figure 8-23. In Palm Desktop, drag fields up or down the left column until they match the data shown in the right. Uncheck PalmPilot fields that don't correspond to the incoming file's fields.

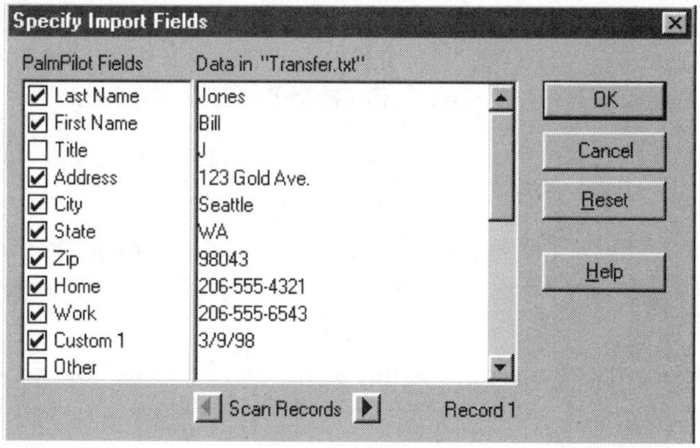

Figure 8-24. When you're finished dragging fields and turning off checkboxes, each PalmPilot field (left) should correspond to the correct kind of information (right).

Now Palm Desktop imports the list. When it's finished, you return to your Palm Desktop Address Book screen—but the newly imported names are high-lighted. (See Figure 8-25.) Now is a really bad time to click the mouse, thus losing the highlighting; as long as the fresh names are still highlighted, if you discover an egregious error, you can press the Delete key to get rid of all of them (and then you can start over).

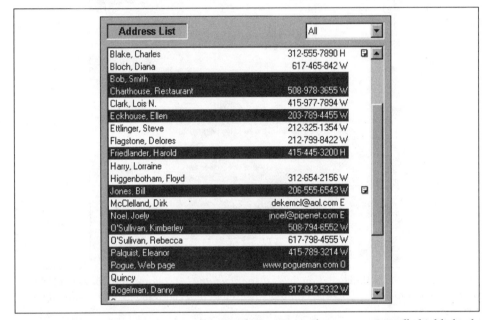

Figure 8-25. Just after importing new names, the new arrivals are automatically highlighted. If you discover a mistake in your import-field mapping, press the Delete key and begin again.

As you can see in Figure 8-25, this importing job was successful: the imported addresses fall into the correct spots in the PalmPilot's little brain.

Exporting data *from* Palm Desktop *to* another program works in much the same way:

1. Select the records you want exported (by Shift-clicking or Ctrl-clicking, as shown in Figure 8-18). If you want to export your *entire* Address Book, skip this step.

2. Choose Export from the File menu; in the next dialog box, type a name for the export file (such as "Transfer"). Specify what kind of export file you want (such as tab-separated text) by choosing from the pop-up menu at the bottom of the window. Also click either All (records) or—if you want to export only the addresses you had highlighted in Step 1—Selected. Click OK.

A Free Stash of Useful Travel Information

This book's CD-ROM contains some ready-to-import lists of phone numbers and other travel information.

To load it into Palm Desktop for Windows (in readiness for a subsequent HotSync to your PalmPilot), click the Address Book icon in Palm Desktop. (If you're smart, you'll now take a moment to create, and select, a special category for the incoming info, such as *Travel #'s.*)

From the File menu, choose Import. Make sure you've inserted this book's CD-ROM; navigate to it; open the Travel Info folder. At the bottom of the Import dialog box, use the "Files of type:" pop-up menu to choose the comma-separated option.

You'll see four files ready for importing: two that contain airline toll-free numbers, and one each for auto-rental and hotel-reservation numbers. (These numbers work in the U.S. and Canada.) Double-click the one you want. In the next dialog box, you'll be asked to assign the incoming information to fields in your Address Book. There are actually only two fields in the incoming text files; line them up with the PalmPilot fields called Last Name and Work Phone, turn off all the other checkboxes in the PalmPilot field list (at the left side of the window), and click OK. After a moment, you'll see your new phone numbers neatly in place.

The CD-ROM contains another set of handy trivia, too: worldwide phone numbers for the offices of major credit cards such as Visa, MasterCard, and American Express. Because these lists aren't formatted in fields, however, you must import these into your Memo Pad, not the Address Book.

To do so, switch to the Palm Desktop's Memo Pad module. Repeat the importing steps above, but this time open the folder (in the Travel Info folder on the PalmPilot CD) called Global Info, and this time choose Text as the file type.

You'll see five files available to import: Amex, Mastercard, and Visa (phone numbers for these cards' overseas branches), plus one called Country Codes (a list of country codes for placing overseas calls) and one called Weights (a lengthy list of measurement conversions, such as "1 foot = 12 inches = 30.48 cm"). Double-click the one you want. Each appears as a single "page" in your Memo Pad; at your next HotSync, off they go to your PalmPilot.

3. In the next box (see Figure 8-26), drag fields up or down the list to change their export order; turn off checkboxes to prevent data from being exported at all; and click OK.

4. Switch to the program you want the addresses brought into, and use its File menu's Import or Open command to bring the data home.

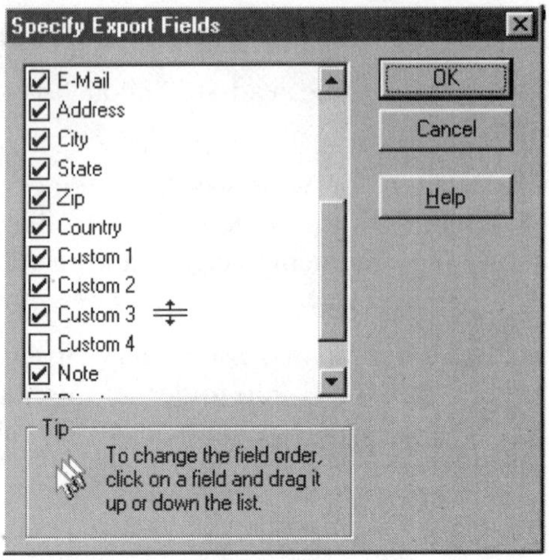

Figure 8-26. When you export Address Book data, you are offered once again the chance to rearrange the order of the outgoing fields.

To Do

Palm Desktop's To Do module, shown in Figure 8-27, is virtually identical to the PalmPilot's (see Chapter 4 for a complete description). Here, as on the PalmPilot, you can:

- Add new To Do items directly to the list by clicking the New button.

- Denote that you've completed an obligation by clicking its checkbox (either in the master list or on the right side of the screen, where it says Complete:).

- Opt to have the date recorded when you click off an item (by clicking the Show button and turning on "Record completion date"—but note that this setting must be turned on independently on the PalmPilot).

- Prioritize items by choosing 1, 2, 3, 4, or 5 from the pop-up menu beside the checkbox.

- Assign a category to each to do task, using the Category pop-up menu on the right side of the screen.

- View only to do items belonging to one category, using the Category pop-up menu *above* the master list.

- Add new category labels, or edit the existing ones, by choosing Categories from the Tools menu.

- Flag a to do item as Private by clicking the Private checkbox.

- Set a deadline for an item, using the Due pop-up menu.

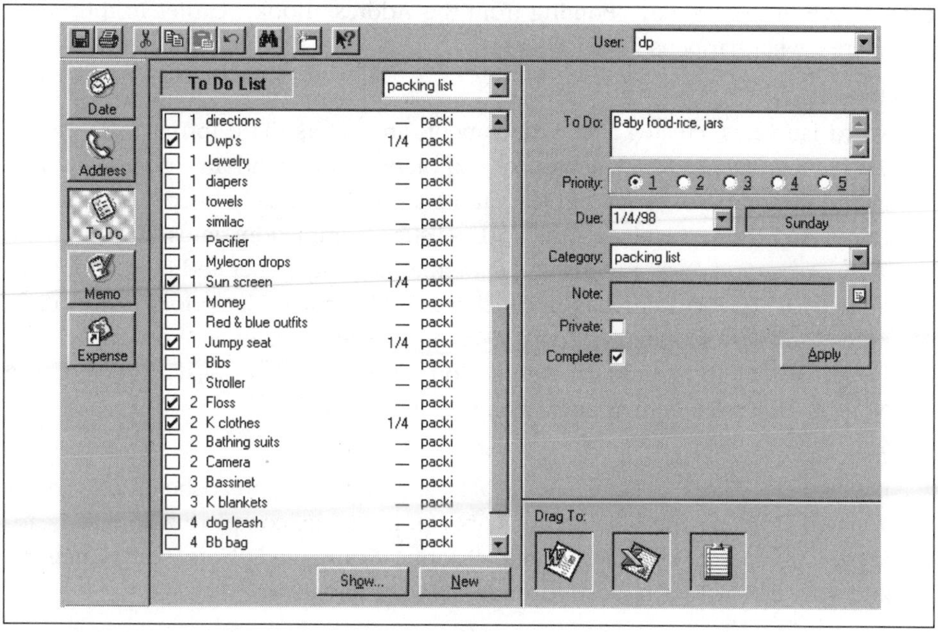

Figure 8-27. Palm Desktop's To Do program offers more than just the master list—at right, it shows a closeup view of whichever item is currently selected. In this illustration, two additional columns have been turned on: the Completion Date and the Category columns.

- Add a page or two of annotations to a to do item by clicking the Note icon (or double-clicking the Note field itself) on the right side of the screen.

- Control which extra columns of information (Priority, Due Date, Category) appear in the main display by clicking the Show button. (Your column-showing settings in Palm Desktop are independent from the identical options on the PalmPilot.)

Figure 8-27 illustrates all of these controls.

The sole difference between the PalmPilot's To Do program and your PC's is the screen size: on your computer, there's enough room to see *both* the master list of to-do items *and* a detail view (of the current selection) off to the right. Actually, though, there are only two things you can do in the detail view that you can't do in the master list: add a Note and specify a due date.

The Drag To Icons

You can also drag a To Do item—or a bunch of selected To Do items—from the master list onto one of the "Drag To" icons in the lower-right corner of the screen (see Figure 8-27). (For hints on selecting multiple list items, even if they're not consecutive in the list, see "Printing from the Address Book," earlier in this chapter.) Here's what happens if you drag to:

The Word icon

Word launches, creates a new document, and offers three formatting options. *Task Progress Report* generates a complete "Memorandum" document that includes a title, To, From, Subject, and Date fields (mostly filled out automatically), and a line between one To Do listing/completion status and the next. *Task Delegation Form* is similar: it's an automatically generated memo, but this time each To Do item has a checkbox and displays its priority, due date, notes, and so on. Finally, *Leave Data as a Table* creates a Word table with these five column headings: Description, Due Date, Priority, Completed, and Note. Each To Do item appears as a row in this table.

The Excel icon

If you have Excel, it launches, creates a new blank spreadsheet, and pastes your To Do items into it. You get a six-column table, complete with row headings: Item Description, Due Date, Priority, Completed, Note, and Category, and your actual To Do items form the rows of the table.

The Clipboard icon

Your dragged To Dos are copied to your PC's invisible Clipboard; now you can switch to any word processing program on your PC and paste them. You get a tab-separated, five-column table that displays each to do's name, priority, "Completed:" status, category name, and note.

Purging Completed Tasks

After you check off a To Do item, it remains visible in your list (unless you've clicked the Show button and turned off "Show completed items"). To cleanse your To Do list of finished tasks, you can use the Purge Completed To Dos command (in the Tools menu).

You'll be offered the chance to have your completed tasks saved in a backup file called an *archive,* so that they're not gone forever. For details on archives, see the section "Archived Records," later in this chapter.

Printing Your To Do List

Before choosing Print from the File menu, you can make a number of adjustments to control exactly what you'll get on the printout:

To control which categories print

Make a category selection from the pop-up menu above your To Do list. (Choose All if you want the whole enchilada to print.)

To include private To Dos in the printout

Choose Show Private Records from the View menu. (In other words, if private To Dos are hidden on the screen, they're also omitted from the printout.)

To print an extra "Due Date" line for each To Do item

Turn on the Due Date *column* in the To Do master list. To do so, click the Show button beneath the list; in the next dialog box, turn on "Show due dates."

To omit already checked-off items from the printout

Click the Show button. Turn off "Show completed items."

To group your printed To Do items by priority

Click the Show button. At the top of the dialog box, where it says "Sort by," choose Priorities. Make sure the Show Priorities checkbox is *also* selected. Your printout will contain an attractive banner heading ("Priority 1," "Priority 2," and so on) for each group of To Dos.

To sort your printout by deadline

Click the Show button. At the top of the dialog box, where it says "Sort by," choose Due Date.

To print notes beneath each To Do item

Choose Print from the File menu; you'll see the option for "Print Notes" (see Figure 8-28).

To hand-pick which To Do items print

Highlight them by Ctrl-clicking. Or, to select a consecutive group, Shift-click the first and last items. (See the previous section "Printing from the Address Book" for specifics.) Then, when you choose Print from the File menu, click the Selection option (see Figure 8-28).

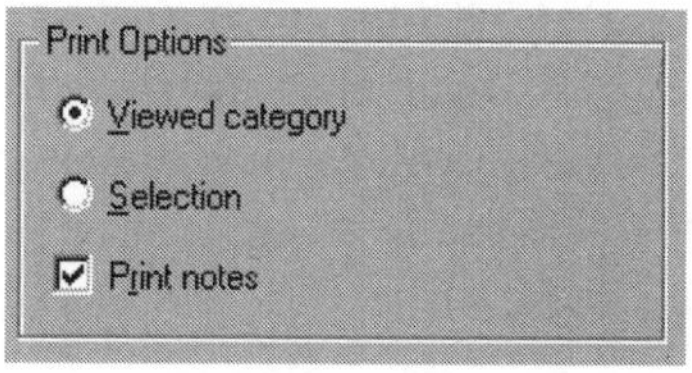

Figure 8-28. These options, shown here on the Macintosh, are added to the usual printing options.

By the way, there's no way to suppress the Category line beneath each To Do item you print; even if you turn off all the options listed above, the minimum To Do printout still contains the actual task in bold, followed by a nonbold Category name. That's a shame, especially for people who've *already* indicated that they want only one particular category to print out (and would prefer a more compact listing). Figure 8-29 shows what a printed To Do list looks like.

To Do List for Marv   **All Items**

Priority 1	**Priority 5**
Dog food for Bullwinkle	**Find nanny for Genevieve**
Due Date: 10/9/98	Due Date: None
Category: Unfiled	Category: Friends
Rotary Club directory!!	Note: She says she's already
Due Date: 10/9/98	asked at the Hungarian
Category: Unfiled	embassy, suggests going
Return tax form to Clyde	through an agent
Due Date: 10/19/98	
Category: Money	

Priority 2
Samples back to storeroom
Due Date: 10/9/98
Category: Unfiled
Library books X 3
Due Date: 11/9/98
Category: Money

Figure 8-29. The full To Do list, complete with Notes and priority headings, prints like this.

Memo Pad

Palm Desktop's Memo Pad repeats the pattern of its other modules: it's exactly the same as its counterpart on the PalmPilot (described in Chapter 4), except that the larger screen offers you the chance to see both the master list and the full memo page simultaneously (see Figure 8-30).

All the usual features work just as they do on the PalmPilot, such as defining, assigning, and viewing categories; clicking a master-list item to view its full text on the right side of the screen; marking memos as Private; and changing the sorting order (either alphabetically or in the order you've dragged items into on the PalmPilot) using the List By button. Delete a memo just as you'd delete anything from Palm Desktop: click its name in the master list, and then choose Edit → Delete.

There are only two features unique to Palm Desktop's Memo Pad. First, you can import or export text files—which can be important to anyone who, for example, wants to slurp reading material into the PalmPilot before a plane ride. (See the sidebar "A Free Stash of Useful Travel Information" earlier in this chapter for step-by-step instructions.)

Second, you can drag a memo, or several selected memos, from the master list onto one of the "Drag To" icons in the lower-right corner of the screen. (To select multiple list items, see the section "Printing from the Address Book," earlier in this chapter.) This time, however, you have only two icons from which to choose:

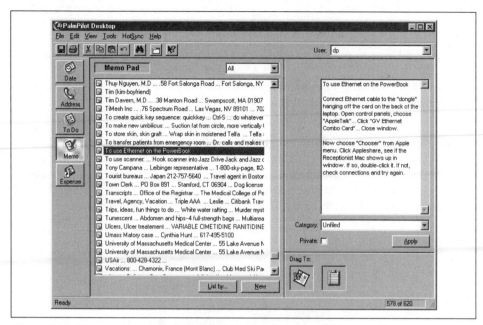

Figure 8-30. The Memo Pad module of Palm Desktop closely resembles the Memo Pad on the actual PalmPilot.

The Word icon

Word launches, creates a new document, and pastes in your dragged memos, one per page. The first line of each memo becomes a *header* for the page, complete with a horizontal line separating it from the body; then comes the category, followed by the entire memo (including a repetition of the first line).

The Clipboard icon

Your dragged memos are copied to your PC's invisible Clipboard; now you can launch your word processor and choose Paste from the Edit menu. You get only the text of the memos this time—no headers, no category labels—and, if you're pasting into a common word processor, each memo appears on a different page.

Printing Your Memos

You have exactly one decision to make when printing memos: *which ones* to include. The usual conventions for limiting the printout apply: private memos don't print if they're hidden onscreen; you'll only print memos belonging to the category you're currently viewing on the screen; and you can Ctrl/Command-click and Shift-click to select a subset of memos manually. (See the section "Printing from the Address Book," earlier in this chapter, for specifics.)

The Least Useful Button on Earth

Two Palm Desktop programs—the Memo Pad and the To Do list—offer a button not found on the PalmPilot: the Apply button. In theory, you're supposed to click it after editing a memo or to do on the *right* side of the screen, in order to update the info in the master list on the left.

The Apply button's usefulness is primarily psychological, however. It serves no real purpose, because any changes you make are *automatically* "applied" when you do *anything else* in Palm Desktop. The moment you switch to a different memo or to do, switch to a different Palm Desktop module, change your view, save your file, HotSync, quit Palm Desktop, and so on, your changes are instantly "applied" and locked in.

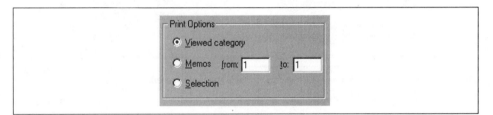

Figure 8-31. Which memos do you want to print?

What's especially odd is the options that then appear when you actually choose the Print command (see Figure 8-31). Here's what they do:

Viewed category

Even if you hand-selected specific memos to print, this option prints *all* memos currently displayed on the screen—that is, all memos in the currently selected category.

Memos from __ to __

This option prints a specified number of *consecutive* memos. In a way, this feature is unnecessary—if you wanted a consecutive batch, wouldn't it be easier to Shift-click them in the master list and then print only the selection (instead of having to memorize the memos' *numbers*)?

If you do decide to use this option, note that it prints the memos in the order they appear on the screen. (You control this order by clicking the List By button below the list.) In other words, memos 1 through 40 when sorted *alphabetically* may be very different from memos 1 through 40 when sorted by *creation order* (that is, the order into which you've dragged memos on the PalmPilot itself).

Selection

Choose this option to print only the memos you highlighted before using the Print command.

Regardless of which memos you finally decide to include in your printout, the result looks something like Figure 8-32. Note that the *first line* of each memo is printed in boldface and close to the left margin of the page; a category name appears next; and then, finally, the entire memo appears (including a repetition of the first line). In other words, the Memo Pad's printouts work best if you're in the habit of writing a "subject" phrase on the first line of each memo, so that the bold-face entries serve as an index-at-a-glance.

Memo Pad for Alyce

Flank steak recipe
   Category: Home Stuff
   Flank steak recipe

   juice of 1 lemon
   1/2 cup soy sauce
   1/4 cup dry red wine
   3 T vegetable oil
   2 T Worcestershire sauce
   1 large clove garlic, sliced
   Pepper
   Chopped chopped dill weed, celery seed
   1-1.5 lb flank steak, trimmed

   Mix all in marinating pan. Marinate steak, turning occasionally, for 2-12 hrs in fridge. Broil over hot coals for 5 min. per side for rare, 7 for med. rare. Slice meat on the diagonal across the grain and serve.

Stamford office phone extn's
   Category: Business
   Stamford office phone extn's
   EDITORIAL
   Linda Cramer 3314
   Allyson Brown 3148
   Epler 3297
   Abes 3244
   Chip Coultis - Lab Manager 3144
   Courteau 3114
   PR dept 3148
   Lab 3176

Directions to Flagstone Resort
   Category: Business
   Directions to Flagstone Resort

   Take I-95 north to Exit 8 ("Atlantic St.").
   2nd light: turn R onto Canal.
   Next light: turn R onto Magee.
   Next light: go straight; the road becomes Smythe Ave. Address is 802 Smythe.

Safe combination 38-96-32
   Category: Business
   Safe combination 38-96-32

Parks Dept. meeting 4/9
   Category: Stamford
   Parks Dept. meeting 4/9
   Meeting was called to order at 4:30 pm.
   Absent: Jenkins, Wilcox, Abernathy.
   March meeting minutes read and approved.

   Meeting abruptly canceled because of asbestos scare one floor up.

nonfat milk
   Category: Groceries
   nonfat milk
   Dannon Raspberry Yogurt
   oranges
   vanilla
   Boston lettuce
   fennel (ask Jennifer)
   VCR tapes

Figure 8-32. The Memo Pad printouts have few formatting options, but that's OK—they look quite nice as they are.

If the built-in printouts of the Memo Pad, To Do list, or Address Book aren't to your taste, remember that you can always transfer your data to a regular word processor or page-layout program for upgraded formatting features. You can use either the Export command (in the File menu), the Drag To Microsoft Word icon, or the Drag To Clipboard option (and then you can paste into your favorite word processor).

Expense

The Expense icon at the left side of the Palm Desktop screen shouldn't fool you: there *is* no Expense program in Palm Desktop. Unlike the other four programs, which appear on both the PalmPilot and Palm Desktop, the Expense program exists *only* on the PalmPilot. You can't create, edit, or even *see* your list of expenditures in Palm Desktop. You're expected to do all your expense-data work in Microsoft Excel.

If you click the Expense icon in Palm Desktop, one of two things happens:

- If you've never used the Expense program on your PalmPilot (or never HotSynced it), you get an error message.

- If you *have* used the Expense program on the PalmPilot and then HotSynced, Microsoft Excel launches.

Click the Expense icon once, not twice, unless you want to launch Excel twice and stare at a rude error message. And if Excel doesn't launch, and you get an error message instead, 3Com has a delightful multistep registry-editing procedure available that fixes the problem.

Transferring Expense Data to Excel

Now you're shown the box in Figure 8-33. If, as suggested in Chapter 4, you use your categories to group your expenses by trip or by project, you're all set: select the category you'd like to turn into an expense report. That, of course, is the ultimate aim of this entire exercise: to print out your expenditures, turn them in to your employer, and get reimbursed.

Of course, you can click All (to send *all* categories' expenses to Excel). You can also select a *subset* of the categories listed by Shift-clicking their names in this list.

Before proceeding, you can also specify an ending date for the transactions you're about to transfer by typing it into the End Date blank. For example, if it's now February 15, and you're preparing January's expense reports, you might type 1/31

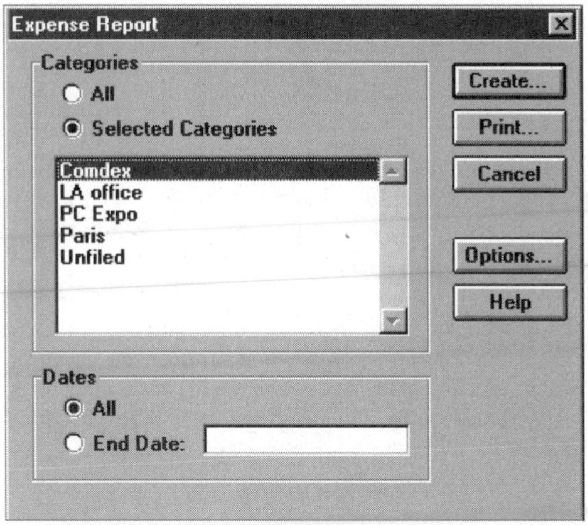

Figure 8-33. Specify which category (or categories) of expenses you want sent to Excel.

into this blank. Otherwise—if you leave the date setting on All—Palm Desktop will send *all* recorded expenses to Excel—at least, all that it knows about (up to your most recent HotSync).

If you'd like to tailor your expense report a bit, click the Options button. You'll see the dialog box in Figure 8-34. If you like you can fill in any blanks your reimbursement process requires (Project, Bill To, and so on), although you can also type this information directly into Excel when the import process is over.

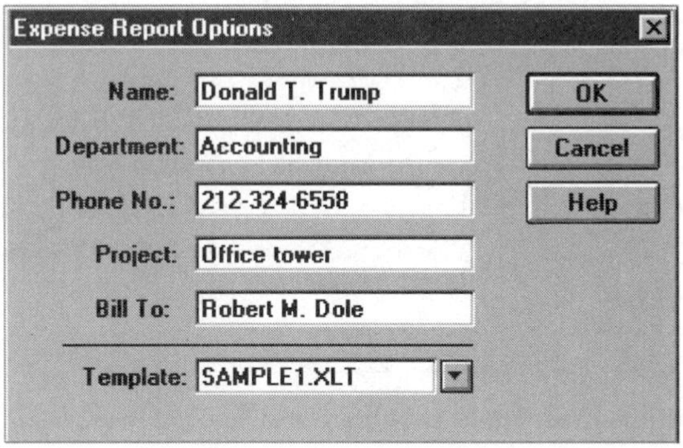

Figure 8-34. Choose an Excel spreadsheet design here.

More important is the pop-up menu at the bottom of the window, where you can specify *which* of the five Excel spreadsheet styles you'd like to use for your expense report. (These four spreadsheet templates, named Sample 1 through Sample 4, plus DATALIST, are normally installed onto your hard drive by the PalmPilot software installer. They're in the *Palm\Templates* folder.) To see what these spreadsheet designs look like, consult the appendix at the back of your *Palm Handbook* manual—or just open them manually in Excel some afternoon.

None of the standard Excel templates provided with your PalmPilot, Sample 1 through Sample 4, incorporates *all* your Expense data. For example, all four ignore anything in your PalmPilot's "Attendees" field, which could be very important to your reimbursement prospects.

If those drawbacks are frustrating you, consider using the blacksheep Excel template—so strange it's not even mentioned in the PalmPilot manual—called DATALIST. This layout, too, is attractive, ready-to-print, and self-calculating, but it has columns for *all* the data you input on the PalmPilot . . . attendees included.

After setting these options, click OK; click Create in the next dialog box; and welcome to Excel. You should now see your expenses properly filed in the correct cells of this spreadsheet (Figure 8-35). Tweak as necessary, print out, turn in, and enjoy your reimbursement. (You may want to return to your palmtop's Expense application at this point to clear out the HotSynced expense items—just tap Menu → Purge and then specify which expense category you'd like emptied.).

If none of the five provided Excel sheets is even close to what you're supposed to turn in for reimbursement, you can design one from scratch. See Appendix C of your *Handbook*, or Appendix B of the *Applications Handbook*, for the not-very-exciting instructions, and set aside at least a full weekend—remapping the PalmPilot's data to the individual cells of your preferred spreadsheet is wildly tedious to all but the die-hard programmer.

Of course, a little money can also solve the problem. If the included Excel spreadsheet templates don't look or work enough like your company's standard expense reports, ChemSoft, Inc. will be happy to custom program a template for you at prices from $200 to $400. (Contact Doug Weitz, 408-615-1001, or email *dweitz@chemsoft.com.*)

If your list of expenses is so long that it doesn't fit on one page of your Excel spreadsheet, you wind up with *multiple* spreadsheets—as many as it takes to accommodate all your lavish spending.

If you're not careful, you might not realize that each page is totaled *separately,* and that it's up to you to rig the formulas so that your grand totals incorporate the totals from *all* the spreadsheets.

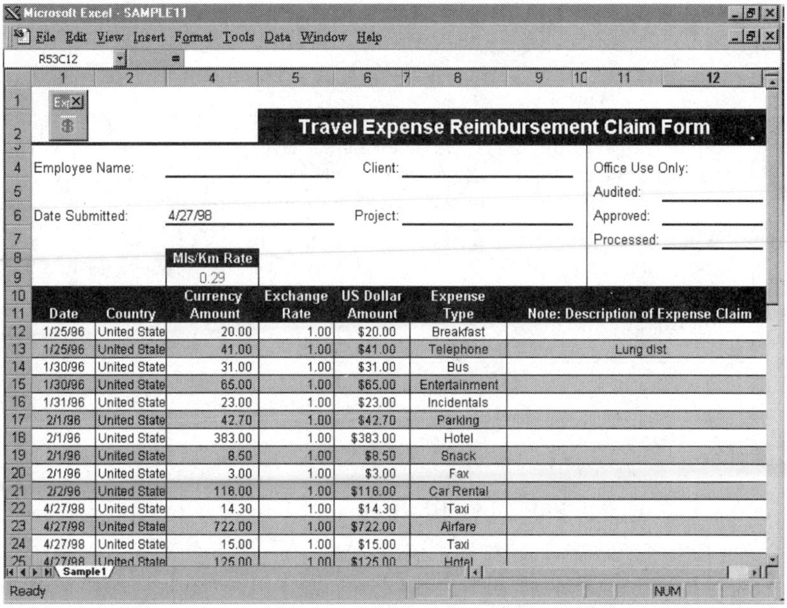

Figure 8-35. Once in Excel, your Palm data turns into a neatly formatted expense report. Note the tiny floating $ tool palette in the upper-left corner; click it to reopen the dialog box shown in Figure 8-33, in case you need to adjust some settings and reimport.

Palm Desktop's Sneaky Storage Mechanism

As noted above, Palm Desktop doesn't let you see, create, or edit expense items. However, it obviously stores this information *somewhere*. Indeed, in a pinch, you *can* view the expense data.

Launch a word processor. Choose File → Open. Navigate to the *Palm* folder on your hard drive; open your user-named folder; open the *Expense* folder; and open the text file called *Expense* (or *Expense.txt*). Although you may not be crazy about the way it's formatted, your data is there, all right—nicely lined up in tab-separated table format (the columns are category, date, description, currency, and amount). In case of disaster, you could copy this information and paste it into Excel or some other document.

Here's another situation where Palm Desktop's awareness of your Expense data (despite its inability to *show* it) could be useful. Suppose your PalmPilot crashes. Suppose the batteries die, you drive for three hours with *no* batteries in the device, and you lose all your data. Or suppose, for some reason, that you're forced to *hard reset* your PalmPilot (a drastic troubleshooting measure described in Chapter 17, *Troubleshooting*).

If you HotSync your PalmPilot, you'll discover that all your Expense data is automatically restored. Palm Desktop feeds it right back to the PalmPilot.

A cell in Excel 5.0 can't hold more than 256 typed characters. Unfortunately (or fortunately), the PalmPilot's Expense program lets you write far more than that in two of its important fields: Attendees, where you make notes about a certain expenditure, and Notes.

When your data arrives in Excel, therefore, any data beyond the first 256 letters of these fields will be chopped off. To retrieve it, use a word processor to open the *Expense.txt* file and copy the missing information manually.

Archived Records

If you've used your PalmPilot much—or read Chapter 4 much—you're familiar with the routine of *deleting* a record from your Address Book, Memo Pad, Date Book, or To Do list. You may also have tried *purging* obsolete events from your Date Book or checked-off tasks in your To Do list. (See Chapter 4 for instructions on deleting and purging.)

As in most computer programs, you're asked if you're *sure* you want to proceed with the deletion or the purge. But as Figure 8-36 shows, there's an added twist to deleting PalmPilot data: a checkbox called "Save archive copy on PC." (You see this same message when deleting information from Palm Desktop itself.)

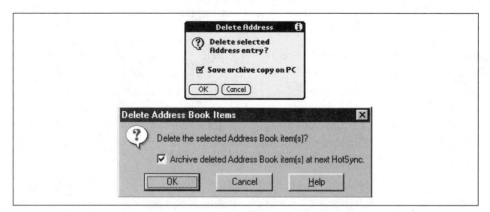

Figure 8-36. When you delete information from the PalmPilot (top) or from Palm Desktop (bottom), you're offered the chance to save them into a backup file.

That option refers to a strange and useful feature of Palm Desktop: its ability to create files full of deleted information—backup files on your PC, one per module, for each user, in each category. At any time, you can use the Open Archive command in the File menu to view this deleted information; and, in a pinch, you can copy and paste it *back* into your primary Palm Desktop file. From there, at the next HotSync, it will be restored to the PalmPilot from whence it came.

Archive files consume only a minuscule amount of disk space on your PC, and are completely invisible and out of your way until you need them. Thousands of PalmPilot users at this very moment are probably unaware that their *Palm* folder even *contains* archive files. Therefore, when deleting or purging information, there's almost no downside to leaving the "archive" checkbox turned on; you never know when you might need the deleted information again. (The only reason you might *not* want to archive a deleted record is for reasons of security or potential embarrassment.)

How to Archive Deleted Data: From the PalmPilot

Sending data you delete from your PalmPilot into archive-land is easy: when you encounter the dialog box shown in Figure 8-36, make sure the checkbox ("Save archive copy on PC") is selected. When you click OK, your data seems to disappear from the PalmPilot, but actually it's just been moved to an invisible holding area awaiting the next HotSync.

When you do HotSync, the deleted data is transferred to your PC; stored in an archive file; and, finally, *truly* deleted from the PalmPilot. Only now does the PalmPilot reclaim the memory that data was using up.

How to Archive Deleted Data: From the PC

Archiving data on the PC works much the same way. Select some data, choose Delete from the Edit menu, and leave on the "Save deleted items" option. As on the PalmPilot, the information now vanishes.

What's especially odd, however, is that even in Palm Desktop, the deleted information doesn't appear in your archive file *until your next HotSync!* In other words, it's easy to understand why deleted PalmPilot information doesn't become an archive on your PC until the next HotSync—after all, it has yet to be transferred. But when you delete data from Palm Desktop and indicate that you'd like it archived, you might expect it to appear in your archive file *on the spot.* Here again, though, your data is held in some invisible storage area until you HotSync with the PalmPilot; only then will you find archive files on your hard drive.

How to Restore Archived Data

To view the information you've deleted or purged (and archived), choose Open Archive from Palm Desktop's File menu. Now another oddity awaits you: you'll discover that Palm Desktop has created a separate archive file for *each* PalmPilot program, user, and category. That's right: if you HotSync two different PalmPilots with your desktop computer, you use all four primary PalmPilot programs, and you've created 15 categories in each program, you'll find *120* archive files (2 X 4 X 15) on your hard drive!

Retrieving exactly the lost data you're interested in, therefore, takes some thinking. Here's what you need to do:

1. In Palm Desktop, click the appropriate module icon at the left side of the screen (Memo Pad, Address Book, and so on).

2. Choose Open Archive from the File menu. Navigate to your *Palm* folder. Inside, you'll see your user-named folder, as described in Chapter 6—actually, one for every PalmPilot you HotSync with this PC. Open the one that you suspect contains the data you want to retrieve. (If you stop to think about it, you can see now that it's perfectly possible to retrieve archived data originally deleted from *one* PalmPilot—say, Frank's—and restore it to someone else's. Simply open the appropriate user-named folder during this step.)

3. Inside the user-named folder, you'll find yet another set of folders, one for each Palm program (called *memopad, datebook, todo,* and so on). Open the one that matches the module you're in (as selected in Step 1). Inside, as shown in Figure 8-37, you'll see individual files named for this module's categories, often with a telltale three-letter extension, such as *.mpa* (Memo Pad archive) or *.aba* (Address Book archive). For example, you might see files called *Unfiled.mpa, Business.mpa, Personal.mpa,* and so on (corresponding to your category list for the Memo Pad). Double-click the one you suspect contains the data you want. (If you guess the wrong file, no big deal; choose Open Archive from the File menu again and repeat Step 3.)

4. Now you're viewing what appears to be a normal Palm Desktop screen (see Figure 8-38)—but notice the title bar of the window. Instead of simply showing the name of the module (such as Memo Pad), it now says "Memo Pad (Editing Archive)." That's your cue not to panic when you see only a handful of records, instead of your usual masterful list of several hundred. This *isn't* your data; it's your *deleted* data, raised from the dead.

5. Select the item or items you want to retrieve, using any of the usual Palm Desktop list-selection methods (see the section "Printing from the Address Book," earlier in this chapter). From the Edit menu, choose Cut (to remove it from the archive file) or Copy (to leave a copy behind in the archive).

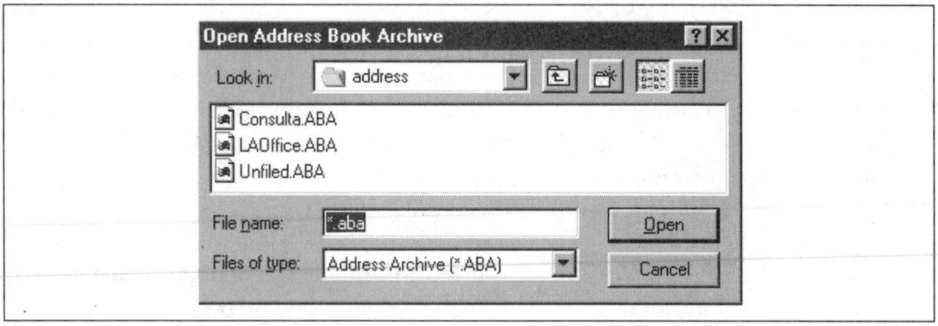

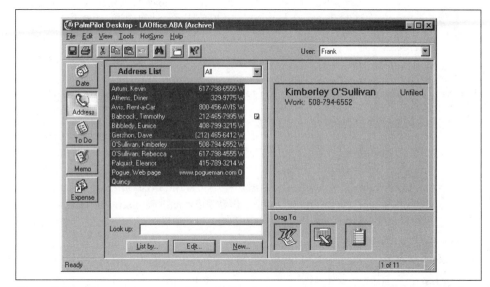

Figure 8-37. Inside your Palm folder are user-named folders; inside each are folders for each Palm program. And inside each of them is a list of archive files, named after the categories from which they were originally deleted or purged.

Figure 8-38. After opening an archive, the key feature is the title of the window. It reminds you that you're not looking at your regular data anymore, but instead a resurrected batch of deleted information.

6. All you have to do now is return to *your* Palm Desktop file and paste the retrieved information into place. From the File menu, choose Open Current. (Doesn't sound familiar? You're right—under most circumstances, this command doesn't even exist. It appears in the File menu *only* when you're editing an archive file. It's your ticket back to your own data file. Of course, all of this would be easier to understand if you could view two windows simultaneously, your data in one and the archive in the other—but let's not quibble.)

You're back where you were in step 1: viewing your own data.

7. Select the user name (upper-right pop-up menu) and the category name (top middle pop-up menu) to indicate where you'd like to put this restored information. You're under no obligation to paste the archive material into the *same* user name or category it came from; if you found the missing data in *Business.mpa*—the Business category—there's nothing to stop you from pasting it into your Personal category, for example.

8. Choose Paste from the Edit menu. The archived data appears in front of you.

As far as your PalmPilot knows, this restored information is actually *new* information typed into Palm Desktop; at the next HotSync, it will be restored to your PalmPilot.

 If you're using Palm Desktop 3.0 or later, you may find it easier to restore archived Memo Pad and Address Book data using the *file linking* feature, described at the end of this chapter.

Profiles and File Linking: Standardized Data, Multiple PalmPilots

In corporate environments, where the PalmPilot is becoming a piece of standard-issue equipment, technology managers face an interesting puzzle: how do you load up multiple PalmPilots with the same set of standard company information? And how do you update them all when that information changes? These aren't trivial questions when the data in question is the company phone list, or price list, or manual that must be consulted in the field.

3Com has accommodated this corporate need in two ways: with *Profiles* and with *file linking* in later models.

Profiles

Pilot Desktop 2.0 and later let you load up new, or newly erased, PalmPilots with a prepared set of information—*before* the PalmPilots get named or HotSynced by your employees.

For example, suppose you're about to issue 15 PalmPilots to your sales force. You want each PalmPilot to contain your company's complete phone directory (in the Address Book); company holidays and other important dates (in the Date Book); detailed descriptions of your company's products (in the Memo Pad); and a sales-call checklist (in a special To Do list category). You also want to install a couple of new programs (such as a shareware database program and a web browser) onto every single PalmPilot.

All of this information is, in Palm Desktop parlance, one *Profile*. With just a few steps, you can preload this Profile onto as many new PalmPilots as you like. After the PalmPilots are loaded up, their happy new owners can take them back to their computers, install Palm Desktop, name their PalmPilots, HotSync, and so on—never guessing how all this useful data managed to appear, fully formed, on their palmtops.

Install a Profile (a set of standard data to be loaded into multiple PalmPilots) *only into an empty PalmPilot*. The Profile-installation process will otherwise *erase* whatever's in the PalmPilot.

You create a Profile in much the same way as you'd create a new user in Palm Desktop.

1. From the Tools menu, choose Users. You see the window shown in Figure 8-39; click New, name the Profile (for example, Price Lists), and click OK in both dialog boxes.

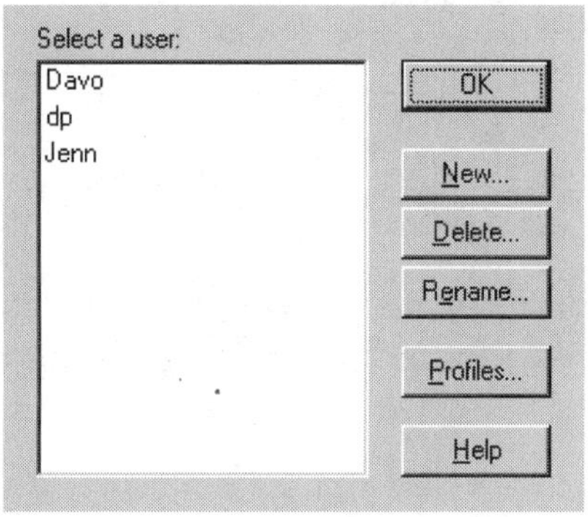

![Select a user dialog box with list showing Davo, dp, Jenn and buttons OK, New..., Delete..., Rename..., Profiles..., Help]

Figure 8-39. This is the control center for setting up Profiles.

2. You return to the usual Palm Desktop window. (Note that the User pop-up menu in the upper-right corner now says Price Lists.)

   Fill the screen up with your canned set of data in the usual way: by importing, by typing, or by HotSyncing with a master PalmPilot (and then copying and pasting the data into your newly named Profile).

3. Insert the first new (or newly emptied) PalmPilot into the HotSync cradle. When you press the HotSync button (see Chapter 6), you'll get the window show in Figure 8-40. Click Profiles, choose the one you want (in this example, Price Lists), and click OK.

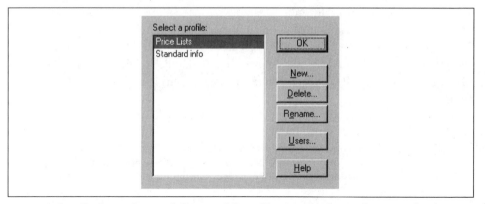

Figure 8-40. Which set of canned data would you like to preload onto the virginal palmtops?

 Behind the scenes, when you create a Profile, Palm Desktop creates a new folder in your Palm folder bearing the name of the new Profile—exactly as it creates folders for each user name. Inside this folder is the usual assortment of Palm program-named folders (memopad, datebook, todo, install, and so on).

You can manipulate Profile-named folders exactly as you manipulate user-named ones, as described in Chapter 6.

The new PalmPilot is now loaded and ready to distribute to its new user; repeat step 3 with any other PalmPilots.

As you can probably tell, it's perfectly possible to design *multiple* Profiles, each filled with standardized data for a different group of employees. As you load up their PalmPilots, simply choose the appropriate Profile name in the dialog box shown in Figure 8-40.

File Linking

Beginning with Palm Desktop 3.0 (which debuted with the Palm III), an intriguing new feature is available—file linking. In this scenario, you can place a constantly updated file in a fixed place on your hard drive or network—and designate that it be loaded automatically onto your PalmPilot at each HotSync. When the file on your hard drive changes, your PalmPilot's copy is automatically updated to match (at the next HotSync).

What kinds of data can you upload in this way? Memo Pad and Address Book data. And how can you use this feature? The possibilities are endless:

- Suppose you use address-book software on your PC that isn't supported by any of the HotSync-conduit programs described in Chapter 6. Before each

---

The Detritus of Profile Installation

You can designate a standard set of add-on Palm programs to be part of a Profile, using the Install Tool program as usual (see Chapter 6). The difference: when choosing a PalmPilot's name (user name) as the destination for the newly added programs, choose your *Profile's* name instead.

Installing programs using the Profile feature works just like installing programs normally: a switch is flipped in your Windows registry informing the HotSync software that programs are waiting to be installed, and these programs are copied into a folder called *Install* (inside your *Palm* folder, inside the user-named folder or Profile-named folder).

There's one difference between installing programs onto a *named* PalmPilot and installing them as part of a Profile: after installing the Profile, the programs you're adding to the PalmPilots *remain* in that *Install* folder. (Rationale: Because you're using Profiles, the HotSync software assumes you plan to use these programs again—for the next PalmPilot.)

If you're finished using a particular Profile, you must drag these Palm programs (*.prc* documents) out of the *Install* folder manually.

HotSync, export your current address book list as a comma-delimited text file, as described below. It gets uploaded to the PalmPilot's Address Book module automatically.

- You oversee a team of PalmPilot-wielding employees. You want to keep them all up-to-date with your company's ever-changing telephone list or price list. So you dump the list every week into a specified server on the network, updated as necessary; every time your PalmPilot users HotSync, their Palm-Pilots' existing price-list or telephone-directory document gets updated.

- You like to read the technology column in *The New York Times* on your train ride to work. So you download it from the Web, always saving it as a text file with the same name into the same hard drive folder, and HotSync. The text of the article always shows up in your Memo Pad.

Since this feature is designed to *replace* data on the PalmPilot at each HotSync, you may be wondering what prevents these uploads from overwriting important memos or your own address-book data. The answer is sneaky and clever: the File Linking feature gets its own private category. Each HotSync does wipe out the previous contents of your Memo Pad and Address Book—but *only* in the designated category, and *only* if the memo's name (or address-book information) matches the file on your hard drive.

Don't edit the memos and addresses in your file-link category on your PalmPilot. Every time you HotSync, you'll get a fresh copy of the original data from the linked file—in addition to the modified records. The result will be a chaotic mix of duplicate records with conflicting information, and you'll have no way of recognizing which is current.   .

(It's OK to add new memos or addresses in this special category, however.)

Before beginning the setup, prepare the information you want uploaded to the PalmPilot each time. You can choose any of the following file formats:

- For uploads into the Memo Pad, create a plain text file; a comma-separated (.CSV) text file (a common export format from database programs, in which each field is separated from the next by a comma); or a Memo Pad archive. See "Archived Records" earlier in this chapter for instructions on creating such an archive; for now, simply note that the only way to create archived data is to *delete* it, either from Palm Desktop or the PalmPilot.

  If the imported file is more than 4000 characters long, the Memo Pad will break it up into multiple "pages" called Corporate Price List 1, Corporate Price List 2, and so on.

- For uploads into the Address Book, create either a .CSV file, as described above, or an Address Book archive file, as described in "Archived Records" earlier in this chapter.

For now, let's assume that the document is a text file called *Standard Prices.txt*.

1. If you're in Palm Desktop, choose File Link from the HotSync menu. If not, click the HotSync Manager icon in your Windows system tray. From the menu that appears, choose File Link.

2. The dialog box shown in Figure 8-41, left, appears. Choose the name of the PalmPilot from the pop-up menu; make sure that "Create a new link" is selected; and click Next.

3. In the next dialog box—also shown in Figure 8-41—specify where you want the uploaded information sent: to the PalmPilot's Memo Pad or Address Book. In this example, we'll use the Memo Pad.

4. Click the Browse button. In the Select File box that appears, use the pop-up menu to choose one of the file formats described above. For the Memo Pad, you can choose from CSV files, Memo Archive files, or Text files. For the Address Book, you can choose either CSV files or Address Book Archive files.

   Now navigate to the *Standard Prices.txt* file and double-click it.

5. In the final empty blank (Figure 8-41), name the special category that the file-link feature will consider its very own.

   Click Next.

6. In this final dialog box (see Figure 8-42), click Update Frequency to specify when the HotSync process should perform the uploading (Figure 8-43). In most cases, you'll want the default—update the PalmPilot whenever the hard-drive file is updated. To save time, however, if you know that the hard-drive file (a price list, product list, or phone list, for example) is only updated at certain intervals—every day, week, or month—you can choose those options instead.

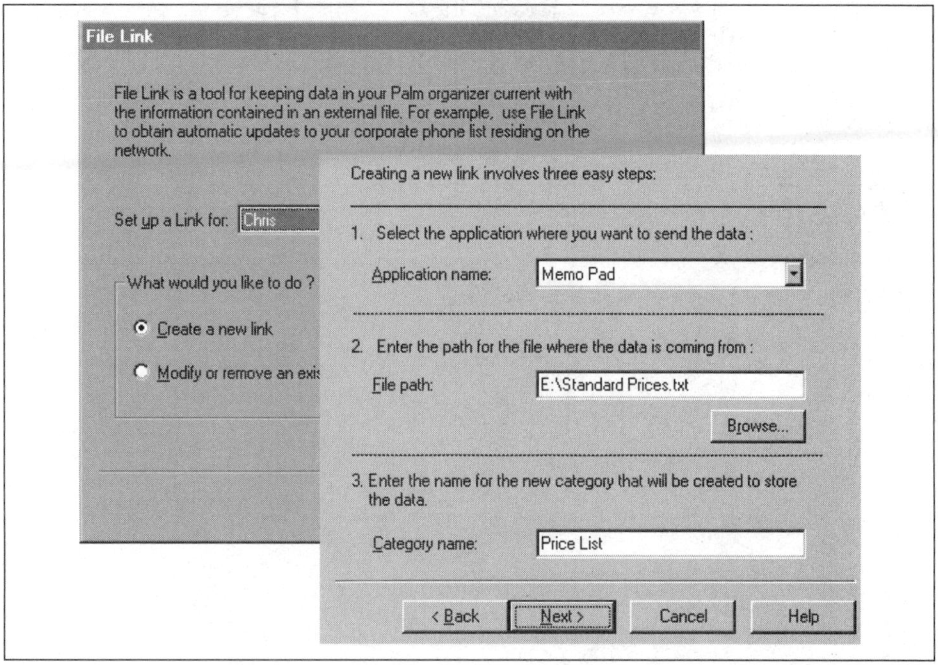

Figure 8-41. Setting up a file link begins with you. Specify whose PalmPilot you're linking to (left) and then describe the location, name, and category of the linked file (right).

This dialog box also contains the useful "Disable the link temporarily but maintain the settings" option. It turns off the file-link feature until you return to this dialog box and switch it on again—which can be handy if your phone list is updated only, for example, every six months.

7. Click OK, and then click Done.

The setup is complete. After the next HotSync, check out your PalmPilot. You should see the new category in your Address Book or Memo Pad—with the hard drive data safely transferred. Make some changes to the hard drive file and HotSync again to experience the full magic of the file-linking feature.

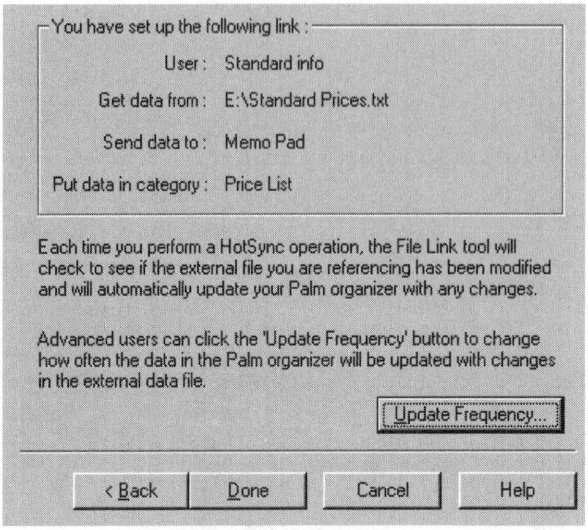

┌──┐
│ ┌─You have set up the following link :──────────────┐   │
│ │   │   │
│ │   User :   Standard info   │   │
│ │   │   │
│ │   Get data from :   E:\Standard Prices.txt   │   │
│ │   │   │
│ │   Send data to :   Memo Pad   │   │
│ │   │   │
│ │ Put data in category : Price List   │   │
│ │   │   │
│ └──┘   │
│   │
│   Each time you perform a HotSync operation, the File Link tool will │
│   check to see if the external file you are referencing has been modified │
│   and will automatically update your Palm organizer with any changes. │
│   │
│   Advanced users can click the 'Update Frequency' button to change │
│   how often the data in the Palm organizer will be updated with changes │
│   in the external data file.   │
│   ┌────────────────┐ │
│   │ Update Frequency...│ │
│   └────────────────┘ │
│   │
│   ┌─────────┐ ┌─────────┐ ┌─────────┐ ┌─────────┐   │
│   │ < Back │ │ Done   │ │ Cancel │ │ Help   │   │
│   └─────────┘ └─────────┘ └─────────┘ └─────────┘   │
└──┘

Figure 8-42. The Update Frequency button is the key to setting up an update schedule.

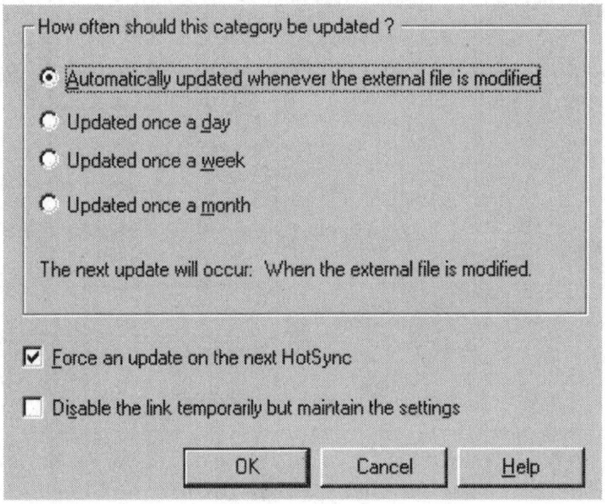

┌──┐
│ ┌─How often should this category be updated ?──────────┐ │
│ │   │ │
│ │   ⦿ Automatically updated whenever the external file is modified │ │
│ │   │ │
│ │   ○ Updated once a day   │ │
│ │   │ │
│ │   ○ Updated once a week   │ │
│ │   │ │
│ │   ○ Updated once a month   │ │
│ │   │ │
│ │   The next update will occur: When the external file is modified. │ │
│ │   │ │
│ └──┘ │
│   │
│   ☑ Force an update on the next HotSync   │
│   │
│   ☐ Disable the link temporarily but maintain the settings │
│   │
│   ┌─────────┐ ┌─────────┐ ┌─────────┐   │
│   │   OK   │ │ Cancel │ │ Help   │   │
│   └─────────┘ └─────────┘ └─────────┘   │
└──┘

Figure 8-43. Deep in the nested dialog boxes lurks the control for turning file linking on or off.

The specialized features described in this chapter—profiles and file linking—depend on which version of Palm Desktop you're using, *not* which version of the PalmPilot itself.

In other words, if you download the latest desktop software, you can use these features with whatever PalmPilot model you own.

Executive Tip Summary

- Palm Desktop is your PC's central clearinghouse for data going to and from your PalmPilot, even if it isn't your regularly scheduled address book/calendar program.

- In Palm Desktop, you can create new appointments in your Date Book by dragging Address Book names or To Do task items from the lower-right corner of the screen directly onto the day-view display.

- You can drag an event from the day-view list directly onto a tiny month-view square to reschedule it to a different date.

- Click a time-slot label at the left side of the day- or week-view display to create a new appointment at that time.

- Switch among day, week, and month views by pressing D, W, or M along with the Alt key.

- Create a blank line at the end of each address's data. That translates into a nice blank line after each address when you print out your contact list.

- In the Edit Event dialog box, each press of the + key sets the time ahead 15 minutes, and the – key sets the time earlier by 15 minutes.

- When entering new addresses into Palm Desktop, don't bother clicking OK to close the dialog box after finishing each address. Instead, press Alt-N to enter the address and refresh the dialog box to its empty, ready-for-the-next-one condition.

- Want more features? Every version works with all previous PalmPilot models. Get the latest version of Palm Desktop from Palm's web site.

9

*Palm Desktop:
Macintosh*

You might expect the Macintosh to get special treatment by the people behind the PalmPilot. After all, over 60 percent of Palm employees once worked at Apple. Inside the PalmPilot is a Motorola processor, just as in the Macintosh; the menus, buttons, and dialog boxes are modeled after the Mac's; the original Palm operating system was written on Macs (using the CodeWarrior professional software-writing kit); the Palm OS's clock calculates time from the same starting date as the Mac (1/1/1904); and so on. Furthermore, with 30 million ardent Mac fans unlikely ever to use a Windows CE palmtop, you might think that cultivating Mac-friendly tools would be a high priority for Palm Computing.

Yet until the beginning of 1999, the story of the PalmPilot's relationship to the Macintosh was an unhappy one. For years, Palm Computing upgraded and enhanced Palm Desktop for Windows—but Mac users had to slog along with the aging Pilot Desktop 1.0. Windows users happily HotSynced all information to their PCs, including email and expense-tracking data—but Mac users could HotSync only the four basic programs (address book, calendar, and so on).

Most limiting of all, for the first years of the PalmPilot's existence, there was no standard HotSync conduit technology for the Macintosh. No outside software companies could create HotSync links to their programs; where Windows users could choose from any of dozens of calendar or Rolodex programs with which to HotSync their palmtops, Pilot 1.0 Desktop was the only Macintosh software that could communicate smoothly with the PalmPilot.

Fortunately, a small but passionate group inside Palm Computing eventually persuaded the company's top brass to devote programming and financial resources to the Mac issue. After a long delay, the new Palm Desktop for Macintosh 2.1 debuted at the beginning of 1999. And, more importantly, so did a standardized

HotSync conduit that made it possible for many other kinds of Mac programs—Quicken, FileMaker, and so on—to exchange data with the PalmPilot.

This book assumes that you're using this dramatically improved software, known collectively as the MacPac 2.1. (It's available on this book's CD.) To make a new PalmPilot work with the Mac, you still need to make one additional purchase—either the $15 MacPac kit (which includes the MacPac software, a printed manual, and an adapter for your HotSync cable that fits a standard Macintosh modem port) or the $6 cable adapter by itself (which assumes that you already have the software and an electronic manual). But the resulting system is a true delight: sophisticated, fast software on the Macintosh talking to the greatest palmtop on Earth.

In attempting to track the popularity of the PalmPilot among Mac fans, Palm Computing once tallied the sales of the MacPac. The company assumed that every PalmPilot sold went to a Windows user—except when a MacPac was also purchased.

Today, however, Mac fans don't actually need to buy the MacPac. They can download the software for free and buy the necessary cradle adapter for $6 from Palm Computing (or, because it's a standard serial-port adapter, from an electronics shop). Palm Computing's once accurate gauge of Mac/PalmPilot usage is gone.

Therefore, Palm now relies on two other Mac-interest gauges. First, it watches subscription requests for InSync Online, its free email newsletter. You can sign up for it at *http://www.palm.com*—and specify that you're interested in Mac information.

Second, Palm carefully studies the registration cards for newly purchased Palm devices. If you care about the future of Palm's support for the Macintosh, mailing that card is among the most important gestures you can make. (You won't wind up on junk mail lists if you check the "I prefer not to receive mailings" checkbox.)

The Story of Palm Desktop

When Palm set out to create Palm Desktop for the Macintosh, it realized that writing such a program from scratch would take years. Instead, the company got both lucky and smart: it learned that Claris Organizer, a popular, easy-to-use calendar/address book program for the Mac, had become orphaned when Apple Computer dismantled its Claris subsidiary. Ironically, Palm's original software designers had, years earlier, used the four modules in Claris Organizer—Calendar, Contacts, Tasks, and Notes—as models for the PalmPilot's primary four programs.

Palm couldn't resist; it did the right thing and purchased Claris Organizer outright from Apple. After a year of enhancement by Palm Computing, Claris Organizer became the new Palm Desktop 2.1.

Palm Desktop is loaded with time-saving features, many of which have nothing to do with the PalmPilot. For example, Palm Desktop can:

- Dial the phone automatically, using either your Mac's modem or the speaker

- Create reminders for your appointments and to do items that pop up on your Mac's screen at the appropriate time

- Perform automatic data entry as you type: capitalizing your address book information as you enter it, completing long city and state names as you begin to type, adding parentheses and dashes to your phone numbers, and so on

- Print mailing labels, portable phone books, and DayRunner-type pages in every conceivable orientation and size, including double-sided pages—even in color

- Attach Macintosh documents on your hard drive to various names, appointments, and so on in Palm Desktop (so that you can, for example, double-click your to do item called "submit quarterly report" and launch the actual report in your word processor)

- Communicate, via AppleScript, with such programs as Outlook Express, Eudora, Claris Emailer, ClarisWorks, and so on (for automatic form-letter or email generation, for example)

Palm Desktop for Windows, Mac fans may be pleased to learn, doesn't offer any of those features.

The Problem with Too Many Features

Despite the luxuries of using Palm Desktop, this long list of features poses one challenging problem: the four Palm Desktop modules aren't identical to the corresponding PalmPilot applications. For example, Palm Desktop has room for secondary mailing addresses in your address book, but the PalmPilot doesn't. Palm Desktop lets you place a person, a memo, or to do item in more than one category simultaneously; the PalmPilot can assign only one.

Fortunately, Palm Desktop's programmers decided to leave the extra features in the Mac software, rather than ripping them out purely for the sake of making them match the PalmPilot. But that decision means that not all information is HotSynced in ways that you would expect; much of this chapter is designed to help you understand the differences between Palm Desktop and the PalmPilot's own software.

What Palm Desktop Is Good For

Remember, the PalmPilot was originally designed not to be a standalone computer, but instead to be a satellite of the computer you already have. Palm Desktop, therefore, is the central station for information going to or from the PalmPilot. For example, you use Palm Desktop to:

- Import addresses or memos from another program, ready to upload into the PalmPilot

- Retrieve data you deleted long ago from the PalmPilot

- Manage the backing up (or loading up) of many different PalmPilots from the same Mac

- Print your PalmPilot data (one of the few things that are difficult to do with the PalmPilot alone)

Getting Your Older Data into Palm Desktop

The manual that accompanies Palm Desktop (which is in electronic form on this book's CD) goes into detail on importing information into Palm Desktop from such programs as FileMaker, Now Up-to-Date/Now Contact, QuickDex, Touch-Base, DateBook Pro, DynoDex, and so on. The steps essentially follow those in Chapter 8, *Palm Desktop: Windows*, in the section "Importing Addresses from Other Programs."

The most frequently asked questions, however, are "How do I bring my old Claris Organizer data into Palm Desktop?" and "How do I bring my information into Palm Desktop from Pilot Desktop 1.0?"

Claris Organizer

Launch Palm Desktop. Choose File → Merge, locate your old Organizer file, and double-click it. All your old information is now incorporated into Palm Desktop.

Pilot Desktop

Because Pilot Desktop is nothing more than a brain dump from your PalmPilot, simply HotSync once. Then install the new MacPac, and HotSync again—all your data is now safely at home in the new Mac software.

Controlling Palm Desktop

Palm Desktop, the application itself, is the center attraction of the MacPac. You'll understand it better, however, if you first get to know its two ancillary software helpers: the Instant Palm Desktop menu and the Palm Desktop toolbar.

Instant Palm Desktop

One of the most attractive features in the 1999 Mac software suite is the small, green menubar icon shown in Figure 9-1. Its official name is Instant Palm Desktop; its purpose is to give you instant access to the best parts of the new software. The lower half of the menu shows a list of today's appointments and dated to do items (those that are due or overdue), along with your most important phone numbers.

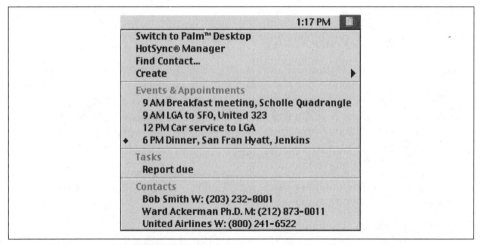

Figure 9-1. The Instant Palm Desktop icon on your menu bar gives you access to all of the PalmPilot-related functions on the Macintosh—and even shows your most important phone numbers, appointments, and to do items.

The upper half of the menu, however, contains four powerful commands that control the Palm Desktop data and save you steps:

Switch to Palm Desktop

> This command is the quickest way to launch the Palm Desktop program itself. It saves you from having to burrow into your hard drive to find the Palm folder, where the actual Palm Desktop program sits.

HotSync Manager

> This command launches the extremely important HotSync Manager program, described later in this chapter. (HotSync Manager installs new programs onto

your palmtop, controls which data gets exchanged with your Mac, allows you to use your modem port for other functions, and more.)

Find Contact...

Use this command to look up a phone number—without actually having to launch Palm Desktop.

Create

This command lets you add new appointments, phone numbers, to-do items, and memos on the fly, instantly, no matter what program you're using at the time—without having to launch Palm Desktop. Efficiency nuts adore this feature.

If you click the Instant Palm Desktop icon and see only the words "Starting Up," your Mac may not know which PalmPilot's data it's supposed to be showing. For example, this is the case when you first install the software and have not yet HotSynced.

To solve the problem, launch Palm Desktop. Choose File → Open, and then locate and open your Palm folder → Users → [your Palm-Pilot's name] → User Data file. When you quit Palm Desktop, the menu-bar icon should now produce a menu that reflects your newly selected PalmPilot data.

The Palm Desktop Toolbar

Once you are in the actual Palm Desktop program, the toolbar at the top of the screen roughly corresponds to the Application launcher on your PalmPilot. Figure 9-2 identifies its icons. (You can also point to one of these icons with the cursor to reveal its name in the status area of the toolbar.)

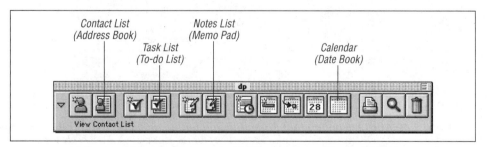

Figure 9-2. The Palm Desktop toolbar summons the various information displays.

You'll read more about the toolbar icons later in this chapter. For now, note the four buttons identified in Figure 9-2; they correspond to the four basic Palm applications—address book, to-do list, memo pad, and date book.

If your monitor is small or unusually shaped, you're not condemned to viewing the toolbar in its default shape. Click the tiny triangle at its left edge, for example, to hide the status area, thus conserving vertical screen space. Or choose Edit → Preferences → General, where you'll find a pop-up menu that lets you hide the toolbar completely (choose None) or turn it into a floating strip that you can drag anywhere on your screen (choose Floating).

Date Book (Calendar)

Whenever you launch Palm Desktop, the calendar comes up first. As you can see in Figure 9-3, you get a far more informative display on the Mac than on the PalmPilot's tiny screen. This calendar, like the PalmPilot's, offers three views, here called Daily, Weekly, and Monthly; switch by clicking the tabs of the right side of the screen. Instead of gray bars, as on the PalmPilot, the actual titles of your appointments are readable.

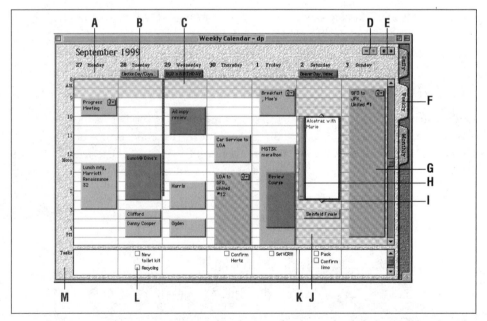

Figure 9-3. To see your appointments and to-do items for the week, click the Weekly tab at the right side of the screen (or press Command-Shift-W).

You can click the View Calendar icon (indicated at right in Figure 9-2) repeatedly to switch among Daily, Weekly, and Monthly views.

Weekly View

You create and edit events in Palm Desktop primarily by using the mouse. Here are a few examples of places you can click in the Weekly view (most of these elements also appear in Daily view):

A. Double-click a date header to add a new untimed event (which is called a banner in Palm Desktop, even if it spans only one day), such as a birthday or anniversary.

B. Untimed events (banners) appear at the top of each day, like this. (This area grows taller to accommodate multiple untimed events.)

C. This area is a map of your day. The white areas represent your working hours, as defined in Edit → Preferences → Calendars. The fat black or colored line at the left edge of the appointments area is like a sundial, growing longer as the day goes by. (The bottom end of this fat line indicates the current time.)

D. In Weekly view, you can control how many days are shown in a single screen, from seven days down to a single day. Click these buttons to add or subtract "day slices" from the display.

E. Click here to view the next or previous week's schedule. (In Monthly view, these buttons shift the calendar by a month.) To view a week that's too far away to be worth clicking these buttons, choose Locate → Go To Date (or click the corresponding toolbar icon). A tiny calendar display appears, much like the one in Figure 4-4 (back in Chapter 4, *The Four Primary Programs*). By tapping on that calendar display, you can jump to any day, anywhere in the past or future. (See Chapter 4 for instructions on using this display.)

 If you've been viewing your schedule for some past or future week, choose Locate → Today, or click the corresponding toolbar icon. The current day is always indicated by a blackened vertical bar, as shown in Figure 9-3, or (in Monthly view) date number..

F. These tabs switch between Daily, Weekly, and Monthly views.

G. To reschedule an appointment, drag it to another time slot or another day. To move it to a date not visible on the screen, double-click it, and then read "Editing an Event," later in this section. To delete it, click once and then press the Delete key.

H. The gripper. Click an appointment to make this vertical handle appear. Double-click this vertical strip to display the dialog box in Figure 9-4, where you have the opion to change an item's time, repeat schedule, and so on. Alternatively, drag this handle up or down to reschedule the event to a different time; drag it horizontally or diagonally to move the event to a different day during the week.

I. The duration handle. These small triangles appear only when an event is selected—that is, when you've clicked on it. If you move your cursor carefully over the duration handle, the cursor's shape changes to a double-headed arrow. You can now drag up or down to make this event taller or shorter (that is, stretching over more or less time), as shown in Figure 9-4.

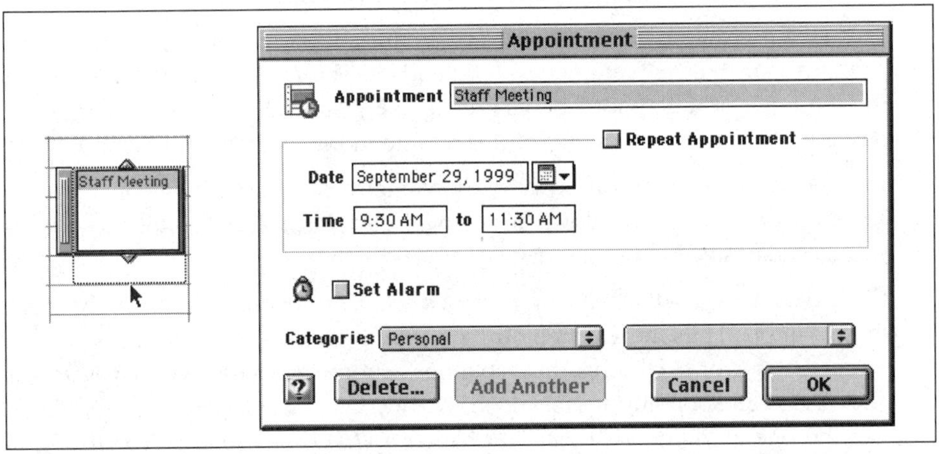

Figure 9-4. Don't you wish it were this easy to shorten actual staff meetings in real life? At right: the Appointment dialog box.

J. The quickest way to create a new event is to drag vertically in any unoccupied area, corresponding to the beginning and ending times of the appointment you're making. Palm Desktop creates a blank appointment rectangle. Type a description for the event—don't worry if you type past the bottom of the little text area; the display scrolls automatically—and then press Return or Enter to complete your entry (and deselect the appointment block).

Thereafter, you can double-click the appointment to adjust the starting, ending, or repeat characteristics of your event.

K. Drag this border up or down to adjust the relative amount of space devoted on your screen to the calendar and the to-do items.

L. Beneath each slice of day is a list of any to-do items that are come due on that day. (Normal, non-time-limited to-do items don't show up on your calendar at all; see Chapter 4 for details on assigning due dates to your to-do tasks.) To indicate that you have completed a to-do item, click its checkbox.

M. Palm Desktop lets you change its background color, texture, and typeface scheme according to your mood. Choose Edit → Preferences → Decor, and click to select an interior design scheme that pleases you.

Keyboard shortcut–lover's note: You can press Command-right arrow and Command-left arrow to change the calendar display by one day, week, or month at a time (depending on which view you're looking at). If you press Option at the same time, you jump seven days at a time in Daily or Weekly views.

Command-up and Command-down arrows also accomplishes something useful: in Daily and Weekly views, they scroll the appointment display.

Daily View

To open Daily view, click the Daily tab at the right side of the screen, or press Command-Shift-D. This view closely resembles a single slice of the Weekly view, except that your to-do items appear to the right of your appointments. Otherwise, this view works exactly the same as Weekly view: drag vertically to create a new appointment, click the Create Event Banner toolbar icon to create an untimed event, drag an appointment to reschedule it, and so on.

When you first run Palm Desktop, it displays a time grid in half-hour increments. That may not be enough precision for a dentist who needs to schedule patients for, say, 10-minute appointments.

If you fall into that category, choose Edit → Preferences → Calendars. Use the Time Interval pop-up menu to specify 10-minute increments, 15, 30, or whatever.

Monthly View

Palm Desktop's month view is a dramatic improvement over the PalmPilot's own month display; on the Mac, you can actually read the titles of your appointments and create new ones right on the calendar squares.

In this view, shown in Figure 9-5, you can manipulate your information in any of the following ways:

- Drag an appointment onto a different calendar square to reschedule it.

- Double-click an empty place on a square to produce the dialog box shown in Figure 9-6. Specify whether you are adding an appointment, a to-do item whose deadline is the square you clicked, or an event banner (untimed event) that begins on the square you clicked. You then proceed to the dialog box shown in Figure 9-7.

- Double-click the number of a certain date (in the upper-left corner of each calendar square) to jump to the Daily view for that date.

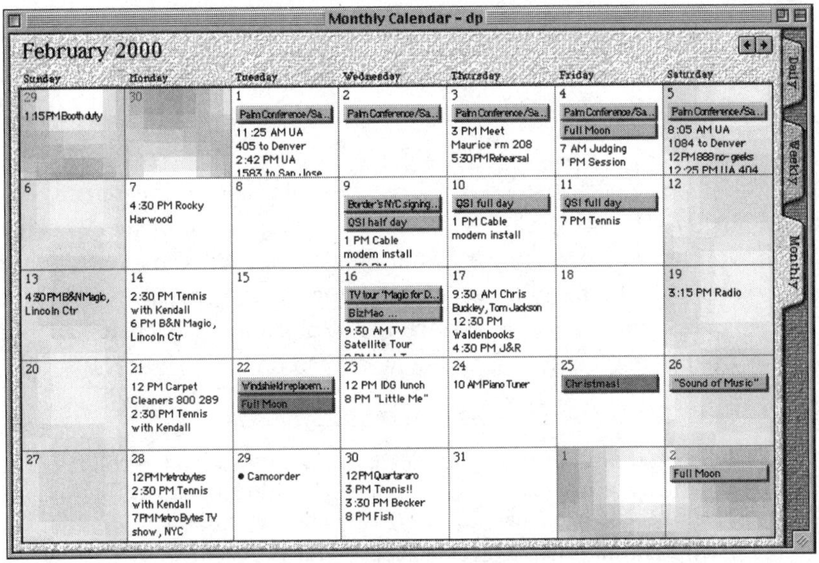

Figure 9-5. In Monthly view, up to five weeks at a time are visible in one glance.

Editing an Event

As Palm Desktop becomes an increasingly important part of your organizational life, you'll become familiar indeed with the dialog box shown in Figure 9-7. It appears whenever you create a new appointment, or whenever you edit an appointment by double-clicking it or its gripper handle.

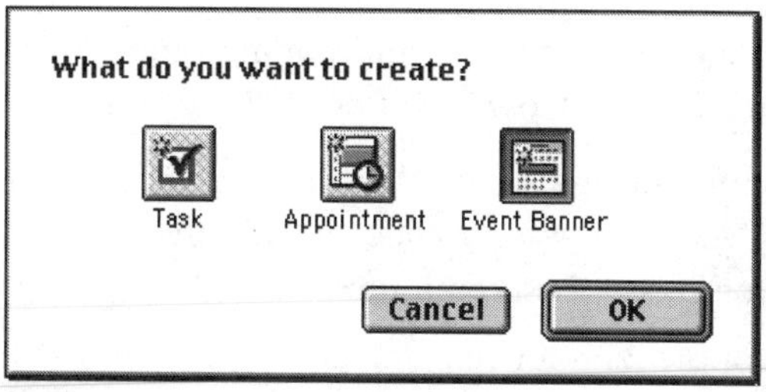

Figure 9-6. Specify what kind of event you are adding to the monthly view calendar. You don't have to click the icon you want—you can type the first letter of its name and then press Return.

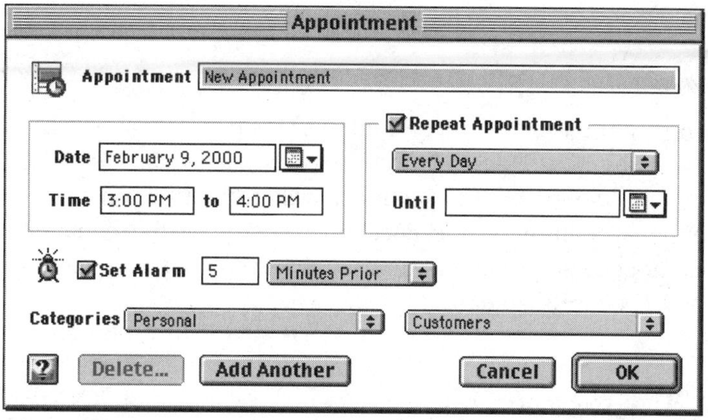

Figure 9-7. You specify an appointment's begin and end times and alarm, repeat, and category status in this dialog box.

As in any Macintosh dialog box, you move from blank to blank in this box by pressing the Tab key. Start by typing the description of your event, such as "Dinner with Chris downtown." (This description can be 255 characters long, exactly as on the PalmPilot.)

Changing the date

Then tab your way into the Date blank; you'll generally have summoned the Appointment dialog box by clicking a calendar square, so you'll very rarely actually type out a date here. But if your aim is to change the date, click the tiny icon to the right of the Date blank to make the pop-up calendar appear, which is generally faster than typing out the full date. (You can also press the + and – keys to choose later and earlier dates.)

Changing the time

Finally, you can change the beginning and ending times by tabbing into the Time boxes. Various typing shortcuts await you here. For example:

- Type the minimum necessary—8a suffices to indicate "8:00 a.m.," and 135 indicates "1:35." As soon as you click outside the box or press Tab or Enter, Palm Desktop completes the typing for you.

- These boxes support 24-hour military time for increased efficiency. That is, if you type 2115, Palm Desktop understands you to mean 9:15 p.m.

- The + and − keys on your keyboard set the currently selected hour forward or backward. Add Shift to adjust the minutes.

- You can use the period instead of a colon. To specify 6:20, for example, you can type 6.2 and be done with it.

Repeats and alarms

The Set Alarm feature lets you set up reminder beeps that will go off both on your PalmPilot (after the next HotSync) and on your Macintosh. (The Macintosh must be turned on at the time; the PalmPilot will turn itself on at the appointed moment.) When you turn on the checkbox, you'll see the controls that govern when the alarm goes off: 10 minutes before the event begins, 3 days, or whatever, exactly as described in Chapter 4.

When you create a new appointment in Palm Desktop, you have to turn on the Alarm option if you want one. Furthermore, Palm Desktop always proposes "5 minutes before" as the alarm setting. That is, the PalmPilot (and the Mac) will begin chirping five minutes before the actual appointment.

But what if *most* of your appointments require an alarm? If you like, you can specify that all events should start out with an alarm—and then turn the alarm setting off on the appointments that don't need one. Furthermore, you can change the default advance-notice time if "5 minutes" isn't appropriate.

To change these defaults, choose Edit → Preferences → Calendars. Turn on the "Set alarm on new appointments" checkbox, and adjust the advance-notice controls (to, say, "1 hour before"). From now on, whenever you create a new appointment in Palm Desktop, it will automatically be set to have an alarm—and the "time before" setting will be preset to your new preference.

The Appointment dialog box also contains a Repeat Appointment checkbox that, when selected, lets you specify that this event happens more than once (every day, once a month, and so on)—exactly as described in Chapter 4. Exactly like the PalmPilot, the Mac also lets you specify an ending date for this cycle of repeating events.

In Palm Desktop, you can set an appointment up to repeat multiple times each month, such as "Disco class" on the first and third Tuesdays of the month. The PalmPilot, however, offers no such option; it can schedule an event to repeat only once every month (or, of course, on specific days every week).

Therefore, when you HotSync, the PalmPilot doesn't treat these events as part of a two-per-month repeat. Instead, it stores two separate monthly repeating events—in this example, a first-Tuesday-of-the-month repeating event, and a third-Tuesday-of-the-month repeating event. In other words, all of the appointments get transferred; all you lose is the behind-the-scenes association of repeat information. This effect is evident only when you want to edit one of these events on the PalmPilot—you'll discover that changing the time for a first-Tuesday dance class, for example, changes all the PalmPilot's first-Tuesday classes, but leaves the third-Tuesday editions untouched.

Printing Your Calendar

Unlike its Windows counterpart, Palm Desktop for the Macintosh is an absolute genius at printing (see Figure 9-8). The built-in online help (choose Help → Search Index For) contains extensive instructions, under the heading "printing," for specifying what appointments you want to print, and in what format. You can specify how many virtual pages you want to print per sheet of paper; single-sided or double-sided pages; special formats for Franklin, DayRunner, Day-Timer, and other paper organizers; daily, weekly, or monthly calendars; simple lists of appointments; what font and size you prefer; what auxiliary information (such as banners and to-do items) you want included; and much more. (The Palm Desktop user guide includes not only instructions, but illustrations and examples.)

What Doesn't Get HotSynced

All the essentials are updated in both directions when you HotSync: the names, times, and dates of your appointments; alarms; repeating-event information; untimed events (that is, one-day banners in Palm Desktop); and so on. A few aspects of the data exchange may take you by surprise—see Table 9-1.

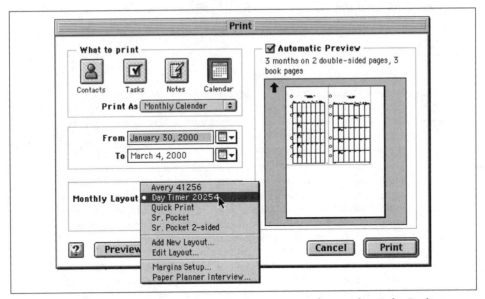

Figure 9-8. These options appear on the Mac when you print from within Palm Desktop.

Table 9-1. Mac-to-Palm Eccentricities (Calendar)

On Palm Desktop	On the PalmPilot
Categories	The PalmPilot's Date Book doesn't offer a category feature, so no category information is HotSynced.
Events that repeat within the month	As noted earlier, this kind of appointment will correctly show up in your PalmPilot's Date Book, but will be stored as multiple once-per-month repeating events.
Multiday banners	The PalmPilot can't create events that span more than one day, so it turns a Palm Desktop banner into a series of consecutive one-day untimed events (such as "Chicago trip").

Interestingly, the PalmPilot itself offers a few features that Palm Desktop doesn't. Here, too, you should be aware of some discrepancies when HotSyncing (see Table 9-2).

Table 9-2. Palm-to-Mac Eccentricities (Calendar)

On the PalmPilot	On Palm Desktop
Repeating untimed events	Palm Desktop's banners can't be made to repeat (except annual ones, such as birthdays, holidays, and anniversaries). If your Palm-Pilot contains untimed events you've set up to repeat weekly or monthly, these events don't get transferred to your Mac at all. (A HotSync error message will tell you so.)

Table 9-2. Palm-to-Mac Eccentricities (Calendar) (continued)

On the PalmPilot	On Palm Desktop
Repeating daily untimed events	As noted above, the PalmPilot offers no banner feature that lets you indicate that some event, such as a trip, lasts more than one day. Instead, you must create an untimed event that repeats daily. When transferred to Palm Desktop, however, such daily repeating events are intelligently and automatically converted into multiday banners.
Alarms on untimed events	Palm Desktop doesn't offer alarms on untimed events, so this information doesn't get transferred to the Mac—except, oddly enough, if the untimed event has been set to repeat. (If you really want an alarm for a one-time-only untimed event on your Mac, therefore, set it to repeat every fifty years!)

Address Book (Contact List)

The gem of Palm Desktop is, without a doubt, its Address Book module. Learn to understand its shortcuts, and you'll be astounded at how quickly you can input and manipulate large amounts of address book information.

To open the address book, click the second icon on the toolbar, or press Command-Shift-C. You're shown your contact information as a giant list, as shown in Figure 9-9. You can find somebody's name extremely quickly—just type the first couple of letters of the last name, exactly as on the PalmPilot; Palm Desktop scrolls to the closest match and highlight's the name for you. You can open the editing screen shown in Figure 9-10 by double-clicking any row of the list.

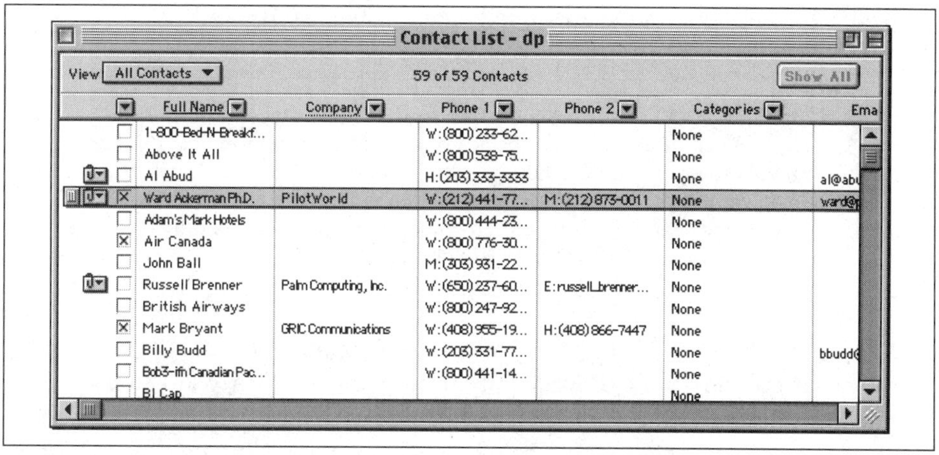

Figure 9-9. The Address Book, or Contact List, in Palm Desktop lets you rearrange or adjust the widths of all columns.

Entering New Contacts

Most people begin life in Palm Desktop by importing their collection of addresses and appointments from an existing program, or from the PalmPilot itself. If, however, you're required to type names and addresses into Palm Desktop directly, you'll be delighted by the time-saving tricks.

- Start by clicking the very first icon on the toolbar. The Contact editor dialog box appears, as shown in Figure 9-10. Go to work typing in each piece of information, pressing Tab to jump from blank to blank, and keep in mind these conveniences:

- Don't bother pressing the Shift key; Palm Desktop capitalizes the first letter of each name automatically. (The on/off switch for this feature is in Edit → Preferences → Contacts.)

- When you're finished filling in one block of information, such as the Phones section, press Return or Enter twice; your cursor jumps into the next information area. Palm Desktop is designed so that you never have to take your hands off the keyboard when entering information.

- You don't have to format your phone number with parentheses and hyphens, and you don't have to type in the area code when the phone number is local. By choosing Edit → Preferences → Contacts, you can select an automatic formatting option for your phone numbers, such as (###) ###-####. If you also specify your default area code in this preferences box, such as 707, you'll be able to type as little as 8290515 when entering phone numbers; Palm Desktop will automatically reformat that number as (707) 829-0515.

 In Figure 9-10, note the checkbox to the right of each phone number. When selected, this checkbox adds the corresponding phone number to your Instant Palm Desktop menu, as shown in Figure 9-1. You've just designated this phone number as one for which you'd like quick access from within any Mac program, saving you the trouble of having to look it up or launch Palm Desktop.

- Certain fields, such as the City, State, and Country blanks, offer a pop-up menu. It contains a list of frequently used entries (which you can edit using the Edit Menu command of this pop-up menu). You can select any of these entries by typing only the first couple letters—AL for Albuquerque, for example; Palm Desktop automatically completes the term for you. (Press Tab or click outside the field to accept the entry, or keep typing to override it.) You can also choose such entries from the pop-up menu itself, but that thwarts the speed freak's desire to keep hands on the keyboard at all times. The on/off switch for this feature is in Edit → Preferences → Contacts → Auto-completion.

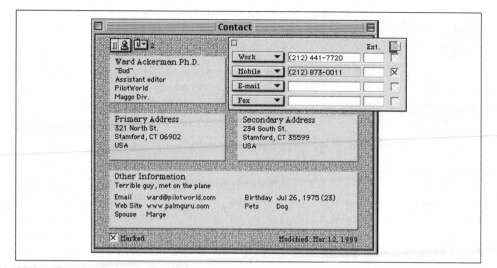

Figure 9-10. While editing an address, you can press Return to open each successive block of information.

> If you enter a birthday on a person's contact card, Palm Desktop automatically creates an untimed event (banner) on your calendar for that birthday.

Categories

Exactly as on the PalmPilot itself, you can assign each name in your address book to a category (such as Business, Personal, NYC Xmas Cards, and so on)—two different categories, in fact. (See Chapter 4 for a complete lesson on the use of categories.) Use the two pop-up menus in the Other Information area of the Contact dialog box.

You can edit your list of category names by choosing Edit Categories from either of these pop-up menus. Your new category names will be transferred to the PalmPilot at your next HotSync, up to the PalmPilot's limit of 15 categories (and 15 characters per category name).

Anticipating the HotSync Process

Taking care during the data-input stage can save you headaches later when you HotSync. For example, on the PalmPilot, the *first* phone number you enter becomes the "main" phone number, the one displayed on the Palm Address Book's "home page" for each person. In Palm Desktop, however, the *top* phone number will become the main display phone number. (You're still free to select a different arrangement of phone number labels—such as Home, Work, and Fax— for each person in your address book, however.)

Another caution: resist the temptation to use the Email label in the first block of four phone numbers in Palm Desktop. Instead, enter each email address in the Email field at the bottom of the Contact window (in the Other Information area). Only this field is HotSynced to the corresponding Palm Address Book email field.

Finally, note that Palm Desktop, like the PalmPilot itself, offers a choice of Custom fields, which you're free to rename in any way you see fit—Spouse name, Pets, Favorite Wine, whatever. Using Edit → Preferences → Contacts → Custom Fields, you can specify that you'd like up to 11 such fields in Palm Desktop—but remember that the PalmPilot only has room for four; any others will be displayed only on the Mac. Also remember that, as on the PalmPilot, the Custom fields' labels apply to everyone in your contact list—unlike the phone number labels, they can't vary by person. (You change a Custom field's label by choosing Field Options from the pop-up menu to its right. Any change you make will be transferred to the PalmPilot at the next HotSync.)

Fields, Sorting, Categories, and Other Options

Once you've imported or typed in your list of names and addresses, you can easily manipulate, sort, and find names using the main list view. (To open this list, click the second toolbar icon.)

Sort order

> You can sort your list by any criteria: name, company, Zip Code, and so on. To do so, simply click the name of the corresponding column so that an underline appears, as shown in Figure 9-9 under the Full Name column header.

 You can create a secondary sort by Shift-clicking or Option-clicking a column name. For example, suppose you want to view your list of contacts alphabetically by company name, but sorted by name within each company group. Click the column heading Company, and then Shift-click the Full Name column heading. A dotted underline indicates the secondary sort criteria.

Filtering

> Palm Desktop's powerful filtering feature lets you see only the names that match certain criteria, such as those belonging to a particular Zip Code. Here again, the secret lies in the headings above each column of information. To

view only your Business contacts, for example, choose Business from the Categories pop-up menu; all other contacts are hidden. (To view your entire list again, click the Show All button at the upper-right corner of the window.)

Using the Custom Filter command from that column-header pop-up menu, you can even choose to view contacts in several categories at once—Business and Travel, for example. (There's nothing to stop you from using the Filter commands of several columns simultaneously—to view your Business contacts only in area code 212, for example.)

Adjusting your columns

You can drag a column header horizontally to rearrange the columns in your contact list. You can also drag the thin gray dividing lines between columns to adjust their relative widths.

Hiding unused columns

Double-click the gap between column names to open the Column dialog box. Click to make checkmarks appear or disappear, and drag column names up or down to change their order.

Memorizing views

Suppose you've spent several minutes setting up filters that show a very specific list of people: those with last name Smith, with area code 310, in the Owe Me Money category, for example. And suppose you need to call up this list every month. Instead of re-creating this elaborate filter every month, choose Memorize View from the View pop-up menu (at the upper-left corner of the Contact List window). Palm Desktop offers to memorize this particular arrangement of filters (and, if you like, the sorting order, column arrangements, and window positions, as well). In the future, simply choose that view's name from the Views pop-up menu to restore the saved list and filter configuration.

Printing and Copying Addresses

Palm Desktop can do much more with your address book information than send it to the PalmPilot. For example, don't miss the Edit → Copy Special command, where you'll see several commands that let you copy neatly formatted, ready-to-paste mailing addresses to the Clipboard. The online help offers elaborate instructions for printing mailing labels and paper address books. You can even integrate your contact list with such AppleScript-savvy word processors as AppleWorks or ClarisWorks and email programs like Claris Emailer (for generating form letters, for example), as described at the end of this chapter.

Selecting Multiple Items in Palm Desktop Lists

Suppose you're cleaning up your address book. As you look through your list, you find a surprising number of people whose entries you'd like to delete. Rather than deleting them one at a time, you can select individual names or clumps of names, and then delete them all at once. Mastering the art of selecting from Palm Desktop's lists pays off in many ways—this is also how you select a group of items to print, duplicate, drag to another item as an attachment, assign to a different category (using the Edit → Categories command), and so on, in any of Palm Desktop's four modules.

The scheme is simple: click once to select one item. Shift-click to add individual items to the selection. Command-click to select a group of consecutive list items (everything between the Command-click and your original click is highlighted). For example, to select items 1–10 and 12–20, you'd click item 1, then Command-click item 10; you'd then Shift-click item 12, and finally Command-click item 20.

What Doesn't Get HotSynced

Palm Desktop's Address Book holds more kinds of information than the Palm-Pilot's own Address Book. It's worth noting, therefore, that only essential information—name, four phone numbers (and their labels), primary address, category, and comments—gets transferred to the palmtop. Other categories of information require special treatment (see Table 9-3).

Table 9-3 Mac-to-Palm Eccentricities (Address Book)

On Palm Desktop	On the PalmPilot
Categories	You can assign each contact to two different categories in Palm Desktop, but only the first category is recorded on the PalmPilot—and then only if that category is among the first 15 in Palm Desktop's address book.
Prefix, suffix, nickname, division	The PalmPilot has no fields to hold this information, so it doesn't get transferred.
Comments	Anything you type into the Comments field of a contact card becomes a Note attached to the address on the PalmPilot.
Second address	Because the PalmPilot lacks fields for a second address, this information is also stored as a Note associated with the address on your PalmPilot.
Birthday, age, web site	These tidbits, too, become Notes on the PalmPilot.

Table 9-3 Mac-to-Palm Eccentricities (Address Book) (continued)

On Palm Desktop	On the PalmPilot
Custom fields	The first four of these, with their labels, get transferred to the PalmPilot. If you've created more custom fields than this in Palm Desktop, that information remains on the Mac.
Attachments and notes	See "Attachments and Notes," later in this chapter.

As you can imagine, the Palm Desktop/PalmPilot HotSync scheme entrusts a lot of information to the Notes attached to your addresses. The finished note might well look like this on your PalmPilot:

```
[Secondary address]
526 North Avenue
Cleveland, OH 44122

[Birthday] July 26, 1975 (24)
[Web site] www.palmguru.com

[Comments]
Nice guy with eye patch, met on the plane to Detroit
```

Although this information doesn't appear in individual fields on the PalmPilot, you can actually edit it. At the next HotSync, the original fields in Palm Desktop will reflect the changes you've made, exactly as you would hope.

To Do List (Task List)

To view your to-do list in Palm Desktop, click the fourth icon on the toolbar, or press Command-Shift-T. The list that then appears bears many similarities to the address book list; see "Address Book (Contact List)" in the previous section for details on sorting, rearranging, or changing the widths of these columns, and using Palm Desktop's filters to selectively hide to-do information.

In general, this list works exactly the way you'd expect. Click the checkbox to indicate that you've completed a task; click an item and then press the Delete or Backspace key to get rid of one; double-click an item to open the dialog box shown in Figure 9-11, where you can change its priority, reassign its category, and so on.

To create a new task, click the third toolbar icon (or press Command-Option-T). The dialog box shown in Figure 9-11 appears, where you can name your task, assign it a priority from Highest to Lowest (corresponding to the PalmPilot's priorities 1 through 5), and so on.

Dialing the Phone from Palm Desktop

Suppose that, while in the middle of a Microsoft Word session, you decide to call your Aunt Martha. Without even launching Palm Desktop, you choose Find Contact from the Instant Palm Desktop menu (see Figure 9-1). You type only three letters—MAR—and Martha's phone number appears in the dialog box. You press return (or click the Display button) to view her full card of information—and a click on the Work telephone icon dials her number. You pick up the phone and begin your conversation.

By default, Palm Desktop dials using your Mac's own speaker; simply holding your handset up to the Mac's speaker during the dialing works amazingly well. If both your telephone and your modem are connected to the Mac, however, you may find that the modem dials the phone faster and even more accurately. To set this up, launch Palm Desktop. Choose Edit → Preferences → Dialing; from the Dial Through pop-up menu, choose Modem Port. On this screen, you'll find other options pertaining to dialing, such as long-distance prefixes and suffixes.

When it comes time to dial, just pick up your telephone handset as soon as you hear the modem finished dialing. As far as your phone company is concerned, you simply dialed the phone yourself—with impressive speed.

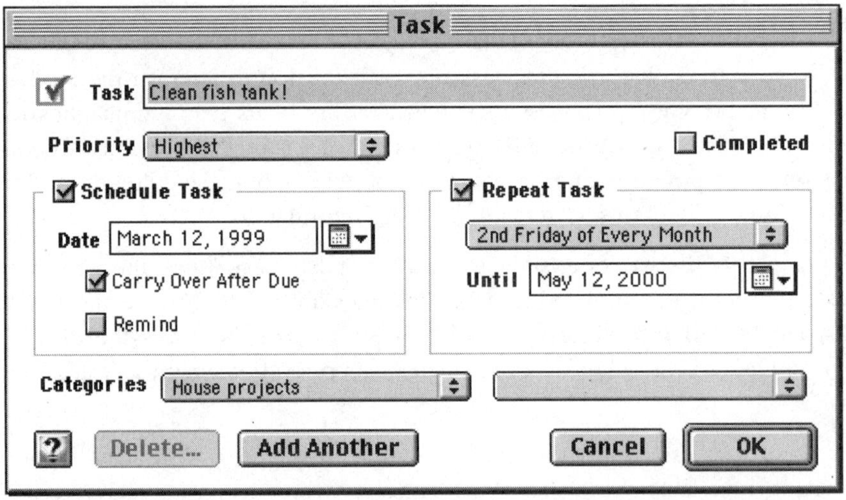

Figure 9-11. Palm Desktop's To Do list offers more features than the PalmPilot's own.

If you're in the habit of assigning due dates to your to-do items, such tasks show up on your calendar, too. As a shortcut to creating a new to-do item, double-click any empty area of the to-do list region of the Weekly or Daily calendar displays. (In Monthly view, double-click a calendar square and then click the Task icon in the dialog box that appears.)

What Doesn't Get HotSynced

As in the other modules, Palm Desktop's To Do module offers more features than the PalmPilot itself does, which can create some surprises when you HotSync. See Table 9-4 for examples.

Table 9-4. Mac-to-Palm Eccentricities (To Do List)

On Palm Desktop	On the PalmPilot
Alarms	Without add-on shareware, the PalmPilot doesn't let you associate alarms with to-do items. Although these alarms work great on the Mac, they don't get transferred to the palmtop.
Categories	As with other information in Palm Desktop, you can assign your to-do items to two different categories, if you like. But only the first category is recorded on the PalmPilot.
Carry Over After Due	This checkbox, shown in Figure 9-11, is available only on to-do items for which you've scheduled a deadline. This option ensures that such a task will continue to appear on your Palm Desktop calendar until you check off the task, even when the deadline has already passed. Because the PalmPilot *always* displays overdue to-do items (marked by an exclamation point, as shown in Chapter 4), it ignores this Palm Desktop setting.
Repeating to-do items	If you've set up a task to appear, say, once each month, all occurrences appear in the PalmPilot's To Do module after a HotSync. But the PalmPilot treats such events as unrelated; if you edit one on the PalmPilot, the others don't change. The PalmPilot's built-in to do list program doesn't offer a repeat feature.
Attachments and notes	See "Attachments and Notes," later in this chapter.

Memo Pad (Note List)

To view the list of Notes, as shown in Figure 9-12, click the sixth icon on the toolbar (or press Command-Shift-N). This list's sorting, filtering, and selecting features are the same as those described in "Address Book (Contact List)," earlier in this chapter.

To create a new memo, click the Create Note icon on the toolbar or press Command-Option-N. Type a title for the memo—this will become the first line of the memo as it shows up on the PalmPilot—and then tab into the main text box to type the body in the memo.

The first-time user of Palm Desktop is inevitably surprised. There, nestled among the familiar memos from the PalmPilot's Memo Pad module, are long lists of strange items called "Handheld Note: Date Book," "Handheld Note: Address Book," and so on. Don't let these items disturb you; they're all part of the master plan, described in "Attachments and Notes," later in this chapter.

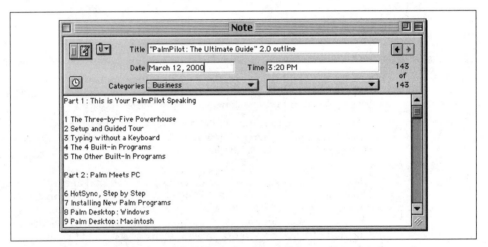

Figure 9-12. The Memo Pad module of Palm Desktop holds much more information per page than the actual PalmPilot.

What Doesn't Get HotSynced

Not all of Palm Desktop's Notes data gets transferred to the PalmPilot at HotSync time. See Table 9-5 for examples.

Table 9-5. Mac-to-Palm Eccentricities (Memo Pad)

On Palm Desktop	On the PalmPilot
Date and time	The PalmPilot Memo Pad doesn't have date and time fields, so this information isn't transferred to the palmtop. On the other hand, if you create a memo on the PalmPilot, Palm Desktop automatically fills in these fields with the date and time of the HotSync during which the memo was sent to the Mac.

Table 9-5. Mac-to-Palm Eccentricities (Memo Pad) (continued)

On Palm Desktop	On the PalmPilot
Categories	As in the other Palm Desktop modules, the PalmPilot permits only one category affiliation per memo; if you associate a second category with a Palm Desktop note, that information is ignored when you HotSync. (And as always, your category selection is only transferred to the PalmPilot if it's among the first 15 you've created in Palm Desktop.)
Long notes	Although Palm Desktop can accommodate a huge amount of text in each memo—about 24 pages' worth—only about the first 4K (about a page and a half, the limit of a Palm memo) gets transferred to the PalmPilot. (Be careful editing such memos on the PalmPilot; when you HotSync again, the truncated memo replaces the full-length one on Palm Desktop.)
Attachments and notes	See "Attachments and Notes" later in this chapter.

Expense Module

Palm Desktop ignores any data you recorded in the PalmPilot's Expense program, as described in Chapter 5, *The Other Built-In Programs*. But the MacPac comes with a clever little program called Informed Filler that turns your expense data into properly totaled and categorized expense reports, ready to print and submit to your boss. Here's how to use it:

1. Before you begin, make sure you have, in fact, created some expense data on your PalmPilot (see Chapter 5)—and have HotSynced it to your Mac. (Behind the scenes, doing so creates an important file called *ExpenseDB.PDB* in your Palm → Users → *your name* → Backups folder. The expense report program consults this file when it creates its report.)

2. If you got the MacPac on a CD-ROM, such as this book's disk, locate the Palm Extras folder. If you downloaded the MacPac software from the Palm web site, be sure to download the Palm Extras item as well.

3. Open the Palm Extras folder, open the Shana Corporation folder, and run the Informed Palm Expense Installer.

4. When the installation process is over, you'll find a new folder on your hard drive called Informed. Open the Informed folder → Palm folder. Launch the Expense Creator program.

5. After the two introductory screens, you arrive at the dialog box shown in Figure 9-13. The important thing here is to help the program find your Palm data file. Click Setup → Select, and navigate to your Palm → Users folder. Click once on the folder with your name on it, and then click the Select button below the directory list. You return to the Expense Creator dialog box.

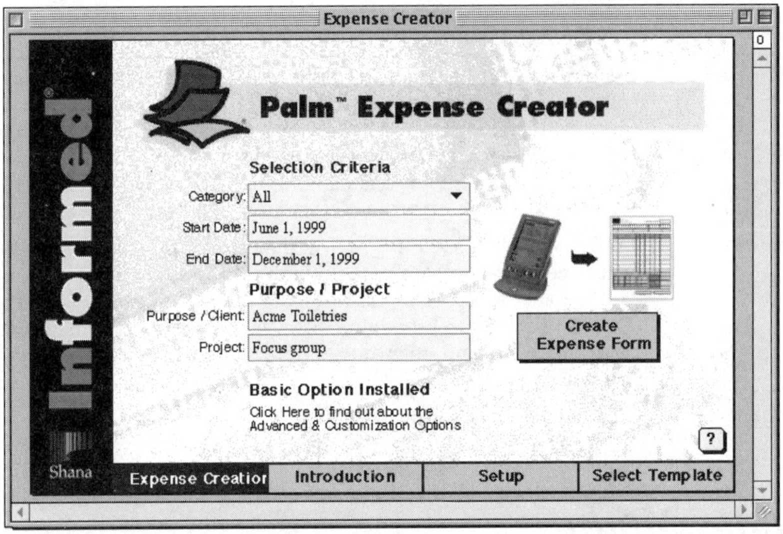

Figure 9-13. The Expense Creator program gives you a great deal of control over the expense reports your Mac generates from the PalmPilot data.

6. Take a moment to customize your expense report-to-be by clicking each of the buttons at the bottom of this window—Personal, Mileage, Currency, and so on—and setting up the corresponding preferences.

7. Click Select Template. From the first pop-up menu, specify which of the expense report designs you prefer. (The Preview button shows you what they'll look like.) If you decide to pony up $30 for the advanced version of this program, you'll be offered many more choices of design.

8. Finally, click the Expense Creation button at the bottom of the screen. Fill in the start and end dates, client name, and any other information you want to appear on the finished expense report. When you click Create Expense Form, the finished expense report appears on your screen, properly categorized and totaled.

After the first time you've created an expense report, create subsequent ones by launching Expense Creator and then following only steps 7 and 8 above.

The Informed product is actually far more advanced than this; it's a full-fledged database program that retains all your expense reports and lets you search, summarize, and organize them. As noted above, the $30 advanced version offers even more features.

After successfully creating an expense report from your PalmPilot's Expense application, you may want to delete the recorded items from the palmtop. The best way to do that is to use the Record → Purge command. It deletes from your PalmPilot all expenses that belong to a particular category. (See Chapter 5 for details on the Expense program, and Chapter 4 for more on categories.)

Attachments and Notes

If you live with Palm Desktop long enough, one significant difference between it and the PalmPilot reveals itself. On the PalmPilot, you can attach a Note to an appointment on your calendar (driving directions to your meeting, for example). In Palm Desktop, however, this note-attaching feature doesn't exist—or rather, it exists in such a powerful and flexible form that it overwhelms the PalmPilot. But with a little bit of planning and understanding, you should be able to master both Palm Desktop's attachment feature and its relationship to the PalmPilot.

Attaching Items Within Palm Desktop

On the PalmPilot, you can attach a note to, say, a calendar appointment. But in Palm Desktop, you can attach *any* item to any *other* item. You might attach an address book entry to a calendar entry, for example, so that your lunch partner's phone number is handy if you need to reschedule. Or you might attach several to-do items to the name of somebody in your address book, such as a list of gift ideas for your mother. All of these associations can be extremely handy as long as they reside on the Macintosh.

You can attach items in several ways, as described in the sections that follow.

Drag one existing item onto another

Drag the "gripper" handle of any item directly onto any other item. Figure 9-14, for example, shows how you might attach a phone number to a calendar entry.

Use the Attach Existing Item menu command

The previous method works well only if you can position the windows in Palm Desktop so that both items—the note you want to attach and the appointment you want to attach it to, for example—are visible. If you'd rather not spend time moving and arranging windows, you can use the Attach Existing Item menu command.

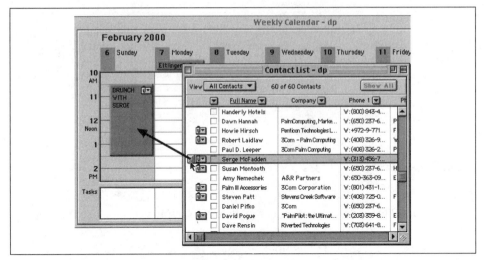

Figure 9-14. You can drag any kind of palm desktop item onto any other.

To do so, locate the item you want to attach—the note you intend to fasten to an appointment, for example. Now press Command-L, or choose Create → Attach To → Existing Item. The peculiar window shown in Figure 9-15 appears; open and close Palm Desktop windows, or use the Find command, until you can see the target item. Now drag the miniature gripper onto it, as shown in Figure 9-15.

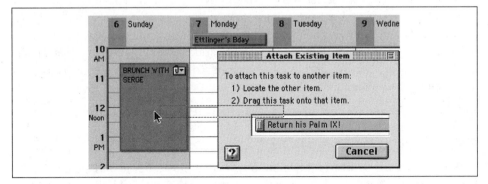

Figure 9-15. If the item you want to attach is visible, but the target item isn't, use the Attach Existing Item command, and then drag the miniature gripper.

Drag an existing item onto the toolbar

Both of the previous methods are useful only in attaching one existing item onto another. But if you want to attach a new item—such as a note you intend to type up—to an appointment, drag the appointment's gripper handle from the calendar onto the Create Note icon on the toolbar, which is the fifth icon in Figure 9-2.

You can even attach Macintosh files to the various appointments, names, notes, and tasks in Palm Desktop (your thesis document to the to-do item that says "Complete thesis," for example). Click the item to which you want to attach the file—and then choose Create → Attach To → File. The standard Macintosh Open File dialog box opens; locate and double-click the file you want. Thereafter, you can open such an associated file by choosing its name from the Attach menu, as shown in Figure 9-16.

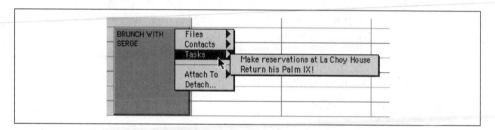

Figure 9-16. You can attach multiple items to a single Palm Desktop appointment, note, task, or address book entry.

Using attachments

After you've attached something in this way, a tiny paper-clip icon appears in the upper-right corner of the attachee, as shown in Figure 9-15. Click this icon to view the pop-up menu of all items you've attached in this way. As Figure 9-16 shows, you can open the attached file or other Palm Desktop item by choosing its name—or detach any of these items using the Detach command.

Remember that attachments are primarily confined to Palm Desktop. In only one instance are such relationships between items transferred to the PalmPilot and back again, as described in the next section.

Attaching Notes on the PalmPilot

Fortunately, there's very little to worry about when you attach notes to appointments, address book entries, and to-do items on your PalmPilot. When you HotSync, these notes are automatically transferred to Palm Desktop, where they show up as attachments to the correct items, exactly as shown in Figure 9-16. The only oddity you'll encounter is a series of items in your Palm Desktop Notes list called, for example, Handheld Note: Address Book. If you ignore these items, your life will proceed blissfully. (You may even want to use the Palm Desktop Filter command, described earlier in this chapter, to hide these Handheld Note items from your lists.)

Attaching Notes in Palm Desktop

Although attaching notes to items on the PalmPilot works the way you'd expect, creating notes destined to HotSync in the other direction requires a great deal more work. If, for example, you attach a Palm Desktop note to a calendar entry using one of the three methods described in the previous section, that note will never appear on your PalmPilot, no matter how many times you HotSync.

There is a way in Palm Desktop to create notes that get HotSynced to the Palm-Pilot, but some planning is required. First, you must name such a note exactly the way Palm Desktop does it, using one of these special titles:

- Handheld Note: To Do Item

- Handheld Note: Address Book

- Handheld Note: Date Book

After creating your note in this way, *then* you can attach it to a calendar, address-book, or to-do item as described in previous section—and it will indeed get HotSynced to the PalmPilot as a note attached to the corresponding item.

HotSync Manager

Palm Desktop is a surprisingly flexible home base for your data on the Mac. Believe it or not, however, Palm Desktop has nothing to do with the actual HotSync process. All communication with your PalmPilot is performed by another important program: HotSync Manager.

To open this program, choose its name from the Instant Palm Desktop menu (see Figure 9-1). You see HotSync Manager's main screen, a glorified on/off button for your ability to HotSync. And why would you ever want to select Disabled, which tells your Mac to ignore the HotSync cradle? Because when HotSync Manager is Enabled, you can't use its Macintosh jack for any other purpose. No other gadget—no MIDI, modem, or digitizing tablet—will work when it's plugged into that port while HotSync Manager is enabled.

This primary screen also offers the "Enable HotSync software at System startup" checkbox, described in Chapter 6, *HotSync, Step by Step*. And its Serial Port Settings tab lets you specify which Macintosh jack the cradle is plugged into, also as described in Chapter 6.

The HotSync Manager program is also used for several important administrative functions:

Adding, deleting, and renaming PalmPilots

Once you've named your PalmPilot, there's only one way to change its name (short of erasing it completely): launch HotSync Manager and choose Users → Show Palm User List. Click the existing name of your PalmPilot, click the Edit button, and then type a new name.

Similarly, you can also delete a PalmPilot's data from your Mac if, for example, you have since sold or lost that device. Click the user's name and then click Delete. Finally, if you're preparing to welcome a new PalmPilot into the family, click the New User button. Each of these actions, of course, creates, edits, or deletes correspondingly named folders in your Palm → Users folder on your hard drive, as described in Chapter 6.

Specifying which direction to HotSync for each Palm program

As described in Chapter 6, in special cases, you can request one-way Hot-Syncing; by choosing HotSync → Conduit Settings, you can dictate that the Macintosh information should completely replace the PalmPilot information for, say, your Address Book.

Installing new programs onto your PalmPilot

As described in Chapter 7, *Installing New Palm Programs*, the HotSync → Install command is the loading dock for new programs you want on your PalmPilot. (Note to people with multiple PalmPilots: Before using this command, be sure to choose Users → Select Current Palm User to specify which PalmPilot you want to receive these programs!)

Viewing the HotSync log

HotSync Manager keeps a diary of your last several HotSyncs, complete with a list of any errors, duplicate records, and so on. Choose HotSync → Log to view it; Chapter 6 has more on this topic.

One Mac, Multiple PalmPilots

Provided you've given each PalmPilot its own name, which you were asked to do the day you installed Palm Desktop, you can't go wrong HotSyncing more than one PalmPilot with the same Macintosh. HotSync Manager, as described in the previous section, lets you control which one the Mac will be talking to when, for example, installing new programs.

Switching Palm Desktop Files

Choosing which PalmPilot's data you want to view in Palm Desktop, however, is another matter. Suppose that you and your sister each HotSync with the same

Macintosh. Now you launch Palm Desktop, only to discover that *her* calendar shows up. To view a different set of data—your own—follow these steps:

1. Choose File → Open. As shown in Figure 9-17, the standard Mac Open File dialog box appears.

2. Navigate to the Palm folder on your hard drive. Open it, then the Users folder inside it, then the folder with your name on it; finally, double-click the User Data file (as shown in the figure). Your data now appears in Palm Desktop.

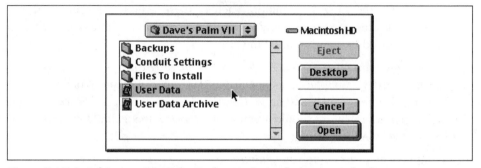

Figure 9-17. Switching users in Palm Desktop isn't simple, but it can be done.

Knowing how to switch Palm Desktop data can be very useful in other situations, as described in the following sections.

You can also switch to a different Palm Desktop file from the Finder. Open your hard drive → Palm folder → Users → the folder with your name on it; double-click the file inside called User Data.

The savvy Macintosh owner with multiple PalmPilots, therefore, performs the following clever trick: make an alias of the first User Data file. Rename the alias, for example, "Dave's PalmPilot," and stash it in your Apple menu. Repeat the process with the User Data file from your other PalmPilot, this time calling the alias, say, "Jennifer's PalmPilot."

From now on, you can switch Palm Desktop files simply by choosing the appropriate name from your Apple menu, cutting many steps out of the usual procedure.

Restoring Archived Data

As you may remember from Chapter 4, whenever you delete information from the PalmPilot, you're offered the opportunity to "Save archive copy on PC." In other words, the deleted appointment or memo isn't gone forever; at the next HotSync, a backup copy of it will be saved onto your Macintosh.

This backup process may give you a rosy feeling of safety, but the means of getting at your archived data on the Macintosh later is by no means straightforward. Here's how it works:

1. Open Palm Desktop. Choose File → Open. Navigate to your Palm folder → Users. Open the folder named for the PalmPilot whose data you want to retrieve. (Usually, you'll want to restore data that was originally deleted from your own PalmPilot. But there's no reason you can't retrieve data originally deleted from *one* PalmPilot—say, Frank's—and restore it to someone else's. Simply open the appropriate user-named folder during this step.)

2. As shown in Figure 9-17, inside the user-named folder are two important files. One is called User Data (your main data file); the other is User Data Archive, which contains your archived records. Open it.

   Now you're viewing what appears to be a normal Palm Desktop screen, but this isn't your data; it's your *deleted* data, raised from the dead.

3. Switch to the module—address book, memo, or whatever—that contains the data you want to restore.

If you want to restore only some of the records, not all, you can't simply highlight the ones you want. Instead, you must isolate the data you want using filters, as described earlier in this chapter. For example, you might create a category called Resurrected, apply that category to the data you want to restore, and then choose Resurrected from the Categories pop-up menu. Now only the selected data is visible—and only this data will be restored to your main Palm Desktop file.

---

4. Choose File → Export. In the following dialog box, specify which data you want to resurrect, using the Which pop-up menu. (The default is All; if you've isolated only certain records, choose the other pop-up menu command, which identifies the number of visible records.)

5. Click OK. Save the exported file to your hard drive and title it—"Restored archive," for example.

6. Choose File → Open, and this time open the User Data file. You're back where you were in Step 1: viewing your own data.

7. Choose File → Import. Open the file you just exported, called "Restored archive" or whatever. In the following dialog box, click OK.

At long last, the archived data appears in front of you, now incorporated back into your primary Palm Desktop file.

When you delete records from Palm Desktop for the Mac, you aren't offered the opportunity to preserve the deleted material in an archive file. However, there's no reason you can't create your own archive files, simply by following steps 3 through 5 above, thus preserving any set of Palm Desktop data in a standalone file that can be emailed, backed up, or even imported into another user's Palm Desktop file.

Sharing Palm Desktop Data Between Two PalmPilots

The question is asked in Palm user groups nationwide, month after month: "My spouse and I both use PalmPilots. How can we share certain information, like our common social schedule, without having to enter each appointment and phone number twice?"

In Windows, the answer is, "You can't." On the Macintosh, however, sharing such data is easy. Simply apply a certain category label to all of the information from PalmPilot A that you want to share. Export this data according to steps 3 and 4 in the previous section, saving it to the hard drive as, for example, "Shared calendar." Switch to the PalmPilot B Palm Desktop file (see the previous section, "Switching Palm Desktop files"), and import the "Shared calendar" file as in step 7 above. The originally exported data now appears in both Palm Desktop files.

Profiles

You can read about Profiles at the end of Chapter 8, *Palm Desktop: Windows*; in essence, a Profile is a set of Palm Desktop data and Palm applications that you want to load onto multiple new, *empty and unnamed* PalmPilots before their first HotSync, such as standard company information. While Palm Desktop's online help offers directions for creating and loading Profiles, it leaves out several important steps.

Creating a Profile

To create a Profile on the Macintosh, follow these steps:

1. Launch HotSync Manager, as described earlier in this chapter. Choose Users → Show Palm User List. In the dialog box that appears, click New Profile, type a name (such as "Company Data"), and click OK. Close the window.

2. Choose Users → Select Current Palm User. In the next dialog box, choose your profile's name. Click OK. If you like, choose HotSync → Install and load up any Palm programs you want every device to receive. (See Chapter 7 for details on installing programs.)

3. Choose HotSync → Conduit Settings. Double-click each of the conduits in turn (Address Book, Date Book, and so on); for each one, click "Macintosh over-writes handheld," click Make Default, and click OK. Quit HotSync Manager.

4. Open Palm Desktop. Choose File → New to open a blank Palm Desktop document. Import the standardized data, such as phone directories, memos, and so on, that you'll want sent into every PalmPilot.

5. Finally, choose File → Save As. Navigate to your Palm → Users → Company Data folder (or whatever you called your profile). In the "Save document as" field, type User Data—exactly that name, with no extra spaces—and click Save.

Your Profile is ready to roll.

To load your Profiles onto new PalmPilots

Once you've created a Profile, here's how to load it onto your empty PalmPilots:

1. Put the first PalmPilot into the cradle. Press the HotSync button.

2. A dialog box appears on the screen; from the pop-up menu, choose the Pro-file name, click OK, and click Yes to confirm.

The new PalmPilot is now loaded and ready to give to its new user, who can name it and add to it his or her own data.

More Macintosh Conduits

Palm Desktop wasn't the only piece of software Palm released in early 1999; in some ways, the new Macintosh conduit-management software is even more signifi-cant, because it opens the way for other software companies to create hookups between the PalmPilot and other Mac programs.

You can find a complete and regularly updated list of Mac-compatible conduits at *http://www.palm.com*. But see Table 9-6 for a few examples to get you started.

Table 9-6. Palm/MacIntosh Conduit Products

Mac Program	Conduit for PalmPilot	Details
FileMaker Pro	FM Sync synchronizes your FileMaker Pro database information with JFile, a popular Palm database; see Chapter 12, *Database and Number Crunching*.	Tsuk Software, *http://www.fmsync.com* ($38)
Eudora, Out-look Express, Claris Emailer	MultiMail Conduit lets you use your favorite Mac email program to send and receive mes-sages, as described in Chapter 13, *Email Anywhere*—and then HotSyncs it to the built-in Palm Mail program on your palmtop.	Actual Software, *http://www.actualsoft.com* ($30 for the conduit, $40 for MultiMail)

Table 9-6. Palm/MacIntosh Conduit Products (continued)

Mac Program	Conduit for PalmPilot	Details
BrainForest	BrainForest is an outliner/thought processor for both Macintosh and the PalmPilot, with two-way HotSyncing.	Aportis, *http://www.aportis.com* ($30, or $39 for the professional edition)
Chronos Consultant	Chronos Consultant is an excellent, full-fledged calendar/address book program, along the lines of Palm Desktop itself—but with more features, such as a built-in journal, speech features, and networkability.	Chronos, *http://www.chronosnet.com* (free trial, $50 shareware with Palm sync software)
Excel, Word	You can drag-and-drop Microsoft Excel spreadsheets and Word documents onto the Documents To Go icon; they're instantly converted into Palm-readable form and made ready to HotSync (see Chapters 10 and 12).	Data Viz, *http://www.dataviz.com* ($40)
Quicken	Pocket Quicken runs on your PalmPilot; at HotSync time, your PalmPilot automatically feeds any new transactions into your Mac's Quicken 98 file.	LandWare, *http://www.landware.com* ($40)
Meeting Maker	This corporate scheduling and calendar program will speak to the PalmPilot, uploading schedules over any corporate network.	On Technology, *http://www.on.com* (price not yet set)
TeamAgenda	This fast, powerful, networkable, cross-platform group calendar program now syncs to the PalmPilot.	TeamSoft, *http://www.teamsoft.com*; price varies with quality
Informed Filler	You can HotSync your PalmPilot's Expense data (see Chapter 5) with the Macintosh at last, as described earlier in this chapter.	Shana, *http://www.shana.com* (included with MacPac; advanced version is $30)
Excel, File-Maker Pro, Informed Manager	Here's a more sophisticated way to track your expenses: use Expense Plus on your PalmPilot instead of the built-in Expense program. At HotSync time, you can choose among several popular programs, such as Excel, to collect and print your expense report.	WalletWare, *http://www.walletware.com* ($69)
TealPoint Software	Most of this popular Palm software company's programs can now be HotSynced to corresponding Mac utilities, including TealDoc (see Chapter 10), TealPaint (see Chapter 11, *The Secret Multimedia World*), TealMeal, and TealInfo.	TealPoint, *http://www.tealpoint.com* (prices vary)

The Palm Extras

As though to atone for its former neglect of the Macintosh community, Palm Computing includes an assortment of delicious add-ons with the MacPac. (They're in the Palm Extras folder, on this book's CD-ROM.)

Some of the software is described by Palm as "unsupported," which means "Works for us, but you're on your own if it doesn't work on your setup." Just look at all you get.

Faster HotSync

Once installed on your PalmPilot, this software module nearly doubles the speed of HotSyncing to a Macintosh (to 112 Kbps instead of the usual 56). Be sure to choose the appropriate version of this file—a separate file is included for the Palm V, for example—and perform a soft reset of your PalmPilot after the installation (instructions in Chapter 17, *Troubleshooting*). (But don't install this amazing utility if you HotSync the same PalmPilot to Windows PC and the Macintosh.)

Infrared HotSyncing Software

If you're the proud owner of a PowerBook or an original iMac model, you can actually HotSync simply by pointing your Palm III or later model at your computer's infrared jack—no cradle needed. This kit consists of four files you drag onto your Mac's System Folder icon, plus four files you install onto your PalmPilot (their names end with the usual *.prc* suffix). Sure enough, you can now HotSync through the air, provided the infrared jacks are facing each other and within a few feet.

AppleScripts

Palm Desktop is extremely AppleScript-savvy. AppleScript is a simple programming language that lets you automate many Mac programs. Note, for example, the tiny button beside the Email and Web Site fields that appears when you're editing an entry in Palm Desktop's address book. You can click this button to trigger the AppleScript of your choice. When you click the Email icon, for example, Palm Desktop can launch your favorite email program, create a new outgoing piece of mail, and type in the email address of the person whose address you were viewing—automatically.

In fact, any of your custom fields in the Palm Desktop address book can show AppleScript-triggering buttons. Simply double-click the custom field's name, as shown in Figure 9-18, or choose Field Options from the pop-up menu to the right of such fields. In the dialog box that appears, follow these steps:

1. Turn on the AppleScript Button checkbox.

2. Choose a Script File from the pop-up menu. This menu's contents depend on the files in your Palm folder → Scripts folder on your hard drive. That is, to install a new AppleScript into these menus—such as the sample AppleScripts

that come with the MacPac—drag the script's icon into the Palm → Scripts folder.

3. Using the Button Icon pop-up menu, specify which icon picture you'd like to appear on the button.

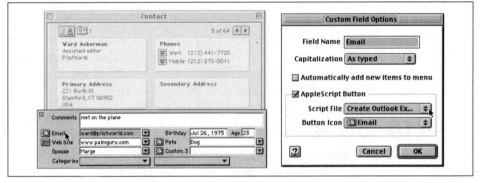

Figure 9-18. To unleash the power of AppleScript, double-click a custom field's name (left) and then set up the script options in the resulting dialog box (right).

So what can AppleScript do? If you're a talented programmer, almost anything. But the most common examples, such as the ones included with Palm Desktop and the Palm Extras folder, follow the lines described in the next sections.

ClarisWorks Letter Link

This is the script whose icon appears in the upper-right corner of the Primary and Secondary Address blocks in Palm Desktop. When you click this icon, you're offered a choice of ClarisWorks letter templates—form letters—plus a Personalize button that lets you create your own. (AppleWorks or ClarisWorks 4 or later must be on your hard drive.) When you click Attach, a new form letter is automatically generated, completely addressed to the person whose contact you were perusing in Palm Desktop.

Create Claris Emailer Message

This script copies this person's email address into the To: field of a new outgoing Claris Emailer message. (The Outlook Express script works similarly.)

Open in Web to URL

Copies the contents of the Web Site field, launches your web browser, and goes to the corresponding web site.

PowerBook Palm Assistant

If your PowerBook has Mac OS 8.5 or later, this script gets your laptop's modem/printer port ready for HotSync. It turns off AppleTalk (networking technology that prevents HotSync manager from using the port) when you run the script before HotSyncing; after the HotSync, run the script again and click Reset to restore your original AppleTalk settings. (You'll want to trigger this script from the desktop, not from within Palm Desktop.)

To Do List for Palm Desktop 2.5

Although Palm Desktop 2.1 is a dramatic improvement over what came before it, a few rough edges remain. For example, you may have noticed that Palm Desktop has no facility for viewing or even honoring the records designated as Private on your PalmPilot. The program could use an easier method of switching among Palm Desktop user files, too. Network HotSyncing, as described in Chapter 6, is also a Windows-only exclusive.

Finally, Palm Desktop for Macintosh doesn't support the File Linking feature offered in Windows, which permits multiple PalmPilots to load a standardized set of address book and memo data (described near the end of Chapter 8). Version 2.5, anyone?

Executive Tip Summary

- Palm Desktop is your Mac's central clearinghouse for data going to and from your PalmPilot. The easiest way to launch the program is to choose Switch to Palm Desktop from the green Instant Palm Desktop icon at the upper-right of your screen.

- You can quickly and easily switch Palm Desktop files—if you HotSync multiple PalmPilots to a single Mac, for example—by choosing the names of their aliases that you've stashed in your Apple menu.

- Create a new appointment by dragging through the appropriate hours in the Palm Desktop calendar; create a new untimed event by double-clicking above the Daily or Weekly time grid; create a new to-do item by double-clicking in an empty spot of the task list in Daily or Weekly views.

- Switch among day, week, and month views by pressing Command-Shift-D, -W, or -M. Fast-forward or fast-rewind through the days, weeks, or months by pressing Command-right or left arrow; add the Option key to jump a week at a time.

- In the Edit Event dialog box, pressing + and – adjusts the hour; Shift-plus and Shift-minus adjusts the minute. When specifying a time, furthermore, you can use a period instead of a colon, and you can use military time instead of specifying a.m. or p.m.

- You can sort any Palm Desktop list—of tasks, addresses, or notes, for example—by clicking a column heading; create a secondary sort by Shift-clicking or Option-clicking a column heading.

- You can share PalmPilot data with another PalmPilot owner—a family member, for example—by exporting the data, switching Palm Desktop files, then importing that data. That's useful if you want to share, for example, a set of social appointments with your spouse.

III

The Undiscovered PalmPilot

10

PalmPilot: The Electronic Book

In this book, you'll read about turning your palmtop into a pager, a music synthesizer, and a graphics tablet. But one of its most popular impressions has nothing to do with interactivity or stylus-tapping: the PalmPilot can serve quite deftly as a *book*.

Thanks to tiny programs called Doc, AportisDoc, TealDoc, and so on, you can load up your palmtop with text to carry with you for reading en route (or en hotel room). As for *what* to read, your options are the same as they are at home: today's newspaper, your favorite web pages, classic works from Shakespeare to Jane Austen, the Bible, your company's latest white paper, or modern poetry and fiction. Any text sitting on *your* hard drive can be turned into a PalmPilot book, too.

About Doc

Programmer Rick Bram originally wrote the shareware program called Doc to get around the 4K-per-document limit of the PalmPilot's built-in Memo Pad program, which put a damper on the prospects of reading longer documents. And, while he was at it, he added all kinds of other features designed exclusively to make reading easier:

- A choice of type styles and sizes
- Many different ways to "turn the page" (scroll down)
- A pop-up menu of bookmarks to facilitate jumping directly to chapter or section beginnings
- A Find command
- A memory-saving compression scheme

Suddenly, the Palm world went Doc-crazy. Palm fans sat up late at night converting classic books (that is, old ones whose copyrights have expired) into Doc format. Doc-library web sites sprouted, crammed with downloadable Doc documents. Other web sites featured downloadable news and region-specific weather reports in Doc format, so that you could load up your PalmPilot before heading away on a trip. Email, reports, price lists, statistics, meeting minutes, speeches, and hundreds of other text documents became Doc fodder, making Doc among the most popular programs that *didn't* come built into the PalmPilot.

Soon enough, programs like MakeDoc became available for both Mac and Windows; they let you convert documents of your own into Doc format, ready for loading onto the PalmPilot. (You'll find instructions at the end of this chapter.)

AportisDoc

In November 1997, the software company Aportis bought the rights to Doc, renamed it AportisDoc, and made a few cosmetic changes. AportisDoc is available today in three versions (the first two are on the CD-ROM that comes with this book):

AportisDoc Reader
> A free program, just for reading, scrolling, and navigating using bookmarks already in the files you're reading. You can choose from either of the two original Palm fonts. This program is pretty stripped—it doesn't even have a Find command. Correction: it *does* have a Find command, plus commands for all the features you'll read about in the next two paragraphs—but choosing them simply displays an advertisement for the more expensive versions.

AportisDoc Mobile Edition
> A $30 shareware program that adds several additional features: working Find and Copy commands, categories, the ability to generate bookmarks (as described later in this chapter), a long list of preference options, a teleprompter mode, and a choice of four typefaces.

AportisDoc Professional Edition
> The PalmPilot software for the $40 Professional edition, under development at this writing, is essentially the same as the Mobile (it adds the ability to insert your own notes into Doc files). The Pro package, however, will come with a drag-and-drop converter for your Mac or Windows PC that turns any Microsoft Word, HTML, or text document into a Doc document.

TealDoc

As an alternative to AportisDoc, consider its attractive, inexpensive upstart rival: TealDoc. As you'll see in this chapter, it offers most of the same features but at a lower shareware price ($17). Current versions of TealDoc read not only standard Doc files, but also a special, TealDoc-only format that can contain graphics embedded with the text. This special kind of file can even contain Web-like hyper-links that jump instantly to predefined locations within the current document or even in other documents. (You could, for example, create a tappable table of contents at the beginning of each of your TealDoc files.) There's even a password option to protect your private documents.

TealDoc, too, is included on the CD with this book.

SmartDoc

Your $20 shareware fee buys you a fast, solid, feature-rich Doc reader that can also *edit and save* Doc files, right on your PalmPilot. (AportisDoc and TealDoc can only read Doc files, not make changes.) This Doc reader also offers Find and Replace commands, beaming ability, and four font choices (including the extra-large type that debuted with the Palm III).

Other Doc Readers

The leading Palm software web sites, and this book's CD-ROM, are filled with other Doc readers. Worth exploring, for example, are:

J-Doc
($10) This program's distinctive features: it can read Japanese text, and it can rotate the text 90 degrees. (On one hand, it's neat to be able to rotate the page you're reading. On the other hand, the Palm screen is a perfect square, so you don't actually gain any page-width space by rotating the text.)

QED
($23) This powerful, word-processor like program both reads and edits Doc files, right on the PalmPilot. QED also lets you create a virtual page that's wider than the actual Palm screen, for those instances when, for example, you want to read a large table that's too wide for the screen. Its icon-based interface isn't the world's clearest, however.

CspotRun
This one isn't big on features, but it's free and consumes only 10K—a no-brainer for people who want to keep a Doc reader installed for occasional use.

What's Up with Doc?

Because there are so many different Doc readers, this chapter emphasizes the three with the richest feature list—AportisDoc Mobile/Professional, TealDoc, and SmartDoc. To save ink and the trees of the rain forest, I'll refer to them generically as Doc readers—even though the original shareware program called Doc is rapidly fading from the scene.

Reading E-books

To use electronic reading materials on your PalmPilot, you need two software components: a Doc reader and the actual documents you want to read. Install both of them as you would any Palm program (see Chapter 7, *Installing New Palm Programs*).

Now, to open your loaded-up document and begin reading, follow these steps:

1. Tap the Applications button. On the Applications screen, tap the Doc reader icon, as shown at left in Figure 10-1.

2. You'll see a list of whatever books or chapters you installed in step 1 (see the right side of Figure 10-1). Tap the one you want to open.

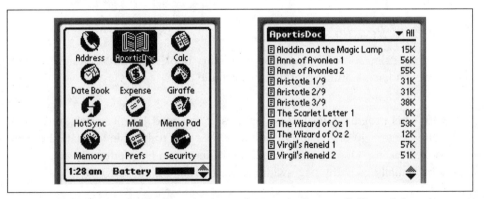

Figure 10-1. To open your electronic book, tap the Doc reader icon (left), and then choose from the documents you've loaded (right).

Once the document is open on the screen, adjust the typeface to suit your eyes by tapping one of the A icons at the bottom of the screen (Figure 10-2). The program automatically reflows the text so that whatever sentence was at the top of the screen remains roughly in place, despite the different type size.

Maximizing Reading Space (AportisDoc)

Once you've selected a pleasant typeface for reading, you may as well maximize your screen space by hiding the row of font-selection buttons—a useful Aportis-Doc feature. To do so, write /L in the Graffiti writing area (slashing from the bottom)—or, the long way, tap Menu → Display → Larger Text Window, as shown in Figure 10-3. The row of controls at the bottom of the screen disappears, turning your PalmPilot into a clean, lean reading machine. (You can still change

Aunt Em dropped her work and came
to the door. One glance told her of
the danger close at hand.
"Quick, Dorothy!" she screamed.
"Run for the cellar!"
    Toto jumped out of Dorothy's arms
and hid under the bed, and the girl
started to get him. Aunt Em, badly
frightened, threw open the trap door

(Done) 5% (F)(G)(A)(A)(A)(P) ▼

Aunt Em dropped her
work and came to the door.
One glance told her of the
danger close at hand.
    "Quick, Dorothy!" she
screamed. "Run for the
cellar!"

(Done) 5% (F)(G)(A)(A)(A)(P) ▼

Aunt Em dropped her work
and came to the door. One
glance told her of the danger
close at hand.
    "Quick, Dorothy!" she
screamed. "Run for the cellar!"
    Toto jumped out of Dorothy's
arms and hid under the bed, and
the girl started to get him.

(Done) 5% (F)(G)(A)(A)(A)(P) ▼

Aunt Em dropped her
work and came to the door.
One glance told her of the
danger close at hand.
    "Quick, Dorothy!" she
screamed. "Run for the
cellar!"
    Toto jumped out of
Dorothy's arms and hid

(Done) 5% (F)(G)(A)(A)(A)(P) ▼

Figure 10-2. Depending on the age and exhaustion level of your eyes, you may prefer a different one of the four included Palm fonts. (The fourth font isn't available on Palm III and later models.)

typefaces, by the way, using the Display menu, as shown in Figure 10-3. The four A icons you've just hidden correspond to the menu commands Regular Font, Big Font, Bold Font, and Monospaced.)

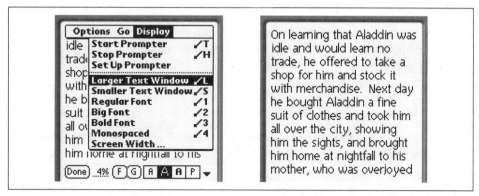

Figure 10-3. Once you've chosen a typeface, hide the controls using the Options menu (left). The result is a screen maximized for reading (right). To restore the buttons at the bottom of the screen, return to the Display menu and tap Smaller Text Window.

Fixing ragged right edges (AportisDoc)

Some e-books, especially those downloaded from the Internet, are preformatted to the width of a standard computer screen. The original typist pressed the Return key at the end of each line. When you read such documents using the smallest type size (the leftmost of the four A icons at the bottom of the AportisDoc screen), they may look fine—but using any of the other type sizes, the irregular line wrapping makes smooth reading nearly impossible. (See Figure 10-4 for proof.)

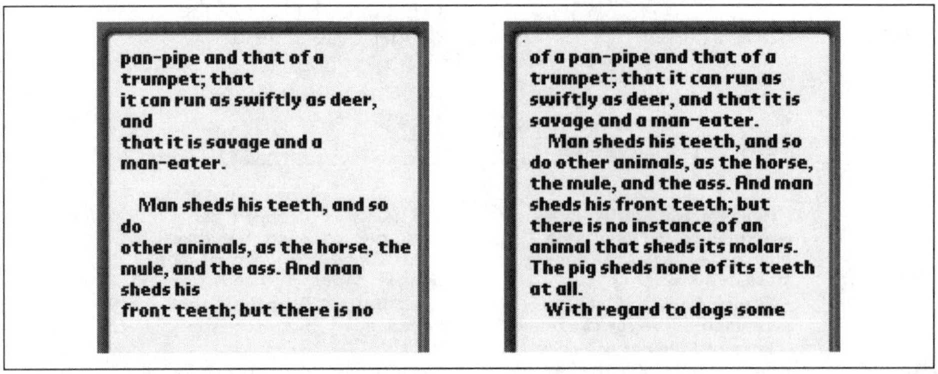

Figure 10-4. Some downloaded e-books, such as this light reading from Aristotle, have invisible "linefeed" (Return) characters in odd places, causing ragged line lengths when viewed at larger type sizes (left). The solution lies in the Preferences command: "Strip Linefeeds" (right).

To solve the problem, tap Menu → Preferences, and turn on the Strip Linefeeds option. When you tap OK, you'll see that all *single* Return characters are being ignored, creating a smooth column of text (see Figure 10-4 at right). (All *double* Returns are preserved, so that paragraphs are still separated by a blank line.)

Changing documents (all Doc readers)

When you're finished reading one document, tap the Done button. You return to the Doc reader "home page" list of documents, from which you can select another document to read by tapping its name.

Scrolling

When you first use a Doc reader, it's set up to scroll a screen at a time. That's just the beginning of your scrolling options, however.

Scrolling a Page at a Time

To "turn pages," you can press the plastic up/down scroll buttons at the bottom of the PalmPilot; alternatively, you can *tap* (with the stylus or, more conveniently, with your finger). Tap below the screen's midline to scroll downward; tap above the midline to scroll to the previous page.

If you find yourself mostly scrolling downward, consider changing the settings so that a tap *anywhere* on the screen turns to the next "page." (If you do need to refer back to something you've already read, you can always press the plastic scroll-up button.) To do so in AportisDoc, tap Menu → Preferences → Tapping Only Scrolls Down; tap OK. In SmartDoc, tap Menu → Options → Preferences → Down Only; tap OK.

You may quickly notice one disconcerting aspect of scrolling in your Doc reader: using the PalmPilot's "page down" mechanism doesn't *repeat* the bottom line of the previous screen at the top of the new screen, unlike word processors on your desktop computer. You're expected to remember "He reached into the box and pulled out" when you see "a grisly dismembered muskrat" at the top of the next screen.

Fortunately, you can change this behavior. *AportisDoc:* Tap Menu → Preferences → Overlap Screens → OK. *SmartDoc:* Tap Menu → Options → Preferences → Overlap Line → OK. *TealDoc:* Tap Menu → Preferences → Part (under the Screen Tap heading); then tap OK. From now on, you'll see the last line of the previous screen repeated at the top of each new screen, making mental continuity much easier.

Scrolling Smoothly

Even if you turn on the "last line overlap" option, scrolling a screen at a time can still be an interruption to your train of thought; your eyes must jump from the bottom of the screen to the top, and you have to find your place in the stream of text.

A handy alternative: you can opt to make the text scroll *smoothly* for as long as you're touching the screen. To set up this arrangement in AportisDoc, tap Menu → Preferences → Tap Scroll One Line Only. In SmartDoc, tap Menu → Options → Preferences → Line (under the Scroll/ Tap setting). In TealDoc, tap Menu → Preferences → Line (under the Screen Tap heading).

Tap OK. Now, if you briefly tap the screen (with the stylus or your finger), you advance the text by one line. But if you *hold* the stylus or finger against the glass, the scrolling continues smoothly until you release.

If you have the smooth-scrolling option turned on in AportisDoc or TealDoc, you can control how fast the scrolling goes. The farther from the screen's horizontal midline you tap, the faster the Palm-Pilot scrolls.

And in all three of the Doc readers described in this chapter, you can scroll *down* by tapping below the screen midline, and up by tapping above it.

Teleprompter Mode (Auto-Scrolling)

One of the cleverest features of Doc reader programs is the auto-scrolling mode, in which the text scrolls slowly up the screen automatically. In the TV news and corporate speech-making worlds, this kind of machine is known as a *teleprompter*. You get to consult a prewritten script without having to muss with papers, index cards, or even a laptop computer; the PalmPilot, perched inconspicuously on the podium or table in front of you, slowly scrolls the text, freeing you to look up from your script whenever you want to make eye contact with your audience.

AportisDoc

Tap Menu → Display → Set Up Prompter. The dialog box in Figure 10-5 appears. The top of the window offers a choice: "1 Page" or "1 Line," referring to how big the scrolling jumps should be. Near the bottom of the window, the "seconds" blank lets you specify how *often* this auto-scrolling should be. (You can even specify fractions of a second by writing a number into the "ticks" blank; ticks are hundredths of a second.)

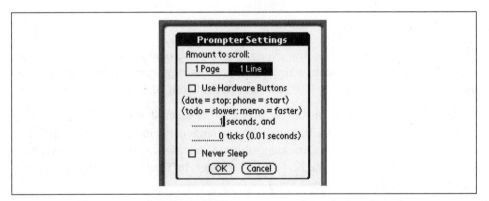

Figure 10-5. The Prompter Settings dialog box sets you up for embarrassment at your speech—unless you change the default settings.

Clearly, the factory setting (auto-scrolling one page per second) is a recipe for disaster, unless you're planning to speak to the Evelyn Woods Speed-Reading Society. For better results, use the "1 Line" option, which is less likely to throw you during your speech. Even this option seems silly, however, because it provides no means of controlling the scrolling speed or pausing the text flow. If one of your jokes goes over big, you don't want to interrupt your audience's laughter by barging ahead with your speech.

Therefore, the most useful option in the Prompter Settings box is the Use Hardware Buttons checkbox. It turns the four rounded plastic PalmPilot buttons into a control center for the scrolling, as shown in Figure 10-6. Now you can speed up, slow down, or even pause the scrolling as suits the moment, turning the Palm-Pilot not just into an excellent teleprompter, but an *interactive* one.

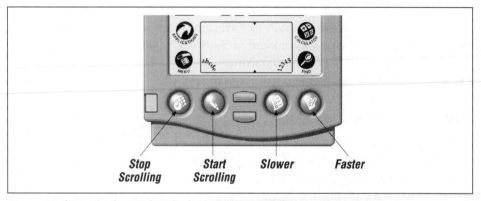

Figure 10-6. Use the four PalmPilot buttons to control the rate of scrolling during your speech (or during your novel-reading).

 If you really are going to use the PalmPilot as a teleprompter, turn on the Never Sleep checkbox, shown in Figure 10-5. It prevents the PalmPilot's battery-saving auto-off feature from leaving you speechless during your big presentation.

TealDoc

Tap the % symbol at the bottom of the screen to summon the auto-scroll controls. Now you can control the scrolling using the hardware buttons, as indicated in Figure 10-7, or by tapping the tiny black buttons at the very bottom edge of the screen. (The tiny bar between these buttons shows a black segment when scrolling is turned on; its length and direction indicate the speed and direction of scrolling.)

SmartDoc

To start auto-scrolling, tap the triangle button at the bottom middle of the screen, or press the Date Book button as shown in Figure 10-7. You control the speed of scrolling using the Slower and Faster hardware buttons, again as shown in Figure 10-7; to stop, press the Date Book button a second time (or tap the bottom-center button, whose triangle changes to a square while scrolling is going on.)

Jumping Around in Your Document

Every Doc reader offers numerous methods of skipping from place to place in the text instead of scrolling.

Many of the commands that pertain to navigating your document lie in Aportis-Doc's Go menu, TealDoc's View menu, or SmartDoc's Navigate menu. For example, the To Top and To Bottom commands are there. Learning to use them (or their Graffiti ShortCut equivalents) will serve you well.

The % Box or Scroll Bars

Understanding where you are in a SmartDoc file is easy, thanks to its standard vertical scroll bar. (You can choose to place it on the left side of the screen if you're left-handed). TealDoc, too, has a scroll bar, although it's placed horizontally at the bottom of the screen. (Tap the % symbol if you don't see it.) In AportisDoc, you see, next to the Done button, a percentage indicator. It shows how far you are through the current document; if it says 50%, for example, you're about in the middle.

What you may not realize, however, is that you can use this blank to jump around in your e-book:

1. Tap the number in the "%" blank.

2. In the dialog box that appears, write a new percentage and tap OK.

The PalmPilot jumps instantly that far into the document.

Bookmarks

At the lower-right corner of the AportisDoc/TealDoc/SmartDoc screen is a small black triangle—your cue that a pop-up menu awaits. In this case, the pop-up menu lists *bookmarks:* predefined spots in the book to which you can jump by choosing their names from this menu. (See Figure 10-7.)

If you've opted to hide the bottom row of controls (see Figure 10-3) in Aportis-Doc, you can still jump to a bookmark; just write /B (slash from the bottom), which is the shortcut for the Go menu's Go To Bookmark command. A list of bookmarks appears, from which you can tap your selection.

To add a bookmark of your own, scroll to the correct spot in the document. (It's the *top line on the screen* that counts as the actual marker.) Tap the pop-up menu triangle at the lower-right corner of the screen; from the pop-up menu, choose Add a Bookmark (see Figure 10-7) or, in TealDoc, New Bookmark. Type a name

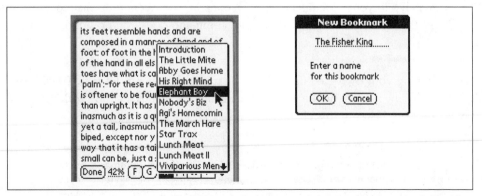

Figure 10-7. Tap the Bookmark triangle to produce a pop-up menu of bookmarks (left). (If there aren't any in this document, the menu contains only a single command: Add A Bookmark. If there are more than 12 bookmarks, the tiny black arrow appears in the pop-up menu—tap it to scroll the list up or down.) If you choose Add A Bookmark, you're asked to name your new placeholder (right).

for your bookmark—maximum 15 letters and spaces—and tap OK. Your new bookmark's name appears immediately in the pop-up menu, ready for action.

Ironically, one thing bookmarks are *not* good for is marking the place where you stopped reading. All three Doc readers *automatically* remember where you stopped; the next time you open something you'd been reading, you're taken directly back to the place where you stopped—no bookmark needed.

Automatic bookmarks

If the document you've loaded into your PalmPilot has no bookmarks, but its chapters or sections are labeled in a consistent way (such as "Chapter 1"), your Doc reader can create a bookmark list for you automatically.

In AportisDoc, tap Menu → Go → Auto Bookmark. A dialog box appears in which you can specify the form your document's chapter headings take. You might write, for example, *Chapter* into the main blank; in the "followed by __ characters" blank, you'd write the maximum number of characters used in the chapter numbers (*2*, for example); and in the Bookmark Name(s) field, write what *you'd* like to use as the bookmark name (such as *Ch.* or *Chap.*). The program automatically fills your bookmark pop-up menu with bookmarks: Chap. 1, Chap. 2, and so on.

The TealDoc Procedure is similar—use the Custom Scan command in the Marks menu. In SmartDoc, tap Menu → Navigate → Scan Custom Bookmarks. In both cases, in the resulting dialog box, you'll see the same kinds of controls described for AportisDoc: what text to look for (such as "Chapter"), how many characters may follow it, and so on.

Unfortunately, if your document *doesn't* contain consistently formatted section headings, the Auto Bookmark/Custom Scan command does you no good.

Prefab bookmarks

When making your own Doc files, if you plan ahead, you can let your Doc reader generate nicely named bookmarks automatically. See the section "Making Your Own Doc Files," later in this chapter.

To delete a bookmark, use the Delete Bookmark command in the Go menu (AportisDoc), Marks menu (TealDoc), or Navigate menu (SmartDoc). A confirmation box appears, listing your bookmarks—tap the one you want to delete.

The Find Command

To search for a particular phrase of text in the document you're reading, tap the F button, or TealDoc's magnifying-glass button, at the bottom of the screen. The Find box appears—the Doc reader's Find box, not the PalmPilot's own; write what you're looking for.

When you tap OK, the program highlights the first occurrence of the text you sought. (If it can't find the text you're looking for, the PalmPilot beeps.)

The Find command searches *from the currently displayed text to the end of the file*. In other words, it doesn't begin searching from the beginning of the document.

If you want to be sure you haven't missed something, then use the Go menu's Go To Top command before searching.

Searching your entire PalmPilot

The onscreen Find command searches only the document you're reading. If your PalmPilot is loaded up with documents, however, and you're desperately trying to remember where you read something, you can use the PalmPilot's own global search option instead. As you may recall from Chapter 2, *Setup and Guided Tour*, this super-Find reads all of the documents on your PalmPilot—not just the Memo Pad, Address Book, and so on, but Doc Files too—in its hunt for the sought-after phrase.

Editing with SmartDoc

The beauty of SmartDoc is that, unlike the other Doc readers discussed in this chapter, it can both read and edit Doc files. After opening a Doc file, you'll see an icon at the top of the screen that looks like a pencil with the slash through it. Tap this icon (see Figure 10-8) to make the slash disappear, which makes the Doc file editable. (Alternatively, you can tap the New button on SmartDoc's "home page" list to create a new Doc file from scratch.)

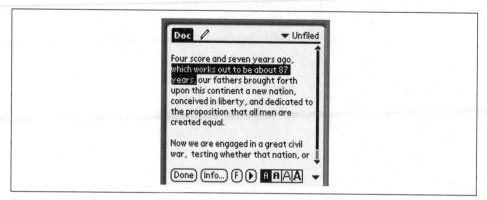

Figure 10-8. Using SmartDoc, you can create new Doc files or edit the ones you already have.

You can make changes using any of the techniques described in Chapter 3, *Typing Without a Keyboard*—writing, copying, pasting, dragging through text and then deleting it, and so on. To save your changes, tap Done. The editing you've done is now part of the Doc file, even when viewed by another Doc reader. (And SmartDoc, as the only Doc reader reviewed here that offers a Beam command, makes sharing such files easy.)

Avoiding Compression Delays

One of the principal virtues of a Doc file is that it consumes only a tiny amount of memory on the PalmPilot, thanks to a clever compression scheme. When you open a Doc file—which is all most people do with Doc files—it decompresses instantaneously.

But Doc compression is asymmetrical—you don't wait when you open a Doc file, but compressing the file to begin with is very time-consuming. Every time you try to save a file in SmartDoc, you'll wait for quite a while (sometimes several minutes) while the PalmPilot performs this compression.

If you plan to make major edits, therefore, begin by tapping Menu → Compression. You'll be asked if you want to decompress the file; tap Decompress. Now the document takes up more memory on your palmtop, but you don't wait for compression every time you tap Done (thus saving your changes).

When you're finished with all your edits, tap Menu → Compression again, and this time tap Compress. You'll still have to wait a long time, but at least you have to do this only once, when you're completely finished editing.

 Bookmarks, described earlier in this chapter, aren't attached to particular text in the file. Instead, they're positioned by a certain number of characters from the beginning of the file. As a result, if you make changes to an early paragraph, all later bookmarks will shift into the wrong places. Therefore, don't add bookmarks to a Smart-Doc file until you're completely finished editing or creating it.

Where to Get Doc Books

You can get e-books to pour into your PalmPilot from three primary sources: the CD-ROM that comes with this book; the World Wide Web; and your own hard drive.

E-books Included with This Book

On the CD-ROM that accompanies this book, you'll find several years' worth of reading material for your PalmPilot—nearly 600 e-books. The nearly complete works of Shakespeare; philosophy; poetry; science-fiction novels; and thick sheaves of traveler information await your perusal. See the database on this book's CD-ROM for a complete list.

(If it seems to you that the preponderance of e-books for the PalmPilot are ancient classics, you're right: the copyright on these works has expired, making them free for distribution without payment to anyone. Aristotle's descendants don't get a nickel.)

E-books on the Web

Every week, more electronic texts are posted online. If you have Internet access, the following electronic libraries, in the form of *.prc* or *.pdb* files (see Chapter 7, *Installing New Palm Programs*), await your browser. (As with anything Internet-related, these sites' existence is confirmed only as of this writing.) All of it's free.

MemoWare.com (http://www.memoware.com)
> The big Kahuna of the e-book sites, having merged with rivals The Lending Library and The PalmPilot E-Text Library in the last year. Highlights of the Fiction category include a huge assortment of Sherlock Holmes titles, plus samplings of Tolstoy, Melville (*Moby Dick*), Dickens, Jack London, Jane Austen,

and Willa Cather. The Short Fiction listings, which may be more appropriate for PalmPilots of limited memory, reads like a Who's Who of famous dead authors: Roald Dahl, William Faulkner, Ernest Hemingway, O. Henry, George Orwell, James Joyce, Oscar Wilde, Virginia Woolfe, and many more. Shakespeare is represented by 39 of his most famous plays; the Poetry category includes the best of Robert Frost, T.S. Eliot, and Robert Service. (For a hilarious, grisly read en route to L.A., read Robert Service's *The Cremation of Sam McGee.*)

If you're seeking some heartbeat acceleration, MemoWare also has the Tarzan series (Edgar Rice Burroughs), *Treasure Island* (Robert Louis Stevenson), *The Adventures of Tom Sawyer* (Mark Twain), grisly Edgar Allen Poe tales, much Sherlock Holmes, some Agatha Christie, a little Jane Austen, all of H. G. Wells's classics (such as *The War of the Worlds*), and even *The Hacker Crackdown* by Bruce Sterling.

This site also includes an enormous library of reference texts, featuring over 300 downloadable lists of holidays, area codes, zip codes, phone numbers, HTML tags, Internet access-company access numbers, medical reference, sports-team schedules, metropolitan subway maps, hotel/air/car reservation numbers, international holidays and so on. Bring extra batteries.

Peanut Press (http://www.peanutpress.com)

The prices to download these files can be steep—$15 for *Monica's Story*, for example—but you get books by popular living authors, including current best sellers. A special kind of Doc reader, one that supports fonts, bold, and italic, is included, and makes the book reading experience much nicer.

Mary Jo's Pilot Library (http://www.dogpatch.org/etext.html)

A no-frills download site filled with classic novels, most aimed at children: 23 *Wizard of Oz* novels; *Peter Pan*; *Little Women*; the Brothers Grimm Fairy Tales; *Pinocchio*; *Hans Brinker*; *Dr. Dolittle*; the Peter Rabbit tales by Beatrix Potter; Kipling's *The Jungle Book*; and a collection of "silly and gross songs." (If all this makes your PalmPilot feel too lightweight, you can also get such moral tales as Hugo's *Les Misérables* and Hawthorne's *The Scarlet Letter.*)

PalmPilot Entertainment Zone (http://www.fidalgo.net/~ram)

Adult e-texts.

The Daily Pilot Newspaper (http://www.vu.union.edu/~cohenr/pilotnews/)

A fascinating use of the PalmPilot, the Web, and Doc files. Dial into the web page, either with your PalmPilot—see Chapter 14, *The Web in Your Palm*—or your desktop computer. Construct your own "newspaper" by choosing from such elements as headlines, health, sports, tech news, and weather. Download a personalized Doc document containing exactly the information you specified. See Figure 10-9 for an example of a Palm-based newspaper.

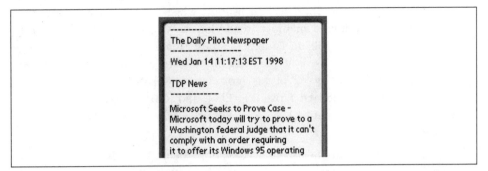

Figure 10-9. The Pilot Daily News gives you news, sports, weather, and even classified ads—and dumps it directly into the PalmPilot. Load up before heading off to a new city, so you'll know what to expect from the weather.

The Pilot Book Depository (http://www.teleport.com/~jleonard/)

A small fiction site, rich in titles not found elsewhere, including novels by Dickens, H. G. Wells, Voltaire, Mark Twain, Robert Louis Stevenson, and so on.

Online Originals (http://www.onlineoriginals.com/welcome.html)

If the oldness of the Web's *free* offerings is getting you down, this site offers books written by *living* authors—but you're asked to pay. An interesting assortment, Pilot-ready, at $7 per title.

Mind's Eye Fiction (http://tale.com)

Here's another alternative for the contemporary-fiction fan: a web site filled with short stories by such modern authors as Larry Niven, David Brin, Spider Robinson, Fred Saberhagen, and Bud Sparhawk. You pay about 60 cents per story.

E-books of Web Pages

Instead of just downloading Doc files *from* the Web, a few clever web pages let you make Doc files *of* the Web. In other words, it's possible to grab the text of your favorite web pages and put *that* onto your PalmPilot, ready for the road. You might want to perform this stunt if, for example, you spot a long article from today's Yahoo news; or you want to proof the text of your company's new web page; or you want to study some statistics just published online.

To make this possible, go to the PalmPilot Internet File Converter web site at *http://pilot.wiw.org*. Here you're asked to type in the web address of the web page you want to convert.

For example, suppose you make a regular practice of reading the Evening News column at the Motley Fool, the sassy investment site, and you'd like to start reading this column on the train ride home from work each day instead of taking up after-dinner time to do so.

Here's how you should proceed:

1. At the office, on your desktop computer, visit *http://pilot.wiw.org*. In the URL box (see Figure 10-10), type the web address of the Motley Fool column you're interested in: *http://www.fool.com/EveningNews/EveningNews.htm*. If you wish, in the right-hand box, type a title for the Doc file you're about to create (see Figure 10-10 again).

2. Click Submit. After a moment, a file called *Convert.cgi* is saved onto your hard drive.

3. Using any of the installation methods outlined in Chapter 7, install the *Convert.cgi* file into your PalmPilot (via a HotSync).

4. Turn on the PalmPilot. Launch your Doc reader, such as SmartDoc. You'll see the name of your new reading material, Motley Fool, listed; tap it to begin reading (as shown in Figure 10-10).

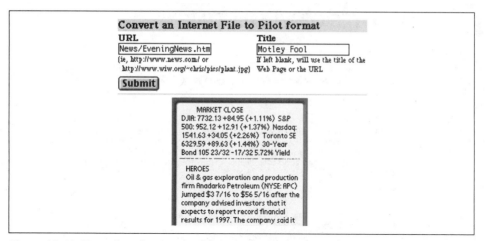

Figure 10-10. Using the Pilot Internet File Converter web site (top), any web page can be turned into a Doc file for easy reading on the PalmPilot (bottom).

Making Your Own E-books

Though many people use the PalmPilot as a glorified paperback, many others load their *own* material onto the PalmPilot for later review. Unfortunately, the Palm-Pilot doesn't display bold, italic, style sheets, and other formatting niceties from your word processor documents; but at least you retain the text itself, which is good enough for shifting many important reading tasks into more convenient time slots (particularly when traveling).

The program you use to turn your own word processor files into Doc files is called MakeDoc. In the shareware world, there are several versions, one each for the Macintosh, Windows, DOS, and Java. (These versions are included with this book.) A superior, but costlier, avenue, is Documents to Go, which offers drag-and-drop conversion for Word documents.

Here's a step-by-step guide to turning your own word processor files into Doc files, complete with formatting tips from a battle-scarred veteran.

Preparing the Original Word Processor File

The original document is shown in Figure 10-11. Note that it's full of formatting: some paragraphs are indented, some are bolded, others italicized. All of this will be lost in the conversion to the PalmPilot. Therefore, note that the preparer has cleverly typed the title of the document in capital letters; as you can see in Figure 10-13, all-caps phrases are great for PalmPilot headings, because it's the only distinctive treatment you can give a headline on the formatting-free PalmPilot.

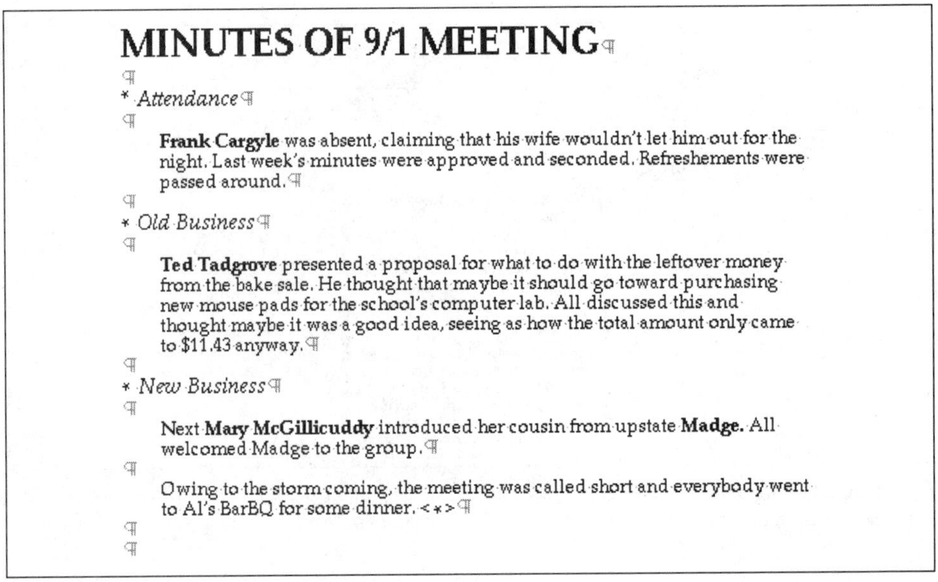

MINUTES OF 9/1 MEETING¶
¶
* *Attendance*¶
¶
    Frank Cargyle was absent, claiming that his wife wouldn't let him out for the night. Last week's minutes were approved and seconded. Refreshements were passed around.¶
¶
* *Old Business*¶
¶
    Ted Tadgrove presented a proposal for what to do with the leftover money from the bake sale. He thought that maybe it should go toward purchasing new mouse pads for the school's computer lab. All discussed this and thought maybe it was a good idea, seeing as how the total amount only came to $11.43 anyway.¶
¶
* *New Business*¶
¶
    Next **Mary McGillicuddy** introduced her cousin from upstate **Madge.** All welcomed Madge to the group.¶
¶
    Owing to the storm coming, the meeting was called short and everybody went to Al's BarBQ for some dinner. < * >¶
¶
¶

Figure 10-11. The original document, shown here in Microsoft Word, has been prepared intelligently. The headline's in all caps, double returns are used between paragraphs, and a consistent symbol has been used to introduce each heading. (These symbols will turn into bookmarks automatically.)

Notice something else about the original Word document: the word processor's automatic blank-line-before-each-paragraph option has been turned off. To create a blank line between paragraphs, the typist has instead pressed the Return key twice (as illustrated by the light gray ¶ symbols in Figure 10-11). That's because the PalmPilot doesn't offer indenting or blank-line-before-paragraph features; a double Return is the only way to produce blank lines in the final product.

How to Let the PalmPilot Create Bookmarks Automatically

SmartDoc, AportisDoc, and TealDoc can generate bookmarks automatically from your word processor document, producing a handy pop-up menu of section names for easy navigation. To make that work, however, you must plan ahead when preparing the word processor file.

First, create one-line section *subtitles*, as shown in Figure 10-11. Second, precede each section name with a consistent symbol or word. In Figure 10-11, an asterisk (*) has been used to denote a heading; but you might prefer to use two spaces, a hyphen, the word *Chapter,* or any other snippet of prefix text.

How does the PalmPilot know that these symbols are supposed to generate bookmarks? At the very end of the document, you *tell* your Doc reader what symbol you've used by placing it between <these symbols>. Inspect Figure 10-11, for example, and you'll see that the document ends with <*>, which tells your Doc reader that the asterisk is the section-denoter.

If you've set up your document correctly with these symbols, the bookmarks are generated automatically when you first open the document (in AportisDoc) or when you use the AutoScan command (TealDoc) or Scan Custom Bookmarks (SmartDoc) command.

Using MakeDoc

When the original document is in good shape, use the File menu's Save As command; save your file as a text-only or ASCII Text document. (In the Save As dialog box, you should see a pop-up menu below the file's name, which you can use to specify that you want a text-only document.) The result is a text file on your hard drive. At this point, the steps depend on your computer:

Macintosh

Drag the text file onto the MakeDocDD icon. If you have Palm Desktop 2.1 or later installed (see Chapter 9, *Palm Desktop: Macintosh*), version 1.0.4 of MakeDocDD asks you to choose your PalmPilot's user name. The deed is done; when you HotSync, the new Doc file is loaded onto your palmtop.

Earlier versions of MakeDocDD aren't MacPac 2–aware; they place the completed Doc file on your Macintosh desktop and display an error message. You can still install the newly created *.prc* file, however, as you would any Palm program.

A promising alternative to MakeDocDD, in testing as this book went to press, is Mac Palm Doc (*http://www.softplum.com*). It offers several unique features, including the ability to splice together multiple text files into a single Doc file. And if you have MacPac 2 or later, this program can automatically install the resulting Doc file onto your palmtop.

Windows

Double-click the MakeDocW icon. The window shown in Figure 10-12 appears. Click the Browse button to locate and select the text file you want to convert. Use the Auto-Install pop-up menu to specify whose PalmPilot you want this file installed onto. You may also, at this point, click the various other dialog box tabs to explore your options (for example, you can specify which of AportisDoc's 15 categories this file should be preassigned to). When you're ready, click Convert.

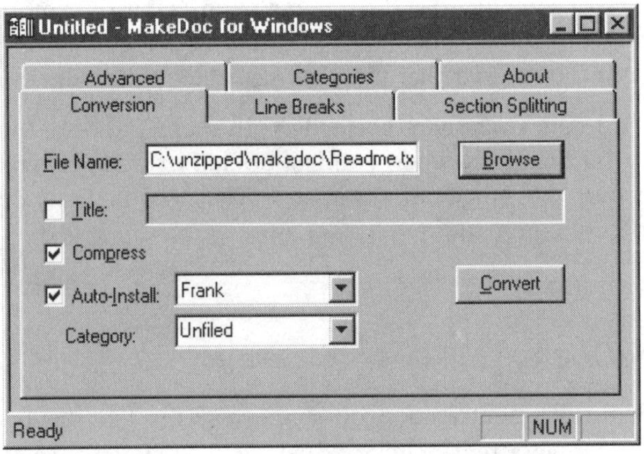

Figure 10-12. *MakeDoc's primary dialog box requires that you select the text file for conversion—and a PalmPilot for installation.*

Note that all of this setup (for Macintosh and Windows) is required only the *first* time you convert a text file. The *next* time, simply drag a text file onto the Make-Doc icon. It will perform the conversion without requiring you to specify any settings.

MakeDoc places the converted file into the Install folder in your user-named folder (see Chapter 6, *HotSync, Step by Step*); on Windows, it also flips the requisite invisible flag that tells the HotSync software that files are waiting. The next time you HotSync, your new Doc file will be automatically installed (see Figure 10-13).

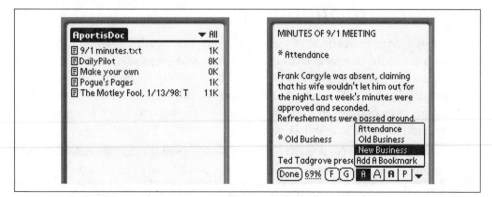

Figure 10-13. When the conversion is complete, and your HotSync is finished, tap the Applications icon; open your Doc reader; and check out the list of Doc files waiting (left). Tap the one you want to read. It opens (right).

Compare, incidentally, the final product in Figure 10-13 with the original word processor file in Figure 10-11. You can see that much formatting is lost, but that judicious use of capitals, section names, and blank lines produces an eminently readable pocket document.

From Microsoft Word to PalmPilot in One Step

Doc files constitute by far the most frequently used word-processing format for the PalmPilot. But it isn't the only one. Documents to Go, a $40 Macintosh or Windows program from DataViz (*http://www.dataviz.com*), converts any Word file into a Doc-like format in a single step. It comes with its own reader program for your PalmPilot, WordView, that can read both its own proprietary format as well as standard Doc files.

All you have to do is drag any Word (or ClarisWorks) document onto the Documents to Go icon on your Mac or PC desktop. The formatting is automatically stripped out, a blank line is automatically placed between paragraphs for easier reading, the text is converted into the Doc-like format, and the resulting file is placed in your Install folder, where it will be transferred to your PalmPilot at the next HotSync.

In the initial release of Documents to Go, you can't edit these documents once they're on your PalmPilot. However, the desktop software is smart enough to monitor changes to the original Word documents—and if they change, Documents to Go can automatically generate an updated file for upload into your PalmPilot.

(Documents to Go can also convert Excel spreadsheets, as described in Chapter 12, *Database and Number Crunching*.)

Executive Tip Summary

- Take the time to learn about each of your Doc reader's scrolling features, which are more complete than in any other word processor—you can scroll a line at a time or a page at a time; only when you tap or only when you press the PalmPilot's scroll buttons; continuously as you hold the stylus down; faster or slower depending on how far you are from the middle of the screen; or even automatically in teleprompter mode.

- The Web, and this book's CD, are filled with great works of ancient fiction. You can download modern works, too, but you'll have to pay for them.

- When preparing your own text for use as Doc reader-ready material, use only capitals—no other formatting—for headings or emphasis. Use two Return-key presses to create a blank line between paragraphs. Use a standard two-letter code wherever you want a bookmark to appear—and place that code within <angle brackets> at the very end of the text.

11

The Secret Multimedia World

Considering that it lacks color, stereo speakers, or CD-ROM drive, you might wonder how the PalmPilot could possibly be mentioned in the same sentence with the word "multimedia." Clearly, the PalmPilot was designed to be fast, stingy with batteries, and expert at sucking *textual* information out of your desktop computer—but to play music, show graphics, and play animations? Never.

Indeed, the average PalmPilot purchaser probably never suspects what this palmtop is capable of; no sound or graphics programs came with it. But with the right shareware add-ons, the PalmPilot can do a creditable job of putting a cultural studio in your pocket.

Photos on the PalmPilot

Here's a shocking fact about the Palm screen: it *isn't* black-and-white! It's actually capable of displaying 4 or 16 different shades of gray, much like an inexpensive laptop. So, how come you've never seen this feature? Because, except for a few Palm VII Web applets (see Chapter 16, *Palm VII: Wireless Email, Wireless Web*), the built-in software doesn't take advantage of the screen's grayscale abilities. The add-on software described in this chapter, however, does; see Figure 11-1 to see what's possible.

To *view* grayscale photos in this way, you need a program called ImageViewer; or a free program called TinyViewer; to *create* grayscale photos, you need a Windows program called ImageConverter. Both programs are included with this book. (If you have a Macintosh, see the sidebar "Creating Image Viewer files on the Macintosh.")

And why would you even want photos on your PalmPilot? Some PalmPiloteers simply like to carry around a digital photo of their loved ones. Others load up

Figure 11-1. You might not suspect that your PalmPilot can display photos—more or less. (The Palm IIIx and Palm V can show up to 16 shades of gray, as shown at left.)

with work-related diagrams, such as the medical painting shown in Figure 11-1. The Web is increasingly full of ImageViewer documents portraying maps of various cities, subway systems, and famous buildings.

Getting a Photo Ready for the PalmPilot Using ImageConverter

ImageConverter lets you grab images from any of three sources: something you're seeing on the screen, something you've copied to the clipboard, or a graphic file sitting on your hard drive (see Figure 11-2).

Suppose there's a graphic file on your hard drive that you'd like to transfer to the PalmPilot. Most PalmPilot models are capable of displaying only four shades: black, dark gray, light gray, and "white" (the color of the screen background). The IIIx, V, and related models can display 16 shades. For best results, then, do some processing manually in a program like Photoshop: change your image to grayscale mode, for example, and fiddle with the brightness and contrast. To get a preview of how the photo will look on the PalmPilot, use Photoshop's Posterize command, and specify 4 or 16 levels of gray. (This is all optional, but it's designed to let you control how the final image appears—otherwise, ImageConverter will simply use its own inflexible conversion scheme.) When you're finished experimenting, save your graphic in one of these file formats: GIF, JPG, PCX, DIB, RLE, or TGA.

Now launch ImageConverter and click the Open button (see Figure 11-2). Locate the image file on your hard drive; double-click it; in the Image Title box, name the graphic as you'd like it to show up on the PalmPilot. Use the Auto-Install pop-up menu to specify whose PalmPilot this file should be installed onto.

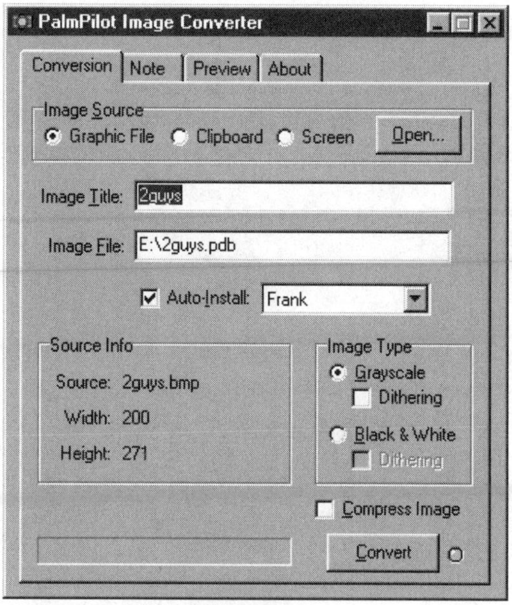

Figure 11-2. ImageConverter turns any graphic into a 4- or 16-shade grayscale image, ready for the PalmPilot.

Before you wrap things up, click the Preview tab to see what the PalmPilot is about to do to your lovely photo. You'll probably discover that turning on both the Grayscale and the Dithering options (on the Conversion tab) produces the best results, as shown in Figure 11-3 and Figure 11-4.

When you click the Conversion tab and click Convert, your image is instantly placed into the Install folder (inside your user-named folder, in the *Palm* folder), ready for HotSyncing.

After the HotSync, tap Applications → TinyViewer (or ImageViewer) on your PalmPilot. Now you're shown a list of the graphics you've installed; tap one to see it in all its 160-pixel-square glory (Figure 11-4). If the image is larger than the PalmPilot's screen, scroll it by dragging with your finger or stylus—right in the middle of the image—or press the four rounded application-launching buttons to scroll the page in each direction. (ImageViewer lets you view pictures up to 640 by 400—about three or four times the size of the PalmPilot's own screen.) When you want to open a different image, tap the Menu icon.

Once you're viewing the image, ImageViewer lets you adjust the darkness of the gray levels, which can often dramatically improve the clarity of your images. To do so, return to the file-list screen, if you haven't already (by tapping the Menu icon). Tap Menu → Options → Adjust Colors. In this dialog box, you can tap the arrows above or below each gray block to change its darkness.

Figure 11-3. The Preview tab lets you see the original photo (left) as compared with the four-gray Palm version (right). Better yet is the dithered four-gray Palm version, shown in Figure 11-4.

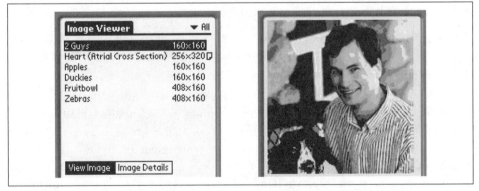

Figure 11-4. Tap the name of a picture (left) to view it (right).

 In TinyVewer, if the image is too large to fit on a single screen, press one of the plastic scroll buttons on the PalmPilot. After a moment of computing, you're shown the original graphic at half its size. To zoom in again, press the scroll button again.

To rename, delete, or annotate an image—or to flag it with a category label—tap the Image Details button on ImageViewer's main listing screen, and then tap one of the images in the list. The resulting dialog box offers Rename, Delete, Note, and Private buttons, plus a readout of size and memory statistics for the graphic you tapped. (In TinyVewer, tap the Info or Delete button on the main listing screen, and then tap the name of an image.)

Creating ImageVewer Files on the Macintosh

The Image Converter application described in this chapter works in Windows only. On the Macintosh, you need the ImageVewer Plug-in, which comes on this book's CD-ROM, and the shareware graphics program called Graphic-Converter. (You can get GraphicConverter from *http://www.shareware.com* or any similar web site.)

To set up this plug-in, put it into the Plug-ins folder, which is inside the GraphicConverter folder. Launch GraphicConverter, choose File → Preferences → Plug-ins → Set Folder, locate the Plug-ins folder, click it once and click Select "Plug-ins." Click OK. Quit GraphicConverter.

When you're actually ready to convert a graphic to ImageVewer formats, open it in GraphicConverter. Use the Picture → Grayscale → 4 Grays command to reduce it to PalmPilot-ready, four-shades-of-gray mode. Follow-up with the Picture → Brightness/Contrast command, which can help a great deal with the clarity of the photo. Resize the photo as desired, using the Picture → Size → Scale command. (The picture doesn't have to be 160 pixels square, like the PalmPilot's screen, but 160 pixels square is as much of the photo as you'll see on the palmtop without scrolling or zooming.)

Finally, choose File → Save As. In the resulting dialog box, choose Format → ImageVewer. Save the new file into your Palm → Users → [your name] → Files To Install folder, making sure to add the suffix *.pdb* to the filename.

At the next HotSync, your photo will appear in the TinyViewer or ImageVewer photo list on the PalmPilot!

(You'll find that GraphicConverter can now open ImageVewer files on the Mac, to—just use the File → Open command as usual.)

Painting and Drawing

There are two ways to create graphics on a computer: by *painting* or by *drawing*. The difference has to do with how the *computer* thinks of your art. In the case of painting programs, the PalmPilot thinks in one-dot units. To display a "painting" (such as a photo), the PalmPilot must memorize the exact status—black, white, or one of the gray shades—of each pixel (screen dot) on its screen. In other words, it stores a *map* of your screen. Painting programs, it's therefore said, generate *bit-mapped* graphics.

When you lay down some "paint," you turn white pixels some other color. You can erase them, but you can't change the original shape you painted—a circle, say, or a letter of the alphabet—because the PalmPilot no longer thinks of them as a circle or a letter of the alphabet. On the other hand, you have control over each individual dot.

Drawing programs, on the other hand, create what are called *object-oriented* graphics (sometimes called *vector* drawings). When you draw a circle in one of these programs, the PalmPilot doesn't store it as a map of black dots; instead, it remembers that you drew a circle of a fixed shading and size. In a drawing program, objects remain objects; after you draw a circle, you can return to it later and move it by dragging it. You can overlap another object on top of it—and later change your mind. You can change a circle's shading long after you drew it.

Both kinds of programs are available on the PalmPilot; here are some of the best.

Getting Your Art on Paper

On desktop computers, drawing programs have a gigantic advantage over painting programs: their printouts. A printout from a painting program looks every bit as jagged on paper as it did on the screen. But when you print from a drawing program, the PalmPilot doesn't tell the printer "three black dots, then a white one . . . ." Instead it says, "A square, one inch tall." The printer can now put on the page a square, one inch tall, at its (the printer's) much higher image quality.

You're probably protesting that the PalmPilot can't print at *all,* so what's the point? Actually, the PalmPilot's premiere drawing program, PenDraw, *can* print if you hook up a standard printer to the HotSync cradle (or cable). See Chapter 15, *Paging, Faxing, Printing, and Beaming,* for details on printing. And your paintings can be transferred to Windows and printed from there.

Painting Programs

The world hasn't been the same since DinkyPad debuted. DinkyPad introduced the simple concept of *drawing* on the PalmPilot's surface as though it were a penny pad, exactly as you can on the Apple Newton (which costs four times more than the PalmPilot). Today, the world is crowded with painting programs. For example:

DinkyPad

> The first sketchpad program. Offers pen, circle, line, rectangle, and eraser tools in five different line thicknesses. By pressing the PalmPilot's scroll buttons, you can actually draw on a much taller "virtual canvas" than fits on a single screen, as Figure 11-5 illustrates. The home-page index view shows a thumbnail of all the different drawings on your palmtop and lets you name and add a note to each drawing. This program uses 23K on the PalmPilot. The companion program, DinkyPad Conduit, transfers your finished artwork to a Windows 95 PC or Macintosh.

Figure 11-5. DinkyPad (upper left) makes quick sketches possible on the PalmPilot, including these examples posted on the Web by Nathan Black (lower left) and Steven Lue (right).

Doodle

> This 25K sketching program has only two tools, a pencil and an eraser; without straight lines and rectangles, it's harder to draw, say, maps than in rival DinkyPad. Doodle also cries out for an index "home-page" view, as DinkyPad has; you can move from one drawing to the next only by choosing Next or Previous from a menu. However, Doodle offers many different pen thicknesses and "nib" shapes, a selection of ink "colors" (various shading patterns), and makes possible sketching styles that would be impossible in DinkyPad.

TealPaint

By far the most complete and professional painting program for the Palm-Pilot. (It's $18 shareware.) TealPaint is the only one, for example, to offer a "marquee" tool (for selecting portions of the drawing and dragging them around), Undo and Revert commands, a "fat bits" super-zoom-in mode for detail work, and even a screen-capture command that takes pictures of other Palm programs. Pop-up menus let you choose from 16 fill patterns, 12 different brush shapes, and 16 drawing tools (including a text tool with choice of typefaces).

To make life easier, you can work on a canvas larger than the actual screen; a thumbnail "index" view lets you choose from among your finished works; incredibly enough, an Anim menu lets you create cel-based animations that play right on the screen; and it all fits in 50K (see Figure 11-6). A utility program for converting HotSynced TealPaint artwork into standard Windows 95 .BMP graphics is included.

PenDraw

Despite the name, PenDraw is for painting, not drawing—and it's great. Weighing in at only 15K, PenDraw's clever interface offers pop-up icons that offer eight shading patterns, eight brushes, seven painting tools, and an Undo command. There's no index page, but a click on the Previous or Next arrows scrolls your other drawings into view (see Figure 11-6).

Pocket Paint

A clever $10 shareware hybrid program that both creates simple sketches, especially maps and diagrams, and displays its own grayscale photo format. Macintosh fans will especially appreciate the accompanying PPaint for Mac application, which lets you turn any standard Macintosh graphics file into a grayscale Palm graphic, much like the GraphicConverter plug-in described earlier in this chapter.

QPaint

The companion to Qdraw, described in the next section. Features a similar interface; in 17K, all the essentials are here—eight painting tools, eight shading patterns, three line-widths, and a choice of two text styles—but not much in the way of bells and whistles.

HDSketch

Like TealPaint, this one includes a text tool, an Undo command, a virtual canvas, and a thumbnail "index" view. It also includes a converter program for Windows and, remarkably, a two-way conduit that keeps your graphics collection constantly updated via normal HotSyncs.

Capturing the Uncapturable

Many of the screenshot illustrations in this book never existed on a PalmPilot at all. Instead, they were captured from a Macintosh or Windows program called POSE (Palm OS emulator), available from this book's CD-ROM. It's a Palm *emulator*, allowing Palm programs to run right on the PC (in a window shaped like the PalmPilot itself), where it's a simple matter to capture the screen image.

Some programs, however, crash Palm OS Emulator. Others use special graphics routines that don't show up on the emulator—only on a real PalmPilot. And software that requires dialing into the Internet, such as the email and web programs described in this book, sometimes can't be captured from POSE. How are you supposed to take pictures of such software for use in, for example, books about the PalmPilot?

Three clever solutions are available (and included with this book): first, there's the free program Snapshot. It creates ImageVewer files, as described in the beginning of this chapter, that depict whatever was on the screen at a precise moment. The program lets you specify how many seconds you want to elapse before the photo is taken, much like the self-timer on cameras. The resulting ImageVewer file will then be HotSynced to your Windows PC or Mac, where you can view and edit.

The second solution, TealPaint, also offers a time-delay screen-grab feature; it gives you 10, 20, 30, or 40 seconds before capturing the Palm screen. After the countdown, if you return to TealPaint, you'll see your newly created painting document, which perfectly resembles the PalmPilot's screen at the designated moment.

Getting this picture onto your computer is another matter. When you HotSync, a new file (by default called Pictures) is placed into the Palm → *your name* → *Backup* folder. Using a supplementary Windows 95 utility program— included with TealPaint—called Paintmgr, you can open and display the TealPaint database of pictures, at which point you can export them as Windows *.bmp* files.

If sitting around and waiting for the countdown to elapse is too boring or too imprecise for you, install ScreenShot Hack instead. As described in Appendix A, *100 Programs Worth Knowing About*, this program is a HackMaster file, meaning that it also requires the HackMaster utility program (included with this book). To set the program up, launch HackMaster, turn on the ScreenShot checkbox, and tap the tiny + symbol to the right of its name. Here you're offered the choice of two ways to capture a Palm screen image: you can write a certain Graffiti symbol, or you can tap the dot beneath the "1 2 3" at the

—Continued—

lower-right corner of the Graffiti area. Either way, whatever is on the screen at that instant is captured as a graphic. Once the graphic is HotSynced to your Windows PC, you can use the accompanying ScreenShot2BMP application to convert the captured images into standard Windows *.bmp* files.

Then you'll be ready to illustrate your own PalmPilot book.

ScratchPad

> With no choice of tools or line thicknesses, the minimalist ScratchPad would be barely worth mentioning except for its tiny RAM appetite: 5K. (Similarly: Scribble, which is even barer-bones.)

SketchPad Palm

> Very Palmesque, complete with home-page index view, category and Private options, a menu command to display the PalmPilot's keyboard, and so on (see Figure 11-6). The actual drawing tools, however, are minimal: one pencil, one width, plus an eraser. SketchPad consumes 17K of RAM, but feels far more professional than its Spartan rival ScratchPad.

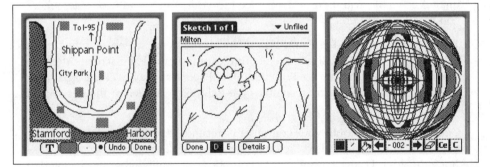

Figure 11-6. Heirs to DinkyPad include the impressive TealPaint (left) and SketchPad (middle). At right, PenDraw's unique Spyrograph tool lets you create geometrical designs that would be impossible in other programs.

Drawing Programs

You don't find paintbrush, pencil, and eraser tools in a *drawing* program; instead, lines, circles, and rectangles are the primary tools. As noted earlier, however, the advantages are considerable: you can change any shape you've drawn at any time. Drawing programs, with their solid, straight lines, free from human shakiness, are perfect for maps, electrical diagrams, architectural drawings, and so on.

At this writing, there are only two drawing programs for the PalmPilot: PalmDraw and QDraw (see Figure 11-7).

PalmDraw

True to its breed, PalmDraw features an arrow tool that lets you adjust the size or position of any line, arc, circle, rectangle, or text block you've drawn. You'll wind up wishing the program let you change line thicknesses or shading patterns—but then again, you can always export your work as a PostScript or EPS file to your computer, and touch it up there. (PalmDraw comes with an accompanying utility program that converts PalmDraw pictures to Windows Metafiles (WMF) or Enhanced Windows Metafiles (EMF) formats.)

PalmDraw even lets you print directly to a PostScript printer with a standard serial port; just connect your HotSync cradle to it directly and use PalmDraw's Print to Serial command.

Although PalmDraw isn't quite MiniCad, in some respects it represents an impressive feat in Palm programming and hints at the promise of the next generation of pocket-sized graphics software.

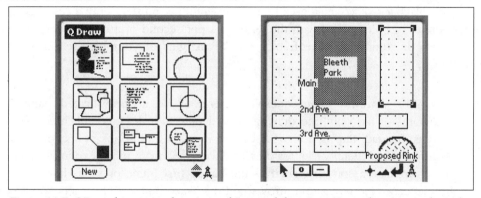

Figure 11-7. QDraw lets you make crisp architectural drawings. Tap a drawing on the index page (left) to open it (right). Tap an object to show its handles, which you can drag to reshape or resize.

QDraw

A muscular, full-featured drawing program that manages to squeeze four menus into the PalmPilot's tiny menu bar. These menus offer such standard drawing-program commands as Group, Ungroup, Send to Back, and Bring to Front, along with Cut, Copy, Paste, and Duplicate. The pop-up tool icons feature the usual arrow, circle, rectangle, and text tools, along with a rounded-rectangle tool whose degree of roundedness you can actually change. Another palette lets you change the fill pattern of any shape (which is lacking from PalmDraw). You can zoom in and zoom out, turn the "snap to grid" option on or off, and view a thumbnail index of all drawings (see Figure 11-7). Not bad for 28K.

Palm Animation Software

The notion of creating the next *Fantasia* or *The Little Mermaid* on your palmtop may strike some as taking the PalmPilot can-do attitude just a hair too far. And yet several useful programs prove that, in fact, this computer is as good as any for creating simple animations.

TealPaint

TealPaint is much more than a painting program, as described earlier in this chapter; it can actually create smooth full-screen animations. Start by drawing the first frame of your cartoon. Tap Menu → Anim → Replicate Frame to create a second frame—a duplicate of the first, which you can now edit slightly to show movement of the first frame's elements. Continue using the Replicate Frame command, each time moving, adding, or distorting the elements to indicate their progress.

When you're finished with this hard part, Menu → Anim → Go Play to enjoy the playback of your little cartoon. The PalmPilot musters only a few frames per second (compared with the 24 frames per second of a real movie), but it beats drawing successive frames on the margins of your high-school math book.

Flip

This $10 shareware item doesn't pretend to be a sophisticated painting program—it has only one drawing tool, a pen in your choice of three thicknesses. Instead, Flip is designed solely for creating flip-book animations (see Figure 11-8). Several of its features are borrowed from more expensive computer animation software, such as the handy first frame/previous frame/next frame/last frame navigation arrows and the Trace button (which lets you see, in ghosted form, what was on the previous frame).

PalmSmear

If you've ever used the goofy, bizarre Mac or Windows program called Kai's Power Goo, you already understand the concept behind PalmSmear. You start by converting a photo under Windows PC into PalmSmear format, using an included converter program. Once the photo is on your PalmPilot, you drag your stylus on the screen to twist and distort the image as though it's printed on a sheet of Silly Putty (see Figure 11-8). Then, after having turned the image of your favorite movie star or relative into a hideous gargoyle, a tap on the Play button creates a smooth animation, morphing the original photo slowly and smoothly into the finished monster. Finally, you can beam the whole affair into another PalmPilot.

Only you can decide whether the novelty value of this bizarre and astounding little program is worth the massive 223K of RAM consumed on your palmtop.

Figure 11-8. You can animate either your own drawings (using Flip, left) or a photo of someone you love or loathe (using PalmSmear, right).

Music on the PalmPilot

You might think that the PalmPilot's chirpy little speaker would nip this palmtop's musical future in the bud. Actually, though, the music software for the PalmPilot excels at many musical tasks: serving as a tuning fork, metronome, ear-training instructor, or simple tape recorder for composers, for example. Here's a rundown:

PalmPiano

Features an attractive four-octave piano keyboard and easy-to-use Record, Stop, and Play commands (see Figure 11-9). The good news: yes, you can actually record your own little melodies by tapping them out on the piano keyboard. The bad news: at this writing, the program remembers only the pitches you play, not the rhythms. You can record as slowly as you like, but everything plays back at a standard speed, without regard to the timings you used (every note gets the same rhythmic value). That's no problem if you're recording the fast part of "Jesu, Joy of Man's Desiring" or "Twinkle, Twinkle, Little Star" (there is a "rest" button to insert a silent beat), but "What's Love Got to Do With It?" is out of the question. If the next version records note rhythms as well as pitches, PalmPiano will be a knockout program.

PocketSynth

A terrific little songwriter's tool that lets you record and play back single-line melodies (see Figure 11-9). You specify the pitch by tapping piano keys and the rhythm by choosing from a row of note values (quarter note, half note, dot, etc.). The program uses its own textual notation for recording your melody: C22, for example, means to play the note C in the second octave for a quarter note—but all of this is generated automatically. It's useful to understand the notation, though, in case you want to compose a longer masterpiece by simply writing into, say, the Memo Pad.

The onscreen piano shows only about an octave, but the Octave button gives you access to three more octaves. There's even a Tempo slider to control the playback speed. As a bonus, the Metronome feature turns your PalmPilot into an outstanding visual and sonic electronic metronome—essential to performers, conductors, and composers. It can even accent the downbeat of each measure, no matter what the meter, and you can turn off the sound if you want.)

Figure 11-9. At left, PalmPiano, which looks better but doesn't record note rhythms—only their pitches. At right, PocketSynth, which does a great job of recording and playing back melodies.

If you repeatedly tap the plastic Scroll Up button at the bottom of the PalmPilot while using PocketSynth's metronome mode, an amazing thing happens: the program actually calculates *your* tempo, displaying the numerical metronome marking for the rate you're tapping. (This feature alone adds about $50 to the cost of the electronic metronomes on sale at your local music store at this very moment.)

EbonyIvory

Tap on the piano keyboard to hear a note and see it represented on the musical staff. What's it for? "If you are in the middle of nowhere and inspired with a tune, EbonyIvory helps you lock down the notes," says the Read Me file. Also good, it says, for "Impressing young children." Seriously, though, EbonyIvory works best as an interactive flash card program: for learning the relationships between the way notes sound, the key on the piano that produces them, and the way they look when notated on sheet music.

FretBoard

If you're a guitarist, this free program is indispensable. FretBoard displays the correct fingerings for any note, scale, or chord. Actually, any musician can benefit from FretBoard; just being able to listen to the cleanly played chords and scales is great ear-training practice. Have somebody change the pop-up menus, and see if you can identify the key, chord, or scale being played. A polished piece of work for real musicians.

McChords

This free program closely resembles FretBoard—its purpose is to show and play the notes of any chord type you select—except that it's designed for pianists. It plays and shows the chords on a graphic piano keyboard instead of the guitar fretboard.

Metronome

A simple but effective electronic metronome, much like the Metronome feature of PocketSynth (see Figure 11-9). This program has two advantages: a big, easy-to-use, idiotproof interface (including a scrollbar to adjust the tempo) and a readout of the musical marking (such as Allegro or Andante) that corresponds to the current tempo setting. (Best in-joke yet: if you drag the scrollbar all the way to the bottom, you learn that you're playing "Mucha too slow-issimo!") Metronome lets you turn on the visual flashing and the audio beeping simultaneously, but lacks PocketSynth's accented downbeat, selectable beep pitch, and auto-tempo calculator.

Tuning Fork

For serious musicians only: serves as an electronic tuner for your tunable instrument. As shown in Figure 11-10, this program does only one thing: plays an A—but lets you adjust to various hertz settings, letting you tune to A-440, A-442, or whatever your orchestra settles on.

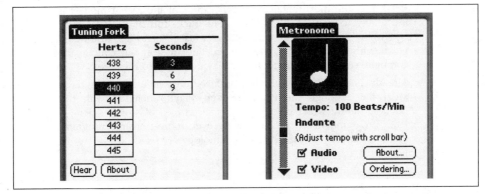

Figure 11-10. The PalmPilot is the perfect toolkit for the performing musician, serving splendidly as either a tuning fork (left) or a visual/audio metronome (right).

M-Tools

This superb, all-in-one program includes three modules. Two closely resemble Metronome and Tuning Fork; the third is a handy reference that instantly displays the key signature for each key you tap in a graphic Circle of Fifths.

PocketBeat

Although you'll never mistake it for Phil Collins, this program is a drum machine, producing various drum sounds by making a surprising variety of different speaker sounds. Make up your own patterns, adjust tempo, switch between preset tempos by hitting a scroll button, and more. Neatest feature: you can specify the tempo by tapping.

Where to Get More Art and Music

The Internet and this book's CD are good starting points for building up your Palm-Pilot's collection of images and music. The database on this book's CD-ROM lists the applications included here; on the Web, visit the Pilot Entertainment Zone, *http://ns1.fidalgo.net/~ram/indexreg.html,* for plenty of both ImageViewer and PocketSynth documents. The PocketSynth documents come as Doc files, described in Chapter 10, *PalmPilot: The Electronic Book*; you're supposed to copy the textual music information out of the Doc file, switch to PocketSynth, and paste it into the Compose area. (Caution: Some of the Pilot Entertainment Zone offerings are rated R.)

The future of music with the Palm platform is looking bright. Although there's no visible sign, the music and sound features in the Palm III and later models have been quietly enhanced. For example, the speaker is still the piezo-style chirper found on previous models, but it's louder. You now get a choice of seven built-in alarm sounds—and programmers can add more to its repertoire.

But by far the most tantalizing new feature of the recent models is the ability to play back standard (one-track, format 0) MIDI files, which are something like text files for music. Such files, distributed by the thousands on the Internet, are tiny in size, but contain the complete computer instructions for playing prepared melodies.

Already one Palm program has surfaced that actually plays these MIDI files through the Palm speaker—PlayIt, included with this book. It surely won't belong before the armies of "road coders"— Palm programmers of the Net—write even more polished programs that can harness this new built-in technology.

Executive Tip Summary

- Unbeknownst to almost everyone, the PalmPilot is not, technically speaking, a black-and-white computer. Its screen is actually capable of displaying up to 16 shades of gray. Programs like ImageViewer can therefore bring half-decent photos to your palmtop.

- Try TealPaint for a surprisingly complete painting program, QDraw for drawing, and PocketSynth as a musician's song-noodling tool.

12

Database and Number Crunching

Because the PalmPilot was designed from Day One to be a bucket for desktop data, it should come as no surprise that Palm databases and spreadsheets abound. You can easily shuttle files between the PalmPilot and databases like Microsoft Access or FileMaker Pro, or between Palm spreadsheets and Microsoft Excel; for thousands of businesses, large and small, Palm data- and number-crunching software opens up new portable possibilities.

All of the programs described in this chapter are included on this book's CD-ROM, in either shareware or trial form.

Palm Database Software

As usual, the best software in the database category isn't sold in stores—it's shareware. In decreasing order of power and sophistication, the three best-known database programs are HanDBase (pronounced "handy base"), JFile, and MobileDB; all three are excellent.

First, however, an important caution: except for FM Sync (described later in this chapter), these programs don't offer genuine HotSync conduits. That is, they don't HotSync with your desktop database on a record-by-record level. (A record is one entry in your database—one card in the catalog.) When you HotSync, your entire database gets transferred to or from the PalmPilot, but individual entries within that database aren't compared with the desktop PC. At all times, you must keep track of where the "live" database file is: either on the PalmPilot or your desktop computer. (Contrast with the built-in Palm programs, where you can make changes both on the palmtop and on your PC, confident that the next HotSync will make sense of everything.)

HanDBase

The features of this shareware gem (*http://ddbsoftware.com*) are impressive enough: the kinds of fields (blanks) in your database can include text, numbers, pop-up menus, checkboxes, serial numbers, and even pictures (such as signatures). Like most Palm programs, HanDBase displays your data as a list view (shown at left in Figure 12-1); when you tap any row of the list, you open the editable, full-screen Record View (at right in the figure). HanDBase's numbers are even more impressive—the entire program fits in 83K on the PalmPilot and costs only $20.

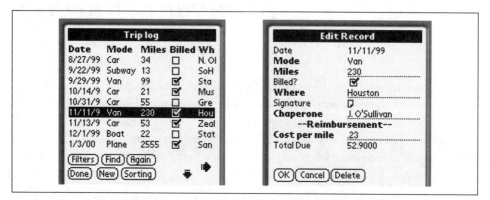

Figure 12-1. Most Palm databases open as a list view (left); tap one row to open its full-screen Record View (right).

Creating a database

When you launch HanDBase, you're shown the Choose Database screen; tap New. As shown in Figure 12-2 at left, you can now write in the name for this database—in this example, Trip log. Also as shown in the figure, you can protect this database from prying eyes by assigning a password, or file this database using the Category menu.

The main attraction of this screen, however, is the Edit Fields list. Your database can have up to 30 fields, such as Name, City, State, and so on. Tap Field 1, for example, to open the Edit Field dialog box (Figure 12-2 at right); name the field and specify what kind of data it will contain. Your choices, as listed in the Field Type pop-up menu, are:

Text

> When the database is finished, you'll be able to write up to 255 characters into this field; it's ideal for most fields, such as names, cities, part descriptions, and so on.

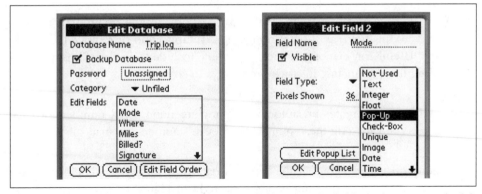

Figure 12-2. Name your database on the screen (left); name the fields on the next one (right).

In setting up your HanDBase fields, you might be surprised to see the Edit Popup List button—you wouldn't expect to find an advanced user-interface feature like pop-up menus in a tiny Palm database program. But this option does exactly what you'd expect: it turns a field into a pop-up menu, listing predefined choices (as shown at left in Figure 12-1). This mechanism saves you (or whoever will be using your database) from having to write using Graffiti to enter data—just choose from the menu. (And if none of the options in the pop-up menu is what you want, you can also write in your own entry.)

It's a quirk of HanDBase, however, that you're not actually allowed to specify the choices in this pop-up menu until after you've finished setting up the database. The easiest workaround: tap OK just after naming the database, before you've actually created any fields. Now, if you tap Done → Properties → the name of your newly created database, you'll be allowed to generate the pop-up menus as you create your fields.

Integer

This kind of field holds whole numbers—useful for Zip Codes and part numbers numbers, for example.

Float

Use this kind of field for numbers that include commas and decimal points, such as money amounts.

Pop-Up

This kind of field is identical to a Text field that you've set up as a pop-up menu, except that it doesn't offer an Edit Popup Menu option. In other words, no write-in choices are allowed when entering data.

Check-Box

> Your finished database will display a checkbox in the column that corresponds to this field, as shown in Figure 12-1; tap to add or remove the checkmark. Useful for marking names you want included in your Christmas-card mailing list, designating in-stock products, and so on.

Unique

> This field type creates an automatically incrementing serial number for each record. You can't edit these numbers—they're stamped automatically.

Image

> When you tap a record in the finished database, this kind of field will take you to a miniature drawing window (at right in Figure 12-3), where you can make a sketch, sign your name, and so on—a feature not found in any other Palm database. (This field doesn't appear in List View; you only see it when you tap a list-view row to open the full-screen record view, and then tap the tiny piece of paper, as shown at left in Figure 12-3.)

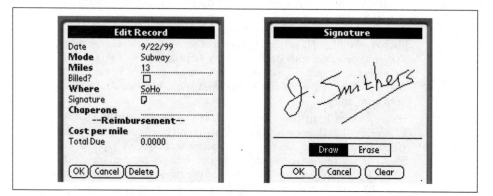

Figure 12-3. HanDBase's Image fields let you capture a signature or other graphic as part of each database record.

Date and Time

> These fields hold a date or time. Using the Behavior pop-up menu, which appears when you set up this kind of field, you can specify what date or time this field should hold: when each record was created, when it was last modified, or a date or time that the database user inputs using the standard Palm calendar and clock-setting controls.

Link and Linked

> HanDBase isn't technically a relational database; that is, if you edit somebody's phone number in one file, it isn't automatically updated in another. Still, HanDBase does let you link files together, letting you view records in one file that pertain to records in another. For example, you might have one

file called *Client List* and another that contains customer orders. When viewing the name of one of your clients, with a single tap, you could summon a list of every order that person has made.

To perform this stunt, you must create a Link field in the first database and a corresponding Linked field in the other. Doing so takes patience and a good deal of time with the program's manual, but the result is much like using the Palm's own Phone Lookup command described in Chapter 4, *The Four Primary Programs*. When you tap the link field in database 1, you're instantly shown a list of matching records from database 2.

Note

This field type is exactly like the Palm's own Notes feature—tap the tiny notepad icon (which appears in Record View, not in List View) to open a Memo Pad-like screen. Here you can input up to 2,000 characters' worth of note information. There's even a pop-up menu that you can load up with commonly used phrases and boilerplate text; a tap on the pop-up menu inserts that text chunk into the note. (Are you listening, physicians and lawyers?)

Heading

This item isn't a field type at all; instead, it creates a centered, boldface heading in Record View, as shown at left in Figure 12-3.

DB Pop-up

This useful option creates a pop-up menu composed of choices from another HanDBase file. When filling out a record in your Orders database, for example, you don't need to write the customer's name. Instead, you can select from a DB Pop-up that offers a list of the names in your Customers database; you save time and prevent misspellings. (If you've read Chapter 13, *Email Anywhere*, you'll recognize this mechanism. It's the same one used by Palm Mail, in which you select an email address from your Address Book when filling out the *To:* blank of a new email.)

Calculated

Amazingly enough, HanDBase even lets you create calculation fields—fields that are automatically filled in according to a formula. Your *Total* field, for example, could show the sum of the Subtotal and Tax fields. Pop-up menus make it easy to incorporate existing fields into the calculation you set up on the Edit Field screen.

After you're finished lining up your fields, tap OK → OK. You arrive at the actual database, where you can now begin creating data.

Governing Field Widths

If you've ever worked with a database before, such as Access or FileMaker, Palm database field types should be familiar. One option of every Palm database, however, may strike you as odd: the Pixels Shown control. Because screen real estate is so limited on the PalmPilot, you'll probably spend a good deal of time tweaking how much horizontal space each field takes on the screen. What makes gauging this number difficult is that it's measured in pixels, or screen dots, of which there are 72 per inch—not a number most of us work in every day.

As a rule of thumb, one letter of the alphabet is about 6 pixels wide. You'd need to write in *12* to accommodate a two-digit serial number, *56* to show the average person's first name, and so on. You can·even hide a field from List View altogether by setting the field width to *0*. (The field will still be visible in Record View.)

Recording data

HanDBase defaults to showing you your data in a list view, as shown at left in Figure 12-1. When you tap New to begin entering your first record, however, you arrive in Record View (at right in Figure 12-1). Use the usual Palm techniques for entering data—Graffiti, the on-screen keyboard, plus any pop-up menus, checkboxes, or time/calendar pop-ups you've established. (As in the built-in Address Book, you can write more text than fits in the visible field—you can continue writing for several lines. The field will automatically grow to accommodate your text.)

You don't have to enter Record View to change the status of pop-up menus and checkboxes—if you like, you can edit these elements directly in List View just by tapping.

The secret is the Preferences screen. Tap Menu → Prefs → Preferences. Turn on the checkboxes for "Checkbox selection in List View" and "Pop-up selection in List View." When you tap OK, you'll find that your pop-up menus and checkboxes are now "live" in List View. (Technically, only Pop-up field types pop up in List View—not other field types for which you've enabled a pop-up menu.)

If, when setting up your fields, you created pop-up menus to accelerate your data entry, you may not immediately understand how to summon your list of choices. Solution: In Record View, tap the boldfaced field name itself (such as City or Product). The pop-up menu appears; when you tap a selection, that text appears in the field itself. You can see some of these boldface field labels in Figure 12-3. This interface mechanism—boldfaced lettering being your cue to tap—is a peculiarity of Palm databases. But it's worth getting used to, because all Palm databases employ it.

> When you're doing a lot of data entry, don't miss the *Copy Record to New* command (in the File menu). It duplicates the current record; you can then edit the newly created duplicate. This technique saves you tedious data input when most of the information stays the same from one record to the next.

Manipulating your data

After you've entered a number of new records, you can manipulate this data in a number of useful ways:

Scroll around

Use the on-screen arrow buttons (in the lower-right corner of the screen), or the plastic Palm scroll buttons, to move up and down through List View. You can scroll right and left by tapping the horizontal on-screen arrow buttons. (If you turn on the corresponding option in HanDBase's Preferences, you can scroll horizontally by pressing the inner hardware buttons—the Address Book and To-Do buttons—instead.)

Find

Tap the Find button in List View to search for text—in one particular field or anywhere in the database.

Filters

This powerful command lets you view only those records that meet certain criteria—everyone who owes you money in New York City, for example. (All other records are hidden from view.)

To set up a filter, tap Filters in List View. Tap to turn on the Filter 1 checkbox, as shown at left in Figure 12-4. Use the Select Field to specify which field contains information you want to match—the City field to specify only records in New York City, for example—and then fill in the corresponding information, as shown in Figure 12-4. You can even set up a second filter on the same screen, further narrowing the results. When you tap OK, all your data will be hidden except those that match the filters you've set up.

To return to viewing all your records, tap Filters again and turn off both checkboxes.

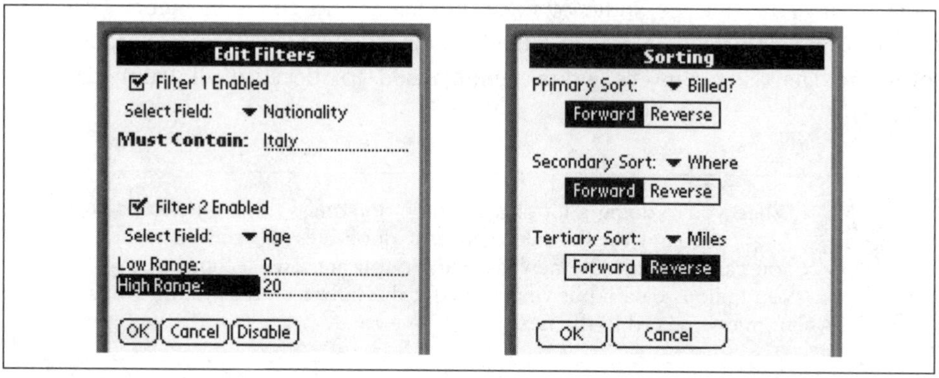

Figure 12-4. This pair of filters finds only Italians who are under 21 (left). At right, you can sort your records up to three different ways at once.

Sort

Tap the Sorting button to summon the dialog box shown at right in Figure 12-4. As the illustration makes clear, you can sort your records alphabetically or in reverse, by up to three fields at once. Using the three different sort commands, you could sort your client list by company name, by subsidiary within each company, and by employees within each subsidiary grouping.

For simple sorting, you may find it faster to tap the heading of any List View column. A pop-up menu appears, offering commands that instantly sort your database.

This pop-up menu also offers a Field Properties command. It gives you direct access to the field-creation characteristics described at the beginning of this section—a great feature when you're fine-tuning the widths of your various fields in List View, for example.

Export data to the Memo Pad

Tap Menu → Actions → Export Records to send the currently filtered and sorted data into, of all things, your Memo Pad. This clever mechanism creates neat, tidy, list-like memos, suitable for reading, editing, or beaming to the PalmPilot of a friend who doesn't have HanDBase.

Run a report

HanDBase can generate useful statistics—minimum value, maximum value, average, and so on—about the contents of a number field. Tap Menu → Actions → Run Report (or tap a column header → Run Report) to create such a report screen.

Transferring a HanDBase Database to the Desktop

After painstakingly collecting your database information with the PalmPilot, you'll probably welcome the fact that transferring it to your Windows PC or Macintosh is fairly straightforward.

HanDBase Desktop (for Windows)

When you pay for your shareware copy of HanDBase, you're also registered for the accompanying program called HanDBase Desktop. As shown in Figure 12-5, it's like a miniature Microsoft Access program that lets you view and edit your HanDBase data on your Windows PC.

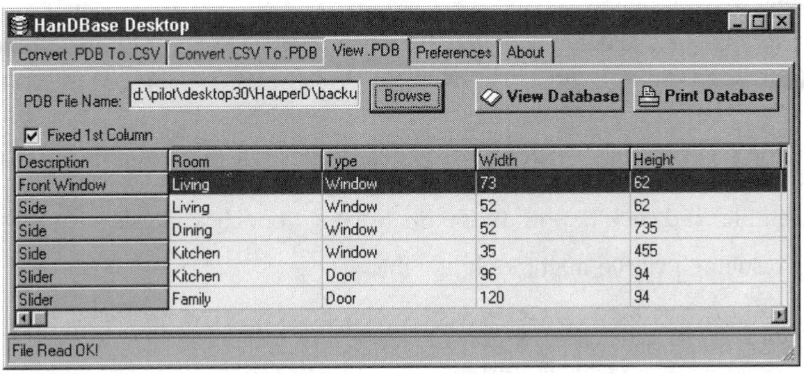

Figure 12-5. HanDBase Desktop converts files going to or from the PalmPilot and lets you view and edit your HanDBase data on the PC.

The program can also convert standard CSV files into HanDBase files, ready to install on your PalmPilot, and vice versa (see the sidebar "Trafficking in CSV"). This option offers tantalizing possibilities for anyone with PC-bound database information.

(At this writing, HanDBase Desktop doesn't perform automatic two-way, record-by-record HotSyncing of Windows database information. Version 2, however, due in mid-1999, is scheduled to make the process automatic.)

HanDBase Desktop (for Macintosh)

If your desktop computer is a Mac, you need HanDBase Desktop for Macintosh, or HDM (*http://www.semicolon.com*). This shareware converter turns CSV files, or tab-delimited text files, into HanDBase files—and vice versa. Simply drag the CSV file (which you have presumably exported from FileMaker, Excel, AppleWorks, or a similar program) into the HDM window. That data is instantly converted into

Trafficking in CSV

Once you begin working with Palm database programs, you'll quickly get to know CSV files. The acronym stands for "comma-separated values" or "comma-space-value," depending on whom you ask, but the principle is always the same: a CSV file is simply a text file containing database information. The field contents, such as Name, Address, or Telephone, are separated by commas, and each record appears on its own line (separated by a return character). (And what if the field itself contains a comma? In that case, you must enclose the contents of the field "in quotes." Alternatively, most modern database programs let you substitute a different character, such as a tab character, for the comma.)

Every Windows or Macintosh database program ever written can read and create CSV files. You'll generally use a command in the File menu called Export or Save As. In FileMaker Pro, for example, choose File → Import/Export → Export Records, and choose Comma-Separated Text from the Type pop-up menu.

In Access, choose File → Save As/Export and click OK. In the following dialog box, choose Text Files from the "Save as Type" pop-up menu, name your export file, and click Export. In the final dialog box, click Finish.

The resulting text file might look like this:

```
Media,Artist,Album Title,Date of Purchase,Duration in Minutes
CD,Louis Armstrong,Satch Plays Fats,4/22/1998,63
Tape,Fink St. Five,"So Long, Sucker",10/19/1982,87
LP,South Frisco Jazz Band,"Too ""Hot"" To Handle",7/4/1985,45
```

Such a file can be opened by any word processor, database program, spreadsheet program—or Palm database-conversion program. If your chosen Palm database doesn't yet offer an automatic, behind-the-scenes HotSync feature, you'll have to endure this intermediate step of creating a CSV file every time you want to move your data to or from the PalmPilot.

HanDBase format and placed in your Files to Install folder (see Chapter 7, *Installing New Palm Programs*). At the next HotSync, you'll find your data safely ensconced in HanDBase on your palmtop.

HDM can also work in reverse, generating Mac database files from an existing HanDBase file. Locate your HanDBase file (see the sidebar "Where to Find Your Palm Database Files on the PC"). Drag the one you want into HDM's Make CSV window; after the conversion, open the resulting text file with your favorite Mac database or spreadsheet program.

HanDJet

Microsoft Access can directly read, edit, and save changes to your HotSynced HanDBase files—as long as you've installed the shareware HanDJet (*http://t-online. de/home/consultus/handjet.htm*). HanDJet is itself an Access application, so you can use all of Access's querying and relational-file features, all in an interface that's designed to resemble HanDBase itself.

One especially pleasant aspect of HanDJet is that it can HotSync your database data directly, without requiring an intermediate CSV file. In fact, in one regard, HanDJet represents the Holy Grail of Palm database software—you can collate the data from multiple PalmPilots into a single Access database. This arrangement is ideal for survey taking, scientific field experiments, inventory checking, sales-force automation, and so on; at the end of the day, the data collected by various employees can all be gathered in a single central Windows database.

Remarkably enough, HanDJet remembers which data came from which PalmPilot, so a subsequent HotSync can actually send edited database information back to the PalmPilots from whence they came.

Where to Find Your Palm Database Files on the PC

Whenever you use one of the conversion programs described in this chapter, you'll be prompted to select the HanDBase, Mobile DB, or JFile database you want to convert. That's fine, as long as you know where to look.

In Windows, after a HotSync, you'll find your Palm database files in Palm → *your PalmPilot name* → Backups. On the Macintosh, the files are sitting in Palm → Users → *your PalmPilot name* → Backups.

If you wind up doing a lot of database conversion, consider creating a shortcut on your Desktop of that deeply buried Backups folder. The time you save could be your own.

JFile

HanDBase may be the most powerful Palm database program, but JFile (*http:// www.land-j.com*) was the first, and it has become extremely popular. It, too, can be outfitted with conversion programs that exchange its data with Microsoft Access (Windows) or FileMaker Pro (Macintosh).

Creating a database

On JFile's opening screen, tap New DB. The resulting screen (see Figure 12-6) lets you name both the database itself and the fields it contains (up to 20). To change the field type, tap the word String to the right of a field. The resulting pop-up menu offers these choices:

String

    This most common kind of field means "any text."

Bool

    Select this item to create a checkbox in your finished layout.

Date and Time

    These fields, when tapped in your finished database, will make the standard Palm calendar-picker or clock-setter appear, so that you can conveniently input a date or time.

Popup

    Choose this item to create a pop-up menu on your finished database screen.

Int and Float

    These fields hold numbers: Use *Int* for whole numbers and *Float* for numbers containing a decimal point.

When you're finished setting up the fields, tap Done.

Figure 12-6. Set up your database on this screen (left); start entering data in the record-view screen (middle), and tap OK to return to the List View (right).

Recording data

Tap the name of your database to open it. The List View that appears may be disorienting, because it doesn't yet contain any information. You'll fix that; tap the Add button to enter Record View, where you can enter the data for your first record, as shown in Figure 12-6 (middle).

If you designated one of your fields as a pop-up menu, the data-entry screen (Record View) is where you create the choices for your pop-up menu. Tap the boldfaced name of the field itself to make the Modify Popup List button appear.

Thereafter, tap that same boldfaced field label to view the pop-up choices—a great time saver for entering predictable pieces of text.

When you're finished entering the data for one record, tap OK to return to the list view. There you'll find a Done button (which returns you to your list of databases), Add (for adding a new record), Find (to search one field, or all the fields, for a certain piece of text), a + button (which means "Find Again"), and a strange, square Del button. When this button is highlighted, you're in Delete mode, and any record whose row you tap in the list view disappears. Tap the Del button again to exit Delete mode.

In general, you edit a record by tapping its List View row (thus entering Record View). Fortunately, you can edit some kinds of fields without having to open the Record View screen—if you know the secret. Tap Menu → Options → App Prefs; there you'll see the useful "Edit in place in column view" checkbox. When this feature is turned on, you'll be allowed to make changes to pop-up menu fields, date fields, time fields, and checkboxes directly in the List View.

Manipulating your data

Most of the data-manipulation commands in JFile resemble those in HanDBase:

Sorting

To sort your database, tap Menu → Tools → Sort Items; you'll be offered the chance to sort your database on three different fields at once. If you don't need that level of control, just tap the boldfaced heading above any column. The pop-up menu offers simple commands that sort your database by that column's contents.

Adjusting column widths

If you find that JFile is too liberal in setting the widths of your fields—by default, only two fields fit per List View screen—adjusting their widths is easy, if not obvious. Tap the boldfaced heading above a column and tap Change Column Width from the pop-up menu that appears. You'll be offered the opportunity to adjust that field's width, in pixels.

Filtering

You can filter your database, too, exactly as described in the HanDBase discussion earlier in this chapter. Tap Menu → Filter Records to view the Filter dialog box.

Transferring a JFile Database to the Desktop

Once again, your Palm database would do you little good if it couldn't be brought home to your desktop computer. With the proper add-on, doing so is easy.

JFTrans

This remarkable program (*http://home.ica.net/~shawkins/jftrans.htm*) imports, export, and massages your JFile data with aplomb. Your data shows up in a standalone Access application (you don't actually have to own Microsoft Access), where you can edit it, change field names, and adjust column widths. You can append the imported Palm data to an existing Access database, let the Palm data wipe out the existing data, or create a new database on your Windows machine—and everything can be easily exported back to JFile. You must click your way through several dialog boxes when sending the data back to the PalmPilot, but you're spared the inconvenience of having to export an intermediary text file, as in other programs.

JConvert

As shown in Figure 12-7, this fast, simple, almost interface-less program comes with JFile (*http://www.land-j.com*). It translates databases both ways between JFile format and CSV formats (see "Trafficking in CSV," earlier in this chapter). Like most of these conversion programs, however, this one requires that you know where to find the JFile database once it's been transferred to your computer. See "Where to Find Your Palm Database Files on the PC" for details.

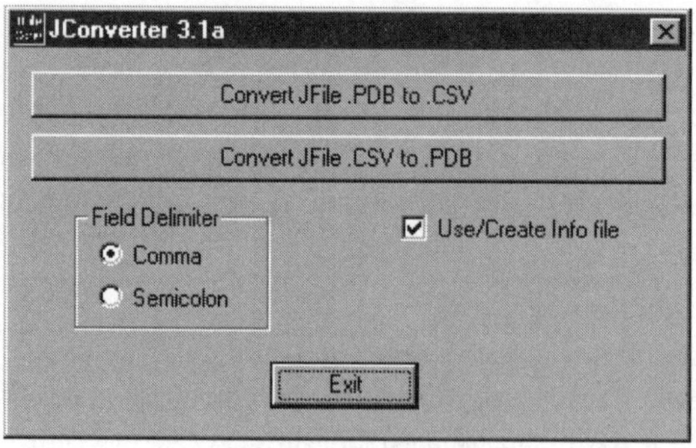

Figure 12-7. JConvert comes with JFile; converts your desktop database files into PalmPilot format.

JetFile Plus

Like HanDJet, described earlier in this chapter, this shareware from the same authors takes the form of a Microsoft Access application (*http://home.t-online.de/*

home/consultus/jetfile.htm). And like HanDJet, this program's power lies in its ability to import the data from numerous PalmPilots into a single central desktop database, where all the querying and searching tools of Access are at your disposal.

JFile View

As the name implies, this program (*http://www.k.shuttle.de/zarba*) is for viewing, sorting, and printing your JFile data on your Windows computer—not for editing. But what it lacks in features, JFile View makes up in speed, stability, and simplicity; you don't even have to install anything. Just run the program, navigate to the previously HotSynced JFile document you want (see "Where to Find Your Palm Database Files on the PC," earlier in this section), and double-click. Your JFile database is instantly on view on the PC, where you can rearrange the columns, make them wider or narrower, or export the database as a CSV or tab-delimited text file.

FMSync (for FileMaker on the Macintosh)

In many ways, FMSync (*http://www.fmsync.com*) is the most sophisticated database software for the PalmPilot—at this writing, it's the only one that actually performs a full, two-way, record-by-record HotSync. If you make it change your JFile database on the road, and your partner simultaneously changes another record on the Mac back at home, both databases will be intelligently updated at the next HotSync. In short, FMSync is a genuine conduit, unlike the other programs described in this chapter (see Figure 12-8).

The FMSync Installer places its conduit into your Palm → Conduits folder. Now, from the Instant Palm Desktop menu (see Chapter 9, *Palm Desktop: Macintosh*), choose HotSync Manager. Choose HotSync → Conduit Settings. You'll see a dialog box, where you specify which FileMaker file you'd like synchronized with JFile. In fact, you can, and must, also specify one layout in that FileMaker file that contains the fields you want sent to JFile. (Even if your FileMaker database contains 300 fields, remember that JFile can accept only 20. Therefore, it's usually best to create a FileMaker layout—of 20 fields or less—exclusively for use by FMSync.)

That's all there is to it. At the next HotSync, FMSync automatically creates a JFile database on your PalmPilot, complete with named fields of the correct type and in the correct order. (Your savings: 30 minutes of tedious setting-up in JFile.) From now on, any changes you make to the database on the palmtop will be reflected in your FileMaker database after a HotSync, and vice versa.

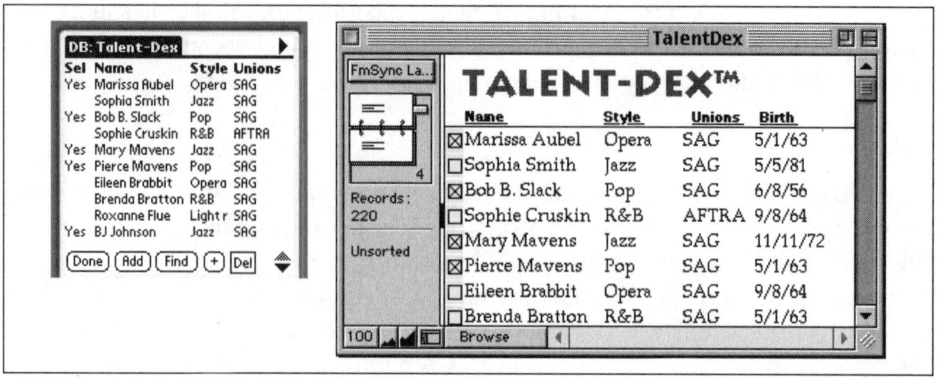

Figure 12-8. FMSync for Macintosh is the only genuine HotSync conduit for the PalmPilot, seamlessly updating a FileMaker database with JFile on a record-by-record basis.

MobileDB

MobileDB (*http://www.mobile generation.com*) is by far the simplest database for the PalmPilot. It's limited to 20 fields, text-type only, and you can't delete a field once you've created it.

On the other hand, MobileDB's speed, small size (36K), and simplicity have endeared it to thousands of Palm fans who want an easy way to carry basic database information away with them. (MobileDB Lite, a free version that lets you look at, but not edit, databases, is even more Spartan.) In some ways, you could argue that MobileDB best embraces the PalmPilot's own philosophy: in mobile computing, speed and simplicity outweigh a long feature list any day.

Creating a database

Tap New to begin the process of creating a new database. You'll be asked to name your new database, and then you'll be shown the list of 20 fields. On each blank, write in a field name. (The small arrow at the right end of each field is a universal MobileDB symbol. It means, "Tap here to expand this blank into a full-screen memo writing area.") Tap Done when you're finished. You arrive at the main list-view data screen.

Recording data

Tap New to enter Record View, exactly as in the other databases described in this chapter. Because a MobileDB field can't hold anything but text, your Graffiti skills get a great workout in this program. Tap Done after filling out each record to return to the list view.

Manipulating your data

The Find, Sort, and Filter commands (in the Tools menu) work exactly as they do in JFile, described in the previous section. You can adjust the column widths (in pixels, as in HanDBase and JFile) by tapping Menu → Options → Edit Column Widths. The only peculiarity you may encounter is when you try to delete an entire database—there's no such command on the master list of databases. Instead, you must open a database; once in List View, you can tap Menu → Options → Delete Database.

Transferring a MobileDB Database to the Desktop

Because a MobileDB file is itself little more than a tab-separated text file, MobileDB converters abound. The MobileDB web site, in fact, contains a page of links to MobileDB conversion utilities for Windows, Macintosh, and various flavors of Unix. These converters translate data between MobileDB and CSV text files, of course, and some can also accommodate Microsoft Access files and even HTML (web-page) tables.

A Database of Your Own

The inexpensive programs described in this chapter are great, ready-made solutions for most database projects. But you probably won't find JFile running on the PalmPilots on the General Motors factory floor. Instead, corporate users are much more likely to build their own custom database applications. For that purpose, consider Satellite Forms ($370, *http://www.pumatech.com*) or Pendragon Forms ($100, *http://www.pendragon-software.com*).

These development tools let you construct database-like, standalone Palm programs, but they require that you dip your toe into the world of programming. (If you've worked in Microsoft Access or Visual Basic, you've experienced this level of complexity.) Furthermore, you're required to pay the company a licensing fee every time you install your finished handiwork on another PalmPilot—$90 per palmtop for Satellite Forms applications, for example.

The advantage of doing so, however, is that you can design your own dream databases—full-fledged Palm applications, really—assured that they will exchange data with your corporate databases in Microsoft Access, Oracle, Lotus Notes, and so on.

Spreadsheet Software

Many a jaded computer user becomes a PalmPilot convert only when they first see a Palm spreadsheet, complete with pie charts. "If that little box can do Excel," they reluctantly conclude, "I guess it really can do anything."

You'll have to learn a few tricks for scrolling on the tiny Palm screen. But if you want to view your Excel files while on the airplane, or perform some what-if analyses on the restaurant table before dessert, the programs described here won't let you down.

Quicksheet

Like Palm databases, Palm spreadsheets range from fully featured (but slower, bigger, and more expensive) to simple (but quicker, smaller, and inexpensive). In the former category is Quicksheet, the 800-pound (or 149K) gorilla of Palm spreadsheets (see Figure 12-9). Your worksheets can be up to 996 by 254 cells in size, although the program bogs down dramatically if more than about 500 cells are occupied. The program offers style sheets, three cell-justification choices, password protection, cell linking across multiple sheets, search-and-replace, draggable column widths—and 38 number, currency, logical, and time functions, from AVEDEV to YEAR. A charting module is even available at extra cost from the same designers (*http://www.cesinc.com*).

Perhaps most useful of all, however, is the program's synergy with Microsoft Excel. Thanks to a Quicksheet add-in, you can open and save Quicksheet files directly from within Excel for Windows (or, in mid-1999, Macintosh). Most formulas and even cell formatting survive the translation. (Note that when you HotSync, the program doesn't perform cell-by-cell comparisons; you with your PalmPilot and your partner on the PC shouldn't edit the same spreadsheet simultaneously. Instead, the most recent version of a spreadsheet "wins" when you HotSync, regardless of what specific changes were made.)

Pilot MiniCalc (PiMC)

At only 42K, Pilot MiniCalc is a surprisingly powerful spreadsheet (*http://home. pacbell.net/abootman*). Capable of 254-cell-square worksheets, this program falls squarely in the midrange of Palm spreadsheets. It's the only candidate that offers, for example, a pop-up on-screen palette of frequently used math symbols—ideal for building formulas. It's also the only Palm spreadsheet that lets you adjust row heights (individually or globally). As in Quicksheet, you can drag to adjust column widths. The program comes with an Excel plug-in that, Quicksheet-like, lets you open and save Pilot MiniCalc spreadsheets directly from within Excel. (There's even a CSV-to-MiniCalc application, in case Excel isn't your spreadsheet of choice.)

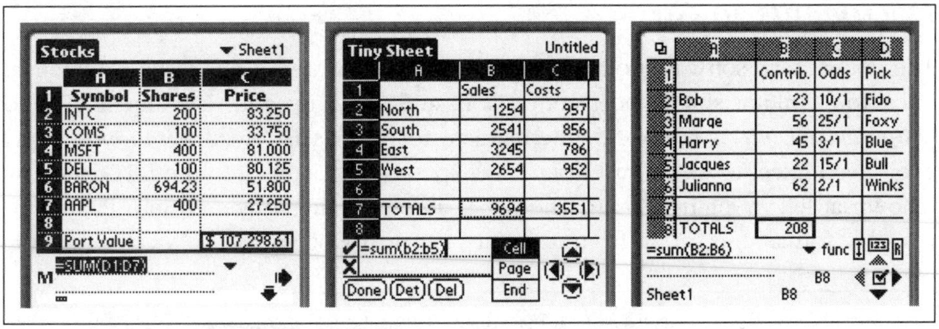

Figure 12-9. Three of the better-known Palm spreadsheets are Quicksheet (left), TinySheet (middle), and Pilot MiniCalc (right).

Pilot MiniCalc doesn't win any awards in the ease-of-use department. Only the terse manual will help you understand the tiny icons that clutter the screen, and the program's default tendency to trail 15 zeros after any number you write in is disconcerting (until you read the tip below). Otherwise, however, Pilot MiniCalc is a compact, inexpensive ($15), admirable performer.

When you first use it, Pilot MiniCalc insists upon using 15-decimal-point precision—in its world, 2.000000000000000 plus 2.000000000000000 equals 4.000000000000000. Fortunately, you're not forced to live with all those superfluous zeros. If you'd prefer to view the actual numbers you write in, and nothing more, tap Menu → Sheet → Global. In the dialog box that appears, set the format to Decimal, and change the number in the "Frac" field to 0 (or the number of decimal-point places you prefer).

You can also adjust the precision of specific cells using the same mechanism—but this time, highlight the cells and then tap Menu → Edit → Format.

TinySheet

As the name implies, this Palm spreadsheet (see Figure 12-9) has nowhere near as long a feature list as Quicksheet. TinySheet's maximum worksheet size is 26 by 99 cells; it offers no cell formatting (such as bold or currency style); and there's no easy way to exchange spreadsheet information with Excel. (You can import and export tab-delimited text with the PalmPilot's own Memo Pad, but that's it.)

On the other hand, the program is quick, inexpensive ($10 shareware—no web site), small (about 70K), and adequate for many quick calculation jobs. Its 31 functions, good navigation tools, and Series command (for automatically generating, say, sequential check numbers) make the overall program feel friendly and powerful despite its limitations.

Documents To Go

The commercial software company DataViz has dedicated itself to the problem of Excel-to-PalmPilot spreadsheet conversion, and come up with Documents To Go (*http://www.DataViz.com*). No intermediate text file is involved here—you don't even need Excel to use it; just drag Excel spreadsheet icons into the DTG window (shown at left in Figure 12-10). The file is automatically converted into PalmPilot-readable format and set up for transfer at your next HotSync.

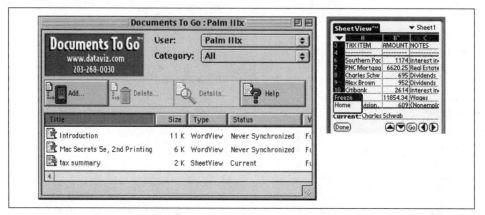

Figure 12-10. Drag Excel spreadsheets into the Documents To Go window (left); they're instantly converted to Palm-readable format (right).

Once the converted spreadsheet is on your palmtop, you read it using the included SheetView program (at right in Figure 12-10). The operative word here is *read*—you can only look at, not edit or create, spreadsheets on the PalmPilot. That's a shame, because SheetView has juicy features that would be welcome in any of the other Palm spreadsheets. For example, you can split the window into two or four individually scrolling panes. You can freeze any row or column, so that you can scroll the spreadsheet without losing the row or column names. A useful Full Screen View hides the various controls, thus dedicating as much screen as possible to the spreadsheet itself, and a choice of fonts makes SheetView eye-friendly.

Most interesting of all, Documents To Go automatically translates comments you've added to Excel cells into SheetView bookmarks, making it easy to jump around to various important spots on your Palm-based spreadsheet. For the person who wants to study, but not edit, Excel data file on the road, DTG is an ideal solution—and DataViz hasn't ruled out the possibility of editable SheetView spreadsheets in a future version.

Quicken in Your Pocket

If managing your financial data is your thing, but spreadsheets aren't, the world of Palm software is filled with personal-finance programs. (See Appendix A, *100 Programs Worth Knowing About*, for capsule reviews.)

For many Palm users, the personal-finance dream was some version of Quicken running on the PalmPilot—after all, you make most of your financial transactions, such as cash-machine visits, when away from your desk. Imagine a Palm program that could record this information as you make your transactions, and then transfer this data automatically into Quicken on your Macintosh or Windows PC when you return home.

That's the purpose of Pocket Quicken ($40, *http://www.landware.com*). In some regards, it's a full-fledged Quicken clone, complete with transactions splits, memorized transactions, auto-fill, password protection, and Quicken-like register of transactions.

A single press of your HotSync-cradle button transfers all of your new transactions into your desktop copy of Quicken. It's important to understand, however, that this data transfer is one-way—except for text information like account names, categories, and classes, your desktop Quicken data is never sent to the PalmPilot. Pocket Quicken is designed to be a sophisticated, electronic scratchpad for recording transactions that you pour into your desktop computer when you return from your travels.

Or consider a longtime favorite of Palm fans: Qmate, a $20 shareware program (available on this book's CD-ROM). Its feature list is long and hardy—32 accounts, multiple currencies, memorized transactions, and so on. Note, however, that Qmate doesn't send the transactions you record directly into Quicken when you HotSync; instead, it creates an intermediary *.QIF* file that you then import manually into Quicken for Macintosh or Windows (or Microsoft Money for Windows).

Executive Tip Summary

- Database and spreadsheet programs for the PalmPilot range from full-featured and large (HanDBase and Quicksheet) to tiny and bare-bones (MobileDB and TinySheet). Install accordingly.

- You don't have to open a List View row to edit pop-up menus, checkboxes, dates, and times. JFile and HanDBase let you edit these data in place, right there in List View. To enable this feature, however, you must visit the Preferences screen and turn on the corresponding checkboxes.

- Pilot MiniCalc is a compact, useful midrange spreadsheet, but its default decimal-point precision (15 zeros) may drive you crazy. Change its Global preferences to the Decimal format with a "Frac" value of 0 to eliminate the extra zeros.

- You can exchange your Palm data and number-crunching work with almost any Mac or Windows database or spreadsheet program. Convenient converters automate the process—and as a last resort, you can import and export comma-separated text files as an intermediate step between Palm and Desktop.

IV

*The PalmPilot
Online*

13

Email Anywhere

Today's PalmPilot works perfectly well as an email machine. True, Graffiti handwriting isn't the world's best system for composing long replies. But the PalmPilot is ideal for reading email—and for writing short responses—because it lets you time-shift. Thanks to the PalmPilot, your down time on the plane, train, or automobile can be productive work time. (Or entertainment time, if you're on somebody's humor mailing list.)

If you have a Palm VII, see Chapter 16, *Palm VII: Wireless Email, Wireless Web*, for details on iMessenger, the Palm VII's built-in program for sending and receiving short messages wirelessly. This chapter covers email retrieved from your desktop computer or from the Internet using a traditional, plug-into-a-phone-jack Palm modem.

The Two Routes to Email

The most important concept to understand about Palm email is the two methods of retrieving it. They're illustrated in Figure 13-1; each has distinct advantages and drawbacks.

Setup 1: Getting Email from Your PC

Under this scheme, the PalmPilot gets and sends mail via your Mac or Windows PC. This method doesn't require a modem for the PalmPilot, ensures that you're never confused as to which machine downloaded which mail, and means that you never lose file attachments. Your PC is the Grand Central Station for email, and your hard drive is the landing point for email attachments.

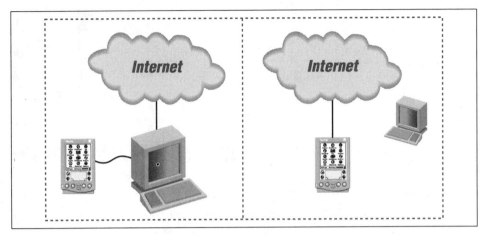

Figure 13-1. There are two ways to get email to and from the PalmPilot: directly, with a modem attached (as shown at right), or via HotSync with your desktop computer (left).

When you HotSync, new mail that's already in your favorite PC email program, such as Microsoft Outlook, Outlook Express, or Eudora, is copied onto the Palm-Pilot. When you HotSync again, any responses you've written on the PalmPilot are copied back to your PC and placed in your email program's Out Box, ready to send. The PalmPilot itself never does any actual sending or dialing.

At this writing, several programs work with your PC in this way. Most people in the Palm world used Palm Mail, which comes built into the PalmPilot Professional and later models; it retrieves email from almost any Windows email program. Another candidate is the $40 shareware called Palmeta Mail, which works on any PalmPilot model. Some email programs, including pdQmail and MultiMail, can retrieve email either from your desktop computer or directly from the Internet. All of these programs are described in this chapter.

Just because your desktop computer is the clearinghouse for email doesn't mean you can't check your email from the road. If you have a modem for your PalmPilot, you can still perform a modem HotSync with your computer at home, as described in Chapter 6, *HotSync, Step by Step,* picking up your fresh email (and sending any replies) that way. In other words, you can have all the advantages of a one-mailbox setup—using your desktop PC as the one mailbox—without sacrificing the ability to travel with your palmtop.

Setup 2: Getting Email Directly from the Internet (or AOL)

Using this email method, your PalmPilot needs a modem. For the Palm V, you need the $170 Palm V clip-on modem (see Appendix B, *PalmPilot Accessories*); for other models, the $130, snap-on PalmPilot modem is the logical choice. Any external Hayes-compatible modem, when connected to the $15 Palm modem cable, should also work.

You also need an email program, such as pdQmail, HandMail, MultiMail, One-Touch Mail, or ProxiMail. For America Online accounts, you need HandMail, Pocket Flash, or Trans AOL. (All of these programs are described in this chapter, and trial versions are included on this book's CD-ROM.)

While getting your email directly from the Internet might seem to be an obvious and natural solution, it does pose some potential problems. For example, suppose you sometimes check your email with your desktop PC and sometimes with your PalmPilot. How will you remember which machine contains which email? On which machine did you read the memo from your boss? And what if somebody sends you an important Microsoft Word document attached to an email? Your PalmPilot, short on storage space as it is and hard-drive free, can retrieve only the body of the message; the file attachment might be lost forever.

Solution 1: Dedicate a special email account just to the PalmPilot.

Solution 2: Leave your email on the email server (your Internet service provider's computers, for example), placing a *copy* onto the palmtop. (Doing so is an option in most direct-to-Internet Palm email programs.) Later, you can download this mail again with your desktop PC, confident that you're not missing anything—and hoping that you remember which messages you've already answered.

Getting Email from Your PC

If you'd like to use Setup 1 (where your desktop computer is the Grand Central Station for email), you have your choice of several email programs. This section tackles them one by one.

Palm Mail

For most people, the obvious email solution is the one built into every PalmPilot (except the original Pilot models)—the program called Palm Mail. It's well designed. It's built into the ROM chips, so it doesn't eat up any precious RAM. And it's a very *official* method of getting email—if something's not working, 3Com's tech-support staff awaits to help you troubleshoot.

PilotMail: The Service

If you decide to give your PalmPilot its own private email account (to keep its email straight from your desktop PC's), consider PilotMail, an Internet access provider that's just for PalmPilots and just for email. The service costs $7 per month, plus ten cents per minute of connection time; you use your PalmPilot's modem to dial a toll-free number that works anywhere in America. (There's also a non-toll-free number you can dial when you're overseas—if you're willing to pay the long-distance charges.) Your PalmPilot gets its own email address, which is along the lines of *billsmith@pilotmail.net*.

Setup is straightforward; to trigger an email send/receive session, you simply press the HotSync button on your PalmPilot modem (or tap the HotSync icon on the screen). The modem rapidly dials the number, retrieves and sends your messages, and hangs up. You read your messages in the Memo Pad, where you'll find them automatically tagged with special category labels: Inbox and Outbox. (If you have a PalmPilot Pro or a more recent model, you can choose instead to have your mail routed into the built-in Mail program.)

As a bonus, the PilotMail service also lets you fax from the PalmPilot (for an added fee). In the To: field of your outgoing message, instead of an email address, you just write the fax number, with area code, followed by the suffix *@fax*. When you connect, your fax is transmitted to the PilotMail servers; from there, the number you specified is redialed automatically until a fax machine connects and accepts your fax.

One other intriguing feature: if you have an alphanumeric beeper, you can set the PilotMail service (for 10 cents a shot) to page you when email (or just email marked *URGENT*) has arrived for your PalmPilot. The page even shows the subject and sender's address.

Visit *http://www.pilotmail.com* for details and signup, or call (888) 447-4568.

The Palm Mail program assumes that if you have a Windows computer, you're running Eudora, Lotus cc:Mail (versions 2.5, 6.0, and 7.0), Microsoft Outlook, Outlook Express, Microsoft Exchange 4.0, Windows Messaging 4.0, Microsoft Mail 3.5, or Windows for Workgroups Mail. For the Macintosh equipped with the MultiMail Conduit, described later in this chapter, you need Outlook Express, Eudora, Eudora Lite, or Claris Emailer; other email programs are scheduled to be added to later versions of the MultiMail conduit.

Setting Up Palm Mail for Windows

The procedure for setting up your email conduit in Windows was once a convoluted affair. But when 3Com discovered that a huge majority of tech-support calls came from PalmPilot owners having trouble setting up Palm Mail, the company decided to address the complexity problem. The result: Mail Setup, a standalone program that comes with Palm Desktop 3.0 and later (which is a free download from *http://www.palm.com*).

This program runs automatically when you install Palm Desktop. You can also run it any time later by choosing Start → Programs → Palm Desktop → Mail Setup. In essence, Mail Setup is a tiny "wizard"—a series of dialog boxes that walk you through the process of hooking up your PC email program. All you have to do is choose your email program from the pop-up menu (see Figure 13-2). Click Next.

If you chose Microsoft Outlook, Eudora, or one of the other programs at the top of the pop-up menu, you're done. If you chose Lotus cc:Mail, however, you arrive at a second dialog box, where you're asked to fill in your user name and password. Click Next, and the setup is really over.

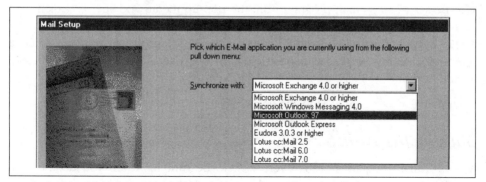

Figure 13-2. On current models, setting up the email system consists of choosing from a pop-up menu.

Setting Up Palm Mail for Macintosh

To exchange email with your Mac, you need Actual Software's MultiMail conduit (*http://www.actualsoft.com*, $30). Just drag the conduit file itself into the Palm → Conduits folder. Then, from the Instant Palm Desktop menu (see Chapter 9, *Palm Desktop: Macintosh*), choose HotSync Manager, and then choose HotSync → Conduit Settings. In the resulting dialog box, double-click MultiMail Conduit; you'll see the dialog box shown in Figure 13-3.

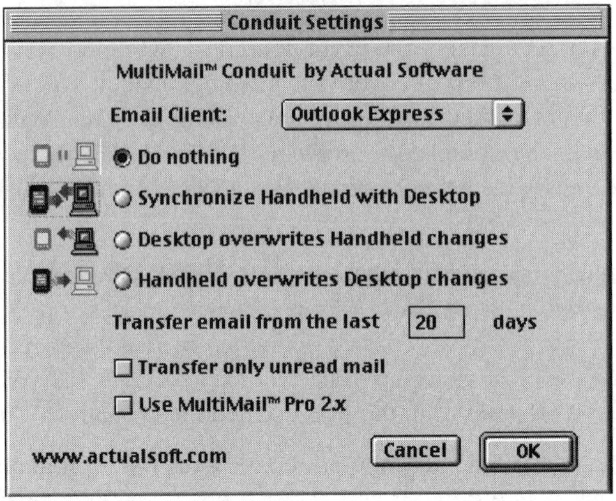

Figure 13-3. Setting up the Mac to exchange email with Palm Mail is as easy as specifying which email program your Mac uses.

Choose your Mac's email program from the pop-up menu, and specify which mail you want HotSynced—only unread mail, or mail a certain number of days old. (If you're using Eudora or Eudora Lite, you also need to launch that program, choose Special → Settings → Miscellaneous, and turn on "Use old-style .toc files" before clicking OK.)

Your Mac is now ready to HotSync email.

Making the Transfer

Your PC mail program doesn't even have to be running when you do the mail transfer. Put your PalmPilot in its cradle and push the HotSync button; during the HotSync, you'll see a new item in the status box that says "Synchronizing Mail."

If you're using Outlook 97 or an earlier Microsoft email program, your PC may now begin dialing the Internet in an attempt to update its mailboxes. Click Cancel; the HotSync will proceed normally.

When the "I'm done!" chirp indicates that the HotSync is complete, you're ready for the road. Read on.

Reading and Answering Messages in Palm Mail

To see the mail that's been transferred from your desktop PC, turn the palmtop on; tap Applications → Mail. The list of waiting mail appears, as shown in Figure 13-4.

If you use the PalmPilot's email feature a lot, take the time to reprogram one of the PalmPilot's buttons to launch the email program, as described in Chapter 1, *The 3 × 5-Inch Powerhouse*. You'll save several stylus-taps per session.

Or, at the very least, install the LaunchHack program (see Appendix A, *100 Programs Worth Knowing About*), which lets you jump directly to any Palm program.

You'll notice several interesting things about this list. For example, the PalmPilot does what it can to strip off the distracting and unhelpful suffixes from the senders' names: *Skibunny@aol.com* is listed simply as Skibunny, for example. Furthermore, if the PalmPilot recognizes the sender's email address as one that's already in your Address Book, it thoughtfully shows the plain-English name (Bob Smith) instead of the email address (*bobs3487@netcom.net*).

If a message's name in the Message List appears in boldface and at the top of the screen—then it's been marked High Priority. Of course, you won't see this boldface at all unless both the sender's email program and your email program have a Priority-marking feature. (Microsoft Outlook is one such program.)

The "folder menu"

If you tap the tiny pop-up menu triangle in the screen's upper-right corner, you'll immediately grasp the Mail program's design concept. There, where you'd ordinarily see a list of categories (for your Memo Pad or Address Book, for example), you'll see a pop-up menu listing Inbox, Outbox, Deleted, Filed, and Draft. The Palm Mail program uses these "folders" as different windows to store your email messages as they travel through their life cycle. Although these labels work exactly like the PalmPilot's usual categories, the software refers to them as *folders*, and this pop-up menu as the *folder menu*.

If you decide to reassign one of the four plastic hardware buttons to the Mail program, as described in Chapter 2, *Setup and Guided Tour*, a secret feature awaits you: repeatedly pressing your newly defined hardware button lets you cycle through the contents of Mail's different "folders."

To begin reading your email, tap a message's name. As shown at right in Figure 13-4, the message opens up. If the message is taller than the screen, you can use the scroll bar to scroll up or down in any of the usual ways (see "Memo Pad" in Chapter 4, *The Four Primary Programs*). On the Palm III and later models,

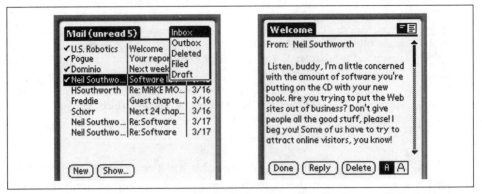

Figure 13-4. The Palm Mail program shows the list of mail waiting for you (left); the folder pop-up menu, listing your Inbox, Outbox, and Deleted mailbox, appears when you tap the triangle in the upper-right corner. Tap a message's name to view its contents (right). At upper right: the Hide Headers/Show Headers icons.

tap Menu → Options → Font to view your choice of type styles. (On the PalmPilot Personal and Professional models, the two *A* icons at the bottom of the screen provide a choice of type styles, exactly as in the Memo Pad.)

The PalmPilot mercifully omits the usual page of Internet routing gobbledygook at the top of the message, showing only the sender's name—but if you really want to see all the header info, tap the tiny icon in the upper-right corner of the screen.

When you're finished reading a piece of mail, you have a choice of three buttons to tap: Done, Reply, or Delete.

 Palm Mail does a good job of collecting the email from your desktop email program, with one exception: it doesn't accept files attached to your incoming mail. That is, if somebody sends you an Excel spreadsheet as an attachment, it won't be transferred to the palmtop—after all, you wouldn't be able to see it on your PalmPilot.

Instead, you'll see a message in your Inbox that, when opened, says simply: "*There are 1 file(s) attached to this message on your Desktop." Whatever was attached to the message is waiting back in your Downloads folder (or wherever your email program puts file attachments). Go home, turn on your PC, and inspect the attachments there.

The Done button

Tap Done to return to the main index screen shown at left in Figure 13-4. The message you've just read remains there, but now a checkmark appears beside its name to indicate that you've looked at it.

The Reply button

If you decide to reply to a message you're reading, tap Reply. You're shown the dialog box in Figure 13-5. Here's what the options at the top of the screen mean:

Sender

> This default choice does just what you'd expect: creates a new, empty email message pre-addressed to the person who emailed you.

All

> Tap this button if you were one of a group of recipients of the message you're reading, and you want your response sent to the entire group. This is the option you'd use, for example, if you're subscribed to a mailing list or newsgroup.

Forward

> Tap this button if you want to remail the message to a new individual. You'd use this option, for example, to forward to another lucky recipient a great joke you've received.

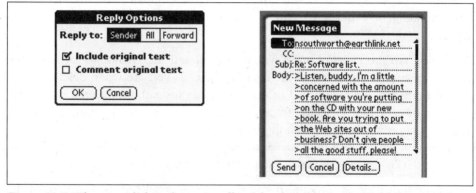

Figure 13-5. When you click Reply, you're offered the chance to "quote back" the original text in your response (left). The "comment" option adds > brackets at the beginning of each line, as shown at right.

The PalmPilot can, if you wish, paste the message you've just read into the top of the reply message, as is typically (and politely) done in standard email correspondence. If that's your wish, turn on the "Include original text" checkbox.

If you'd also like "commenting brackets" added to the pasted text, as shown at the right in Figure 13-5—to help distinguish it from your own reply—also turn on the lower checkbox, "Comment original text." To proceed, tap OK.

Now you find yourself in a Memo Pad-like screen. The idea, of course, is to scroll down below the quoted text (if you selected that option) and then to write in your reply. This is the moment of truth: the ultimate test of your Graffiti skills. Most people can identify email at a glance that was sent from a PalmPilot—it's the email that's *unusually* short and to the point.

The Excessive Quote-Back Feature

The problem with Palm Mail's reply mechanism is that it pastes the *entire* contents of the incoming message at the top of your reply. You can't simply highlight a portion of the message for quoting back, for the sake of conciseness and clarity, as you can in some email programs. Your email correspondent is likely to be a little bewildered that you're sending back the complete original email message, even if the part you're responding to is a single sentence somewhere in the middle.

To simulate the missing feature, you have no choice but to quote back the entire message, and then—in your reply—manually highlight and delete unwanted portions of the original message.

Delete

The third option available to you when reading fresh email is the Delete button. Understanding how deleted email works is one of the Mail program's trickiest aspects.

When you tap the Delete button, you're not offered the chance to "archive" the deleted message on your PC at the next HotSync, as you are when deleting information from, say, the Memo Pad or Address Book. Instead, the deleted message is simply moved to the Deleted "folder." At this point, you're welcome to view it again (by choosing Deleted from the folder menu shown in Figure 13-4). You can even move it back out of the Deleted folder—as long you to do this before you've HotSynced. (Figure 13-6 shows the steps for rescuing a piece of deleted mail.)

One thing, however, is for sure: If you don't move a deleted message out of the Deleted category, it will disappear for good at the next HotSync—from both your PalmPilot and your desktop PC. This time, there's no archive to bail you out if you decide you shouldn't have deleted something.

 If you delete a piece of Palm Mail mail, don't instinctively press the Scroll Down button to read the next piece. Whenever you delete a message, the PalmPilot automatically brings the next message into view—pressing the Scroll Down button would actually make you skip an unread message.

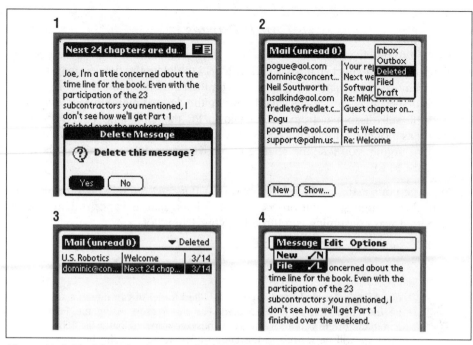

Figure 13-6. The life cycle of a piece of deleted mail. (1) After reading a piece of email, you tap the Delete button. You're asked to confirm the deletion; you tap Yes. (2) You change your mind and want to resurrect that message. You tap Done, and return to the main Message List screen. From here, you use the folder pop-up menu in the upper right to choose Deleted. (3) Now you're viewing all messages you've deleted since your last HotSync. You tap the mistakenly deleted message. (4) When the message opens, you tap Menu → File (or just tap the Undelete button). The deleted message has now been rescued. It will reside safely in the Filed category of your Mail program (if you used the File command) or your Inbox (if you used the Undelete button)—at least until you change your mind again.

The Filed folder

After reading a message, you have three options: delete it, leave it in your Inbox, or move it to a special Palm folder called Filed. Once it's in the Filed folder, it's neither susceptible to deletion (as it is in the Deleted folder) nor cluttering up your list of unread mail (as it is in the Inbox folder).

To file a message you're reading, tap the Menu icon and tap File in the Message menu. (Alternatively, you can use the Graffiti shortcut /L; draw the slash from the bottom.) Your message gets moved into the Filed "folder," accessible by choosing Filed from the folder menu. From there, you can do two things about a filed message: delete it or reply to it.

Email Purges

Because so much email is junk mail these days and because deleted mail consumes a lot of memory, Palm Mail offers a way to delete the deleted mail—that is, to remove it permanently from the PalmPilot's memory even before your next HotSync. (This process is called purging the deleted mail.) Purged deleted mail will still disappear from your desktop PC the next time you HotSync, exactly as though you merely deleted it without purging; the only difference is that by purging, you lose the chance to recover your deleted mail (as shown in Figure 13-6).

To purge your mail, tap Menu → Options → Purge Deleted. You're asked to confirm the purging. If you proceed, your deleted mail is vaporized, and the memory it was consuming is returned to your PalmPilot.

Once you've moved a message to the Filed folder, it can never again be moved; it can only be deleted. For this reason, using the File command offers you a safeguard. A message appears that asks: "This message will be moved to the Filed folder. Keep it in the Inbox as well?"

If you tap Yes, you now have two copies of the message, one each in the Inbox and the Filed folder.

Composing a New Email Message

Replying isn't the only time you'll be writing email messages, of course; sometimes you'll want to initiate an email exchange yourself. Doing so is only slightly different from replying—for example, when starting a round of email, you have to write in the recipient's email address. (When replying, it's filled in automatically.) Fortunately, Palm Mail offers a variation of the Phone Lookup feature described in Chapter 4, saving you several steps.

To open a new, blank email form, tap New on the main index screen. (Alternatively, choose New from the Message menu from anywhere in the Mail program; the Graffiti shortcut is /N.) The form shown in Figure 13-7 should look familiar if you've ever used an email program before. Put your recipient's address in the *To:* blank, a short title of the message in the *Subj:* blank, and the actual message in the *Body:* blank. (The *CC:* stands for carbon copy; put the email addresses here of anyone else you'd like to receive this message. However, because the PalmPilot lets you specify multiple *To:* addresses anyway, as shown in Figure 13-7, the *CC:* field isn't terrifically useful.)

There are a couple of hidden tricks that make starting a new email easier on the PalmPilot, however.

Expandable fields

Tap the names of the blanks (*To:, CC:, Subj:,* or *Body:*) to expand them to a full page, as shown in Figure 13-7. If you're sending the same piece of mail to many different email addresses, for example, tap the *To:* label; on the resulting full-screen page, write each email address, separated from the next by a comma. Similarly, many Palm Mail users reflexively tap the *Body:* tab when composing messages so that they don't feel confined to a portion of PalmPilot's screen, and instead have the full height and width of the glass surface to use.

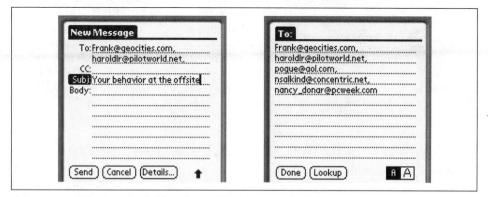

Figure 13-7. To expand a field so that it fills the screen (right), tap its label, such as To: (left).

Email address lookup

If you've been using your Address Book program to store email addresses along with other contact information, your diligence is about to pay off. In the *To:* or *CC:* blanks of a new email message, you can command the PalmPilot to write in the person's email address, no matter how long or complicated, automatically—with just a couple of Graffiti strokes.

Here's how the feature works:

Selecting from a list:

> If you simply want to select your recipient's name from a list, plant your cursor in the *To:* or *CC:* fields, and then invoke the Lookup command. The quickest way is to use the Graffiti stroke /L. If you prefer to use menus, tap Menu → Options → Lookup (see Figure 13-8, top left).
>
> The Address Book master index list appears (Figure 13-8, left)—but instead of showing phone numbers on the right side, it shows email addresses. Better yet, it shows only the names of people who have email addresses, so you're not forced to wade through a list cluttered by unconnected Luddites.

Tap somebody's name and then tap Add. You return to your message in progress, but now the person's email address is correctly written into the address field.

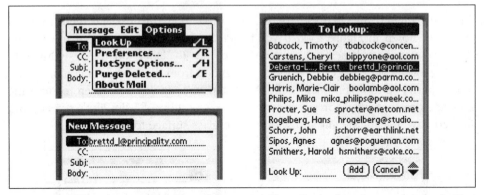

Figure 13-8. To grab an email address from your Address Book when the cursor is in the To: field, use the Lookup command (top left). The Address Book screen appears (right); tap the name you want and then tap Add. You return to the email form, where the email address of the person you selected is automatically filled in (lower left).

Auto-complete

Another way to use the Lookup feature is to write your recipient's last name— actually, write only as much of the name as necessary to distinguish it from the other names in the list. If your recipient's last name is Sununu, Sunu is probably enough. After writing the name (or portion of a name), invoke the Lookup command (/L).

This time, the Address Book never even appears. The complete email address of the name you wrote simply appears in the address field, fully formed.

(If you misspell the name or otherwise write a name for which there's no match in your Address Book, the PalmPilot displays your full Address Book list. It's saying, "I don't get it, but here—tap the name you meant." Tap one and then tap Add.)

Note that you can use either facet of the Lookup command repeatedly within a field. For example, if you're sending a piece of mail to four people, use the Lookup routine; write a comma and a space; do the Lookup routine again; and so on. Remember, too, that you can invoke the Lookup command in either of the views shown in Figure 13-7—that is, either in the full email form or one of the expanded, full-page field screens (which you get by tapping a field name).

Other email-sending options

Before you send your reply or newly written message on its way, you can turn on any of several options that affect how it's sent. To access these options, tap the

Details box at the bottom of the main email-writing screen. The Message Details dialog box appears, as shown at left in Figure 13-9.

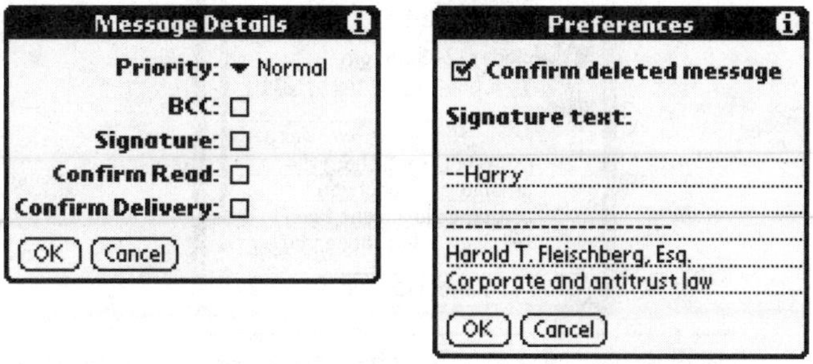

Figure 13-9. The Message Details box (left) controls whether or not your "signature" is automatically appended to the end of each message you send. To edit this "signature" text, choose Preferences from the Options menu (right).

Here's what these options mean:

Priority

As noted earlier, this feature may be meaningless to your recipient. A message is only flagged Normal, High, or Low priority if both your desktop email program and your recipient's email program offer a Priority feature. (Note: when you use this pop-up menu to change the message's priority, you're affecting only this message. Contrast with some of the other options in this dialog box, which affect this message and *all* subsequent messages.)

BCC

Stands for blind carbon copy. If you turn on this checkbox and tap OK, you'll discover that a new line has been added to your message, up at the top: a field labeled BCC. Any email addresses you write into this field (using exactly the same techniques described under "Email address lookup," above) are sent copies of the message.

How is this different from the regular CC field? Addressees in the BCC receive copies of the message secretly. (See Figure 13-10.) People whose names are listed in the To: and CC: fields will never know that there were additional recipients. When you add email addresses to the CC field, by contrast, each recipient sees the addresses of everyone else you sent the mail to. (Now you know why most of the junk email you receive has your name listed as a BCC: recipient—the junk mailer doesn't want you to know how many thousands of people got this same email!)

There's no way to leave the BCC option on permanently. Beginning with the very next message you write, the BCC field will be absent once again. You must turn this field on, using the Message Details dialog box, each time you want it.

Figure 13-10. Names you write in the BCC field don't show up in the email message after it's sent.

Signature

Because your signature is generally the same on every message, the PalmPilot (like most email programs) lets you write it just once, and then offers to stamp it at the end of every message automatically.

To store your signature, tap Menu → Options → Preferences. Now you're in the dialog box shown at right in Figure 13-8. You have plenty of space to write your email signature, including any witty aphorisms you like to append to your messages.

This signature won't get tacked onto your emails, however, unless you also turn on the Signature option. After writing an email message, tap the Details button to view the dialog box shown at left in Figure 13-8. Tap to make a checkmark appear in the Signature box.

From now on, every message will have your prepared signature text added to the end. You won't see this text—even if you open up a message in the Outbox—because it's not actually added until the message is sent. But your recipients will see the signature.

If you ever want Palm Mail to stop adding your signature text, open the Details box once again and uncheck the Signature box.

Confirm read and Confirm delivery

If you turn on these options, new mail will eventually appear on your Palm-Pilot which simply confirms that your recipient has (a) received the message ("Confirm delivery") and/or (b) opened it ("Confirm read"). Note that this confirmation message may take a long time to arrive. For example, it can't arrive until you've HotSynced, sent the mail with your desktop PC, waited for enough time to elapse that your recipient receives and opens the mail, checked your email account with the desktop PC again, and HotSynced again.

Be careful with these options, by the way. They stay on for all subsequent messages—until you uncheck these checkboxes. If you're not careful, you'll gum up your memory with dozens of confirmation messages.

When you're finished setting these options, tap Done. And when you're finished composing your email, tap the Send button (see Figure 13-5). The message disappears from the screen (it's moved to the Outbox category), and you're returned to whatever list you were viewing (Inbox, Outbox, and so on) at the moment you tapped the New button.

The Draft Folder

If you're midway through writing a message when some important visitor arrives at your door, what are you supposed to do? Or suppose you're all done writing to someone, but you can't remember the email address and won't have it until you return to the office tomorrow. The solution in both cases: stash your message in the Draft folder. You can return to the message later, complete it, and send it (or delete it).

When you've got a newly written message on the screen, there are three ways to stash it as a Draft:

- Tap Menu → Save Draft.

- Use the Graffiti shortcut /D.

- Tap the Cancel button. A dialog box asks if you'd like to save the message in the "Draft Folder"; tap Yes.

In all three cases, you return to the message list, and your message-in-progress is stored in the Draft category. To view the list of drafts, tap the folder menu in the upper-right corner of a list view, and tap Draft.

What can you do with drafts? To finish one up and send it, tap its name (in the list of Draft messages). It opens up in a non-editable form; tap Edit, make any final changes, and tap the Send button. You've just moved your message into the Outbox, from which it will be sent to your PC at the next HotSync.

If you decide instead to get rid of one of your drafts, tap its name; on the next screen, tap Delete.

Messages in your PalmPilot's Filed and Draft folders are never transferred to your PC's email program. (They are backed up onto your
PC at a HotSync, but you can't access them.) Only the contents of
the Inbox and Outbox folders are ever HotSynced to the corresponding folders of your desktop email program. (The contents of your
Deleted folder are simply deleted from your PC.)

Finally, note that outgoing messages you write on your PC don't get
HotSynced to your PalmPilot's Outbox—what would be the point?

The Outbox Folder

After you compose a message and tap the Send button, the message is placed in
the Outbox folder. When you HotSync, all Outbox messages are transferred to
your PC email program's own Outbox. To see a list of such waiting-to-be-sent
messages, choose Outbox from the folder menu. (Figure 13-4 shows this menu.)

At any time before HotSyncing, however, you can edit, delete, or set aside any of
these Outbox messages. To do so, tap a message's name. The message opens up
in a non-editable form. At this point, you can:

Read the message

When you're finished, tap Done to return to the Outbox list.

Edit the message

Tap the Edit button to return to the message-writing screen described above.
And when that's done, tap the Send button. You return to the Outbox list.

Delete the message

To do so, tap Delete; if you tap Yes on the confirmation screen, the message
is moved to the Deleted folder, as described under "Reading and answering
messages in Palm Mail" earlier in this chapter.

Save it as a draft

If you decide you're not quite ready to send this message, move it to the Draft
folder, as described earlier. Tap Edit → Menu → Message → Save Draft. From
the Draft folder, you can always make changes to your message and, finally,
move it back into the Outbox folder, ready for sending.

File the message

Tap Menu → Message → File. Shortcut fans: Just write /L. (Yes, /L is also the
shortcut for the Lookup feature, described earlier in this chapter; fortunately,
the Lookup command doesn't function in this context. Apparently the designers were going for simplicity, not logic.) Your message gets moved into the
Filed folder.

Remember, though, that there's not much you can do with a message once you've filed it. You can't, for example, move it back into the Outbox. (If that's your intention, move the message into the Draft folder instead.)

Understanding the Folder-Movement Possibilities

If you've read this much of the chapter, you might be left with the impression that you can move messages freely among Palm Mail's five different folders. As Figure 13-11 makes clear, however, there are some exceptions. For example, you can't move incoming mail back to the Inbox once you've moved it to the Filed folder.

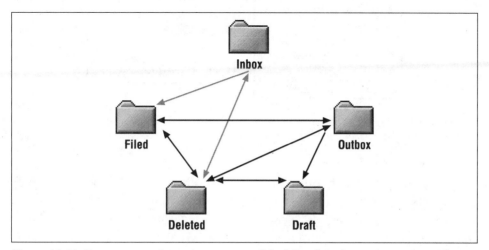

Figure 13-11. You can move incoming messages (black lines) and outgoing messages (gray lines), but some restrictions apply.

On the other hand, you can think of your desktop computer as a last-resort backup. For example, if you've made a mess of things on your PalmPilot, remember that everything is still safe on your desktop computer (assuming you haven't made a similar mess of things there). Using the "Desktop overwrites handheld" option while performing a HotSync (see "The Concept of Conduits" in Chapter 6), it's possible to reinstate messages that you've prematurely deleted or moved out of your Inbox.

Unless you've already HotSynced, that is. In that case, the damage is done.

HotSync Options

One limitation of the PalmPilot as an email gadget is its storage capacity. If you receive, store, or reply to a lot of email, your palmtop's memory can get quickly swamped.

For that reason, the HotSync Options dialog box lets you exclude or include mail from certain people, chop off messages longer than a certain size, or limit your HotSyncing to sending replies only. You can also control these options independently for local HotSyncs and modem HotSyncs (see Chapter 6).

To change these options, tap Menu → Options → HotSync Options. The dialog box shown in Figure 13-12 appears.

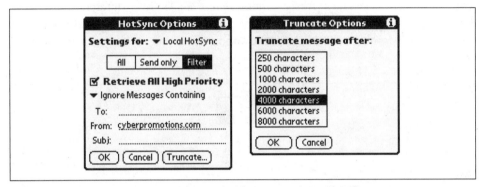

Figure 13-12. The HotSync options let you hold your email—and HotSync times—to a minimum (left). The lower your email length limit (right), the more messages your PalmPilot can store.

Begin by choosing either Local HotSync or Modem HotSync from the pop-up menu at the top of the screen; the settings you're about to make apply only to the HotSync method you've just selected. Now you can change the controls as follows:

Truncate

> The Truncate option lets you chop off the ends of especially long email messages. When you tap this button, a new dialog box appears (at right in Figure 13-12) that lets you specify a maximum length for incoming emails. True, even at its highest setting, any message longer than 8,000 characters will be chopped off in the middle when transferred to your PalmPilot—but, of course, the complete message is still on your desktop email program, if it turns out the missing text is important.

All

> This setting, the default, means that when you HotSync, you'll get all new messages from your PC and send to the PC all email you've written on your PalmPilot.

Send only

> If you're in a hurry, or performing a modem HotSync (and trying to minimize long-distance charges), you might choose to shorten your HotSync time by sending all the messages you've written on the palmtop, but not downloading new messages to read.

Filter

This option gives you some control over which messages are transferred to your PalmPilot. As shown at left in Figure 13-12, you're allowed to either include or exclude messages from a certain address, to a certain address, or containing specific text in the subject line.

Unfortunately, the Filter command isn't as flexible as you might like. For example, you can't set up a number of separate, complex filtering rules, as you can in desktop email programs ("block all mail from *cyberpromotions.com except* if the subject line contains my name—*and* block mail from hotmail. com that contains *'Make money at home'* in the subject line"). For that kind of power, consider one of the commercial email programs described later in this chapter.

Nor, however, is the PalmPilot's filtering quite as lame as it seems; you can combine several factors into your filtering. For example, write several words on the "From:" line, each separated by a space, to block email from multiple addresses. Example: *SkiBunny@aol.com bclinton@whitehouse.gov.* (Need more room? Tap a field label, such as "From:", to expand the blank to full-screen size.) The PalmPilot will block (or include) email from any of those addresses. In other words, the space means "or."

If you write on more than one line here—for example, on the "From:" blank and the "Subj:" blank—Palm Mail looks for messages that meet *both* specifications. (Writing on more than one line means "and.") To block all but urgent email from your brother, for example, you'd write his email address on the "From:" line and the word Urgent on the "Subj:" line. And then you'd choose "Receive Only Messages Containing" from the pop-up menu.

Why do you need a control to filter mail that's *to* a specific email address? After all, isn't all the mail you're downloading addressed to you?

Not necessarily. The To: filter lets you add somebody else's name to the exclusion list. In other words, you can block email that's been mass mailed to a circle of addresses that also includes the name you write into the To: filter field.

Retrieve All High Priority

This checkbox on the Filter screen should really say, "Retrieve Messages Marked 'High Priority,' *Even* if They'd Normally Be Screened Out by the Filtering Settings I've Made Here."

Finally, here's a relaxing thought about the filtering options: they govern only email that's *transferred to your PalmPilot.* These controls don't prevent you from seeing all your mail when you return home and turn on your desktop PC.

Unread

This option, which debuted on the Palm III, gathers only email from your desktop PC that you haven't opened there—a good way to prevent large amounts of email from arriving on the palmtop. Moreover, you get only copies of those messages; they remain on your desktop PC (unless you process them on the palmtop, of course, in which case their desktop-PC status is updated).

Ordinarily, you wouldn't expect to find printing features in any Palm email program. But if you equip your palmtop with the $40 Palm-Print software (*http://www.stevenscreek.com*), you get a special version of Palm Mail that lets you print any message to a compatible printer. (PalmPrint requires either an infrared-equipped printer, such as those from HP, Canon, and Citizen, or a special cable available from the company.)

MultiMail and One-Touch Mail, described later in this chapter, are also PalmPrint-ready—you can tap a menu command to get a hard copy of whatever email is on your Palm screen.

Palmeta Mail

If the concept of getting your mail from your PC (instead of directly from the Internet) appeals to you, an alternative to Palm Mail awaits: Palmeta Mail. Depending on your circumstances, Palmeta Mail may be a more attractive alternative. For example:

- Palmeta Mail doesn't require a PalmPilot Pro; it works on any PalmPilot model, old or new.

- Palmeta Mail doesn't install anything onto your PalmPilot; your email shows up in the Memo Pad. To keep it separate from your actual memos, your email is tagged with three new category labels: Inbox, Outbox, and Sent. (You can change these default labels.) You can use the remaining 12 category labels to flag your processed email with any tags you want.

- Palmeta Mail accepts email messages of any length, breaking them into separate Memo Pad "pages" if necessary. (Just press the plastic Scroll Down button to continue reading.) Palm Mail, by contrast, chops off and discards the last part of any message longer than 8,000 characters.

- If your desktop email program's address book lets you record real names (Bob Smith) along with email addresses, you can address your outgoing mail on the PalmPilot using the plain-English names.

- The program also offers some useful options and controls not found in the built-in Palm Mail program, as you can see in Figure 13-13.

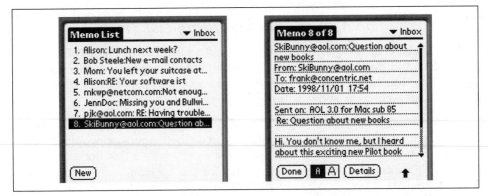

Figure 13-13. Palmeta Mail's interface is the familiar Memo Pad. (A nice touch is the "include name" feature, which adds the sender's name to the name of each message, as shown at left.) Tap a memo's name to read the email (right).

On the other hand, Palmeta Mail requires Windows 95 or NT 4.0 and costs $40 (if you download it from *http://www.palmeta.com*) or $45 (by faxing your credit card number to 603-425-2492).

After you set up Palmeta Mail, perform a HotSync, exactly as you do with Palm Mail. When the HotSync is over, however, you don't launch any special program; instead, you go to your Memo Pad. Using the category pop-up menu (see Chapter 4), choose Inbox. There you'll see your incoming mail; tap the subject line to open the message. (See Figure 13-13.)

The simplicity of Palmeta Mail's concept—the familiar Memo Pad is the interface for reading mail—is also the program's greatest downfall. There are, for example, no automatic features for replying, quoting back text, looking up email addresses, forwarding mail, or adding a standard signature to the end of your messages. In fact, you must actually write the words "To:" and "Subject:" if you want to send a piece of mail. Copying and pasting—and using the Graffiti ShortCuts described in Chapter 4—becomes a fact of life.

pdQmail

If you're lucky enough to own a pdQ phone, then you're already familiar with pdQmail. It's the email program built into that combination PalmPilot/cell phone. You'd expect an email program designed for such an expensive gadget to be of a very high caliber; in this case, you'd be right. PdQmail is an extremely full-featured, well-designed email program (see Figure 13-14).

Among its most remarkable aspects: it can handle email using either of the two methods described at the beginning of this chapter. If your PalmPilot has a modem, pdQmail can get your mail directly from the Internet. If not, pdQmail can

The Address Book Mailing-List Trick

Some Palm email programs can retrieve email addresses from your PalmPilot's existing Address Book; others can't. You won't last long without this feature, however; having to copy-and-paste each address from your Address Book into your mail program is about as thrilling as watching C-SPAN.

If you do use a program with an Address Book lookup feature, here's a spectacular tip. If you sometimes send email to predefined groups of people, create one entry in your Address Book. As the last name, write a description ("Sales Reps," for example). As the email address for this "person," enter all of your group members' email addresses, one after another, separated by commas (for Palm Mail or One-Touch Mail), semicolons (for Palmeta Mail), or returns (for HandMail). For example, you might write into the email field:

```
SkiBunny@aol.com, pschorr@earthlink.net, hcooperman@micronet.com,
jc112@aol.com
```

From now on, whenever you choose Sales Reps (using your email program's Address Book Lookup feature), all of those names will be automatically pasted into the To: blank of the message you're creating.

HotSync your messages with your Windows PC, so that you can read them, and reply to them, on the road.

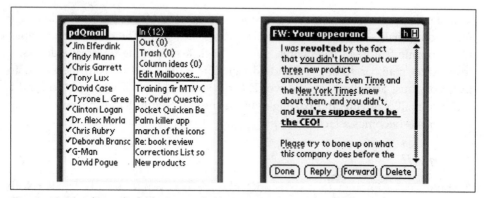

Figure 13-14. pdQmail's folder menu (left) gives statistics about the number of messages in each folder. Right: pdQmail is the only email program for the PalmPilot that shows text formatting. (The dotted underline means italic.)

PdQmail via PC

If you choose to HotSync your email to the PalmPilot, run the included pdQmail Conduit application. To your standard list of conduits (see "The Concept of Conduits" in Chapter 6), it adds a pdQmail conduit containing the usual choices—Synchronize, Handheld overwrites Desktop, and so on.

During the installation of this conduit, you'll be asked to specify your Windows email program. PdQmail can handle Eudora, Outlook Express, Outlook 98, or any generic MAPI email program. (The 1.0 release of pdQmail can't HotSync with Netscape products, America Online, Lotus Notes, or cc:Mail.)

When the installation is over, the pdQmail conduit synchronizes your email beautifully with your Windows email program. Messages from your PC's Inbox are automatically copied to pdQmail on the PalmPilot, replies you write on the PalmPilot are delivered to your PC's Outbox, and messages you delete on the PalmPilot are also deleted on the PC.

The pdQmail feature list

At 216K, pdQmail isn't what you'd call petite. But in power and features, the program is unmatched:

- pdQmail is the only Palm email program that displays text formatting, such as bold and italics, which is often included in HTML-formatted messages (see Figure 13-14, right). (This formatting shows up only on directly downloaded mail, not mail HotSynced from your PC.)

- You can sort your list of messages by date, subject, sender, thread, priority, and so on. (Tap Menu → Options → Sorting and Columns.)

- As in other Palm email programs, you can specify that you'd like a standard signature appended to the end of each email you send. But in pdQmail, you can choose to have this signature included either globally or on a message-by-message basis.

- You can assign a priority to each outgoing message, for the benefit of those email programs (such as Outlook) that display priority information in the recipient's Inbox.

- pdQmail uses "excerpt bars," which help to identify portions of messages that have been forwarded or quoted back—a less distracting alternative to the greater-than symbols (>) that generally precede each quoted line. (See Figure 13-15, left, for an example.)

- The program's filters offer extensive control over what messages are fetched at each online session or HotSync. In order to conserve time and Palm memory, you can specify that you want to get only the first, say, 20 lines of each message. You can also limit your downloading to the most recent X number of messages you've received.

- Those same filtering commands let you omit messages from certain people, with certain subject lines, to certain recipients, and so on—or include only messages that meet those criteria (Figure 13-15, right). You can also use filters to automatically file downloaded mail into the pdQ mailboxes you've set up. (To see your options, tap Menu → Options → Filters → New.)

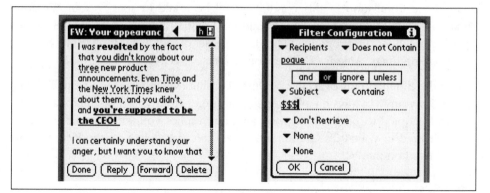

Figure 13-15. Left: The vertical bar at the left edge of a message indicates material that is being quoted or forwarded. Right: pdQmail filters at work screening out spam junk mail.

A trial version of pdQmail is included with this book. It's also available from *http://www.qualcomm.com/pdq* as shareware, or with the Qualcomm pdQ PalmPilot/cell phone itself.

MultiMail

Like pdQmail, MultiMail is an impressive, full-featured, commercial email program that can handle your email in either of two ways—directly from the Internet using a Palm modem or, with the added-cost MultiMail Conduit, directly from your desktop PC.

If you choose the latter method, you'll find that MultiMail can exchange messages with such Windows programs as Netscape 4.x, Eudora Pro, Outlook Express, Pegasus, or any desktop email program that offers MAPI compatibility.

On the Mac, as noted earlier in this chapter, you have a choice not only of Mac email programs—Eudora, Eudora Lite, Outlook Express, and so on—but also of which Palm program you want your messages HotSynced to: the built-in Palm Mail application or, for more features, the MultiMail application itself, described next.

MultiMail features

MultiMail (see Figure 13-16), the program that runs on your PalmPilot itself, is available in two versions. Both require a PalmPilot Pro or later model:

MultiMail Discovery

This $10 version sends and receives email, offers Reply and Forward buttons, and lets you file your mail in any of 15 "folders." You might miss, however, such standard features as automatic signatures and a link to your Address Book for inserting email addresses, as well as such desirable features as attachments and direct-HotSync potential.

MultiMail Pro

Costs $30. Lets you download longer messages; sorts your email by sender, date, or subject; handles much longer messages than the Discovery version; offers a "headlines only" mode, which downloads only the subject (and sender) names of your messages; lets you set up a blob of standard signature text that's automatically appended to your sent messages; and, most important, links to the PalmPilot's Address Book program for selecting email addresses.

The derivation of MultiMail's name is no secret—the program can handle multiple email accounts (up to eight), multiple email filing folders (up to 16), multiple email protocols (SMTP, POP3, and IMAP4), a choice of fonts for better readability, and so on. The program can handle massive email messages—up to 60K, substantially larger than other Palm email programs' capacity.

Most remarkably, however, MultiMail can handle file attachments. With the necessary plug-ins, available for free from *http://www.actualsoft.com*, you can send and receive files to other PalmPilots along with your text messages. At this writing, plug-ins are available for attaching, receiving, and viewing these kinds of files:

Text

In other words, you can send pages from your Memo Pad.

Palm programs (.prc files)

Only in MultiMail can you send a message that says, "Hi Chris. Attached is that really cool PalmPilot chess game you asked me about"—and be confident that Chris will be able to start playing that game the instant he receives the message, because the *.prc* file will be attached and automatically installed on his palmtop.

Quicksheet files

See Chapter 12, *Database and Number Crunching*, for details on this Palm spreadsheet.

VCard attachments

This file type lets you email Palm Address-Book entries to other people; the recipient can drop your contact information directly into the Address Book.

Using MultiMail

Tap a message to read it. If you tap Reply, the program automatically pastes the contents of the original message, > bracketed (in the Pro version), in a new reply screen. The Pro version lets you tap the *To:* or *CC:* labels to open your Address Book's list of email addresses, exactly as in the other programs described in this chapter.

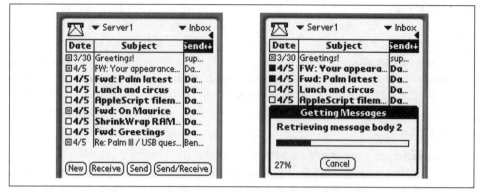

Figure 13-16. MultiMail is the only Palm email program that lets you adjust the widths or order of the columns on the main email-listing screen (left); just drag. To save connection expense, MultiMail lets you download only message titles, tap the checkboxes (which turn black) to indicate the ones you really want to download, and then go online again to retrieve the bodies of the messages you want (right).

One of MultiMail's claims to fame is its support for IMAP4 protocols, a geeky way of saying it can do some fancy tricks when connected to the right kind of Internet service provider (ISP).

If your email account is IMAP4-compatible, you get a special button called Quick Sync at the bottom of your main MultiMail index screen. Its four checkboxes control exactly which "syncing" operations the PalmPilot should perform with your Internet account. To save time, for example, you could turn off the "Sync Server Changes" option, which brings your list of mailbox names up to date. You might also turn on the "Headers Only" option, which downloads only the subject and senders' names of your email, so that you can choose which full messages to download the next time.

Getting Email Directly from the Internet

Most people get email onto the PalmPilot by HotSyncing it there. But the true road warriors enjoy the ultimate perk of pocket computing—doing email directly from the palmtop. This scenario requires that you purchase a Palm modem or Palm V modem, as described at the beginning of this chapter and in Appendix B; that you have an Internet email account—a PPP account with an ISP (Internet service provider) such as EarthLink, Netcom, AT&T, Mindspring, and so on; that you travel with a piece of telephone wire; and that you can find a phone jack wherever you go.

It also requires a Palm email program that's designed for dialing into the Internet—such as HandMail, One-Touch Mail, pdQmail, MultiMail, or ProxiMail, all of which are described in this section.

Configuring Your Palmtop for Internet Access

By far the biggest problem with using a direct-to-Internet mail program is that you need a full afternoon just to set it up. You're asked to fill in a long series of dialog boxes like the ones in Figure 13-17, filled with cryptic Net codes. Unless you're a telecom guru yourself, you'll probably have to call your ISP (or burrow around on its web page) to learn what codes belong in these blanks.

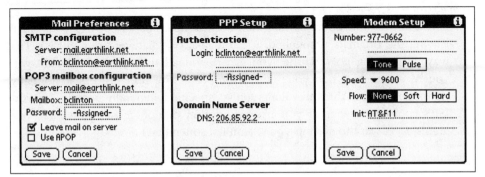

Figure 13-17. The setup boxes for HandMail.

Here's a walkthrough of some typical fields you'll be asked to fill in. (These are the ones from HandMail; you'll find similar ones in every Palm direct-dial email program.)

SMTP Configuration

In the following discussion, let's say that the name of your Internet provider is EarthLink.

Server
> An *IP address.* Such an address usually looks like *mail.company.com* or *mail.company.net,* where *company* is the name of your Internet provider. For EarthLink, for example, the correct address here is *mail.earthlink.net.*

From
> Your email address. It might look like this: *bclinton@earthlink.net.*

Name
> Put your colloquial, noncoded name (such as Bill Clinton) here. Your correspondents will see this name after your email address; for example, they'll see *bclinton@earthlink.net (Bill Clinton).*

POP3 Configuration

Server

This address generally follows the form *pop3@company.com* or *mail.company. com*. For EarthLink, it's *mail.earthlink.net*, again.

Mailbox

Write your "screen name" or "user name" here—that is, your email address before the @ symbol. If your email address is *bclinton@earthlink.net*, write *bclinton* here.

Password

Tap this box; write in your password.

Leave mail on server

If you turn on this option, your PalmPilot will download a copy of your email, leaving the originals untouched at EarthLink (or whatever your ISP is). That way, if anything goes wrong, you can download that same mail again with your desktop PC when you return from your trip, and process it normally. (Messages longer than the limit you've specified generally remain on your ISP's computers whether you use this option or not; most Palm email programs don't want to swamp your PalmPilot's memory.)

Palm email software's "Leave mail on server" option makes one very attractive email lifestyle possible: it lets you read and think about your email during your commute or plane flight with the PalmPilot—but put off responding (because Graffiti is too clumsy for lengthy replies). When you return to your desk, you're already familiar with the email's contents and can get right to work responding.

Modem setup

You'll also need to set up your modem—what its startup string is and what number it should dial. For a discussion of these topics, see "Setting up the PalmPilot" in Chapter 6.

PPP Setup

Here, you're asked to write in, once again, your name (everything in your email address before the @ symbol) and your password. You are also asked to write in your domain name server (DNS) number. It's a string of four sets of numbers separated by periods, such as 44.151.06.15. There's only one source of this information: your Internet service provider's tech-support department or web page.

Connection Script

This most daunting element of typical Palm email programs' setup requires a few minutes of actual programming—or actual talking to your ISP's tech representative. Using the pop-up menus in the dialog box pictured in Figure 13-18, you must build a script for the PalmPilot to follow. You tell the PalmPilot what your ISP's computer will say, and what it should say in return. The most common sequence is shown in Figure 13-18. (Fortunately, the script isn't required for most popular email services.)

Connection Script

▼ Send ¶: ....
▼ Wait for: login: ....
▼ Send ¶: bclinton ....
▼ Wait for: password: ....
▼ Send ¶: prezman96 ....
▼ End: ....

Figure 13-18. Some email services require a connection script.

If you're getting nowhere trying to figure out what codes to plug into your Palm email program, visit *http://www.jpsystems.com* and download the demo of One-Touch Mail. The included Quick Start manual is extremely useful in determining your ISP's correct settings, featuring field-by-field information for connecting to AT&T, IBM.net, GTE, CompuServe, EarthLink, MindSpring, MCI 2000, Netcom, and other services.

HandMail

One of the first direct-to-Net email programs was HandStamp, which to this day works on modem-equipped original Pilot and PalmPilot models. Its $50 successor, HandMail, is far more sophisticated, capable of extensive filtering, letting you preview message headers before downloading, checking up to five different email accounts, attaching Memo Pad pages, and even connecting to America Online. (The older HandStamp comes in the same package from SmartCode, *http://www.smartcodesoft.com.*)

In general, HandMail's design is clear. That is:

- The "category" pop-up menu in the upper right switches between the Inbox, Outbox, Draft, Trash, and any filing folders that you set up.

- Tap a message's name in the Inbox to read it; tap View in the pop-up menu (see Figure 13-19). Once it's open, you can tap the Rep (Reply), Fwd (Forward), or Del (Delete) buttons at the bottom of the screen; Reply and Forward open up a preaddressed blank message.

- When you're writing a new piece of mail, tap the *To:* button to open a large screen where you can add multiple email addresses (one per line). Tap Lookup to view a list of names from your Address Book, so that you don't have to write in addresses manually

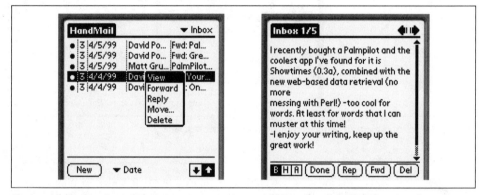

Figure 13-19. Use the pop-up menu to open a piece of HandMail (left). When reading a message, the icons in the lower-left let you view the body of the message (B), header information (H), or text attachments in the form of Memo Pad pages (A).

Unfortunately, because the French company SmartCode has few overseas representatives, it has earned a reputation for ignoring its English-speaking HandMail customers. Attempting to get a response from the company by email or telephone—even sales inquiries, let alone technical help—is generally an exercise in frustration. (Perhaps Palm Computing's 1998, multimillion dollar purchase of SmartCode will produce some positive change in this regard.)

One-Touch Mail

As the PalmPilot's popularity explodes, enterprising software companies continue to push the state of the art in email software. Among the most recent direct-to-Net entries is the formidable One-Touch Mail, a $50 commercial program from JP Systems (*http://www.jpsystems.com*). Like most modern Palm email programs, it can get your mail from multiple accounts, apply filtering rules, and so on. But One-Touch Mail offers a few exclusives of its own:

- Canned messages, available from a pop-up menu, save you the agony of trying to scratch out an email reply as your taxi pounds over the New York City pot-holes. A pop-up menu lets you slap predefined phrases into the message you're trying to write. (Of course, this feature is available to any email program, in the form of ShortCuts; see Chapter 3, *Typing Without a Keyboard*, for details on this built-in Graffiti shorthand. But One-Touch Mail's feature is more convenient, because you don't have to leave the program to edit your boilerplate phrases.)

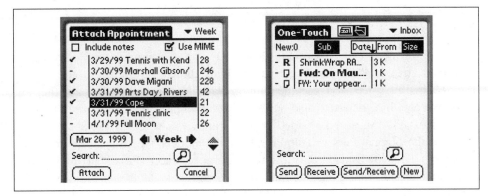

Figure 13-20. One-Touch Mail's attachments feature lets you choose Date Book appointments, for example, that you want to send to another PalmPilot or Windows desktop computer via email (left; the selected appointments have checkmarks). When you are reading messages (right), R indicates that you've replied, F means you've forwarded this message, and bold means you haven't read the message yet.

- One-Touch Mail's attachments feature isn't as broad as, say, MultiMail's. On the other hand, it has charms of its own—to any outgoing message, you can attach any memo, datebook, to-do, or address book entry from your own PalmPilot—or an entire category of such items. When your recipient receives the message you've sent, one tap on the tiny double-page icon above the screen opens the dialog box shown in Figure 13-20. The Save button automatically files the attachment into the corresponding Palm application on the recipient's PalmPilot—Datebook, Address Book, or whatever.

- Like the other state-of-the-art Palm email programs, One-Touch Mail can quickly download only a list of your waiting mail; just tap the ones whose full-length bodies you'd like to download the next time you go online.

Technically, One-Touch Mail sends your Palm attachments as *vCard* and *vCalendar* files. Although you don't need to know what this format means, it's useful to note that the PalmPilot's programs aren't the only ones that can read such files. Netscape Communicator and Microsoft Outlook can also recognize them, making One-Touch Mail's attachments feature even more promising; now you can email appointments, electronic business cards, and other information directly into the Windows calendar and address book programs of your recipients.

ProxiMail

ProxiMail (formerly called Top Gun Postman) is an ingenious hybrid of programs described in this chapter. It gets your mail directly from the Internet, like HandMail—but it lets you use the built-in Palm Mail program to read, file, and compose email. You get to use software that's already built into the PalmPilot, uses no extra RAM, and is loaded with features. (As a result, ProxiMail doesn't work on the original Pilot or PalmPilot Personal models, which lack the Palm Mail program.) The downside: you must use one application (ProxiMail) to get your email and another (Palm Mail) to read and reply to it.

ProxiMail offers a unique (optional) feature: a real-time interview about each piece of mail that comes in while you're connected. As shown in Figure 13-21, you're shown the size, subject line, and sender of each message; for each one, you can choose to download the complete message, to skip it and leave it on your ISP's computer (to deal with later), or to skip it and delete it from your ISP's computer (if you know that it's junk mail).

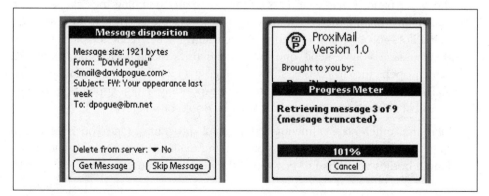

Figure 13-21. ProxiMail shows you the header information of each message as it comes in (left); it then downloads the full message only if you request it (right).

After the session is over, you read, reply to, and file your mail exactly as described in "Palm Mail," earlier in this chapter. You benefit from all the features built into that program: automatic signatures, Address Book lookups, and so on. ProxiMail can accept messages as large as 32K (four times bigger than Palm Mail's own limit).

One final bonus: the program is free (from *http://www.proxinet.com*).

pdQmail and MultiMail

These two outstanding email programs are described earlier in this chapter. They're mentioned here as a reminder that they're particularly smooth performers when dialing directly to your ISP account, even though they do double duty as HotSync-to-your-desktop-email-program programs.

Closing the Connection

No matter which email software you choose, getting your mail (on your PalmPilot or any other computer) involves two steps. First, your modem dials and establishes a *PPP link*—a communications pathway. Once that road is paved, then you can run your telecom software over it, whether it's an email program, web browser, or whatever.

When you're finished using the telecom program, however, the PPP connection is still open. The modem doesn't hang up automatically. The official way to end the call is to tap Applications → Prefs → Network → Disconnect.

A much better idea: simply turn your PalmPilot off momentarily. Doing so gracefully closes the PPP connection and hangs up the call, sparing you that long sequence of steps.

America Online

In general, America Online's mail system isn't compatible with the usual email standards used by the rest of the Internet. That's why so few Palm email programs can get mail from America Online. However, if your email account is with AOL, you're not necessary out of luck.

PocketFlash

PocketFlash ($25 from *http://www.powermedia.com*) does one thing very well—it dials your local AOL access number, grabs your email, and deposits it into the built-in Palm Mail application. From there, you can process, file, and reply to this email exactly as though it had arrived from the Internet or via HotSync, as described earlier in this chapter.

Like other polished email programs, PocketFlash can fetch only the message subjects, saving connection time, and then later download the full messages you
select. As a bonus, setting up PocketFlash is far simpler than setting up a full ISP-
access program. All you have to tell the program is the local phone number and
your AOL screen name, as shown in Figure 13-22; the program does the rest.
(PocketFlash can check email from all five of your AOL screen names in a single
call.)

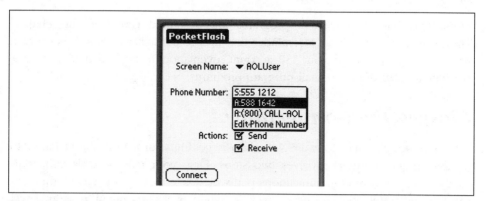

Figure 13-22. PocketFlash is a no-brainer to set up for America Online email.

TransAOL

TransAOL (*http://members.aol.com/VinceDeb*) doesn't dial AOL directly. Instead, it
uses your desktop PC as the home base for email and simply uses a HotSync to
shunt your AOL mail onto the palmtop. On the PalmPilot, you can read and compose email from any of your screen names; in fact, you can send and receive
newsgroup messages this way. Any replies you write on the PalmPilot get sent
back to the PC at the next HotSync, and from there your email is sent the next
time your PC goes onto America Online.

TransAOL uses the PalmPilot's Memo Pad program as its "front end." As a result, it
has no built-in features for looking up email addresses from your Address Book.
On the other hand, the program is free; download the accompanying registration
program to unlock it.

HandMail

HandMail, described in the previous section, comes with an accompanying Palm
application called HandMail AOL. Beyond its affinity for America Online, the program is identical to HandMail itself, except that it doesn't offer filtering and it's far
easier to set up before connecting for the first time.

> ### *CompuServe*
>
> No special Palm software is required to get CompuServe mail, because it follows standard Internet email format. When properly configured, any of the Internet email programs described in this chapter should be able to get your CompuServe mail, whether by dialing directly with a Palm modem or by HotSyncing with your desktop PC. (Either way, ask CompuServe's tech-support staff if you need help with the settings.)

Executive Tip Summary

- Any PalmPilot model, old or new, can do email. You may require a shareware program and a modem for the PalmPilot to do so, but it's possible.

- Each commercial Palm email program has distinct advantages. MultiMail lets you attach Palm applications, Quicksheet spreadsheets, Memo Pad pages, and many other kinds of files to your outgoing email. One-Touch Mail lets you attach PalmPilot records—appointments, address book entries, to do items, and so on—to your email, which can then be automatically filed on the recipient's palmtop. ProxiMail (which is free) offers the familiar features of Palm Mail—but gets your mail directly from your ISP account using a Palm modem. And pdQmail correctly displays HTML-formatted messages, such as bold, italic, and underlined text.

- If you use one of the direct-dial-to-Internet email programs, consider establishing a separate email account just for your PalmPilot. Otherwise, you may get into the nightmare of having duplicate messages on your palmtop and PC, and you may never be quite clear on which ones you've answered and where you read something.

- If your PalmPilot email program offers a lookup feature that grabs email addresses from your Address Book, you can write the email addresses of everyone in an entire group on a single email-address field—just separate them by commas, or returns (depending on the program). Thereafter, choose the name of the group when addressing a message to have all of those addresses pasted into the *"To:"* field automatically.

14

The Web in Your Palm

In five years, or even two, we'll think nothing of surfing the Web on a piece of gadgetry smaller than an index card. Today, however, most Piloteers are shocked to hear that this tiny gizmo can browse the Internet's most famous feature, complete with graphics, bookmarks, and hotlinks. After all, the Palm's manual, advertising, and web site say not a word about this capability.

But not only is there such a thing as a Palm web browser, there are *several,* each with a different assortment of useful features. (They're all on the CD that comes with this book.) And setting up a PalmPilot for web browsing is much easier than setting it up for email; this time, all you need is the name, password, and phone number of your Internet account—no fancy codes necessary.

To use any of these programs, you need a fairly recent model; alas, the original Pilots and the PalmPilot Personal are forever barred from the Web (unless you upgrade, as described in Chapter 18, *The Palm Family, Model by Model*).

You also need a modem attached to your PalmPilot (if you have a Palm VII, also see Chapter 16, *Palm VII: Wireless Email, Wireless Web*, for details on Web access without a modem). Once again, you can either buy the tiny snap-on Palm modem (which has its own batteries) or you can attach any external PC modem via a Palm modem cable. If you're rich enough to have the Novatel wireless modem (see Appendix B, *PalmPilot Accessories*), you can pack your sunscreen, put on your bathing suit, and head to the beach for a pleasant afternoon of surfing.

Web surfing, that is.

The Principles of Palm Web Browsing

In many ways, surfing the Web with your PalmPilot is like surfing it with, say, Netscape Navigator or Microsoft Internet Explorer. For example, you can't view the Web unless you've signed up for an account with an ISP—an Internet service provider, a company that provides an Internet account in exchange for a monthly fee. EarthLink, IBM, AT&T, Netcom, and Concentric are some popular ISPs.

Cached Pages

On your PC, the graphics from each web page you visit are saved, or *cached,* onto your hard drive. If you visit that same web page again—even if it's only a minute or two later—the page appears on your PC's screen almost instantaneously, because the computer doesn't have to redownload that information from the Internet. Instead, it just coughs up the graphics it previously cached.

On the PalmPilot, caching is more important than ever. This is, after all, a mobile device; you spend most of your time using it when it's *not* hooked up to a phone line. Consequently, the Palm web browsers store entire pages, complete with text and graphics, so that you can view them again later without dialing.

In fact, most Palm browsers are so cache-dependent that they seem to be surprised when you access a page that *hasn't* been previously saved. For example, if you enter a new web address and tap Connect, each of the Palm web browsers displays a message like those shown in Figure 14-1. That's your warning that the PalmPilot is about to begin trying to dial, and you'd better hook up the modem and phone line. (If you're already hooked up and online, just tap Connect and go on your way.)

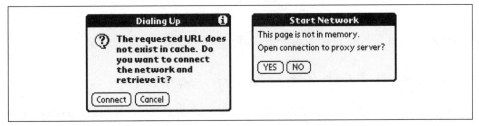

Figure 14-1. Your warning that you're about to go get a web page, as shown in HandWeb (left) and ProxiWeb (right).

Setting Up the PalmPilot for Web Browsing

To prepare your PalmPilot, tap Applications → Prefs; from the upper-right pop-up menu, choose Network. You're shown the screen in Figure 14-2. Tap the pop-up menu labeled Service; if you see your ISP among the list (at right in Figure 14-2), tap it.

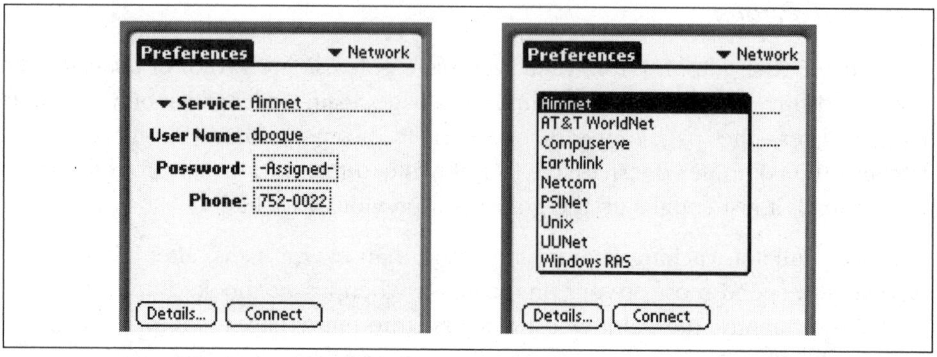

Figure 14-2. The Network Preferences screen lets you inform your PalmPilot about your choice of ISP.

If not, tap Menu → Service → New. Write the name of your ISP into the Service blank; write your User Name (usually some variation of your name, such as *bclinton*) into the second blank; tap the Password box and input the password your ISP provided; and, finally, tap the Phone box to write in the local phone number you dial to access your ISP.

For basic web browsing, you won't even need to tap Details and fill in the DNS blanks. (If you do need this information, however, only your ISP can provide it.)

Your PalmPilot is now ready for the World Wide Web!

ProxiWeb (Top Gun Wingman)

You wouldn't think that the PalmPilot could be capable of showing the *graphics* from the web pages you visit; after all, its screen is supposedly black-and-white. But if you've read Chapter 11, *The Secret Multimedia World*, you already know about the PalmPilot's secret grayscale feature, which does a reasonable job of displaying color images using only 4 or 16 different shades of gray. ProxiWeb uses that secret feature to good advantage, actually showing you web pages with mixed graphics and text (see Figure 14-3).

ProxiWeb can even download Palm (*.prc*) applications and install them onto your palmtop (even if they're compressed as *.zip* files!). The program is so fast, attractive, and powerful, you'll be astounded that it's free.

For the first year of its existence, ProxiWeb was known as Top Gun Wingman. Written by a bunch of guys at UC Berkeley, Top Gun Wingman swept the Palm community like a hurricane, amazing everyone who downloaded it.

In 1998, the programmers formed a new company called ProxiWeb, upgraded the program, and renamed it. Top Gun Wingman is still floating around—on the Web, for example, and even on this book's CD-ROM—but its development life is over. ProxiWeb, its noble descendant, is the one you want.

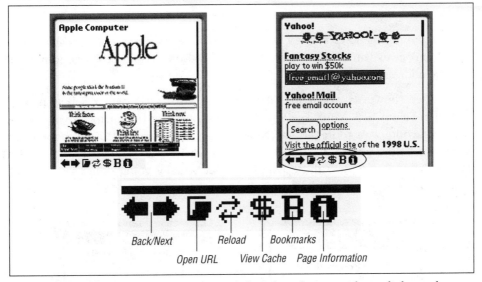

Figure 14-3. ProxiWeb can show graphics side-by-side with text—with very little speed penalty (top). Bottom: the toolbar demystified.

Install ProxiWeb as instructed in Chapter 7, *Installing New Palm Programs*. When you launch it (by tapping its icon on the Applications screen), a welcome screen appears. At the bottom of the screen is the ProxiWeb toolbar; you can find out what each button does by tapping it with the stylus. A label, in plain English, appears to the right.

At this point, you can proceed in one of two ways. You can tap the Open URL button, shown in Figure 14-3, and then write in the address of the web page you

---

How It Works—and How It's Named

How is it that a palmtop computer the size of a playing card actually feels *faster* at downloading web pages—at 14.4 Kbps, in fact—than a $3,000 computer? And what's this "proxi" stuff?

Turns out ProxiWeb performs its high-speed, high-quality magic by cheating: it intercepts your PalmPilot's requests to see each web page. A computer in California—a *proxy server*—processes that web page's data by stripping out all kinds of unnecessary information and passes the streamlined result along to you. Your PalmPilot doesn't have to contend with any of the usual junk that makes web browsing so slow: color, frames, blinking GIFs, animations, and so on.

That's how the software is able to do what it does—and why it's named what it is.

---

want; a pop-up menu of canned web address pieces (such as *http://, www., .com,* and so on) saves you a lot of writing (Figure 14-4, left). Just choose one to insert it into the address you're writing.

More often, however, you'll probably want to tap the Bookmarks button, also shown in Figure 14-3. You'll see ProxiWeb's list of starter bookmarks; to add some of your favorite web addresses, tap New (at right in Figure 14-4). (Any bookmarks shown in bold type are those that have been cached, as described later—which means that you can view those pages without actually going online or having a modem attached.)

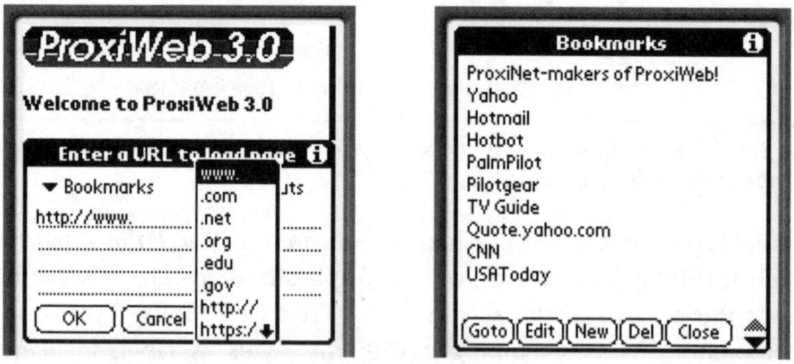

Figure 14-4. To visit a page not in your Bookmarks list, use the Enter a URL dialog box (left). To edit your bookmarks, use the Bookmarks dialog box (right).

To visit a page, tap the name of a bookmark and then tap Go to. The message shown in Figure 14-1 appears, reminding you that this page has not yet been stored on the PalmPilot; tap Yes. Now your PalmPilot dials; a progress bar appears (no web browser would be complete without a progress bar); and, at last, an actual, miniature web page appears. (Once online, you can bookmark a page without going through the Bookmark mechanism described above—just tap Menu → Go → Bookmark Page.)

You can, of course, press the PalmPilot's plastic up/down buttons to scroll up or down on a web page you're viewing. You can also use the vertical scroll bar on the right side of the window, which is probably so skinny you didn't even realize it *was* a scroll bar. (There's a horizontal scroll bar on the bottom of the screen, too, so that you can see entire Dilbert cartoons on your screen.)

But the easiest way to scroll in ProxiWeb is simply to drag your stylus around in the middle of the page. The image moves under your pen as though attracted by a magnet.

In PalmPilot's attempts to represent the web page the way it actually looks, the graphics can get pretty tiny. That's why, if you tap a graphic, the pop-up menu in Figure 14-5 appears; tap View Full Size to have a better, bigger look at the image. What's especially amazing is that if the blown-up graphic contains an image map—that is, areas of the picture you can tap to summon other web pages—ProxiWeb works exactly the way you'd expect.

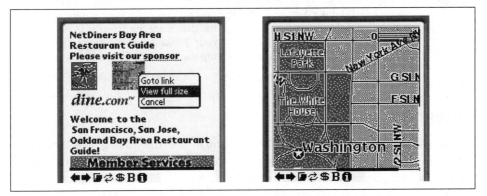

Figure 14-5. To get a better look at a graphic, tap it (left) to enlarge it (right).

Whenever you see a dotted line under some text (such as the word *sponsor* in Figure 14-5), you're looking at a link—the equivalent of blue underlined text on your PC's browser. Tap it to open the web page it refers to.

While you're visiting the menus, you may be startled to see the View Source command in the View menu, which opens up the HTML programming code that underlies every web page. If you're a student of web-page design, you'll find this feature (which no other Palm browser has) extremely useful.

Storing Web Pages

Whenever you're looking at a web page you'd like to save for a time when you're not actually online, tap Menu → Go → Lock In Cache.

Thereafter, if you use the View menu's Cache command, you'll see the list of pages you've stored. Tap one to view it—whether your modem is connected or not. On the other hand, remember to delete pages you won't need again. Tap Menu → View → Cache → the name of the web page you want to delete → Del.

Forms and Buttons—They Work!

Forms are *blanks,* such as the search field into which you'd type what you're looking for at Yahoo.com, for example. When you see a blank on a web page to "type into," just tap there—and begin writing in the Graffiti area. You can also tap on web-page buttons, such as Submit or Search buttons, choose from Web-based pop-up menus, and click to select checkboxes.

ProxiWeb's status bar (at the bottom of the screen) generally keeps you apprised of what's going on. But in every PalmPilot web browser and email program, including ProxiWeb, the tiny, three-pixel-tall, blinking | mark in the upper-right corner of your screen is also a helpful indicator—it tells you that data from the Internet is still arriving. If that blinker is blinking, your PalmPilot hasn't frozen or given up; it just hasn't finished receiving the page you're going for.

Preferences

If you tap Menu → ProxiWeb → Prefs, you'll see the dialog box shown in Figure 14-6. Many of the controls here have to do with the proxy server's Internet address, which you generally won't need to change.

Some of the controls, however, are worth noting. For example, you can prevent ProxiWeb's cached pages from taking over your PalmPilot's memory by setting the Cache Size limit to something reasonable (the default is 100K).

Even more useful is the "Map Phone/ToDo as Prev/Next" checkbox. When this option is turned on, the plastic hardware buttons corresponding to the Address

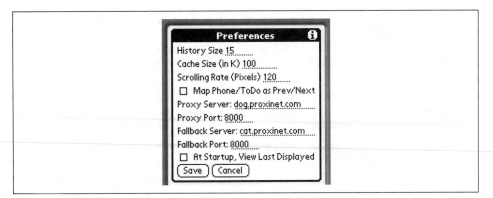

Figure 14-6. Most of ProxiWeb's Preferences are worth leaving alone.

Book and To Do programs become Previous and Next page buttons. You may find that it's easier to navigate the web with your thumbs than by using the stylus.

Not bad for a web browser that takes up only 84K of space, eh? Microsoft could probably learn a thing or two.

HandWeb

In some respects, HandWeb's design is better than ProxiWeb's—for example, getting at your bookmarks is easier (in fact, they're the startup screen). The current version can even display grayscale graphics, just as ProxiWeb does.

Unfortunately, HandWeb doesn't offer the crown-jewel feature of ProxiWeb: its proxy servers in California, which filter out all of the useless Web clutter that makes web browsing slow. As a result, using HandWeb with "load images" turned on is unbearably slow—minutes per page, as compared with seconds per page for ProxiWeb. Unfortunately, the delay can be so great that the PalmPilot itself shuts off before your Web page has fully arrived, a victim of the palmtop's three-minute power-saving circuitry—which also hangs up your connection. HandWeb is also expensive ($50) and a memory hog (162K).

That's too bad, because HandWeb otherwise has much to recommend it—when images are turned off.

Using HandWeb

When you start up HandWeb, the master home page view is a list of bookmarks, as shown in Figure 14-7. In the lower-right corner, a pop-up menu lets you switch the view from a list of web page *titles* (such as "The Whitehouse") to web page *addresses,* or URLs (such as *http://www.whitehouse.gov*). The New button lets you add new bookmarks.

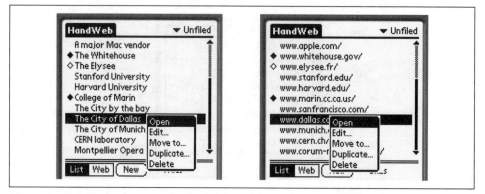

Figure 14-7. You can view HandWeb's bookmark list either as web-page titles (left) or URLs (right). Either way, tap in the list to make the pop-up menu appear—and then tap Open to view that page from the Web.

Going Online

To begin your web session, tap an item in the bookmark list. The PalmPilot dials (if it hasn't already) and a progress bar appears at the bottom of the screen.

After a moment, the text of the desired page appears. If you have turned off graphics, you see the *name* of each missing picture enclosed in a box, as shown in Figure 14-8. As with all Palm browsers, a dotted underline indicates that the text is a "hotlink" (tap to open a different web page). Graphics, too, are sometimes hotlinks on the Web; even when HandWeb displays only a graphic's name in a rectangle, you can still tap there. Don't miss the vertical scroll bar at the right side of the window, which lets you bring other parts of the web page into view.

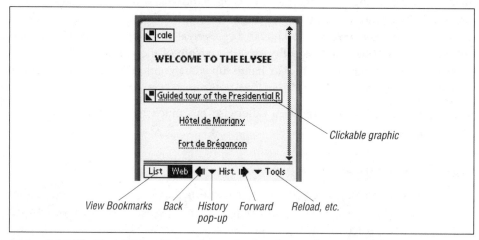

Figure 14-8. The HandWeb toolbar is the navigational control center.

The HandWeb toolbar at the bottom of the screen (Figure 14-8 again) offers the usual web-browser amenities: Back and Forward buttons, and a button to take you back to the bookmark list. And where, you may ask, are the Reload and Stop buttons? The Stop button is visible only while a page is actually downloading; the Reload command is hidden away in a pop-up menu. Tap the word Tools (Figure 14-8) to see it (Figure 14-9). This menu also contains an Info command (which identifies the current page's address), an Add URL command (which adds the current page to your list of bookmarks), and a Save Page command, discussed later.

The word History on the HandWeb toolbar is actually a pop-up menu. As shown in Figure 14-9, it lists every web page you've visited during this session; just tap a page's name to revisit that page.

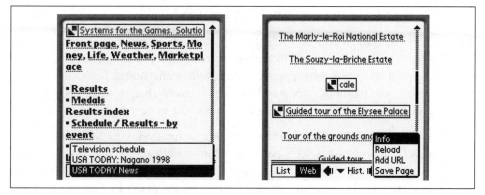

Figure 14-9. HandWeb's two useful pop-up menus. The History list (left) shows your recently visited pages; the Tools list (right) offers four handy page-related commands.

Saving Pages

Exactly as with ProxiWeb, you can grab whole web pages and save them for offline reading. Whenever you find yourself viewing a page you'll want to inspect later, tap the word Tools in the lower-right corner of the screen; from the pop-up menu, choose Save Page (see Figure 14-9).

Once you've done so, a small black diamond appears next to the web page's name in your bookmark list, as shown in Figure 14-7—your reminder that this page is safely stored.

If you see an *empty* diamond beside a page's name, the page is being held in the PalmPilot's temporary cache, which HandWeb maintains without any action on your part. These pages pop up instantly if you summon them again—but they'll be gradually replaced by more recent pages as you continue to browse the Web.

Like any desktop-computer web browser, HandWeb maintains a cache of recently visited pages in memory, so that revisiting them will be quick. But on a memory-strapped PalmPilot, 40K (the factory setting) can be a lot of RAM to be occupied by dead web pages when you're not even using HandWeb.

To flush them, thus freeing up that RAM for other uses, tap Menu → Options → Cache → Purge.

And if you, the proud owner of, for example, a memory-packed Palm IIIx, think 40K is too *little* to set aside for caching web pages, open Preferences in the Options menu. You'll see 40K listed as the "Recent" pages cache size, which you can edit accordingly.

Forms, Pop-Up Menus, and Saved Text

Like ProxiWeb, HandWeb lets you interact with web pages. For example. if you visit a page where you're asked to type in your name or a search phrase, tap the field. A special text-entry box appears—complete with Graffiti input and (if you use the menu) the PalmPilot's popup keyboard. HandWeb also shows you pop-up menus and checkboxes on web pages; they work just as you'd expect.

One last feature of HandWeb is worth noting: whenever you see some useful facts, figures, or prose on a web page, you can easily capture that text into your PalmPilot's Memo Pad program. Just tap Menu → Options → Save as Memo. As shown in Figure 14-10, you can now hop over to your Memo Pad program, where the saved web text is first in the list, ready for reading, editing, or beaming to a friend.

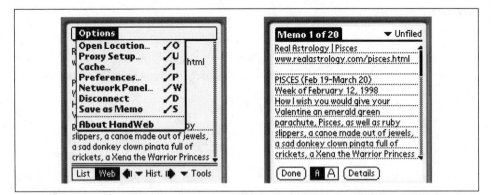

Figure 14-10. To preserve some text forever, use the Save as Memo command (left). Switch to your Memo Pad to see the captured prose (right).

Signing Off HandWeb

When you're finished with your web session, you don't have to disconnect the phone call by returning to your Network Preferences panel, as you do with Proxi-Web. Instead, just use HandWeb's Disconnect command (in the Options menu, as shown in Figure 14-10).

> HandWeb can download files, just as ProxiWeb can. Of course, they won't do you much good unless they're PalmPilot files—*.prc* and *.pdb* files, as described in Chapter 7. But if you *do* find such PalmPilot-downloadable documents and programs, you can install them onto the PalmPilot directly from the Web, with no installation or HotSync-ing necessary.
>
> To locate web pages with ready-to-download PalmPilot files in the correct format, visit Appendix C, *Piloteers in Cyberspace.*

pdQbrowser

If you've read the previous chapter, you've met pdQmail, pdQbrowser's email-related sibling. The programs cost $40 for the pair; they're the email and web components of the Qualcomm pdQ Smartphone (a combination cell phone and PalmPilot).

pdQbrowser's primary virtues are speed and clean design—but don't buy it hoping for a long feature list. For example, the program can't display graphics, offers no History list, and lacks such basic commands as Stop and Reload. On the other hand, if you're willing to do without graphics, you'll enjoy the browser's ability to display buttons, forms, pop-up menus, scrolling lists, and so on (see Figure 14-11, left). PdQbrowser is also the only browser that uses both boldface and different font sizes to simulate the original page's layout (Figure 14-11, right).

When you first launch the program, you see your bookmark list (see Figure 14-12). (If you see the last web page you visited, tap the Bookmarks button at the bottom of the screen.) To visit a web page, tap its name in the bookmark list—or if you'd like to visit a web page not in the list, tap Menu → Options → Visit Location, and write in the URL you want (at right in Figure 14-12).

As with the other browsers reviewed here, you can adjust how much Palm memory the program devotes to storing pages you have visited (tap Menu → Options → Preferences). However, the program offers no indication of which pages have been cached; to find out, you have no choice but to try visiting the page. If your modem starts dialing, the page hasn't been cached.

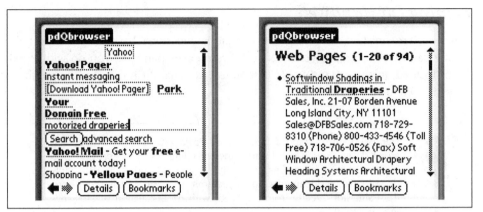

Figure 14-11. Web pages show up in pdQbrowser with all their components intact, such as buttons, links, and fields (left). You don't get graphics, but you do get a very good approximation of the original page's layout (right).

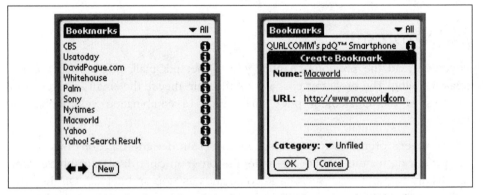

Figure 14-12. To edit a bookmark in pdQbrowser, tap the I button to the right of its name (left). As you write the URL, the program is nice enough to fill in the Name field automatically (right), automatically extracting what you write between "www" and "com".

AvantGo

Imagine a web browser that's lightning fast, shows full graphics and text styles, and doesn't even require a modem for your palmtop. That's the beauty of AvantGo, a free Windows program with a matching component for the PalmPilot. This combination offers a clever twist on bringing the Web to the PalmPilot, one that's become a hit among corporate users.

AvantGo Via the Desktop

You can use AvantGo in either of two ways. First, you can get your web pages via your PC. At HotSync time, the AvantGo desktop-PC software dials the Internet (or hooks into your company's intranet), rapidly grabs the web pages that you're interested in, and compresses them into PalmPilot-ready format. (You can specify how many pages "deep" you want to be able to follow links in the downloaded web pages.) At the next HotSync, the pages are transferred to the PalmPilot. Thereafter, on your own time, you can call up those pages and read them without pressure—and without a modem (see Figure 14-13).

Figure 14-13. With AvantGo, you can do your browsing while not connected to the Net. Links (represented by dotted underlines, left), work to summon subsequent pages (right), complete with graphics and text.

Because all of this information is formatted as HTML web pages, it can contain graphics, fonts, styles, and other nuances that make it look good—a vast improvement over the plain-text Doc format described in Chapter 10, *PalmPilot: The Electronic Book.* Yet because these documents are HotSynced onto your palmtop (and not slowly downloaded), speed isn't an issue.

You can set up the program to regularly download your favorite web pages; in fact, when you install the free program, you're offered the chance to sign up for "channels" of data that get automatically downloaded, such as sports, humor, science, travel, weather, PalmPilot news, and so on. The partner companies that provide data for this purpose will sound distinctly familiar when you read Chapter 16; they're *Weather.com*, Fodor's travel guide, Bloomberg news, the Merriam-Webster Dictionary, the Yellow Pages and White Pages, and so on. You can subscribe to even more channels at *http://www.avantgo.com.* The software, information, and service are all free.

AvantGo as a Direct Browser

The original AvantGo, through version 1.1 (see Figure 14-14), works as just described. New in 2.0, however, is the ability to go online directly with a Palm modem, using AvantGo as a normal browser. As with ProxiWeb, described earlier in the chapter, AvantGo.com's proxy computers preprocess the web pages you request, stripping out unnecessary color, Java, frames, and so on. Your PalmPilot is sent only compact text and grayscale graphics. (In fact, if you have a 16-level grayscale screen, like that on the Palm IIIx and Palm V, the thumbnail graphics show up in 16 levels of gray instead of the usual four.)

In other words, AvantGo combines some of the best features of ProxiWeb, the Palm VII, and the original AvantGo. As a result of its many advantages and stability, the AvantGo system has found applications far beyond its original conception as an offline web page browser. Corporations distribute manuals and other documents in AvantGo format, taking advantage of HTML's formatting potential (and buying the AvantGo Server software). At the Palm Developer's Conference each year, attendees stuff their PalmPilots into loading stations, where AvantGo-formatted guides to the show (including seminar schedules) are automatically uploaded.

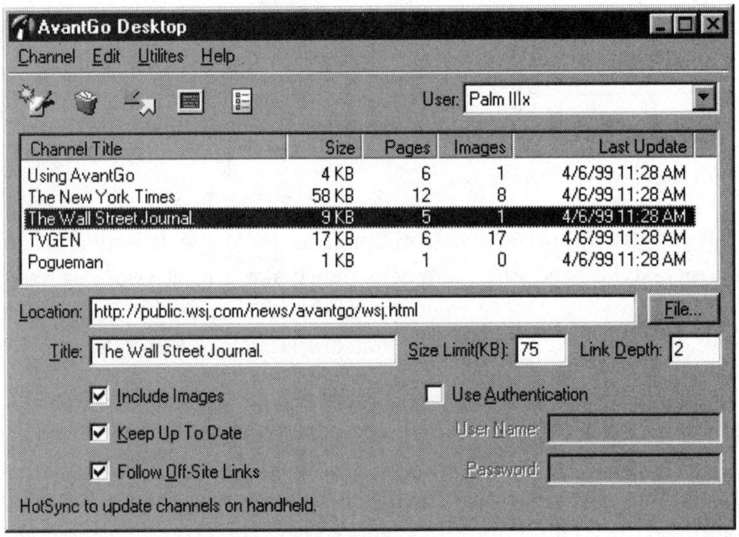

Figure 14-14. AvantGo Desktop (shown here in version 1.1) lets you specify which web sites you want transferred to your palmtop and how many links "deep."

How to Make Your Web Site Palm-Friendly

If you're designing web pages, you can take a few simple steps to make visiting your site a pleasant experience for fellow Piloteers.

First, of course, never use a clickable graphic button without a text hotlink that does the same thing. Second, if you must use Java or frames on your page, provide an alternative set of pages that work without these Palm-hostile features.

Third, wherever you do use graphics, provide an <ALT> tag in the HTML code for each image. If you know HTML, you know what this means. If you don't know HTML, and you make your web pages using a program like Claris HomePage or Adobe PageMill, use the View as HTML command. Among the nest of computer codes, you'll find a line of text like this for each graphic on your page:

```
<IMG SRC="BostonMap.gif" WIDTH=216 HEIGHT=264 ALIGN=bottom
naturalsizeflag="3">
```

Your job is to insert a plain-English label for the picture; this label will show up on PalmPilot web browsers as the *name* of the missing picture, as shown in Figure 14-8.

To create such a label, type the words *ALT="Text label here"* into the HTML code just after the name of the picture file. The result should look like this (the insert is marked in bold here for clarity):

```
<IMG SRC="BostonMap.gif" ALT="Map of downtown Boston" WIDTH=216 HEIGHT=264
ALIGN=bottom naturalsizeflag="3">
```

Finally, if you plan to offer downloadable files on your page, don't compress them or encode them; for example, don't use Base64 or a similar "Content-transfer-encoding" scheme. The only Palm browser that can download files (at this writing) are ProxiWeb and HandWeb, and they work best with files whose names end with *.prc* or *.pdb,* as described in Chapter 7.

Executive Tip Summary

- ProxiWeb is by far the most elegant and satisfying PalmPilot web browser. Check Preferences to remap the plastic PalmPilot buttons to Previous Page/ Next Page buttons for best surfing results.

- While in ProxiWeb, get into the habit of dragging your stylus up and down the screen. This method of scrolling is smoother and more controlled than whacking the plastic scroll buttons.

- PalmPilot web browsers are optimized for offline viewing; take advantage of that fact. Hastily visit the web pages you'll want to read later and *cache* them—then read them on the plane, train, or automobile.

- If nothing seems to be happening, check the nearly microscopic vertical bar in the upper-right corner of the screen. If it's blinking, your web page is still loading.

- If you don't need to surf the Web "live," use Avant Go to download web pages with your PC, to be read on your palmtop later.

15

Paging, Faxing, Printing, and Beaming

This chapter shouldn't exist at all. As originally conceived, the PalmPilot was never intended to serve as a beeper, fax machine, infrared transmitter, or printout-generating computer. You were supposed to let your *desktop* computer do all of that stuff, and use the PalmPilot to look up the occasional phone number or appointment.

But the fans wouldn't sit still. Today, you can find software or hardware that lets the PalmPilot perform all of those amazing connectivity stunts, taking it far beyond the realm of simple data bucket.

Paging

Talk about technology convergence: thanks to a collaboration of 3Com (who makes the PalmPilot), Motorola (who makes beepers), and PageMart (who sells pager subscriptions), your PalmPilot can also serve as a beeper. You've got one less gadget to clip to your belt.

The concept is simple enough: for $170, you get the Synapse Pager Card, a replacement for the *memory card* in any Pilot, PalmPilot, or early WorkPad model; just slide off the plastic cover for this card (on the back of the PalmPilot), pull out the existing memory card, and slide in your new, pager-enhanced card. As a bonus, the replacement card has two megabytes of memory, doubling or quadrupling the memory of all Pilot and PalmPilot models. You also get a replacement *door* for this memory-card slot—a door that bulges out slightly to accommodate the bulkier electronics on the card itself. Unfortunately, the pager card isn't available for the Palm III or later models, and rules out the possibility of adding infrared to your older palmtop.

After installing the software (see Chapter 7, *Installing New Palm Programs*), you're ready to receive pages.

How Paging Works

To send a page, your friends, loved ones, and business associates call a special 800 number; after a beep, they punch in your ID number. At this point, they can send one of two kinds of pages:

Numeric

> The person trying to reach you simply types in his phone number, exactly as with standard beepers everywhere. (You won't know what the call is about until you call the person back.)

Text

> The person trying to reach you dictates a message to an operator, who types it into a transmitting computer. Length limit: 300 letters and spaces, about twice the length of this paragraph.

A few seconds later, your PalmPilot turns itself on and begins to beep. (You can choose from among eleven beeping sounds—in fact, you can choose a *different* beeping sound for each priority level.)

To stop the beeping, press any of the PalmPilot's plastic buttons. Now the actual message appears on your screen (see Figure 15-1). It's up to you to return the call, take action, or whatever. You can discard or file away the page, just as though it's a note in, for example, your Memo Pad.

Figure 15-1. With the PageMart card installed, your PalmPilot can receive text pages.

At this writing, the PageMart service costs $14 per month (for pages in your area) or $20 per month for nationwide service. For that money, you get 100 text pages, or 400 numbers-only pages, per month. (If you *really* travel a lot, you can get a $100-per-month deal that covers all of North America, Canada, and parts of Central and South America.) The other expense is batteries: leaving the pager card on 24 hours a day drains the batteries much faster than the PalmPilot alone would.

No Vibrations

The downside of using your PalmPilot as a beeper, of course, is that it can't *vibrate,* as traditional beepers can; it doesn't have a buzz mode. If you're attending a symphony concert when your PalmPilot goes off, you'll either miss the page entirely (because you turned off the audible alarm feature) or annoy everyone else in the audience.

There is hope, however. If you're truly dedicated to the cause of turning the PalmPilot into a full-fledged beeper, consider the TaleVibes. It's a tiny, $40 plug that snaps onto the HotSync jack (at the bottom of the device) and vibrates whenever one of your alarms or pages goes off. (See Figure 15-2.) Point your browser to *http://members.aol.com/gmayhak/tcl/vibes.htm* for details.

Figure 15-2. Snap this thing onto your PalmPilot for vibrating alarms and pages.

More Ways to Page

The Synapse pager card isn't the only paging technology available for the Palm-Pilot—which is fortunate, because that product is restricted to original Pilot and PalmPilot models. You might also consider one of these products:

BeamLink

$50 buys you this fascinating software, which transmits pages by infrared between your palmtop (Palm III or later) and a Glenayre AccessLink I or II pager. In other words, the beeper itself is used to send and receive messages, but now you can read them, file them, address them, and compose them on the palmtop (see Figure 15-3, left). As part of your outgoing text pages, you can send Palm records, such as Memo Pad pages, addresses, to-do entries, and so on. Your Palm Address Book itself can be transmitted to the pager—up to 1500 names. You can also use your pager to send text messages as email, as described in Chapter 13, *Email Anywhere.* For an extra cost per page, you can even send pages to a system that telephones your recipient and reads what you've written out loud, in an electronic voice.

Of course, BeamLink requires that you point the pager at the palmtop, which isn't quite the same as having your PalmPilot turn on and vibrate when a message comes in—but the pager itself can do the vibrating. (JP Systems, *http://www.*

jpsystems.com, sells the software either alone or with the pager. BeamLink is an updated version of what used to be called One-Touch, which required a cable to connect the PalmPilot to the pager.)

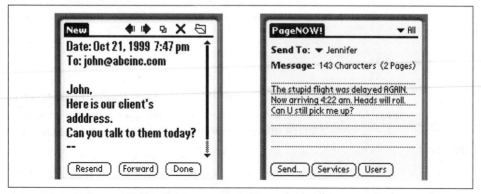

Figure 15-3. BeamLink (left) sends and receives pages via your infrared beeper. PageNow (right) is for sending only.

PageNow

This $30 software (*http://www.markspace.com*) has only one mission in life: to send pages (Figure 15-3, right). It connects to the national paging network by dialing a paging server using your Palm modem or wireless modem; it can even send your page text by infrared to an infrared-equipped cell phone, such as the Ericsson 888, which then transmits the message. PageNow automatically splits long messages into successive pages, can handle elaborate dialing strings, and lets you stamp each outgoing page with a greeting or signature.

Pilot Pager

If all this talk of infrared pagers and $170 pager cards sounds like overkill, consider this tiny, aging, free software. It's not so much a paging program as a simple dialer. With a modem attached to your PalmPilot, Pilot Pager automates sending a numeric page—it dials the necessary number (the paging service's 800 number, for example), pauses, punches an optional touch-tone (to specify voice or numeric message, for example) and extension number, and finally plugs in your own call-back number. Your index finger and brain are spared the stress of dialing all of that manually.

Faxing

If you're a PalmPilot owner, you're probably more technologically advanced than most of the people around you. Although email is the most common method of transmitting written messages these days, a few old-timers aren't yet online. Fortunately, your PalmPilot can accommodate them—by sending faxes.

To turn your PalmPilot into a faxer, it needs a modem (see Chapter 12, *Database and Number Crunching*) and software, described next. (These fax programs work with any model.) Nobody will confuse the resulting faxes with laser printouts—the fonts that PalmPilot uses are bitmapped, meaning that you can see the individual dots that make up each letter—but what do you expect from a three-by-five-inch fax machine?

HandFax

The first commercial Palm faxing software was HandFax (from the makers of HandStamp and HandWeb, described in Chapter 13 and Chapter 14, *The Web in Your Palm*). The price is $50. (A demo version is included on the CD-ROM with this book.)

HandFax works like a charm. It saves you effort—and avoids reinventing the wheel—by letting you write fax messages in the Memo Pad and grab fax numbers from your regular Address Book. Here's the step-by-step:

Setting up HandFax for the first time

After installing HandFax, launch it from your Applications screen. Begin by tapping Menu → Options (see Figure 15-4) and setting up your configuration. These commands get you ready:

Fax Setup
> This command's settings govern whether a company name or logo should appear at the top of each fax you send.

Phone Setup
> Here, you specify the usual dialing options (see Chapter 6): whether your PalmPilot should dial 9 before the number, whether to turn off call waiting, whether to bill the call to a calling card, and so on.

Modem Setup
> Use this command to specify your modem if you're not using the clip-on Palm modem. (See "Setting up the PalmPilot" in Chapter 6, *HotSync, Step by Step*, for details on these specs.)

Sender Information
> Write in your own name, fax number, voice number, and address—all optional information that will, if you wish, appear at the top of every fax you send.

Sending a fax

Now you're ready to fax. Connect your modem to the PalmPilot and the phone wire to the wall jack. As you can see from Figure 15-4, HandFax's main screen shows a list of your Memo Pad's contents (the first line of each memo appears).

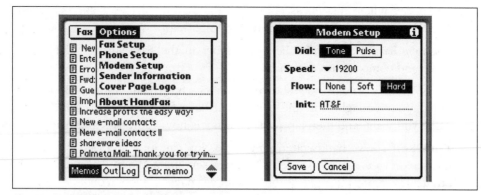

Figure 15-4. HandFax's opening screen shows a list of your Memo Pad contents, ready to send (left). Begin your setup using the various commands in the Options menu, such as Modem Setup (right).

1. Specify what the fax message is, as follows:

   To send a Memo Pad page: Tap the Memo Pad item you want to send, and then tap Fax Memo.

   To write a fax by hand: Tap Menu → Fax → New Fax.

2. Now you arrive at the screen shown in Figure 15-5. Specify whether you want a cover page automatically generated by tapping the "Use cover page" checkbox. (The cover page will include your own Sender Information, the word FAX in large letters, the recipient's information, the date and time, number of pages, and subject line.)

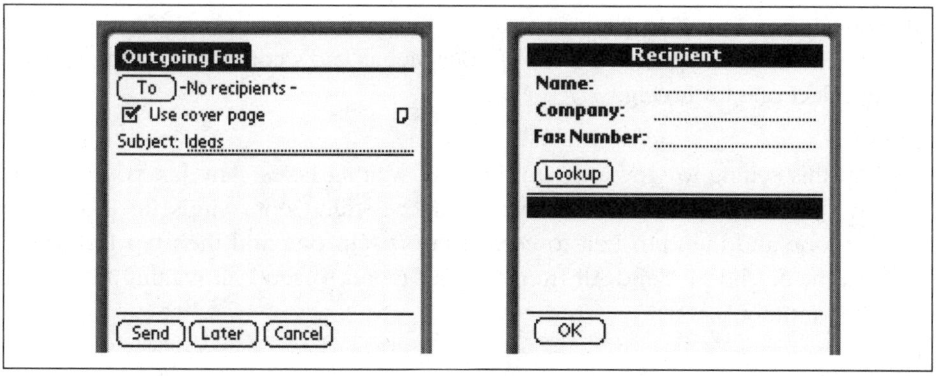

Figure 15-5. This screen is where you write your actual message if you're not planning to fax a page from your Memo Pad (left). Tap the To button to view the recipient screen (right).

3. Tap the Subject line, if you wish, and write a name for the fax. If you're *not* sending a Memo Pad page, tap in the large blank area at the bottom of the window and write out your message. (See Chapter 3, *Typing Without a Keyboard*, for Graffiti tips.)

4. To specify where this fax is going, tap the To button (see Figure 15-5, left). The address screen shown in Figure 15-5 (right) appears.

The long way: Hand write the fax number in the Fax Number blank. (The name and company are optional.)

The short way: You're now shown the names from your Address Book—but, thoughtfully enough, only the names that have fax numbers appear. Tap the name you want, and then tap Add. Your fax is now addressed and ready.

Tap OK. If you've handwritten a message, you can look at it one last time on this screen (see Figure 15-5, left). If you're sending a Memo Pad page, tap the tiny page icon to the right of the "Use cover page" option. You'll be shown a preview of the outgoing memo (which you can't edit here—only in the Memo Pad).

5. Tap Send. If you've hooked everything up correctly, a small status window appears to keep you apprised of the fax's progress. You'll hear the modem dialing, you'll watch a "Sending 1/3" page-count progress bar fill up, and you'll thrill that you've just used the world's tiniest fax machine.

(Alternatively, you could tap Later—a useful option if you're modemless or phonelineless at the moment. Your fax is saved in the Out Box, described next; you can edit it or send it later.)

The three lists

You may have noticed the three rectangular buttons at the bottom of the main HandFax screen (see Figure 15-4). They are:

Memos

This default setting shows a list of your Memo Pad's contents, making it easier to select one for faxing.

Out

Tap this setting to view an "Out box" of waiting faxes. Any fax you chose to save for later, or any fax that wasn't successfully sent, winds up in this list. Tap one and then tap Edit to correct errors; tap one and then tap Del to discard it; or choose Send All from the Fax menu to send all waiting faxes, one after another.

Log

Tap this box to view a list of faxes you've sent (or tried to send). A tiny "thumbs up" or "thumbs down" icon appears next to each fax, indicating whether or not the transmission was successful.

If a fax *wasn't* successful, tap it; tap Details; and tap Send Again.

Your graphic logo

Believe it or not, HandFax even lets you draw a graphic rendition of your logo or letterhead—if you're a pixel Picasso. Choose Cover Page Logo from the Options menu to enter a crude painting program.

Here you can draw your logo or signature, dot by dot, using the simple drawing tools on the palette: pencil, circle, rectangle, line, and eraser. While you're in the drawing mode, the four plastic buttons at the bottom of the PalmPilot don't perform their usual program-launching functions; instead, they scroll the picture horizontally. (The outer buttons scroll left and right by one dot; the inner ones scroll it by *four* dots at a time.) To scroll the picture vertically, use the PalmPilot's usual up- and down-scroll buttons.

You won't find it easy to reproduce your corporate logo using only these tools, particularly while riding any form of bouncy transportation. Still, if you manage something worth including at the top of each fax you send, choose Save from the HandPaint menu—and then choose Quit from that same menu. (That's probably the only time you'll ever use a Quit command to exit a program into another part of the *same* program.)

DB Fax (Fax)

The shareware world's programmers—Road Coders, as they're affectionately known in the PalmPilot world—have been busy, too. The conservatively named DB Fax, for which $14 is requested, lets you vary the font and formatting of your faxes—and even lets you insert graphics. It's on this book's CD-ROM. (The author, David Bertrand, sometimes refers to the program as Fax, and sometimes as DB Fax.)

 DB Fax comes in two pieces, *FAX203U.PRC* and *LIBF203U.PRC.* (The version number in the middle—2.0.3 in this example—may change.) You must install both pieces to use this program. See Chapter 7 for installation tips.

Setting up Fax

You set up Fax almost the same way as you do HandFax—by choosing commands from what here is called the Config menu (see Figure 15-6). The User Config command lets you specify your name and fax number (which will appear at the top of each fax you send) and also lets you specify a dialing prefix (such as 9).

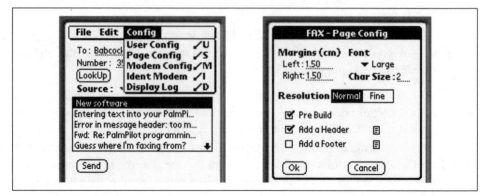

Figure 15-6. Use the Config menu (left) to set up such parameters as the page margins, font size, and header options (right).

The Page Config command is particularly interesting; it offers several options that even HandFax lacks. For example, you're offered a choice of three font styles: Standard (what you normally see on the PalmPilot), Bold (what you see at the tops of Palm windows), and Large (a vertically stretched form of the standard font). You can also determine the page margins here, and indicate whether or not you want headers or footers attached to each fax.

Sending a fax with Fax

You can't handwrite a fax message directly into Fax. However, you do have a choice of source material for your outgoing fax. Choose one of these from the pop-up menu shown in Figure 15-7:

ClipBoard
> This option lets you fax text from *any* Palm program. Suppose, for example, that you want to fax a To Do item. Highlight the text of the item; use the Edit menu's Copy command (which places the text on the PalmPilot's invisible Clipboard); switch to the Fax program; and choose Clipboard from the pop-up menu.

MemoPad
> If you choose this option from the pop-up menu, the first lines of every page in your Memo Pad appear in a scrolling list. Tap the one whose contents you want to send.

Other
> If Fax catches on, other software programmers may add faxing features to their Palm software; this option waits for that day.

After specifying what you want to fax, specify the recipient. You can, of course, write the fax number (and, optionally, the recipient's name) by hand on the blanks

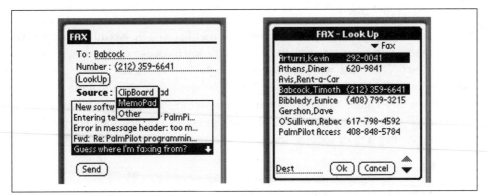

Figure 15-7. Specify what you want to fax (left), and whom you want to fax to (right).

shown in Figure 15-7. If the recipient is already in your Address Book, however, it's much faster to tap the LookUp button. As shown at right in Figure 15-7, your Address Book list appears.

At this point, you can check to see if the target individual *has* a fax number by making sure the pop-up menu (at upper right) says Fax. (This pop-up menu controls which phone number appears in this mini-list: Work, Home, or Fax.) If the list is long, begin writing your recipient's name in the blank at the bottom of the screen; the program scrolls automatically to the nearest match, exactly as the Lookup feature does elsewhere on the PalmPilot (see Chapter 4, *The Four Primary Programs*).

When you've tapped the person's name, tap OK to return to the main screen.

Now tap Send. Status messages on the screen keep you posted while the program creates the fax image, dials, and transmits the fax.

If the PalmPilot takes too long to send faxes from Fax, the receiving fax machine will "time out," meaning that it will wait so long for your PalmPilot to begin sending that it hangs up out of impatience.

The solution lies in the Page Config dialog box: turn on the Pre-Build option. Now Fax will compute the fax image *before* dialing. As a result, your phone call will be shorter (which could save you money), you lessen the likelihood of timeouts, and you render Fax compatible with more kinds of modems and fax machines.

The downside of the Pre-Build option is that your palmtop's available memory limits the length of the outgoing fax. (When Pre-Build is *off*, Fax continuously creates the fax image, page by page, as it sends, so that there's no limit to the fax's size.)

Formatting your faxes

You might not think that a piece of software that fits in 57K would permit formatting of the text in your fax, but Fax does. The interface isn't what you'd call elegant—in fact, you must write geeky codes right into the text of your fax—but it can be done. Table 15-1 and Table 15-2 show what you should write to trigger each effect, and Figure 15-8 shows what your Memo Pad might look like with the codes in place. (Note that you can plant these codes not just into your message, but into your headers or footers, too.)

Table 15-1. Codes to Insert Text or Pictures

Code to Insert Text	Action
&SNAME	Inserts your name.
&ID	Inserts your Fax ID.
&SPHONE	Inserts your phone or fax number.
&DNAME	Inserts the recipient's name.
&DOODLE.0 through &DOODLE.9	Inserts a drawing that corresponds to the Doodle drawing program's page. Numbers are offset by one—&DOODLE.0 inserts Doodle page 1.

Table 15-2. Codes to Format Text

Code to Format Text	Action
&<	Aligns the line with the left margin.
&-	Centers the line.
&>	Aligns the line with the right margin.
&s	Uses the standard font.
&b	Uses the bold font.
&l	Uses the enlarged, taller font.
&1 through &5	Specifies the font size. &1 is smallest; &5 is enormous, with letters nearly an inch tall.

In these codes, capitalization matters. Note that each code begins with an ampersand (&); to make this symbol using Graffiti, tap once and then draw a figure 8.

Each of these codes will be replaced, in the actual fax, with information you enter in the User Settings command (in the Config menu). For example, if you write, "This fax is for &DNAME only," the resulting fax will say, "This fax is for Frank Simcox only" (or whatever the name is).

If you have the graphics program called Doodle installed in your PalmPilot (see Chapter 11, *The Secret Multimedia World*), you can go HandFax one better: you can actually insert drawings into your faxes. At the point where you want one of your Doodle drawings to appear, insert the appropriate code.

Figure 15-8. Here's what a correctly coded Memo Pad page looks like before faxing.

Each of these codes changes the format of the line of text on which it appears. (In other words, you can vary the type size and alignment only once per line; you can't make just one word of a paragraph boldface.) If you put several conflicting tags in a row (such as the code for the smallest font followed by the code for the largest font), the last one on the line counts.

For still more codes, including those necessary for inserting graphics into your faxes, see the Fax manual (included on the CD-ROM that comes with this book).

Don't forget that a subscription to PilotMail, described in Chapter 13, automatically gives you fax capabilities. When specifying the "email address" for a message you've written, write the fax number followed by the phrase *@fax*. Your message will be sent as a fax—the PilotMail server keeps trying until it gets through—and a confirmation message is e-mailed back to your palmtop.

Mobile WinFax

As this book went to press, Symantec Corporation announced that it had begun beta-testing its Mobile WinFax, a Palm faxing program that can send and receive faxes on your palmtop.

The program's cleverest feature is its integration with your Windows PC. In conjunction with its desktop component, Mobile WinFax lets you pull off these stunts:

- Your PC can generate fax images of graphics, cover pages, or documents of any kind—and then store them on your palmtop. (You might prepare, for example, résumés, prices lists, or maps to your office in this way.) Once on the road, you can incorporate these elements into faxes you create on the PalmPilot. If you have a modem attached to your palmtop, you can then send faxes directly from it.

As you might expect, the drawback is memory: each desktop-document page or cover page takes up 70K of RAM on the PalmPilot. (The PalmPilot can send or receive a maximum of 16 pages per fax.)

- Instead of storing images, cover pages, and document pages on your palm-top, you can choose instead to store only a *list* of them on the PalmPilot. As you write faxes while on the road, you can indicate that you'd like these documents incorporated into the fax.

  Then, following a local HotSync (or, if your PC has two modems, even a long-distance modem HotSync), your PC does the actual faxing, sending the indicated documents along for the ride.

- You can incorporate Memo Pad pages into faxes you send directly from the PalmPilot. You can even sign faxes you create on the palmtop, or otherwise mark them up.

- After your PC software has received faxes, they can be sent to your PalmPilot, so that you can study them on the road.

- Your PalmPilot can actually receive faxes. (You must manually tell it when to answer the phone—you can't let it sit on your bureau all night long, collecting one fax after another.) Only a couple square inches of the received document fits on the Palm screen; fortunately, you can scroll around, zoom in or out, and even rotate the image.

- Because Mobile WinFax can both send and receive faxes, you can forward a fax you've received to somebody else (after marking it up, if you desire).

You can find details at *http://www.symantec.com/mobile/winfax.*

Printing

Most people assume that the PalmPilot can't print directly to a printer. But two shareware programs let you hook up certain kinds of printers directly to the PalmPilot. Both are included on the CD-ROM that comes with this book.

PalmPilot printing isn't nearly as seamless as faxing or beaming, however. The PalmPilot's only port is its HotSync jack (at the bottom of the unit), and its only cable is the HotSync cradle (or HotSync cable). This cradle acts as a *serial port;* unfortunately, most printers today have *parallel ports* instead.

If you want to make your PalmPilot access your printer, then, these are your options:

- Use Your PalmPilot's infrared feature. If your printer also has an infrared transceiver, such as those from HP, Canon, or Citizen, this is an ideal setup—just point the palmtop at the printer to create your printout. PalmPrint, described in the next section, does an excellent job of this kind of wireless printing.

- Hope that your printer also has a serial port. Many do, even though they're largely unused.

- Even if your printer has a serial port, it's likely to have the wrong number of pins. The usual printer serial port is a *female DB-25* connector, which has two rows of pins (13 and 12 in each row). The end of the HotSync cradle cable is, alas, a *DB-9,* with 5 and 4 rows of pins, respectively. It's your job to buy the appropriate adapter (from an electronics or computer store)—a *DB-9 male to DB-25 male* adapter—that lets you connect the HotSync cable to the printer jack.

- If your printer has only a parallel port, no simple adapter will help. You need a more expensive contraption: a serial-to-parallel converter. If you're still interested, visit *http://www.stevenscreek.com/pilot/palmprint.shtml* for a list of such converters.

Finally, once you've straightened out your cabling problems, there's one more caveat: printing from the PalmPilot involves mucking around in some user-hostile variables, and a great deal of trial-and-error may be involved.

As laptop owners have long known, there's no particular reason to think of printers when you need hardcopy of something you've written. Instead, consider the fax machine that awaits in virtually every hotel and office in the world.

Suppose you've written notes for an upcoming meeting in your Memo Pad. Instead of fretting about how you're going to print from the PalmPilot, consider faxing that page—using the fax software described earlier in this chapter—to the hotel's front desk, for example.

You'll probably find doing so far faster and easier than hunting down the appropriate printer cables, praying that you locate a serial printer onsite, and fiddling with the settings until you make the printout happen.

PalmPrint

PalmPrint ($40 from *http://www.stevenscreek.com*) is the unchallenged leader in Palm printing software. More and more third-party Palm programs are equipped with a Print command, which requires PalmPrint to work. Several of the email programs described in Chapter 13 rely on PalmPrint in this way, and PalmPrint itself comes with special, print-enabled versions of the PalmPilot's built-in Mail program (see Chapter 13) and Address Book (see Chapter 4).

After installing PalmPrint and launching it (and writing in your serial number, if you've paid for the shareware), you arrive at a screen like the one shown in Figure 15-9. Now comes the critical part: You must adjust the pop-up menus to correctly match a printer language your printer can accept. This isn't always as straightforward as it seems; the HP setting, for example, may be the correct option for an Epson or Apple printer. Only experimentation, your printer's manual, or your local guru will help you find the correct match.

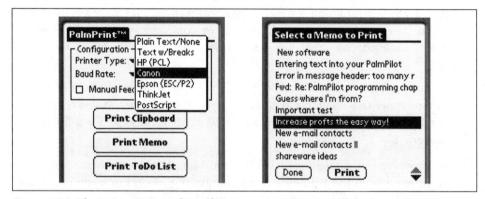

Figure 15-9. The Printer Type and Baud Rate pop-up menus are all-important in getting printouts from your PalmPilot (left). If you choose to print a Memo Pad page, a list of your Memo Pad contents appears; tap the memo you want (right).

The baud rate pop-up menu is similarly fussy; make sure it matches your printer's baud rate, as indicated by its manual or control panel. Use this same pop-up menu to specify Infrared printing, if that's what you plan to do.

To make a test print, tap Print Clipboard (to print whatever you've most recently copied from a Palm program); Print Memo (to print a page from your Memo Pad—see Figure 15-9); or Print To Do List (to print your entire list of to-dos, including category, notes, priority levels, and due dates (if any).

 Infrared printing is one of the most attractive PalmPrint features, but it can be tricky. Your PalmPilot's batteries should be relatively full—even if they're strong enough to power the palmtop, they may not be strong enough to transmit your printout. The distance is critical, too—between 4 and 20 inches is usually best.

IrPrint

This $25 promising newcomer (*http://www.iscomplete.org*) communicates exclusively with infrared-equipped printers. In its first release, it prints only from the five built-in Palm programs (Memo Pad, Address Book, Mail, and so on); the program's open architecture holds the potential for other software companies to print-enable their future products, too.

The program offers three ways to print:

* Tap Menu → Record → Print in the specially modified Memo Pad, Address Book, Date Book, or To Do programs that come with IrPrint (see Figure 15-10, at left).

* On IrPrint's main screen (Figure 15-10, right), tap the name of the built-in Palm application from which you want to print. A list appears, showing the names of the individual memos, to-do items, and so on; tap the one you want to print.

* Use the included add-on software AltCtrlHack to make a printout of the current screen image, no matter what software you're using.

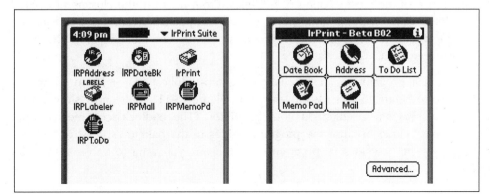

Figure 15-10. IrPrint lets you print from specially modified Palm programs (left), or specific records from your existing Palm programs (right).

Beaming

The 1998 PalmPilot model, the Palm III, introduced an ingenious and useful new feature: an infrared transmitter/receiver. Now you can point your palmtop (Palm III or later) at somebody else's—and *beam* programs or data through the air, from one palmtop into the other. (Previous models equipped with the Palm III upgrade—officially called the "Palm Computing 2MB Upgrade Card," as described in Chapter 18, *The Palm Family, Model by Model*—are invited to the party, too.)

Right out of the box, the infrared feature means that you can share programs with friends, exchange complete electronic business cards in seconds, send the minutes of the last meeting to everyone present, share your outline for the next presentation, or conveniently back up your painstakingly input data to another PalmPilot. As the Palm III and its descendants become the majority players, beaming will become a standard feature in every piece of Palm software.

What You Can Beam

You can't beam just *anything* from one PalmPilot to another. For example, you can't beam any of the programs that are built into the ROMs, such as the Address Book or Memo Pad. (Then again, why would you want to?) Nor can you beam data from your Expense or Mail programs.

But you can beam any programs *you've* installed, as well as data from the other standard Palm programs, as follows. (See "The Beaming Process, Step by Step," later in this chapter, for specific instructions.)

Programs

Here's one of the most exciting possibilities. From now on, the clusters of excited PalmPilot users on trains, in airports, and at computer conventions won't just be *talking* about the latest shareware programs they've downloaded; now they'll be *distributing* them.

To beam a program to another PalmPilot, tap Applications → Menu → App → Beam (see Figure 15-11). Also as shown in Figure 15-11, you're now shown a list of every program installed on your PalmPilot. (The padlock icon means "non-beamable," either because the program resides in the palmtop's ROM or because it's a protected commercial program.) Tap the one you want to transmit; then tap Beam.

Memo Pad pages

You can beam either a single Memo Pad "page" or *all* memos in a particular category. To beam one page, bring it up on your screen. Tap Menu → Record → Beam Memo. (See Figure 15-12, right.)

To beam an entire category, tap Done, so that you're viewing your "home page," table-of-contents view. From the Category menu at the upper-right corner of the screen, choose the category whose memos you want to transmit. Tap Menu → Record → Beam Category.

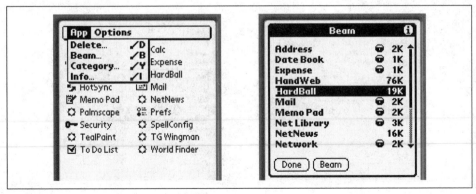

Figure 15-11. Choose Beam from the App menu (left) to view a list of beamable—and nonbeamable—programs (right).

The Importance of Being BeamBox

You'll fall in love with the ability to beam programs to your friends. And then one day, there you'll be on the Alaskan tundra, sealing the important real estate deal with a native Kwakiutl Indian by offering to beam him your favorite Hack-Master module—and it won't work. The program you intend to beam simply won't show up in your list of beamable applications. You'll stand there tapping until you're frozen solid, but the deal will never go through.

If you had read this sidebar, you'd have known that not every Palm application is beamable. HackMaster modules (described in Appendix A, *100 Programs Worth Knowing About*) support databases, and other specialized files don't show up in the normal list of applications to beam. In such cases, launch BeamBox, which *does* show HackMaster files and similar items in a list of items that you can then beam to another PalmPilot.

But BeamBox must be on both PalmPilots for the transfer to work. So how do you get BeamBox onto your friend's PalmPilot? Simple—*beam* BeamBox to the other PalmPilot, using the normal Beam command on your Applications screen. In other words, BeamBox doesn't require BeamBox to beam itself.

 When you beam a category, all beamed records arrive in the recipient's Unfiled category. To file them en masse, suggest to your recipient the shareware programs Mass Transit (*http://www.io.com/~mmoss*) or SuperCat (*http://www.iscomplete.com*).

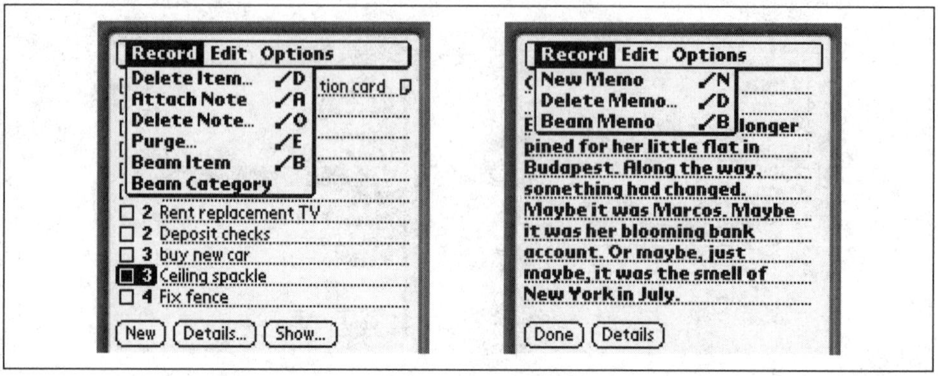

Figure 15-12. In the To Do program, you can beam either one to do task or all to dos in a particular category (left). The Memo Pad can beam either a single page (right) or, in its home-page view, an entire category's worth.

To Do items

As with the Memo Pad, you can beam either *one* to-do or an entire *category* of them. To send just one, tap it, and then choose Beam Item from the Record menu (Figure 15-12, left). To send a whole category-full, switch to that category (from the Category pop-up menu in the upper-right corner of the screen) and then choose Beam from the Record menu.

Date Book appointments

Tap an appointment in the Day View of your Date Book program (see Chapter 4 for details). Use the Beam Event menu in the Record menu to transmit this appointment—a handy way to ensure that all parties due at a meeting have the identical information. (There's no way to beam more than one appointment at a time.)

Address Book entries

You can beam an *entire* Address Book entry into another PalmPilot, compete with all phone numbers, email addresses, mailing addresses, and everything else. Oh, the joy! Can you imagine a world where *everyone* carried a PalmPilot? Trade shows would be pure happiness—no more business cards to collect, sort, and painstakingly type into your PC. Can you imagine business meetings? In ten seconds, everyone in the room would have everyone else's contact information safely (and accurately) stored. Even dating would be vastly improved; a blind date would be considered a success only if one party asked for an Address Book beam from the other's PalmPilot.

Because this feature is such a huge time- and headache-saver, you get a choice of three ways to beam address information:

One address

> Launch your Address Book. Tap the address you want to beam; from the Record menu, choose Beam Address. (See Figure 15-13, right.)

One address category

> To send all addresses in a particular category, you must begin at the home page, table of contents Address Book list (Figure 15-13). Choose the correct category from the upper-right pop-up menu, and then tap Beam Category in the Record menu.

Your business card

> The ability to beam *your* business card quickly and conveniently is among the most successful new features of the Palm III and later models.
>
> Before you can make it work, however, you must teach the PalmPilot which Address Book entry *is* your business card. That entails creating a record for yourself, filling it in accurately, and then choosing Select Business Card from the Record menu (see Figure 15-13, right).
>
> After you've designated that address to be your business card, you'll see a tiny icon above your name (see Figure 15-14, right).
>
> Beaming your business card is simple, thanks to a striking new interface feature: *hold down* the Address Book plastic button for two seconds. (Sure, you *could* choose Beam Business Card from the Record menu instead, but who's got the time?)

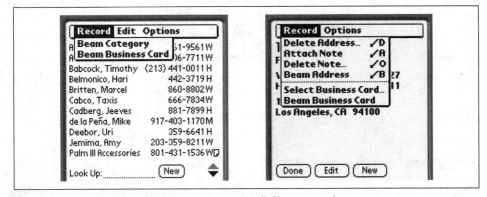

Figure 15-13. From the Address Book master list (left), you can beam an entire category's worth of addresses. You can also beam just one person's information by opening it (right) and using the Beam Address command.

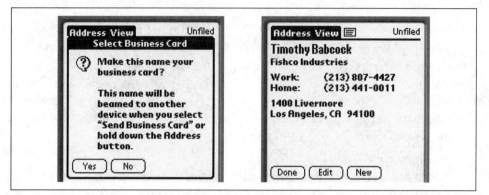

Figure 15-14. Open the Address Book entry that contains your information. From the Record menu, choose Select Business Card (see Figure 15-13, right). The message shown here at left appears; tap Yes. From now on, a special icon appears on your own Address Book entry (right), to the right of the "Address View" label. You've just set up your electronic business card.

If you do a lot of beaming, the Preferences screen offers a handy shortcut.

In Chapter 2, *Setup and Guided Tour*, you may have read about the Ronomatic stroke, the PalmPilot's giant vertical penstroke shortcut, in which you drag your stylus straight up the *entire* glass surface of the palmtop. This gesture can trigger your choice of action: Turning on the backlight, displaying a Graffiti cheat sheet, and so on. On the Palm III and later models, this gesture can also mean: "Beam the currently selected memo, address, appointment, or to-do—without making me tap menus."

To set this up, tap Applications → Preferences → Buttons → Pen → Beam Data.

For safety's sake, this penstroke never beams an entire *category* of data; for that feature, you must still use menu commands.

The Beaming Process, Step by Step

The procedure for beaming is almost always the same. (In the following steps, Frank is the person you're beaming to.)

1. You and Frank place the top ends of your PalmPilots between 2 and 20 inches from each other, head-to-head, level with each other. (If the PalmPilots are too close, you'll get a "Beam interrupted" message. That's good to remember when troubleshooting—more infrared beams fail because the PalmPilots are too close than too far.) If you inspect the top edge of your palmtop, you'll see

the tiny, dark-red plastic cover of the infrared transmitter. That's where the signals enter and exit. (On an upgraded Pilot, WorkPad, or PalmPilot model, the transmitter is on the underside of the Pilot instead—it's the little bulge on your memory-slot door.)

2. Choose the Beam command from the appropriate program. (See "What You Can Beam," earlier in this chapter.)

3. Your screen says "Searching," and then "Sending"; Frank's says "Preparing," then "Waiting for Sender," and finally "Receiving" (plus the name of whatever you're sending). When this actual transmission begins, Frank's PalmPilot makes a beep; when the transmission is finished, it beeps an octave lower.

   Frank's palmtop is smart enough to identify what *kind* of data it's just received. It knows which Palm program this new data belongs in. The Palm-Pilot asks him: "Do you want to accept 'New Data' (or whatever you've just beamed) into (whatever program it belongs in)?" (For example, if you've just beamed your business card, Frank is asked if he wants your name entered into the Address Book program.)

   Frank can tap Yes or (if he's paranoid) No.

From now on, the beamed data is safely duplicated on the second PalmPilot, indistinguishable from data that was handwritten—or HotSynced—into it.

Being able to get unsolicited beams from others is an extremely cool feature, but some people may consider it a bit creepy. After all, who knows what kind of grisly data is being rammed down your palmtop's throat? Sure, you're always asked to *confirm* that you want the data—but only *after* it's been beamed to you.

If paranoia is taking the fun out of the PalmPilot for you, tap Applications → Prefs, and (from the upper-right pop-up menu) choose General. At the bottom of the screen, you'll see the choice for Beam Receive—On or Off. Switch it off; you've just disabled your ability to receive beams at all.

Other Uses for the Infrared Port

Beaming Palm data between palmtops is only one way to use the IR transceiver on Palm III and later models. Enterprising Piloteers have come up with an astounding assortment of other uses for this jack, listed in the following sections.

Communicating with your desktop PC

As described in Chapter 6, you can HotSync an infrared-equipped laptop or desktop PC with your PalmPilot by IR—no cable or cradle needed. IR Sync (*http://www.iscomplete.com*) software offers this feature; IBM WorkPads come with a similar program; and IR syncing software is included free with the MacPac (see Chapter 9, *Palm Desktop: Macintosh*).

If infrared HotSyncing to your infrared-equipped PC is your goal, Palm Computing offers a free solution: the Enhanced Infrared Update. (It's available from *http://www.palm.com/custsupp/downloads/irenhanc.html.*)

Technically, this patch lets your palmtop speak the IrCOMM protocol, a special dialect of the IrDA language. Not only does it make IR HotSyncing possible, but it's also a necessary patch to let your palmtop communicate with Ericcson cell phones (the software described later is also required).

Communicating with your cell phone

With the right software, you can harness the power of your Address Book to dial your infrared-equipped cell phone, such as the Ericsson SH888, 600/700 series, or the Nokia 8810. Some of the programs in this category include HandPhone (*http://www.smartcode.com*), IrLink (*http://www.iscomplete.org*), and the shareware D127 Infrared Dialer (*http://home.t-online.de/hom/Martin/Renschler*).

Communicating with your pager

BeamLink, described earlier this chapter, lets you send and receive text messages—even email—from your two-way, infrared-equipped pager.

Communicating with your printer

Earlier in this chapter, you'll find descriptions of programs that let you print simply by pointing your PalmPilot at any infrared-equipped printer, such as those from HP, Canon, Citizen, and Seiko.

Communicating with your boss

Imagine having an interactive whiteboard in your hand. You could sketch or type messages, product designs, or maps to the airport—any of which show up an instant later on a neighboring PalmPilot, thanks to an infrared transmission. That's exactly the idea behind IRP2PChat (*http://www.iscomplete.org*), shown in Figure 15-15.

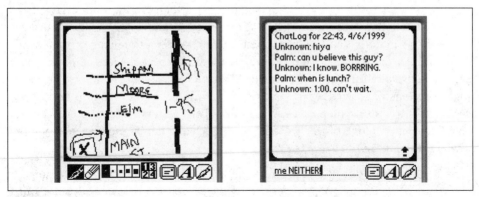

Figure 15-15. Using IRP2PChat (short for "infrared PalmPilot-to-PalmPilot chat"), you can collaborate on drawings (left) or carry on silent conversations (right) via infrared with another PalmPilot.

Communicating with your TV

The thought of turning the PalmPilot into a TV remote control must have occurred to almost every owner at one time or another. But Pacific Neo-Tek (*http://www. pacificneotek.com*) has actually done it. OmniRemote ($20) lets you draw buttons onto the screen of the size and location you prefer (see Figure 15-16). You train each button by pointing your existing TV remote control at the PalmPilot. When you're finished, you can actually control your home entertainment system by tapping virtual buttons on your Palm screen. You can also remap the six plastic hardware buttons at the bottom of the palmtop—you could define the scroll buttons to adjust the volume up or down, the outer application buttons to adjust the channels, and so on.

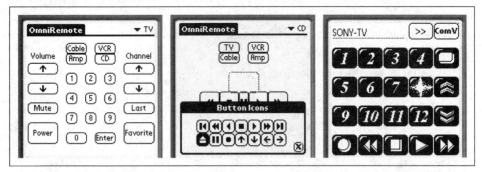

Figure 15-16. OmniRemote (left) lets you control your entertainment system using your PalmPilot; you can design your remote control as you see fit (middle). The similar PalmRemote (right) is better looking, but hampered by its not-quite-English documentation.

Using the standard Category pop-up menu, you switch among button layouts for up to 15 different appliances—VCR, DVD player, TV, and so on. You can also create macros—buttons that, when tapped, trigger longer sequences of commands. For example, one button could power up three different devices, flip the sound system into Dolby mode, and start the DVD player playing. A timer feature can trigger buttons or macros at appointed times, turning on the palmtop and issuing commands to your entertainment system. (This assumes that you've left the PalmPilot within range of the TV, and no dog, cat, or family member has bumped it while walking by.)

OmniRemote users quickly discover the limits of infrared technology. The range of your PalmPilot's infrared signal can very wildly, from two feet to 25—but it's usually on the short side. The strength of signal, from weakest to strongest, comes from these sources:

Any PalmPilot with weak batteries
> As noted earlier in this chapter, your infrared circuitry is the first to die when battery juice is low. Just because there's enough power to keep your palmtop humming doesn't mean there's enough to power the IR feature.

Palm III and family
> This original incarnation of the infrared transceiver is the weakest of all. You may need to sit close to your entertainment system—or buy the OmniRemote Module, described below.

Palm V, Palm VII
> The infrared technology on these models is stronger than the III family.

An upgraded Pilot or PalmPilot model
> If you bought the upgrade card for these older models (described in Chapter 18), you have the most powerful built-in infrared of all. For some reason, the upgrade card's signal is far stronger than the built-in signal of more recent models.

Any PalmPilot with the OmniRemote Module
> The OmniRemote Module is a tiny ($20) gadget that clips onto the HotSync jack of any PalmPilot model except the Palm V. This transmitter is four times stronger than the built-in Palm III transmitter, ensuring problem-free channel surfing for the devoted couch potato. Because the module requires that you point the bottom of the PalmPilot at your TV, a handy Flip command in OmniRemote turns the entire button display upside-down on the screen, so that the controls remain right-side up in your hand.

OmniRemote is the most famous Palm remote-control program, but it isn't the only one. PalmRemote ($20) is not only better-looking (see Figure 15-16), but offers predefined remote settings for popular brands of equipment, saving you the trouble of training individual buttons. PalmRemote's primary obstacle to attaining remote-control celebrity is the roughness of its translation from Japanese (both the manual and text in the software itself)—and the fact that it's not trainable. (The web site is *http://hp.vector.co.jp/authors/VA005810/ remocon/premocce.htm*.)

The Great PalmPilot Car-Unlocking Myth

When USA Today first published the article in 1998, a buzz went through the PalmPilot community: could it really be true that thieves were using the palm-top's infrared transceiver, in conjunction with a trainable IR program like OmniRemote, to unlock and steal parked cars?

As delicious as the rumor sounded, it turned out not to be true. Most American cars' keyless transmitters use radio signals, not infrared. The few models that use infrared transmitters rely on *code jumping*, in which the infrared signal needed to unlock the door changes every time you do it.

Then there's the small problem of training the PalmPilot—you would have to have the car's original keyless transmitter to train your PalmPilot to begin with. And if you had the original key, why would you bother with the PalmPilot?

In short, the rumor proved to be just a rumor—not a single case of a PalmPilot unlocking a car has ever been reported.

Beaming Ear to Ear

Despite all this talk of cell phones, pagers, and remote controls, one of the most satisfying uses of the PalmPilot's beaming feature is IR games. There's no more natural, entertaining way to kill time on a plane, train, or automobile ride than playing Battleship with the passenger in the seat in front of you. You watch only your screen, she watches only her screen; and yet, as each move you make is transmitted by infrared into the opponent's palmtop, you both feel the rush of par-ticipating in something communal.

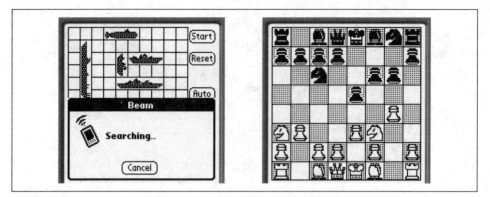

Figure 15-17. Games like Battleship (left) and Chess (right) make some of the best use of the PalmPilot's IR features.

At *http://www.iscomplete.org*, and on this book's CD, you'll find a complete line of interactive, two-person, infrared games, such as IRChess, IRBattleship, IRHangman, IRGin (card game), IRCheckers, IROthello, IRConnect, and others (see Figure 15-17). As PalmPilots appear in ever more corporate pockets, more and more people in meetings will be forced to wonder: are those two guys across the table diligently taking notes—or blowing up each others' submarines?

Executive Tip Summary

- Don't let conventional wisdom get you down. The PalmPilot can indeed receive pages, send faxes, make printouts, and transmit information wirelessly.

- Your paging options are a PageMart card (which replaces the memory card door on a Pilot, PalmPilot, or original WorkPad model), which can receive pages; or a OneTouch cable/software kit that lets your PalmPilot plug into your existing beeper. Need your PalmPilot to vibrate instead of beep? Get a TaleVibes doodad that plugs into your PalmPilot's HotSync jack.

- You *can* print from the PalmPilot. You may have better luck, however, by getting into the habit of *faxing* yourself whenever you need a hardcopy—fax software for the PalmPilot is sure-fire and cable-free (although it requires a modem).

- If you do much beaming, consider changing the Prefs/Buttons application so that a penstroke up the face of the PalmPilot begins a beam (instead of, for example, summoning the Graffiti cheat sheet).

The Secret Infrared "Dot Commands"

You can read about the PalmPilot's secret dot commands in Chapter 17, *Troubleshooting*; in short, they're undocumented commands that perform sometimes useful, sometimes pointless functions.

When it comes to beaming, three dot commands may all be useful under certain circumstances. To invoke one, start by drawing the ShortCut symbol. (See Chapter 3 for details on using ShortCuts; the symbol looks like a loop, a lowercase cursive L, as shown on the table inside this book's covers.)

Follow the ShortCut loop with a period (a double tap) in the Graffiti writing area, and then write one of these letters:

I   This magic stroke permits your PalmPilot to receive one beam, one time—even if you've turned off the Beam Receive feature. Suppose, for example, that you've heard that leaving your Beam Receive checkbox turned on drains your battery slightly faster than when Beam Receive is turned off. (That's true, by the way.) Terrified, you've tapped Applications → Prefs, chosen General from the upper-right pop-up menu, and turned off Beam Receive. But now somebody wants to beam you! Smiling confidently, you write this dot command. Your PalmPilot instantly displays the "Waiting for Sender" message, opening a very temporary (five-second) window of beaming opportunity. If no beam arrives from another PalmPilot, the message disappears from your screen, and you're once again incapable of receiving beams.

S   When you write the S, the period and shortcut symbol you've just drawn disappear. From now on, any beams you generate aren't sent through the infrared lens. Instead, they're sent to a serial cable (such as the Palm HotSync cable, described in Appendix B) that you've used to connect your HotSync jack with another computer. A programmer might use this feature, for example, to capture IR-sent data to a Mac or PC that's running a communications program. (To return to normal infrared beaming, make this shortcut a second time. And don't forget to do so; otherwise, next time you HotSync, your palmtop will insist that its HotSync port is "in use by another application." A soft reset, described in Chapter 17, will also cure this condition.)

T   This dot command turns on Beam-to-Yourself mode. (When you make the T, your shortcut symbol and period disappear; that's the only confirmation you get.) Now you can play infrared games against yourself, send addresses and memos to yourself, and otherwise experiment with beaming single-handedly. You get to see all the usual symptoms of beaming—both sending and receiving—but you don't need a playmate. Among other things, this mode is useful for taking screenshots of infrared-savvy software in action (for the purposes of, say, writing a PalmPilot book chapter about beaming).

16

Palm VII: Wireless Email, Wireless Web

Mankind's quest to connect to the Internet without wires would be comical if it weren't such a tragic expenditure of effort and money. People buy $5,000 laptops equipped with $400 wireless modems attached by $129 cable adapters that dial into $50 per month wireless services—just so they can check their email without a wire to the wall. Even everyday PalmPilots can be connected to wireless modems, such as the Novatel Minstel described in Appendix B, *PalmPilot Accessories*; but even that arrangement entails enough additional bulk and complexity to threaten the PalmPilot's famous pocketability.

That's why the Palm VII is such a revelation. For the first time, everything is self-contained—the computer and the wireless modem—in a gadget that's only a half-inch taller than the traditional PalmPilot. Everything about this machine has been given the trademark Palm streamlining: signing up for the service takes less than a minute, activation of your account is instantaneous, and the email and Web experiences are smaller, simpler, "lite" versions of the real thing.

Palm VII: The Hardware

In most respects, the Palm VII (see Figure 1-8) is identical to the PalmPilot models discussed in the other 17 chapters of this book. It runs the same programs, HotSyncs the same way, uses the same Graffiti alphabet, and runs on the same AAA batteries.

But the Palm VII's wireless circuitry makes this palmtop dramatically more complex than its predecessors, featuring hundreds more components. (That's why you can't upgrade a Palm III or other previous model to a Palm VII—inside the case, it's a whole new jungle.) Some of these new components are worth getting to know.

The Palm VII represents the first time Palm Computing has capitalized on its own grayscale technology (as you know from Chapter 10, *PalmPilot: The Electronic Book*, all PalmPilots have grayscale screens, even though the vast majority of Palm software is black-and-white).

As you'll notice in this chapter's illustrations, the web clipping feature of the Palm VII features attractive grayscale graphics. They enhance the illusion that you're actually visiting real web pages.

The NiCad Battery

The Palm VII is a half-inch taller than its closest sibling, the Palm IIIx. The extra height is required by the NiCad rechargeable battery that's nestled inside, just above the screen. (If you look at the Palm VII from its left side, you can see the rounded contour of this battery.)

This battery doesn't power any standard PalmPilot functions. It's dedicated to a single component—the internal two-way radio that communicates with the nearest cellphone base station. The standard AAA batteries still power the rest of the PalmPilot; by serving as the exclusive energy source for the transmitter, the NiCad permits the AAAs to last for two or three weeks (but not as long as in other Palm models).

When you remove your AAAs to change them, most PalmPilots preserve the contents of memory for only a couple of minutes, as described in Chapter 17, *Troubleshooting*.

But the Palm VII's built-in NiCad battery acts as a backup when the AAAs are low or dead. When you've removed your AAAs to change batteries, the NiCad (if it's charged) can keep your data safe for hours or even days—a totally undocumented bonus.

Charging the NiCad

The NiCad battery gets its charge from AAA batteries. Generally, this trickle of charge is so small that you won't notice much of an impact on the AAAs' longevity—except the day you take a brand-new Palm VII out of its package. At that point, the NiCad battery is dead; the first pair of AAAs takes an hour or so to charge up the NiCad. (You can't go online with your Palm VII until the NiCad is charged.) That's why your first pair of AAA batteries gets used up so quickly on a new Palm VII.

Thereafter, the Palm VII trickle-charges the NiCad battery with power from your AAA batteries whenever necessary. This recharging is automatic and often takes place when the device isn't even turned on. (You can't go online during the recharging, but all other PalmPilot features work. A message will tell you so.)

Want to see how your NiCad charge is holding up—and when the Palm VII next intends to recharge it from your AAA batteries?

Tap Applications → Diagnostics (on the Palm.Net category page of applications). Tap Details. You'll see not only the current charge level of your AAA batteries (full is 3.0) and NiCad battery (listed as "Transmitter Charge"—5.0 or higher is full), but also the ID number of the closest BellSouth base station, the current signal strength, and when your Palm VII anticipates needing to charge the NiCad again.

The Antenna

Use the PalmPilot long enough, and you begin to marvel at how much effort has been put into reducing the number of steps required to perform any task. So it's no surprise that the antenna on the Palm VII is itself an On button—a feature that earned a patent for Palm computing. Lift the antenna, and your Palm VII instantly turns on and switches to the Applications screen containing the built-in wireless programs (the contents of the Palm.Net category).

The Palm VII antenna comes set to open your Applications screen when lifted. If you don't go online much, though, you may prefer to have the antenna-lifting action trigger something else—opening the Expense program, say, or launching your favorite Palm game.

To do so, tap the Applications button repeatedly until you arrive at the System or All category. Tap Prefs; from the upper-right pop-up menu, choose Buttons. Use the pop-up menu next to the tiny picture of a Palm VII to choose a different program. From now on, the new program will be launched when you raise the antenna.

Positioning the antenna

As you lift the antenna, you'll feel it click into three preset positions—at 90, 135, and 180 degrees to the PalmPilot. For best reception, the antenna should be perfectly vertical; that's why Palm recommends the 90 degree angle when the palmtop is on a table, or the 135-degree angle when you're holding the Palm VII in your hand. (Close the antenna when you're not planning to go online, so that you don't use up your NiCad battery's juice unnecessarily.)

Removing the antenna

Thanks to its rubbery construction, the Palm VII antenna is flexible enough to withstand being knocked by passersby as you hustle along busy city sidewalks reading your email. You can, however, remove the antenna completely; you'll find instructions in the Palm VII Handbook. (Those instructions are provided for the benefit of those who might need to replace the antenna when it gets damaged. Considering its nearly indestructible nature, however, you're much more likely to need to remove the antenna for use as, say, an emergency finger splint or bite-able mouthpiece during painful surgery.)

Palm VII: The Service

The Palm VII is the first PalmPilot that you may never stop paying for. If you plan to use the wireless features—email and web querying—you must sign up for (and pay monthly for) an online account with Palm.Net, a special kind of Internet service provider run by Palm Computing. This account gives you a new email address to be used exclusively with your Palm VII. It also entitles you to use the Palm.Net web site (from your desktop computer or Palm VII), where you can check your billing statement, inspect maps of national wireless coverage, download new query apps (described later in this chapter), and get help with your palmtop.

Activating the Service

Signing up for this account is remarkably simple and almost instantaneous—you don't have to call any 800 number or mail in any application. Instead, turn the Palm VII on by lifting the antenna. Tap the Activate icon and follow the steps on the screen. You'll be asked for your contact information, credit card information, and first three choices of email address. (Whatever you write here, such as ski-bunny, will wind up as *skibunny@palm.net* in its final form.)

You'll also be asked to make up a password. Fortunately, everyday online transactions don't require this password; you'll need it only when visiting the Palm.Net web site to check your usage and billing statistics.

 If you ever forget your Palm.Net password, visit *http://www.palm. net*. There, with only your credit-card number to prove that you're you, you can make up a new password.

During the signup process, you'll also be asked to choose a service plan. At this writing, you have a choice of two plans: Basic ($10 per month) and Expanded ($25 per month). Choosing one isn't necessarily easy, because what you get for the money is measured in kilobytes (KB)—not a very intuitive unit when you're trying to measure things like emails and web pages.

Instead of trying to weigh the passage of KB through your Palm VII, remember that a kilobyte is 1,024 written characters (the equivalent of this paragraph and the three that precede it—about three Palm screens full of writing).

Therefore, assuming the maximum email message is a couple of screens long—and it is, because the Palm VII initially chops off messages longer than that, as described later in this chapter—here's a better comparison of the two plans:

Basic plan

$10 per month for 50KB, which is good for four or five emails a day, or one message plus a couple of web searches a day.

Expanded plan

$25 per month for 150KB, which ought to cover 15 messages a day, or three emails a day plus several web searches daily.

If you go over your limit, each extra kilobyte you transmit or receive wirelessly (three screens of information, or a couple of emails) costs 30 cents.

The activation may take several minutes, and may even take a couple of attempts to go through; but otherwise, that's the entire process. Your Palm VII is now ready to go online, send and receive email, and query the Web.

Getting Signal

In many ways, the Palm VII is the offspring of a Palm III and a cell phone. And cell-phone technology, as you probably know, is still in its infancy. The BellSouth wireless data network that talks to your Palm VII covers 93 percent of America's "business regions," which is to say the most populous 260 cities in the country. But that means that large areas of the rural United States have no coverage at all. (If you're a Palm fan in Montana, Wyoming, or the Dakotas, see the coverage maps at *http://www.palm.net* for the bad news.)

In other words, there will be times and places when you can't use the online features of your Palm VII. To check your signal strength, turn on the Palm VII by lifting the antenna. If you hear the rapid-fire, five-note chirp, your Palm VII has detected a BellSouth base station in the neighborhood (or up to 20 miles away)—you're in luck. You can perform online transactions.

Weak signals, however, drain your NiCad battery faster and may make transactions take longer. Check the strength of your signal by tapping the Diagnostics icon on your Application screen. There you'll see a graph of the signal strength—five bars and 100% is the best—which updates in real time as you move around the room and change the angle of the palmtop.

The Diagnostics app's often-ignored menu offers some intriguing troubleshooting tests: the Wireless Test, which tests your connection to the base station; the System Test, which tests the entire connection circuit; and the Channel List, which identifies all the base station's channels your Palm VII can receive and their relative strengths. Your Palm VII automatically switches to the strongest channel.

Believe it or not, moving just a few feet can make a huge difference in your ability to go online. As a general rule, also remember that steel blocks the radio signal. You won't get much good use out of your Palm VII in an elevator, a steel-reinforced concrete building, in the subway, and so on. That's why moving close to a window often works to improve the signal strength.

Palm VII: The Software

When using a Palm VII, you'll become acutely aware that data equals money. After all, 50KB isn't much, and every email or web transaction brings you closer to that monthly limit.

Fortunately, the Palm VII software has been designed with a paranoid eye to reducing the amount of data that's transmitted. When you send data, the Palm VII compresses it to a fraction of its actual size before going on the air; data destined to be received by your Palm VII is similarly compressed by the Palm.Net host computers. As you'll read in the following section, full web pages are never actually sent to the Palm VII—only a few characters of text. And special icons on the screen make it very clear which commands actually transmit or receive data, so that you never spend money (KB) without knowing it. (Figure 16-1 should make this clear.)

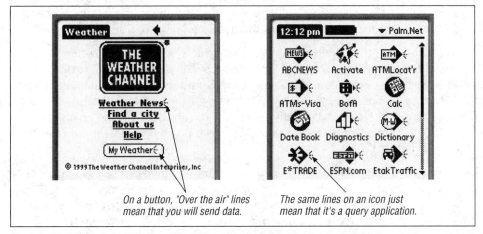

On a button, "Over the air" lines mean that you will send data.

The same lines on an icon just mean that it's a query application.

Figure 16-1. The tiny three-line "broadcast" icon found on buttons (left) lets you know that you're about to spend a few cents by tapping. The same indication on icons (right) just means you're about to open an online-capable program—you won't spend any money.

Wireless Email: iMessenger

The desire to save money by holding down the amount of data transmitted explains why Palm Computing never describes the Palm VII's email feature *as* an email feature—the brochures always say "wireless messaging" instead. That

How Palm.Net Works

The path traveled by your emails and web data from the Palm VII to the Internet is surprisingly convoluted—and requires an impressive amount of state-of-the-art technology.

Inside the Palm VII isn't a cell phone, but rather a two-way radio. Information you send gets transmitted from the antenna through the air to the closest base station of the Bell South Mobitex Network, which is like a cell-phone network except for three differences. First, Mobitex is dedicated to computer data (pagers, wireless modems, Palm VIIs, and so on); second, it carries data at only about half the speed of a cell-phone network; and finally, it covers much more of the United States than a traditional cell network.

BellSouth's computers then send your data onto the Palm.Net server computers. At the Palm.Net data center in California, computers known as Web Clipping Proxy Servers (WCPS) take note of your Palm VII's ID number and location, so that the information you've requested from the Internet will be sent back to your Palm VII and nobody else's.

If the transmission from your Palm VII is email (and not a web query), the WCPS transfers the request to a different set of computers—email servers that connect directly to the Internet and process mail. Otherwise, if you've sent a web request for, say, some Wall Street Journal headlines, the query is sent to the Internet exactly as though a standard web browser had sent it.

After a moment, the information you requested is sent back to the WCPS, which thoughtfully strips out all kinds of web data that's useless to your Palm VII—Java, JavaScript, comments, image maps, and so on. (That whittling down of data saves you money, since you're paying for information by the kilobyte transmitted.) What's left is tightly compressed, sent back up the chain to the BellSouth network, over to the closest base station, and finally through the air to your palmtop.

Many people have wondered whether the Palm VII could be used as a pager—that is, to wake up and start beeping whenever an email has arrived. The answer is no; the Palm VII always *requests* information, and can never receive it unsolicited. Otherwise, the transmitter would have to be powered up all the time, constantly watching the network for incoming messages, which would not only eat up your battery power very quickly a would also require that you keep your antenna up 24 hours a day.

(Shareware programmers are on the case, however: software that checks your email at scheduled intervals is in the works at this writing.)

peculiar wording is designed to reduce the average consumer's expectation that using the Palm VII is the same as using, say, Eudora on a desktop computer, complete with long-winded meeting minutes, replies-to-replies, and file attachments.

As long as you recognize that short messages are preferred, however, it's OK to admit it: no matter what Palm Computing says, the Palm VII does indeed send and receive 100%, Grade A, standard Internet email.

The program it uses to do so is called iMessenger. You'll find this application on the Palm.Net category page of your Applications launcher (see Figure 16-2)—the screen that appears when you turn on the Palm VII by lifting its antenna. If your account has been activated, just tap Check & Send to get your email and send any outgoing messages.

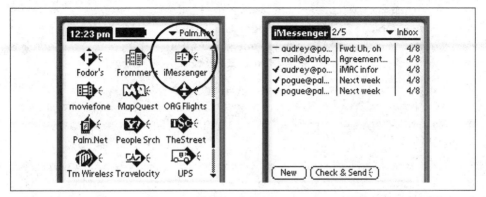

Figure 16-2. Tap the iMessenger icon (left) to open your wireless email program (right).

How iMessenger is like Palm Mail

iMessenger looks for all the world like Palm Mail, the built-in email program described in Chapter 13, *Email Anywhere*. In fact, many of the features are identical; they're explained at length in Chapter 13, but here's a summary:

- The start-up view shows you a list of all waiting email. Tap a message to read it; tap Menu → Options → Font to change the typeface; tap Reply or Delete, if you like; tap Done to return to the list of messages.

- The upper-right category pop-up menu provides access to the five folders—separate lists of messages—of email: Inbox, Outbox, Deleted, Filed, and Draft. To the extent described in Chapter 13, you can move messages freely among these various folders.

- Messages you've filed in your Deleted folder remain there until you remove them using the Message → Purge Deleted command, or until you've accumulated 50KB of deleted mail. At that point, new deleted messages begin to push the old into oblivion.

- If you'd like a standard signature stamped onto the bottom of each outgoing message, tap Menu → Options → Preferences → Signature and write out what you'd like your tag line to be. (Note to the budget-conscious: make it short.) Then, when composing an email message, use the Options → Add Signature command.

- To create a new email, tap New on the main screen. You can include multiple recipients by tapping the word "To:" on the email form that appears—the *To:* blank expands to a full screen. Separate email addresses here with commas. You can also use the Lookup function to grab email addresses from your Address Book program, as described in Chapter 13.

How iMessenger is different

On the other hand, iMessenger differs from the built-in Mail program in important ways. For example, Palm Mail exchanges email with your desktop computer, but iMessenger email doesn't HotSync to any desktop email program. Your wireless messages are locked on the Palm VII, readable only in iMessenger.

Nor can you move messages between iMessenger and Palm Mail. The Palm VII's two mail programs are utterly independent, each with its own private stash of messages. (It surely won't be long before enterprising Palm programmers address this limitation with add-on software.)

Some experimentation will quickly show you that iMessenger is missing a number of useful features you're used to from Palm Mail: CC and BCC address fields, a Reply to All option, and the ability to filter incoming messages. (These features are covered in Chapter 13.) On the other hand, iMessenger offers some unique features of its own:

Contextual menus

When viewing your list of mail, the narrow first column generally displays a checkmark (which means you've read the message), a small black diamond (which means you wrote the message), or a hyphen (which means you haven't read the message yet). But if you tap in this space to the left of any message, a pop-up menu appears, exactly as though you had right-clicked your Windows mouse or control-clicked your Mac mouse. This contextual menu (shown in Figure 16-3) may offer such useful commands as File (which moves the message into your Filed folder), Delete message (which moves it to the Deleted folder), Edit (for messages you've written), and so on.

The message log

Tap Menu → Options → Show Log to view a message-by-message diary of your iMessenger transactions, as shown in Figure 16-3 at right. Messages

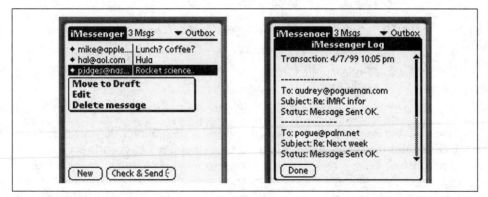

Figure 16-3. Tapping in the narrow left column produces contextual pop-up menus pertaining to the message you're tapping (left). The log (right) helps you monitor your email traffic.

you've sent are listed by addressee and subject; messages you've received are only tallied ("Received 4 new message(s)").

Automatic text attachment viewing

As with Palm Mail, iMessenger generally doesn't download files attached to your incoming emails. But unlike Palm Mail, iMessenger can handle plain text files attached to incoming messages; the contents of the text file automatically appear as part of the body of the incoming message.

Kilobyte Management

In their efforts to avoid swamping your Palm VII with a deluge of expensive, lengthy messages, iMessenger's designers have built in a number of safeguards:

Limited numbers of messages

When you tap Check & Send, the Palm VII sends all email you've written, but *receives* only the first ten incoming messages. If you're told that more email is still waiting to be downloaded, you must tap Check & Send again.

Limited numbers of characters

Again to protect you from expensive email overload, iMessenger also limits the lengths of incoming messages. Only the first 500 characters of each message are ever downloaded (about the length of this paragraph). If you see the words "Message Complete," you're seeing the entire message. If not, tap the More button (see Figure 16-4); a message tells you how much more of the message is still waiting to be downloaded. You can choose whether to download the entire remainder of the message or, if the remainder is more than another 500 characters, only the next chunk.

Sneaking Your iMessenger Mail to the Desktop

As noted in this chapter, there's no easy way to get iMessenger messages onto your desktop computer. Most people assume that iMessenger mail is forever stranded on the palmtop.

Actually, that's not quite true. Two sneaky workarounds await.

First, visit *http://www.palm.net* with your desktop computer. If you click My Account and then iMessenger Blind Carbon Copy (BCC), you'll be asked to sign in. Then you're offered a useful but undocumented feature: you can enter your regular, non-Palm email address. Thereafter, the Palm.Net computers will automatically send to that email address a secret copy of each outgoing Palm VII message. This feature costs nothing, doesn't use up any of your monthly KB allotment, and provides a useful record of your correspondence in the desktop email program of your choice. (Unfortunately, this trick only sends copies of your outgoing messages, not incoming.)

Second, while it's true that your iMessenger messages don't get *HotSynced* to your desktop PC's email program, they do get transferred to your Windows PC (not, alas, Macintosh) at HotSync time. Trouble is, your email is transferred only for backup purposes; it winds up in your Palm → *your palmtop's name* iMessenger folder, in a file called iMessengerDB. Amazingly enough, you can open this file up with a word processor, such as Word (in the Open File dialog box, use Word's All Files option). There you'll see your emails, nicely arranged and formatted except for a line of computer codes after each one; the messages in each folder (Inbox, Outbox, and so on) are separated by a column break in Word.

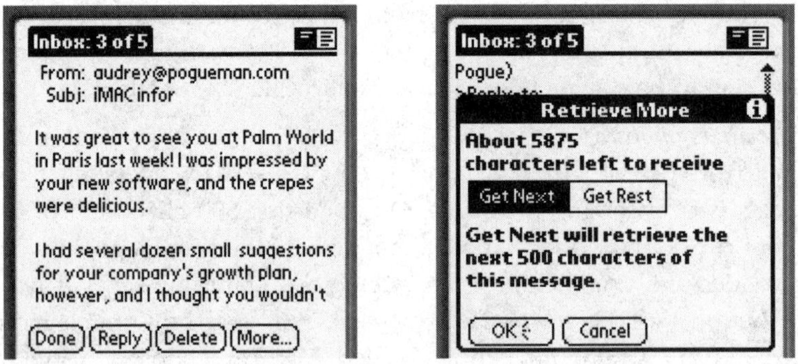

Figure 16-4. If the message is longer than 500 (compressed) characters (left), tap More. You'll be offered the chance to retrieve the rest of the message, or only the next 500 characters (right).

Fortunately, what appears on your palmtop in each "500-character" chunk is actually much longer than 500 typed characters. That's because your messages are compressed by the Palm.Net computers before being sent to your Palm VII, so 500 characters' worth of compressed data goes a long way.

If a look at the beginning of the message convinces you that the remainder isn't worth downloading—for example, if you're the victim of the ultimate Palm VII nightmare: getting spammedef with junk email—don't tap the More button. The remainder of the email remains, unread, on the Palm.Net computers in California. You have a month to change your mind—within those 30 days, you can open the first downloaded chunk and tap the More button to retrieve the rest of the message.

If you receive a very long message, by the way—more than 50,000 characters (about the length of this entire chapter), it's returned to the sender as undeliverable. After all, it's a Palm VII—they should know better

---

Suppose you tap Check & Send one morning, and the Palm VII tells you that after downloading the first 10 messages, 11,528 emails are left to be downloaded. You realize that one of two things must have happened: either you've been email-bombed by some teenager, or your Palm VII email address has been accidentally published on the Baywatch web site.

Fortunately, you're not condemned to downloading 10 of those messages at a time, long into the night, racking up incredible Palm.Net bills. Instead, sit at your desktop computer and visit *http://www.palm.net*. Click the "My Account" link, click iMessenger Mailbox Cleanup, sign in when requested, and marvel at the resulting screen's "Delete ALL Messages" command. You're saved.

As the pop-up menu informs you, this cleanup screen can also delete messages older than two or four weeks, delete all messages you've partially downloaded, and so on.

Limited address lists

Since you're paying for your email by the typed character, you're entitled to be annoyed when you get messages addressed to an endless list of people. For example, if you and 30 other people are the recipients of a particular message, all of their names appear in the *To:* blank (or *CC:* or *BCC:* blanks) of the incoming message. You're paying for the transmission of all those names, which by themselves could take up 500 characters or more.

Fortunately, iMessenger puts its foot down after 300 characters' worth of addressee names—and chops off any list of names longer than that. (There's no way to see the rest of the list.)

Limited reply traffic

Suppose you decide to keep your Palm VII email address somewhat private— to be shared, for example, only with your family and a few important business contacts. And yet every outgoing message identifies your Palm VII as the sender. How do you prevent your recipients from recording that email address as your primary contact information, thus initiating a new flood of nonessential email to your Palm VII?

Simple: tell iMessenger to stamp your outgoing emails with a *different* return address—for example, your regular desktop address. To do so, tap Menu → Options → Preferences. In the "Reply To Address" field, write the public email address you'd like your respondents to use for their replies.

Limited email pile-up.

Your Palm.Net mailbox—that is, the one that resides on the Palm.Net computers in California—follows a "you snooze, you lose" policy. If a message hasn't been checked in two months, it's automatically deleted; you'll never see it. You'd be wise to fire up the Palm VII, therefore, at least once every 60 days.

Furthermore, the Palm.Net computers don't allow more than two megabytes of emails to pile up in your account. If you get so much email that your waiting mail exceeds that amount—which is a huge amount of email—subsequent incoming messages are returned to sender marked "undeliverable" until you take care of downloading or deleting some messages.

The future of iMessenger

Clearly, iMessenger is very well designed for its advertised purpose—the creation and reception of short messages sent by Internet email. In this limited scope—as a sort of email-based pager—iMessenger is fine.

As an actual email program, however, iMessenger has plenty of room to grow, especially when it comes to accessing your messages in other ways. It would be nice, for example, to be able to view your messages on your desktop PC, in the Palm Mail application, or even at the Palm.Net web site, for those occasions when you want to check your email without racking up your Palm.Net bill.

Palm Computing is well aware of iMessenger's fledgling status and is already at work expanding its capabilities. Because the software in the all current Palm models can be upgraded using a software updater, enhancing iMessenger in the future will be a simple matter of downloading an updating program from the Web and running it while your Palm VII is sitting in its cradle.

Wireless Web: Clipper

Almost everyone expresses initial disappointment to learn that the Palm VII cannot, in fact, surf the Web wirelessly. You can't write in any old web address and jump to the corresponding web site. (For that purpose, you'll need a standard Palm modem, wireless modem, or Qualcomm pdQ SmartPhone, plus a web browser like ProxiWeb, as described in Chapter 14, *The Web in Your Palm*.)

The reason: downloading full web pages is slow, clunky, and unsatisfying on the tiny Palm screen, violating every principle that made the PalmPilot a success. (The built-in wireless transmitter runs at only 8Kbps per second; the standard desktop modem runs seven times faster.) More to the point, web surfing would be massively expensive; downloading a single web page can involve the transfer of 100KB or more—an unforgivable expenditure when your limit is 50KB per month.

Palm Computing solved the problem ingeniously: selected web pages, designed specifically for use on the small Palm screen, you can preload onto your PalmPilot via HotSync. These mini-web pages are complete with grayscale graphics, layout, blanks, pop-up menus, and so on. All they lack is the actual data that makes a web page useful. (See Figure 16-5 for an example.)

Thanks to this scheme, you can harness the Web for what it's really good for—delivering up-to-the-minute information—while transmitting and receiving practically no data at all. Because the web pages are already on the Palm VII, no graphics, frames, Java, tables, ads, or blinking animations are ever transferred; only a few characters of text data are actually sent wirelessly, such as stock prices, a news article, movie schedule, sports scores, and so on.

To use one of these miniature web pages, you tap or write to specify what information you want—the weather report, a restaurant listing, flight arrival information, or whatever. The Palm VII transmits your query to the Web, and a few seconds later, the blanks on your screen are filled in with the requested information. Palm calls this process web clipping, and the small screens of filled-in web-page data are the web clippings themselves

Where to Get Palm Query Applications (PQAs)

The miniature web pages that sit full-time on your Palm VII are called Palm query applications, or—if you're an insider or a programmer—PQAs. They look like standard Palm programs, and you launch them the same way—by tapping one on your Applications launcher screen.

But PQAs aren't actually programs—they're documents, web pages, that open into a browser-like application called Clipper. (You can't launch Clipper alone; you must open it by tapping a PQA icon.)

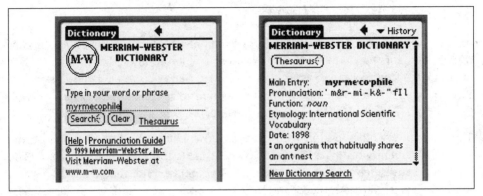

Figure 16-5. You can open up miniature web pages on your Palm VII without actually going online (left). When you request some data, only a few characters of text are returned to your palmtop (right).

A new Palm VII comes with 10 preinstalled PQAs, such as ABC News, ESPN Sports, Weather, and so on. About a dozen more come on the CD-ROM in the Palm VII package. (All 24 of these query applications are described in the following sections.) An ever-expanding list of even more PQAs is available at *http://www. palm.net*. You install PQAs just as you'd install any Palm program, as described in Chapter 7, *Installing New Palm Programs*.

Making Your Own Web Query Applications

But the real beauty of Palm query apps is that you can make your own. Behind the scenes, a PQA is nothing but a small web page written in standard HTML code. If there's a web page you'd like to visit frequently, there's nothing to stop you from creating a PQA of your own and installing it on your Palm VII. Appendix D, *Writing a Palm VII Query Application (PQA)* gives step-by-step instructions.

Using a PQA

To perform a web search, lift the Palm VII antenna. Unless you've reconfigured the device's Preferences screen, the Palm.Net category of your Applications launcher appears (see Figure 16-1). Tap the PQA you want to use, such as ABC News or ESPN.

Now the miniature web page appears. Various buttons and blanks let you specify what kind of information you'd like, as described in the following sections of this chapter. The one consistent interface element is the set of radiating lines on specific buttons—the "on the air" symbol, shown in Figure 16-1—which indicates that an online transaction will take place if you tap there. (Translation: you're about to start using up your monthly limit of wireless transactions.)

When you do tap such a button, thus initiating an online transaction, you'll see the status of the transaction displayed in the black tab—the title bar—at the top of the screen. It will say Sending, then Waiting, and finally Receiving. The information you requested should now appear on the screen.

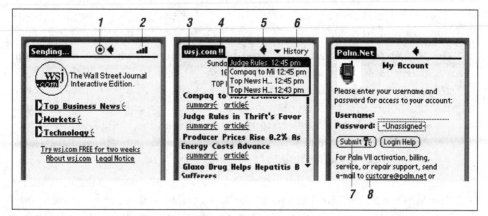

Figure 16-6. The miniature browser known as Clipper is filled with secret buttons.

Although only a few of these items are mentioned in the Palm VII Handbook, Clipper offers various hidden buttons and useful displays that let you control the web clipping process, as shown in Figure 16-6:

1. *The animated stop sign.* While your request is being processed, this stop sign fills and empties, fills and empties. If you decide that the process is taking too long, or that you'd rather do something else, tap the stop sign itself. It's your Cancel button.

2. *The signal strength meter.* During the connection process, these bars indicate the strength of the signal your Palm VII is getting from the BellSouth network. Five bars is the best. If you're seeing one or two bars, consider moving to a better location, as described earlier in this chapter.

3. *The PQA title.* After search results appear, hold the stylus tip down on this black tab to see exactly how much this web clipping cost you, in bytes (of which there are 1,024 in a kilobyte).

4. *Double exclamation points.* When you've finished downloading a screen of web information that's longer than 1KB, this symbol !! appears in the title bar, as shown in Figure 16-5. That notation is designed to warn you that the data you've just received is a kilobyte hog. Next time you use it, you'll be aware that, relatively speaking, this one's an expensive download.

5. *The Back button.* Exactly as in a standard web browser, tap this left-pointing arrow to step back through the pages you've seen. Eventually you can tap your way all the way back to the Applications launcher. Tapping the Back button doesn't entail transmitting or receiving any data. The antenna doesn't need to be up, and you don't eat up any of your monthly data allowance. (Once you launch another PQA, your most recent trail of information screens is lost.)

There isn't any Forward button, by the way. For that purpose, use the History menu, described next.

6. *The History pop-up menu.* Each time you make a web clipping request, the results are cached, or stored, on the Palm VII. Up to 50KB of data can be stored this way; then new information pushes out the oldest. (Note, however, that this 50KB is shared among all of the web-query apps on your palmtop. When you're at that limit, it's entirely possible for an incoming ABC News article about Bill Gates's mansion, for example, to push into oblivion the directions for a prize-winning soufflé.)

At any time, you can choose from this pop-up menu to view a list of previous clippings you've received in this PQA. Tap the one you want to see; it returns instantly to the screen. Using the History pop-up menu doesn't involve going online or spending any money. You've already spent the money and the time to retrieve this information.

7. *The Key icon.* When this icon is present on a button, it means that the information you're about to send will first be encrypted. This means that the transaction will take slightly longer. It also means that nobody can intercept the data you're sending, which generally involves your credit-card number, password, or other private information.

8. *Email addresses.* Now and then, a PQA screen will include a button to tap to send an email message. When you do so, an empty outgoing iMessenger message screen (described earlier in this chapter) appears automatically.

When you're finished viewing the information that's been summoned to your screen by a PQA, don't miss the Copy Page command (in the Edit menu). It grabs all the text on the screen you're viewing. You can then switch to another program, such as the Memo Pad, to paste it for viewing—and subsequent HotSyncing to your desktop PC.

There's otherwise no way to transfer web-captured data to your desktop.

The Preinstalled PQAs

Out of the box, the initial release of the Palm VII comes with 10 Palm query applications already in your Applications launcher. When you lift the antenna, it's this list of icons that first appears, as shown in Figure 16-1.

Each of these query applications is based on an existing web site, and each has been created by a different partner company—*USA Today*, the *Wall Street Journal*, the Weather Channel, and so on. As a result, they vary dramatically in quality, design, and usefulness. Unfortunately, the Palm VII package includes very little information about these PQAs. It's up to you (or the rare Help screen) to figure out how they work; one disadvantage of the Clipper mechanism is that it doesn't let the creator of each PQA add custom menus, such as a Help command.

Let this section and the next be your guide, then, to understanding this most powerful feature of the Palm VII. (This discussion covers the PQAs included with the original release of the Palm VII.)

ABC News (real-world web page: http://www.abcnews.com)

The "Front Page" screen appears when you launch the query application, listing categories of articles—Science, Travel, World, and so on. Tap one of these categories to go online to retrieve the list of news stories in that category. When the headlines appear, tap the one whose article you'd like to read (see Figure 16-7).

You go online again; this time, you're shown the opening paragraph of the article in question. Tap Full Story to retrieve the rest, Front Page to return to the list of topics, or Back to return to the list of headlines.

Figure 16-7. Using a news PQA like ABC News involves drilling down from section names (left) to headlines (middle) and finally to the news stories themselves (right).

This structure—baby steps toward the full article—should remind you of iMessenger, the Palm VII's wireless email program. In both cases, you're given plenty of control over the downloading process, ensuring that you never wind up downloading more material than you had anticipated (or want to pay for).

Activate (real-world web page: http://www.palm.net)

This tiny PQA is useful only on the day you activate your account, as described earlier in this chapter. After you've signed up for a Palm.Net account, tapping this icon produces nothing except an error message.

E*trade (real-world web page: http://www.etrade.com)

On the home page, write in the stock symbol whose current share price you'd like to check, such as AAPL for Apple or C for Citigroup (see Figure 16-8). Then tap either Sum (for a summary—just stock price, net change, and today's trading volume) or Detail (for a complete list of statistics—bid and asking price, daily highs and lows, earnings per share, PE ratio, and so on). The Detail view even offers a Chart command that retrieves a graph of your chosen stock's price over the last day, five days, month, half-year, or year.

As on most free stock-quote services, E*Trade provides share prices that are 20 minutes old.

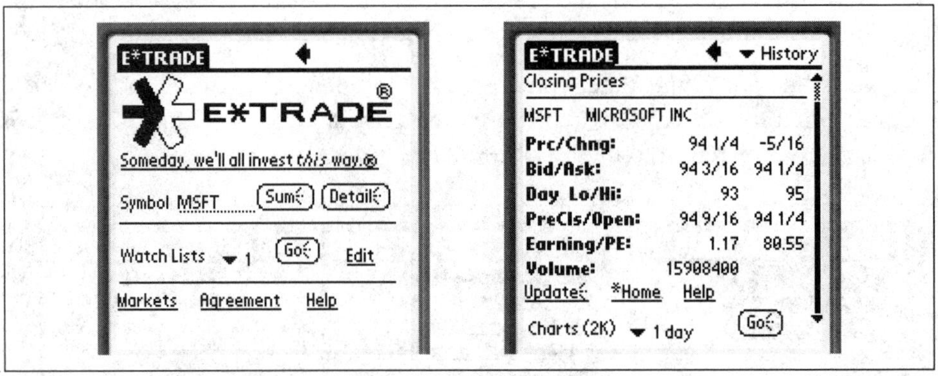

Figure 16-8. The E*trade query application at work. Specify a stock symbol or list of stock symbols (left), get the current prices and statistics (right).

The home page also offers a Watch List feature. A watch list is a set of stock prices you'd like to check every day, without having to write down the stock symbols over and over again. To build your list, tap the Edit link; the resulting screen lets you list eight securities. (In fact, using the pop-up menu above the list, you can actually build five different watch lists, each with a different set of securities.) When you're finished writing the stock symbols, scroll down and tap the Send button.

Now return to the home page and tap Go. (If you've set up more than one watch list, choose the corresponding number from the pop-up menu first.) The stock prices for all items on your watch list are retrieved simultaneously and displayed in a neat list.

The remaining useful item on the trade PQA home page is the Markets button. It summons a screen on which you can request either news, statistics, or graphs for the major stock markets—Dow Jones, New York Stock Exchange, NASDAQ, and so on.

ESPN.com (real-world web page: http://www.ESPN.com)

Sports fans never again need to interrupt dinner to get up and go check on the game score. The ESPN query application could not be simpler—tap the sport whose scores you want to check, and then, on the following screen, tap News, Scores, Standings, Schedules, or whatever else will satisfy your craving. (See Figure 16-9 at left.) An astounding range of sports are represented here—not just baseball and football, but auto racing, golf, college sports, boxing, tennis, hockey, extreme sports, and much more.

Figure 16-9. The Palm VII gives you everything from sports scores (left) to driving directions (middle and right).

MapQuest (real-world web page: http://www.MapQuest.com)

If you write in two addresses, MapQuest will give you turn-by-turn driving instructions from the first to the second. Unfortunately, the driving instructions frequently aren't the most direct and don't take road construction into account; frankly, you're sometimes better off just asking directions. In any case, it's fun to play around with, and may occasionally get you out of a bind.

To use the PQA, write in the starting and destination addresses, as shown at middle in Figure 16-9. (For driving directions to or from an airport—choose Airports from the pop-up menu—enter only the city and state of the airport; leave the street address blank.) When you tap Directions, you'll see extremely detailed driving directions on your screen, complete with exits, turns, notifications of tolls, and so on (Figure 16-9, right).

Palm.Net (real-world web page: http://www.palm.net)

This simple PQA offers two buttons. The first, My Account, asks for your Palm VII user name (your email address without the *@palm.net* portion) and password, and then shows you how many kilobytes you've used up this month. (See Figure 16-6 at right.)

The second button, Customer Support, simply offers a list of help topics, such as a glossary and reception tips. Most of these topics don't involve going online at all—the help screens are preloaded on your Palm VII. The sole exception: the Contact Us item, which offers tappable hotlinks for sending email help requests to the Palm.Net team.

The Last Easter Egg

Despite Palm Computing's explosive growth and massive success, its employees haven't lost their small-company spirit. Case in point: they're still allowed to plant the occasional Easter egg into their software.

To view the Palm VII's secret surprise, make the graphic Easter egg appear on the Preferences screen, as directed in Chapter 2, *Setup and Guided Tour.* This Easter egg is the On switch for several other Palm Easter eggs.

Now switch to the Palm.Net PQA. Tap a few pixels above the lower-left corner of the screen; when you land on exactly the right spot, you'll be treated to a list of the Palm VII's designers. (Bonus Easter egg: Tap just above and to the right of each name. Four of them trigger full-screen photos.)

People Search (real-world web page: http://www.yahoo.com)

When it works, Yahoo People Search can be among the most useful applications on your Palm VII. In essence, it's a White Pages telephone book of the entire United States. As is typical of this kind of collection, however, you may find that you're successful only about two-thirds of the time, even when searching for numbers you're sure are published.

Just write in as much information as you can about the person whose number you're looking for. If you want to know the mailing address too, tap the Show Addresses checkbox—but remember that the address means more data to transmit. Finally, tap the Search button to see if you'll get lucky (see Figure 16-10).

Figure 16-10. Write the name of the person you're looking for (left); when it works, People Search gives you a list of matching names, addresses, and phone numbers.

Speaking of poor odds, the home screen also offers an Email option. The theory: that you should be able to look up somebody's email address, like a global White Pages for email. In practice, however, this feature almost never works. Be sure to turn on the Email Links On checkbox—that way, if the search turns up any valid email addresses, you'll be able to send a message to that person with a single tap.

Travelocity (real-world web page: http://www.travelocity.com)

If you want a PQA that works the first time and every time, this is it (see Figure 16-11). Your Palm VII can look up flight arrival and departure information, flight numbers, schedules, and even gate numbers. If you've ever called an airline during bad weather to find out whether or not a flight will be on time and waited on hold for 45 minutes, you'll appreciate the value of having the entire Sabre flight/reservations system in the palm of your hand.

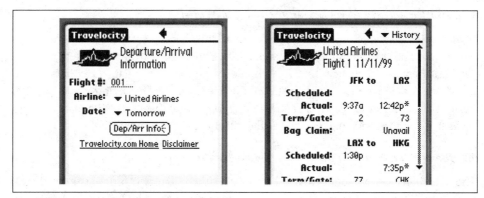

Figure 16-11. Ask for a flight number (left), Travelocity shows you the departure and arrival times, and, sometimes, even the gate numbers.

The options on the Travelocity home screen are:

Departure/Arrival Information

>   Write in the flight number, airline, and date; Travelocity tells you the times, terminal, gate, and even baggage claim carousel of that flight.

Flight Schedules

>   Specify the airports you're flying from and to, the airline you prefer (if any), and when you want to fly. Like the world's smallest travel agent, Travelocity offers you a list of every flight that meets your criteria, complete with flight numbers and times.

Existing Itineraries

>   This option is available only to existing Travelocity members. (Becoming a Travelocity member is free—just visit the web site with your desktop PC and make up a name and password.)

>   Using this button, you can look up the details of any travel you've previously booked on the actual Travelocity web site—a great feature when in the cab on the way to the airport.

Flight Paging Reservation

>   If you have an alphanumeric pager with national coverage, the Travelocity PQA offers a remarkable feature. Tap this button, and then specify your paging service, PIN number, and the flight you're worried about. A setup screen appears, where you can specify when you want your pager to go off with reminders: only when the flight schedule changes, a certain amount of time before the flight leaves (to remind you to go to the airport) or before it arrives (to remind you to pick up your spouse), and so on. At the appointed time, your pager will ring and display the news about your flight.

Wsj.com (real-world web page: http://www.wsj.com)

PQAs don't get much better designed than this: tap a category (Top Business News, Markets, or Technology) to see a list of headlines from today's *Wall Street Journal.* Beneath each headline is a choice of buttons: Summary (a concise paragraph) or Article (the full article); see Figure 16-12, left. Considering you'd pay $60 per year to access the real-world *Wall Street Journal* web site, having access to the biggest 30 or so stories each day is a delightful Palm VII freebie.

Weather (real-world web page: http://www.weather.com)

The Weather PQA, brought to you by The Weather Channel, provides news headlines, plus weather reports for any city in the United States. (Tap Weather, News, or Find a City, respectively).

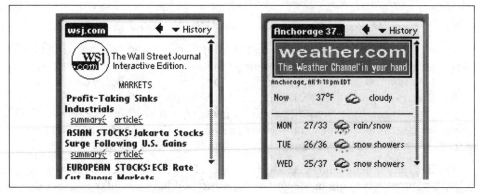

Figure 16-12. The Palm VII lets you fold up today's Wall Street Journal smaller than anyone else on the subway (left). At right: the amazing Weather PQA. Don't get dressed without it.

By far the most interesting aspect of the Weather PQA, however, is the My Weather button. Tap it for an instant five-day weather forecast for the spot where you're standing, as shown in Figure 16-12. (Don't worry about paying for the wireless transmission of the little sun/cloud graphics; they're pre-loaded on your Palm VII, not actually transmitted wirelessly.) The sidebar "The Palm VII Knows Where You Are" explains how it pulls off that impressive feat.

PQAs on the Palm VII CD

To prevent you from getting Wireless-Access Compulsive Kilobyte Overload (WACKO), Palm chose to place only a handful of PQAs on the out-of-the-box Palm VII itself. If you've been able to use restraint in your over-the-air pursuits, however, you can install the next batch of 13 that come on the Palm VII CD-ROM. During the installation of Palm Desktop, you were shown this list (see Figure 16-13) and offered the opportunity to install them. If you declined, you can always reinsert the CD-ROM and run the installer again, this time opting to add the extra PQAs. Here's a rundown.

ATM Locator (real-world web page: http://www.mastercard.com/atm)

Enter your current Zip Code (or as much of your address as you like), tap Find ATMs (Figure 16-14, left), and this PQA returns the street addresses of every MasterCard-compatible cash machine in the area. You can also search for ATM locations in various worldwide cities, or—this time without going online—view a list of airports in any country that offer cash machines.

ATMs—Visa (real-world web page: http://www.visa.com/atms)

This PQA, too, offers a list of close-by cash machines—this time with a slant toward those that accept Visa cards. You can search by address, phone number,

The Palm VII Knows Where You Are

Some of the PQAs included with the Palm VII offer a creepy but amazing feature: they provide information that pertains to the area where you're standing at this moment, wherever you may be in the country. For example, the Weather PQA gives the local forecast, the ATM Locator tells you where the closest cash machine is, and Moviefone gives you the remaining show times for the closest movie theaters. As they say at Palm Computing, your Palm VII is a "poor man's GPS" system. How does the thing know where you are?

Simple: at all times, your Palm VII must be within range of BellSouth wireless base stations, which are hidden on hilltops and building tops all over the country. At all times, the Palm VII also knows which base station is the closest. (In fact, you can look up the exact ID of the base station you're currently connected to by tapping Applications → Diagnostics → Details.) When you use a PQA that's location-dependent, the Palm.Net network simply notes which base station is doing the requesting and sends back local information accordingly. (If this auto-detection system sometimes gives you goofy results, remember that the closest base station may be up to 20 miles away.)

Note to the paranoid: No human is paying any attention to your online transactions; all of this tracking is done automatically by software. But if you, a Witness Protection Agency participant, are bothered that your Palm VII is transmitting your location every time you look up the weather, tap Applications → Prefs and choose Wireless from the upper-right pop-up menu. Turn on the "Warn when sending ID or location information" checkbox.

From now on, a message will appear on the screen whenever your Palm VII is about to transmit your location. You'll be offered the chance to decline—but, of course, you won't know what the weather's going to be.

Zip Code, or airport. The best part is that each listing (shown in Figure 16-14, right) offers a little Map button that shows you, more or less, the location of the ATM.

BofA (real-world web page: http://www.bofa.com)

This little PQA is of no value unless your bank is Bank of America. But it's a tantalizing taste of things to come—just enter your name and password, and you're shown your account balances and transaction history, exactly as though you were standing at a sophisticated cash machine. Beats calling up the 800 number and crunching touch-tones.

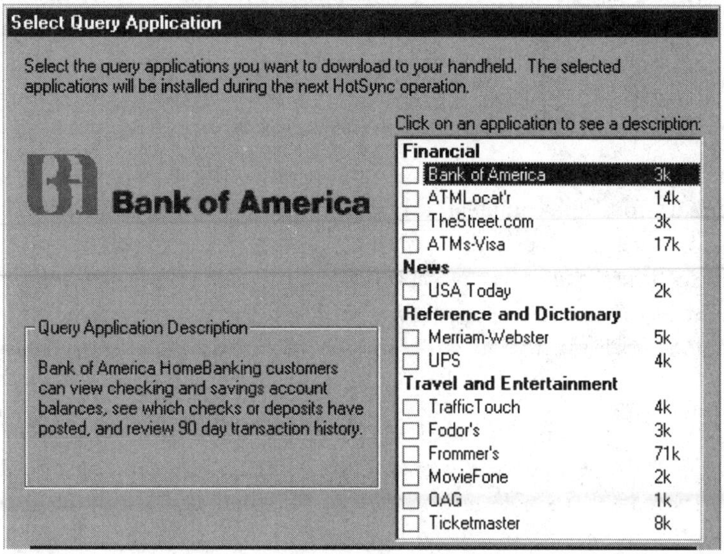

Figure 16-13. The Palm VII installer CD offers you the chance to install additional PQAs. If you've got a Mac, just stick the Palm VII CD into your drive, open the Query Applications folder, and install the included PQAs as though they're normal Palm programs (see Chapter 7).

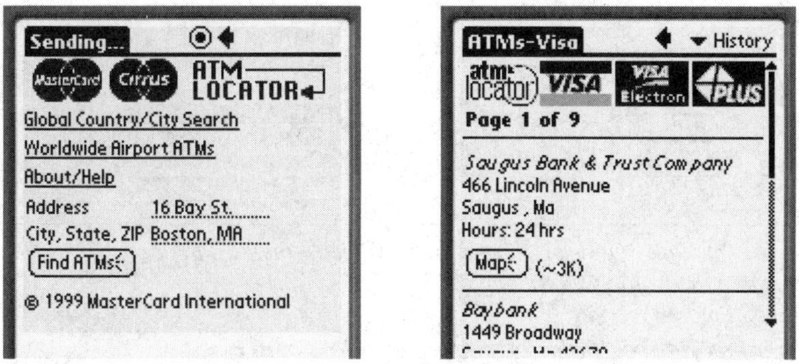

Figure 16-14. Tell the Palm VII where you are (as shown with the MasterCard-sponsored ATM Locator, left), and you find out where the closest cash machines are (as shown at right in the Visa-sponsored ATM Locator)

Dictionary (real-world web page: http://www.m-w.com)

Here's another brilliant idea—just write in a word, tap Search, and read the complete Merriam-Webster definition, including pronunciation guide and etymology. (Figure 16-5 shows the effect.) Or tap Thesaurus for a list of synonyms. The Dictionary PQA is essential for anyone who writes, reads William F. Buckley, or plays

Scrabble, and it really, truly works. (It's probably best not to ask why a dictionary publisher is making its crown jewels available for free—without even showing you ads in the process.)

EtakTraffic (real-world web page: http://www.etak.com)

Out of the box, this PQA is only somewhat useful—the Traffic pop-up menu provides detailed, up-to-the-minute traffic reports from a canned list of 21 cities (see Figure 16-15, left). The resulting accident reports are extremely specific, listing exact intersections, the severity of accidents, when the obstructions will be cleared, and so on (Figure 16-15, right). And you get the news when you want it, without having to listen to the radio for the next 20 minutes hoping for a traffic report.

It's only after you promise to pay $60 per year at *http://www.etak.com*, however, that this PQA becomes especially useful; you can specify the exact route of your commute. Thereafter, a single tap on the My Personal Traffic button gives you the traffic scoop for the precise roads you travel.

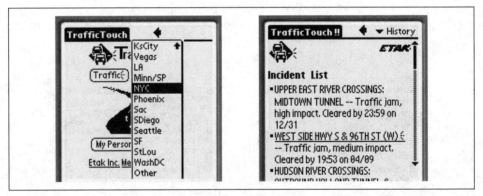

Figure 16-15. The Etak PQA lets you specify a city (left), then an area of the city, to find out exactly how bad the traffic is there (right).

Fodor's (real-world web page: http://www.fodors.com)

This electronic version of the famous Fodor's travel guidebooks offers restaurant and hotel listings and reviews for 100 of the world's top travel destinations, from Acapulco to Zurich. Tap either Dining or Lodging, choose from the list of cities, specify your price range (Figure 16-16, left), and up pop listings of restaurants or hotels that meet your criteria (Figure 16-16, middle). From there, tap one of the resulting establishments to view complete contact information, description, and even a detailed review excerpted from the famous guidebooks. (Example: "The accommodations are simple and without TV, but clean and very spacious. Half the rooms were repainted in 1996.") This is, if you think about it, ideal material for a traveler's companion like the Palm VII.

Figure 16-16. Fodor's guide (left) shows you a list (middle) of restaurants or hotels in the area you specify; tap the name of the place to read a professionally written review. Frommer's (right) is similar, but lets you specify exacting criteria for the kind of attraction, hotel, or restaurant you're looking for.

Frommer's (real-world web page: http://www.frommers.com)

This electronic city guide is broader than Fodor's, since it finds and describes not only restaurants and lodging, but also shopping, night life, and attractions. On the other hand, this guide is strictly North American, offering information about only 27 cities. (Only three cities in the entire Midwest and two cities in Canada rate inclusion.)

To use the PQA, tap a region, then tap the city you want, and finally the kind of information you're looking for (Accommodations, Shopping, and so on). Now you're shown a gargantuan checklist of criteria: Type, Price, Neighborhood, and so on (Figure 16-16, right). (Hint: Tap many more checkboxes than you're inclined to do, or you won't turn up any matches at all.) The resulting list offers both detailed contact information as well as concise, extremely useful reviews.

moviefone (real-world web page: http://www.moviefone.com)

If you've ever dialed 777-FILM (or the equivalent) in your city, you're already familiar with the macho singsong of the guy they call Mr. Moviefone. Guided by your touch-tones, he tells you the remaining showtimes of the movies you want to see in your neighborhood.

The PQA edition deprives you of his mellifluous voice, but doesn't waste your time with ads either. In fact, you don't even have to indicate where you are—just tap the This Zip Code button. After a moment, you're shown a list of all local theaters; tap one to see the remaining showtimes of its movies today (Figure 16-17, left). You can also tap Other Zip Code to find out what's showing elsewhere in the country.

Figure 16-17. Mr. Moviefone shows you today's remaining showtimes (left). TheStreet offers short, snappy financial-news articles (right)

OAG Flights (real-world web page: http://www.oag.com)

As with the more useful Travelocity PQA, this one lets you input a departure and arrival city, and airline, and a time; it fetches from the Online Airline Guide web site a list of flights that match those criteria. As a bonus, the program also offers to look up city, airport, and airline codes (SFO for San Francisco, and so on).

TheStreet (real-world web page: http://www.thestreet.com)

Tap a financial-news category (International, Markets, Tech, and so on) to view a short article—almost gossip-columny in tone—on that topic. (See Figure 16-17, right.) Unlike the other news PQAs, such as ABC News and the Wall Street Journal, this one is only one level "deep"—there's no option to start by retrieving only headlines, because there's only one short article hiding behind each category name.

Tm Wireless (Ticketmaster) (real-world web page: http://www.ticketmaster.com)

This interesting PQA is one of the few that actually let you buy something over the air—in this case, tickets to a Broadway show, circus, rock concert, sports event, or other Ticketmaster-handled event.

Write the name of the show into the Act Name blank (Figure 16-18, left). (If you don't know the name of the act, you're out of luck.) You're shown a list of showtimes—tap Info for details on the performance, or Buy It (if it's not sold out) to begin the ticket-buying process (Figure 16-18, middle). You'll be asked how many seats you want, what price range, whether you want the tickets held for you or mailed to you, and so on—and finally, you'll be offered a seat selection and asked for your credit card number.

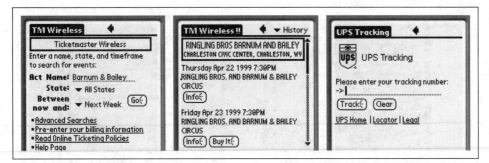

Figure 16-18. Ticketmaster is one of the most sophisticated PQAs—it actually lets you specify a show (left) and even buy tickets for it, if available (middle). UPS package tracking is much simpler, but can be extremely useful (right).

UPS (real-world web page: http://www.ups.com)

If you use United Parcel Service to send packages, this handy little query application could be useful indeed. You write in the number from the shipping label of a package you've sent (Figure 16-18, right). The PQA tells you the precise status of that package—where it is at this moment, and if it's been delivered, who signed for it.

You can also tap Find UPS Drop-off Locations to locate the closest UPS package drop-off office or box.

USA Today (real-world web page: http://www.usatoday.com)

This PQA works much like the other news services described in this chapter— except the content, of course, comes from today's *USA Today* newspaper. Tap the name of a newspaper section (Nationline, Lifeline, Tech News, and so on) to view corresponding headlines, which you can then tap to retrieve the full article (see Figure 16-19).

"Full article," in this case, is stretching it; what you actually get is short blurbs, almost teasers, no more than three paragraphs long. Still, you're getting free news with no ads and very little scrolling.

Yellow Pages (real-world web page: http://www.uswestdex.com)

If you're ever forced to justify your Palm VII purchase to a family member, just point out how compact your palmtop is compared to the stack of physical Yellow Pages books it can replace using this query application—every single Yellow Pages in the country.

Specify your city; from the pop-up menu, specify the category you want, from Accountants to Veterinarians (see Figure 16-20, left). If the kind of business you're looking for isn't in the pop-up list—which is often—write it into the blank; the

Figure 16-19. After choosing a section of today's USA Today *newspaper, tap a headline (left) to read a condensed version of the story (right).*

program is surprisingly smart about prompting you for the Correct category heading (Figure 16-20, middle). The result is almost always an on-target, useful list of local merchants and their phone numbers/addresses.

Figure 16-20. If it's out there, it's in here. Choose a city and a Yellow Pages category (left); choose from the pop-up menu if the program asks you to be more specific (middle). The results (right) are satisfyingly useful, every single time.

Life in the Wireless Age

Owning a Palm VII isn't Nirvana. The service can be expensive, the transmitter sometimes fails to connect even when the signal is strong, and constantly having to worry about your kilobyte count detracts from the overall thrill of living wirelessly.

On the other hand, there's nothing like the Palm VII—nothing small enough for your pocket that can connect to the Internet wirelessly in any form. Furthermore, Palm Computing is dead serious about perfecting this science; over the last couple of years, the company has been quietly acquiring wireless-technology companies both in the U.S. and in Europe. Clearly, we haven't seen the last of the wireless PalmPilots.

The PQA Explosion

The future of the Palm VII and its descendants lies not just in new models and new technology, but also in new software—namely, the new Palm query applications that are cropping up like dandelions. Within a week of the Palm VII's release, the *http://www.palm.net* web site was overrun with new PQAs. They include Bloomberg (financial news), Prudential Real Estate (search its homes-for-sale database), My Excite (personalized weather, news stories, horoscopes, stock portfolio, and so on), Techdirt (computer-industry news and gossip), United Airlines (flight schedules), Ajaxo and MySimon (comparison shop online stores), Horoscope (yours daily), and so on.

Some of the PQAs are genuinely revolutionary—and brillianty suited to use on a wireless palmtop. The Go Network PQA, for example, translates any text (including email and web pages) into any of five languages, doing a passable job (for software, anyway). The SkyTel, MobilComm, Paging Services, and PageNet PQAs let you send messages to your friends' beepers; almost every available paging service is represented here.

Among the most thrilling possibilities: BarPoint. Write in the UPC barcode number from the back of any product—a computer you see in a store, a book on the bookshelf, a box of Cheerios—and this PQA consults BarPoint.com's multiterabyte database of prices from stores around the country. Instantly, you're shown the lowest price on your Palm VII.

This information gives you terrific bargaining power—or confidence in knowing that the price you're about to pay is low enough. Retailers have every reason to be nervous about this development; consumers stand to save enormous amounts of money; and Symbol, who makes barcode-scanner-equipped PalmPilots, is working on saving you even the effort of writing in the UPC code of the product you'd like to price-check.

Executive Tip Summary

- To save battery juice, keep the Palm VII antenna folded when you're not actually going online.

- If reception is a problem, try to give the device access to the sky. Move closer to a window—or just move a few feet in one direction or another. Keep the antenna vertical.

- In theory, there's no way to transfer your iMessenger wireless email to the desktop. In practice, however, you can visit *http://www.palm.net* web site to request that a blind carbon-copy of each outgoing message be sent to your regular desktop email address. You can also open your iMessenger backup file in any Windows word processor to view the text of all iMessenger messages, albeit separated by a line of computer garbage.

- Hold the stylus tip down on the title bar of a results screen to see how many bytes it cost you.

- To cut down on the amount of expensive data you're transmitting, use a different "reply-to" address on your outgoing iMessenger emails. You can also save data by quoting back only the minimum in your replies—not the entire incoming message.

- The 24 Palm Query Applications (PQAs) provided with the Palm VII are only the beginning. More are available at *http://www.palm.net*—and you can even make your own, following the instructions in Appendix D, *Writing a Palm VII Query Application (PQA)*.

V

Troubleshooting and Upgrading

17

Troubleshooting

Part of the PalmPilot's wild success has come from the fact that as computers go, it's uncomplicated. It doesn't have to boot up. It doesn't have a system folder. It doesn't need Norton Utilities. And in this world, "uncomplicated" usually means "trouble-free." (When's the last time you called for technical support with your mouse pad?)

But the PalmPilot is still a computer, and as such, it still displays the occasional glitch. Fortunately, a PalmPilot hangs or freezes far less often than a "real" computer. In fact, if you use only the built-in applications, you'll probably *never* encounter freezes or hiccups, and you'll quietly wonder what all the fuss is about. Still, it's wise to be prepared.

Palm snafus are almost never serious. Thanks to the HotSync concept, even if your palmtop croaks completely, you *always* have a backup on your desktop machine. Still, if you're one of the unlucky ones, let this chapter be your guide to recovering smooth operation of your palmtop.

 In a perfect world, *everything* on your PalmPilot would be backed up when you HotSync—including any add-on programs you've installed. That's true, however, only if the programmer correctly wrote the add-on program. A few applications, unfortunately, don't get backed up automatically during a HotSync because the programmer neglected to turn on one subtle internal software switch.

This issue, and others like it, explains why 3Com instituted the "Platinum Certification" program described in Appendix A, *100 Programs Worth Knowing About*. Platinum Certification is awarded only to programs that have been written to 3Com's guidelines for well-behaved PalmPilot programs. (This issue also explains the need for shareware like Backup Buddy, which backs up everything during a HotSync.)

What to Do When Disaster Strikes

If none of the suggestions in this chapter helps fix your PalmPilot, call 3Com's technical-help center at (847) 676-1441. If the PalmPilot is actually broken (and can't be fixed using the steps outlined in this chapter), 3Com will send a prepaid, cushioned box to you by overnight courier; pick it up; and return the device to you a couple of days later, all fixed.

If the disaster struck during the first year you owned the PalmPilot, and the damage wasn't caused by something *you* did (like dropping it), all of this is free. Otherwise, this luxurious service costs $100.

If you accidentally drop your PalmPilot, your heart may stop as you see pieces flying everywhere.

However, as my own accidental testing has shown, most of the time the pieces flying everywhere are the battery door, batteries, stylus, and (in pre-Palm III models) maybe even the memory door. The glass screen, the electronics inside, and the dark-gray case usually withstand desk-height drops.

All of those smaller pieces are easily snapped back together. If the PalmPilot doesn't turn on right away after such a trauma, do a soft reset, described next. Unless the fall was especially high or the angle was especially wrong, the PalmPilot usually picks right up from where it left off before the accident.

The Importance of Resetting

Every kind of computer offers a means of restarting in case of lockup, plus a means of starting up without any startup add-ons. The PalmPilot is no exception. The following techniques—the soft reset in particular—are amazingly useful. They can get you out of an impressive majority of hangs, freezes, glitches, and other software-based anomalies.

Soft Reset

A *soft reset* of the PalmPilot means turning it off and on again. But when some piece of buggy software has *frozen* the thing, you can press the on/off button from now until doomsday with no effect: the PalmPilot simply stays on, with a frozen screen. In such a case, you need to do a soft reset—a method of *manually* turning the device off and on again.

To do so, unfold a paper clip. Or, if you own a Palm III or later model, unscrew the plastic top (not the point) of the stylus to reveal a *built-in* "unfolded paper clip" pin. Use the paper clip, or the unscrewed stylus cap pin, to press the button in the Reset hole on the back of the palmtop, gently. (This hole is identified by the word RESET).

When you do a soft reset, the palmtop automatically turns on again. Your programs and information are 100% intact.

The true Piloteer, possessing a pre-Palm III model without an unscrewable stylus, carries a paper clip *inside* the PalmPilot, ever ready to do a soft reset when necessary.

There's a perfect place to stash it, too: in the battery compartment. Slip it, or even tape it, in the groove between the two batteries, replace the battery-compartment door, and you're in business.

And what if you have a Palm V, which has neither an unscrewable stylus cap nor a battery compartment? Well, you could always carry around a paper clip in your sock.

Warm Reset

A soft reset, as you now know, is the equivalent of turning the PalmPilot off and on again. But suppose the problem you're having is caused *by* the startup procedure—by a system-update patch (see Chapter 18, *The Palm Family, Model by Model*), a HackMaster file (see Appendix A), or another startup file, for example. In such cases, a soft reset won't solve the problem. What you need to do is restart the machine with a virginal, untouched "System Folder," with no patches or add-ons—the equivalent of starting up a Macintosh with the Shift key down or Windows in Safe Mode.

To do this *semisoft* or *warm reset*, hold down the Scroll Up plastic button on the front of the unit. With this button down, press a paper clip's unfolded end, or the stylus's pin, into the Reset hole on the back of the unit, as described earlier.

If this procedure solves whatever problem you were having, do a HotSync to back up your data. Now do a soft reset, as described earlier, to start up the PalmPilot *with* all of its various startup add-ons.

Suppose you're encountering some strange software behavior on the PalmPilot. A soft reset doesn't eliminate the problem, but a semisoft reset does. In other words, you've established that the problem is caused by a HackMaster program (Appendix A) or an operating-system patch (Chapter 18). How do you remove whatever's causing the problem?

Removing HackMaster files is easy: Tap Applications → HackMaster, and turn off the checkboxes of any "hacks" you want to remove. Turn the PalmPilot off and on again.

Removing Palm OS update patches is only slightly more involved. Perform a semisoft reset to turn all the patches off. Now you can remove these patches just as you'd remove any add-on program (see Chapter 7, *Installing New Palm Programs*).

Hard Reset

A *hard reset* is a drastic step—the equivalent of erasing your hard drive. It *deletes all of your information,* restoring the PalmPilot to the condition it was in when you bought it. Perform a hard reset only if you've done a HotSync to back up your data, and only if:

- You've tried soft and semisoft resets, and neither solved whatever problem you're having.

- You get a Fatal Error message after performing a soft or semisoft reset.

- You're giving or selling your PalmPilot to somebody else—or *getting* a Palm-Pilot from someone else—and want to wipe it clean.

To hard-reset your PalmPilot, hold down the on/off button at the lower-left front corner. While this button is down, insert a straightened paper clip or the stylus-cap pin into the Reset pinhole on the back, as described in "Soft Reset."

A message appears on the screen: "Erase all data? YES = 'up' button. NO = any other button." In other words, press the plastic Scroll Up button to perform a hard reset. (If you press any other plastic button, the PalmPilot simply turns on normally.)

Now the PalmPilot is in its factory-fresh condition, without any add-on software programs, system patches, or data except what came with it when you bought it. (If you experience strange behavior *now,* your PalmPilot is definitely broken. See "What to Do When Disaster Strikes," earlier in this chapter.)

To copy your data back onto this virginal palmtop, launch Palm Desktop (Windows) or HotSync Manager (Mac). From the Options menu, choose Custom (Windows)—or from the HotSync menu, choose Conduit Settings (Mac). As shown in Figure 6-8, you can now double-click each of the conduit names—Memo Pad, Address Book, and so on—to open a customization dialog box (see Figure 6-9). Choose *Desktop Overwrites Handheld* in each case, and then HotSync; when it's over, your data will be restored to the palmtop.

Graffiti-Recognition Problems

See Chapter 3, *Typing Without a Keyboard*, for help with getting the PalmPilot to understand your Graffiti handwriting.

But if you're confident that you're drawing your Graffiti strokes correctly, it's conceivable that your digitizing circuitry has become corrupted, or that the touch screen's cable has come loose inside the machine. Do a quick test: install Teal-Echo, described in Chapter 3 (and included on this book's CD-ROM) to see exactly what shapes the PalmPilot is "seeing" when you write. If the circuitry is obviously nutso, detecting lines that you're not actually drawing, call Palm Computing; the repair is free if you're still under warranty.

HotSync Problems

3Com's studies indicate that a huge percentage of technical-support calls the company receives are about HotSyncing. No matter how well designed the PalmPilot may be, HotSyncing involves hooking up to a *desktop computer*—a beast hundreds of times more complex and balky. As you'll see in this section, nearly all of HotSync troubleshooting procedures involve work on the *PC*, not on the PalmPilot.

The First Steps to Take

If you can't get a local HotSync (where the PalmPilot is directly connected to your computer) to work, double-check the cabling and HotSync settings described in Chapter 6, *HotSync, Step by Step*. If HotSyncs still don't happen, here are some additional troubleshooting experiments to conduct.

1. Turn off any startup programs or system extensions that may be interfering with your ports. Fax software is especially suspect, because its purpose is to monitor your serial ports constantly.

2. Quit any telecom programs that may be running (America Online, Internet software, and so on).

3. On the Macintosh, if you've connected the cradle to the printer port, make sure AppleTalk is off. (To do so, choose Chooser from the Apple menu and click AppleTalk Inactive.) And if you have a Wacom drawing tablet, consider turning its control panel off when HotSyncing to avoid sluggishness.

4. On Windows, if you have an internal modem or PC card modem, it may be assigned to the COM port you're trying to use with your PalmPilot. (You'll see nothing plugged into the actual COM port, but the port is "stolen" by the internal modem.) Reassign the internal modem to a different COM port. For details on COM ports, see "The Windows Nightmare: COM Port Management" later in this section.

5. Try quitting the HotSync software and restarting it. On the Macintosh, this means opening the HotSync Manager program and clicking Disabled, and then Enabled. On Windows, this means exiting the HotSync Manager program and relaunching it.

6. Check to make sure you've plugged your cradle into the serial port you specified. To change the HotSync software's concept of which port it's plugged into under Windows, launch Palm Desktop; choose Setup from the HotSync menu; and select a different COM port. On the Macintosh, open the HotSync Manager program, click the Local tab, and choose the correct jack (modem or printer) from the Serial Port pop-up menu. (Don't be confused by the term Modem on the HotSync Manager's startup panel—it's not referring here to your modem *port,* but rather to performing HotSyncs over the phone line, as described in Chapter 6.)

7. Try a lower HotSync speed, especially if you're having trouble syncing with a laptop. On the Macintosh, this means opening HotSync Manager, clicking the Local Setup tab, and changing the Speed pop-up menu. On Windows, launch Palm Desktop, choose Setup from the HotSync menu, tap the Local tab, and change the Speed pop-up menu.

8. On either kind of computer, reinstall the Palm software.

9. Don't use any PalmPilot in a HotSync cradle designed for a different Palm-Pilot model. For example, don't use a Palm III in the cradle that came with a PalmPilot Professional, nor a WorkPad in the cradle that came with an original Pilot 1000 or 5000 model. You can *sometimes* get such setups to work, but you're asking for trouble. Each generation's cradle is slightly different.

10. If you can't HotSync to your laptop computer, the laptop's power-saving sleep mode may have closed its serial port. Quit and restart the HotSync monitoring software, as described in step 5.

11. Macintosh models with G3 processors—as well as 5400, 6400, 4400, Power-boat 3400, and many clones from Power Computing, Umax, Motorola, and APS—have a well-known hostility toward successful HotSyncing with the original Pilot software. When you try to HotSync, you get a message that "The connection between your PalmPilot and the Desktop was lost," or "could not be established."

    Solution: Upgrade to MacPac 2.1, included on this book's CD-ROM.

12. If you're HotSyncing a lot of data, or if you're connecting to an older, slower Mac or PC, you may get a message that indicates that the PalmPilot has "timed out" waiting for a response from the PC. In other words, the PC took too long in responding to the PalmPilot's signal. The PalmPilot gives up in disgust, and the HotSync never takes place.

    If this happens to you, and trying step number 5 again doesn't solve the problem, try this workaround. It's a sneaky feature, a "back door," intended primarily for programmers (also known as developers)—that's why it's called the Developer's Backdoor. In short, this feature tells the PalmPilot to wait *forever* for the PC to respond.

    To invoke it, tap the Applications icon, and then the HotSync icon. Here's where things get strange: while pressing the scroll-up button (Palm III and later), or *both* scroll buttons (previous models), tap the upper-right corner of the screen until you see the message: "DEVELOPER'S BACKDOOR: DLServer Wait Forever is ON." Tap OK, and then try to HotSync again.

    The PalmPilot will stay in "wait forever" mode only for one HotSync; if the PalmPilot shuts off or you cancel the HotSync, the PalmPilot returns to its normal impatient self. Sometimes, by the way, this special treatment is necessary only for the *first* HotSync; thereafter, HotSyncs work fine.

13. If you're still getting time-outs—your PC never "answers" the HotSync message—and even the developer's backdoor doesn't work, it's conceivable that your HotSync cradle is actually defective—for example, a couple of its metal contact points may be sunken in slightly.

    If you can *see* that the contacts are messed up, contact 3Com. If not, try pressing the lower part of the PalmPilot forcibly backward against the back of the cradle (where the contacts are). (Also try cleaning the palmtop's contacts with a pencil eraser.) If the HotSync is now successful, you've found your problem.

14. If these steps still haven't produced positive results, consider testing your HotSync cradle to make sure it works. (See "Testing the HotSync Cradle," next.)

The Second Backdoor

While the purpose of the "Developer's Backdoor" is immediately useful—it makes your PalmPilot wait forever for the PC to respond at the beginning of a HotSync—there's a second backdoor that's a bit more mysterious, but highly entertaining (and perfectly safe).

Tap the Applications button, and then tap HotSync. To summon the first Developer's Backdoor, as you know, while pressing the scroll-up button (or, on older models, both scroll buttons), you tap the upper-right corner of the screen.

But if you tap the *lower*-right corner of the screen (while pressing the appropriate scroll buttons), you get Developer's Backdoor #2—a screen full of extremely impressive-looking technical gobbledygook, as shown above. Technically, they're low-level communications statistics—but the deeply impressed person looking over your shoulder on the airplane never needs to know that.

According to 3Com's tech-support staff, one of the most frequently heard complaints is that customers' Palm data doesn't show up in Palm Desktop, on your desktop computer, after a HotSync.

Actually, it's probably there. Check the User Name pop-up menu in the upper-right corner of the screen (Windows) or the name at the top of the toolbar or calendar (Mac). If it doesn't show *your Palm-Pilot's name,* then you're not looking at the results of your HotSync. (Remember, Palm Desktop can switch among many different Palm-Pilots' contents; some may even show up empty. See Chapter 8, *Palm Desktop: Windows,* and Chapter 9, *Palm Desktop: Macintosh,* for instructions on switching user files.)

Another source of confusion: capitalization matters in choosing a User Name. FRANK is not the same as Frank. Make sure you're viewing the one that really designates your PalmPilot.

Testing the HotSync Cradle

If you've tried every possible means of solving your HotSync problems on the *computer* end, it's faintly conceivable that your HotSync cradle itself is defective. Here's how to check.

Begin by quitting the HotSync Manager program (Windows) or by clicking the Disabled button in HotSync Manager (Macintosh). Then:

Windows 9x

1. Locate your HyperTerminal program (called *Hypertrm* on your hard drive). Launch this program. Type a name, such as *HotSync test,* and click OK.

2. At the Phone Number screen, choose "Direct to COM 2" (or whatever COM port your HotSync cradle is connected to) from the bottom pop-up menu. Click OK.

3. At the Port Settings screen, choose *9600* as the bits per second, and *None* for Flow Control. (The data bits, parity, and stop bits should already be set at 8, None, and 1.) Click OK.

4. Now you arrive at a blank white screen. Put the PalmPilot into the cradle; press the HotSync button.

5. If gibberish starts filling the screen, your PalmPilot and cradle are working correctly. If not, check your COM ports, as discussed above; and if *that* isn't the problem, your cradle may need to be replaced.

Macintosh

Use Zterm, a popular shareware terminal program, for this. (You can get it from *http://www.shareware.com,* among other places.)

1. Open HotSync Manager. Make sure HotSync monitoring is off (so that the button says Disabled).

2. While pressing Shift, launch Zterm. In the Port Selection dialog box, choose the appropriate port (modem or printer); click OK.

3. From the Dial menu, choose Directory. Click New.

4. Type in a Service Name, such as *HotSync test.* Leave everything else blank.

5. Choose 19200 as the speed. The data bits, parity, and stop bits should already be set at 8, None, and 1. Local Echo should be off, and Neither should be selected for Flow Control. Click OK.

6. With the HotSync test name highlighted, click Dial. A blank window appears.

7. With the PalmPilot in the HotSync cradle, press the HotSync button.

If you see gibberish filling the screen, all is well. If not, tap the Cancel button on the PalmPilot, and then tap the Local Sync icon. And if *that* doesn't send gibberish characters to the Mac, try repeating this test using whichever port you *didn't* select in step 2.

If you still can't HotSync, and you've tried the other steps in this chapter, your cradle may need replacing. Call 3Com.

The Windows Nightmare: COM Port Management

One of the most common causes of HotSync problems in Windows is the mis-assignment of your PC's *COM ports*. If your HotSync cradle isn't attached to an available COM port—and if the HotSync Manager software hasn't been informed as to *which* COM port that is—the HotSync process won't work at all.

Your PC probably has one or two COM port jacks on the back; you're supposed to plug such *serial devices* as mice, modems, PC-card adapters, and other computers into them. To complicate the issue, your PC may have additional, *internal* COM ports with no corresponding jacks on the back panel. If your PC has an internal modem, for example, it's probably connected to one of these internal ports.

But just finding a free COM port won't necessarily solve your HotSync problems. Internally, your COM ports speak to your PC's brain by making an Interrupt Request (an IRQ). The PC has a limited number of "channels" over which these communications can take place, so some COM ports (1 and 3, for example) generally *share* an IRQ channel. If any action takes place on COM ports 1 and 3 simultaneously—mouse movement and HotSync activity, for example—the result is the dreaded *IRQ conflict*. Both gadgets wind up temporarily dead. Your manual, the PC manufacturer's help line, or local PC guru should be able to help you out of such messes.

 If you're running short of COM ports, and your PC can handle it, here's a quick way out: install a BUS or PS/2-style mouse instead of one that uses up a COM port. Such mice use IRQ channel 2, which frees up a COM port so that you can keep your HotSync cradle, mouse, and modem permanently connected.

Finding out about your COM ports

How do you find out what COM ports you have?

Windows 3.1

Run the program on your hard drive called Microsoft Diagnostics. At the DOS prompt, type MSD (and then press Enter). The screen that now appears tells you how many COM ports you have. It also tells you if you have a *serial* mouse; if so, it's using COM port 1. Moreover, if you have an internal modem, it's probably using COM port 2. When it comes to configuring your COM ports for use by the HotSync cradle, now you know which two COM ports you *can't* use successfully.

Windows 9x

Right-click My Computer; choose Properties from the pop-up menu. In the System Properties dialog box, click the Device Driver tab, and then click Ports (COM & LPT) to see how many COM ports your computer has.

Getting more ports

So what happens if you have no COM ports left over for your HotSync cradle?

- If you have an external modem, of course, you can unplug it and replace it with the HotSync cradle when you want to HotSync. You can also buy an A/B switch box for about $25 that lets you keep *both* the HotSync cradle and the external modem connected; you just turn a knob to switch between them.

- Laptop PC-card slots are generally treated as COM 2 ports. On some models, you can switch them off, thus freeing up COM 2 for use by your HotSync cradle (check your manual).

  In general, laptops have more COM-assignment problems. If yours has an infrared transceiver, for example, it's probably using up one of your precious COM ports; fortunately, you can generally disable it.

  If you do manage to free up a COM port for your HotSync cradle, your laptop still may have problems HotSyncing unless you choose a lower HotSync speed (see Chapter 8). Also remember that if your laptop goes to power-saving sleep mode while you're HotSyncing, the transfer will be interrupted; you may have to restart the machine (and certainly the HotSync Manager program) to try again.

- If one of your back-panel jacks is occupied by a network cable, you can replace it with the HotSync cable. (Be sure to turn off the networking *software,* too.)

- For about $50, you can buy a serial-port expansion card that gives you additional COM ports. (Installing it involves assigning IRQ channels, however, which is not for the novice.)

- If you have a Palm III or later model, consider installing the Palm OS 3.3 updater described in the next chapter. It lets your copy of the HotSync Manager see all available COM ports.

Secrets of the Dot Commands

Drop in on a Palm trade show or discussion group online, and you're sure to hear Piloteers drop references to the *dot commands* into their conversation.

That term refers to seven mysterious, for-programmers-only, undocumented commands. Most are useless, although fascinating; numbers 3 and 6, however, can be helpful under certain circumstances.

To trigger one of these commands, write the Graffiti ShortCut symbol (see Chapter 3 for details on ShortCuts)—which resembles a cursive, loopy, lower-case L drawn from the lower-left; then a period (two taps), and then one of the following numbers:

1. Puts your PalmPilot into a program-debugging mode—or just freezes it. Also opens the internal connection to the serial (HotSync) port, which may quickly drain the batteries. To exit this mode, perform a soft reset, as described at the beginning of this chapter.

2. A different debugging mode, much like 1.

3. The words No Auto-Off appear; you've just turned off your auto-power-shutoff feature. In other words, now your PalmPilot won't go to sleep after one, two, or three minutes (whichever is your Prefs setting, as described in Chapter 2, *Setup and Guided Tour*)—it stays on until you turn it off. This setting could be useful if, for example, you're reading a speech from notes on the screen and don't want the thing shutting off in the middle of your meeting. (To restore the auto-shutoff feature, do another soft reset.)

4. Briefly displays, in bold type, your PalmPilot's user name and secret internal number. Reported to be flaky and not worth trying.

5. Deletes your HotSync log and user name. Unfortunately, also deletes your PalmPilot's record of which information is current with your PC. As a result, the next time you HotSync, you'll get duplicates of every record (address, appointment, to-do item, etc.) on the palmtop!

6. Shows your PalmPilot's birthdate—the day its ROM chips were created. Kind of fun, actually.

7. Makes the word NiCad appear. You've just adjusted your PalmPilot's battery gauge (on the Applications screen) so that it more accurately reflects the state of AAA NiCad (or NiMH) batteries, if you're using them (see the end of this chapter). Repeat this ShortCut again to make the word Alkaline appear—you've just restored the original setting, which is for AAA alkaline batteries.

—Continued—

See Chapter 15, *Paging, Faxing, Printing, and Beaming,* for three more dot commands (which control beaming) or Chapter 18 for a special dot command that reverses the strange backlighting of the Palm IIIx, V, and VII. Now that you know about the dot commands, go forth with new confidence—you're a *real* insider now.

Modem HotSync Troubleshooting

Modem HotSyncs almost never work perfectly on the first try. Don't be discouraged if you're not successful at the outset. Instead, try these steps:

- Turn up the speaker volume (on PalmPilot and WorkPad models; see Figure 6-15) so that you can hear where the dialing is going astray. You may need to insert commas into the dialing sequence if you're using a calling card, for example.

- Try choosing a slower speed, both on your PalmPilot and on your desktop PC modem.

- Confirm that the desktop computer you're dialing into hasn't gone into power-saving sleep mode, been turned off, had its modem turned off, or had its power strip turned off. And, of course, make sure that the HotSync software is up and running on the desktop computer. Confirm that no fax or other telecommunications software is interfering with the modem port.

- If your modem has a power-saving "sleep" feature but no actual on/off switch, you're out of luck. Once you're away from your computer, you have no way to wake the thing up to receive your PalmPilot's call.

- Try to recall whether or not your internal PC modem is a Megahertz or Hayes Accura brand. These models have known problems answering HotSync modem calls.

  Solution: Launch a modem program, such as HyperTerm; follow steps 1 and 2 of "Testing the HotSync Cradle," earlier in this chapter. Once your PC is successfully communicating with the internal modem, type ATSO=1&W and press Return. You've just issued a command to your internal modem that should solve the problem.

Palm Desktop Problems in Windows

Palm Desktop, described in Chapter 8, is the PalmPilot's home-base software on your PC. Because it must interact with your other programs—such as Microsoft Excel and Word, not to mention Windows itself—it's substantially more susceptible to problems than the actual PalmPilot. Here are some of the ways out of trouble.

Can't Reclaim the Port?

When you've completed a modem HotSync, your desktop computer remains on the alert for your *next* HotSync from the road. In other words, the HotSync software continues running so that you can dial in the next time.

In fact, on Windows, even if you exit the HotSync Manager program by double-clicking on the system tray icon and choosing Exit, HotSync Manager continues running, despite the disappearance of its icon from the system tray.

So who cares? You will, if you now try to use that modem port with any other program. To reclaim the port, either restart the computer or press Ctrl-Alt-Del to bring up the Close Program and shut down the communications port. In fact, do that *twice*. Your port should now be free.

Word and Excel Macro Icons Not Visible or Not Working

Under Windows 95, using Pilot Desktop 2.0, you're supposed to see icons for Microsoft Word and Excel (if you have them installed on your PC). They let you drag-and-drop data from your Palm Desktop window to create automatically formatted reports, as described in Chapter 8.

If the Word and Excel icons don't show up, or nothing happens when you drag data onto them, maybe it's because you have Office 97, but you're using Pilot Desktop 2.0 (which doesn't work with Office 97). Upgrade to Palm Desktop 3.0 or later, available at *http://www.palm.com*.

If that's not the trouble, then your Windows registry is probably confused. The lengthy but effective repair process is described at *http://palmpilot.3com.com/custsupp/helpnotes/desktop/macronst.html*.

Excel Doesn't Launch When You Click the Expense Icon

If you get an error message when you click the Expense icon in Pilot Desktop ("Microsoft Excel could not be found"), then your Windows registry has gotten confused, as it's wont to do. The solution is long and complex, but it works like a charm; it, too, is described at *http://www.palm.com*.

Error Message: "Word Basic Err=513 String Too Long"

You get this message when you try to drag-and-drop too much Address Book or Memo Pad information onto the Word icon in Pilot Desktop 2.0 or later. (The limit is 65,536 characters.) Drag less material to avoid the message.

Some Expense Categories Don't Show

This problem occurs when, in Palm Desktop, you click the Expense button to launch an expense report—but when you inspect the resulting Expense Report in Excel, some of your Category names don't appear.

The problem is that you created a category called *Expenses* in your PalmPilot's Expense program. That's a no-no; "expenses" is a keyword used internally by the PalmPilot software, and you're not allowed to use it in your category names.

The solution is simple: rename the category on your PalmPilot. (If the problem persists, you'll have to paste the records from the Expenses category into another category.)

Error Message About "AWFXCG32.DLL Problems"

AWFXCG32.DLL is a Microsoft Fax Mail file. Check the internal version number of your copy of Microsoft Fax—in Windows Explorer, use the Properties command. You need version 4.0.962 or later.

Goofy Text at the End of Email Messages

If, after HotSyncing, your PalmPilot shows a bunch of header-like information at the bottom of your email messages, you're probably using Microsoft Exchange version 4.0.837.0 as your PC email program. Update to a later version, such as the one that's been renamed Windows Messaging.

Error Messages with Microsoft Exchange

If you're still using Microsoft Exchange as your desktop PC's email program, you can prevent HotSync error messages by taking these steps:

- Don't HotSync more than 100 emails at a time.

- If the PC starts dialing to get new mail before proceeding with the HotSync, hit the Cancel button.

- Make sure there aren't any email messages saved into Microsoft Exchange's Draft folder.

For what it's worth, subsequent generations of Microsoft mail programs (such as Windows Messaging or Microsoft Outlook) don't have these limitations.

Macintosh: Problems with the MacPac 2

Palm Desktop 2.1 and its accompanying software, included with this book, is so dramatically improved from what came before it that the number of things that go wrong is very small. Chapter 9 covers some of these quirks, such as the peculiar relationship between notes and other records in Palm Desktop. Here are a few other items worth noting.

HotSync Gives Up

If you're HotSyncing a lot of information, you may need to give HotSync Manager (in your Palm folder) more memory. Highlight the icon, choose File → Get Info → Memory, and increase the Preferred Size. Try adding about 25 percent at a time until the problem goes away.

You Bought the 2MB Upgrade Card and Can't HotSync to Your Mac

Early versions of this upgrade card were buggy. Call Palm Computing for a free replacement.

Software Troubles on the PalmPilot

Many of the PalmPilot's potential pitfalls are relatively minor (and very rare). This section covers a few of them.

Mail Messages Deleted

This problem must baffle hundreds of PalmPilot users all over the world. The symptom: You HotSync email from your PC to your PalmPilot's Mail program. But when you read the messages, any that have the same *subject line* have disappeared (except one)!

That's just the way life is with Palm Mail. Only the first message with any particular subject line gets transferred to the PalmPilot; others are ignored. You'll have to respond to *those* messages on your desktop PC.

To Do Items Shift by One Day

If you're using an original Pilot model (the 1000 or 5000), you may be susceptible to this bizarre bug. It crops up when Windows adjusts its clock for Daylight Savings Time, believe it or not. The result: To Do items in Windows Pilot Desktop 1.0 (not on the PalmPilot itself) suddenly appear a day early. (Lord knows we can't have *that*—you wouldn't want to finish your tasks early!)

The solution is to replace your *TODO.DLL* file with a repaired one, which is available from *http://palm.3com.com/custsupp/helpnotes/palmapps/todost.html.*

Ignoring the Dial Tone

Under normal circumstances, a PalmPilot modem doesn't begin dialing until it "hears" a dial tone. Sometimes, however—especially when you're traveling overseas, where the dial tones sound different—it's helpful to turn that "wait until you hear it" feature *off.*

To do so, tap Applications → Preferences; from the upper-right pop-up menu, choose Modem. Add *X3* to the end of the existing codes in the String field. From now on, the modem won't bother waiting for a dial tone; it will simply begin charging ahead, dialing whether there's a dial tone or not.

Wrong Answers in Calculator

The Calculator in the Pilot 1000 and 5000 models occasionally gave mathematically questionable results. The solution is to install the "SlimCalc" replacement. See the "Pilot: Return of the Pentium Bug?" sidebar in Chapter 5, *The Other Built-In Programs,* for instructions.

HotSyncing Takes Longer and Longer, and ShortCuts Are Incredibly Slow

This particular snafu primarily affects power users, or other people who frequently perform a soft reset, described at the beginning of this chapter. It affects every PalmPilot model, and goes like this:

Every time you reset your palmtop, three invisible ShortCuts are added to your list, even though they're already there. (See Chapter 3 for details on ShortCuts.) Oddly enough, these are the three beaming *dot commands* described at the end of Chapter 15. If you reset your palmtop enough, these superfluous ShortCuts will accumulate, eventually numbering in the dozens or more. Every time you HotSync, of course, your shortcuts database must be transferred to your desktop computer, which takes longer and longer as the invisible ShortCuts list grows. And if you try to open your actual ShortCuts screen, as described in Chapter 3, you'll find that the palmtop grinds to a halt as it sorts its massive list of invisible text entries.

The solution is to run dbScan, a utility program included on this book's CD. The latest version neatly prevents your invisible ShortCuts from building up.

I'm Worried About the Year 2000

Don't be. The PalmPilot is built on the same Motorola chip family as the Macintosh, and therefore, as on the Mac, all functions will run smoothly until the morning of February 6, 2040. (A simple software patch will extend the chip's useful life to the year 20,000.) And besides, if you're still keeping your data in the PalmPilot you're using today in 2040, you've got bigger problems than the year 2000 bug.

Disappearing or Shifting Date Book Entries

If you travel with a laptop and your PalmPilot, don't change the laptop's time-zone settings (in Windows' Regional Settings or Date/Time control panels) as you arrive in each new city! If you do, when you HotSync, times and dates of your Palm-Pilot's dialog box appointments can shift in bizarre ways. Recurring events may disappear entirely, and discrepancies between the appointments on your Palm-Pilot and on your laptop may appear.

To end the chaos, reset your laptop's time zone to its original setting; your Date Book entries should sort themselves out at the next HotSync. If you must know what time it is in your new city, change the time zone on the *PalmPilot,* but not on your laptop.

The shifting Date Book syndrome isn't limited to laptop travelers. *Anyone* who has the wrong time zone selected (or no time zone at all) may experience shifting appointment times on the PalmPilot. (This means you, too, network users. The network's time should also be correctly set.)

On the Macintosh, you set the time zone in the Date & Time control panel. In Windows 95, check the Regional Settings or Date/Time control panel. (In Windows 3.1, the process is long and complex; see *http://palmpilot.3com.com/custsupp/helpnotes/palmapps/timefix3x.html* for step-by-step instructions.)

Hardware Troubles

This section covers some hardware difficulties you may occasionally encounter and their solutions.

My Screen Is Completely Blank!

The completely black or completely white syndrome strikes many a Piloteer. In most cases, the problem is simple: while jostling around in your pocket or briefcase, the contrast knob at the edge of the unit got turned *all the way* to black or white. (That's probably why, on the redesigned Palm III and all later models, the contrast knob is much harder to turn accidentally.)

My Screen Is Still Completely Blank!

If the contrast knob isn't the problem, it's conceivable that your memory card has come loose inside the palmtop (after being dropped or swapped, for example).

If you checked the memory card, tried a soft reset (described earlier in this chapter), and checked the contrast knob, but the screen is still empty, your PalmPilot probably needs to be repaired.

Finally, hold the palmtop up to your ear and listen for the faint buzz. If you don't hear it, your batteries, or your palmtop, may be dead. If you hear the buzz, the screen's connector cable may have come loose inside. Contact 3Com.

Humming Sounds from the PalmPilot

If you've never heard this hummy, hissy sound, try it right now: Hold the Palm-Pilot right up to your ear and turn it on. (Turn the backlighting on for a much louder hum.)

The sound is perfectly normal, and there's nothing you can do about it; it's made by the gadget's electronics. (As 3Com explains it: "The humming is caused by the power supply coupling with the speaker circuit.")

You may also hear, by the way, a tiny, occasional *tick* sound. That, too, is normal; it's the battery circuitry checking out the sound circuitry.

Beaming Problems

If you can't get beaming to work (see Chapter 15), remember that both the sending and receiving units must be infrared-equipped. They must be between two and 20 inches apart, and their infrared panels should be able to "see" each other. The recipient's Beam Receive option must be turned on, too.

Finally, note that the receiving PalmPilot must have at least *twice* as much memory free as the transmitted item it's receiving (50K free for a 25K beamed application, for example).

Power Button Needs to Be Pressed Twice

If your PalmPilot won't turn on with a single press of its on/off button, your batteries may be low. If that doesn't solve the problem, and you have an original Pilot model, install System Update 1.0.6, included on this book's CD-ROM.

Screen Taps Don't Do Anything

If tapping onscreen elements doesn't seem to work, try re-aligning the screen layers, as explained at the beginning of Chapter 2.

One of the Silkscreened Button Icons Doesn't Do Anything

If you tap, for example, the Menu icon and nothing happens, chances are that everything's fine—there simply *aren't* any menus in whatever program or screen you're using. Similarly, tapping the Calculator icon doesn't do anything if the Calculator is *already* on the screen, the Find icon does nothing if the Find box is already open, and so on.

Buttons Stick

On original Pilot models, this was a known design problem. 3Com will fix it for you—or at least would have during the first year you owned the Pilot.

Oily or Sticky Film On the Screen

If diluted Windex on a soft cloth doesn't get rid of this goop, contact 3Com to request a replacement PalmPilot.

The Battery Drains Too Fast

Do you keep your palmtop in its cradle your desk? Bad idea. Palm fans on the Internet were quick to discover what's certainly the most egregious design flaw in the Palm world: whenever your palmtop is sitting in its cradle, even turned off, the serial connection is open—and your battery juice quietly drips away, like car oil onto the garage floor.

Various radical solutions have been proposed, from keeping a piece of plastic wrap over the connector to dismantling the cradle and cutting the offending pin (at this writing, instructions are at *http://www.conklinsystems.com/pilot/drainfix. shtml*). The best solution, of course, is not to leave your PalmPilot in the cradle. Unless it's a Palm V, of course—in that case, the cradle is the *best* place for the PalmPilot to be when it's not turned on.

There's a Dark Spot on the Screen

Pity the hundreds of people who bought 3Com's leather slimline case, inserted the PalmPilot, closed the cover, and pressed with their thumbs to make the Velcro adhere to the palmtop. Doing so has one traumatic side effect—it creates a dark spot where you pressed with your thumbs.

This screen damage recovers somewhat over the ensuing hours, but never completely. 3Com may or may not consider this a warranty-covered repair, depending on its mood.

The Palm V Turns On by Itself and Chatters

You'll find a discussion of this disturbing problem in the next chapter.

The Palm IIIx Screen Has a Ghosting Grid

You probably noticed this disturbing problem in the Week or Month views of your Date Book program. No amount of fiddling with the contrast control gets rid of these faint gridline extensions that shoot all the way off the screen.

Fortunately, the solution is easy: download and install the OS 3.1.1 update from the Support area of *http://www.palm.com*. No more ghosts!

Understanding Palm Memory

The PalmPilot uses memory (RAM) in some remarkable ways. For one thing, RAM takes the place of the hard drive on a traditional computer. All of your data, as well as any programs you install yourself, reside permanently in memory. Only the battery juice keeps these programs and data from vanishing into the ether. (The built-in programs—Memo Pad, Address Book, Mail, and so on—are permanently burned into the ROM circuitry, so you never need to fear losing them.)

Because the built-in programs are stored in the device's ROM, you can't delete them. The Memo Pad, Address Book, To Do, Date Book, Mail, and Expense programs are permanently part of your PalmPilot.

On the other hand, even if you never use some of these programs, you shouldn't be bothered by their undeletability. Because they're etched permanently in silicon, they use up no RAM at all.

In this day of PCs that come with 64MB of RAM, you might have been startled when you first learned that your new palmtop came with only half of a megabyte (original Pilots) or, at most, four megs (on Palm III*x* units).

But the truth is that PalmPilots—and Palm programmers—use RAM far more efficiently and compactly than desktop computers. A chess program that might require 4 megabytes of memory in Windows requires only 17K on the PalmPilot. It's the rare PalmPilot owner, therefore, that ever comes close to exhausting the RAM that came built into the palmtop.

The memory-management center on a Pilot or PalmPilot model is the Memory application. Tap Applications → Memory to launch it. On the Palm III and later models, the Applications screen's Delete and Info commands replace the Memory application.

Chapter 5 includes a complete discussion of the Memory and Applications screens; for now, note that they're what you use to see how much RAM each of your programs is using up, and delete programs you no longer need.

Memory Troubleshooting

If you're trying to install onto a pre-Palm III model a new program that should fit into your remaining RAM, but the installation fails when you run a HotSync, your memory may be *fragmented* (broken into smaller pieces, each of which is too small to accommodate the program you're trying to install). For example, Hack-Master, the powerful feature extender described in Appendix A, locks itself into a certain spot in your PalmPilot's memory, effectively breaking up the memory on either side of it into smaller fixed pieces.

To dislodge this plug in your memory pipes, tap Applications → HackMaster and turn off all the checkboxes. Launchpad and PowerFix are other utilities that may create memory blocks; if they're creating new-program installation problems for you, delete them.

Now your HotSync (complete with new-program installation) should proceed smoothly. Re-enable your HackMaster modules (or whatever other utilities you disabled).

Where's My RAM?

If you launch the Memory program, you may be startled to see that your PalmPilot has only a fraction of the memory it was advertised as having. A Palm III, for example, seems to have only 1952K free (instead of 2048).

The "missing" RAM is being set aside by the Palm OS itself, which reserves a blob of memory—the *dynamic heap*—for use by your applications. In the latest models, such as the Palm V, this reserved space has been increased from 96K to 128K—in other words, the "2MB" Palm V has less usable RAM than the "2MB" Palm III! (The larger heap space is preferable, however, since it lends greater stability to the machine.)

Consider yourself lucky; 6 percent is a far lower percentage of the Palm-Pilot's RAM than your desktop computer's OS uses of *its* memory.

The Greatest Memory Secret Ever Told

The operating system on original Pilot and PalmPilot models came on a ROM chip, exactly as on any normal computer—that is, permanently etched in silicon. But the Palm III and subsequent models come with *flash RAM*—a reprogrammable ROM chip. The beauty of this arrangement is that when Palm Computing releases an improved version of the operating system, you'll be able to upgrade your machine without having to exchange circuit boards, as you did on the original models.

In effect, your "2MB" Palm III, Palm V, or Palm VII actually has 4MB of memory. And the Palm IIIx, advertised to have 4MB of RAM, actually has six. In each case, an unadvertised 2MB is reserved for the operating system and built-in programs.

But the Palm OS, as you may have heard, is famously compact; so are the built-in programs. Even 2MB would seem generous for these small programs—and it is. In fact, they only consume 1224K of the space set aside for them. Wouldn't it be nice if the remaining 824K, currently sitting there wasted on every Palm III and later model, were available for you to use for your own stuff?

This long-winded explanation is why the $30 FlashPro program (*http://www.trgnet. com*) is such a great value. Its sole purpose is to let you access that wasted RAM, in effect turning your 2MB PalmPilot into a 2.8MB PalmPilot.

At shown in Figure 17-1, you just tap the names of the programs you want copied into flash RAM (or back again). The copying takes only seconds. You can consider the newly available flash RAM as either extra storage space or as a backup of important programs in your main memory (not that PalmPilot main memory is particularly prone to failure).

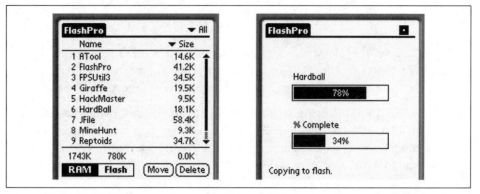

Figure 17-1. The FlashPro program on your Palm device shows where each program is stored—in actual RAM or in flash RAM (left). You can easily move programs back and forth (right).

The single fly in this otherwise exciting ointment is that not every program runs when launched from flash RAM. A handful give you error messages; others actually crash. HackMaster files, in particular, shouldn't be copied into flash RAM while they are turned on. (See Appendix A for details on HackMaster.) Some older email and web programs crash when run from flash RAM; so do data files, those whose names end with *.pdb* (such as Doc files described in Chapter 10, *PalmPilot: The Electronic Book*). Although the vast majority of Palm programs are flash-friendly, the careful FlashPro user occasionally drops into the *http://www.trgnet.com* web site to consult the compatibility list.

Your first instinct is probably to consider FlashPro a gift of *additional* memory. Remember, however, that flash RAM is *nonvolatile*; like the built-in Palm programs stored there, this information doesn't need battery power. It's permanent until you change it.

Therefore, consider making *backup copies* of your most important programs—including FlashPro itself—in your flash RAM. Keep backup copies of your Date Book and Address Book data files there, for example. (Generally, such data files don't run from flash RAM, but there's nothing to stop you from storing them there.)

That way, even if you drop the device and the batteries fly away, or you take the batteries out for more than 10 minutes, your most important data is still preserved in the nearly indestructible flash RAM.

Battery Management

The PalmPilot sips battery juice at a slower rate than nearly any other computer you can buy. A color Windows CE device runs through its pair of AA batteries in a matter of *hours*—not weeks, as with the PalmPilot. Even people (such as 3Com employees) who use their PalmPilots constantly—especially people who do a lot of HotSyncs and infrared beaming—get nearly a month out of each set of batteries.

You might assume that the PalmPilot has two basic operating modes—on and off. Actually, though, it's constantly lapsing into a third mode called idle, in which the processor is shut down, using no battery power; that's the state your palmtop is in whenever you're reading something on the screen (as opposed to writing or punching buttons). The instant you begin tapping or writing, the processor wakes up. Since most people spend more seconds studying what's on the screen than manipulating it, idle mode is one of the great secrets of the device's long battery life.

What Happens as the Batteries Run Down

A fresh pair of AAA batteries generates 3 volts of power. (You can track your current pair's remaining charge by viewing the "fuel gauge" on the Applications screen.)

When the batteries are down to 2.1 volts and then 1.8 volts, low-battery warning messages appear on the screen. Even then, you still have several days' worth of typical use left in your current pair of AAAs.

When the remaining juice is *very* low, you may begin to encounter bizarre operational problems. The PalmPilot may take longer to translate your Graffiti gestures into text, programs may take longer to launch or operate, and you may need to press the on/off button twice to turn the palmtop on. At this point, you should HotSync and replace the batteries.

Still, there's no call for paranoia; even when the batteries enter hibernation mode at 1.6 volts, your data is safe in the PalmPilot for weeks (or one week on the Palm V). You can't even turn the PalmPilot *on,* but your data is still preserved, and all will be well after you insert fresh AAAs. (If the PalmPilot won't turn on even after it has fresh batteries, perform a soft reset, as described at the beginning of this chapter.)

For reams of fascinating PalmPilot battery information, visit *http://www.pstech.de.ppp.*

Your data is only jeopardized, in fact, when there are *no* batteries installed. In that event, your data is erased in a matter of *minutes*. (The Palm VII is a special case, as described in Chapter 16, *Palm VII: Wireless Email, Wireless Web.*)

How to Change Batteries

HotSync before you change batteries. Insert the replacement pair within a minute or two of removing the dead pair. 3Com suggests replacing the batteries one at a time—that is, take out dead battery A and replace it, and then take out dead battery B and replace *it*, although nobody's ever shown an advantage over replacing both at once.

If you jump to the Applications screen just after installing new batteries, by the way, you might be alarmed to see that the battery "fuel gauge" graph is still on "empty." Give it time; the bar will gradually fill up again as it notices the fresh batteries.

Of Alkalines, NiCads, and Renewals

3Com recommends disposable alkaline batteries for the PalmPilot—not just because of their long life, but also because they are depleted at a smooth rate. When the remaining voltage in them reaches a certain level, the PalmPilot's circuitry can accurately show you "low battery" warnings when there's still enough charge to give you time to seek out fresh ones. (PalmPilots, Palm III, and subsequent models show these warnings earlier than the original Pilot models.)

You might suppose that rechargeable batteries would be ideal for the PalmPilot. When one pair of AAAs runs down, you can simply charge them up instead of buying a fresh pair. And the most common kind of rechargeable batteries—the nickel-cadmium (NiCad) type, such as those made by Panasonic—can be recharged hundreds of times before requiring replacement.

Unfortunately, NiCads have a significant drawback: their voltage drops off abruptly at the end of their charge. They're likely to drop dead so fast that the PalmPilot doesn't have a chance to warn you. The result: you don't have time to replace them. And remember that once your PalmPilot's batteries are *completely* dead (NiCads lose their remaining charge *very* quickly once depleted), you have only a matter of minutes to replace them before your data is erased.

One type of rechargeable battery doesn't suffer from the NiCad quick-dropoff syndrome: rechargeable *alkalines,* such as Rayovac Renewal batteries. Unfortunately, you can't recharge these as many times in their lifetimes—25 times or less. And their charge doesn't last nearly as long as disposable alkalines. But they behave exactly like regular alkalines, complete with a smooth voltage dropoff at the end of the charge. There's a wrinkle here, too, though—Renewals like to be "topped off." They last longest, and gain the most charge, if you never let them drain fully, and instead frequently recharge them in midstream.

Squeezing More Life Out of Your Batteries

If you rely on the auto-shutoff feature, you can squeeze more juice out of each pair of batteries by setting the PalmPilot to turn itself off after only one minute (instead of two or three). To do so, tap Applications → Prefs → General. Tap the "Auto-off after:" pop-up menu to make your choice. (If you switch your PalmPilot off promptly whenever you're finished consulting it, of course, this trick won't help you.)

Some perfectly natural actions make the batteries drain much faster: using the backlight, HotSyncing, beaming, and even leaving the PalmPilot in its cradle, as described earlier in this chapter.

Finally, if you're willing to pay the higher price for "ultra" alkaline batteries, introduced by most battery companies in 1998, you'll find that they power your PalmPilot longer than any other kind of battery.

The NiMH Future

The most promising battery technology for the Palm platform is not NiCad or rechargeable alkaline, but nickel-metal-hydride (NiMH). These rechargeables, made in AAA sizes by Panasonic and others, have much higher capacity than their rivals and have no memory effect. Their charge does drop off rapidly when exhausted, but the timing of the PalmPilot's warnings can be adjusted with software, such as the shareware Voltage Control, so that you're still given plenty of warning. Palm Computing is enthusiastically studying NiMH technology for inclusion in new products.

Executive Tip Summary

- A *soft reset* is among the most useful troubleshooting tips you can know—for use when the PalmPilot is frozen. To perform one, insert the unscrewed stylus-cap pin or a straightened paper clip gently into the Reset hole on the back panel until the device turns on again.

- Carry a paper clip in the battery compartment so you'll be ready to do a soft reset when necessary, or use the unscrewable stylus end-cap.

- If you think it might be helpful to erase your PalmPilot completely, perform a *hard reset*. While pressing the power button, push a paper clip or the stylus cap pin into the Reset hole on the back panel. When the message on the screen tells you to do so, press the scroll-up plastic button. Your PalmPilot is now as empty as the day you bought it.

- If you don't want your PalmPilot to shut off automatically to save battery power, use one of the secret Dot Commands: draw the ShortCut symbol (a lowercase cursive L), a period, and then the number 3. Now the palmtop will only turn off when you actually turn it off yourself. (To restore the auto-off feature, return to the General screen of the Preferences application and choose something, anything, from the "Auto-off after" pop-up menu.)

- If you're having trouble HotSyncing, the problem is most likely related to fax or modem software or, on Windows, confusion about which COM port the HotSync cradle is attached to.

- Your information is safe in the PalmPilot for several minutes when the batteries are removed. Even with drained batteries, though, your PalmPilot data is safe for several weeks (even if the PalmPilot won't turn on).

- Consider rechargeable NiMH batteries if the idea of rechargeables is attractive to you. Avoid NiCads, however; at the end of each charge, they deplete too quickly for your PalmPilot to warn you.

- If you have a Palm III or later model, $30 buys you 40 percent more RAM in the form of FlashPro, ingenious commercial software from TRG.

18

The Palm Family,
Model by Model

Palm Computing has been introducing new PalmPilot models at an increasing rate. No longer does the "one generation per year" policy seem to apply. Here are the details of the 12 PalmPilots and clones that have been released up through the middle of 1999, along with the upgrade options for each. (See Chapter 1, *The 3×5-Inch Powerhouse*, for photos.)

First Generation: Pilot 1000, Pilot 5000

These original models debuted in 1996, introducing the world to the principal Pilot principles: small size, extremely focused software, long battery life, and simple design. They offered these features:

- Built-in *programs* (Date Book, Address Book, To Do list, calculator, and Memo Pad; see Chapter 4, *The Four Primary Programs*)

- 128K (on the Pilot 1000) or 512K of memory (on the Pilot 5000)

Of course, 128K may not seem like much memory. But the Pilot gets a lot of mileage out of a kilobyte. 128K is enough to hold 2,500 addresses, memos, and calendar entries; 512K holds 5,000 such entries.

Still, if you're feeling claustrophobic, you can upgrade your Pilot 1000 or 5000 to the Palm III for $130. After you install the new circuit board, your upgraded machine will become a Palm III in every significant respect, including its 2MB of RAM and infrared beaming, except one: you'll lack the backlighting feature. Visit *http://www.palm.com* for details.

You can upgrade these original models in a less expensive manner, too—you can ensure that they're running the latest possible version of the Palm operating system. To find out what version of the OS you have, tap Applications → Menu →

App → Memory. If you don't have version 1.06, install it; if you have Palm Desktop 3.0 or later, you'll find it in the Update folder in your Palm folder. Otherwise, you can download it from *http://www.palm.com*. You'll gain improved reliability and eliminate memory fragmentation problems (see Chapter 17, *Troubleshooting*).

Second Generation: PalmPilot Personal, PalmPilot Professional

The 1997 PalmPilot models added several important features to the original design—in addition to the word Palm at the beginning of the name:

- *Backlighting*, as described in Chapter 1. A tiny light-bulb design adorns the on/off switch to remind you of the switch's dual function.

- *Palm OS 2.0*. This improved version of the built-in software offers dozens of welcome enhancements to the built-in programs. For example, the Calendar program now offers a month-at-a-glance view; you can reschedule Calendar events by dragging them to different days of the week; you can reorder items in the Memo Pad's table of contents; and individual Memo Pad screens now have scroll bars that let you move easily through longer documents. You'll read about these enhancements in Chapter 4.

- *512K of memory*.

- *Expense*. A program for recording your expenses while on the road, suitable for submitting to your boss for reimbursement when you return (see Chapter 5, *The Other Built-In Programs*).

- *Palm Game Pack*. HardBall (otherwise known as Breakout), SubHunt, Puzzle (slide the tiles back into the correct square matrix), and MineHunt. More about these games in Chapter 5.

PalmPilot Professional

The Professional model offers everything you've read about so far, plus:

- *Mail*. An Internet email program that doesn't actually dial into the Internet, but rather scoops up any unread mail from your desktop computer's email program. See Chapter 13, *Email Anywhere*, for details.

- *TCP/IP capability*. In other words, your PalmPilot can access information over company networks or the Internet. For example, you can perform HotSyncs from any cradle attached to your company's network or by dialing into such a network from the road. Having TCP/IP features also means you can browse the World Wide Web with your PalmPilot, an amazing feat described in Chapter 14, *The Web in Your Palm*.

- *1MB of memory*. That's enough for 10,000 names, calendar dates, and so on.

Smaller Enhancements on Both Models

But along with those big-ticket improvements came a host of smaller enhancements, warmly welcomed by PalmPilot fans:

Universal features

- Dots at the lower corners of the Graffiti writing area summon the Graffiti keyboard (if you tap the left one) or number pad (if you tap the right one).

- The Lookup command, described in Chapter 4, lets you grab phone numbers from the Address Book program without having to launch it.

- If you highlight some text—in any program—and then tap the Find icon, the selected text is automatically placed into the "Find what" blank.

- The dark gray plastic of the case is sturdier and less brittle than on the original Pilot models.

- The free carrying case is made of a nicer, more leatherlike material.

The Date Book

- The Date Book program now has a month-at-a-glance view (see Chapter 4). In the Week view, you can drag events from one date or time to another and if you tap a time bar, a popup box appears at the top of the screen to identify the appointment. Furthermore, tapping the date (at the top of the screen) changes it to show the current time.

- You can now set up alarms for nontimed events. These alarms take the form of an alert message that appears when you turn on the PalmPilot on the designated day.

- A new preference option lets you hide empty time slots in Day view.

- Tiny icons now appear beside the names of appointments that have alarms, notes, or repetition associated with them.

- If you write a number, the Set Time dialog box appears automatically, so that you can tap the specific beginning and ending times for a new appointment.

- Alarms repeat every five minutes until you dismiss them.

The Memo Pad

- The Memo Pad's table-of-contents "home page" has scroll bars, and you can choose how you'd like it sorted—alphabetically or in an order you create by dragging items up or down the list.

- Each memo in the table-of-contents list is numbered.

Graffiti and stylus gestures

- You can control which function is performed when you draw a straight line up the face of the PalmPilot: display the keyboard, turn on backlighting, show a Graffiti cheat sheet, or "turn off and lock."

- A Graffiti Help command is available in all of the built-in PalmPilot programs.

- You don't have to install the Giraffe game; it's now stored in the PalmPilot's ROM chips, saving you that much free RAM.

- The Caps Lock indicator (that appears when you draw the "caps lock" Graffiti stroke) now looks like the Caps Lock indicator on the Macintosh—an arrow with a small pedestal—rather than two upward-pointing arrows.

Memory, the Applications screen, and Preferences

- The Memory program lists your installed programs alphabetically, and the Delete Applications screen can be scrolled by pressing the up/down plastic buttons on the PalmPilot.

- You can turn sound on or off independently for alarms, error beeps, and game sounds.

- A new option lets the Address Book "remember last category" (see Chapter 4).

- You can scroll to an application by writing its initial in the Graffiti area.

To Do

- You can control how your to do items are sorted.

- You can opt to have the date of completion recorded when you check off a to do item.

- You can, if you wish, view a column that shows each to do item's category.

Pilot Desktop 2.0

The 1997 models were accompanied by new Windows desktop software, now called Pilot Desktop 2.0. This program, too, was dramatically enhanced:

- You can print your weekly or monthly calendars, dial phone numbers (if you have a modem) from the Address Book, and view your To Do list while using the Date Book.

- You can insert the current date or time (anywhere you can type) by pressing predefined keystrokes.

- The Profiles feature described in Chapter 8, *Palm Desktop: Windows*, lets you preload canned data into multiple new PalmPilots.

- You can import text files into the Memo Pad that are larger than 4K. (Such files are split into multiple memos, each within the 4K limit.)

How to upgrade a PalmPilot

As with the first Pilots, these models' OS versions have been upgraded several times. At this writing, the most recent version is 2.05. If you check your version number (tap Applications → Menu → App → Info or Memory) and find that you have some earlier version, install the 2.05 patch (it's in your Palm → Update folder, or you can download it from the Palm web site).

Or, if you crave the infrared transceiver and updated OS of the Palm III, you can order the Palm III memory-card upgrade (for $130).

Programs that worked fine on original Pilot models should work fine on Palm-Pilots and Palm III models. The reverse, however, may not be true—new programs may not be backward-compatible with earlier PalmPilot models.

But there is one caveat for ugpraders to new PalmPilot models: Any version of Pilot Desktop or Palm Desktop can open the files created by previous versions (on your desktop computer). But once you save your data from the newer version, you can't open your files with the previous version again.

Third Generation: Palm III

After having so carefully cultivated a recognizable brand name, 3Com adopted a new and confusing name for the third generation of its famous palmtop. Threatened legal action by the makers of Pilot *pens* explain the move.

This model introduced infrared beaming, a sleeker case shape and 2MB of memory. A matching desktop application for Windows, Palm Desktop 3.0, accompanied the Palm III.

Once again, though, those major items accompany a longer list of minor enhancements:

- The screen is clearer and higher-contrast than any previous PalmPilot model. To prevent accidental screen changing, the contrast wheel is now recessed into the edge of the unit.

- A sturdier stylus with a metal shaft has replaced the flimsy plastic model—and the end cap unscrews to reveal a pin that's perfectly sized to fit the Reset hole (see Chapter 17, *Troubleshooting*). There's also a new, removable, flip-up protective lid that can lock into either of two open-position angles. (You can't remove or insert the stylus while the lid is fully open—get into the habit of removing the stylus before opening the lid.)

- The HotSync jack (the serial port) is now protected by a spring-loaded shutter; the power button is 50% larger; and the HotSync cradle has been redesigned to fit the Palm III's tapered bottom end. (You can get a Palm III to

Going In and Out of Stylus

The stylus provided with the Palm III and its III-series successor is superior to the previous plastic Palm stylus in every way except one—early versions have a way of dropping out of the stylus pocket. The metal shaft provides little friction, and is susceptible to expansion and contraction with temperature.

Online Palm fans were quick to share their various solutions, most of which involved holding either the stylus or the PalmPilot over an open flame, melting the stylus pocket or the stylus itself into a shape that would provide more friction. The most effective solution is far less dangerous: wrap a piece of tape around the shaft. The added width will keep the barrel securely in the stylus pocket.

And while we're talking about stylus tricks, consider this: the clip at the top of the Palm III/IIIx stylus is cleverly shaped to guide the stylus into the pocket without much aim on your part. Put the tip of the stylus into the pocket, give it a sloppy shove, and watch in amazement. As long as the clip isn't fully rotated away from its outward-facing position, it will automatically straighten the stylus into correct alignment with the pocket on its way in, snapping satisfyingly into its secure position.

work in a previous model's HotSync cradle if you use both hands to hold it in place, but older models won't mate with the Palm III cradle.)

- You must now remove four tiny screws and remove the back panel to get at the memory card.

- When you tap the Applications button, a dramatically improved Applications application appears. Using menus, you can now assign your various programs to categories and choose whether to view them as icons or in a list. (Press the Applications button repeatedly to cycle through the different categories of programs.) The Memory program is gone, having been replaced by Info and Delete commands in the Applications program's menus.

- Each Palm program now offers one or two Beam commands: for example, Beam Item or Beam Category. You can beam a memo, a to-do item, a Date Book appointment, a person's Address Book entry, or an entire category of any of the above. You can also transmit add-on programs to people equipped with Palm III or later models, as described in Chapter 15.

- If you hold down the plastic Address Book button at the bottom of an infrared-equipped Palm Pilot, your designated "business card" (an Address Book entry you've designated as yours) is instantly beamed to any Palm device with range.

- All of the built-in programs (except Expense) offer a Font menu command that lets you choose from among three typefaces: Standard, Bold, or Large. More important, the behind-the-scenes software can accommodate new fonts that you install yourself.

- The Mail program's Preferences dialog box offers a new mail-filtering option: Unread, which sucks in only unopened email from your desktop computer when you HotSync.

- On the PC, there's now a folder called Add-On (in the Palm folder). This is the "waiting room" for freshly downloaded PalmPilot programs you may want to install later. The PC software—now called Palm Desktop 3.0—also offers file linking, as described in Chapter 8.

- The speaker is louder and offers a choice of seven alarm sounds. Palm programmers can now add new sounds, too. They're actually little standard MIDI music files, available by the thousands from the Internet. (See Chapter 11, *The Secret Multimedia World*, for details.)

- Palm Desktop now offers an Install button. It replaces the InstallApp that came with previous PalmPilot models, letting you select multiple programs at once for installation at the next HotSync. The new dialog box that appears shows the size of the file you're about to install, too.

  Similarly, a new Palm Mail setup wizard/program greatly simplifies setting up HotSyncing with your Windows email program.

You can turn your Palm III or III-family palmtop into a self-standing, upright desk ornament, suitable for reading notes, consulting your calendar, or showing off a photo of your spouse.

The trick is the removable hard cover, a feature not found on any other models. By pulling the hinge pins away from the machine, you'll find that this cover comes off easily. Take the stylus out, too. Now flip the cover around (so that the inside surface faces the Palm III), move it to the back of the device, and reattach it to the hinge holes.

Finally, reinsert the stylus into its pocket as far as it will go. You'll find that the plastic lid acts as an easel, propping up the device at a perfect viewing angle, and the top of the stylus acts as a hinge brake to prevent the A-frame arrangement from collapsing. Call up your speech notes, driving directions, or family photo, and enjoy your handy, hands-free handheld.

How to upgrade a Palm III

One of the most remarkable features of the Palm III and later models is that the code that stores the PalmPilot programs, as well as the OS, is stored in flash RAM, as described in previous chapter. This code can be updated via software as necessary, without having to replace the chips themselves.

For example, as of the end of summer 1999, you can flash-update any Palm III or later device to Palm OS 3.3 (available from the *http://www.palm.com* web site). The update comes with a utility program that backs up your programs and data, installs the 3.3 software, and then restores your stuff. (When running this kind of ROM updater, you'll need to leave your Palm device in the cradle for up to 10 minutes, so make sure your batteries aren't on their last legs.)

You can also upgrade the Palm III's memory, as described at the end of this chapter.

IBM WorkPad

IBM produces clones of the Palm III (called the WorkPad 86022X), Palm IIIx (called the WorkPad 80230X), and Palm V (called the WorkPad 86040U). These devices are identical to their 3Com equivalents except for the case colors, which are black instead of gray. (Details are at *http://www.pc.ibm.com/us/workpad/index.html.*)

Symbol SPT 1500

In 1998, Symbol Technologies (*http://www.symbol.com/palm*), a long-standing manufacturer of bar-code-reading machines, designed an impressive $590 handheld that adds, to the basic Palm III, an integrated laser-beam barcode reader. The resulting device holds great promise for warehouse inventory-takers, forward-thinking grocery stores, doctors and nurses, and anyone else for whom data collection in the field is important.

Alas, the SPT 1500 doesn't come with any such software; finding it, or getting it written for your purposes, is up to you. (Every major Palm programming kit—Satellite Forms, CodeWarrior, CASL, Pendragon, GCC, plus Symbol's own Penright and Ideam EZTrack, let you create scan-ready applications. Some ready-to-use programs are also available, such as Stevens Creek Software's Take an Order, and On Hand order-entry and inventory programs.)

In the meantime, you can have a blast just drawing on the walls using the laser beam as a pointer (not into people's eyes, please).

Qualcomm pdQ SmartPhone

In the interest of continued briefcase-lightening, Qualcomm licensed the Palm operating system for inclusion in its most intriguing cell phone, the pdQ (*http://www.qualcomm.com/pdQ*). Picture a PalmPilot nestled into the handset of a CDMA-format (digital) cell phone, and you'll get the idea. Any number in your Address Book can be dialed automatically, wherever you are; likewise, email directly from your Address Book is instantaneous and wireless. (All other features of the PalmPilot portion are identical to those described in this book.)

1999 saw the release of two SmartPhone models: the pdQ 800 (a dual-mode, analog/CDMA digital cell phone) and the pdQ 1900 (a CDMA digital Sprint PCS phone). Neither is nearly as compact as, say, a cell phone or a PalmPilot. But for Palm fans trying to consolidate the number of gadgets they carry around, the ingenious, expensive pdQ is a tantalizing prospect.

Fourth Generation: Palm IIIx, Palm V

Two new models debuted in February 1999: the Palm IIIx and Palm V. Aside from the physical characteristics described in this section, one of the most important internal changes was the introduction of a new processor—the Motorola Dragonball EZ (instead of the traditional Dragonball). While similar to its predecessor in many ways, this chip accepts less expensive memory modules, which means that these models' list prices may well slip downward even more rapidly than usual.

The new chip requires a new Palm OS to accommodate it: Palm OS 3.1. The changes are invisible to you; except that the screen can now display 16 shades of gray instead of 4, they don't offer any new features. (You can't install this new OS on any previous model, not that it would do you any good.)

Unfortunately, several dozen popular Palm programs proved to have incompatibilities with the new OS. Because software authors generally scramble to solve such problems, use the web links on this book's CD-ROM to check for updates of any programs that seem to cause problems for your Palm IIIx or Palm V.

Palm IIIx

The Palm IIIx looks and works almost exactly like its older brother, the Palm III. But it offers a few bonuses:

Much clearer screen
> The new screen technology, made possible by a new, ultrathin 3M film placed behind the display, makes the background lighter gray-green and the images much crisper.

4MB memory

Enough for 40,000 names, notes, dates, and so on.

A more rugged design

The memory module inside is no longer a separate card that can come loose. Instead, memory is fastened directly to the main circuit board.

An interior slot

Moving the memory module onto the main circuit board means that an available slot remains on the circuit board. You can fill the slot with still more memory—or add-on circuitry not even imagined yet.

Free HotSync extras

The Palm IIIx package includes the Network HotSync software (described in Chapter 6, *HotSync, Step by Step*) and a software module that lets you HotSync with Microsoft Outlook for Windows. Both were once extra-cost options.

Palm Computing designed the Palm IIIx to be the expandable workhorse, the one corporations will likely buy for distribution to their employees.

Palm V

At its release, the Palm IIIx's impact was overshadowed by the simultaneous unveiling of the flashy, fashionable, slimline Palm V (see Figure 1-8). This $449 gadget is intended to be the Mont Blanc pen, or the Lexus automobile, of handhelds: it's half as thick as previous models, slightly shorter, 25% lighter, and—with its heat-blasted, anodized aluminum case—much more fashionable than the plastic models, too. A leather cover closes over the front of the screen.

Carefully protecting its crown jewel—the simplicity of the software design—Palm made no software changes to this device. But the hardware changes are plenty:

Built-in rechargeable batteries

The new design does away with the AAA batteries that have been a fact of PalmPilot life. Instead, a built-in lithium-ion battery recharges whenever the device is sitting in its matching, equally cool-looking HotSync cradle. (A charge lasts for about a month of typical use.) The charging goes quickly, from totally drained to fully charged in a couple of hours; in fact, just HotSyncing once a day is enough time in the cradle to keep the Palm V perpetually charged.

A $50 travel adapter is available for those who'd rather not lug the cradle along. It includes a standard AC power cable/cradle, plus a handful of prong adapters for overseas use.

Solving the Backlight Problem on the 1999 Palm Models

The screen used on these latest PalmPilot models is almost universally beloved. It's so superior to previous screen technologies that it's almost painful to go back to using, say, a Palm III.

The one glaring exception is the backlighting. For some reason, 3Com's designers chose to do something radical with the backlight of such models as the Palm IIIx, Palm V, and Palm VII backlight. Instead of merely illuminating the light gray-green background of the palmtop, as on previous models, the backlight also inverts the image, black-for-white. Now you get glowing gray-green text against a solid black background.

In pitch-black darkness, this arrangement is arguably clearer than the previous backlight system. In dusk or shadow, however, it makes the display nearly unreadable. Across the land, upgraded owners of previous models are cursing the seemingly arbitrary change.

Fortunately, switching your palmtop back to the old, much clearer backlighting system takes only one second and costs nothing. It requires the use of a *dot command*, such as those described in Chapter 17. Unlike some of those commands, however, the backlighting-reversal dot command is rock-solid and perfectly safe.

All you have to do is launch a program where you can do writing, such as the Memo Pad (or, for quicker access, the Find dialog box). Make the ShortCut symbol (which looks like a cursive lowercase L), make a period (tap twice), and write the number 8 (on the right side of the Graffiti area). You'll see the words *[Normal Backlight]* appear; you've succeeded in restoring the clearer illumination scheme to your palmtop.

If you ever want to restore the default, inverted-image backlighting setting, repeat the ShortCut. This time, you'll see the words *[Inverting Backlight]*, indicating that your ShortCut worked.

(Backlight dot command not working? Then maybe you fall into this specific category: you've been using an older model and decided to transfer its data into your newer PalmPilot simply by dragging the data from one user-named folder on your hard drive into another, as described in Chapter 6. In such cases, the dot command doesn't work. To solve the problem, do a complete backup using a program like Backup Buddy, which is included on this book's CD-ROM; do a hard reset, as described at the beginning of Chapter 17; finally, open your Palm → Users → *your PalmPilot name* → Backup folder and throw away the file called *Graffiti_Shortcuts.prc*. After the next HotSync, the backlight dot command will work properly.)

Powered HotSync cradle

> The Palm V HotSync cradle is also an AC adapter. Palm V fans have quickly learned to leave the device on, in its cradle, all day long, serving as the best-looking desk clock, calendar, or family-photo frame ever made.

Best screen yet

> The Palm V's screen clarity is breathtaking, slightly better than even the Palm IIIx's.

Stylus channels on both sides

> Left-handers can rejoice at last, because the stylus may now be tucked into either channel. The remaining channel opens a world of possibilities: for example, it can be used as the hinge slot for a cover, such as the included leather cover. (This slot could also accommodate the hinge of the beautiful, but overpriced, brushed-aluminum hard cover, which Palm discontinued soon after customers noticed the aluminum peeling away from the plastic shell.) Palm also markets a combination ball-point/stylus whose pocket clip slides into the channel; the pen itself hugs the side of the device. (Details on these add-ons in Appendix B, *PalmPilot Accessories.*)

For some PalmPiloteers, the Palm V harbors a single downside: the new design of its HotSync jack renders it incompatible with all previous serial-port gadgets. You can't, for example, hook up any of the gadgets described earlier in Chapter 1, such as the GPS receiver or the TaleVibes vibrator, to the Palm V. (Nor can you use the HotSync modem from other PalmPilot models with the Palm V; see Appendix B for more on the Palm V's special modem.)

History tells us, however, that the legions of Palm engineers won't take long to offer those products in Palm V format—or to design an adapter.

Fifth Generation: Palm VII

In early summer 1999, Palm Computing revealed a dramatic new direction for its wildly popular palmtops—wireless Internet. Only half an inch taller than a standard Palm IIIx, the Palm VII nonetheless houses far more components, including a two-way radio transmitter, antenna, and NiCad rechargeable battery designed to power the transmitter. The result is a PalmPilot that can check and send email or check web pages without having to plug into a wall.

Complete details on the Palm VII, including tips and troubleshooting, are in Chapter 16, *Palm VII: Wireless Email, Wireless Web.*

Palm V and the Self-Activating Power Switch

In an effort to ensure that your Palm V won't turn on by itself in your pocket, 3Com redesigned the power button. It's now at the top of the unit, where a forceful finger push is required to turn the device on.

Those designers, however, overlooked the other four power buttons, the Memo Pad, Address Book, and other buttons. Because the device is so thin, and because the included leather cover is so flexible, such buttons have a tendency to get pressed in your pocket, thus turning on the Palm V. Then there's the problem of alarms, which turn the device on without any button being pressed.

None of this would ordinarily be a problem, since disposable-battery cost isn't an issue. The real problem is that, once turned on, continued pressure on the face of the Palm V presses the scroll buttons, which are the highest protrusions from the face of the palmtop. The scroll buttons do what scroll buttons are supposed to do when they reach the end of the scrolling area—they chirp. And as long as pressure is applied, they chirp rapidly over and over again, resulting in a chipmunk-like chattering. The sound of happy rodents in your pocket doesn't connote quite the same degree of style and class you were probably hoping for when you bought the Palm V.

You have a couple of options. First, you could consider cutting a hole in the leatherette flap cover to accommodate the two scroll buttons. This solution certainly isn't elegant or good-looking, but it does neatly solve the problem of pressure being applied to your scroll buttons in your pocket.

Second, you can glue one-third of a rubber O-ring to the inside of the leather flap, just above the scroll button, thus protecting the scroll button from pressure. There are software solutions, too: the Palm OS 3.1.1 update (from the Support area of *http://www.palm.com*) disables the Scroll Up button whenever an alarm message is on the screen.

Finally, if you find your Palm V waking up in your pocket from button pressure, not just when alarms go off, consider StayOffHack, included on this book's CD-ROM; it turns off the Palm V immediately after a hardware button turns it on. (This, of course, deprives the device of that convenience—being able to turn it on using, say, the Memo Pad or Address Book button—but for many V fans, it's that or the chipmunks.)

Memory Upgrades

Just because your PalmPilot came with, say, 2MB or 4MB of RAM doesn't mean you're stuck with that little. Believe it or not, the circuitry is designed to accommodate up to 12MB of RAM on 256 different cards (although you'll have a tough time getting them to fit in any current model). In fact, the OS is designed to handle a theoretical limit 4GB of memory—that's a *lot* of Doc files.

If you'd like more RAM, and the FlashPro trick described in Chapter 17 isn't enough, the next step is to buy a memory upgrade. For example, Technology Resource Group (TRG)'s catalog includes the Super Pilot upgrade, which brings the memory total of a Pilot, PalmPilot, Palm III, or WorkPad to either 3MB or 8MB (for $200 to $250). For the Palm IIIx, there's the Xtra Xtra upgrade, which gives you a total of 8MB (for $150). (The company ships you a complete memory/ROM card; you install it yourself. Visit *http://www.trgnet.com* for current deals.)

The Palm V is a tougher nut to crack, because its circuit board has no memory slot, and the ultra-slim case itself offers very little interior room. Still, EFIG (*http://www.efig.com*) is willing to cram 8MB into your tiny palmtop (for $250). The result isn't perfect—tiny traces of white glue are visible around the seams of the case, and your battery charge gets used up almost twice as fast when the machine is not in use. (The storage capacity of dead batteries drops, too—when the Palm V is out of juice, your data is normally safe for another week; with this upgrade, it lives for only two and a half days.)

This latter upgrade, by the way, invalidates your warranty.

Executive Tip Summary

- For $130, you can turn any Pilot or PalmPilot model into a Palm III, complete with all features except backlighting.

- Free updates for each Palm OS version are available on this book's CD-ROM (and from the 3Com web site). They're well worth installing, if you don't already have them, for reasons of stability and memory management.

- If a Palm program is causing problems for your Palm IIIx, Palm V, it's probably because of an incompatibility with the new Dragonball EZ processor (or the Palm OS 3.1 that accommodates it). Check the software author's web site for an updated version.

VI

Appendixes

A

100 Programs Worth Knowing About

On the CD-ROM with this book, you'll find over 3,100 programs for the PalmPilot. All of this software comes from PalmCentral.com, the largest Palm-software web site on the Internet.

Accompanying all the software on the CD-ROM is a catalog program, called the PalmCentral CD Catalog, that lists, illustrates, describes, and even installs each of these programs onto your PalmPilot. If you're hunting for, say, beekeeping software or a graphic that illustrates the third cervical vertebra, you should begin your quest by searching this program.

The purpose of this chapter is to bring about 100 of those programs to your attention—100 of the most useful, most important, or most unusual. Some of these, such as HackMaster, SwitchHack, and DateBk3, are worth installing immediately. The appeal of the others depends on you and your lifestyle.

But all of them serve as testimony to Palm Computing's wisdom in making the PalmPilot an open, easy-to-program platform. You'll note that the vast majority of the programs listed here and on the CD-ROM were written by individuals—and cost nothing or very little. That should show you something else, too: that the world of PalmPiloteers is a true community. That's why the web home pages for each program are listed—and linked to—in the PalmCentral Catalog; true, some may go out of date or change, but at least you have a first resort when it comes to downloading newer versions of these programs or getting help with them.

How to Use This Appendix

The software descriptions in this appendix are organized by category, exactly the same way this book's CD-ROM, the PalmCentral CD Catalog, and the Palm Central. com web site are organized. If you find something that looks interesting, launch the PalmCentral CD Catalog program on this book's CD-ROM to read more about it, visit the author's web site, or install it onto your palmtop. Along the way, you'll also find capsule reviews of some of the most interesting commercial Palm software.

Most of the programs listed here, however, are shareware. In other words, you're free to try out the software, but if you keep using it beyond, say, 30 days, the honor system compels you to send the author a check for the requested amount. (Instructions for payment are generally found within the software.)

Platinum Certified

Most of the programs listed in this chapter are shareware or freeware, but commercial software is also plentiful. As you peruse ads, catalogs, and web sites, you may run across one of two logos that pertain to PalmPilot software: one that says Palm Computing Platform Compatible and another called Platinum Certified.

That first logo, Palm Computing Platform Compatible, means that the software company has agreed to avoid several technical programming no-nos. This program is run on the honor system, but it's better than nothing.

A harder logo to qualify for is the Platinum level. This kind of certification is awarded by 3Com to software programs that have been inspected (by a company called Product Quality Partners, *http://www.qpqa.com/qp3com.html*). PQP tests the software not just for clean programming, but also to make sure the program follows PalmPilot user-interface guideline—how menus, checkboxes, and other interface components work.

In general, a piece of software bearing the Platinum mark should be stabler and more consistent with 3Com-written programs. (There's a list of current Platinum software at *http://www.palm.com/software/pilosoft.html*.)

Applications

This category features general-purpose Palm programs: launchers, enhancements for the built-in Palm programs, and so on.

Actioneer

This fascinating commercial program uses artificial-intelligence techniques to translate hastily written instructions, such as "call Bob tomorrow 2 p.m.," into full-fledged entries automatically recorded in the correct Palm application—memo, to do list, and so on—or even several of them simultaneously. One version ($20) goes on the palmtop; a corresponding version ($40) works in Palm Desktop for Windows. Actioneer, Inc. (See Figure A-1.)

Figure A-1. From left to right: Actioneer, Launch 'Em, and ToDo Plus.

Launch 'Em

You can use this program to replace the standard Applications screen on your palmtop. The advantage, as shown in Figure A-1, is the tabs across the top that make it easier to file and find your apps. You can drag and drop the icons as well as the tabs, password protect certain tabs, and so on. Synergy, $10.

ToDo Plus

As noted earlier in this book, one of the limitations of the built-in To Do program is that you can't create repeating tasks, and you can't associate alarms with to-do items. This clever enhancement eliminates those drawbacks (see Figure A-1). Hands High Software, $20.

Calculators/Math

The calculators listed here are only the most general-interest programs; see the Palm Central CD Index program on the CD-ROM for calculators that convert time, tides, sunrise and sunset, body mass, wind chill, coin totals, file downloads, video time code, planet positions, RF impedance, and much more.

EZ Tip

The world has waited too long for a program like this: you specify how much the restaurant bill was, what percent tax and tip, and how many people ate—and the program tells you what everyone owes. Unlike the simpler programs Big Tipper, TipMe, TipCalc, QuickTip, and so on (also included on the CD-ROM), this program even lets you input each person's order amount, for those awkward times when splitting the tab evenly wouldn't be fair to the guy who had nothing but a salad. Jane Halfond, free. (See Figure A-2.)

Foreign

A quick and easy foreign-currency calculator, one of several included on the CD-ROM. Edmund Seto, $7.

Kalk

Now the PalmPilot can be an RPN calculator, thanks to this program and many like it. Hoger Klawitter, free.

One+One

Throw away that old HP scientific calculator. This algebraic financial and scientific calculator offers dozens of functions and 20 memory registers. Palm-Calc, $15. (See Figure A-2.)

Palm III Converter Pro

Converts every conceivable unit of measurement into any other—pressure, area, volume, temperature, velocity, length, time, and much more. ZingWare, $10.

Pilot MiniCalc, TinySheet, Quicksheet

Surprisingly powerful Palm spreadsheets, described in Chapter 12, *Database and Number Crunching*.

Stamps

A postage calculator for U.S. mail. Simple and invaluable; handles both domestic and international shipping prices. Koichi Terada, free.

Taco Bell Calorie Counter

If there's a symbol for the astonishing breadth of Palm software, it's got to be this program, which quickly and easily displays calories and fat for meals at Taco Bell, as shown in Figure A-2. Shawn Kresal, free.

VCR+ Calculator

Write in the VCR+ code from your newspaper, and this simple calculator tells you what it means—the starting date, time, channel, and duration of the TV show. Laurent Chardonnens, free.

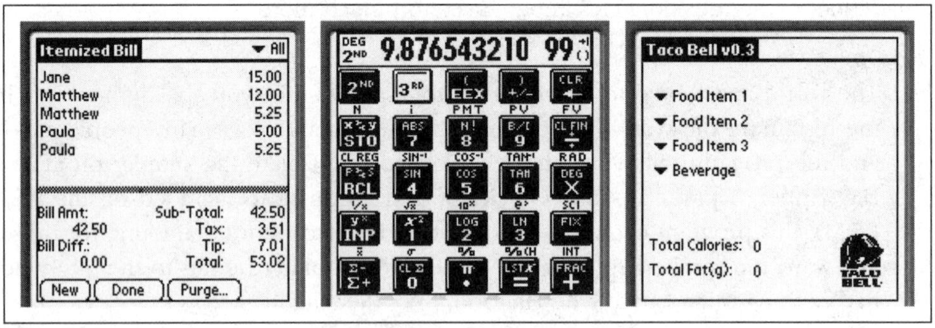

Figure A-2. From left to right: EZ Tip, One+One, Taco Bell Calorie Counter.

Cutesy

These fun-only programs may not make you more productive, but they're probably responsible for selling more PalmPilots than any other category.

BuzzWord

A buzzword generator. Do you need to baffle your clients, or just make yourself sound more intelligent? Try dropping "mandatory fault-tolerant knowledgebase" or "right-sized homogeneous intranet" into conversation. You know Dilbert's boss uses this one. David MacLeod, free.

BioRhythms

Check your physical, emotional, and mental cycles before committing to that big business or relationship deal, as shown in Figure A-3. Jeff Jetton, $5.

Eliza Pilot Psychologist

Your own psychoanalyst on the PalmPilot. She actually responds to your handwritten questions. DDH Software, free.

McRazor

This gag was funniest when the Palm V, code-named Razor, was still under wraps, but it's still hilarious: it turns your PalmPilot into a handheld electric razor, complete with buzzing sound and on/off switch. Mike McCollister, free.

Mirror

Mirror simply turns your entire screen black. Don't laugh—it actually makes your PalmPilot work beautifully as a mirror, suitable for checking makeup or seeing over your shoulder. Bill Westerman, free.

SoftGPS

"My PalmPilot is amazing," you tell friends at a party. "I have a GPS program that can tell me exactly where I am to within one foot of where I'm standing." And then you show them, as you hold out your PalmPilot to show that huge X and the words "YOU ARE HERE." Brad Goodman, free.

Thumb Scan

You explain to your friends that the PalmPilot won't work except when anyone but you places a thumb on the designated spot—and you demonstrate to prove it. (See Figure A-3.) (Actually, it works for you not because of your thumb, but because you're holding down a secret button at the same time.) HeadRUSH Software, free.

Tricorder II

Sure, the PalmPilot's great for keeping track of appointments, but you can't scan for tachyon emissions with it... until now! The hi-tech-looking screen pretends to "scan" your environment for a wide variety of geological, meteorological, and biological phenomenon, as shown in Figure A-3. If you have a Palm

III or IIIx (which has a flip-up front cover), the illusion of the Trek gadget is complete. Jeff Jetton, free.

Figure A-3. From left to right: BioRhythms, Thumb Scan, Tricorder II.

Communications/Internet

This category includes web browsers, email programs, faxing programs, Telnet apps, infrared programs, terminal emulators, pager software, and so on.

DB Fax, HandFax, Mobile WinFax
> As described in Chapter 15, *Paging, Faxing, Printing, and Beaming*, these programs let you send faxes from your modem-equipped PalmPilot.

HandWeb, ProxiWeb, pdQweb
> See Chapter 14, *The Web in Your Palm*, for complete details on these impressive Palm Web browsers.

HandStamp, MultiMail, pdQmail, OneTouch Mail, PocketFlash
> These full-featured email programs for the modem-equipped PalmPilot are described in detail in Chapter 13, *Email Anywhere*.

IRP2PChat
> As described in Chapter 15, now you can send secret instant messages back and forth across the table during important business meetings, and nobody will be the wiser. Lets you beam both text and graphics to any other Palm-Pilot with this program. IS/Complete, $15.

NetNews
> If your PalmPilot has a modem, you can read Internet newsgroups (bulletin boards) with simple programs like this one. Written by Palm Computing's own Gavin Peacock (free).

OmniRemote
> This is the astonishing software that turns your PalmPilot into a remote-control unit for your home entertainment system. Details in Chapter 15.

Palm IRC

The PalmPilot might not seem to be the ideal platform for online chats using the Internet Relay Chat protocol, but this software makes it possible. Hiroyki Okamoto, $10.

Database Programs

For a complete discussion of FileMaker or Access-type database programs on the PalmPilot, see Chapter 12. But this category also includes software to track every other conceivable kind of data—car mileage, beer/wine/cigar collections, commuting schedules, frequent-flyer mileage, hospital patients, telephone calls, videocassettes, shopping lists, and much more.

JFile, HanDbase, Mobile DB

These are the leading Palm database programs, as described in Chapter 12.

AirMiles

As the Read Me file notes, 20 percent of frequent-flyer miles are never redeemed. This program tracks your mileage for various airlines. Hands High Software, $30.

AutoLog

One of several useful car-expense trackers. Logs your gas purchases, oil changes, insurance and other payments, calculates mileage for different day ranges, and can handle multiple cars. John Wolstad, $13.

KarKare

Calculates your gas mileage and tracks your maintenance schedule. (See Figure A-4.) Lee Golden, $15.

TealMeal

One of the classic PalmPilot apps. A database engine that you load up with files containing restaurant databases for your favorite cities. Once thus loaded, you can easily search for local restaurants meeting exacting criteria, such as cheap Italian outdoor restaurants that take Visa. (See Figure A-4.) TealPoint Software, $14.

Time Reporter

The ultimate tracker of time and clients. This program HotSyncs your time/client records directly into the popular TimeSlips Deluxe desktop software. (See Figure A-4.) Iambic, $120.

Development

This category contains nearly 200 useful tools for programmers: assemblers, icon editors, PocketC libraries, CASL modules, and much more. (For a full discussion of

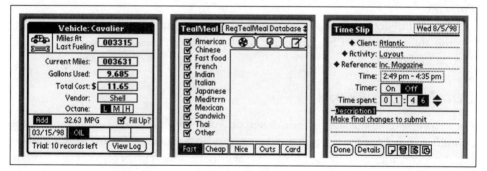

Figure A-4. From left to right: KarKare, TealMeal, Time Reporter.

writing Palm applications, see *Palm Programming: The Developer's Guide*, also from O'Reilly & Associates.)

The Most Useful Program on the CD-ROM

Unless you've upgraded your PalmPilot to 256MB of RAM, you won't be able to install every program on this book's CD-ROM onto it simultaneously. How, then, are you supposed to try the included programs out without having to painstakingly HotSync them one by one onto your palmtop?

Do it the way the programmers do—by running such programs on your desktop computer, in a PalmPilot lookalike program called the Palm OS Emulator, or POSE. This program comes in a Windows version and a Mac version, and looks and acts exactly like an actual PalmPilot—except you can type on your computer keyboard instead of having to use the mouse to crank out Graffiti strokes. There's no better, faster way to try out new programs before you actually install them on your PalmPilot. It's included on this book's CD-ROM. Don't miss it!

Document/Memo/Editors/Outliners/Viewers

If you're looking for word processors or outliners, you've found the right category. This group includes the Doc readers—that is, the closest thing the PalmPilot has to word processors—described in Chapter 10, *PalmPilot: The Electronic Book*, along with various related programs.

AportisDoc, TealDoc, SmartDoc, QED, RichReader
See Chapter 10 for full descriptions of these popular Doc-reading programs.

AvantGo
This powerful and elegantly designed Windows program automatically grabs web pages and converts them to Palm-readable format, complete with graphics and hotlinks. See Chapter 14 for more details. AvantGo, free.

BrainForest

An intriguing cross between an outliner and to do list. HotSyncs directly to BrainForest for the Macintosh or for Windows. Aportis, $30.

Hi-Note

This program is a popular shareware hybrid—a hierarchical memo pad that lets you organize your memos in outline form. You can even make little drawings part of your outline. Cyclos, $20.

Drawing/Graphics

It surprises many people that the PalmPilot is such a good graphics machine. But the programs in this category, and those described in Chapter 11, *The Secret Multimedia World*, prove it.

Backdrop

This fascinating utility lets you use any Image Viewer graphics file (see Chapter 11) as a desktop background for all your Palm programs. Backdrop EZ, for the Palm IIIx and Palm V, can even handle four-color background pictures. Josh Freeman, $18.

DinkyPad, Doodle, TealPaint, PalmDraw

These classic doodling programs are described fully in Chapter 11.

ImageViewer

This classic program lets you convert your desktop-based photo files into Palm-viewable graphics, as described in Chapter 11.

Flip

Just as you doodled in the margins of your high-school math book to make simple animations, so this little program lets you turn your PalmPilot into a flip book. Andermation, $10.

PalmSmear

As described in Chapter 11, this bizarre program lets you distort photos—and even animate the distortions. Mark Chauo-Kuang Yang, free.

Snapshot

When it comes time to write your own Palm book, you can use this program to take "snapshots" of Palm screen images. Joseph Strout, free.

TinyViewer

A more memory-conservative viewer of ImageViewer files. Ken Shirriff, free.

Educational

In this category, you'll find flash-card programs, tutorials, and lessons for math, languages, Morse code, and more.

FlashCard!

> Your basic flash card program, based on the Memo Pad, for drilling yourself on any topic you desire. Martin Wilber, free.

Finance

> Track your finances, compare loans, track stock prices, convert currencies, and perform other financial tasks with these programs.

ExpensePlus

> This commercial program is quick, smart, and far more flexible at expense tracking than the built-in Palm Expense program, as shown in Figure A-5. Example: When you tap Meal, it proposes Breakfast, Lunch, or Dinner according to the current time of day. WalletWare, $70.

Financial Consultant

> This program is designed for real estate and banking people who could use a powerful financial calculator on the road. (See Figure A-5.) LandWare, $30.

Loan Wizard Pro

> Another calculator, this one geared toward comparing loans. Don't get a mortgage without it. MindWeave, $25. (The $15 non-Pro version doesn't let you store the statistics of multiple loan offers.)

Pocket Quicken

> A nearly full-fledged Quicken clone, complete with transaction splits, memorized transactions, auto-fill, password protection, categories and classes, and Quicken-like transaction register. (See Figure A-5.) You go about your day, recording transactions—and they all appear automatically in your Quicken file (Windows or Macintosh) at the next HotSync. (The transfer is one-way—transactions you record on the desktop aren't sent back to the PalmPilot.) LandWare, $40.

Portfolio Manager

> A handy pocket-sized place to record your stock holdings, so that you can look at them and gloat at any time of the day or night. Kenneth Tsang, $25.

Foreign Language

These programs include dictionaries, fonts, and localized operating system versions for using your PalmPilot in dozens of non-English languages.

Dictionary

> This powerful two-way translation program accepts foreign-language modules, many of which are also included on the CD-ROM—English/Spanish, English/ Dutch, English/French, English/German, English/Japanese, and so on—that turn it into a nearly universal phrase book. Evolutionary Systems, $18.

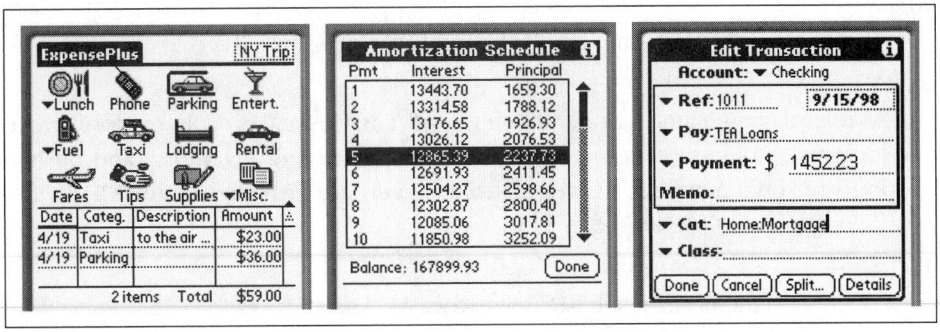

Figure A-5. From left to right: ExpensePlus, Financial Consultant, Pocket Quicken.

Games

You know when your electronic gadget has truly arrived when the legions of programmers worldwide turn their attention to making it a game machine. Over 350 games are included on this book's CD-ROM. Here are a few highlights.

IR Battleship, IR Checkers, IR Chess, IR Hangman, CodeFinder, IROthello
> These are excellent versions of all the famous games—made all the more amazing by the fact that you're playing your opponent by infrared, PalmPilot-to-PalmPilot, whether across the boardroom table or up to the front seat of the car. ISComplete, $50 for the whole pack, or $15 per game.

Crossbow
> An impressive crossword-puzzle program. You load crossword puzzles into the Memo Pad program; then you can view the crossword grid on the Palm-Pilot's screen and use Graffiti to enter the answers. Converters are available that can read the format of *The Times* cryptic puzzles and *USA Today*'s theme crosswords, which you can download. Harry Ohlsen, free.

Niggle
> Scrabble. Play against the PalmPilot or against up to three other people. Built-in 80,000-word dictionary, timer, score history—and it's all free from Steve Bennett. (See Figure A-6.)

Guess Me
> You probably know it as Mastermind: a game of luck and logic deduction, in which you make successive attempts to guess the hidden pattern of four pegs. Tan Kok Mun, $12.

Jookerie
> A clever word game where you trick your opponent into believing that your ludicrous explanation is real! (You probably know this game as Dictionary.) Land-J technologies, $12.

Klondike

    The classic solitaire game; engaging and fun. Bill Kirby, $12.

Kyle's Quest

    A role-playing game, along the lines of Final Fantasy. You explore great-looking graphic worlds, meeting characters, managing inventory, and designing your own new levels (over 20 bonus levels are provided on this CD-ROM). (See Figure A-6.) Kyle Poole, $15.

OXO

    Nicely designed four-level 3-D tic-tac-toe. Ak Analytics, $7.

Palm Jongg

    Mah Jongg, the ancient games of tiles. Tan Kok Mun, free.

Pocket Chess

    Not Deep Blue, but great fun. Play against the PalmPilot and lose! Amazingly, this complete computer-chess game consumes less than 30K of memory. (See Figure A-6.) Scott Ludwig, free.

Pocket Gammon

    Classic backgammon. Shuji Fukumoto, $15.

Ted-Truss

    Tetris. Tony Leung, $12. (Note the seven other Tetris clones on the CD, too.)

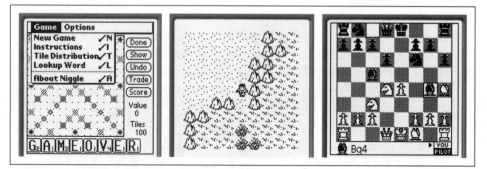

Figure A-6. From left to right: Niggle, Kyle's Quest, Pocket Chess.

Gaming/Sport Rules/Aids

This category includes helpers, such as scorekeepers, for real-world games by the dozen: gymnastics, golf, tennis, baseball, Keno, skating, car racing, and more.

DivePlan

    Lets scuba divers plan their dives. You specify your tank capacity, safety stop depth and time, and so on; it calculates maximum bottom time based on your air consumption, previous dive history, surface interval, and so on. Bill Ezell, $10.

Golf Scoring System

> The ultimate golf-game scorekeeper. Ideal for carrying around on the links—then HotSyncs the data to the desktop. Richard Hocking, free. (See the many other golf-score programs on the CD-ROM, too, including a demo of the best-selling commercial IntelliGolf.)

RaceTime

> Billed as the first car-race timer for the PalmPilot, which isn't very surprising—but this happens to be a very nice racing-car timer. Fred Raub, $15.

Hacks

One of the most important programs you can install is HackMaster—a sort of master switch for all kinds of extremely useful, time-saving, power-leveraging add-on modules for the PalmPilot. (Don't be daunted by the word Hack—in general, these programs are as "official" and stable as any other.)

HackMaster

> This is the master On switch and control panel that makes *hacks* possible—additions to the Palm operating system. Offers a convenient list of checkboxes that let you turn various hacks on and off. Daggerware, $5.

AppHack

> Lets you use two sequential button presses to launch up to 24 predefined Palm programs, saving you a traipse to the Applications screen. Daggerware, $5.

Battery Control Hack

> Adds a tiny battery-gauge display to the corner of your PalmPilot at all times. Dovcom, free.

ClockHack

> Puts the current time on your screen at all times. Haus of Maus, free.

CorrectHack

> Lets you define a list of abbreviations that will be automatically replaced with the expanded versions as you write. Also great for setting up auto-corrections. In other words, does what Microsoft Word's AutoCorrect does. For example, you can set up CorrectHack to automatically replace teh with the, or to replace your initials with your full name. The expansion takes place automatically as you write. Dovcom, $12.

FindHack

> Indispensable! Beefs up the PalmPilot's Find command in numerous ways, as shown in Figure A-7. (a) Lets you locate text even in the middle of words. (b) Remembers the last six searches you did. (c) Lets you select where the search

will be performed: in all applications, in built-in applications (Memo Pad, Date Book, To-Do List, Mail, Expense), or in the current application. (d) Permits using wildcards—using the question mark (?) or dot (.) to mean "any character." Florent Pillet, free.

MagicText

Lets you drag-and-drop text between Palm applications and double-tap to highlight a word. Also adds a system-wide contextual menu for easy access to Email Lookup, Copy/Cut/Paste, check the time, and so on. (See Figure A-7.) Synergy, $18.

MenuHack

Lets you pull down PalmPilot menus by tapping at the top of the window, just as you do on your PC or Mac, instead of having to tap the Menu icon at the bottom of the screen. One of the most useful hacks of all time. Daggerware, free.

ScreenWrite

Lets you write Graffiti directly on the screen (instead of only in the writing area beneath the screen), as shown in Figure A-7.

SwitchHack

With one click, switches between the currently running program and the last one you used. Also creates a pop-up menu of the ten programs you've most recently used—an incredibly valuable time-saver. Requires HackMaster. Deskfree Computing, $5.

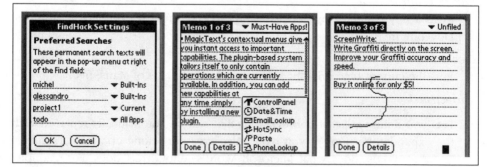

Figure A-7. From left to right: FindHack, MagicText, ScreenWrite.

Health/Fitness

These programs let you track yourself—your heartbeat, diet, and so on.

DietLog

> An amazingly comprehensive and professional database/diet tracker that lets you input what you eat as you eat it—by tapping. At any time, you can then summon statistics about what you've eaten and how you're proceeding toward your goals. SoftCare, $60.

Info

Here are 450 listings of reference information: birthstones, coffee drinks, recipes, Furby trivia, jokes, web addresses, tips and tricks, and many more. Most must be opened using a Doc reader (see Chapter 10) or a Palm database (see Chapter 12).

Law

Reference texts, mostly for U.S. Federal law statutes. Most must be opened using a Doc reader (see Chapter 10).

Literary

Looking for a good book? Here are 569 of them, in Doc format (see Chapter 10): Jules Verne, Mark Twain, T.S. Eliot, the complete works of Shakespeare, and hundreds more.

Mapping/Navigation

If you're lost, these files may help. They're maps (and other navigational aids) that cover major cities and subway systems.

Medical

These 100 programs are primarily of interest to physicians. They're reference documents concerning drug doses, lab tests, diagnostic databases, and so on, plus a healthy allotment of medical diagrams.

Music/Sound

Chapter 11 offers complete descriptions of the leading music programs for the PalmPilot, including PocketSynth (lets you record and play back single-line melodies), PalmPiano (features a tappable piano keyboard), EbonyIvory (shows each note's position on sheet music when you tap a piano key), FretBoard (displays guitar fingerings for any note, scale, or chord), Metronome, Tuning Fork, and more.

Religion

If you've got a Doc reader (see Chapter 10), various editions of the Bible and other religious texts await in this category.

Restaurants

Most of these restaurant city guides require TealMeal, described earlier in this chapter. Load them up when travelling to a new city, and you've got a miniature Fodor's guide on your palmtop; search by price, cuisine, and so on.

Synchronization/Installation

See Chapter 6, *HotSync, Step by Step*, for a description of the leading commercial HotSync programs, which include IntelliSync, PilotMirror, Desktop To Go, and many others. These additional HotSync utility programs are generally designed to run on the Desktop, not the PalmPilot itself.

Backup Buddy

> Backs up your entire PalmPilot, including the programs—such as HackMaster files—that aren't normally backed up by the standard HotSync process. You can also perform scheduled as well as transparent incremental backups. Separate versions for Windows 95/NT and Macintosh. Alexander Hinds, $20.

IrSync

> This surprising utility lets you HotSync an IR-equipped PalmPilot by infrared with any desktop computer (such as a laptop) that has an infrared jack. IS/ Complete, free.

Mac Pac 2

> This is the long-awaited Macintosh HotSync software that includes the version of Palm Desktop described in Chapter 9, *Palm Desktop: Macintosh*.

Palm Buddy

> For Macintosh. Shows a Finder-like window that lets you drag and drop programs to install and back up. Features automatic conversions of Doc, JFile, and MobileDB databases. Florent Pillet, $20.

Ripcord

> Can install an entire set of programs and databases into your PalmPilot in one pass. In addition, Ripcord attempts to organize the files that are installed, in an attempt to minimize memory fragmentation. Ripcord Home Page, $10.

Support Apps

These desktop-based applications help to create and manage data for your Palm-Pilot.

FMSync

As described in Chapter 12, this amazing Macintosh conduit translates your FileMaker database into JFile format on the PalmPilot—and keeps the two files HotSynced. Rob Tsuk, $38.

Image Converter

This is the Windows program that converts your favorite photographs into Image Vewer format (see Chapter 11). Art Dahm, free.

Make Doc

The CD-ROM includes many different versions of this program, for Windows, DOS, Macintosh, Unix, Java, and more. They're all designed to do the same thing: turn text files on your desktop into ready-to-install Doc files for the PalmPilot, as described in Chapter 10.

Time/Date

Because the PalmPilot is something that, presumably, you always carry with you, programmers have seized upon it as the modern-day pocket watch. Here are some of the ways Palm software can help you keep track of your time and schedule.

Action Names

This enhancement for the built-in Palm applications gives you new ways to access your data. It offers new calendar views, graphic displays of your schedule, and several clever means of integrating your data—adding a meeting note to somebody's card in your Address Book, or displaying your to do list with your calendar. (See Figure A-8.) Iambic, $20.

AnaClock

Run this program to turn your PalmPilot into a stately analog desk clock. Particularly useful if you have a Palm V and you leave it in its cradle on your desk, turned on, all day long. PalmAdd Software, free.

BugMe!

You can quickly jot a note on the PalmPilot (either Graffiti or your actual handwritten scrawl, stored as a graphic) and set an alarm to have the note pop up and bug you at the appropriate time, as shown in Figure A-8. BugMe! is great when you need to remember something in an hour or so but don't want to bother with setting an alarm in the Date Book. Haus of Maus, $10.

Clock III

A wonderfully designed, useful multi-function clock, stopwatch, countdown timer, and alarm. Can show a second time zone and battery meter. Little Wing Software, $25.

DateBk3

As described in Chapter 4, *The Four Primary Programs*, this beloved replacement for the built-in Palm calendar has a feature that will blow you away: weekly view, two-week view, yearly view, to-do items that can repeat and have alarms, a daily journal, appointments that go beyond midnight, and many other improvements. Pimlico Software, $20.

LClock

This is as simple a travel alarm clock as you'll find. Giant numbers tell you what time it is, and the time you set for your morning alarm is simultaneously visible. LinkeSoft, $9.

TealGlance

Shows an elegant screen full of important information (date, time, battery condition, Date Book entries for today and tomorrow, to-do items, and more) whenever you turn on the PalmPilot. TealPoint Software, $12.

TZones

Want to know the time in four different locations simultaneously? This program does it. (See Figure A-8.) William Ball, free.

Figure A-8. From left to right: Action Names, Bug Me!, Tzones.

Travel/Entertainment

The vast majority of files in this category are listings—in Doc or JFile formats (see Chapters 10 and 12)—of movies, airport information, train information, TV show episodes, hotel and rental-car phone numbers, and so on. Here are a couple of exceptions:

Aramis City Guides

These little programs are miniature travel guides for popular tourist destinations—demo modules for Boston, Chicago, Los Angeles, San Francisco, New York and Washington are included on the CD-ROM. Tap a category—Dining, Children's Activities, Nightlife, Sights, and so on, as shown in Figure A-9—to view full listings and reviews for the city in question. Aramis, $18 per city.

Gulliver

This commercial program is heaven-sent for the frequent traveler. With the minimum of tapping and writing, you can record your complete itinerary—hotel and car reservations, flight schedules, frequent flyer numbers, and phone numbers of airlines, hotels, and so on. (See Figure A-9.) Features like auto-fill and beamability make the program even more likable. LandWare, $30.

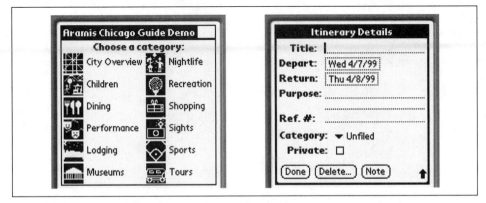

Figure A-9. From left to right: Aramis City Guides, Gulliver.

Utilities

The 120 programs in this category are mainly for use on the PalmPilot itself. They help you manage battery usage, memory, backlight, beaming, and so on.

Beam Box

As described in Chapter 15, this handy little program lets you beam software to other PalmPilots that would not normally be beamable—HackMaster files, for example. Jeremy Radlow, $5.

FlashPro

Chapter 17, *Troubleshooting*, explains why this remarkable program blesses your Palm III or later model with 824K more RAM—and you don't even have to take the thing apart. TRG, $30.

PalmPrint

Use this impressive software to print any of the built-in Palm apps to any infrared-equipped printer, as described in Chapter 15. Stevens Creek Software, $30.

TealScript, Jot, Fitaly, T9

These replacements or enhancements for the Graffiti alphabet are described in Chapter 3, *Typing Without a Keyboard.*

Undupe

Somewhere, somehow, someday, you or somebody you run into will need this program. With one tap, it removes duplicate records that have cropped up in your built-in Palm applications. Stevens Creek Software, $5.

B

PalmPilot Accessories

As with any computer, the PalmPilot itself is likely to be only the beginning of your expenditures. A rapidly growing industry of add-ons and accessories awaits your credit card.

The purpose of this appendix, then, is to alert you to the most interesting and surprising add-ons. Who could have guessed that there's a pocket-sized scanner that can read business cards directly into the Address Book program? Who wouldn't be intrigued by the EarthMate, a gadget that calculates your exact position on the face of the earth by receiving signals from satellites now in space? And who among us couldn't use a replacement for the carrying case that comes with the PalmPilot?

Consider this chapter a directory, a wish book, or a mind-expander when it comes to contemplating the potential of this tiniest of computers.

3Com Attachments

All of the 3Com/Palm-branded gadgets listed below are available at the Palm web site, *http://www.palmorder/modusmedia.com.*

Palm Modem

A small, lightweight modem, about the size of a bath-size Camay, for surfing or email; see Chapter 13, *Email Anywhere*, and Chapter 14, *The Web in Your Palm*. An AC adapter is available for $20 more. 3Com, $120 (or $170 for the Palm V model).

HotSync Cable

A cable to replace the HotSync cradle (see Chapter 6, *HotSync, Step by Step*), for those for whom briefcase space is at a premium. 3Com, $20.

HotSync Cradle

A duplicate of the cradle that came with your PalmPilot. Why? In case you plan to HotSync regularly with a second computer. 3Com, $30.

Macintosh Serial Adapter

Don't buy the $15 Mac Pac—that's for suckers. Instead, use the Mac Pac software (included on this book's CD-ROM) and just buy this inexpensive cable adapter, which connects the standard HotSync cradle to a Mac modem port. 3Com, $6.

Modem Cable

Use with pocket and external modems to back up and synchronize with your office PC. 3Com, $20.

Other Attachments

TaleLight

This may seem incredible, but Tech Labs actually sells a tiny, acrylic-covered light—in your choice of colors and styles— that snaps into your HotSync port, as shown in Figure B-1. It's billed as a "silent alarm" because, with the addition of the freeware program FlashHack, you can set up your Date Book alarms to flash this tiny light instead of sounding an alarm. Or use it as a flashlight for reading theatre programs. Or install the goofy Tricorder program (see Appendix A, *100 Programs Worth Knowing About*) to control the TaleLight (in "photon emitter" mode, of course), and the freeware program TaleLight Hack can even operate the TaleLight as a metronome or—in the event you're lost at sea in a life raft—a Morse code generator. Tech Labs, $12 to $25 (depending on model and color). *http://members. aol.com/gmayhak/tcl/light.htm.*

Figure B-1. The TaleLight is amazingly neat-looking. Use it as a flashlight, an alarm, or just to impress your friends.

TaleVibes

From the makers of the TaleLight comes this tiny clip-on device that gives your PalmPilot or Palm III-family device a "buzz mode," like a pager, so that your alarms going off won't disturb everyone else in the theater. A tiny LED even blinks to get your attention if you happen to be looking at the thing. The module protrudes a half inch beyond the bottom of the palmtop. Tech Labs, $50, *http:// members.aol.com/gmayhak/tcl/vibes.htm.*

Minstrel Wireless Modems

By purchasing a 3×5-inch computer, you've gone halfway toward ultimate porta-bility. For $370, you can go the rest of the way with a five-ounce, 19.2Kbps wire-less modem that lets you check email or browse the Web without being plugged into anything. (The Minstrel III is for the Palm III family; the original Minstrel is also available for the PalmPilot Pro.) Uses a NiMH rechargeable battery; an AC adapter is also included. You can choose from among different service plans, but the least expensive are from GoAmerica ($50 per month, unlimited use) or Bell Atlantic Mobile ($55 unlimited). Novatel, $370 (plus monthly charges); *http://www. novatelwireless.com.*

Earthmate

This two-pound, PalmPilot-sized, yellow plastic-housed gadget is a GPS (global positioning system) add-on for the PalmPilot (see Figure B-2). After HotSyncing a chosen driving route to your palmtop from the Street Atlas CD-ROM (included), you hook the receiver up to your PalmPilot. As you drive, it tells you exactly where you are in the world to within 100 feet by picking up signals from tracking satellites. Don't forget to buy the special PalmPilot cable, which doesn't come with the Earth-mate itself. And while you're spending, consider adding $20 more for the Solus Pro software, which continuously updates the PalmPilot screen to show your position on a map (instead of a text readout). Delorme, $200; *http://www.delorme.com.*

CardScan

A tiny scanner for business cards (see Figure B-3). The CardScan reads your pals' business cards into a special Rolodex program on your Windows PC. (The pro-gram does a surprisingly good job at placing the correct info—name, city, email address, and so on—into the correct blanks, but vertically-oriented cards, shaded backgrounds, and speckles throw it for a loop.) From there, at the next HotSync, the program can feed the scanned-in, edited contact information to your Palm-Pilot's Address Book. Corex, $300; *http://www.corex.com.*

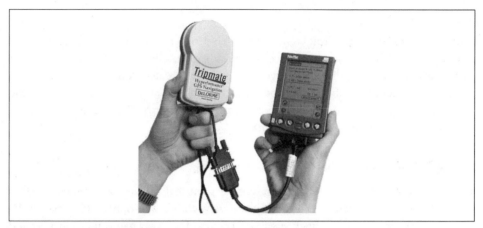

Figure B-2. The EarthMate (left) shows where you are in the world (right)

Figure B-3. The CardScan Plus is bigger than the PalmPilot, but not much. Its relevance: its corresponding Windows address book can HotSync with your PalmPilot.

GoType Keyboard

For many PalmPiloteers, this compact, full-featured, fold-up, portable keyboard is the best $80 they've ever spent. The 1999 and later models (including the special Palm V edition) double as HotSync cradles. (See Chapter 3, *Typing Without a Keyboard*, for a photo.) Landware, $80; *http://www.landware.com.*

Palm Navigator

This gadget looks exactly like the Palm snap-on modem—but it's a compass. The accompanying software provides the display, and add-on software lets you download maps from the Web that talk to the Navigator module. If you're a Boy

Scout, what are you waiting for? Precision Navigation, $30; *http://www. precisionnav.com.*

Unimount

If your cell phone isn't keeping you quite distracted enough while driving, here's the solution: a mounting bracket that holds your PalmPilot in place as you drive (see Figure B-4). (Models to hold it in place at the office or on the golf cart are also available.) The thing is amazingly cleverly designed, featuring a right-side slider that hovers over the screen for operating scroll bars and tapping buttons without having to pull out the stylus. Prices vary, but $50 to $100 is the range. Revolv, *http://www.revolvedesign.com.*

Figure B-4. The UniMount holds your palmtop in place when it's not on your palm.

JetTalker

Who'd want one of those Windows CE palmtops? They're slow, they guzzle batteries, the interface is hopelessly convoluted—but hmm, they've got that nice voice-memo feature . . . . If being able to record and play back voice recordings on your PalmPilot is important to you, the JetTalker clip-on module has your name on it. The device looks like a Palm clip-on modem, but houses a mike, speaker, and enough RAM to store 34 minutes' worth of talking. The corresponding software lets you assign categories (and a password, if you like) to the messages you record. Dynafirm, $170; earpiece/mouthpiece privacy set $25; *http://www.dynafirm.com.*

Screen Protection and Stylus Replacements

Note to the wise: Ask before you buy. Only a few of the stylus replacements listed here fit into the PalmPilot stylus slot.

Concept Kitchen Stuff

Concept Kitchen sells a line of inexpensive accessories for your screen. Write-Rights are clear plastic screen overlays that are said to reduce glare and offer a nicer writing surface. (12 per pack; each lasts a month; $28 per package.) PDA ScreenClean, a cleaning kit designed to restore the original finish to the PalmPilot screen, is $20 and includes both a Karma Cloth (do you need it? Not unless you're out of old T-shirts) and 12 BrainWash wet-dry cleaning towelettes (these really work). Concept Kitchen, $15; *http://www2.conceptkitchen.com.*

Scotch Tape

The kind that comes in a blue dispenser (bearing either the name Magic or the product number 811) is perfect for placing on the Graffiti writing area—at a fraction of the cost of other screen-covering products.

Combination Pen/Stylus

Many companies sell combination ball-point pen and PalmPilot stylus devices—just don't twist the barrel the wrong way before writing on the screen. Some fit the PalmPilot stylus slot, others don't.

For example, fashionable Throttle is available in a $10 Classic model (in PalmPilot gray or WorkPad black), whose pen clip goes into the stylus pocket; the rest of the stylus hugs the outside of the palmtop. (The $30 Executive model, in Nickel or "stealth" matte black finish, is similar, but doesn't lock into place when in the pocket.) Then there's the $15 Slimline model, which fits completely into the stylus pocket (not the Palm V); its head unscrews to reveal a reset pin, exactly like the standard Palm III stylus. Ttools, *http://www.ttools.com* (which offers many a photo).

PDA Panache sells stylus replacements for the Pilot/PalmPilot family ($14), the Palm III/IIIx/VII family ($16), and the Palm V ($18). Made of solid brass (in a chrome or black finish), it fits entirely inside the stylus pocket. The Palm V model offers a neat feature: it clicks both fully into the pocket and halfway, for those times when you're using the thing a lot. (All of these models have an unscrewable cap to reveal the standard reset pin.) PDA Panache, *http://pdapanache.com.*

Speaking of the Palm V: 3Com's own chubby Dual Action Stylus slips its pocket clip into the Palm V stylus well; the matching brushed-aluminum pen itself hugs the outside of the palmtop. Twist to convert from a stylus to a ball-point pen. $40 at *http://www.palmorder.com/modusmedia.com.*

Finally, Cross (*http://www.cross-pcg.com/pcg*) and (ironically) the Pilot Pen company (*http://www.pentopia.com*) both make attractive lines of styli, many of which are also ink pens. Most, however, don't fit the palmtop itself; you're supposed to carry them in your pocket, under separate cover.

The Color Pack

If you're a Palm III-family owner, you've got options nobody else has. You alone can graduate beyond the hopelessly drab PalmPilot Gray color of the case and stylus. For $19, 3Com will sell you the Palm III Color Pack. It includes two replacements for your hard plastic flip lid, one in teal and one in dark blue. As a bonus, you also get two replacement styluses—and their plastic ends are color-coordinated to match the replacement flip lids. *http://www.palmorder/ modusmedia.com/P3/P3-stylii.htm.*

Carrying Cases

For many aficionados, replacing the carrying case that comes with the PalmPilot is the first order of business. The Palm III's flip cover helps protect the screen, but won't do you much good if you drop the device on a kitchen floor; the Palm V's leatherette front flap makes the palmtop susceptible to inadvertent turn-ons in your pocket; and the Palm VII's case is too tight a sleeve, and one more thing to lose.

Fortunately, the world's carrying-case manufacturers are huge PalmPilot fans. You could dedicate an entire web site just to reviews and photos of the array of PalmPilot carrying cases on the market today.

In fact, one person has (*http://www.fredlet.com*). For several years running, her personal quest has been to examine, photograph, and review every PalmPilot carrying case in existence. For a summary of all of the available cases and their specs, and links to their makers' web sites, visit *http://www.fredlet.com/pilot/cases/table.htm.*

What you quickly find out, however, is that most cases come in one of the following designs:

Slip-In
> Imagine a pocket without pants. The Pilot and PalmPilot lines included a slip-in case; you push the PalmPilot itself into a sheath as though it's a sword. The downside is that the case isn't attached to the PalmPilot itself, making it one more thing you might lose.

Flip-up
> These cases are hinged at the top. To see your PalmPilot's screen, you lift the front cover upward and fold it back, as though it's a legal pad. (See Figure B-5.)

Figure B-5. The Flip Case (http://www.synsolutions.com) is a $23 flip-up leather wrap that covers the front and back faces of the PalmPilot. You can easily HotSync with the case on the PalmPilot.

Book

This kind of case is "hinged" on the left side; the PalmPilot is generally fastened to the inside of the case with Velcro, as shown in Figure B-6. A cover closes over the front of the PalmPilot when not in use, fastening on the right edge with Velcro, a snap, or a leather loop. (This is the design of the ill-fated Palm V hard case.)

Figure B-6. 3Com's Slimline case for the PalmPilot (left) and Deluxe case (right) make your classy-looking palmtop look even classier.

Portfolio

If you've ever seen a Day Runner, Filofax, or other personal (non-electronic) organizer, you get the idea (Figure B-7). These cases are much larger than the PalmPilot; they're designed to hold your papers and credit cards along with the PalmPilot itself.

Flip-down

These cases are hinged at the bottom. To see your PalmPilot's screen, you flip the front cover downward, as though it's one of those fold-up cell phones. (See Figure B-7.)

Figure B-7. Case Logic's $15 PLT-1 leatherette case doesn't cover the top of the unit, so you can get at your stylus, but there's also a leather loop for a stylus on the side of the holster.

Extreme Protection

If you're an adventurer whose PalmPilot is likely to get dropped or whacked, you need a case with a durable, hard outer shell. Nothing protects your Palm-Pilot from the most extreme shocks, of course, but the Rhinoskin Cockpit gives it a fighting chance. Made of titanium (atomic number 22, atomic weight 47.90), this case looks like what it is: a machine-folded piece of sheet metal. And it isn't cheap: it's around $100. However, its users swear by it, telling frightening tales of dropping PalmPilots from the roofs of cars or rock climbing—and the Palm-Pilot, in its Titanium case, survives, thanks to the rubber pads on the inside. The accompanying Clip Pak (no atomic number available) adds a belt clip-option to the titanium case (*http://www.rhinoskin.com*).

C

Piloteers in Cyberspace

Why did the PalmPilot become such a runaway hit? When you get right down to it, the thing shouldn't have clobbered Windows CE devices on the market (outselling them four-to-one, at this writing). After all, the PalmPilot is mostly black-and-white. Its screen is 160 pixels square. And it doesn't run Microsoft programs.

One big part of the answer is the sense of community it engenders. Owning a PalmPilot isn't like owning, say, a Micron PC clone, where you've made a purchase and that's it. Instead, owning this gadget is more personal; you feel as though you're part of something bigger, an inner circle of the enlightened, some exciting underground family. At trade shows, on planes and trains, and at computer clubs, you can spot clusters of animated PalmPilot-wielding enthusiasts comparing notes, exchanging tips on cool new shareware, and reporting on (or beaming each other) what they've found online recently.

The largest convocation of such zealots is, in fact, online. Hundreds of web sites have cropped up for the propagation of software, news, reviews, and general evangelism. This chapter offers you a few starting points for finding great Palm material on the Web.

Electronic Newsletters

Thanks to the Internet, you don't have to go hunting for news and reviews about the PalmPilot and its descendants—you can choose to have them emailed directly to you at no charge.

As with all email newsletters, save the "unsubscribe" instructions for the newsletters described here so that you can turn off the faucet of email if it ever becomes overwhelming.

InSync Online

As important a free email newsletter as ever existed, because this one is run by Palm Computing itself. Every day, a message arrives in your inbox, featuring a trick, tip, or other useful blurb about your favorite palmtop. (The tips and tricks are often excerpted from this and other PalmPilot books.) Better yet, you can specify what kinds of information you want to receive—tips but no product announcements, Macintosh-only information, and so on. To sign up, visit *http://www.palm.com* and choose InSync Online from the Quick Index.

The NewNews Digest

A daily email listing of new products, software, and developments, with a special emphasis on the release of new shareware. To sign up, go to *http://www.pilotgear.com*. Click the News button. Choose Subscribe to Mailing List and type in your email address. The rest is automatic.

PalmPower Tips

A free weekly email Palm tip or trick. Sign up by inputting your name and email address at *http://www.palmpower.com*.

Shopping

Where do you buy new stuff for you palmtop—carrying cases, modems, stylus replacements, business-card scanners? After all, you won't exactly find Palm stores in your local mall.

The answer is: at these web sites. They take credit cards, are constantly updated, and feature photos of the stuff they're selling.

PilotGear HQ

One of the first and largest Palm-only shopping sites (*http://www.pilotgear.com*). Each product is featured in a photo and has a link, where possible, to the manufacturer's web page. You can register hundreds of shareware programs here—the legendary proprietor has even begun marketing new software under the PilotGear label.

Palm.com

When it comes to accessories developed by Palm itself, you can't beat Palm's own web site, *http://www.palm.com*. Carrying cases, modems, covers, stylus replacements, cables, power adapters, and other basic accessories are illustrated and sold here.

Software

The sole purpose of these web sites is to stock every shareware and freeware program ever written. Thanks to their categorization and Find commands, these sites make it easy to find goodies to download. And the beauty of downloading Palm programs, of course, is that they're tiny—they take only seconds to download.

PalmCentral.com (http://www.palmcentral.com)
> The daddy of them all (see Figure C-1). This site, created by the programmer who wrote the popular StuffIt compression program for the Macintosh, is so popular that its contents have been duplicated at mirror sites around the world. You can browse by category or search for a particular word in the title or description. The results are presented in a tidy list that includes descriptions, Download buttons, and links to the authors' own web sites. For the truly Palm-obsessed, the lists of the most recently released 25, 100, or 200 programs are continuously updated. (This web site, of course, is the source of the files and information on this book's own CD-ROM.)

The Pickled PalmPilot (http://www.pickled.com)
> Here's another primary source to search when you're on the prowl for something specific. Includes instructions for installing new Palm programs, links to other sites, and more.

EuroCool (http://www.eurocool.com)
> The highlight of this software-download site is the user-feedback screens. You and your fellow PalmPilot owners can rate and review what they download—a great way to warn future users away from dogs, and endorse the really great programs.

Reading Material

The Web is crawling with web sites containing reading material you can dump into your palmtop and (using a Doc reader such as AportisDoc) read on the road. For complete descriptions, see Chapter 10, *PalmPilot: The Electronic Book.*

PalmPilot Magazines

Several hundred pages of *PalmPilot: the Ultimate Guide* not enough reading for you? Then dial up these info-packed sites:

PalmPower (http://www.palmpower.com)
> One of the best online Palm magazines. Includes useful how-to articles, tips for getting the most out of the PalmPilot, excellent news coverage, and links to other web pages of interest.

Figure C-1. Palm Central is one of the most up-to-date and well-organized Palm software sites.

PalmZone (http://www.palmzone.com)

PalmZone is an attractively designed, free online "magazine" filled with reviews, short articles, and "experiences" working with various Palm add-ons (Figure C-2). Includes a large software library, too.

Tap (http://www.tapmagazine.com)

An actual paper magazine, mailed to you by U.S. Mail; $20 per year. Reviews, tips, tricks, and how-to articles.

The Piloteer (http://www.pmn.co.uk)

This intriguing British publication is subscription-based, like a paper magazine ($25 per year), but electronic—each month, you download a set of web pages. The writing and reporting are high-quality; each issue features news, reviews, features, tutorials, and commentary. Even if you don't subscribe, the web site is worth a daily visit just to read the concise industry news posted there.

The Gadgeteer (http://www.the-gadgeteer.com)

In theory, this web site covers all palmtops, but the coverage is predominantly Palm-related. The writing isn't magazine-quality, but you'll get a lot of the reviews—they're definitely worth reading before buying a Palm program or accessory.

A Guide to Downloaded Palm Goodies

If you have problems downloading software, you're not alone. The bizarre rituals involved in getting software off the Internet have plagued computer users since the Internet began. The problem isn't finding files to download—it's figuring out what to do with them once they've been downloaded. You wind up with a folder full of files bearing strange names and bizarre suffixes.

The key is that suffix, the three or four letters that end the file's name after the period. Here's the scheme:

.zip

> This is a Zip file, a file that was compressed into smaller form before being put up on the Web. If you have a Macintosh, you need the free StuffIt Expander to decompress and use it (*http://www.aladdinsys.com*); for Windows, you need any "unzipping" program, such as PKZip *(http://www.pkzip.com)* or WinZip *(http://www.winzip.com)*.

.sit

> This is a StuffIt file, the Macintosh equivalent of a Zip file. Both Macintosh and Windows users need a program like StuffIt Expander (*http://www.aladdinsys.com*) to turn the downloaded file into usable form.

.prc

> This kind of file, a Pilot resource code file, isn't compressed at all. It's a standard Palm application, ready to download and install as described in Chapter 7, *Installing New Palm Programs*.

.pdb

> This kind of file, too, is ready to download and install on the PalmPilot. It's a Pilot database file—that is, a support file or data file that accompanies an actual Palm application.

.htm or .html

> Because the PalmPilot is enjoyed equally by Mac and Windows users, an increasing number of software authors provide their instruction manuals in web-page format—that is, as HTML files. After downloading some Palm software, look in its folder for something called *Index.html, Getting Started.htm*, and so on. Launch your favorite web browser, choose File → Open File, and open this HTML file. That's your manual.

.pdf

> Another instruction-manual format that can be opened on both Mac and Windows—one that's especially popular among commercial software companies—is the PDF (portable digital file) document, better known as an Adobe Acrobat file. To read it, you need the free Acrobat Reader program, available at *http://www.adobe.com*.

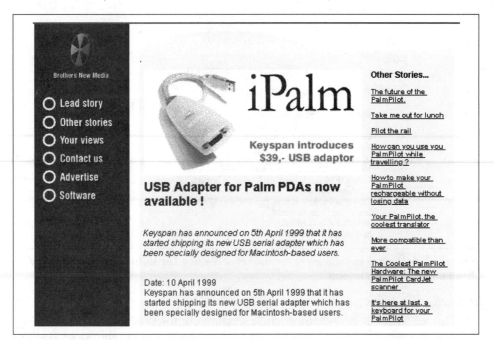

Figure C-2. PalmZone is typical of web magazines: colorful, current, and free.

Palm Discussions

Nowhere is the sense of Palm community stronger than in the online discussion groups. Here's where you can ask questions of the general Piloteering multitudes, share timesaving discoveries, and find out others' experiences with various products and techniques.

The PalmPilot Mailing List

A mailing list, in this case, means "a discussion conducted by email"; you can both read and respond to messages you receive. This particular mailing list has thousands of participants; in dozens of messages per day, they discuss every conceivable aspect of PalmPiloting. Any of these messages are technical, but many are amusingly obsessive (see Figure C-3).

To sign up: go to *http://www.ultraviolet.org*. Click Pilot Mailing List Info. There you'll find instructions for subscribing either to the one-message-at-a-time version (which fills your email box with individual messages throughout the day) or the "digest" version (which sends you one message per day, a neatly compiled collection of the day's individual messages). Instead of signing up to receive these discussion fragments by email, you can also go read them, including past issues, at the web site (*http://www.ultraviolet.org/mail-archives/pilot-mail.html*).

```
From: pilot-pda-digest-help@freeside.ultraviolet.org
To:   pilot-pda@freeside.ultraviolet.org
--------------------

pilot-pda Digest 17 Jul 1999 10:00:01 -0000 Issue 240

Topics (messages 8687 through 8715):

Syncing mail from Eudora's boxes?
PocketMirror 2.0.4 Upgrade - Website problems?
Contact management software
Transfer Data & TRG 8 meg
3Com Ad Campaign
Warranty if you upgrade with TRG?
Using the PalmV contrast button to launch an application...
Pilotgear down?
Do some Palm V screen problems as IIIx
installing in flash RAM
palmIIIx / switchhack
best launcher for IIIx?
```

Figure C-3. Each day's installment of the PalmPilot Mailing List begins with a summary of the topics you're about to read.

PalmPilot developers list

This email list is a discussion circle exclusively for programmers. It's run by 3Com, who admit you to the list only if they deem you worthy. Send email to *devsupport@palm.com* to apply.

PalmPilot newsgroups

A newsgroup is an electronic Internet-based bulletin board. You can access it from your desktop computer; you use such programs as Netscape Communicator, Microsoft Internet Explorer, or Newswatcher to read and respond to the messages.

PalmPilot discussions are everywhere online. Some are devoted solely to Palm OS machines, such as *comp.sys.palmtops.pilot*, but much chatter also goes on at *comp.sys.pen*, *comp.sys.handhelds*, and *comp.sys.palmtops*.

PalmPilot power boards

Part of the PalmPilot Power online magazine described earlier, these boards aren't as overwhelming as some of the higher-volume discussion areas, and the help you get is generally excellent. Go to *http://www.palmpower.com* (click the Palm Power Power Boards button).

Live chats

There's a live chat session for Palm owners and programmers twice a week via IRC (Internet Relay Chat) every Wednesday and Sunday night at 8:30 Central Standard Time. (Wednesday nights feature online giveaways of software and hardware.) To join these chats, you need an IRC client program such as mIRC (for Windows) or Ircle (for Macintosh), which you can get from *http://www. shareware.com*, among other sources. Once you're running this IRC program, type */server irc.us.openprojects.net* into its command-line area and press Return; then, using the Channel command, join channel #palmchat. You should see the discussion under way; even when it's not Wednesday or Sunday night, a few hardy souls are almost always hanging out.

And if you haven't got time to wait for live typing, visit *http://www.palmlife. com/palmchat.html* to read the transcripts of past chats.

Help and Answers

If you're having trouble making something work, the online world contains roughly 11 million times more information than the original Palm manual.

The official 3Com Pilot web site (http://palmpilot.3com.com)
Palm Computing maintains an extremely helpful web site. Click Support for a vast and comprehensive help area, complete with answers and workarounds for hundreds of tweaky little problems. Highlights include a Frequently Asked Questions list, articles describing the various upgrade offers, and—most precious of all—instructions on emailing Palm Computing for free technical help. (Hint: the email address for this tech-support service is *support@palm.com*— and type 0000 as the subject of your message.)

America Online and CompuServe
Each of these online services has its own discussion area for Palm topics, with actual 3Com tech-support reps responding to your message-board postings. On America Online, go to keyword PALMPILOT. On CompuServe, GO PALMB. Libraries 5 and 8 contain Palm software.

Calvin's PalmPilot FAQ (http://www.pilotfaq.com)
FAQ stands for Frequently Asked Questions, which is exactly what you find on this famous information site: several dozen answers to common questions, especially on troubleshooting early models.

Pilot Exploration: the Web Ring

The web sites listed in this chapter are only tip of the tip of the iceberg; the Web's PalmPilot offerings number in the thousands. Many of the information sources listed above provide jumping-off points—lists of web links—to other useful sites.

If you have a few hours (or months) free, though, you might consider letting chance be your guide. Hitch your exploration to the wagon of the PalmPilot Web Ring, a software invention by which hundreds of Palm web sites are linked, one to the next, in a vast circle; each such page features Web Ring navigation buttons (such as Previous, Next, Random, and so on) that take you around the ring. (See Figure C-4.)

Figure C-4. At the bottom of every PalmPilot Web Ring page are controls that propel you farther around the great community of PalmPilot web pages.

To begin your journey around this ring—and to find out how to make your web site part of this ring—visit *http://www.palmcentral.com/webring.html*, which is the Ring's home base. You can also use the find command to jump directly to a site.

PalmPilot User Groups

Getting software, help, and information about your palmtop is by no means an Internet-only proposition. Informal PalmPilot clubs are springing up worldwide. At this writing, for example, you're free to attend monthly meetings of user groups in Chicago, Kansas City, Denver, Boston, New York, Philadelphia, Stanford, Ontario, the Netherlands, and many other places. (Visit *http://www.palm.com/resources/ usergroups.HTML* for a starter list.)

User groups represent an exceptional opportunity to exchange tips and tricks, get troubleshooting help, and see accessories and hardware add-ons that you can't see on the Web except in low-resolution photos.

D

Writing a Palm VII Query Application (PQA)

—written by Dave Menconi,
Palm Clipping Project Lead, Palm Computing

As explained in Chapter 16, *Palm VII: Wireless Email, Wireless Web*, a Palm Query Application (PQA) appears to the Palm VII owner as just another application, much like the Memo Pad or Calculator. But in reality, it's a database that's given special treatment by the operating system. When you tap it, the operating system opens it with a program you can't see (called Clipper, although you'll never actually see that name displayed).

In addition, a PQA is different from other applications in what it can do. It can collect and display information, but it can't process information like most programs. Since it connects to the Internet, its inability to actually crunch data is not as great an impediment as it seems—there are literally thousands of computers that can do processing for you!

A PQA usually consists of a form (or query) that you're supposed to fill out. The Palm VII sends the form data to a server on the Internet, which processes the query and returns information in the form of a tiny web page. But that's not the only use for PQAs, as you'll see in this appendix; a PQA can also serve as a single-screen application launcher or even as an illustrated, attractively designed electronic book, complete with tappable hotlinks to other chapters (or even other PQAs).

This appendix provides a brief overview of making your own PQAs. This discussion assumes that you know what HTML is, that you're able to create simple web pages already, and that (for commercial-quality PQAs) you know what a CGI script is and how to interact with one. For a more complete discussion of writing Palm VII query applications, see the forthcoming book *Developing Palm Queries* (O'Reilly & Associates).

The query applications (PQAs) described as examples in this Appendix are on this book's CD-ROM. They're in the sample Palm VII Apps folder.

General Procedure

To create a PQA, you start with an HTML web page on your desktop computer. The page can contain standard HTML 3.2 codes plus small, four-color grayscale graphics. You run your finished web page through a free Windows program called QABuilder, which converts the HTML and images into a PQA. (You can sign up for access to QABuilder from *http://www.palm.com/devzone/palmvii.*) You can then install the PQA onto your Palm VII and run it like any other application. Details on these steps are given later in this discussion. (QABuilder is available in separate versions for Windows and Macintosh.)

In designing the web page, you'll probably want to use a standard web browser and editor; more sophisticated HTML generators tend to be harder to control. Many of the things you can do with HTML are very inefficient for a Palm VII—and some HTML tags don't work at all on the Palm VII, as described later in this appendix.

Three Kinds of PQA

There are essentially three levels of complexity in PQAs, corresponding to the complexity of the Internet server with which they communicate.

Self-Contained

Although few people realize it, the PQA format is ideal for creating electronic documents that don't connect to the Internet at all. Instead of using the Doc electronic-book format described in Chapter 10, *PalmPilot: The Electronic Book,* consider creating a PQA for this purpose. The huge advantage is that, unlike plain-text Doc files, a PQA can contain pictures, a wide variety of text formatting, layout formatting such as tables and headers—and, best of all, hyperlinks. These links, in the form of buttons or underlined text, can link to other spots within the same document or even to other PQAs.

The CD-ROM accompanying this book contains two examples of these self-contained PQAs. The Guess PQA is a frivolous guessing game (see Figure D-1). The DevPQA query application is this appendix itself in PQA form.

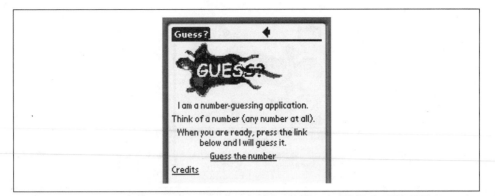

Figure D-1. The PQA format makes a terrific electronic document format, complete with graphics, formatting, links, and even some phony interactivity, as this guessing game demonstrates—even if you never go online.

WWW Links

Another kind of PQA can consist solely of links to the web, without much of a Palm VII-based form at all. This sort of document is like a Doc file that does nothing but retrieve information from the World Wide Web, instead of taking up space on your Palm VII. Such a document is especially useful for accessing data that changes over time.

Be careful, however, when creating links to ordinary web pages. The Palm VII doesn't handle everyday, graphic-filled pages well. Even a simple page can contain thousands of bytes of information—and the Palm VII user is paying for every byte. It's better to link to special web pages designed for the purpose that contain minimal graphics.

On the CD-ROM, you'll find a PQA called BBC, a good example of this kind of document. It links to the BBC interactive news page, as shown in Figure D-2. (Use these links with discretion—some of the news articles can be very large.) Another example, also on the CD-ROM, is the Pogue PQA, which contains links to various parts of the *http://www.davidpogue.com* home page. (Don't miss the computer-industry song spoofs.)

Server-Supported

The most useful PQAs, and almost all of the professionally designed ones, involve setting up a CGI on the server of your Internet service provider. ISPs often provide scripts that their customers can use for their own web pages. For example, you could construct a PQA that requests customer information, which then gets emailed to you. Ask your ISP what other CGIs are available. You can find thousands of other CGI scripts on the Internet itself. In general, it's easy to install a CGIscript once the system has been configured correctly.

Figure D-2. A PQA can contain links to web sites, which is especially useful when the links point to pages that change over time.

Another possibility: use an existing server that's already operating correctly, and direct your PQA to it. That is, you can rework the form of an existing web page (not necessarily your own page), turning it into a PQA. Again, though, caution is advised—most unmodified CGIscripts send complex HTML codes back to your Palm VII that it may not be able to interpret.

Zip4, included on this book's CD-ROM, is the perfect example: write in an address, and the U.S. Postal System computers will send back the complete nine-digit Zip Code for that address (see Figure D-3).

Figure D-3. It's possible to link to one of the thousands of existing server programs— wirelessly.

Step 1: Create the HTML Document

There are two components to a Palm Query Application. The form (or "query"), which is originally written in HTML, and the server CGI program that replies to the query. Entire books are devoted to each of these topics, but this section offers a few helpful notes.

Guaranteeing a Good-Looking PQA

On this book's CD-ROM, you'll find several example PQAs; install one onto your Palm VII, and then load the corresponding source HTML into your browser, as shown here in Netscape Navigator. Adjust your browser window until it's as narrow as a Palm VII screen.

Now load the HTML into a web-page editing program, make changes to your taste, and load it back into your browser. When it looks good in the browser, it should look good on the Palm VII, too.

Keep It Small

As you design your PQA-bound HTML document on your desktop computer, you should have at your side the invaluable—but free—Palm VII Content Style Guide. (The latest version is at *http://www.palm.com/devzone/palmvii*). This guide provides powerful lessons in design, simplicity, and reducing the amount of data that travels to and from the Palm VII. (Remember that a low-data-rate PQA is an inexpensive PQA, and therefore one that will be a hit with your target audience.)

Keep the PQA layout as simple as possible: what minimum information must the user provide to get the answer he or she wants? If possible, design a form that fits on a single Palm VII screen—that's the core of the PQA. Add some help and information text, a mailto link for feedback, and a small logo, and you've designed a basic PQA.

Creating the CGI Script

Making a CGI script is much more difficult. A CGI is a program that runs on a web server and provides answers to the queries a PQA creates. The results are then displayed on the Palm VII. As described above, many ISPs provide generic CGI programs. However, most professionally designed PQAs require a custom-written program. In designing it, remember that the resulting HTML should be simple and short. The screen is small, the connection is slow, and the Palm VII user wants only the requested information, nothing more.

A logo or other small graphic at the top of the first page adds interest and sets the PQA apart, but otherwise, use graphics sparingly on the Palm VII. Graphics built into your PQA don't cost the Palm VII user anything, of course, because they're not transmitted over the air—but they do use up screen space quickly. Your customers won't appreciate having to scroll past the graphics to get to the form elements.

Use graphics even more sparingly in the downloaded response, because graphics are very expensive to download. In fact, you should only download pictures if the user asks for them (for example, by tapping a View Chart button).

Icons

Every application on the Palm VII needs two icons—a large icon for use in the application launcher's Icon view and a small one for use in List view (see Figure D-4). You can create your own icons, or you can let QABuilder provide default generic icons: a small and large solid black diamond with the familiar "over the air" lines on the right side.

Notes for HTML Coders

Most of the commands and controls in the HTML 3.2 specification work on the Palm VII. However, a few common codes don't work: vertical alignment (the VALIGN attribute to various tags), nested tables, subscripts, superscripts, small text, the LINK tag, the APPLET tag, and the ISINDEX tag.

Only four colors are supported: BLACK="#000000", SILVER="#C0C0C0C0" (light gray), GRAY="#808080" (dark gray), and WHITE="#FFFFFF". If you enter any other color number, it will be "rounded off" to the closest of these four colors, often with unfortunate results. Graphics can't be bigger than 153x144 pixels, and sequential *.gif* animation is not supported (thank goodness).

The BODY tag supports only BGCOLOR and TEXT tags. There are also limitations on the types of fonts—Clipper does a decent job of differentiating among the various subtle font variations allowed in the 3.2 HTML specification (such as <SAMP>,

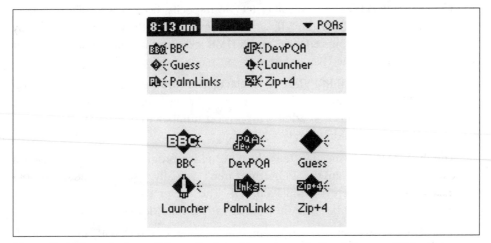

Figure D-4. Create both small icons (top) and large icons (bottom) for your PQAs. If you don't want to bother, you can use the default solid black diamond (as shown on the upper-right PQA in the lower illustration).

<STRONG>, and <EM>), but there are only so many different fonts that will work with so few pixels. Therefore, for example, <SAMP>, <CODE>, and <KBD> are all translated into TD Monospace. And <FONT> attributes like "Arial" are ignored.

A few HTML tricks that aren't actually in the 3.2 specification, but have become widespread, also don't work on the Palm VII: FRAMES, any form of image maps, and any kind of scripting (like JavaScript).

Cool New Tags

On the other hand, the Palm VII accommodates a number of new tags that, while not part of the standard HTML vocabulary, take advantage of the Palm VII's special capabilities:

- Two new input types—DATEPICKER and TIMEPICKER—allow the user to select a date and time in the standard Palm fashion (illustrated in Chapter 2, *Setup and Guided Tour*). The date and/or time information will be passed on to the server in standard Internet formats—YYYY-MM-DD and hh:mm, respectively.

- Several META tags are specific to Palm VII web clipping, too. These all have the form <META NAME="TAGNAME" CONTENT="VALUE"> and go into the <HEAD> section.

  The "PALMCOMPUTINGPLATFORM" metatag (with a content of "TRUE") tells the Palm VII server that you have a "Palm-friendly" site. If you don't include this metatag, your PQA won't display your graphics!

The "HISTORYLISTTEXT" metatag lets you specify how pages will appear in the History List on the Palm VII, as shown in Chapter 16. You can specify any text. The special strings &DATE and &TIME indicate that you want the date or time inserted into the History List.

The "PALMLAUNCHERREVISION" metatag lets you set the revision date on your PQA as it appears in the version list of the the Palm application launcher. As any developer knows, adding a revision number to a program can save a great deal of confusion later.

The "LOCALICON" metatag tells the QABuilder program to include files (for example, graphics) in the PQA that aren't actually used by the PQA, but instead are elsewhere on the Palm VII. The server can reference these files much more cheaply because they are already on the device.

- You can use two special strings in your coding: "%ZIPCODE" and "%DEVICEID." The Palm VII server will replace the first with the current Zip Code of the device, and the second with the device's unique ID number. You can use the first to return location-specific information (such as the nearest store) and the second to track information about the user (for example, which stocks he has in his portfolio).

  Use caution with both of the special strings. The zip code is based on the location of the radio base station, but a particular Palm VII might use base stations across several zip codes. Furthermore, the Palm VII's unique ID can be "spoofed" using a web browser, which contacts your server directly without going through the Palm VII servers.

- The tag pair <SMALLSCREENIGNORE> and </SMALLSCREENIGNORE> can be used to identify portions of a web page that you don't want to show up on a small screen. In other words, thanks to these tags, you can design just one web page (or CGI) that will work for both a standard browser and a Palm VII. Just make sure to mark with these tags all the material you don't want transmitted to the Palm VII.

- You can even create links in your PQA to other Palm applications, in effect turning your PQA into a launcher. If you put a tag in your HTML like this:

  ```
  <A HREF="PALM:ADDR.APPL">ADDRESS BOOK</A>
  ```

  then "Address Book" will appear in your PQA as a link. When the Palm VII user taps it, the Palm VII launches the Address Book! (Figure D-5 shows this effect.)

All the standard applications on the Palm VII have four-character abbreviations. You can look them up either in the table below, in the Palm VII Content Style guide, or in the Launcher sample PQA included on this book's CD-ROM, which uses these tags to create a launching pad on a single PQA screen (see Table D-1).

Figure D-5. A PQA can launch other Palm applications.

Table D-1Palm VII HTML Launch Codes

HREF Code	Application Called
PALM:calc.APPL	Calculator
PALM:secr.APPL	Security
PALM:pref.APPL	Preferences
PALM:addr.APPL	AddressBook
PALM:todo.APPL	To Do
PALM:date.APPL	Date Book
PALM:memo.APPL	Memo Pad
PALM:sync.APPL	HotSync
PALM:mail.APPL	Mail
PALM:exps.APPL	Expense
PALM:lnch.APPL	Launcher (Applications Screen)
PALM:clpr.APPL	Clipper
PALM:setp.APPL	Setup
PALM:memr.APPL	Memory

Random notes

When you build a link into your PQA, the Palm VII automatically adds an "over-the-air" symbol (three little lines facing to the right, as shown in Figure 16-1) to indicate that tapping will expend some of the user's monthly kilobyte allowance. For this reason, be sure to leave a character's worth of space at the end of your links. Similarly, to use use a graphic as a link, include an over-the-air icon in the lower-right corner of the image. (The Palm VII doesn't automatically add this icon to graphics.)

The Palm VII supports HTTPS, the secure version of the hyperlink protocol. When a link will cause a secure over-the-air link, a little key icon appears on the corresponding button, indicating that the link will be secure (see Figure 16-6). Therefore, leave space in your design for both the over-the-air and the secure icon. Naturally, if you use a graphic as a link, you should include the secure icon in the lower-right corner of the graphic.

Step 2: Run QABuilder

Once you've created all the pieces of your web document, run the QABuilder application. Choose File → Open Index, and then open the main HTML file. QABuilder will read this file, automatically tracking all other HTML files and graphics that will be incorporated into the finished PQA.

To compile the PQA, choose File → Build PQA. In the window that appears, you can specify where you want the finished PQA saved and what you want it called (see Figure D-6). You can also use the Install to User: command to specify a Palm VII onto which you would like this PQA installed at the next HotSync. You can use the Large, Small, and Default buttons to select the icons you want for your PQA as it appears on the Palm VII launcher. Finally, when everything is to your liking, click Build. QABuilder will build the PQA, store it in the directory you specified, and even set it up to install on your Palm VII the next time you HotSync.

Your PQA is ready to fly.

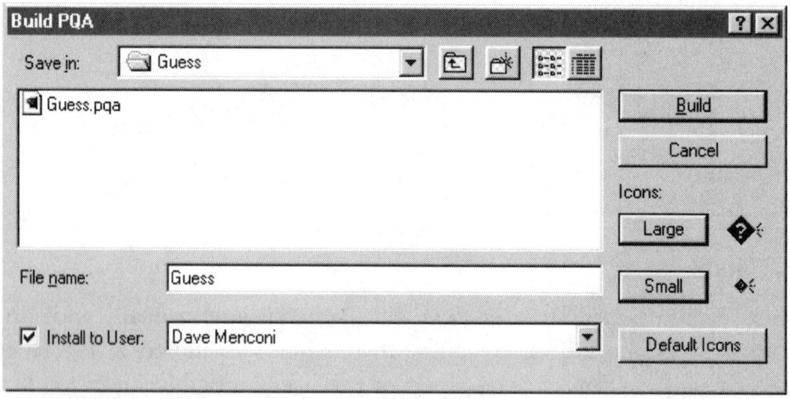

Figure D-6. QABuilder lets you specify what you want to call the PQA, where you want to save it, and what icons you want to use.

Conclusion

The Palm VII is a phenomenon, and everyone who has one wants more PQAs. The opportunities are as great as when the original PalmPilot debuted—this is your chance to get in on the ground floor and really make a mark. All you need is some HTML, a few graphics, and enough imagination to fill an area 160 pixels square.

E

Unix, Linux,
and Palm

—written by Brian Pinto,
Senior Staff Engineer, Logikos Inc.

The vast majority of desktop software, talk, and tips in the Palm world assume that your desktop computer uses Windows or the Mac OS. But the growing legions of the technically adventurous who use Unix or are adopting Linux shouldn't feel left out. Although Palm Computing itself officially ignores these alternative operating systems, the Unix/Linux online community has rushed to fill the void. Here's a look at the state of the art in the Unix and Linux environments. (Almost all of the programs described here are on the CD-ROM that accompanies this book.)

Desktop Alternatives

Palm Desktop, provided by Palm Computing only for the Macintosh and Windows, provides three important functions. It mimics the functions of the PalmPilot on your computer, so that you can edit and create data in bulk for the palmtop. It also backs up the data from the Palm device. Finally, the Desktop lets you install new applications onto the palmtop.

As is so often the case, there are many choices of Palm connectivity in the Unix world. In addition to traditional command-line interface tools, you can choose from at least three graphical Palm Desktop alternatives.

Most of the software described below should be considered in beta or even pre-beta. The momentum in the Linux world is so great, however, that the software will probably have advanced considerably by the time you read this.

The pilot-link Package

The *pilot-link* package is a suite of 34 single-purpose, command-line interface programs for interacting with the PalmPilot. Some provide the communication layer between the PalmPilot and the PC; others are used for PalmPilot development. (For information on writing Palm software, see O'Reilly's *Palm Programming: The Developer's Guide.*)

Installation Directions and "Gotchas"

The *pilot-link* package is distributed under the GNU Public License as source code "tarred and zipped" (*.tar.gz*) in a single file. After you download the file from the Web—or copy it from this book's CD-ROM—the file is unzipped and extracted into a directory called */pilot-link-0.9.1* (or whatever the current version number is). You must now compile the source code files by first running *configure* and then *make.*

The programs then rely on two environment variables being set: *PILOTPORT* and *PILOTRATE.* If you don't set these variables, *PILOTPORT,* the serial port with which to connect, will default to */dev/pilot,* and *PILOTRATE,* the speed of your PC's serial port, will default to 9600 bps. You can also override *PILOTPORT's* default by explicitly specifying the serial port on the command line.

At this point, you should create a pilot device file (*/dev/pilot*). Doing so will simplify things and, once created, will serve other PalmPilot desktop packages, such as *KPilot,* that you may install later.

To create a pilot device file, use superuser (root) privileges to create a symbolic link called *pilot* to the appropriate serial port in the */dev* directory. For example, if the cradle is attached to the second serial port (or COM2) of your PC, type:

```
/dev$ ln -s /dev/cua1 pilot
```

In addition, change the permissions on the file so that it can be read from and written to by all programs by typing:

```
/dev$ chmod 666 pilot
```

or:

```
/dev$ chmod a+rw pilot
```

pilot-link Advantages

If you're mainly interested in HotSyncing your data to a safe place (your regularly backed-up PC), then *pilot-xfer* is the program you want. Typing *pilot-xfer -h* at the prompt will give you all the options available, listed in Table E-1.

Usage

```
pilot-xfer [-p port] -option target
```

Table E-1. Options for HotSyncing

Option	Meaning	Target
b	Back up all databases to a directory	Backup directory of choice
u	Update; backs up only changed or new databases	Backup directory of choice
s	Sync; remove database if deleted on the PalmPilot	Backup directory of choice
r	Restore database to PalmPilot from directory	Backup directory of choice
I	Install a file onto the PalmPilot	Filename of file(s) to be installed
m	Merge files	Filename of file(s) to be installed
f	Fetch a database from the PalmPilot to your PC	Database name with no extension
d	Delete a database on the PalmPilot	Database name with no extension
e	Exclude a filename	Filename of file(s) to be excluded
P	Purge deleted records from databases	
l	List all databases in RAM	
L	List all databases in RAM and ROM	
v	Version information	
h	Help; list this table	

Example

```
pilot-xfer -b MyData
```

Or, alternatively, type:

```
pilot-xfer -p /dev/cua1 -b MyData
```

The above example backs up the data from your PalmPilot to the PC, placing it in a directory called *MyData/* relative to your current directory. If the directory you specify for the backup doesn't exist, it will be created before the backup process begins.

In general, to run any specific utility, place the PalmPilot in its cradle, type the command with the appropriate or desired options at the command prompt, press the Return key, and then press the HotSync button on the cradle.

When using *pilot-xfer*, after the return key is pressed, you'll see this message:

```
Waiting for connection on /dev/pilot (press the HotSync button now)...
```

Other specialized programs deal with each of the PIM functions of the PalmPilot, including Expense and Mail. You can also find programs to synchronize with other Unix-specific calendar/address book programs like *ical*, an X Windows–based calendar, and *netplan*. The *pilot-link Read Me* file offers explanations of all the utilities available.

pilot-link Disadvantages

While the *pilot-link* package is feature-rich, you may miss the integrated feel of a GUI application. You may also miss the specialized HotSync options available within the official Palm Desktop program. On the other hand, pilot-link gives you individual utilities that work with importing and exporting PIM data to and from text files. These text files can then be modified using editors or other automated scripts, and then exported back to the PalmPilot database format and downloaded onto the device.

Like all the other tools discussed in this chapter, the *pilot-link* package is a work in progress. In fact, the most recent release version is labeled 0.9.2!

KPilot

KPilot is a graphical Palm Desktop–type program that comes bundled with the *K Desktop Environment (KDE)*. KDE is one of the newer desktop windowing environments available for Unix or Linux. *KPilot* and its companion program, *KPilot-Daemon*, are conveniently located on the Utilities submenu of the K Start Menu. However, it is also available as a standalone package and, with the appropriate libraries, could be installed under other X Window managers. The most recent version available is labeled 3.0 and is based on the *pilot-link* package.

Installation Directions and "Gotchas"

If you're not using KDE and must install it separately, the package comes in RPM format, which makes it easy to install. After installation, using superuser (root) privileges, you must create a symbolic link called *pilot* to the appropriate serial port in the */dev* directory.

For example, if the cradle is attached to the second serial port (or COM2) of your PC, type:

```
/dev$ ln -s /dev/cua1 pilot
```

You should also change the permissions on the file so that the KPilotDaemon can read and write to the port, exactly as you do with the pilot-link package. Type:

```
/dev$ chmod 666 pilot
```

or:

```
/dev$ chmod a+rw pilot
```

At this point, running either *KPilot* or *KPilotDaemon* brings up the Options dialog box (shown in Figure E-1). Most of the default settings are fine; be sure, though, that `Pilot Device:` is set to */dev/pilot* (the default) and that the `Speed:` setting matches the speed of your serial port. The only other setting to check is the `Sync Files` box under Sync Options. You'll also notice the *Address Settings* tab; while interesting, it's of little use at this point. The KPilot Options dialog box is also available within *KPilot* by choosing File → Settings.

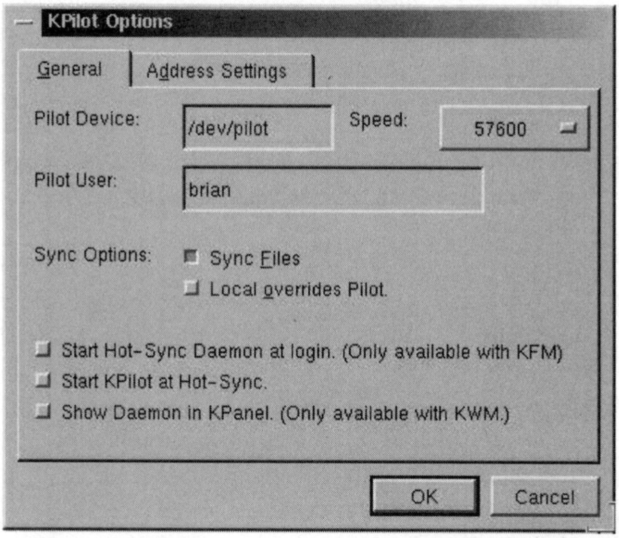

Figure E-1. The KPilot Options Dialog box lets you get KPilot ready for use.

Before going any further, fully back up your PalmPilot by choosing File → Backup within KPilot. (If you don't, and you try to HotSync before doing a backup, you will be forever lost—the message `"Hot-Sync in Progress..."` will appear, but the HotSync will never complete. Recovering from this situation involves hunting down and deleting certain files in a process too painful to describe here.) Interestingly, unlike with the Palm Desktop, backing up with *KPilot* is a very thorough process. It backs up *everything* on your PalmPilot, including HackMaster files, third-party applications, and their associated data. (See Chapter 6, *HotSync, Step by Step*, for more on the standard backup process and what it doesn't back up.)

KPilot Advantages

After the first backup, HotSyncing your PalmPilot is as easy as pushing the HotSync button on the cradle. At this writing, KPilot only lets you see and edit Address Book and Memo Pad data, not To Do or Date Book information. It does recognize categories and Private data. Unfortunately, at this writing, a known bug prevents the editing or importing and exporting of Address Book and Memo entries.

Fortunately, KPilot does let you synchronize your email with the Palm Mail program (see Chapter 13, *Email Anywhere*). To set this up, choose Conduits → Setup. When the Conduit Setup Dialog box appears, install the *popmail_conduit*; then click Setup to reveal the Popmail Conduit dialog box, where the email settings are revealed in gory detail.

KPilot also provides a file installation utility: choose Pilot Application → File Installer. Drag-and-drop file installation is available when using KDE. You can even drag and drop a file onto the KPilotDaemon icon if it's displayed on the KDE dock.

KPilot Disadvantages

Apart from the most obvious limitation of KPilot—missing support for your To Do and Date Book data—the next areas most in need of support are the Sync options. Unlike the Palm Desktop, which gives you finer control over the HotSync process (see Chapter 6), Kpilot only has two settings in the Options Dialog box: Sync Files and Local overrides Pilot; you have no option to overwrite the Palm-Pilot's data with your desktop PC's data.

PilotManager

Originally developed on Sun SPARCstations running Solaris, *PilotManager* now runs on a variety of Unix platforms. Written in Perl with the Tk extension, *PilotManager* has a user-extensible HotSync daemon containing individual conduits. (It, too, is based on the *pilot-link* package.) *PilotManager* requires Perl to be installed; Tk is also necessary, but you can download it with the other packages available on the web site if you don't have it already.

Installation Directions and "Gotchas"

Installation involves selecting the right "package" for your system. Depending on your hardware, operating system, and installed software, the package for you consists of two or three separate "tarred and zipped" (*.tar.gz*) files. Everybody needs the Basic package, which consists of the platform-independent Perl code, and one of the Small package files, which contain binary files based on your hardware, operating system, and the installed version of Perl. You may also need the Tk package, depending on your installed software configuration. Unzipping and untarring the packages creates the files in a directory called *pilotmgr/* relative to your current directory.

Change to the *pilotmgr/* directory and type *PilotManager*. A setup script takes over and checks your environment and installation. If you're not running CDE or Open-windows, or you don't have *plan* installed, you'll have to rename *SyncCM* and *SyncPlan* so that they're not called by the startup script.

Assuming everything went well, PilotManager should now be executed again; a Welcome Message dialog box appears for the first execution of the program. You can now configure PilotManager using the Properties dialog box (choose File → Properties), as shown in Figure E-2. Set the port and communication speed and double-click conduits to move them from the Inactive to the Active conduit list. You can now individually configure each conduit.

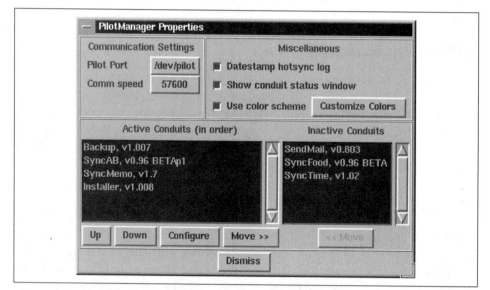

Figure E-2. The PilotManager Properties Dialog box in KDE should be one of your first stops.

PilotManager Advantages

PilotManager has a well laid-out graphical interface, and most settings are just a click or two away. HotSyncing is as easy as pushing the button in the PilotManager main window and then hitting the HotSync button on your cradle. The package can both back up the PalmPilot and install new PalmPilot files. Other PIM conduits synchronize the Date Book, Address Book, and Memo Pad. In addition,

PilotManager supplies two other interesting conduits: *SyncTime* and *SyncFood*. *SyncTime* allows you to keep your PalmPilot's clock in sync with your workstation, and *SyncFood* synchronizes your restaurant database with Food, an application by Alan Harder.

PilotManager does not provide an integrated desktop program, as the real Palm Desktop or KPilot does. Instead, it excels as a broker, synchronizing your Palm-Pilot information with various other PIM programs running on the workstation. As a consequence, most of your time will initially be spent configuring conduits. The conduit configuration for SyncMemo, for example, is quite involved.

PilotManager has a very informative web site, which provides the latest version for downloading, complete with detailed instructions and FAQs. In addition, you may subscribe to a mailing list, and all messages currently posted to the list are available for your perusal.

PilotManager Disadvantages

Unfortunately, PilotManager lacks conduit support for the To Do program on your PalmPilot. Furthermore, the SyncCM conduit synchronizes your Date Book with the Openwin or CDE calendar manager, which isn't available for Linux. (Instead, consider using a different Date Book conduit, such as *SyncPlan*, which synchronizes your Date Book with plan, an alternative X Window/Motif calendar package available for Unix. If you don't have either of these calendar packages installed, you won't be able to view or edit your Date Book data from your workstation.)

The design decision to make PilotManager a broker, while a good one, has a downside—you can't interact with data for which no program on the workstation is installed.

gnome-pilot

Part of the GNOME project, gnome-pilot is the package of utilities for HotSyncing your PalmPilot to a PC. Similar to the KDE, GNOME, which stands for GNU Network Object Model Environment, is one of the new windowing interfaces competing for mind-share in the Unix/Linux world. At this writing, gnome-pilot's development is lagging behind other implementations. And yet, when completed, it promises to have the most ambitious feature list.

gnome-pilot intends to provide a daemon that will support multiple PalmPilots and users. In addition, the conduits will sync the PalmPilot PIM functions to specifically tailored GNOME applications. The current version of gnome-pilot can back up your device, install files, and HotSync Memos. gnome-pilot, like all the desktop programs described thus far, is based on the pilot-link package.

Other Tools and Software

There aren't many PalmPilot-oriented programs being developed for Linux or Unix workstations, but that situation may change once the connectivity suites are mature. Development tools exist, but they're traditional command-line drive tools, which are less attractive to developers accustomed to the GUI-driven Integrated Development Environments.

Pyrite

Pyrite (formerly called PalmPython) is one of the more exciting new tools. It's an extension of Python, the object-oriented scripting language, and was developed on a PC running Linux. Pyrite requires *Python* 1.5 or newer and pilot-link 0.8.11 or newer running on Linux. It should also work with little or no modification on most Unix platforms.

MakeDoc

If you'd like a tool to convert your text files to Doc format (see Chapter 10, *PalmPilot: The Electronic Book*), use makedoc, included on this book's CD-ROM. makedoc is a C++ program, and you can compile it with gcc. Once files are converted to the DOC format, you can send them to the PalmPilot using pilot-xfer. (Also worth trying: txt2pdbdoc, which converts text to and from Doc format, as well as from Doc to HTML format.)

Z-doc

Z-doc is a Doc reader developed under Linux and released under the GNU GPL.

Linux on Palm

Where does this all lead? What's the natural progression for the PalmPilot and Linux? Why, Linux running on the PalmPilot itself, of course! A group of enthusiasts has ported the Linux kernel to the PalmPilot's Dragonball microcontroller. So, if you want to impress your friends, you can replace PalmOS on your PalmPilot with Linux. You won't be able to do anything with your Palm device running Linux yet . . . but stay tuned.

Where to Go from Here

The best resource for the rapidly evolving world of Palm/Unix/Linux information is, of course, the World Wide Web.

Linux/Unix based PalmPilot tools (ftp://ryeham.ee.ryerson.ca/pub/PalmOS)

 The mother ship for distributions and various packages. *pilot-link* and make-doc can be found here. The page is just a long list of files with version numbers and dates.

KPilot Homepage (http://www.slac.com/pilone/kpilot_home/mainpage.html)

 Home of KPilot. The latest versions of KPilot may be found here. A mailing list is also available.

PilotManager (http://www.moshpit.org/pilotmgr)

 Home of *PilotManager*. Very informative site with a lot of detail about Pilot-Manager.

Gnome-pilot (http://www.gnome.org/gnome-pilot/)

 Home of *gnome-pilot*, the PalmPilot utilities for the GNOME desktop.

Unix Pilot Software Repository (http://www.pilot.pasta.cs.uit.no)

 Mainly a site for development tools. This site has versions of *pilot-link* and PalmPython; each package is followed with a mini-list of instructions on how to build and install it.

Z-Doc/PalmPilot (http://www.geocities.com/Area51/7689/zdoc.html)

 Home of Z-Doc, a freeware Doc-format file reader.

CQ Codeworks: Pyrite (http://www.concentric.net/~N9mtb/cq/pyrite/pyrite.html)

 Home of Pyrite (formerly PalmPython), the extension to the Python programming language.

Linux/Microcontroller Home page (http://www.concentric.net/~N9mtb/cq/pyrite pyrite.html)

 Home of uCLinux—Linux for the Dragonball microcontroller.

F

About the CD-ROM

The *PalmPilot: The Ultimate Guide* CD-ROM works best with Macintosh or Windows 95/98. In the main CD-ROM window, you'll find the following items:

PalmCentral CD Catalog

The *PalmPilot: The Ultimate Guide* CD-ROM contains over 3,100 PalmPilot programs, ready to install—a treasure trove of applications in every conceivable category. The disc's collection includes almost every piece of software mentioned in the book, plus thousands more—the very best software, handpicked, from the vaults of PalmCentral.com, the Internet's largest Palm software site.

The PalmCentral CD Catalog is a database-like card-catalog program that describes and illustrates the applications on the disc. It offers a complete listing of all the programs, each categorized, described, and illustrated. If you see a program you think you might like, just click the Install button to install it on your PalmPilot, the More Info button to dial up the software's web page (to check for updated versions, for example), or the Show Me button to view the software in its own folder on your desktop.

The program also includes Help, a list view, a Browse by Category button, and a Pogue's Picks button (which shows you the programs described in the book). For complete instructions, see "How to Use the PalmCentral CD Catalog," later in this chapter.

Palm OS Emulator

This amazing program, otherwise known as POSE, creates a living, working, life-size Palm device on your Windows or Macintosh screen. You can push the buttons, tap the screen, type on your keyboard (instead of writing with Graffiti), install programs, or even go online to try out Palm email and web software—all on the screen of your desktop computer. There's no better way to try out Palm software without actually committing them to your palmtop.

The Emulator won't run unless you provide it with one of the ten enclosed ROM files. See the file called *Read Me—Very Important* in the *Emulator* folder for instructions!

Sample Palm VII Apps

This folder contains sample HTML documents and Palm VII web-query applications to accompany Appendix D, *Writing a Palm VII Query Application (PQA)*.

Software

This folder contains the actual software referenced by the PalmCentral Catalog program. If you'd rather browse aimlessly through the software instead of reading about it in the Catalog, feel free to open the various folders inside this one. The software is organized by category.

Palm MacPac 2 (Appears on Macs only.)

This folder contains the complete MacPac 2, the Macintosh front-end software described in Chapter 9, *Palm Desktop: Macintosh*, including Palm Desktop 2.1.

Internet Config (Appears on Macs only.)

Internet Config is a control panel required by the web-connection feature PalmCentral CD Catalog, described later in this appendix. Don't install this if your Mac has Mac OS 8.5 or later, or if your System Folder already contains Internet Config.

IntelliSync Trial (Appears on Windows PCs only.)

The IntelliSync Demo is a 30-day trial version of IntelliSync, a Windows program that lets your PalmPilot HotSync with almost any Windows desktop program—ACT, Daytimer, Goldmine, Lotus Organizer, Microsoft Outlook, Schedule+, Sidekick, and so on. (A discount coupon at the back of this book lets you purchase the full version at a discount.)

Travel Info

Here (Windows PCs only) are the text files of airline, hotel, and car-rental 800 numbers described in Chapter 6, *HotSync, Step by Step*, ready to import into Palm Desktop for Windows.

CD Contents Text Listing.csv

For the benefit of those who can't use the PalmCentral CD Catalog program, such as Unix and Linux fans, here's a *.CSV* (comma-separated values) text file that contains a complete listing of what's on this CD-ROM. Fields include author, title, description, location on the CD-ROM, and more. It's a *.CSV* file, comma-separated, that you can import into any spreadsheet or database.

Support Files

> You can ignore this folder, which contains the software needed to make the PalmCentral CD Catalog run. Mac users can likewise ignore the MacInstaller application, which powers the PalmCentral CD Catalog's auto-install features.

How to Use the PalmCentral CD Catalog

To help you navigate the thousands of programs on the CD, open the Palm-Central CD Catalog.

 Each time you launch the PalmCentral CD Catalog, a message appears reminding you that the program is being run from its CD-ROM—and that, therefore, you won't be able to edit the database. You can safely ignore this message, which disappears after a moment.

Browse Categories

When you first launch the program, you're shown a list of PalmCentral's 28 categories. Click one of these category names (such as Info, Law, or Literary) to view programs in that category, or click The Whole List to view a listing of all programs on the CD-ROM.

Either way, you now arrive in List View, described next. If you spot a program that looks interesting, click its listing to open the Detail View card; from there, you can read about the program, install it, visit its web site, or click the previous/next (arrow) buttons to scroll through the descriptions of other programs.

List View

The best overview of the programs on the CD-ROM is List View, shown in Figure F-1. At this point, you can proceed in many different directions:

1. Click the name of a program to open Detail View, described later.

2. Click to sort the list by title.

3. Click to sort the list by category.

4. Click Browse Categories to return to the list of this collection's categories; click a category name to see which programs are in that category. Or click Pogue's Picks to view a list of programs that are mentioned in this book (or are otherwise noteworthy).

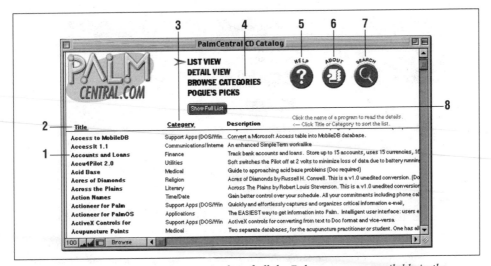

Figure F-1. In List View, you see a concise list of all the Palm programs available in the chosen category.

5. Click Help to read a help screen similar to this appendix.

6. The About screen displays credits for the PalmCentral CD Catalog program.

7. Click here to search the database for programs—by name, category, and so on. You'll be shown a blank form, as shown in Figure F-2. Type what you're looking for and press Return. (If the search produces no results, click Modify Find to set up the search differently, or Cancel to return to the list of software.)

   After a search is complete, the PalmCentral Catalog hides the listings of all programs that didn't match your search criteria. To restore the full list, click Show All Files.

   After using the Search command, the Pogue's Picks button, or the Browse Categories button, the database hides all programs that don't fit your criteria. Click Show Full List to resume viewing the complete list of programs.

Detail View

Once you've clicked a program name, you're shown a detail view like that pictured in Figure F-3.

1. Shareware, author, and other information is provided for each program on the CD. To find out the requested price for a piece of shareware, click the Show Me button and read the Read Me or other instructions that come with the software. (Sometimes shareware payment information is only visible once you're actually running the software, via the Help command, for example.)

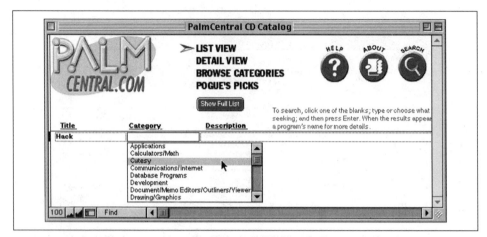

Figure F-2. When searching, you're shown an empty List View screen. Type in exactly what you're looking for, or click in the Category blank to select from a pop-up menu of categories. In this example, you'll find any HackMaster files in the Cutesy category.

Secrets of the Find Command

The Find command in the PalmCentral CD Catalog program, like most computer Find commands, is very literal. (The program is based on FileMaker Pro, and so it inherits all the find features of that program.)

For example, if you search for *ImageViewer,* the program won't find any matches—because there's actually a space in the program's name (Image Viewer). Similarly, a search for *Hack Master* will come up empty-handed, because the actual filename is HackMaster (no space). A few program names even include hyphens. If you're having trouble locating a certain file, therefore, consider searching for only a part of its name (such as *Image* or *Hack*).

Another tip: under normal circumstances, the PalmCentral CD Catalog searches only the *beginnings* of words, exactly as on the PalmPilot. If you're looking for HackMaster, a search for *Master* won't produce the file you want, but a search for *Hack* will. You can find text in the middles of words, however, if you use this trick: precede your search with an asterisk (*), which is FileMaker's wildcard character. A search for *master* will turn up HackMaster.

If the description of a program is so long that it appears truncated, click it. A scroll bar appears.

2. Click More Info, if your computer has Internet access, to visit the web page for this software to check for updates, instructions, and more information.

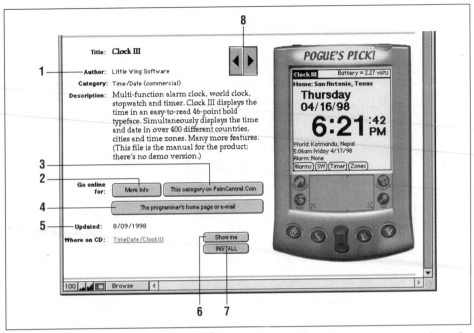

Figure F-3. Detail view provides the specs for the file you clicked, along with buttons that take you to the author's web page and install the program.

 On the Macintosh, in order to go online, the PalmCentral Catalog program requires the control panel called Internet (Mac OS 8.5 and later) or Internet Config (a free program that works on any Mac).

If you don't have such a control panel, install the Internet Config control panel, which is provided in the *Internet Config* folder of your CD.

3. If you have Internet access, click here to visit PalmCentral.com to view its complete listings in the corresponding category.

4. This button takes you to the programmer's home page, if there is one; if not, this button opens up a new, pre-addressed, outgoing email message in your default email program. Either way, the idea is to help you contact the author for more information.

5. In certain circumstances, you may want to locate the actual software on the CD. This field tells you where it is. For example, Clock III's location is shown as "TimeDate/ClockIII." In other words, open the Software folder on the CD, then the TimeDate folder, and finally the ClockIII folder to see the actual icons for this software. (Hint: instead of using this reference information to find the file, just click the Show Me button, or this field itself. The folder in question pops open automatically.)

6. Click Show Me to jump directly to your computer desktop, where the folder containing the program in question is opened automatically. Here you can access the software, read any supporting instruction files, and so on.

7. Click Install to install the currently displayed program onto the PalmPilot. This button works for most of the programs listed on the CD. If you're trying to install a Windows or Macintosh program, however, or a Palm program whose installation is escecially complex, you're better off clicking the Show Me button to jump back to your desktop. From there, you can install the pieces using the usual methods (see Chapter 7, *Installing New Palm Programs*).

Installation notes: If you HotSync multiple Palm devices with your desktop computer, a dialog box appears the first time you click Install. It asks you to specify which PalmPilot you'd like to install onto.

Your choice of PalmPilot will remain in force until you specify a different one. To do so in Windows, choose Commands → Change Palm User. On the Macintosh, Option-Click the Install button. In either case, you'll be offered the chance to switch to a different Palm user.

If, after using the Install button, you decide you'd rather not install a program after all, simply remove it from the Palm Waiting Room. *Wndows:* Launch the Palm Install Tool; click the file's name and then click Remove. *Macintosh:* Open Palm → Users → *your name* → Files to Install folder, and throw away the file you don't want.

Another Macintosh note: The Install button works only if you've installed the MacPac 2, which is included on this CD-ROM (and which requires a Macintosh with a PowerPC chip).

---

8. These are the Previous and Next buttons. Click them to view more programs in the set you're browsing.

Troubleshooting

If the CD-ROM doesn't show up on your Desktop at all when inserted into your CD-ROM drive, it's likely that your computer's CD-ROM system isn't correctly installed. Consider reinstalling the driver software, testing it with other discs, and so on.

If the CD-ROM is missing from this book, or if it was damaged the day you bought it, contact O'Reilly & Associates at (800) 998-9938 for a replacement.

Index

About the Author

David Pogue, a *summa cum laude* Yale music major and former Broadway conductor, writes the award-winning back-page column for *Macworld* magazine. He's the author or co-author of 15 computer, humor, and music books, including *Macs for Dummies*, *The iMac for Dummies*, *Classical Music for Dummies*, *Magic for Dummies*, *Macworld Mac Secrets*, *Hard Drive* (a novel), and *Tales from the Tech Line*. Mia Farrow, Carly Simon, Harry Connick, Jr., and Stephen Sondheim are among his computer students.

He lives with his wife, daughter, and son in Connecticut. Pogue's web page is *http://www.davidpogue.com*; his email is *david@pogueman.com*.

Colophon

Our look is the result of reader comments, our own experimentation, and feedback from distribution channels. Distinctive covers complement our distinctive approach to technical topics, breathing personality and life into potentially dry subjects.

The animal on the cover of *PalmPilot: The Ultimate Guide* is a flying squirrel. This rodent, immortalized in cartoon form as half of Rocky and Bullwinkle, is able to "fly" or glide spread-eagled through the air for distances of up to 50 meters, by means of a "flightskin." This furry skin extends from the front paws to the ankles, and operates as a parachute when flying and landing. The squirrel's tail is used as a rudder, enabling it to change direction in flight. The flying squirrel is less graceful on the ground than in the air, due to this same skin.

Flying squirrels are mostly nocturnal, and live in tree nests or holes in forests throughout Europe and North America, eating insect, nuts, and fruits. They depend on their sight and hearing, as well as their gliding flights, to protect them from enemies—most notably various birds of prey. Flying squirrels are playful and gregarious animals, gliding between trees in groups.

Nancy Kotary was the production editor for *PalmPilot: The Ultimate Guide, Second Edition*; Paulette Miley was the copyeditor; Jeffrey Liggett, Clairemarie Fisher O'Leary, Colleen Gorman, Melanie Wang, and Ellie Maden provided quality control; and Maureen Dempsey provided production support. Mike Sierra provided FrameMaker technical support. Seth Maislin wrote the index, with indexing support from Brenda Miller.

Edie Freedman designed the cover of this book, using a 19th-century engraving from the Dover Pictorial Archive. Kathleen Wilson produced the cover layout with QuarkXPress 3.32 using the ITC Garamond font. The CD label was designed by Hanna Dyer. Whenever possible, our books use RepKover™, a durable and flexible lay-flat binding. If the page count exceeds RepKover's limit, perfect binding is used.

The inside layout was designed by Alicia Cech, based on a series design by Nancy Priest, and implemented in FrameMaker 5.5.6 by Mike Sierra. The text and heading fonts are ITC Garamond Light and Garamond Book. The illustrations that appear in the book were produced by Robert Romano and Rhon Porter using Macromedia FreeHand 8 and Adobe Photoshop 5. This colophon was written by Nancy Kotary.

More Titles from O'Reilly

Hand-held Computers

Palm Programming: The Developer's Guide

By Neil Rhodes & Julie McKeehan
1st Edition December 1998
482 pages, includes CD-ROM
ISBN 1-56592-525-4

Emerging as the bestselling hand-held computers of all time, PalmPilots have spawned intense developer activity and a fanatical following. *Palm Programming*, endorsed by Palm as their official developer's guide, is a tutorial-style book eagerly awaited by developers and experienced C programmers. Includes a CD-ROM with source code and third-party developer tools.

Graphics/Multimedia

Encyclopedia of Graphics File Formats, 2nd Edition

By James D. Murray & William vanRyper
2nd Edition May 1996
1154 pages, includes CD-ROM
ISBN 1-56592-161-5

The second edition of the *Encyclopedia of Graphics File Formats* provides the convenience of quick look-up on CD-ROM, up-to-date information through links to the World Wide Web, as well as a printed book—all in one package. Includes technical details on more than 100 file formats. The CD-ROM includes vendor file format specs, graphics test images, coding examples, and graphics conversion and manipulation software. An indispensable online resource for graphics programmers, service bureaus, and graphic artists.

Photoshop in a Nutshell

By Donnie O'Quinn & Matt LeClair
1st Edition October 1997
610 pages, ISBN 1-56592-313-8

Photoshop 4's powerful features make it the software standard for desktop image design and production. But they also make it an extremely complex product. This detailed reference defines and describes every tool, command, palette, and sub-menu of Photoshop 4 to help users understand design options,make informed choices, and reduce time spent learning by trial-and-error.

Graphics/Multimedia

Director in a Nutshell

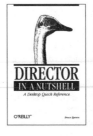

By Bruce A. Epstein
1st Edition March 1999
658 pages, ISBN 1-56592-382-0

Director in a Nutshell is the most concise and complete guide available for Director®. The reader gets both the nitty-gritty details and the bigger context in which to use the multiple facets of Director. It is a high-end handbook, at a low-end price—an indispensable desktop reference for every Director user.

QuarkXPress in a Nutshell

By Donnie O'Quinn
1st Edition June 1998
546 pages, ISBN 1-56592-399-5

This quick reference describes every tool, command, palette, and sub-menu in QuarkXPress 4, providing users with a detailed understanding of the software so they can make informed choices and reduce time spent learning by trial-and-error.

Lingo in a Nutshell

By Bruce Epstein
1st Edition November 1998
634 pages, ISBN 1-56592-493-2

This companion book to *Director in a Nutshell* covers all aspects of Lingo, Director's powerful scripting language, and is the book for which both Director users and power Lingo programmers have been yearning. Detailed chapters describe messages, events, scripts, handlers, variables, lists, file I/O, Behaviors, child objects, Xtras, browser scripting, media control, performance optimization, and more.

O'REILLY®

TO ORDER: **800-998-9938** • *order@oreilly.com* • *http://www.oreilly.com/*
OUR PRODUCTS ARE AVAILABLE AT A BOOKSTORE OR SOFTWARE STORE NEAR YOU.
FOR INFORMATION: **800-998-9938** • **707-829-0515** • *info@oreilly.com*

In a Nutshell Quick References

Web Design in a Nutshell

By Jennifer Niederst
1st Edition November 1998
580 pages, ISBN 1-56592-515-7

Web Design in a Nutshell contains the nitty-gritty on everything you need to know to design Web pages. Written by veteran Web designer Jennifer Niederst, this book provides quick access to the wide range of technologies and techniques from which Web designers and authors must draw. Topics include understanding the Web environment, HTML, graphics, multimedia and interactivity, and emerging technologies.

WebMaster in a Nutshell, Deluxe Edition

By O'Reilly & Associates, Inc.
1st Edition September 1997
374 pages, includes CD-ROM & book
ISBN 1-56592-305-7

The Deluxe Edition of *WebMaster in a Nutshell* is a complete library for web programmers. It features the Web Developer's Library, a CD-ROM containing the electronic text of five popular O'Reilly titles: *HTML: The Definitive Guide*, 2nd Edition; *JavaScript: The Definitive Guide*, 2nd Edition; *CGI Programming on the World Wide Web*; *Programming Perl*, 2nd Edition—the classic "camel book"; and *WebMaster in a Nutshell*, which is also included in a companion desktop edition.

AOL in a Nutshell

By Curt Degenhart & Jen Muehlbauer
1st Edition June 1998
536 pages, ISBN 1-56592-424-X

This definitive reference breaks through the hype and shows advanced AOL users and sophisticated beginners how to get the most out of AOL's tools and features. You'll learn how to customize AOL to meet your needs, work around annoying idiosyncrasies, avoid unwanted email and Instant Messages, understand Parental Controls, and turn off intrusive advertisements. It's an indispensable guide for users who aren't dummies.

Internet in a Nutshell

By Valerie Quercia
1st Edition October 1997
450 pages, ISBN 1-56592-323-5

Internet in a Nutshell is a quick-moving guide that goes beyond the "hype" and right to the heart of the matter: how to get the Internet to work for you. This is a second-generation Internet book for readers who have already taken a spin around the Net and now want to learn the shortcuts.

ASP in a Nutshell

By A. Keyton Weissinger
1st Edition February 1999
426 pages, ISBN 1-56592-490-8

This detailed reference contains all the information Web developers need to create effective Active Server Pages (ASP) applications. It focuses on how features are used in a real application and highlights little-known or undocumented aspects, enabling even experienced developers to advance their ASP applications to new levels.

WebMaster in a Nutshell

By Stephen Spainhour & Valerie Quercia
1st Edition October 1996
374 pages, ISBN 1-56592-229-8

Web content providers and administrators have many sources for information, both in print and online. *WebMaster in a Nutshell* puts it all together in one slim volume for easy desktop access. This quick reference covers HTML, CGI, JavaScript, Perl, HTTP, and server configuration.

Perl in a Nutshell

By Stephen Spainhour, Ellen Siever &
Nathan Patwardhan
1st Edition January 1999
674 pages, ISBN 1-56592-286-7

The perfect companion for working programmers, *Perl in a Nutshell* is a comprehensive reference guide to the world of Perl. It contains everything you need to know for all but the most obscure Perl questions. This wealth of information is packed into an efficient, extraordinarily usable format.

O'REILLY®

TO ORDER: **800-998-9938** • *order@oreilly.com* • *http://www.oreilly.com/*
OUR PRODUCTS ARE AVAILABLE AT A BOOKSTORE OR SOFTWARE STORE NEAR YOU.
FOR INFORMATION: **800-998-9938** • **707-829-0515** • *info@oreilly.com*

How to stay in touch with O'Reilly

1. Visit Our Award-Winning Web Site

http://www.oreilly.com/

★ "Top 100 Sites on the Web" —*PC Magazine*
★ "Top 5% Web sites" —*Point Communications*
★ "3-Star site" —*The McKinley Group*

Our web site contains a library of comprehensive product information (including book excerpts and tables of contents), downloadable software, background articles, interviews with technology leaders, links to relevant sites, book cover art, and more. File us in your Bookmarks or Hotlist!

2. Join Our Email Mailing Lists

New Product Releases

To receive automatic email with brief descriptions of all new O'Reilly products as they are released, send email to:
listproc@online.oreilly.com
Put the following information in the first line of your message (*not* in the Subject field):
subscribe oreilly-news

O'Reilly Events

If you'd also like us to send information about trade show events, special promotions, and other O'Reilly events, send email to:
listproc@online.oreilly.com
Put the following information in the first line of your message (*not* in the Subject field):
subscribe oreilly-events

3. Get Examples from Our Books via FTP

There are two ways to access an archive of example files from our books:

Regular FTP

- ftp to:
  ftp.oreilly.com
  (login: anonymous
  password: your email address)
- Point your web browser to:
  ftp://ftp.oreilly.com/

FTPMAIL

- Send an email message to:
  ftpmail@online.oreilly.com
  (Write "help" in the message body)

4. Contact Us via Email

order@oreilly.com
To place a book or software order online. Good for North American and international customers.

subscriptions@oreilly.com
To place an order for any of our newsletters or periodicals.

books@oreilly.com
General questions about any of our books.

software@oreilly.com
For general questions and product information about our software. Check out O'Reilly Software Online at **http://software.oreilly.com/** for software and technical support information. Registered O'Reilly software users send your questions to: **website-support@oreilly.com**

cs@oreilly.com
For answers to problems regarding your order or our products.

booktech@oreilly.com
For book content technical questions or corrections.

proposals@oreilly.com
To submit new book or software proposals to our editors and product managers.

international@oreilly.com
For information about our international distributors or translation queries. For a list of our distributors outside of North America check out:
http://www.oreilly.com/www/order/country.html

O'Reilly & Associates, Inc.
101 Morris Street, Sebastopol, CA 95472 USA
TEL   707-829-0515 or 800-998-9938
          (6am to 5pm PST)
FAX   707-829-0104

O'REILLY®

Titles from O'Reilly

International Distributors

UK, EUROPE, MIDDLE EAST AND AFRICA (EXCEPT FRANCE, GERMANY, AUSTRIA, SWITZERLAND, LUXEMBOURG, LIECHTENSTEIN, AND EASTERN EUROPE)

INQUIRIES
O'Reilly UK Limited
4 Castle Street
Farnham
Surrey, GU9 7HS
United Kingdom
Telephone: 44-1252-711776
Fax: 44-1252-734211
Email: josette@oreilly.com

ORDERS
Wiley Distribution Services Ltd.
1 Oldlands Way
Bognor Regis
West Sussex PO22 9SA
United Kingdom
Telephone: 44-1243-779777
Fax: 44-1243-820250
Email: cs-books@wiley.co.uk

FRANCE

ORDERS
GEODIF
61, Bd Saint-Germain
75240 Paris Cedex 05, France
Tel: 33-1-44-41-46-16 (French books)
Tel: 33-1-44-41-11-87 (English books)
Fax: 33-1-44-41-11-44
Email: distribution@eyrolles.com

INQUIRIES
Éditions O'Reilly
18 rue Séguier
75006 Paris, France
Tel: 33-1-40-51-52-30
Fax: 33-1-40-51-52-31
Email: france@editions-oreilly.fr

GERMANY, SWITZERLAND, AUSTRIA, EASTERN EUROPE, LUXEMBOURG, AND LIECHTENSTEIN

INQUIRIES & ORDERS
O'Reilly Verlag
Balthasarstr. 81
D-50670 Köln
Germany
Telephone: 49-221-973160-91
Fax: 49-221-973160-8
Email: anfragen@oreilly.de (inquiries)
Email: order@oreilly.de (orders)

CANADA (FRENCH LANGUAGE BOOKS)
Les Éditions Flammarion ltée
375, Avenue Laurier Ouest
Montréal (Québec) H2V 2K3
Tel: 00-1-514-277-8807
Fax: 00-1-514-278-2085
Email: info@flammarion.qc.ca

HONG KONG
City Discount Subscription Service, Ltd.
Unit D, 3rd Floor, Yan's Tower
27 Wong Chuk Hang Road
Aberdeen, Hong Kong
Tel: 852-2580-3539
Fax: 852-2580-6463
Email: citydis@ppn.com.hk

KOREA
Hanbit Media, Inc.
Sonyoung Bldg. 202
Yeksam-dong 736-36
Kangnam-ku
Seoul, Korea
Tel: 822-554-9610
Fax: 822-556-0363
Email: hant93@chollian.dacom.co.kr

PHILIPPINES
Mutual Books, Inc.
429-D Shaw Boulevard
Mandaluyong City, Metro
Manila, Philippines
Tel: 632-725-7538
Fax: 632-721-3056
Email: mbikikog@mnl.sequel.net

TAIWAN
O'Reilly Taiwan
No. 3, Lane 131
Hang-Chow South Road
Section 1, Taipei, Taiwan
Tel: 886-2-23968990
Fax: 886-2-23968916
Email: benh@oreilly.com

CHINA
O'Reilly Beijing
Room 2410
160, FuXingMenNeiDaJie
XiCheng District
Beijing, China PR 100031
Tel: 86-10-86631006
Fax: 86-10-86631007
Email: frederic@oreilly.com

INDIA
Computer Bookshop (India) Pvt. Ltd.
190 Dr. D.N. Road, Fort
Bombay 400 001 India
Tel: 91-22-207-0989
Fax: 91-22-262-3551
Email: cbsbom@giasbm01.vsnl.net.in

JAPAN
O'Reilly Japan, Inc.
Kiyoshige Building 2F
12-Bancho, Sanei-cho
Shinjuku-ku
Tokyo 160-0008 Japan
Tel: 81-3-3356-5227
Fax: 81-3-3356-5261
Email: japan@oreilly.com

ALL OTHER ASIAN COUNTRIES
O'Reilly & Associates, Inc.
101 Morris Street
Sebastopol, CA 95472 USA
Tel: 707-829-0515
Fax: 707-829-0104
Email: order@oreilly.com

AUSTRALIA
WoodsLane Pty., Ltd.
7/5 Vuko Place
Warriewood NSW 2102
Australia
Tel: 61-2-9970-5111
Fax: 61-2-9970-5002
Email: info@woodslane.com.au

NEW ZEALAND
Woodslane New Zealand, Ltd.
21 Cooks Street (P.O. Box 575)
Waganui, New Zealand
Tel: 64-6-347-6543
Fax: 64-6-345-4840
Email: info@woodslane.com.au

LATIN AMERICA
McGraw-Hill Interamericana
Editores, S.A. de C.V.
Cedro No. 512
Col. Atlampa
06450, Mexico, D.F.
Tel: 52-5-547-6777
Fax: 52-5-547-3336
Email: mcgraw-hill@infosel.net.mx

O'REILLY®

SPECIAL OFFER for owners of *PalmPilot: The Ultimate Guide!*

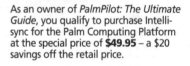

O'REILLY™

O'Reilly & Associates, Inc.
101 Morris Street
Sebastopol, CA 95472-9902
1-800-998-9938

Visit us online at:
http://www.ora.com/
orders@ora.com

O'REILLY WOULD LIKE TO HEAR FROM YOU

Which book did this card come from?

_____

Where did you buy this book?
- ❏ Bookstore
- ❏ Direct from O'Reilly
- ❏ Bundled with hardware/software
- ❏ Computer Store
- ❏ Class/seminar
- ❏ Other _____

What operating system do you use?
- ❏ UNIX
- ❏ Windows NT
- ❏ Other _____
- ❏ Macintosh
- ❏ PC(Windows/DOS)

What is your job description?
- ❏ System Administrator
- ❏ Network Administrator
- ❏ Web Developer
- ❏ Programmer
- ❏ Educator/Teacher
- ❏ Other _____

❏ Please send me O'Reilly's catalog, containing a complete listing of O'Reilly books and software.

Name _____   Company/Organization _____

Address _____

City _____   State _____   Zip/Postal Code _____   Country _____

Telephone _____   Internet or other email address (specify network) _____

Nineteenth century wood engraving
of a bear from the O'Reilly &
Associates Nutshell Handbook®
Using & Managing UUCP.

BUSINESS REPLY MAIL
FIRST CLASS MAIL   PERMIT NO. 80   SEBASTOPOL, CA

Postage will be paid by addressee

O'Reilly & Associates, Inc.
101 Morris Street
Sebastopol, CA 95472-9902